The Great Pyramid Secret

Egypt's Amazing Lost Mystery Science Returns

by

Margaret Morris

𝔖𝔠𝔯𝔦𝔟𝔞𝔩 𝔄𝔯𝔱𝔰
2010
Detroit

10\10

The Great Pyramid Secret: Egypt's Amazing Lost Mystery Science Returns

By Margaret Morris

Copyright © 2010 by Margaret Morris

ISBN: 0-9720434-6-2

Library of Congress Control Number: 2009906129

Science and technology, Great Pyramid, archaeology, Egyptology, ancient mysteries, architecture, engineering, Egypt, geopolymer, history, history of science, pyramids, geology

Margaret Morris' web site: http://www.margaretmorrisbooks.com

First Edition

The reference to "Award-Winning Science" on the front cover alludes to the Gold Ribbon Award from the National Association for Science, Technology and Society (NASTS) and the Federation of Materials Societies, honoring the most significant real advances in Materials Research of the last decade. The award was presented to Dr. Joseph Davidovits on September 26, 1994, at the National Press Club, Washington DC. Joseph Davidovits is the founder of the chemistry of geopolymerization and of the Geopolymer Institute. He is also a Consultant to the European Union Commission. In November of 1998, Dr. Davidovits was honored by French President Jacques Chirac with one of France's two highest honors, the grade of "Chevalier de l'Ordre National du Mérite (National Order of Merit, awarded for distinguished civil achievements),"

Scribal Arts
16863 Lenore St.
Detroit, MI 48219
U.S.A.

Dedication

This book is dedicated to the following people: It is dedicated to the memory of geophysicist, geochemist, and micropaleontologist Dr. Edward J. Zeller (1925–1996). He was a long-term Director of the Radiation Physics Laboratory of the Space Technology Center, a focal point of federal agencies funding, including NASA-sponsored research, at the University of Kansas at Lawrence—a major research university. It is also dedicated to physicist Dr. Gisela A. Dreschhoff, who, for about a decade, also served as Director of the Radiation Physics Laboratory. This book is also dedicated to Dr. Joseph Davidovits, founder of the chemistry of geopolymerization and the Geopolymer Institute, and to igneous rock geologist Robert G. McKinney, and to Michel Barsoum, a Professor of Materials Science and Engineering at Drexel University.

Contents

List of Illustrations and Tables

Photographs and Line Drawings

Tables

Acknowledgements

To write this book, I needed scientific, technical, and other forms of support. I was fortunate to obtain such support from the people listed below. Most of the scientific and technical expertise and assistance applies to the scientific solution presented in Part 2 of this book:

I thank Robert G. Magnuson for tasks involved in the creation of this book. This book would not exist without his long, steady support and assistance.

I am enormously grateful to geologists Robert G. McKinney and the late Dr. Edward J. Zeller. I am greatly privileged to have consulted with them over the years to resolve difficult geological problems. I depended on their in-depth knowledge and great willingness to volunteer their help in the interest of science. The extent of Robert G. McKinney's contributions since 1990 are hard to put into words. I owe him a tremendous vote of thanks.

The same is true for geophysicist, geochemist and micropaleontologist Dr. Edward J. Zeller, who was always very generous with his time although in the midst of his own remarkable contributions to science. As a scientist and individual, Ed was rare and will always be sorely missed by his friends, family, and colleagues in the scientific community.

Geologist Dr. Luciano Ronca was a professor at Wayne State University, in Detroit, Michigan, when I made his acquaintance in 1990. He kindly introduced me to his former professor Ed Zeller that year because of Ed's exceptional qualifications. For this I will always be grateful.

Geologist James Shelton, of SIP Technologies, in Mandeville, Louisiana, has made a fine contribution to this book by providing his insights in Appendix 3.

I thank astronomer Dr. Edwin C. Krupp, Director of the Griffith Observatory in Los Angeles, California, for preparing a statement for this book.

Above all, I owe thanks to the internationally recognized French scientist Dr. Joseph Davidovits. This book is based on his new branch of chemistry and on his pyramid construction theory. He is an award-winning materials scientist. I began working as his historical assistant in 1984, when he founded the Institute for Applied Archaeological Science (IAPAS) at Barry University, in Miami Shores, Florida. The IAPAS was established to revive worthwhile ancient technology and to advance the clarity of ancient history.

I would like to put on record my thanks to my brother, William E. Morris, Jr., for introducing me to the work of Dr. Joseph Davidovits in 1983. This occurred after a presentation at Brookhaven National Laboratory by Joseph Davidovits and Liliane Courtois, the latter of the Center for Archaeological Research, in Paris.

My late Mother wrote letters on behalf of this work, and I extend my love and appreciation for her efforts.

I extend my thanks to materials scientist Dr. Rustum Roy, former Head of the Materials Research Institute, at Pennsylvania State University, for his actions on behalf of this research, and to Dr. Mike Silsbee, Head of the Pennsylvania State University Materials Research Laboratory, for his efforts.

I wish to thank zeolite expert Dr. Robert Colpitts, who has held a number of industrial and university positions, for advising me.

I offer a great many special thanks to materials scientist Dr. Michel Barsoum, Distinguished Professor of the Materials Engineering Department of Drexel University, Philadelphia, Pennsylvania, for his ongoing efforts on behalf of this body of research. He read the unpublished manuscript of this book, and it inspired his subsequent years of research. I sincerely appreciate his wholehearted commitment to expanded research. At the

1. Joseph Davidovits delivering a lecture on Geopolymerization

time of this writing, Professor Barsoum has dedicated more than five years of very devoted and intense research to this project.

Michel Barsoum put together an international team. Their findings on behalf of this body of research have been reported in the scientific literature and in the international media. My thanks are extended to the entire international team (as listed in the *Journal of the American Ceramics Society*, 2006, 89, 3788-3796). They primarily include Michel Barsoum, Gilles Hug, of the French National Aerospace Research Agency, and Adrish Ganguly of Drexel University. Dr. M. Radovic and L. Walker of Oak Ridge National Laboratory conducted scanning electron microscope measurements. Readers can see a summary of the project at the National Science Foundation's web site (Discoveries page; article title: *The Surprising Truth Behind the Construction of the Great Pyramids*).

I wholeheartedly thank Dr. Linn W. Hobbs, Professor of Materials and Professor of Nuclear Engineering in the Department of Materials and Engineering at MIT. Dr. Linn W. Hobbs kindly read a prepublication draft of this book and suggested a number of advanced tests that could be performed on samples of pyramid stone at MIT. Dr. Linn W. Hobbs subsequently worked with other MIT professors to arrange for a class that works with the technology that is the focal point of this book. Their first class, Materials in Human Experience (class 3.094), was taught in the spring of 2008.

I am happy that Dr. Hobbs' continues to work in this new area of Egyptology, and I also thank him for interesting his graduate student Katherine Kershen in designing and conducting a test project with him at MIT. My thanks are also extended to Katherine Kershen for her suggestions and her calculation, which appears in this volume, with regard to building Khufu's pyramid.

I extend my gratitude to Senior Engineer George Gardiner, of the International Chimney Corporation, in Williamsville, New York. George Gardiner kindly provided input concerning engineering problems involving transporting enormous monolithic structures.

I am grateful to Jon Bodsworth for beautiful photographs of Egyptian antiquities. Everyone can enjoy the charm of his on-line collection by visiting his web site: http://home.freeuk.net/egyptarchive/html/home.html

My thanks are extended to precision mold maker Gary Mellinger. When I consulted with Gary, he already had 28 years of precision-casting experience with Spokane Industries, in Spokane, Washington. His valuable contribution appears in this book.

I offer my gratitude to Systems Engineer Mike Carrell, who is now retired after 38 years with the former RCA Corporation, where he held the position of principal member of the technical staff. Mike made a number of valuable contributions to this book, including using zoom lens photography to investigate the obelisk called Cleopatra's Needle in New York City's Central Park. Mike also made rough measurements of the trench next to Khafra's pyramid on behalf of this book.

George Havach, of the U.S. Geological Survey, has benefitted this work. My many thanks are in order for him having consulted specialized geological reference material on behalf of this research, and for his great encouragement and enthusiasm.

I offer my thanks to Sanford Rose, President of Hallco Technologies, in New York City. Sanford applied his skills in manufacturing to inspect Khafra's Valley Temple, at Giza, and a tomb in Zoser's Pyramid complex, at Saqqara, on behalf of this work. I thank him also for photographs used in this book.

I also thank Dr. Gisela A. Dreschhoff, who, for about a decade, served as Director of the Radiation Physics Laboratory of the Space Technology Center at the University of Kansas, in Lawrence. My thanks are forthcoming for her guidance as I developed the conclusion of Chapter 30 of this book.

The ancient names Imhotep, Amenhotep-son-of-Hapu and Kha-em-waset must be included here. We all owe these priestly natural scientists a debt of gratitude for their remarkable contributions to examples of unprecedented architecture. As explained in these pages, they are responsible for some of the largest monoliths of ancient Egypt.

Anticipating reaching you, the reader, has inspired me to continue on through the years despite the opposition and many difficulties involved in completing this work. I sincerely hope you enjoy this book and benefit from it.

Part One
The Mysteries

Chapter 1
A Stunning Secret of the Ages

We are going to explore a super-tantalizing ancient mystery, and experience a whole new way of thinking about it. Sometimes captivating mysteries are unappreciated because experts lack the right kind of expertise. Sometimes the mysteries are appreciated, but still cannot be explained without the right expertise. In these pages, we encounter a stupendous mystery of ancient Egypt that is not fully appreciated. We are going deep into unsolved riddles of the Egyptian pyramids and other ancient stoneworks that qualified experts recognize as masonry marvels unequalled in all of later history. One thing will become conspicuous as we go along: Something is terribly amiss with accepted thinking about the masonry and engineering problems.

The unexplained features of ancient Egyptian stoneworking range from the minute to the gigantic. We will look at an overview in this chapter, and then go deep into the many spellbinding puzzles in later pages. The evidence (based on accepted studies) I present in later chapters proves that the surprising problems I raise here are both real and severe. On the smaller scale, some unexplained ancient Egyptian artifacts (made with very hard stone like diorite and quartzite) defy reproduction when the best modern tools are used against such hard rock. Many thousands of artifacts were fashioned of these materials during the Late Stone Age.

On the gigantic scale, the construction of Egypt's Great Pyramid has long challenged human power to explain or understand. In these pages, we will see that attempts to explain the construction of the Great Pyramid with lifting devices and cutting methods do not withstand scrutiny. Many people are surprised to learn that Egyptians built the Great Pyramids—the most admired and mysterious monuments of all time—when tools and lifting devices were at the Late Stone Age level.

At that time, the strongest widely-available metal was copper, which is relatively soft. Just a few blows to fairly soft limestone will badly blunt a copper chisel. Copper wears off on the stone, and so the copper supply is quickly diminished. But the several million blocks in the pyramid complexes (consisting of pyramids, temples and other sacred architecture) are mostly of medium hardness. The blocks of the Great Pyramid are too hard to cut with copper tools.

Sand is abundant and much harder than copper, and can be used in combination with copper tools to saw rock. But the masonry of the Great Pyramid is characterized by wavy, intricate, interlocking custom-fit joints (with mating protuberances) that are not characteristic of sawing action (which produces even cuts characteristic of back-and-forth motions). This superstructure is built so that its vertical and horizontal joints typically interlock—producing super-stable, custom-fit, interlocking tiers on a gargantuan scale. Besides, the vast amount of copper needed is not accounted for by archaeological findings at the copper mines or any other available source.

If we suppose that copper tools could be sufficiently hardened to cut the pyramid blocks, then we still encounter the staggering problem of insufficient copper supplies. The shortage is that severe. But the tools found in sealed Egyptian tombs are typical, soft copper—and we will see that masonry problems associated with the pyramid complexes go far beyond what can be solved with even the hardest known metals.

Many pyramid blocks are of a hardness that can be cut with a hard form of bronze. But Egyptology has determined that hard bronze was not available to Egyptians when the Great Pyramids arose. Since the inception of Egyptology (more than 100 years ago), most Egyptologists assumed that copper tools were adequate for quarrying and carving limestone into pyramid blocks. Aided by stone-cutting experiments by masons and tool experts, Egyptologists are beginning to recognize that copper chisels are too soft and were too scarce to have been used to quarry and cut most pyramid blocks.

Egyptologists have shown that the backs of the casing blocks remaining on the three Great Pyramids of Giza conform exactly to the intricate irregularities of the front faces of the blocks behind them. The Great Pyramid was originally covered by 20 acres of massive, smooth casing blocks that angled to produce the overall pyramid shape. Before its casing was mostly stripped away in earlier centuries, the Second Great Pyramid at Giza exhibited almost that amount of casing, too. These intricately interlocking casing blocks are not accounted for by the tooling methods proposed by Egyptology. Cutting and fitting them with matching irregular surfaces on all touching sides would require the constant shifting and resurfacing of about 40 acres (this is just counting the surface area) of massive blocks for the Great Pyramids of Giza until this perfection could be achieved.

In the 5th century B.C., the Greek historian Herodotus visited the Great Pyramid when it was fully intact and its blocks were pristine and unblemished. Herodotus reported seeing a myriad of casing blocks 30 feet long covering the outside of the Great Pyramid. We must exercise caution when accepting measurements in ancient texts (the Greek world used different measurement systems). But Herodotus' report matches that of the learned Abd el-Latif of Baghdad, who visited Giza around A.D. 1200. Abd el-Latif also reported seeing a myriad of 30-foot-long blocks casing the Great Pyramid as far as the eye could determine. Ancient monoliths of this length and more still exist in Egypt and elsewhere. But Egypt's only block-lifting method during the Pyramid Age was the use of a mud-brick ramp, which is unable to support the heavy weights found high in the Great Pyramid.

The severe lack of copper or any hard metals has prompted some Egyptologists to propose that pyramid builders must have shaped the millions of pyramid blocks with stone tools—the only other kind available.[1] A critical dilemma results: Experiments show that stone tools are not suitable for producing the blocks of the Great Pyramids, either. The vast pyramid tiers had to be carefully prepared to prevent any distortions that would adversely affect the overall giant pyramid shape—a feat that would be challenging with today's most advanced tooling methods.

The four giant pyramid faces are subtly and evenly bowed inward. This is just one of the intricate, immense design patterns and instances of ultra-accuracy existing on a scale never achieved before or since. On the outer surface of the Great Pyramid, casing blocks produced the accurate angle of the Great Pyramid (most of the casing is now stripped away). Some casing joints were measured and shown to fit snugly at 1/500 inch or in perfect contact. Casing blocks are tightly form-fitted on all touching sides. It is not logical to think that this is the product of stone pounding balls and crude stone axes.

So, a primary question is how vast numbers of pyramid blocks were custom-shaped when no tools existed that are sufficient for cutting medium-hard and harder limestone. Iron was a rare metal even 1,000 years after the Great Pyramid was built, when smelting was finally introduced. Iron smelting sites are rare throughout classical ancient Egyptian history, and none are known from the Pyramid Age (when all Great Pyramids were built). No iron has ever been found within a sealed tomb of that period. The small amounts of iron that could have been available from meteorites is vastly insufficient for completing the monumental tasks. Experts estimate that the Great Pyramid alone contains over two million blocks. The Second Great Pyramid at Giza is almost as large. Besides, iron is inadequate for producing amazing masonry features we will explore.

Almost five percent of the building units found in pyramid complexes were made with granite. The many thousands of tons of small artifacts and huge, precisely-shaped building units made with granite and other hard rock types present even more severe problems that we will also explore—because these rock types are much harder than limestone.

Like the limestone, blocks made with granite in the pyramid complexes fit to the negative imprint of touching blocks on all visible sides, too. Sometimes the custom-fit separations between blocks are so fine that they are hard to detect. These precision separations are appropriately called hairline joints.

Deep in its interior, the Great Pyramid incorporates huge beams—up to 27 feet long—made with granite. There was no steel in ancient Egypt for cutting granite, and so the use of this kind of strong metal cannot explain the tight-fitting building units. These beams typically conform to one another on all touching surfaces. Blocks and beams also typically exhibit flat surfaces. Granite is so hard that today this rock is cut with diamond, which was also unknown in ancient Egypt according to all of Egyptology.

Granite can be shaped by striking it with very hard pounding balls. But the stone can crack, and so the intended granite object can be ruined. The workmanship is also extremely crude. With a great deal of effort, granite can be gradually cut with a copper saw or tube drill and sand. The results are extremely rough. But Pyramid Age artifacts made with granite show long, clean tool sweeps and ultra-precision features that cannot be the result of polishing away crude tool marks. We will explore examples that have amazed experts. Modern experiments using all manner of methods have not come close to replicating the remarkable features of finely-made ancient objects made with granite or diorite.

Some such highly-problematic Pyramid Age artifacts were studied in depth by Sir William Flinders Petrie (1853–1942), one of the founders of Egyptology. The problem is that artifacts he examined, and some that he collected, show signs of super-rapid cutting. His observations left him stunned and debating rapid cutting lines in granite and diorite throughout his whole career.

To provide a sense of what I mean by rapid cutting, consider that it requires about 10 hours of labor to cut less than 1/2 inch into hard, red Aswan granite with devices that combine copper and abrasive sand for drilling. Whereas, as astounding as it may seem, the cutting rate for one of Petrie's artifacts was calculated by a highly-skilled machinist to have been produced 500 times faster than can be performed in granite with today's diamond drills rotating at 900 rotations per minute. I know this sounds incredulous, but the artifact is real and displayed in London's Petrie Museum. Petrie's documentation and debates are found in standard, mainstream Egyptological literature. Besides, this artifact is far from being an isolated case.

Aside from the machinists Petrie consulted with and others who have since studied his findings, some masonry experts claim that crisp hieroglyphics cut into some ancient Egyptian obelisks (made with granite) are of better quality than can be achieved with modern diamond drills.

Some ancient Egyptian sarcophagi (made with granite and other types of hard stone) exhibit surface areas—covering many square feet—that are extraordinarily flat. It is very difficult to achieve the extreme flatness over surfaces larger than a few inches by grinding with abrasives. Today, the huge, flat surfaces on ancient Egyptian sarcophagi astonish masons who work with granite and other hard rocks. Expert masons I discussed the problems with admittedly cannot duplicate these artifacts with their best modern methods.

Hammering hard, tough diorite will ruin the striking surface of a high-quality modern hammer made of tough tool steel, which is stronger than regular steel. Yet, exquisite objects were made to perfection with diorite as far back as the Neolithic Period of the Stone Age. Archaeologists report finding intricately-made diorite vessels amidst the primal rubble of primitive Neolithic camp sites. Egyptologists have marveled over a myriad of ancient Egyptian diorite vessels. These objects routinely exhibit magnificent features that cannot be duplicated when using today's machining devices on diorite.

It is difficult to bore into a bed of quartzite using a tungsten carbide (next in hardness to diamond) drill bit, although thousands of pounds of pressure are applied to the tool bit. But large monolithic objects were made to perfection with quartzite in ancient Egypt. The works include 50-foot-high monolithic statues and beautifully-formed sarcophagi. Their features confounded the Egyptologists who discovered them. Sir William Flinders Petrie's mind reeled when he squeezed through a maze in a pyramid and discovered a massive sarcophagus made with quartzite that exhibits an astounding degree of perfection.

Without the advantage of any hard metals or good tools, ancient Egyptian sculptors routinely rendered diorite, quartzite, basalt and other types of hard rocks into extraordinary works of art. These objects are appreciated as unparalleled today. Some are great artistic masterpieces. Many thousands of tons of hard rock types were superbly rendered.

Other pyramid construction problems are as severe as stone cutting enigmas. Assuming the Great Pyramid was completed (or nearly completed) during the 24-year reign of Pharaoh Khufu (as Egyptologists have determined), its scale is too large to have been built with primitive stone-cutting tools and lifting methods. I am not suggesting that the Great Pyramids took more time to build than Egyptology has determined. When we examine the historical record, we find that we must explain the construction mysteries within the building time allocated by Egyptology. But staying within the historical framework poses problems of logistics and rapid construction that are unfathomable with the building system accepted by Egyptology.

Egyptology has carefully and diligently demonstrated the primitive level of technology that existed when the Great Pyramids were built, too. So, we must stick within the technological capabilities of the ancient Egyptians. The reason is that massive evidence (collected by many generations of Egyptologists) defies the existence of advanced technology in ancient times.

Several books have become popular over the past 40 years or so by asserting the existence of high technology in association with unexplained ancient stone marvels. But quarries associated with the monuments never show the marks of power saws or other high technology. Firsthand inspection in Egypt always uncovers very crude rock extraction techniques, extremely primitive tools, and rudimentary settings. Ancient tombs, writings, and rubbish heaps all show the remains of only ancient culture. Given that stunning artifacts date from the Neolithic Period to over 1,000 years after the Great Pyramid was built — a period of thousands of years — evidence of high technology would show up directly and indisputably in the Egyptian culture if it existed. Without adequate tools or substantial extra building time, or superior mechanical lifting methods, the pyramid construction mystery runs very deep.

Many theories about how the Great Pyramid was built have been offered. But there are several basic requirements any theory must meet. Theories other than the one presented in these pages do not take all of these requirements into consideration, let alone satisfy them. Most theories actually ignore most of them. Most work with a 2-1/2 ton weight average, and thereby avoid dealing with mammoth blocks that represent real weights high in the Great Pyramid. We explore the requirements in these pages to make this aspect of the construction mystery perfectly clear.

The facts I have sketched out so far show that something is fundamentally wrong with the accepted theories of ancient Egyptian masonry. The deeper we delve into details (which are proven by accepted studies described and cited in these pages), the more convincing and astonishing the masonry dilemmas become. The special means used to create the remarkable masonry work has eluded Egyptology.

The first Egyptologists were baffled by hard stone artifacts they excavated from the ruins of ancient Egypt.[2] More than a hundred years of subsequent Egyptological research has failed to explain how these same artifacts were made with the primitive means available to the ancient Egyptians. So, over the past 40 years or so, several best-selling books have proposed technologically advanced methods for explaining mysterious ancient building ruins and smaller stone artifacts that amaze researchers. But these notions are unsatisfying because they do not directly explain the creation of remarkable features of the pyramids, temples or smaller artifacts, either.[3] Caught between their contempt for these Atlantean, space-alien and other high-tech-antiquity books and their own embarrassing inability to provide a proper explanation, Egyptologists now mostly trivialize the very same problems that Egyptology has never explained.

Consequently, the masonry and engineering enigmas I present in these pages are mostly overlooked by contemporary authorities, who simply try to explain away the problems of pyramid construction. As I show in this book, unresolved masonry and construction problems are seriously misrepresented in up-to-date, authoritative Egyptological literature on pyramid building. What has happened is analogous to shoving the Great Pyramid under a rug of garguantian proportions. Once these enigmas are exposed, it becomes obvious that a fundamentally new theory of pyramid construction is imperative.

There are also severe logistical problems to contend with. We will explore some that have been unrecognized until now. We will also consider accepted experiments that have attempted to quarry, carve, hoist, and set limestone blocks with replicated ancient Egyptian cutting implements and lifting devices. When evaluated logically and correctly, these accepted Egyptological studies prove that the prevailing theory of pyramid construction is entirely unworkable. The new light thrown onto the numerous unresolved engineering and masonry puzzles spotlights the gloss with which today's experts have obscured the facts.

Some of the experiments we will explore employed metal and stone tools (often necessarily combined with abrasives like quartz sand and much harder grit) to shape rocks of the types used for ancient artifacts. We will explore specific, startling features and characteristics of artifacts that defy replication.

The solution to the long-standing riddles emerges as self-evident in the pages of this book — because I show that the collective masonry and engineering mysteries can be explained only by the special ancient technology presented here. We will see that using the brute force of machines is really doing things the hard way, and that the Egyptians had a better, far more elegant way. An extremely primitive, but extraordinarily efficient technology allowed for the production of artifacts that cannot be made any other way. The elegant technology allows for super-rapid pyramid construction, and solves all of the logistical and block-raising and cutting problems, and the manufacture of the puzzling artifacts I describe.

The Great Pyramid is the most conspicuous testament to a novel and once-sacred technology that was gradually lost to the world. Even in ancient Egypt, this technology gradually declined to the extent that there remains unsuccessful stoneworks crudely bashed out and abandoned in the Egyptian granite quarry at Aswan. Bashing rock was all they had left when they wanted to attempt to make large monuments of hard stone.

The existence of the ultra-special technology that is the focal point of this book is not speculative or theoretical. It is fully recovered in these pages. Several highly-qualified scientists with specialized expertise, positioned at major university and private research laboratories, and even one U.S. National Laboratory, have freely given their time and expertise to this body of research in the interest of science, collectively over many years. Some use the kind of highly-advanced equipment that can take stone apart atom-by-atom to uncover its secrets. The results have been very impressive, and the research is on-going. An exciting new branch of Egyptology is emerging as a result of this body of research.

With all of the above in mind, let us continue our journey of discovery by returning to the time when this very special sacred technology was at its peak. We start by exploring specifics of stunning masonry features of the Great Pyramid, some of which much later inspired the ancient Greeks to proclaim the magnificent structure as the First Wonder of the World.

✦ Chapter 2 ✦
The Great Masonry Wonder

S ituated in a desert necropolis in what is now the outskirts of modern Cairo, the Great Pyramid is historically unprecedented because of its enormous scale, precision and magnificent design complexities. Experts calculate that the stupendous monument incorporates about 2.3 million massive blocks—totaling an estimated 93.5 million cubic feet of limestone. Before its capstone and upper tiers were removed, it soared to about 500 feet.

The maximum error between the lengths of its sides is less than one percent, although each of the four sides measures 756 feet long at the base of the Pyramid. More stunning, its 13-acre foundation was measured to be level to 7/8 inch from corner to corner (some think the slight imperfection is due to settling). This scale of leveling has never again been achieved in history. Even small stone buildings are difficult to level with modern methods.

Having long studied the technological level of the Pyramid Age, Egyptologists deduce that workers built the Great Pyramid without the use of hard metal tools or the wheel as a means of lifting or transportation. No evidence of the block and tackle exists for the Pyramid Age.

Specifically, Egyptologists found that workers built the Great Pyramid almost a millennium before the wheel was introduced in Egypt for transportation. Given that ancient Egyptian wheels were always very flimsy, they would be useless for making hoists for lifting heavy weights. Ancient Egyptian wheels cannot bear heavy strain. The Great Pyramid was built centuries before the appearance of the block and tackle in Egypt, according to all known archaeological and historical evidence. Bronze, needed for metal tools strong enough to cut medium-hard fossil-shell limestone, was introduced about 800 years after the Pyramid Age. Iron, a much stronger metal, came into use even later. Iron was a precious metal until the Greek occupation of Egypt (after 332 B.C.).

Estimating a ten-hour workday for building the Great Pyramid, Egyptologists calculate that an average of one block was raised and set in place every two or three minutes. This is a staggeringly rapid pace. To complete (or nearly complete) the Great Pyramid within the reign of the pharaoh, this astounding construction rate had to continue for about 23 or 24 years. The reign of its builder, Pharaoh Khufu, lasted that long (from about 2551 to 2528 B.C.). Even for a short duration, modern experiments (placing monoliths that do not even approach the upper end of the range of weights found in the Great Pyramid) have not been able to duplicate this rapid construction rate.

Ignoring Real Block Weights

There is a fundamental problem with almost all studies that calculate lifting blocks for the Great Pyramid: They use averaged block weights of only 2.5 tons each. The pioneering founder of Egyptology, Sir William Matthew Flinders Petrie, calculated this average by estimating the number of blocks in the structure to be about 2.3 million (he arrived at this figure while taking into consideration the 27-foot-high mound of rock incorporated into the base of the Great Pyramid). Petrie averaged the pyramid blocks at 50 x 50 x 26 inches (arriving at about 2.5 tons apiece).[1] While there is nothing wrong with averaging block weights in and of itself, most theorists use average weights instead of real weights. This eliminates

2. The 13-square-acre foundation of the Great Pyramid extends under its edges. Its visible portions show that it was constructed to conform to the uneven bedrock below. Despite settling and earthquakes, the careful measurements taken reveal the near-perfect leveling of the foundation.

the difficulties of proving how thousands of much heavier units, weighing up to 73 tons, can be raised to at least 160 feet. Some of the heaviest blocks on the exterior of the Great Pyramid were incorporated at about 500 feet above ground level.

Read almost any authoritative book on pyramid building and you will be told that raising the blocks poses no serious problems. Some books assert that building the Great Pyramid was relatively easy. But these books present highly distorted facts by not working with real weights (see the beam weights in this chapter and the actual block heights in Appendix 1). We delve deeper into this issue below.

Massive Blocks at Great Heights

Supposedly authoritative literature obscures another truth. It is commonly held that block sizes diminish at a fairly constant rate as the Great Pyramid ascends. The is assumed because from the base to the 17th tier, block heights do progressively diminish from about six down to two tons. But above the 17th tier, some tiers are made of very large blocks. Most calculations ignore these massive blocks higher in the Great Pyramid.

Until recently, the standard book used for Egyptian building methods was *Ancient Egyptian Masonry: The Building Craft* (1930), by Somers Clarke and Reginald Engelbach. Much has been learned since its publication about 80 years ago. The newest and most complete and authoritative replacement is *Building in Egypt* (1991). This new Egyptological standard was written by one of the foremost experts on Egyptian stone masonry, Dieter

Arnold of the Metropolitan Museum of Art in New York. Arnold based his new standard on prominent studies of recent decades. In *Building in Egypt*, Arnold says the following about the diminishing block sizes in Khufu's (Greek: Cheops) Great Pyramid:

> At the pyramid of Cheops, the height of steps (which corresponds to that of the casing) starts with 1.49 meters from the ground and ends with 0.58, 0.56, 0.57 and 0.54 meters near the top.[2]

His statement is technically correct. But it gives the impression that block sizes gradually diminish at a fairly constant rate in the entire Great Pyramid. Whereas, some of the largest blocks were incorporated into tier 201 near the top (almost 500 feet high). Arnold does briefly acknowledge that some of the tiers (courses) in the core masonry (the main building blocks) of the Great Pyramid comprise larger blocks:

> For the casing blocks [remaining casing blocks correspond to course heights] of the Cheops Pyramid, Petrie noticed that the height decreases in general but that some courses in between are considerably higher. Such courses appear in a completely irregular pattern in distances of 6, 7, 8, 9, 10, 12, 14, and 16 courses.[3]

Arnold's book does not specify how tall these larger tiers are or the considerable added engineering problems posed by elevating the taller blocks to great heights. Later in these pages, I quote his assertion that raising blocks to great heights posed no special problems.

Arnold's book does not mention the majority of unresolved difficulties of constructing the Great Pyramid. He wrote the new standard on ancient Egyptian construction from a Middle Kingdom perspective—when no Great Pyramids were built. Middle Kingdom pyramids are mostly mounds of rubble today because of poor construction—built when the so-called Pyramid Age was over. So, few of Arnold's readers will recognize the magnitude of unresolved engineering and masonry problems we are going to see here.

Tier Measurements Show Real Block Weights

Measurements of the tiers establish the exact heights of the Great Pyramid's blocks (see Appendix 1). These tier measurements are critically important because they help show the real weights of pyramid blocks all the way to the top. There are no measurements of the widths or depths of the blocks, and so we can only estimate weights based on their stability of placement and on what is typical for more fully exposed and fallen pyramid blocks.

Tier measurements were first taken when Napoleon and his army were stranded in Egypt during the French Revolution. In 1798, Napoleon and his army invaded Egypt. Napoleon had members of the Commission of Arts and Sciences with him. During their stay in Egypt, savants of the Napoleonic Egyptian Expedition accurately measured the Great Pyramid's tier heights. Later, early pioneers of Egyptian archaeology verified the measurements. These investigators include Colonel Howard Vyse and J.S. Perring. In the 1970s, French Egyptologist Georges Goyon confirmed the tier measurements.[4]

The measurements show that tier 19 increases in block size. This is not apparent from ground level because of distortion created by perspective when we look up from the Great Pyramid's base. At tier 35, block sizes dramatically increase again. Tier 35 is made of blocks just over four feet tall and of varying lengths. Because they are situated so high above ground, their placement presents a much greater challenge than blocks at the base measuring about five feet high and more than seven feet long.

Though not as sharp, sudden increases in block sizes occur in a number of other tiers. Included are tiers 67, 98, 118, 144, 180 and others high in the Great Pyramid. Tier 201 was dismantled since Napoleon's crew measured it. But their measurements show that it was taller than tier four at the bottom. Some tiers have random blocks that take up the height of two tiers. Very heavy beams appear in the interior masonry. Several weighing up to 73 tons are situated 160 feet above ground level and higher, at the level of the King's Chamber and above. To form the tip of the Great Pyramid, a missing capstone of unknown weight rested at nearly 500 feet.

We can appreciate the dramatic difference between calculating with real block weights as opposed to weight averages of only 2-1/2 tons. Keeping in mind that the Great Pyramid was built during the 4th Dynasty, here is an example of this generalization. These are Arnold's remarks about the diminishing block sizes:

> In the period from the Fourth to the Twelfth Dynasty, the shape and size of the casing blocks did not vary significantly. The lowest course usually has the highest steps, starting with 2 to 3 cubits and slowly decreasing with every step upward until it measures about 1 cubit at the top. This was clearly due to the problems of lifting.[5]

Anyone aware of the tier measurements will immediately know that Arnold's statement cannot apply to the 4th Dynasty's Great Pyramid, wherein course 35 is taller than course two—and the upper tier 201 was taller than tier four. In modern times, no one has tackled raising massive blocks nearly 500 feet high on a mud-brick ramp. For reasons we will explore in the chapter on ramps, the task is not feasible.

The Great Pyramid's Design Complexities

To study the Great Pyramid's masonry designs, I put its tier height measurements on a chart. I wanted to see how many tier heights there are. My chart shows that the tiers conform to only 73 heights. This demonstrates a high degree of tier height uniformity, given that there were originally roughly 200 tiers. This dramatic statistic accentuates the Great Pyramid's design complexities and presents a severe challenge to the accepted construction theory. It produces enormous logistical problems (about which I say more below). It also produces precision that has not been properly appreciated by pyramid theorists who claim that building the Great Pyramid by cutting and raising huge limestone blocks was relatively easy.

Giza limestone is craggy and full of fossil shells. This makes cutting it to perfection more problematic than cutting medium-hard limestone that has an even texture. Egyptologist Georges Goyon's measurements show that the tier heights are very precise. He rounded his measurements off to a half centimeter. So, the 73 different tier heights are perfect to a half a centimeter or less. This kind of accuracy on such an enormous scale is beyond extraordinary.

When Goyon climbed the northeast corner of the Great Pyramid in the 1970s and measured its tiers, he produced charts showing the exact same peaks and plateaus recorded by Napoleon's scholars. Like them, Goyon found that the tier heights suddenly increase and diminish in 19 sharp fluctuations. Goyon tried to explain this difficult-to-achieve design pattern.

He proposed that it results from quarrying technique.[6] He reckoned that quarrymen cut along the bedrock's strata* to more easily produce rough building stones. If so, then the blocks could be relatively uniform, with their heights corresponding to the distance between strata. But Goyon's idea does not hold up under investigation.

---

* Strata are sheetlike layers that form in the limestone due to slight interruptions in the sedimentation process.

In 1984, Joseph Davidovits and Hisham Gaber measured the strata in the quarry associated with the Great Pyramid. Their measurements show that the heights of the Great Pyramid's blocks are shorter than the distance between the strata. The same is true for the blocks of Giza's Second Great Pyramid (built for Pharaoh Khafra, c. 2520–2494 B.C.).[7]

So, it makes no sense to cut rock the way Goyon proposed. A quarryman cutting along the strata would have to cut the blocks down more. That would require a double cutting routine. So, Egyptology has not explained how pyramid builders overcame the difficulties of creating the design pattern shown by the tier measurements. Egyptology has not shown how such a super-astounding level of precision could be achieved on such an enormous scale.

Another masonry pattern further complicates matters. In 1984, Joseph Davidovits photographed the south and west faces of Khafra's Great Pyramid at the upper levels. Davidovits clearly photographed the upper levels directly below the casing blocks that still cover the tip.[8] He photographed almost 2,000 blocks in tiers with undamaged masonry. His study shows that long blocks are positioned next to, and above and below shorter blocks. This arrangement staggers the location of joints, creating a stable, interlocking superstructure. The design pattern Davidovits demonstrated also vastly complicates the logistical and technical problems involving cutting, storing, sorting, and selecting pyramid blocks at Giza.

Another pattern shows extreme perfection. The vast, rough faces of the Great Pyramid were exposed when its casing blocks were stripped centuries ago. This damage reveals its stepped structure. Its vast stepped faces are slightly and evenly bowed in. These curvatures are very difficult to detect when standing at its base. From that vantage point, all four faces appear to be flat. The concave curves can only be seen from the air and at certain vantage points at Giza. The curves are regular and very subtle. This design greatly compounds the problems of building the Great Pyramid with the means proposed by Egyptology.[9] It also greatly adds to the logistical problems of cutting, storing, sorting, and selecting pyramid blocks.

Petrie discovered a remarkable design complexity. He surveyed the faces of the Great Pyramid and found that the mean optical plane that touches the most prominent points of the blocks shows an average variation of only 1.0 inch.[10] The near-perfect plane shows how closely blocks conform to the angle of the Great Pyramid's gigantic sides. Although today's Egyptologists advocate that there are few, if any, remaining pyramid construction enigmas, the features we have considered so far are incredible. They show just how much is unappreciated by those who advocate that the construction problems are overrated.

A Logistical Nightmare

We encounter gargantuan problems when considering cutting over 200 tiers to about 73 heights (we do not know the heights of any that were above tier 201) prepared to within 1/2 centimeter. Consider the enormous tasks of quarrying, shaping, hauling, sorting, and storing so many correctly-sized blocks. At Giza, many thousands of blocks are visible to the naked eye. About half of them can be seen on the surfaces of the Great Pyramid. Blocks had to fit into regularly-made, concave faces and conform closely to the enormous outer edges of the tiers.

The inadequacy of Pyramid Age (Late Stone Age) tools for cutting medium-hard to hard fossil-shell limestone blocks to specifications vastly complicates the problem. Limestone has a strong tendency to crack, most especially when quarried by primitive means (like hitting it with stone pounding balls). In that case, salvaging smaller units establishes block sorting and storing on an even larger scale. Given the complexities of such an enormous operation (involving millions of blocks incorporated into the Great Pyramid in less than 25 years), achieving the 19 sharp height fluctuations and other features described would be challenging with the best modern means.

Another consideration is the high rate of breakage that occurs with all limestone quarrying operations. Even if cracked and broken blocks can be pared down for incorporation into smaller tiers, the constant reshaping and shuffling of multiton blocks further complicates the sorting and storing quagmire.

To form the overall giant pyramid shape, blocks had to be prepared and situated so that their top surfaces conform to the tier immediately above. One of the amazing features of the Great Pyramid is the way large tiers, covering acres, correspond to one another other in such a way as to prevent distortion of the overall pyramid structure. The amazing features described below should also be factored into the enormous problems of logistics.

Perfection of the Casing Blocks

The Great Pyramid is famous for its vast number of tight-fitting joints. There are now gaps between some blocks because mortar, used to cushion them against earthquake stress, has disappeared. But there is no room for this durable, thick pink mortar between the tightly-fitted blocks. These custom-fit blocks actually conform to the shape of neighboring blocks. This feature cannot be accounted for by construction solutions accepted by Egyptology.

Many pyramid and temple blocks exhibit joints (the area where two tight-fitting stones adjoin) that deviate from the vertical plane. Some joints are long and wavy or oblique. Some are even L-shaped. But their fit is very snug along the entire lengths of their joints. In some Old and Middle Kingdom (c. 2575–1640 B.C.) structures, 30 percent of the blocks exhibit such formfitting oblique joints.[11] Achieving the placement of massive stones with oblique joints confounded researchers who tried the feat on a small scale.

The main pyramid blocks were made with local limestone. Most of the limestone at Giza is formed by the consolidation of round, flat seashells about the size and shape of coins. Its grade is course and rough. The casing blocks (most of which were removed centuries ago) on the outer surface of the pyramids are very fine-grained. Their surfaces are so smooth and reflective of sunlight that early European travelers often mistook them for polished marble.[12] The casing blocks once covered the coarse limestone tiers, converting these stepped structures into pyramids with smooth, flat faces. The casing blocks were made with corners squared at 90-degree angles to a high degree of accuracy.

Remaining casing blocks on the Great Pyramid weigh from six to 16 tons each. Egyptologists estimate that there were originally an estimated 115,000 casing blocks forming the smooth outer faces of the Great Pyramid. To create these vast faces, workers used about 2,379,842 cubic feet of fine limestone. One of the mysteries of Egyptology is how each casing block was so closely custom-fitted on all sides with neighboring blocks on such a massive scale. Egyptologists have measured the remaining casing blocks on the Great Pyramid to fit to a mean opening of 1/50 inch. The joints fit as closely as 1/500 inch or in perfect contact.[13]

The backs of casing blocks on the three Great Pyramids of Giza conform exactly to the irregular front faces of the backing blocks behind them. This snug, interlocking fit is amazing by modern standards. The scale on which workers applied the casing blocks to the Great Pyramids renders their joints historically unprecedented. Remaining casing blocks on Khafra's pyramid are even larger on average than those on the Great Pyramid. Some built into Khafra's pyramid fit together by interlocking tongue-and groove joints.

In *The Pyramids and Temples of Gizeh* (1883), W.M.F. Petrie discussed casing blocks remaining at the lower north side of the Great Pyramid. He described cement between them that is paper-thin and found between tight-fitting joints that did not need to be filled. Petrie described what he called an "almost impossible" task of controlled handling on a gargantuan scale:

> Several measures were taken of the thickness of the joints of the casing stones…the mean thickness of the joint there is .020; and, therefore, the mean variation in the cutting of the stone from a straight line and from a true square, is but .01 on length of 75 inches up the face, an amount of accuracy equal to the most modern opticians' straightedges of such a length. These joints, with an area of some 35 sq. ft. each, were not only worked as finely as this, but cemented throughout. Though the stones were brought as close as 1/500 inch, or, in fact, into contact and the mean opening of the joint was 1/50th inch, yet the builders managed to fill the joint with cement, despite the great area of it, and the weight of the stone to be moved—some 16 tons. To merely place such stones in exact contact at the sides would be careful work; but to do so with cement in the joint seems almost impossible.[14]

Although the Great Pyramid's casing blocks are now few in number, a much older account reveals that such tight-fitting joints, filled with paper-thin cement, originally existed on an enormous scale. Although paper-thin, this cement is as hard and impervious as the blocks. It proves the existence of a sophisticated cement technology that was lost to Egypt in later times. The older account attesting to casing blocks separated by the highly durable, paper-thin cement is by the accomplished Abd el-Latif (A.D. 1162–1231) of Baghdad, who visited Giza:

> These pyramids are built of large stones between 10 and 20 cubits long by a breadth and thickness each of 2 to 3 cubits; but most especially worthy of admiration is the extreme nicety with which these stones are fashioned and disposed one above the other. The courses fit so exactly that not even a needle or a single hair can be thrust between the joints. They are cemented together by a mortar which forms a layer the thickness of a leaf of paper. With the composition of this mortar I am totally unacquainted.[15]

As el-Latif's report matches Petrie's accurate account of the close jointing and cementing, it is likely very reliable. The hard and extremely durable cement el-Latif witnessed was no longer made in Egypt in his time. By comparison, modern portland cement, from which today's buildings are made, lasts no longer than 150 years under ideal environmental conditions. But the paper-thin cement both Petrie and el-Latif observed has endured for thousands of years.

Like el-Latif, the 5th century B.C. Greek historian Herodotus reported a myriad of casing blocks 30 feet long.[16] Their reports are at odds with the size of blocks seen today at the base of the Great Pyramid. Presumably, in ancient times sand encased the lowest tiers, covering the shorter blocks we see today. Egyptologists speculate that a dense blanket of sand covered areas of Giza so that the 60-foot-high Sphinx was completely buried (and that this may explain why Herodotus did not mention the Sphinx). Today, only a few casing blocks remain on the north and south sides of the Great Pyramid. But el-Latif and Herodotus witnessed the monument when it exhibited all of its formfitting casing blocks, which they reported were up to 30 feet long.

Although we know of monolithic statues and obelisks with a much greater length (in height), we know of one pyramid block that long today. It measures 29 feet long and about six feet high. It is incorporated into the entrance of the 5th Dynasty pyramid of Unas, at Saqqara. Given that the average weight density of limestone is 152.5 pounds per cubic foot, the Unas block must weigh between 450 and 500 tons (I do not have its thickness dimension). The ceiling of the King's Chamber of the Great Pyramid features beams up to 27 feet long, situated at almost half the height of the monument. Consider that blocks at or near that size range were witnessed in great numbers by Herodotus and Abd el-Latif. Compare the problems of raising the heavier weights with those of raising the 2.5-ton block average used in almost every pyramid-building calculation found in "authoritative" books on the construction of the Great Pyramid.

There are actually longer blocks in ancient architecture. Three are found in the Temple of Baalbek, in Syria. One measures 64 feet long and 14 feet square. But hauling a great many huge pyramid casing blocks on barges from across the Nile presents a truly incredible scenario. So does raising, cementing and fitting them to correspond to each other in shape, and so that they produce flat, correctly angled faces covering many acres.

Mammoth-Scale Leveling

The foundation of the Great Pyramid dazzled the first Egyptologists. Slabs of fine-grained limestone are sunk into shallow bedrock. The slabs make up a gigantic square platform that surrounds the Great Pyramid and extends under its edges. The platform has a discrepancy so slight from a true square that its accuracy is extraordinary, given its 13-acre size. What is more remarkable is that this huge platform is so accurately level as to be off only 7/8 of an inch from the northwest to the southwest corner. The slight unevenness might be due to settling.[17] The undersides of the platform slabs conform to irregularities in the bedrock below. That is, platform slabs fit snugly into particular spots in the irregular bedrock, like pieces in a gigantic three-dimensional puzzle.[18]

Although this feature is astounding by today's stone cutting standards, the magnificent platform-foundation of the Great Pyramid is only addressed in Egyptological literature in terms of how level surfaces were measured with ancient means.[19] The same literature ignores the germane question: How could masons accurately level and custom-fit hard limestone slabs on this vast scale with only abrasives and copper and stone tools? There is no doubt that the limestone is hard, because the platform tolerates the tremendous weight of the Great Pyramid.

How could masons cut the undersides of these level platform slabs to conform exactly to irregularities in the bedrock on such an enormous scale? We see this kind of accuracy in the tiers, too, which correspond to each other so that they are level over a vast number of acres. The overall picture astonished early Egyptologists like W.M.F. Petrie. The Great Pyramid exhibits precise right angles on a super colossal scale. A gradual incline from casing block to casing block produced huge, beautifully-formed triangular pyramid faces that measured about five acres each. The four corners of the Great Pyramid each tapered into triangles that rose almost 500 feet high and met perfectly at a point at the top.[20] The ancient workers made it all to unparalleled precision.

ᓚᔎᓫᔲ Chapter 3 ᔲᓫᔲᔎᓫ
Incredible Construction Speed

The speed at which Egyptology has determined the Great Pyramid was built is unrivaled by modern block-raising experiments. Egyptologists use an inscription in the Great Pyramid to help estimate the time it took for the entire monument to be completed. A vault above its King's Chamber shows Pharaoh Khufu's reddish-brown painted cartouche (consisting of his royal names enclosed by an oval-shaped frame). The inscriptions date this cartouche to the 17th year of his reign. Because the cartouche is located at about half of the height of the Great Pyramid, Egyptologists reckon that the monument soared to that level by year 17 of Khufu's reign.

Assuming these hieroglyphic writings are authentic (as Egyptologists believe them to be), by Khufu's 17th year on the throne his pyramid was well underway. Its magnificent Grand Gallery and the exquisite King's Chamber were already completed—so that the most admired features and about half of the height of the pyramid were finished by the time Khufu had reigned for 17 years. Given that two-thirds of the height of the Great Pyramid contains 96 percent of its total bulk, we see that most of the monument was finished by the 17th year of Khufu's reign.

The construction speed is staggering, especially given the overall perfection and design complexities and the amount of material employed. Experts have estimated that the Great Pyramid contains a total volume of 93.5 million cubic feet of limestone masonry. Some contemporary Egyptologists propose that this figure should be modified downward some. Manipulating figures serves as a mechanism for easing engineering problems that are not reconciled by the accepted construction paradigm.

Khufu's dated cartouche works against the idea of doubling or tripling the Great Pyramid's construction time to ease inexplicable construction problems. To reconcile the number of blocks that had to be set per day during Khufu's 23-year reign, Dieter Arnold proposed extending the life span of Khufu and other prolific pyramid-building pharaohs:

> There can only be one solution…namely to increase the lifetime of the pharaoh…[1]

An Egyptologist requires tangible chronological information to adjust the chronology of the pharaohs that was so carefully researched over many years by other Egyptologists. Arnold's proposal lacks such evidence. It also ignores evidence to the contrary—the dated cartouche suggesting that the Great Pyramid was well on its way to completion by year 17 of Khufu's reign.

Egyptology asserts that each pyramid was finished, almost entirely if not completely, during one pharaonic reign. A completed ritual chamber, such as the King's Chamber in the Great Pyramid (situated at about half of the Pyramid's height), was necessary for a pharaoh's funerary rites. Religious doctrine held that the soul of the heaven-sent pharaoh must ascend to his throne among the stars. The ascension point was a ritual chamber in the Primordial Mountain. The pyramids are re-creations of the Primordial Mountain, the rock that religious tradition held was the foundation of the world.

History offers many examples of this long-honored burial custom. For instance, thousands of years after the Pyramid Age, King Herod the Great (73–4 B.C.), the Roman-backed king of Judea, honored this cross-cultural tradition. Herod was buried in a huge structure resembling a volcanic mountain, a re-creation of the Primordial Mountain. A Chinese example is the massive earthen burial mound of the Chin Dynasty's Emperor Shin Huang Ti, built around 210 B.C. in the northeastern province of Shanxi in China.

Ancient Egyptian religious doctrine held that chaos would quickly rule if their god-kings did not safely ascend to the heavenly throne. The Egyptians made every effort to build the pyramids in time, since few ancient Egyptians lived more than 35 years.

The one-reign construction period held by Egyptology badly clashes with an attempt to build a scale model of the Great Pyramid. In 1975, Japanese engineers from Waseda University, in Tokyo, built a 34-foot-high pyramid four miles south of the Great Pyramids of Giza. Their simplified model did not include any interior halls or chambers. Based on their engineering experiment, the engineers calculated that it required not 23 years, but 1,200 years to build the Great Pyramid.[2]

A 1,200-year construction period is far more problematic than Dieter Arnold's mere doubling or tripling of the lengths of the reigns of pharaohs who built Great Pyramids. Ancient Egyptian history could not have accommodated more than a 100-year construction period for the Great Pyramid. A brief historical reconstruction shows why.

Pharaohs of the 5th and 6th Dynasties stripped blocks from the earlier Great Pyramids to build their much smaller pyramids. Within about 100 years of the completion of the Great Pyramid, anarchy and social collapse ensued in Egypt. The end of the 6th Dynasty (c. 2152 B.C.) marked the end of the classical civilization of Old Kingdom Egypt. The next centuries of relative impoverishment were not conducive to pyramid construction. The pyramid necropolis underwent serious decline.

By the end of the Middle Kingdom (c. 1640 B.C.), Egypt was occupied by a foreign power called the Hyksos. During the Hyksos occupation of Egypt, the pyramid complexes were gradually despoiled of masonry and probably plundered of treasure.

Later, the Hyksos invaders were driven from Egypt (after 1550 B.C.), ushering in the period Egyptologists call the New Kingdom. During the 18th Dynasty (which started the New Kingdom), the state treasury neglected the maintenance of northern Egypt, where the pyramids are located. The neglect was by pharaohs who came into power far to the south. The 18th Dynasty pharaohs from Thebes, deep in the south, proclaimed this city Egypt's new capital. Thebes was the focus of many lavish new construction projects. These Theban pharaohs promoting the status of Thebes had little incentive to glorify the area of the old northern Memphite capital that fell to the Hyksos. The pyramids were built in the necropolis that served Memphis and other northern cities like Annu (the city called On in the Bible and Heliopolis by the Greeks). It was not until a millennium after the construction of the Great Pyramid that more work was finally carried out on the badly dilapidated pyramids. The restoration was conducted by the administration of the famous 19th Dynasty Pharaoh Ramses II.[3]

Ramses' family ties were in the north, and he adorned Memphis and the north with some of Egypt's most sumptuous constructions. His administration repaired several pyramids and restored pyramid maintenance cults.[4] We see that history cannot accommodate a 1,200-year construction period for the Great Pyramid.

Two different disciplines (engineering and Egyptology) have examined the pyramid-construction problem from entirely different perspectives—and come to badly clashing conclusions. The tremendous difference of opinion is significant.

Owing to the serious historical constraints, we cannot assume that the Waseda team's estimate of a 1,200-year construction period took place. But had the Waseda team factored in associated monuments at Giza—like the 1/4-mile-long causeway that once led from

Khufu's Valley Temple to his Great Pyramid—they may have estimated an even longer overall construction period. If the Waseda team would have factored in the design complexities covered in the last chapter, the would have estimated an even longer construction period. Whereas, if Egyptology is correct, then a highly-efficient method—one that Egyptologists have not considered—was used to build the Great Pyramids very rapidly.

An estimate by the German Egyptologist Rainer Stadelmann underscores the rapid construction rate: Stadelmann estimated that, in only 60 years, almost 318 million cubic feet of limestone were consumed to build the 4th Dynasty's Great Pyramids.[5]

Some people try to solve the rapid construction puzzle by suggesting that the Great Pyramid is older than the 4th Dynasty. Proponents of this idea speculate that Pharaoh Khufu usurped a far older, pre-Egyptian monument. They suggest that survivors from Atlantis, the fabled sunken island, built the Great Pyramid.[6]

If proponents could prove that the Great Pyramid dates to an earlier period, then the time it took to build it would become an open question. Although some popular books promote an Atlantean origin, there is no sound evidence favoring a construction date before the 4th Dynasty.

Aside from pure speculation, some information comes from a radiocarbon dating test. Bits of wood and charcoal were tested, since these materials appear in the thick pink mortar found here and there on pyramids and associated monuments. The mortar samples came from a number of Old Kingdom monuments, including the Great Pyramid.

A team including Mark Lehner, a faculty member of the University of Chicago's Oriental Institute, undertook the initial project in 1984–5.[7] Lehner collected the samples and suggested the means of testing. The radiocarbon-14 project dated the Great Pyramid up to 400 years older than the 4th Dynasty. But this team did not recognize that pyramid mortar cannot be accurately dated with the radiocarbon-14 method.

A problem is that pyramid mortar was made with carbon-based material, namely sodium carbonate (a salt present in the Egyptian salt combination called natron). Because natron contains a form of carbon, it pollutes radiocarbon dating tests. Carbon pollution can skew test results.[8]

To make pyramid mortar, gypsum, clay, chalky limestone debris and natron were mixed with water. So, natron was carried in solution into the organic debris in the mortar mix.[9] Natron permeated the wood and charcoal bits that were tested. But regardless of the source, the strange results of Lehner's radiocarbon dating project suggest pollution.

In Lehner's tests, the first pyramid ever built, attributed to the 3rd Dynasty Pharaoh Zoser, dated as though it were built later than the 4th Dynasty Great Pyramid.[10] These results sharply conflict with chronology developed through many years of careful Egyptological field and textual research. Worse, one of Lehner's test results indicates that mortar near the top of the Great Pyramid dates older than mortar near the bottom.[11]

Workers applied the mortar at the bottom of the Great Pyramid first. So, this mortar should date as the oldest. The strange results can suggest that the Great Pyramid was built from the top down—which is hardly a likely scenario. Mark Lehner's book titled *The Egyptian Heritage: Based On the Edgar Cayce Readings* (1974) advocates that the Great Pyramid is a 12,500-year-old remnant of survivors from Atlantis.[12]

Lehner promoted an Atlantean origin for the Great Pyramid throughout most of his career as an archaeo-Egyptologist. This notion is fueled by the lack of a sorely-needed, responsible, comprehensive explanation for the Great Pyramid's construction enigmas. Until the true explanation is popularized, Atlantean enthusiasts will interpret masonry features that defy orthodox explanations as the product of a technologically advanced Atlantean civilization—one that they contend the Great Pyramid itself proves must have existed.

Lehner's radiocarbon-14 results (which date the Great Pyramid up to 400 years older than the 4th Dynasty) fit neither the Atlantean nor the orthodox historical framework. We cannot properly construe his flawed test results as evidence justifying a need to lengthen the construction period for the Great Pyramid. So, no rethinking of the puzzle is warranted based on Lehner's tests.

Rather than out of time and place, the Great Pyramid fits perfectly into the evolution of ancient Egyptian architecture. There was a fairly steady increase in block size from the first pyramid (built for Pharaoh Zoser in the 3rd Dynasty) to the Great Pyramid. In general, workers built pyramids increasingly taller from the time of Zoser's pyramid to that of the Great Pyramid, too. The fabulous corbelled walls in the Grand Gallery of the Great Pyramid show another sign of design evolution. They have profiles like giant upside-down staircases. Those in the Great Pyramid are more grandiose than the corbelled rooms in previous pyramids.[13] The elaboration suggests steady architectural progression.

Large pyramids, including Snofru's Red Pyramid at Dahshur, immediately preceded the Great Pyramid. The Red Pyramid is very similar in construction to the Great Pyramid—also suggesting design progression. The enormous Great Pyramid of Khafra at Giza immediately followed the construction of Khufu's Great Pyramid. Khafra's pyramid is almost as tall and massive as the Great Pyramid. Khafra's Great Pyramid represents the beginning of an architectural decline that became increasingly dramatic as time went on.

No solid evidence has been put forth to justify an Atlantean origin for the Great Pyramid. The same is true for the Sphinx. To eliminate any doubt, I evaluate the evidence for redating the Sphinx and Great Pyramid later in this book. Without justification for moving the date of construction of the Great Pyramid backward in time, theorists cannot legitimately explain its rapid construction rate.

When reckoning the problems of constructing the Great Pyramid, experimenters rarely raise heavy stones to appreciable heights. To build their 34-foot-high pyramid near Giza, Waseda University engineers resorted to modern means, including a forklift. They did not attempt to build interior features or cut a level limestone foundation. They poured portland-cement-based concrete to make their foundation. Steel tools were used to quarry blocks.

The Waseda crew increasingly fell behind its deadline. To save time, the team resorted to using dynamite to quarry blocks, trucks to haul them, and a forklift to hoist them into place. So, even with modern means, the crew was unable to keep up with the designated construction pace. Workers had to complete the pyramid by casting concrete blocks. Of the 700 blocks (with a total weight of 25,353 tons), 300 were poured concrete.[14]

The Public Broadcasting System (PBS) science series Nova later attempted and filmed the construction of a much smaller pyramid. The televised Nova program is titled This Old Pyramid. It first aired as a 90-minute special over PBS stations on November 4, 1992. Nova's goal was to address unresolved problems of constructing the Great Pyramid. Nova incorporated fewer than 200 blocks, ranging in size from half a ton to two tons, into an unfinished, 18-foot-high miniature pyramid. The Nova film repeatedly states that their workers used only ancient means to build the miniature pyramid. The film strongly implies this throughout. But only one 1/2-ton stone, needed for the on-camera demonstration, was raised up the miniature ramp manually.[15] The rest were hauled and placed with a front-end loader (a construction vehicle with a hydraulically operated scoop in front).

Compare the over two million blocks in the Great Pyramid, placed hundreds of years before evidence of the use of a simple block and tackle in ancient Egypt. Nova also used heavy steel hand tools to cut and quarry the softest limestone the quarries at Tura have to offer.[16] Compare the exactness of the Great Pyramids, built when only primitive tools were available.

Nova's pyramid blocks had crude tool marks all over their faces. The corners of their blocks were chipped. Gaps between the blocks measured up to 0.2 inch wide. Compare joints as close as 1/500 inch in the Great Pyramid, or in close contact along whole joints. Compare the 13-acre foundation of the Great Pyramid, measured to be 7/8 inch off level. Nova did not attempt to cut a limestone foundation.

For inclusion in this book, Systems Engineer Mike Carrell contemplated the problem of the level foundation and tiers of the Great Pyramid. Mike Carrell prepared this statement stressing the critical importance of a level foundation and accurate tiers:

> Among the remarkable features of the great pyramids are their great weight and the levelness of the tiers. At Giza, the pyramids rest on a hard limestone bedrock, which must have been chosen because it is reasonably level. The first tier of blocks must transmit their weight and the weight of all above them to the bedrock. To do this there must be exact conformity of the lower surfaces of the blocks with the actual surface of the bedrock. Any misfits will concentrate the burden on a smaller area, increasing the stress, and possibly resulting in a fracture.

> The same considerations apply to the horizontal interfaces between each successive layer. They must mutually conform to transmit stress, and they must be level, lest errors accumulating from one tier to the next cause distortions in the shape of the pyramid. Producing these necessary features in limestone with the tools available, within the recorded time, presents a seemingly insurmountable task.

Nova's pyramid building experiment did not attempt to meet these requirements.

It is not uncommon for an engineer to introduce a device and claim that it can solve the construction enigmas of the Great Pyramid. Ingenious devices range from simple to highly elaborate. But most have nothing in common with the technological level of the Pyramid Age. Egyptologists call the 80-year span in which all the Great Pyramids arose (c. 2575–2494 B.C.) the Pyramid Age. It falls into the Late Stone Age's Chalcolithic period (beginning about 4000 B.C.). People of that time had tools made of copper, stone and/or wood, and they had abrasives like sand. The simple modern mechanical devices theorists propose bear no relationship to Pyramid Age implements. Even those that do seem feasible are unworkable because they depend upon a mud-brick ramp, which is entirely unworkable.

Theorists tend to focus on a particular engineering or masonry problem without considering the full range of enigmas. Consequently, proposed solutions are at odds with features of the Great Pyramid and/or with Pyramid Age technology. When responsible new engineering systems are proposed, they come under considerable scrutiny—assuming that they comply with the orthodox paradigm of pyramid construction. Dieter Arnold made this comment:

> But at what point one method or another was used can only—if at all—be determined by detailed technical studies of some of the thirty major pyramids. Before this is accomplished, the most ingenious and scrupulous system developed on the drawing board is nothing but one more example of unproven speculation.[17]

We continue with the magnificent interior features of the Great Pyramid and the conundrums they pose.

🏛 Chapter 4 🏛
Enigmatic Interior Features

T he grand entrance of the Great Pyramid is a prominent feature on its north face at 55 feet above ground level. It is very impressive because of a double layer of conspicuously large beams that form its outer wall. These beams lean against one another at their tops to form a triangular arch. Each of these four beams measures about ten feet in height. In the interior of the Great Pyramid, the flat ceiling of the entrance passage also exhibits heavy beams.

Ascending Passageway and Block Lowering

When entering the Great Pyramid, we soon come to its 129-foot-long Ascending Passageway. Its upper portion is finely executed with tight-fitting blocks made from limestone. Three large blocks made with granite—together 15 feet in length—were placed to plug this remarkable passageway at its lower end. The placement of these plugs has been the subject of much debate. Most theorists think they were stored in the Grand Gallery (above the Ascending Passageway), and then slid down this 129-foot-long expanse into position.[1] But the plug blocks are less than 1/2 inch narrower than the Ascending Passageway itself.[2] So, a realistic way of lowering them into position has yet to be devised or demonstrated.

One problem is that these blocks fit very closely with the ceiling. In some places, there is only 1/10 inch clearance.[3] In general, the gap between the tops of the plugs and the ceiling of the corridor is only about 1-1/3 inch.[4] To prevent them from slipping out of position, workers made the plugs slightly wedge-shaped. The Ascending Passageway is intricately custom-fit to their shape.[5] Large, unbroken portions of these blocks show their custom, precision fit with one another, too. Engineers are mystified: They proclaim it a staggering feat to slide these blocks—each about five feet long and weighing about seven tons—down 129 feet so that they did not become not hopelessly jammed. The blocks are also in exactly custom-fitted positions.

Various pyramids and later tombs exhibit dramatic examples of blocks in narrow spaces at the bottom of long, sloping shafts. These extremely tight places allow only a few men to work at a time. For example, several pyramids are equipped with underground burial chambers containing large, heavy sarcophagi.

The only way into these chambers is through long, sloping rock-cut shafts. Some of the narrow bedrock shafts are fully paved with tight-fitting blocks made with limestone or granite. In several pyramids, blocks plugging sloping corridors filled the corridors very exactly. In the 12th Dynasty pyramid of Pharaoh Senworset I (c. 1971–1926 B.C.), six or seven plug blocks made from granite weigh up to 20 tons each.[6]

The Descending Passageway's Extraordinary Precision

The Great Pyramid's Descending Passageway is famous for its accuracy. Although it is 350 feet long, and runs down into the bedrock at an angle of 26 degrees, it measures only 1/50 inch off square along its entire course.

The floor, walls and ceiling of the Descending Passageway were once very smooth surfaces. But now the floor is so damaged that it is very uneven. The Descending Passageway

3. The Great Pyramid of Khufu is shown in the foreground, with Khafra's Great Pyramid in the background. Casing blocks still cover the upper tiers of Khafra's pyramid.

leads to a rough subterranean chamber called the "Pit." It was crudely bashed out of bedrock and left unfinished.

Enormous Girdle Stones

The Great Pyramid is equipped with massive installations called 'girdle stones.' These hollow blocks, made with limestone, are spaced at intervals along the Ascending Passageway and reinforce it. The Ascending Passageway runs straight through the girdle stones, which range from 12 to 15 feet long.[7] Altogether, there are four full girdle stones and three half girdle stones. They are thought to be a feature unique to the Great Pyramid—and one that makes it far superior to all others. Engineers wince at the thought of raising, installing and fitting the huge hollow blocks so that they can support the Ascending Passageway. These huge masses are never taken into account by studies attempting to explain away construction problems.

The Magnificent Grand Gallery

The Ascending Passageway leads to the most grandiose feature of any pyramid, the Grand Gallery.[8] The Grand Gallery is such an imposing, impressive structure that climbing it leaves an unforgettable impression on the senses. This magnificent construction measures 157 feet long and 28 feet high. Its colossal, finely-executed walls, made with white limestone, were elaborately fashioned with great care. The smooth walls are corbelled and made of seven courses of giant blocks. The magnificent corbelled walls look like great upside-down staircases that start at the ceiling.

The design makes the width of the Grand Gallery at its ceiling equal to half of that at its floor. The Grand Gallery's ceiling is also corbelled—made of overhanging block courses that approach one another from opposite sides. The design leaves a center gap that is bridged by a single block. Engineers recognize the tremendous complexities of building this corbelled ceiling so that it slopes at a 26 degree angle.

The Extraordinary King's Chamber

The Grand Gallery leads up to the famous King's Chamber—an extraordinary room made entirely (walls, ceiling and floor) of blocks that were finely executed with red granite.[9] Its walls incorporate 100 huge blocks made in five courses of nearly equal height. These wall blocks are estimated to weigh up to 50 tons apiece, and are very smooth, flat, and exact.

There are almost 300 joints between the blocks, most of which fit so closely that they are called 'hairline' separations. Many are barely detectable to the naked eye. The King's Chamber measures about 34 feet from east to west, 17 feet from north to south, and it is 19 feet high. The bottom course of wall blocks terminates below floor level. The disconnected construction isolates the floor so that shifting and settling do not cause deformation. The blocks making up the floor are so large that only 21 of them cover the whole floor. The construction of the finely-crafted masonry of the King's Chamber has long posed a glaring mystery.[10]

Pyramid Age copper chisels will not cut hard red Aswan granite, and no harder metal was available. Other options are lapping or sanding. But it is hard to imagine lapping 50-ton granite blocks so that they conform to each on all contact surfaces, with hairline joints, and have flat faces that form smooth walls. A project to reproduce such blocks by sanding granite has not been undertaken. The heavy beams of the King's Chamber, described below, produce one of the most vexing problems of pyramid construction.

Khufu's Sarcophagus and the Rapid Cutting Mystery

The King's Chamber contains no furnishings other than Khufu's hard sarcophagus. It was made with granite and weighs about three tons. It rings like a bell when struck with a hammer. Similarly, the entire King's Chamber is extremely resonant.[11] This is probably because its blocks are very homogeneous.

The prominent early figures of Egyptology, William Petrie and Alfred Lucas, hotly debated enigmatic artifacts like the cutting lines on Khufu's sarcophagus. Petrie was the first to recognize that these cutting lines prove that the ancient masons cut through the sarcophagus at an extraordinarily rapid rate. His observation prompted more recent and unorthodox theorists to assert that highly-advanced power tools must have been used. But this idea has no legitimate correlation with ancient history.

The debate between Petrie and Lucas went on for 35 years. It concentrated on how the Egyptians could have accomplished vexing masonry tasks. We can get an idea of the severity of the problem they debated by looking at experiments preformed since their time. Stonemason Denys Stocks conducted experiments showing that Aswan granite can very gradually be cut with copper tubular drills and abrasive sand.[12] It took his team one week (I do not know the length of their work days) to cut through one inch of granite using a copper tube drill and an abrasive. His crew (consisting of two men per saw) gradually cut a core from granite at Aswan, in southern Egypt. But their core was covered with intersecting striation marks.

The resulting parallel striations were of various widths and depths, and their edges were rough. The means Stocks used do not produce rapid cutting or crisp features. So, how Khufu's sarcophagus was rapidly cut through is unresolved by Stocks' experiments. We will delve more deeply into this problem in a later chapter.

The Exquisite Queen's Chamber

Below the level of the King's Chamber, the so-called Queen's Chamber was built at the 25th course. This room measures 19 feet long x 17 feet wide x 15 feet high. J.P. Lepre eloquently described the Queen's Chamber this way:

> The jointing of the limestone blocks comprising this chamber is so nearly perfect that many of them are practically invisible to the naked eye. Therefore, one receives the mistaken impression that the chamber is carved out of a solid piece of rock rather than built of many individual blocks fitted together. This absolutely perfect jointing is even more astonishing when one considers that the monument is close to 5,000 years old and has experienced numerous earthquakes throughout the centuries.[13]

Enormous Interior Beams

Heavy beams and blocks in the interior of the Great Pyramid pose unresolved engineering problems. One reason is that any construction ramp must be able to support the heaviest building units of the Great Pyramid. Competent engineers recognize that earthen ramps are not strong enough to support the transport of the main blocks, plus the weight of the men needed to raise them, on a massive scale. The construction beams are far larger, and would require much more manpower to raise than the average-sized pyramid blocks.

Highly-experienced engineers who seriously studied the problems believe that only solid masonry could provide the necessary strength to raise numerous blocks on ramps.[14] But the ramp designs consume far too much material for solid masonry to be practical for building the Great Pyramid. A very compact earthen ramp may accommodate a limited number of pyramid blocks. But the ramp will quickly disintegrate when bearing numerous heavy weights. Earthen ramps are perfectly suitable for the bulk of the masonry of small pyramids made mostly of small blocks. But Egyptology is without a workable explanation for how blocks could be elevated to build the Great Pyramid. We will explore this problem in depth in a later chapter.

The problem with ramps becomes most conspicuous when we consider the nine mammoth granite beams making up the ceiling of the King's Chamber. The beams measure up to 27 feet long. Most of these enormous beams are estimated to weigh about 54 tons. Some are estimated at about 70 tons. These are the largest building units of the King's Chamber. Collectively, the weight of the granite slabs that make up the flat ceiling is more than 400 tons.[15]

The ceiling of the entrance passage to the King's Chamber incorporates another large beam made with granite. Measuring 10 feet long by eight feet high, it weighs about 45 tons. The problem of elevating such weights becomes evident when we consider that these enormous monoliths are situated about 160 feet above ground level. The collective problems involve how workers could transport beams up to 27 feet long from the Aswan quarries (about 600 miles south of Giza), and then elevate them to the level above the King's Chamber.[16] The heaviest building units made with granite known at Giza are the 56 built into this general area of the Great Pyramid.[17]

Above the King's Chamber, several cyclopean beams make up the remarkable system of five stress-relieving chambers. The pointed roof of the topmost of these chambers reaches to about half the height of the Great Pyramid. This pointed roof is made of 11 pairs of sloping beams each measuring over 20 feet long. They are each estimated to weigh about 36 tons. Lower in the monument, the ceiling of the Queen's Chamber is made of six pairs of immense beams.

Strong Evidence for Undetected Chambers

I first published this evidence for hidden chambers in 2004, in *The Egyptian Pyramid Mystery is Solved!* (Volume 1). The shafts in the Great Pyramid are extremely long, complex architectural features that required a great deal of extra building effort. These long shafts also provide strong evidence of hidden chambers near the King's Chamber, as follows:

The southern shaft of the Queen's Chamber became famous after a robot (designed by German roboticist Rudolph Gantenbrink) climbed it and found it blocked by a slab made with limestone. Later, another robot drilled through this slab (popularly called Gantenbrink's Door) and found yet another slab behind it.

A 2002 Fox-National Geographic TV special revealed this second slab. After the program was over, one of the technicians involved in the project decided to send the robot up the northern shaft in the Queen's Chamber. He commented in a subsequent news report that the robot found that the northern shaft deviates from its straight course to the exterior masonry to accommodate the corbelled walls of the Grand Gallery. When I learned of his report, I immediately recognized strong evidence of hidden chambers near the King's Chamber.

The evidence of a hidden area near the King's Chamber is based on the above-mentioned news report combined with J.P. Lepre's observation of the shafts of the King's Chamber. He found two bends in the southern shaft of the King's Chamber and four in its northern shaft. We can put two and two together and recognize that these bends should accommodate hidden areas, just as the bends in the northern shaft in the Queen's Chamber bends to run around, rather than through, the walls of the Grand Gallery. Here are J.P. Lepre's valuable observations:

> The north channel is rectangular in form, being 5" high by 7" wide, while the south air channel has a stranger configuration. Within the chamber itself is a dome-shaped, representing a quite wide 18" by 24" opening. After a few feet it maintains this basic domeshape, but is now reduced to a 12" by 18" aperture which, after a few feet more, narrows to approximately 8" by 12". It maintains these dimensions as it passes through the pyramid's masonry to the 101st outside course, but takes two sharp bends in the process. In the first of these turns it changes its shape from dome to oval, and in the second turn (or its third line of travel), from oval to rectangular or oblong. This is a very strange design, to say the least, one which is classically demonstrative of the architect's propensity to dramatically shift design when it is least expected.

> To add to this idiosyncrasy is the fact that, at the first turn or bend, this air channel changes its direction, inclining to the south-southwest from true south; it then alters its direction once more, further southsouthwest, at its second turn. The entire direction and configuration is so bizarre that it has thus far defied any logical explanation. In contrast, the north air channel of the King's Chamber maintains its basic rectangular shape throughout its long journey to the exterior of the edifice. Yet it, too, changes its direction during the course of its travel, and takes, not two, but four distinct bends

or turns. For although its basic upward angle is not altered, it deviates, first to the north-northwest, then back to north, then to the north-northeast, finally returning to true north. Thus it curves in a semicircular pattern, and then returns to its original direction.

The reader may wonder how so many turns in such small channels could possibly be sighted by the author or any other viewer; certainly the apertures spoken of are much too tiny to admit a man—or even a very small child, for that matter. But recall that the beginning 6' section of the southern air channel measures 18" by 24" at its commencement inside the burial chamber and 12" by 18" where it reaches its first bend. In the confines of this space it is possible for a small to medium-sized person to crawl forth, and by stretching, to view the two sharp bends which the channel then takes.

In respect to the northern air duct, it is of course not possible to be afforded such a view from the interior of the burial chamber, as the 5" by 7" duct cannot admit the body of a viewer, and even if it could, then no one would sight four turns of the duct from a single vantage point.

Fortunately for the interested observer—though sadly for the pyramid—although the first 8' of this channel has remained perfectly intact, the distance of the next 30' or so has been excavated by inquisitive explorers who broke through to this section and tunneled northward, following the direction of the channel. They did not begin their excavation where the air channel commences, in the King's Chamber, but broke into the west wall of the short passage leading to that chamber, where an iron grating has now been placed by the Egyptian government to ward off further observation. Within this cavernous tunnel, one can immediately see the first, second and third bends which the air duct takes in this confined area. By stretching one's self at the northern, more narrow end of this tunnel, the fourth bend in the channel can also be seen. Were it not for this fortuitous but barbarous quarrying we would never been made aware of the interesting features of this northern air vent.

While the unorthodox curve in the southern air vent is puzzling, in the northern air channel the direction is even more eccentric, with that channel turning once again to its original direction. One's initial reaction to this deviation is that this duct was shifted and then brought back shortly thereafter in order to avoid something in that area of the King's Chamber north wall. Could we then deduce that there may be a cavity or a passage of a sort in that location that the architect wished to keep secret? This is, of course, pure speculation. Only one thing is certain: that the architect had a purpose in diverting and then redirecting this channel.[18]

In short, putting J.P. Lepre's keen observations together with the *National Geographic* project information revealing that the northern Queen's Chamber shaft definitely deviates its course to avoid the Grand Gallery, we can recognize strong evidence of a hidden area near the King's Chamber of the Great Pyramid.

We continue with very serious challenges to the orthodox theory of pyramid construction that theorists have not previously recognized.

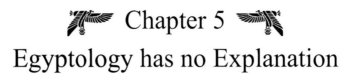

Chapter 5
Egyptology has no Explanation

The size of the Giza limestone extraction sites associated with the Great Pyramid places an intolerable strain on the prevailing construction theory. So does the geology of Giza. Here we explore situations that are strange and impossible when the accepted paradigm of pyramid construction is applied.

The Khufu Quarry Mystery

Some years ago, Mark Lehner conducted a mapping project at Giza.[1] Lehner measured the limestone quarry used to build the Great Pyramid. He found that the amount of limestone in the Great Pyramid roughly equals the amount removed from this quarry. Lehner's calculation convinced him that workers quarried all the main building blocks for the Great Pyramid from this quarry. But neither this conclusion nor his later revision of it compute with the overall picture at Giza.

Block quarrying is a very wasteful process. An estimated four blocks will crack during quarrying for every usable block. This general estimate was provided to me by limestone geologist Robert L. Folk, Professor Emeritus of the University of Texas, in Austin. If we assume that cracked blocks are salvageable for making smaller blocks, then we may arrive at a rate of two cracked per every usable block. In that case, the Giza quarries would be about twice as large as measured by Lehner. But the problem is far from being that simple.

The amount of waste rock will vary considerably depending on the quality of the limestone and the quarrying methods. In the 1800s, quarrymen extracted roughly-shaped blocks by lining up in quarries with eight-foot-long steel bars. They would strike up and down with the bars, and then twist them to break away large chunks of stone. The strength of steel afforded an advantage over ancient Egyptian block quarrying methods.

Today's quarrymen use chain saws to section rock faces into blocks. They detach blocks with wedges and hydraulics or air pressure. Extracting truly large blocks is so cumbersome and difficult that strategically-located dynamite charges are used.

Regardless of the method used, block extraction begins only after waste rock is removed from the top surface of the quarry. Waste rock is unsuitable for making blocks. Today, quarrymen use dynamite to perform this initial clearing of waste rock. Once a face of suitable limestone is exposed, a good limestone quarry will yield 30 percent waste with today's technology. But this 30 percent figure is calculated only after up to 30 feet of top waste rock has been removed. The percentage of waste rock can vary dramatically. A poor quarry might have a 50 percent net yield after the removal of waste rock. But at Giza, we find a whole different scenario: The good-quality limestone was left untouched and remains today.

Almost without exception, the limestone extraction sites at Giza contained only poor-grade limestone. This limestone is not suitable for building construction. It is like the body of the Sphinx, which flakes off constantly and is prone to water damage. Nonetheless, this supply of poor-quality limestone was heavily exploited during the Pyramid Age. But the Great Pyramid is made of good-quality limestone. Owing to the quality of its blocks, the Great Pyramid is expected to remain standing for 100,000 years. The fragile Sphinx is predicted to collapse within generations if something drastic is not done to rescue it. These circumstance may seem very strange, and so we will return to these important topics.

In 1988, Joseph Davidovits and I pointed out that the quarry associated with the Great Pyramid is too small to have furnished enough blocks to build the monument.[2] Mark Lehner, in *The Complete Pyramids* (1997), later agreed:

> The calculated amount of stone removed - c. 2,760,000 cu. m (97.5 million cu. ft) - compares neatly with the total 2,650,000 cu. m (93.5 million cu. ft) in Khufu's pyramid. Too neatly in fact. There should be more missing that this: modern masons and quarrymen estimate that between 30 and 50 percent of stone was wasted in the extraction of stone. However, the quarry extends an unknown distance to the south, beyond the line of Menkaure's causeway...And much stone was taken from the Central Wadi...[3]

Lehner thinks that these other unmeasured areas can adequately satisfy the problem we raised. We will see why his proposal does not even come close.

The Sphinx's Head

Egyptologists are not sure if there were two or three geological layers at Giza. The bottom layer is hard limestone. The middle layer is weakly-bound limestone. It was mostly exhausted in ancient times. The top layer (if such a layer existed) now consists of the head of the Sphinx. Egyptology speculates that the head of the Sphinx is the remains of a layer of hard rock that was all quarried away to build the Great Pyramids.

If we accept this premise, then it is likely that this layer was not very expansive. The reason is that when geochemist Dietrich Klemm and Egyptologist Rosemarie Klemm gathered a great many samples from the Great Pyramids, they found that only 2.5 percent of the blocks are made of stone as hard as the Sphinx's head. So, the theoretical layer does not solve the problem of quarry size. Some geologists think that the Sphinx's head was formed from a small knoll instead of a large layer.

While the limestone body of the Sphinx is very fragile, its head is very hard. Only a tiny percent of the pyramid blocks tested are that hard.[4] The Klemms' findings and what geologists typically see at Giza suggest that any rock layer (or knoll) from which the Sphinx's head was crafted was not extensive.

The Block Quarrying Enigma

Based on the crude tool marks all over quarry walls at Giza, Dieter Arnold deduced that pyramid blocks were quarried with simple stone hand tools.[5] We know from many archaeological finds that hard rocks, including granite, chert, basalt, quartzite, and hard limestone were used to make crude ax heads. Workers affixed ax heads to wooden handles with leather strips.[6]

Stone axes make a different type of impression on the quarry walls than metal chisels with flat cutting edges. So, based on the existing tool marks, Arnold reckoned that stone axes or broken pieces of flint were somehow used to cut trenches in the bedrock until blocks were isolated on all four sides. Next, he suggests, the workers undercut blocks to separate them from the quarry floor. This method generates enormous amounts of waste rock because the trenches have to be wide enough for men to crouch in when separating the blocks from the quarry floor.

Stone axes are unsuitable for quarrying even roughly-shaped limestone blocks. During the filming of Nova's *This Old Pyramid* documentary, Mark Lehner tried to shape a block made from the softest limestone of Tura. Lehner's ax (replicated to Dieter Arnold's specifications) was made of diorite, a very hard, tough rock. The limestone block Lehner worked on

4. *Quarry near Khafra's Great Pyramid: It shows stumps left over from the removal of limestone blocks. It is the only quarry at Giza that looks like this. Its volume equals three percent of Khafra's pyramid. Petrie was the first to notice that there is vastly too little evidence of block quarrying at Giza to acccount for pyramid construction.*

had already been pre-shaped with a modern steel tool before he touched his diorite ax to it. But Lehner's repeated behind-the-scenes cutting attempts were futile. He finally discarded the diorite ax and used a modern steel tool.

Primitive stone ax heads, held to handles with banding, are unsuitable for the much heavier work of making trenches in bedrock to extract blocks. These tools will fly apart when a hard blow is struck.

Flint is very hard, but it is brittle and will break when repeatedly struck against a hard surface. The best tool the ancient Egyptians had for making trenches was the pounder, a heavy chunk of hard rock. Pounding balls will not neatly slice rock. But workers can use them to bash out pits and trenches. Pounding on limestone tends to crack it, and this produces much building waste. Given the enormous amount of rubble generated by pounding balls and other primitive means of quarrying, Giza should furnish evidence of vastly larger worked areas than Lehner has accounted for.

Lehner directs our attention to other potential area of block quarrying at Giza. But the problems are so severe that the overall picture elicits disbelief when the standard pyramid construction paradigm is accepted. The worst problems are these: First, the pyramid blocks are of a better quality than the rock extraction sites at Giza. Second, the pyramid blocks look different than Giza limestone. Third, when we factor in all masonry structures at Giza, the quarry waste would be vastly more than Lehner reckons. Giza had to furnish limestone for three large pyramid complexes. Fourth, there are vastly insufficient signs of blocks quarrying at Giza. So, there is no true accounting of where blocks could have been quarried at Giza. We examine this set of problems. Later in these pages we will take up a fifth problem: How blocks can be quarried with crude picks is not answered by Egyptology.

The Missing Rock Quagmire

Certain that Pyramid Age Egyptians did not have iron tools for detaching blocks from the quarry floor, Egyptologists opt for more primitive methods. Some suggest that quarrymen used long wooden levers. But this system requires much room for men to maneuver in, resulting in an increase in the size of quarry trenches. Some advocate that pounding balls were used. But this method will increase the number of cracked blocks and generate more quarry waste.

A great deal of stone was consumed to build all structures in the Giza pyramid complexes. They include temples and long causeways. Causeways were built to reach from pyramids to their Valley Temples near the Nile. Khafra's causeway is about 1/4 mile long and about 15 feet wide. Khufu's great causeway no longer exists. Herodotus was very impressed with it when he visited Giza in the fifth century B.C.

He reported that Khufu's long causeway was made of smooth, fine-grained blocks. Herodotus wrote nothing about the core blocks in the causeway (these blocks were probably not yet exposed). But they were most likely of a coarse limestone grade like the main pyramid blocks. All of the coarse-grade limestone in Giza structures is presumed to come from Giza. The fine-grained casing, which was not local to Giza, was reserved for the inner and outer facings of monuments. So, we can expect that a tremendous number of coarse-grade blocks were incorporated into Khufu's mammoth causeway: Herodotus considered the enormous structure as, "...not much inferior, in my judgment, to the pyramid itself."

Pyramid complexes were secluded behind high masonry walls. We do not know how large Khufu's walls were because little was left of them in the early days of Egyptology. We know that the walls secluding Zoser's Step Pyramid complex at Saqqara measured a square mile. They were made with limestone, and are 30 feet high. Such expansive structures weigh heavily on the problem of the size of Giza quarries. At Giza, there are three Great Pyramid complexes.

Another consideration adds to the quarry size mystery. The standard theory of pyramid construction assumes that the Great Pyramids were built using enormous construction ramps. Making a ramp for the Great Pyramid requires a staggering volume of material.

Master Builder Peter Hodges determined that a ramp must be made of solid masonry to be strong enough to support the transport of the Great Pyramid's masonry. He had in mind the core masonry, and I already described the larger girdle stones, beams up to 27-feet long, and massive blocks incorporated as high as tier 201. A ramp's masonry must be strongly secured, too, so that blocks do not slip out of place under the heavy loads. Building such a ramp places a tremendous demand on the quarries—vastly more than building the Great Pyramid itself.

The Great Pyramid contains about 93.5 million cubic feet of limestone. The volume of a stone ramp depends upon its slope. Peter Hodges determined that to successfully raise blocks for the Great Pyramid, the slope must be 1:10. He determined that any gradient more steep is unworkable. The Great Pyramid is 480 feet high. Multiply that by ten, and the ramp's length becomes 4,800 feet long—and the whole length must be made of blocks massive enough to create unfaltering stability.

Ramps made of stone rubble cemented with clay have been found attached to some of the smaller pyramids. But these pyramids mostly incorporate blocks small enough to be carried by one or two men. Many Egyptologists assume that a much larger mud-rubble ramp was scaled up to build the Great Pyramid. But engineers who have seriously studied the problems insist that only a solid stone ramp would be strong enough to raise the massive blocks incorporated into the Great Pyramid. Even without factoring a ramp in with all the masonry that originally existed, we have a picture of how badly the accepted theory of pyramid construction is at odds with what we find at Giza in terms of quarry size.

The Geological Mismatch

The Giza areas where rock was extracted consist of weakly-bound limestone, like the body of the Sphinx. The Sphinx's body is so fragile that it flakes off constantly. This is not true for pyramid blocks. The Sphinx's body has such a high clay content that it is prone to water damage. The pyramid blocks are of far better quality. The parts of the Sphinx that are hard limestone are its head and some area at the foot (the bottom geological layer).

Bedrock walls at Giza expose the layers of limestone where rock was removed. So, we know what blocks cut from this bedrock will look like. Various studies showed the fundamental geological differences between the Giza quarries and the pyramid blocks.[7] Collectively, the studies show that the pyramid blocks at Giza look different than the bedrock and are of a different quality. Because of the distinctly different appearance between the pyramid blocks and the quarry walls, some researchers concluded that pyramid blocks must have been transported from a distant site. That would create vexing engineering and logistical nightmares for the accepted methods of pyramid construction. It is not even established that a suitably deep harbor existed at Giza for ferrying large blocks to the site.

The first study was undertaken with M. Edme Francois Jomard (1777–1862), General Commissioner for the Napoleonic Scientific Expedition, with geologist Francoise Michel de Roziere. The observations appear in Jomard's *Description de l'Egypte* (1809–1830).[8] The book includes a drawing of pyramid limestone. It is made of coinlike seashells scrambled in the rock matrix. This drawing is typical of all the blocks in the pyramid and temples of Giza. But scrambled shells do not characterize Giza bedrock. The bedrock is characterized by normal sedimentary layering. In other words, the coinlike seashells lie flat in the bedrock.

Later, W.M.F. Petrie spent many seasons at Giza studying the problems he encountered.[9] Giza quarries were not yet cleared in his day. Had there been matching limestone at Giza, we can expect he may have been satisfied. But he could not find sufficient signs of block quarrying at Giza to account for the Great Pyramid. So, we look at this mystery before considering more geological studies.

Missing Signs of Block Quarrying

Now that Giza is clear of stone rubble, we can closely examine places where rock was extracted. A quarry next to Khafra's Great Pyramid shows the removal of blocks. The quarry has trenches and stubs left over from block quarrying. But the volume of blocks removed equals only about three percent of Khafra's pyramid.

A huge rock extraction site is associated with Khufu's Great Pyramid, too. Lehner showed that it roughly equals the size of the Great Pyramid. The problem is that there are very few signs of block quarrying there.

Petrie recognized that there is not enough evidence of block extraction at Giza, and wanted to know where most pyramid blocks could have come from. He carefully searched for miles around the Giza area for a limestone outcrop where whole blocks were removed. But he found none. He asserted that all of the stones must have come from across the Nile—from more than 15 miles away in the Mokattam hills.

A serious problem arises because Dietrich Klemm later analyzed fossil shells at Giza. He determined a definite match between shell types in the Great Pyramid's blocks and those at Giza where rock was extracted (the area measured by Lehner). So, Klemm concluded that Khufu's blocks were quarried there. But this only deepens the mystery, for the following reasons: First, there are insufficient signs of block quarrying there (Khufu's quarry is not characterized by trenches and/or stumps). Second, this limestone does not geologically match the pyramid blocks. The bedrock is of poor quality; the pyramid blocks are of good quality. The bedrock shows normal sedimentary layering; the pyramid blocks are instead made up of scrambled shells.

Jumbled shells are a striking characteristic of the Giza pyramid complexes. It is difficult to find a nummulitic* block in the Giza pyramid complexes that does not exhibit scrambled shells (the exceptions are bedrock protrusions incorporated into monuments). Both the bedrock and many thousands of building blocks can be carefully inspected at close range at Giza. Fossil shells normally lie flat in sedimentary limestone. So, Giza bedrock is normal and typical in this respect.

In *The Great Pyramid in Fact and Theory* (1932), William Kingsland—who did not always agree with Petrie—agreed that the pyramid blocks do not look like Giza limestone:

> The Core Masonry is composed of limestone of varying quality; some of it as pure as that of the Casing Stones, but a good deal of it is what is known as nummulitic limestone, as it contains large quantities of fossil shells resembling coins. It all appears, however, to have come from the Mokattam Hills on the opposite side of the Nile, from the quarries of Masara and Tura.[10]

So, both Petrie and Kingsland recognized that the main pyramid blocks (with the large coinlike shells) do not match the geology of Giza. Both thought that an enormous number

---

* In limestone, the nummulite shells are fossilized discs, which are shaped like coins. Their appearance inspired their name, which comes from the Latin word nummus, meaning coin. In bunches, they resemble a handful of coins, and those at Giza are unusually large, up to the size of a quarter. These organisms once lived near the bottom of the sea that covered much of Egypt and northeastern Africa 50 million years ago. As nummulites died, their shells built up on the ocean floor, often into large banks. At Giza, their petrified shells are solidified into the limestone layers of the bedrock.

of blocks must have been imported to Giza from elsewhere. Hauling so many blocks from afar puts an intolerable strain on logistics and other aspects of the accepted ideas of pyramid construction.

The closest quarry showing that an enormous number of nummulitic limestone blocks were quarried is far from Giza. It is in Middle Egypt, at the quarry called Zawyet Sultan on the east bank of the Nile, near el-Minya.

Another study was made in the 1980s by geologists from Japan's Waseda University. They wanted to test W.M.F. Petrie's assertion that the Great Pyramid's main building blocks were ferried to Giza from afar. So, they compared Giza bedrock with the Great Pyramid's blocks. The team concluded that the nummulitic blocks of the Great Pyramid are different than Giza limestone:

> [the Great Pyramid blocks are]…hard and highly viscous [and the] characteristics of the limestone are different from those of the limestone of the site…[11]

During their study, the Waseda geologists did not have time to try to determine if matching limestone could be found at another quarry far from Giza.

Another study was made in 1984 by Joseph Davidovits and Egyptian geologist Hisham Gaber. They compared Giza pyramid and temple core blocks with the Giza quarries.[12] Joseph Davidovits' theory of pyramid construction is the focus of this book. It solves all of the enigmas I am explaining. Like the other researchers, Davidovits and Gaber observed that Giza bedrock does not match the nummulitic pyramid blocks. They found that the jumbled shells in pyramid core and backing blocks (immediately behind the casing) contrast sharply with the sedimentary layering that characterizes Giza bedrock.

Given that this is such an important point, in 1990, I arranged for confirmation by Robert L. Folk, a leading sedimentation expert. Folk invited petrographer Donald H. Campbell to join us in our investigation of Giza and Saqqara. Folk and Campbell were unable to find pyramid or temple blocks at Giza with sedimentary layering. Robert Folk confirmed that the shells in the pyramid and temple core blocks at Giza are jumbled. He observed normal sedimentary layering in the bedrock at Giza. We looked closely at the walls of the huge rock extraction sites associated with pyramid construction.

These various studies clearly establish the dilemmas: The accepted paradigm of pyramid construction cannot account for the geological difference between the bedrock and the main pyramid blocks. But transporting a vast number of blocks to Giza from a distant site involves insurmountable tasks. There is no evidence at Giza to support the importation of so many blocks. Excavators have amassed a tremendous amount of evidence about the activities at Giza 4,500 years ago, including many small tombs, a bread factory, and even a myriad of tiny fish bones left over from the meals of workers. But there is no direct evidence of block transport: There is no evidence of heavy river barge transport, or even transport sleds, or of the remains of a huge, solid construction ramp. There is not enough evidence of block quarrying at Giza to account for quarried and carved masonry structures at Giza. The rock extraction sites are too small to account for the masonry structures at Giza, too. Assuming the existence of a solid masonry ramp strong enough to support the raising of heavy weights for the Great Pyramid would place an extra tremendous burden on the problem of quarry size.

The Critical Lack of Building Waste

The lack of building waste at Giza presents another anomaly when the accepted paradigm of pyramid construction is applied. A high amount of breakage occurs during block quarrying. So, there should be millions of cracked and broken blocks at Giza. But they do not exist.

Historical and early Egyptological reports tell of pyramid tiers that were dismantled from small pyramids at Giza. We learn that blocks were torn off and dumped nearby. Collectively, the blocks that fell or were torn from the pyramids are relatively few compared with the great number of waste blocks that should exist at Giza.

A myriad of fragments of 4th Dynasty artifacts have been found at Giza, including bits of vases, sculptures, faience and even perishable mud-brick. Given the presence of these artifacts, how can several million broken blocks vanish without a trace?

The small Queens Pyramids at Giza are made of small blocks. These blocks are of a size that might come from recycling or paring down larger blocks that broke. But these pyramids are too small to have absorbed the vast amount of stone from broken blocks. It is normal for a large number of broken blocks to be found near ancient buildings made with quarried stones. This is not the picture we have for Giza.

The Romans and Arabs removed fine limestone blocks from the nearby ancient capital of Memphis. Romans heated the blocks to make lime for cement. But the nummulitic limestone of Giza is not suitable for calcining into lime. It is too full of large fossil shells to be good for lime making. So, burning limestone to make lime is not the answer to this mystery.

Large scale recycling is not the answer, either. No study, based on actual statistics, has addressed the problem of how much stone could be recycled. But it is hard to imagine recycling so many broken blocks into later buildings: The reason is that the number of broken blocks absent from Giza is much greater than all stone in Theban monuments built over a 1,500-year period in later times. Besides, the Theban monuments are made of sandstone. The normal amount of building waste left from quarrying limestone blocks for Giza walls, causeways, pyramids and temples can be expected to equal vastly more stone than all other Egyptian architecture put together. But this block waste does not exist.

Limestone is prone to cracking and chipping, especially when quarried and shaped with primitive Pyramid Age tools. But blocks had to be very accurately made, given the 73 tier heights (accurate to 1/2 centimeter) of the Great Pyramid and the enormous design patterns I described.

Given that every block-quarrying operation generates a great deal of waste blocks, it may seem strange that evidence suggests that there never were heaps of waste blocks at Giza. Ancient travelers touring Giza did not report heaps of waste blocks. Herodotus did not report cracked, chipped or broken waste blocks in the 5th century B.C. In the 1st century B.C., the Greek historian Diodorus Siculus was struck by the lack of waste blocks:

> ...and the most remarkable thing in the account is that, though the constructions were on such a great scale and the country round about them consists of nothing but sand, not a trace remains either of any mound [construction ramp] or of the dressing of the stones, so that they do not have the appearance of being the slow handiwork of men but look like a sudden creation, as though they had been made by some god and set down bodily in the surrounding sand.[13]

Piles of broken blocks were not reported by the 1st century Roman naturalist Pliny the Elder, either. In 64 B.C., the geographer Strabo reported heaps of fossil-shell rubble, but no piles of abandoned blocks.[14]

It is unlikely that peasants took several million broken blocks to built house foundations. Houses were made of dried mud-brick down to Roman times. Large areas of Giza were covered in sand for most of recorded history, making abandoned stones highly inaccessible. Sand blows in from the Libyan Desert and builds up rapidly. Without constant maintenance, encroaching sands will bury the 60-foot-high Sphinx in short order.

The upshot of all this is that we are confronted with the use of a special construction method that did not generate quarry waste. The real method used to build the Great Pyramid complexes of Giza accounts for the seemingly strange geological circumstances I described at Giza, too. Constructing the Great Pyramid is not as theoretically simple as Egyptology assumes. Building the Great Pyramid was not basically a matter of cutting mostly 2-1/2-ton limestone blocks from a Giza quarry and hoisting them up a mud-brick ramp, and incorporating a more modest number of larger blocks and beams, and ferrying casing blocks from Tura. Giza presents giant, vexing mysteries that dissolve only when the correct theory of pyramid construction is applied.

Chapter 6
Egyptian Masonry Marvels

While the Great Pyramid is by far the best known example of enigmatic masonry, many other examples attest to the use of a special technology that was lost. Egyptologists found the kind of treasure they never imagined possible when exploring regions of Zoser's 3rd Dynasty Step Pyramid at Saqqara. They found vessels so surprising as to cause astonishment and awe. Most of the more than 30,000 vessels found in Zoser's pyramid date to earlier times. These vessels are made of very hard rock types. A great many are made of diorite. Experts marvel at but cannot explain how, with only abrasives and primitive hand-tools at their disposal, Predynastic and Early Dynastic Egyptians fashioned the most perfect and hardest stone dishes of all time.

Pounding hard diorite with the best modern hardened steel hammer will ruin the hammer's striking surface. The remarkable features of these vessels include ultrathin walls that are uniform in thickness. This is among several features that have not been replicated by using abrasive sand and replicas of ancient tools.

In 1999, a team from the German Archaeological Institute in Egypt published the discovery of symbol writings more than 5,000 years old (dating between 3300 and 3200 B.C. and found in the tomb of the Predynastic King Scorpion at Abydos, Egypt). The finding challenges the long-held consensus that writing was first invented in Mesopotamia, at about the same time. But some of the hardest vases, made with either diorite or basalt, date to the Neolithic Period of the Stone Age (at about 7000 B.C.). So, as startling as it may seem, based on all available evidence, dwellers along the Nile produced vessels with hard stone that are unparalleled when using today's best machine tools against comparable hard rock types. Ancient people produced these items long before they had a rudimentary written language (comprising simple line drawings of natural elements like animals, plants and mountains).

Artisans made dishes and other vessels of a number of rock varieties, including diorite, serpentine, schist, breccia, purple porphyry, red jasper, obsidian, quartz, granite and basalt. Some of the rock types used are too hard to be crafted using iron tools (rock types in this category include metamorphic schist, diorite and quartzite). So, the prolonged use of meteoric iron is not the key to their manufacture — and would not suffice to create their extraordinary level of perfection.

There is no mystery to making simple vessels of soft limestone, Egyptian alabaster or other relatively soft rock types. Alabaster can range from soft to hard and compact. An artisan can shape the soft variety called Egyptian alabaster with primitive tools and abrasives. A mild acid like vinegar eases the task. But the several thousand hard-stone vessels I mentioned remain highly enigmatic.

In his *Archaic Egypt* (1987 rev.), W.B. Emery admitted to being baffled:

> Unfortunately, we have no really satisfactory evidence of the method of manufacture of these stone vessels, and, although certain processes of the work are known to us, others remain a complete mystery. How did they achieve such accuracy that when we 'swing' a shallow bowl or dish, no deviation from a perfect circle can be noted? How did they cut rock crystal tubular jars with walls not more than a millimetre [.04 inch] thick?[1]

Relying on Old Kingdom tomb depictions, Emery described methods suitable for drilling soft varieties of stone. For instance, a tomb wall shows a scene that is interpreted by Egyptology as a boring operation—the use of a drill weighted with rocks. It is impossible to bore into hard diorite or quartzite by the method shown. Emery recognized that the known methods cannot explain the difficult-to-achieve crafting of hard-stone vessels. Some have complex features, such as the jars with narrow necks, wide shoulders and round bellies. He examined jars that greatly puzzled him:

> How, for example, was the upward pressure obtained to cut away the interior side of the shoulders? All of these problems as yet remain unanswered and are likely to remain so until perhaps the discovery of a stone vase maker's workshop which will reveal some of his methods.[2]

No one has actually proven any methods by demonstrating them in practice when tooling hard, tough diorite. So, these diorite vessels remain a glaring mystery of Egyptology. German scholar Kurt Lange was awestruck by hard stone vases he examined at Saqqara.[3] Some have long narrow necks and wide bellies, and their necks have perfectly undercut flared openings. Their walls are of uniform thickness. These vessels are even smooth on the insides. But they also show regular cutting grooves that can only be the result of rapid cutting. I quote his description that reflects his astonishment in a later chapter.

Tool experts have not reproduced or demonstrated the tools that can cut these features in hard rock. Many of the vessels are delicately inscribed with the symbols of the Predynastic monarchs (who ruled before the unification of southern and northern Egypt into a nation with its first pharaoh). Some vases made with schist have flawless, paper-thin edges. This amazes experts because schist is a hard, crystalline rock that easily breaks along its closely-set foliations into thin, flaky plates. Its crystalline structure makes this rock brittle, and greatly compounds the problems of working it to this level of perfection.

A vase made of schist in the Cairo Museum has extremely thin, uniform walls. It is difficult to imagine the ancient lathe that could create this vessel in hard schist. In the Cairo Museum, a bowl (nine inches in diameter) made with granite balances perfectly on its small, rounded bottom tip. The tiny round base-tip measures less than .15 inch square. When the bowl rests on a level surface (like smooth glass), its top edge is aligned along the horizontal plane.[4] This speaks to the perfection of this object: Granite is heavy, and so the bowl would tip over without the exact level of perfection achieved.

W.M.F. Petrie pondered long and hard over fragments of 4th Dynasty dishes and other vessels he found at Giza.[5] He believed that the ancient Egyptians made some of them with lathes. Some examples were made from either basalt, diorite or black granite. Narrow, clean cutting lines (which are circular) are conspicuous on the interiors of the bowls. But the primitive lathes known are only capable of shaping far softer materials, like wooden objects.

No one has explained how a Late Stone Age turning device could cut these unprecedented vessels out of hard stone. Today's most advanced lathes would not produce such vessels when worked against hard stone. Ancient vessels commonly have two attached handles that would interfere with lathe turning. Gaston Maspero mentioned the early date at which artisans made vessels with handles:

> As early as the close of the Predynastic period stone vases were worked in the hardest materials, such as breccia, syenite, quartz, crystal, and diorite, and great alabaster bowls were so finely worked as to be transparent. Stone vases intended for suspension were provided with handles carved at the sides and pierced. Some of the finest

of these stone vessels belong to the later prehistoric and early dynastic times; they are found also in porphyry, slate, alabaster, diorite, basalt, and other fine stones in the temples of the Fourth and Fifth Dynasties...[6]

Long before the first pyramid was built, Egyptians produced many kinds of masterful works. Artist Nestor I'Hote (c. 1780–1842) worked with one of the great founders of Egyptology, Jean Francois Champollion (1790–1832). L'Hote was ecstatic about artwork found in three Old Kingdom mastabas by the famous French archaeologist Auguste Mariette (1821–1881) and the distinguished German Egyptologist Karl Richard Lepsius (1810–1884). Mastabas are early-style oblong tombs, with sloping sides and flat roofs. They are older than the pyramids. Describing the sculptured objects in one of the most ancient such tombs (that of the vizier Menefra of Memphis), I'Hote remarked:

> The sculptures in this tomb are remarkable for their elegance and finesse. The relief is so light that it can be compared with one of our five franc coins. Such perfection in something so ancient confirms the observation that the further one goes back in antiquity towards the origin of Egyptian art, the more perfect are the results of this art, as if the genius of these people, unlike others, was formed in one single stroke.[7]

Moving forward to the 1st Dynasty, we find that heavy slabs blocked the entrances of royal tombs at Saqqara. First Dynasty tombs at Helwan, in northern Egypt, are the earliest known burial chambers lined with large slabs made with limestone. The largest slabs measure more than 7 x 13 feet, large enough to cover a whole wall.[8] Early examples like this show Egypt slowly emerging from a history of building with mud-brick. The 3rd Dynasty revolutionized the practice of building with stone. Starting in the 3rd Dynasty, whole pyramid complexes were made mostly with limestone.

The 3rd Dynasty Step Pyramid of Pharaoh Zoser was Egypt's first pyramid. It exhibits very impressive features. The burial chambers (located about 90 feet below ground) are gigantic constructions made with granite. The ceilings of the crypts beneath Zoser's pyramid are constructed of huge beams made with granite. They have round holes in them. These holes are sealed with round plugs, also made with granite, that weigh about three tons each.

Zoser's successors in the Old Kingdom also built impressive features into their tombs.[9] In 3rd Dynasty tombs of Beit Khallaf, in northern Upper Egypt, slabs weighing six to seven tons were installed in shafts about 82 feet deep.[10] Lowering heavy weights in confined spaces presents complex engineering problems that are far more challenging than lifting the same weights on a large ramp able to accommodate more workers.

By the 4th Dynasty, builders were generally using larger blocks than before. Some weigh more than 200 tons. Among the largest surviving units are blocks incorporated into the Mortuary Temple of the Third Pyramid at Giza, built for Pharaoh Menkaura. These blocks, made from limestone, weigh up to 220 tons.

Outer wall blocks of the Valley Temple of Giza's neighboring Second Great Pyramid, built for Pharaoh Khafra, are extremely heavy. Made with limestone, they each measure about 10 x 16 x 26 feet.[11] Some of these large blocks are located more than 40 feet above ground level.

If they had to be lifted with machinery today, the world's largest crane would be required. Few modern industrial cranes exist with the necessary capacity.[12] These cranes are equipped with onboard counterweights (which prevent them from tipping) weighing more than 150 tons. The booms of the cranes reach to 220 feet. The cranes themselves tower 200 feet. They rely on 20-foot-tall, diesel-driven power supplies to drive electric generators and many huge hydraulic pumps.

The early archaeologists Georges Perrot and Charles Chipiez were awestruck by the accomplishments of Khafra's sculptors and others of the Old Kingdom:

> How did the sculptors manage to carve into these rocks which are so hard?...Even today it is very difficult when using the best tempered steel chisels. The work is very slow and difficult and one must stop frequently to sharpen the edge of the chisel, which becomes dull on the rock, and then re-temper the chisel. But the contemporaries of Khafra, and everyone agrees on this, had no steel chisels.[13]

Among the artifacts these archaeologists were marveling at was the somewhat larger than life-sized statue of the 4th Dynasty Pharaoh Khafra.* It is made with rock usually called 'Chephren diorite.' Perrot and Chipiez recognized that tempered steel tools are inadequate for reproducing the crisp detail found on this and other artifacts. As mentioned, hammering hard diorite with the best modern hardened steel hammer will ruin the striking surface of the tool. At Giza, archaeologists have excavated innumerable fragments of finely-executed bowls made with various types of diorite.

The 4th Dynasty workers also perfected fully corbelled rooms. They appear in pyramids at Dashur, south of Saqqara. Magnificent examples appear in the Bent Pyramid and the Red Pyramid, both built for Pharaoh Snofru (c. 2575–2551 B.C.).[14] The Bent Pyramid was named for the dramatic inward slope of its upper tiers. The Red Pyramid was named for the reddish tinge of iron oxide in its limestone. The magnificent three-room burial chamber in the Red Pyramid is considered one of the finest of the Old Kingdom. Built 14 to 16 corbels high and each measuring about 14 x 27 feet in width and length, and 48 feet high, these chambers are beautifully corbelled on all four sides. Only the corbelled ceiling of the Grand Gallery of the Great Pyramid surpassed the length of these remarkable ceilings.

Evidence shows that a pivoting stone door opened and closed both the Bent Pyramid and the Pyramid of Meidum. These structures have sockets in sidewalls near entrances that can accommodate door pivots. W.M.F. Petrie believed that the Great Pyramid was similarly equipped with a huge pivoting stone door. He drew evidence from Strabo's *Geographica*, written at about 64 B.C.:

> [The Great Pyramid] a little way up one side, has a stone that may be taken out, which being raised up, there is a sloping passage to the foundations.[15]

Petrie asserted:

> A self-replacing door, which left no external mark, is absolutely required by the fact of the Arabs having forced a passage. Only a flap door, or a diagonal-sliding portcullis slab, can satisfy this requirement. A flap door is unequivocally shown to have been used at Dahshur. And Strabo's description of the entrance agrees with such a door, and with no other. Such is the evidence for the closing of the Pyramids by doors; equally proving also the absence of any plugging up of the entrance passages.[16]

---

* The Khafra statue rock type has several names. It is technically classified by geologists as an anorthosite (soda-lime feldspar) gneiss (meaning it has a banded or laminated structure). This dark green rock is commonly called diorite and, more properly, diorite-gneiss. It is also often called 'Chephren (Khafra) diorite' by Egyptologists. In ancient Egypt, this highly prized rock was called *"mntt."*

A decline in pyramid construction set in during the 4th Dynasty. The Third Pyramid at Giza is dramatically smaller than those built for Khufu and Khafra. But lesser pyramids of the 5th and 6th Dynasties still incorporated stunning special features. A casing block incorporated into the masonry near the entrance of the 5th Dynasty Pyramid of Unas measures about six feet high. Its length is 29 feet.

The ceilings of burial chambers in the lesser pyramids are made of giant beams leaning against one another at the top (forming constructions called pointed saddle roofs). An example is the roof over the underground burial crypt of the 5th Dynasty pyramid of Pharaoh Djedkara Isesi, located at Saqqara.[17] Another is the roof over the crypt of Pharaoh Niuserra's 5th Dynasty pyramid, at Abusir, north of Saqqara. These pointed saddle roofs are exceptional because of the size and number of their beams.

The 60 blocks roofing Niuserra's crypt each weigh about 90 tons.[18] A roofing block in Djedkara Isesi's pyramid weighs 24 tons. As mentioned, there are several examples of heavy blocks underground in narrow caves and shafts, where numerous workers, ramps and long levers will not fit. Burial chambers were constructed in deep underground shafts for several 5th and 6th Dynasty pyramids, including those of Userkaf, Niuserra, Djedkara Isesi, Unas, Teti, and Pepi II.

At Saqqara, 18 columns made from quartzite appear in a temple court of the 6th Dynasty pyramid complex built for Pharaoh Pepi II.[19] Among the hardest types of rock, quartzite is entirely too dense to cut with copper, bronze, iron, or flint tools.

In quartzite, quartz grains are bound together with natural cement that makes the rock incredibly dense. Quartzite is composed almost entirely of quartz, which can be shaped with topaz, corundum, or diamond. But Egyptologists do not believe that the 6th Dynasty Egyptians had any of these three materials.[20] Besides, the objects are so huge that the quantity of gems or gem dust required for cutting would be staggering. The first undoubted reference to diamond during antiquity appears in Roman literature of the 1st century A.D.[21]

Quartzite is also extremely tough. Using today's technology, it is a very slow and difficult process to drill through a bed of quartzite with a modern tungsten carbide bit, with 950 pounds of pressure on the drill bit's shaft and a drill strength of 5,000 to 10,000 pounds per square inch. The tungsten carbide bit is next in hardness to diamond.

While impressive quartzite items date from the earliest times in Egypt, experts have no viable suggestions as to how the Egyptians quarried quartzite. Shaping huge objects with this material also raises unresolved problems. Some have suggested that quartz sand must have been the cutting medium because it was plentiful. A piece of quartz will indeed scratch another piece of quartz with considerable difficulty because they are of the same hardness. But imagine scratching quartz against quartz to create finely-sculpted, inscribed colossi over 50 feet high.

Explaining the creation of Egypt's inscribed, finely-sculpted 50-foot-high quartzite colossi without the unfathomable task of scratching quartz sand against quartzite is one of the objectives of this book. The solution presented here also solves unfathomable transport problems, and the erection of seven-story quartzite monoliths without the need for a crane or other heavy machinery.

The mundane task of scratching quartz against quartz certainly fits within the technological abilities of ancient people. We can imagine a sculptor spending his years creating a single vase or statuette with this method. But it is logical to suggest that quartzite colossi over 50 feet high alert us to the existence of a more sophisticated technology.

Extraordinary claims demand extraordinary proof, as Carl Sagan used to like to say. In this case, asserting that quartz sand was used to sculpt 50-foot-high monolithic quartzite colossi is an extraordinary claim, and it is not backed by any proof—just assumption.

W.M.F. Petrie was astounded when he discovered the exquisitely-made multiton monolithic quartzite sepulcher in the 12th Dynasty pyramid of Pharaoh Amenemhet III, at Hawara. To find the sepulcher, Petrie squeezed through a dark, water- and mud-filled maze of blind alleys, designed to confound anyone who might enter the substructure of the pyramid. The passageway was so narrow that he had to remove his clothes to squeeze through. Petrie reported:

> The workmanship is excellent; the sides are flat and regular, and the inner corners so sharply wrought that—though I looked at them—I never suspected that there was not a joint there until I failed to find any joints in the sides.[22]

He simply could not fathom how such an item could be made in one piece. This monolithic quartzite sepulcher is box shaped, with no lid. It measures about 22 x eight x six feet. It is thought to have been cut from a block weighing 80 tons. If we were to assume the construction means assumed by Egyptology to be correct, its flat, regular surfaces would vastly compound the enigma of its production.

A large sarcophagus and a second smaller one, each made with quartzite, were found inside of the sepulcher itself. Three 4-foot-thick slabs of the same material, placed side-by-side, sealed the sepulcher. Two stress-relieving chambers, covered by two sloping beams, protect the sepulcher from above. These beams were made with limestone and form a pointed saddle roof and weigh almost 50 tons each.

Among the other sarcophagi made with quartzite are those found in the Valley of the Kings, in southern Egypt. These sarcophagi include those found in the tombs constructed for the later 18th Dynasty Queen-Pharaoh Hatshepsut, Pharaoh Tutankhamun, and Pharaoh Amenhotep II. In 1817, the Italian archaeologist Giovanni Belzoni found the tomb of the 19th Dynasty Pharaoh Ramses I in the Valley of the Kings. The tomb included a huge sarcophagus made with red quartzite.

The long-destroyed 12th Dynasty Labyrinth, one of Egypt's most remarkable structures, was associated with the pyramid of Pharaoh Amenemhet III. In 1843, German Egyptologist Richard Lepsius, one of the most eminent 19th century Egyptologists, identified and explored the Labyrinth site.[23] Although the Labyrinth no longer exists, Lepsius was able to determine that the structure was about 585 feet long and 520 feet wide. The spectacular Labyrinth amazed both the ancient historian Herodotus and the geographer Strabo.

Herodotus acclaimed the Labyrinth as beyond description. He reported that it had 12 roofed courts and 3,000 galleries, half of which were subterranean and not accessible to visitors. He said it was hard for him to believe men could produce such a marvel:

> The Labyrinth has 12 covered courts - six in a row facing north, six south. Inside, the building is of two storeys and contains 3,000 rooms, of which half are underground, and the other half directly above them. I was taken through the rooms in the upper storey, so what I shall say of them is from my own observation, but the underground ones I can speak of only from report, because the Egyptians in charge refused to let me see them, as they contain the tombs of the kings who built the Labyrinth and also the tombs of the sacred crocodiles. The upper rooms, on the contrary I did actually see, and it is hard to believe that they are the work of men; the baffling and intricate passages from room to room and from court to court were an endless wonder to me,

as we passed from a courtyard into rooms, from rooms into galleries, from galleries into more rooms, and thence into yet more courtyards.

The roof of every chamber, courtyard and gallery is, like the walls, of stone. The walls are covered with carved figures, and each court is exquisitely built of white marble and surrounded by a colonnade...It is beyond my power to describe. It must have cost more in labour and money than all the wall and public works of the Greeks put together – though no one would deny that the temples of Ephesus and Samos are remarkable buildings. The Pyramids too are astonishing structures, each one of them equal to many of the most ambitious works of Greece; but the Labyrinth surpasses them.[24]

The marvelous interior of the Labyrinth was a maze of confounding, winding passageways. Once inside, anyone unable to comprehend its fabulous structure could not find an exit route without a guide. The architectural design itself incorporated deep religious significance, perhaps akin to the mazelike patterns depicted on the floors of some medieval churches.[25]

Strabo described the Labyrinth's giant wall blocks and monolithic pillars. He was astounded when he witnessed the ceilings of the rooms, which were monolithic slabs of extraordinary size.

One of Egypt's most praised construction works was built during the 18th Dynasty. Made with quartzite, the twin Colossi of Memnon were originally monolithic and stand 63 feet high (counting their 13-foot pedestals). Despite their name, given to them by the Greeks, they were statues of Pharaoh Amenhotep III (c. 1391–1353 B.C.). They stand at the approach to the now-vanished Mortuary Temple of this pharaoh. They were constructed under the supervision of his architect, Amenhotep-son-of-Hapu of Athribis.

The weathered colossi have endured deliberate damage and natural disasters. Quartzite is the hardest and toughest type of stone used to make Egyptian colossi. During this historical period, iron was rare and very precious because of its hardness. Nevertheless, iron tools are not capable of sculpting quartzite. As mentioned, modern drill bits almost as hard as diamond can penetrate a bed of quartzite only with a great amount of pressure, and the task is considerably difficult.

Aside from the problem of transporting and raising the astonishing 50-foot-high colossi, anyone who has ever tried creating a work of art out of quartzite using any means appreciates the severe problem posed by carving objects this massive. Keep in mind that experts who try to explain away such objects have not actually created anything comparable, and can point out no modern team or company that has.

These remarkable colossal statues were monoliths until the Roman Emperor Septimus Severus (A.D. 193–211) restored the earthquake-damaged southern statue with large blocks. Including their pedestals and crowns, the colossi each measure about 63 feet high. The third fingers of the hands each measure four feet. The widths at their shoulders measure 20 feet. Each statue weighs some 750 tons and rests on a 556-ton quartzite pedestal.[26]

In the 19th Dynasty, the gold-gilded Mortuary Temple that the Colossi of Memnon once guarded was exploited for building material by Pharaoh Menerptah (c. 1224–1214 B.C.), a son of Pharaoh Ramses II. A stele that Menerptah expropriated bears a description of the temple:

...an everlasting fortress of sandstone, embellished with gold throughout, its floor shining with silver and all its doorways with electrum [an alloy of silver and gold]. It is wide and very long, adorned for eternity, and made festive with this exceptionally large stele. It is extended with royal statues of granite, of quartzite and of precious stones, fashioned to last forever. They are higher than the rising of the heavens, their rays are in men's faces like the rising Sun…Its magazines have stored uncountable riches.[27]

We can only imagine the splendor of the interior of this Mortuary Temple.

During the 19th Dynasty, the administration of Ramses II erected an enormous colossus of this pharaoh to adorn a great temple of the god Ptah in Memphis.[28] The Ptah Temple complex, one of the largest in Egypt, extended a third of a mile in length and a quarter of a mile in breadth. It was located near the central quarter of old Memphis, Egypt's first capital. The Temple was founded within the so-called "White Walls" associated with the founding of Memphis in the 1st Dynasty (c. 2920 B.C.). The splendor of Memphis is said to have been beyond belief. Even in the 12th century A.D., the ruins of Memphis were reported to be a collection of such marvelous beauty that the intelligence is confounded. It was said that even the most eloquent man would not be able to adequately describe them.

For the Greeks, the now-vanished Ptah Temple of Memphis epitomized Egyptian architectural genius. Some modern linguists believe that the Greeks named the land of Egypt after it.[29] They indicate that the Greek word for the Ptah Temple is transliterated as Aegyptos, which in English is Egypt.

Today only the Temple's enormous colossus of Pharaoh Ramses II remains. Although it has fallen, the colossus, originally about 40 feet high, is so extraordinary that it remains one of the most famous features of Egypt. It is one of the most outstanding of Ramses II's statues.

Stuart M. Edelson is a sculptor who worked in the Conservation Department of the Metropolitan Museum of Art, in New York. His deep appreciation for this statue arises from his own work with similar limestone for more than 20 years:

> Anyone who has never carved stone might marvel most at the quarrying of the many-ton block, and then at the task of roughly hewing it into shape, tasks which must have been gargantuan. Of course, this impressed me, but the drudgery of rough carving spoke to me of an effort that could have been achieved by any gang of workers sufficiently numerous, supervised, and driven. Persistence on this grand scale is not uncommon. The distinction of the Ramesses colossus lay elsewhere.
>
> The essence of this great statue lies in the many square yards of carved surface. Faced with a task of such magnitude, a cold sweat would form on the brow of any modern worker in stone. I scrutinized a ten-foot-long portion of the royal leg. Along its entire length no flaw distracted from the grace and power of the sinewy, kingly stride, and I knew something of the difficulty with which such perfect surfaces could only be achieved.
>
> Among the many problems presented by this stone, it likes to chip unpredictably to the terror of the sculptor who would shape it. The stone was familiar to me. I had worked on a small piece of similar but softer material the year before, and the twenty years' experience that went into my small sculpture provided an insight into the true greatness of the colossus before me.
>
> I had spent countless hours vainly trying to grind out by machine the countless ripples that had formed in the carving process — on a much smaller expanse of softer stone.

Only after much experimentation with various abrasives and finally with different rhythms of sanding was I able to produce the smooth surfaces essential to the overall impact of the work. Even on the small scale the effort involved was enormous.

When modern, mechanized marble yards cut smooth and polish stone the size of Ramesses, the shapes are either flat or they are featureless columns. It is done with power tools the size of houses and even then the work is painstaking, time-consuming and risky. Here, the ancients achieved perfection with hand-held stones and crushed abrasives applied to sticks. And the shapes wrought were the complex, subtle forms of the human anatomy. How these master carvers achieved perfect surfaces on this scale with simple tools was beyond my comprehension. My own twenty years' experience provided no clue. But clearly this was not the work of slaves. This forty-foot length of stone could only have been brought to life through the sensitive hand and watchful eye of a master sculptor, and with a great deal of loving care.

Unlike so many works on a Herculean scale, this Ramesses allowed for no imprecision in areas the sculptors knew could not be seen. The hidden places were equally finely finished. There were no technical concessions to the many near-insuperable problems that had to be faced. Looking at the supreme craftsmanship that went into the body's hidden recesses as well as its conspicuous visible areas, it was clear to me that all involved in making this image had the integrity and wisdom worthy of the god and the great king it was meant to represent.[30]

The stunning colossus was donated to the British Museum, but it proved to be too heavy to move to London. So, a museum had to be built around it instead.

The administration of Ramses II also greatly expanded a remarkable underground tomb in the necropolis of Memphis. Like several people, places and monuments of ancient Egypt, today it is known by its Greek name. The Greeks called it the Serapeum. It is remarkable for its many heavy sarcophagi situated within niches that form rows along its inner walls. The sarcophagi weigh about 65 tons each. The problem of moving 65-ton and heavier monoliths can be better realized with the help of a famous ancient Egyptian tomb scene dating from about 1850 B.C.[31]

The tomb scene shows 172 men pulling a 60-ton colossus of the nobleman Djehutihotep along lubricated, flat ground. The scene may be impressionistic, given that French architect Henri Chevrier performed an experiment showing that 400 men are required to pull 60 tons on a flat surface. Lowering a 65-ton sarcophagus requires many more men, the number depending upon the steepness of the downward slope. On its inside, the Serapeum's main known corridor is 110 yards wide and flanked on both sides by niches that store the sarcophagi. The niches themselves are relatively small and cannot accommodate many workers. We will return to the Serapeum in later pages because of another special problem: It contains sarcophagi with walls of ultra-precision flatness that today's granite-cutting companies are unable to duplicate.

In certain other underground tombs, heavy sarcophagi rest at the bottom of narrow sloping tunnels where there is not enough room for numerous laborers.[32]

Moving forward to the 20th Dynasty, the New Kingdom Pharaoh Ramses III (c. 1194–1163 B.C.) was buried in the Valley of the Kings, in the Theban necropolis. Costaz, a scholar of the Napoleonic Egyptian Expedition, found Ramses' sarcophagus after entering the Valley of the Kings through its only road. Costaz wrote:

The gate through which one enters the valley is the only opening in its entire contour. As this opening is man-made, the valley must previously have been shaped in the form of an isolated basin which could only be reached by climbing the steep mountains. It was perhaps this remoteness which gave them the idea of placing the royal sepulchers there to make them safe from robbery, which the ancient Egyptians so much feared…High mountains crowned with rock are hemmed in on all sides from the horizon, allowing only part of the sky to be seen. Towards midday, when the bottom of the valley has been in the sun for a few hours, the heat becomes concentrated and excessive. Any tempering wind can find absolutely no way into this enclosure. It is like an oven. Two men from the escort of General Desaix died from suffocation. I do not think that it would be possible to remain there for 24 hours without the shade provided by the catacombs which offer protection from the overwhelming heat.[33]

In the numerous tombs, Costaz encountered plundered and destroyed sarcophagi. Only the one belonging to Pharaoh Ramses III was still intact. Costaz made a compelling observation:

Imagine a long oblong chamber made of pink syenite granite, ornamented inside and out with hieroglyphics and paintings. Its dimensions are such that a man standing inside can hardly be seen by everyone outside. A blow with a hammer makes it ring like a bell…The sarcophagus must previously have been closed by a cover that has since disappeared…The cover would have formed a considerable mass that was very difficult to move…A comparison between the dimensions of the sarcophagus to those of the entrance of the valley yields a big surprise and a new example of the Egyptians' taste for difficult tasks. The entrance of the Valley of the Kings is not wide enough to allow the sarcophagus through, so that the huge mass must have been hoisted with a crane or pulley up the hills that surround the valley and then brought down along their sides.[34]

Costaz's account becomes all the more compelling given the placement of Khufu's sarcophagus in the Great Pyramid thirteen centuries before. No matter how Khufu's sarcophagus is oriented, it is too wide to fit through the doorway of the King's Chamber and its adjoining hall. Egyptologists believe that placing it involved the risky and frightening task of hoisting the sacred object halfway up the pyramid for installation—before the ceiling of the King's Chamber was built. Removing this and other sarcophagi intact requires dismantling tremendous amounts of material in order to enlarge associated exit routes.

We continue by exploring why Egyptology is beginning to abandon its most fundamental ideas about how the Great Pyramid was built.

Chapter 7

It Staggers the Imagination

Egyptology is abandoning a long-held, central tenet of pyramid construction. Since the inception of Egyptology, Egyptologists have asserted that copper chisels and saws were used to prepare several million pyramid blocks. Relatively new findings show that this is not feasible. So, Egyptologists are beginning to propose that primitive stone tools were used for almost every masonry task. But Egyptology provides no explanation of how the extraordinary masonry feats might actually be achieved with such tools.

Dieter Arnold, in his *Building in Egypt*, acknowledged trials in the 1980s that established a new dividing line between the types of rock that can and cannot be cut with copper chisels:

> For some time, the observation of ancient tools, their traces on the stone surface of unfinished monuments, and occasional tests of the hardness of Egyptian copper or bronze tools made it clear that Egyptian masons and sculptors were able to cut softer stones with copper tools but had to use stone tools for dressing hard stones. The line distinguishing the two was between limestone, sandstone, and alabaster on one side and granite, quartzite, and basalt on the other. A series of tests carried out recently by Denys Stocks seems to lower this border line drastically.[1]

The finding drastically impacts the believability of the accepted theory of pyramid construction. Arnold continued:

> We know that hard stones such as granite, granodiorite, syenite, and basalt could not have been cut with metal tools. The tests conducted by Stocks seem to indicate that even hard limestone, sandstone, and alabaster would fall into this category.[2]

Most of the limestone blocks in the Giza pyramids and temples are medium-hard to hard. In the 1980s, geologists from Waseda University conducted a geological survey of the Great Pyramid. They provided this brief, general description of the limestone blocks:

> …hard and highly viscous.[3]

Their finding agrees with other studies. The Great Pyramid would have collapsed from its own weight long ago if its blocks were not sufficiently hard and sturdy. The level foundation on which the Great Pyramid stands is hard and strong enough to support the superstructure. Geologist Kenneth O. Emery examined the rate at which the Great Pyramid weathers, and predicted that it could remain standing for 100,000 years — because of the structural integrity of much of its masonry. He classified the hardest limestone in the Great Pyramid as "gray, hard, dense limestone."

A large percent of the blocks (the main building blocks) of the Great Pyramid are made up of fossil shells that make them difficult to carve. Antoine Zuber conducted experiments and found that he required hard bronze chisels to cut limestone of comparable hardness.[4] But hard bronze tools were not available when the Great Pyramids were built.

The problem worsens when we consider that when Egyptologist Georges Goyon climbed the Great Pyramid with a precision instrument, he recorded tier height measurements for all 73 different heights (making up the 200 tiers) to be exact within less than a half centimeter. Blocks had to be prepared so that they fit into tiers of the desired height and shape. As a result, a myriad of the blocks are shaped so that they actually correspond to the shape of blocks they touch on all sides. Some of the Great Pyramid's blocks had (or still have) mortar between them. Mortar helps cushion masonry against earthquake stress. So, these blocks are exceptions to the overall close fittings.

By comparison, when the PBS Nova pyramid-building experiment used steel tools to cut blocks from much softer Tura limestone, they did not achieve these excellent results. Nova's blocks had gaps between them, and many of their corners were chipped. A custom fit was not achieved, and the blocks were covered with conspicuous tool marks.

A copper arsenate alloy, considered bronze, was known in Egypt during early times. But this is not a hard metal. It is unsuitable for making stone-cutting chisels. It was used to make statues instead. The type of bronze capable of cutting the medium-hard to hard limestone pyramid blocks is an alloy of copper and tin. This is the material Antoine Zuber used in his experiments. Using a cold hammering process, Zuber made chisels with bronze that was alloyed with eight to 12 percent tin. This kind of bronze became available in ancient Egypt at about the end of the Middle Kingdom—roughly 800 years after the Great Pyramid was built.

To solve the problem of how stones harder than copper were cut, Egyptologists long proposed a lost art of tempering copper. Hammering will harden a copper tool to a certain extent, but not nearly enough to allow it to render hard limestone, granite, schist, diorite, basalt, quartzite, or other varieties of hard rock into the objects perfected in ancient Egypt. The hardened tools are immediately ruined when used against these hard stones. Too much hammering makes copper more brittle.

While examples of hammered copper are mentioned in Egyptological literature, the vast majority of copper tools found in Egyptian tombs are typical soft copper.

There is another reason copper chisels, or copper saws combined with abrasive sand, could not have been used to cut the millions of limestone blocks. Shaping the 2.3 million blocks of the Great Pyramid would consume a staggering amount of copper. The Second Pyramid at Giza, built for Pharaoh Khafra, is almost as large as the Great Pyramid. The two large pyramids of Pharaoh Snofru (who preceded Khufu) collectively contain more limestone than the Great Pyramid. Dieter Arnold calculated that the major pyramid complexes build during the 80-year Pyramid Age—the golden age of pyramid construction—contain 12 million blocks. Known copper mining and/or importation does not account for this phenomenal demand. Besides, sawing with copper and sand would produce regular surfaces, whereas the form-fitted pyramid blocks exhibit wavy joints and are characterized by a myriad of minor interlocking irregularities.

In his *Atlas of Ancient Egypt* (1985), Egyptologist John Baines provides an overview of Egypt's copper supply:

> Sinai is also a source of copper, and copper mines contemporary with the Egyptian 18th–20th Dynasties have been excavated at Timna near Eilat. These were probably worked by the local population under Egyptian control; there is no evidence that the Egyptians themselves mined copper anywhere in Sinai.[5]

Native copper mining reached its peak in the New Kingdom, about a thousand years after the Great Pyramid was built. But even in the New Kingdom, the copper yield was only about four tons a year. Copper quickly wears off of a chisel when used against a hard surface like medium-hard limestone—so that the copper is consumed. Khufu's Great Pyramid complex alone included the pyramid itself (utilizing about 93.5 million cubic feet of limestone), the enormous causeway, temples, and expansive retaining walls. Other pyramids collectively consumed more than triple the amount of Khufu's Great Pyramid (not counting their associ- ated causeways, temples and retaining walls). Cutting granite consumes much more copper. Joseph Roder estimated that about one million cubic feet of granite was incorporated into Old Kingdom Egyptian monuments.

Extra copper can be obtained from the labor- and energy-intensive process of reducing copper ores like azurite and chrysocolla. But it is very unlikely that copper was obtained this way. The reason is that native veins of copper ore still exist at the Sinai mines. We can deduce that the real technology used to build the pyramids did not overburden the copper supply.

Having recognized that the consumption of copper would have been far too great, Dieter Arnold concluded that the Egyptians used stone tools for most masonry tasks:

> These observations would again be in accord with the assumption that even "soft" stones were not only dressed but also quarried mainly with stone tools, an assump- tion that would not deny, of course, that metal chisels existed and were occasionally used for special purposes.[6]

So, based on all of the studies, the most up-to-date Egyptology determines a far greater reliance on stone tools for all types of masonry work than has been previously recognized. Arnold deduced that stone tools were more abundant than metal ones from the earliest times to the New Kingdom and perhaps later. Arnold added:

> First, no marks of metal tools have been observed on these stones [hard limestone, hard sandstone, alabaster and other harder rocks]. Second, all known types of copper chisels do not — even after cold hammering — have any effect on these stones; in fact, the tools suffer so much damage that they could not have been used for that work. In addition, near the pyramid of Senwosret I, layers of stonecutters' debris could be studied, and the presence of granite dust indicated that the material was worked there. In these layers, no traces of greenish discoloration from copper could be detected.[7]

The question is clear: How did the ancient Egyptians produce the unparalleled features of the Great Pyramid, and the remarkable features of other objects described in these pages, mostly with stone tools? Egyptology has not answered this question in a manner that will withstand even the most rudimentary scrutiny.

The 1992 Nova film *This Old Pyramid* told its audience that it was using only ancient means to test pyramid construction. On camera, Mark Lehner tested a copper chisel on a block of very soft Tura limestone that had been pre-shaped with a steel tool. Just as the cop- per tools Dieter Arnold mentioned were immediately ruined during testing, a few strokes badly blunted Nova's copper tool. The Nova crew did not attempt to make their soft lime- stone pyramid blocks with copper tools. Instead, modern steel tools were used to quarry and shape all blocks for Nova's miniature pyramid. Nova's pyramid blocks were covered with crude tool marks.

The Nova film shows a quarryman working in the soft limestone quarry at Tura. He is standing so that one of his legs is in a deep trench he made with a heavy, modern steel tool. Although the film's opening narration states that the Nova crew would use only ancient means, the ring of steel resounds in the film.

Nova's quarrymen used steel adzes and steel pry bars. They used heavy steel pickaxes to cut trenches. They would not have made their rate of progress with copper chisels, stone pounding balls, stone pickaxes, or copper saws combined with abrasive sand—the only stone cutting tools Egyptologists have determined were available to Pyramid Age Egyptians.

To separate blocks from the quarry floor, Nova's stonemasons drove steel wedges beneath the blocks and hit these wedges with heavy steel sledgehammers. Comparably, in 1965 Joseph Roder showed that wedges (which fit into rectangular slots made in the stone) were not used in Egyptian quarrying before the Saite Period (c. 500 B.C., when Greek stone working methods had been introduced).[8] The wedge holes were made to accept iron wedges. So, the technique dates to the Iron Age.

Despite this use of modern means—including a front-end loader for placing all blocks except for one 1/2-ton block used for the on-camera demonstration—the Nova film *This Old Pyramid* concluded by saying that the experiments of the Nova crew had solved the problems of pyramid construction.

Likewise, the fairly large blocks used for Waseda University's 34- foot-high experimental pyramid were cut with modern steel tools.

Mark Lehner simply ignores the new Egyptological standard on stone masonry, Arnold's *Building in Egypt* (1991), and other presentations showing that copper tools are not useful for cutting blocks for huge medium-hard to hard limestone structures. In *The Complete Pyramids* (1997), Lehner wrote:

> The many acres of fine Turah limestone which cover the pyramids were dressed using chisels only c. 8 mm (⅓ inch) wide.[9]

This kind of illogical and incorrect information otherwise appears in the older, out-of-date Egyptological sources. When limestone is freshly quarried, it is softer than after being exposed to air. But this does not mean that ancient pyramid builders were able to take advantage of its initial softness. Dieter Arnold recognized that quarried blocks would have dried out and hardened by the time workers could have hauled them to construction sites for custom shaping:

> Blocks intended to be built into foundations and core masonry, which did not need further dressing, could be left waiting, sometimes up to three years, until they were used. The other blocks that needed dressing could not be left too long, for the stone would dry fast and its hardness would increase considerably...Because some time might have elapsed between extracting the stone from the quarry and the final dressing of the surface, the stone would probably have dried out and become more difficult to work.[10]

Arnold's statement implies that the majority of quarried blocks would not need dressing. But this asks us to believe the impossible: Fossil shell limestone blocks cannot be quarried so that they are automatically suitable for forming a level foundation or corresponding, well-fitted tiers that form an enormous pyramid shape. We have already established that the tier heights of the Great Pyramid meet a remarkable degree of accuracy, and that tiers correspond to one another on their upper and lower surfaces, and that the monument is appreciated for its blocks that are form-fitting on all sides.

Accuracy is critically important for building the perfect pyramid shape, and this cannot be over-stressed. The Great Pyramid has great stability, because its 13-acre foundation is almost perfectly level (off only 7/8 inch from corner to corner). Top surfaces of each pyramid course had to correlate with the next tier to be built. The important point Systems Engineer Mike Carrell contemplated bears repeating:

Among the remarkable features of the great pyramids are their great weight and the levelness of the tiers. At Giza, the pyramids rest on a hard limestone bedrock, which must have been chosen because it is reasonably level. The first tier of blocks must transmit their weight and the weight of all above them to the bedrock. To do this there must be exact conformity of the lower surfaces of the blocks with the actual surface of the bedrock. Any misfits will concentrate the burden on a smaller area, increasing the stress, and possibly resulting in a fracture.

The same considerations apply to the horizontal interfaces between each successive layer. They must mutually conform to transmit stress, and they must be level, lest errors accumulating from one tier to the next cause distortions in the shape of the pyramid. Producing these necessary features in hard limestone with the tools available, within the recorded time, presents a seemingly insurmountable task.

Clearly, all blocks required some sort of shaping so that they would fit with the scheme of surrounding masonry. It is not realistic to think that blocks for producing 73 tier heights — exact in height to within 1/2 centimeter — will come neatly out of a craggy fossil shell limestone quarry to form a pyramid of over 200 tiers without shaping being a requirement. This is a critical consideration that Arnold does not address.

Observations by Petrie show us surprising accuracy in the rough building blocks—and this also shows that all blocks required some kind of shaping. He partially surveyed the Great Pyramid, using reference points at both corners of each face:

> The form of the present rough core masonry of the Pyramid is capable of being very closely estimated. By looking across a face of the Pyramid, either up an edge, across the middle of the face, or even along near the base, the mean optical plane which would touch the most prominent points of all the stones, may be found with an average variation at different times of only 1.0 inch.[11]

The idea that pyramid builders took advantage of the initial softness of moist, freshly-quarried limestone does not hold. Dieter Arnold acknowledged that by the time blocks could be moved from the quarry to the construction site, they would have dried and hardened. The glaring problem simply cannot be minimized by stating that most blocks did not require dressing. Dieter Arnold does not recognize the full weight of the block-cutting problem because he assumes that most of the 12 million pyramid blocks did not require dressing.

To solve block-cutting problem, some Egyptologists propose that the Egyptians relied on stone pounders. Dieter Arnold writes:

> The picture is completed by the presence of huge quantities of spherical balls of dolerite and elongated mauls or axes all over Pharaonic construction sites…By bouncing the dolerite balls, which weighed up to 6 kilograms [13 pounds] or more, at a certain angle and rhythm, the surface of a stone like granite was bruised and ground down to powder.[12]

If we follow Arnold's logic, then many millions of pyramid blocks would have to have been shaped to conform to tier heights and other specifications with pounding balls. The pounding balls Arnold has in mind were made of very tough greenish-black dolerite (diabase) or other hard rocks. It defies logic to think that the Great Pyramids could have been built by such means.

Arnold's suggestion suits Pyramid Age technology, and, given enough time, pounding rocks can produce certain results. A team of masons might build a wall this way. Even the giant 60-foot-high Sphinx at Giza (which is relatively small compared with the Great Pyramid) might be sculpted with very gentle tapping and grinding. But the body of the Sphinx is made of a weak grade of limestone. No tight-fitting joints or flat surfaces or corresponding tiers had to be achieved. No massive blocks had to be lifted and fitted to sculpt the Sphinx. But the scale and perfection of the Great Pyramids cannot have been achieved with pounding balls.

It would be impossible to use pounding balls to produce a level 13-acre foundation or 115,000 massive, beautifully-sloped casing blocks that custom-fit as closely as 1/500 inch or in perfect contact. Remember that Petrie measured a flatness of .01 for a length of 75 inches up the face of the Great Pyramid where casing remains. This is accuracy equal to modern opticians' straightedges.

Ancient historians marveled over the many tiers of smooth casing blocks covering the Great Pyramid. The top of Khafra's Great Pyramid at Giza still exhibits such casing blocks. Tight fitting, beautifully angled casing blocks appear on many monuments, and provide us with an idea of how those covering the entire Great Pyramid were fit. The four faces of the Great Pyramid were covered with 2,379,842 cubic feet of casing blocks. Dieter Arnold admits to serious problems with the use of pounding balls:

> It is difficult to imagine, however, how this method was applied to inclined, vertical, or even overhanging planes...We do not know exactly how the masons achieved two corresponding and neatly fitted planes on two neighboring blocks.[13]

We see that Egyptology's last option, stone tools, is unworkable. Something is fundamentally wrong with the standard paradigm of pyramid construction. Precise, intricate features and overall accuracy on such a huge scale cannot simply be the product of men working with stone tools.

Somers Clarke and Reginald Engelbach carefully studied fancy joints, including those in the Great Pyramid, and developed drawings and models. Fancy joints are common in Old and Middle Kingdom architecture. Some joints are L-shaped, and many exhibit oblique masonry angles. In some Old and Middle Kingdom structures, 30 per cent of the joints are oblique. Somers Clarke and Reginald Engelbach tried to demonstrate that these blocks were assembled on chains of so-called rockers.[14] They reasoned that a temporary positioning of blocks on movable rockers would help workers pull blocks close together for adjustment. This awkward procedure requires a tremendous increase in work. It is incompatible with the rapid construction rate reckoned for the Great Pyramid. Dieter Arnold doubts that the rocker system was used:

> ...the evidence for the use of such an instrument is rather weak.[15]

Most pyramid blocks bear no tool marks, making it difficult for Egyptologists to determine the means used to shape them. The absence of tool marks on pyramid blocks should not pass unnoticed. But very telling tool marks are apparent on the backs of Old Kingdom statues and on sarcophagi made with granite. Distinctive tool marks appear on slabs east of the Great Pyramid. These slabs were made with basalt, and formed a platform that originally covered more than a third of an acre. Egyptologists think this masonry is the flooring of Khufu's destroyed Mortuary Temple. About ten percent of the slabs remaining today exhibit saw-mark striations between them that prove they were not made with stone pounding balls or diorite axes.[16]

Basalt is too hard to perfect even with iron saws. Remember Arnold's statement: "We know that hard stones such as granite, granodiorite, syenite, and basalt could not have been cut with metal tools." Some of the above-mentioned slabs in the platform east of the Great Pyramid have notched corners for fitting adjacent blocks. Robert Moores, of the Black & Decker tool company, observed plunge cuts on two of the slabs.[17] According to Moores, the plunge cuts he observed indicate the definite action of a saw blade on basalt. Moores indicates that these plunge cuts eliminate any possibility that slowly shaping the slabs with abrasives made the saw striations. In other words, the plunge cuts suggest a far more rapid cutting process than using abrasive sand. So, a huge and mysterious question is raised: How did ancient workers readily slice through basalt?

It requires many hours of sawing to progress a fraction of an inch through basalt with abrasive sand and a copper drill — the standard tools of the Pyramid Age. These basalt slabs represent a fraction of the Pyramid Age artifacts that show signs of rapid cutting.

During W.M.F. Petrie's research in Egypt, many of these basalt slabs were being broken up for removal. The Egyptians were interested in the thin layer of fine limestone below for lime production. But their hammering and sawing efforts would not produce the plunge cuts or other signs of rapid cutting. The operation in Petrie's time helps us sort out the tool marks on these slabs, so that ancient rapid cuts are not confused with modern hammering or other means used to tear up these slabs.

To address the quandary of the saw marks running through the basalt slabs, in 1991 Robert Moores designed a giant fixed copper drag saw that he theorized might cut basalt. He did not build a prototype to prove his system, but only sketched his design. His sketch shows a notched blade about 13 feet long, requiring nine men to operate. He imagined the huge copper blade suspended by ropes attached to its two ends. Other attached ropes would be used to pull the blade back and forth, producing saw strokes. As the cutting medium, he proposed quartz sand poured onto the blocks at the point of the sawcut. Moores reckons that either the blocks would have to be cut underwater or a slurry of water and sand must constantly be applied to the cut. The blocks must be guided by bearings to keep the cutting edges in exact alignment. A block would also have to be rotated, given that the blade's angle of attack was altered several times on a slab Moores examined at Giza. Moores does not postulate why the Egyptians would have undertaken this additional work, which would complicate an already cumbersome operation.

He does not explain how his proposed mechanism could force the copper rapidly through hard basalt. The amount of pressure would have to be tremendous, and the pressure would bend the copper instead of allowing it to cut into the rock. Moores does not account for how such a device could possibly produce the compelling plunge cuts. His saw does not fit with the known tools of the Pyramid Age, which is not characterized by machinery. The drag saw itself is not thought to have been invented until some two thousand years after the Great Pyramid was built. The first known drag saw was a small, very rudimentary instrument. Ancient Egyptian tomb paintings and texts do not depict or mention the use of any sort of large machinery or anything similar to a drag saw. Egyptology knows only of copper handsaws, suitable for cutting wood. But these tools were used in the Pyramid Age to make wooden furniture.

Ancient Egyptian tools were very rudimentary.[18] Needles, knives, handsaws, chisels, hoes, adzes, and picks with wooden handles date from early periods. The heaviest copper tools were the adz, ax, and hoe blade. Ancient Egyptian chisels have a broad, flat cutting edge, making their shape appropriate for block cutting. But Dieter Arnold observed that a heavy blow with a mallet would drive such a chisel deep into its wooden handle, causing it to split. Ancient Egyptian chisels are not suitable for cutting good quality stone. Tomb paintings show chisels in the hands of leather workers and carpenters.[19]

A wealth of evidence proves that the Egyptians did not cut the pyramid and temple blocks with giant drag saws. The pyramids and temples exhibit innumerable examples of perfectly fitting mosaic and wavy joints. On both its interior and exterior, the Great Pyramid exhibits a tremendous number of highly-irregular joints, which are very closely fit. For instance, blocks lining the interior vaults above the Great Pyramid's King's Chamber are made of large, custom-fit blocks. So is much of the rest of the pyramid masonry. Such blocks hug one another very closely along their whole joints, even though the joints deviate from being purely straight up and down.[20] Such close, wavy jointing, characterized by a myriad of irregularities that perfectly mate between adjoining blocks, is common in pyramid complexes — and such tight-fitting irregularities are not the product of a giant drag saw or any other kind of saw. The back-and-forth motion of a saw blade will instead produce far more regular surfaces, even when saw blades go askew.

Some form-fitted blocks are very crudely shaped. The ceiling and other areas of the entrance passage of the Great Pyramid show examples. The ceiling of the burial chamber of the collapsed pyramid at Meidum is a stunning example.[21] The ceiling units are so crudely shaped that they cannot be considered blocks. They look like stone blobs. But all fit tightly together along their oddly-shaped joints, bringing to mind a finished jigsaw puzzle made of custom-fit blobs. A huge reciprocating (back-and-forth motion) drag saw simply does not produce the wavy, highly-irregular, interlocking custom-fitting joints. The pyramid blocks are not the product of machine tools that tend to make regular planes.

Casing blocks on the three main pyramids at Giza emphasize this point, too: The casing blocks conform to one another on each touching surface, including the irregular faces of backing stones behind them.[22] Experts who have examined some of Khafra's form-fitting casing blocks observed that they fit together with tongue and groove joints. These configurations defy the use of a drag saw. Arnold described Giza's amazing form-fitting casing blocks:

> …the connection of the casing with the backing stones is very close and would have to be carefully prepared. The best examples are the close joints between casing and backing stones at the three main pyramids of Giza. The backing stones were frequently dressed exactly to the shape of the rear face of the casing blocks.[23]

Even casing blocks made with granite, and measuring up to ten feet long on Khafra's Pyramid, are form-fitted. So are those incorporated into Khufu's Pyramid. The rears of these blocks are highly irregular, yet they fit exactly into the irregularities of the front faces of the blocks behind them. The conforming fit cannot result from working with either a saw or stone pounding balls, flint picks, or stone axes.

Paving blocks are another example of this kind of work. They fit tightly, and at all sorts of fancy angles. Their notches receive the corners of adjacent blocks. Dieter Arnold described these blocks:

> In the huge limestone buildings of the Old Kingdom, a pavement of granite is not uncommon. In a few cases, even basalt was used. Since both stones were much harder to work than the underlying limestone, the undersurface of the limestone foundation was chiseled out in a way that allowed the protuberances of the pavement to fit into it. This could be done only by frequently setting and lifting the pavement blocks, a procedure that had to be carried out in any case to fit the mosaic-like blocks together.[24]

Dieter Arnold's proposal is illogical for the following reasons: First, the 13-acre pavement foundation of the Great Pyramid and the irregular bedrock under it are hard and strong enough to support this massive monument. What kind of tools could be used to achieve the flawless correspondence between the foundation slabs and the bedrock? How does one cut hard limestone to match the protuberances with their mating anti-protuberances (on the undersides of granite and basalt slabs) to achieve tight-fitting paving blocks on such a massive scale—and while keeping the tops of the slabs level?

Second, if we follow Arnold's logic, then the same method would apply to the hundreds of thousands of giant casing blocks fitted to the exteriors of the Great Pyramids at Giza and others. These blocks would have to be repeatedly shifted and reset until they conformed exactly to the vast number of protuberances existing all along the irregular shapes of all adjacent blocks. The aforementioned paper-thin cement would have to be applied in the process. We recall Petrie's astonishment, and how he called simply fitting such blocks with the thin cement between them an almost impossible task (he was considering 16-ton casing blocks). The larger the block, the more troublesome this kind of an operation is. It is vastly easier to cut regular blocks in the first place.

Tall monolithic temple columns, made with granite or limestone, have decorated capitals and are sometimes round shafts with cross sections that are true circles.[25] Some columns taper. These cannot be the products of artisans working with pounding balls or drag saws or giant lathes. When explaining 36-foot-high monolithic granite columns, Egyptology can only address simple tasks like measuring roundness. As for the production of such columns, Arnold admitted that Egyptology simply lacks an explanation:

> The dressing of a monolithic column certainly was more difficult, and we have no information about the methods used…Achieving accuracy was difficult, however, if we consider that granite columns nearly 11 meters [36 feet] long had to be manufactured. On a portion of a 6.30 meter long shaft of the granite columns of Sahure, the mean diameter tapers 11.4 centimeters, with an error of only 8 centimeters…By viewing such column shafts, one can see that their diameter is not always a true circle. This observation, the heavy weight of such column shafts, and the missing drill holes for inserting a fulcrum-shaft axle rule out the possibility that the column shafts were hung in a horizontal position and rotated.[26]

We see that the use of giant lathes to make these columns is out of the question. Such a tool would have been very large, powerful, sturdy machinery, and would defy all of the findings of archaeology. No one has demonstrated that huge, perfectly round temple columns can be made by sanding with abrasives. Only the ancient means presented in this book is logical and fits with Stone Age technology.

🕮 Chapter 8 🕮
Iron is not the Solution

Iron tools are not adequate for perfecting the artifacts made with hard stones like basalt, diorite, red Aswan granite, greywacke (schist), or quartzite. Egyptologists used to suggest that masons might have had iron tools for quarrying and shaping the millions of limestone pyramid blocks. An example of this suggestion appears in an older book, Ahmed Fakhry's *The Pyramids* (1969 ed.):

> Both in quarrying and building, workmen used copper chisels and possibly iron tools, as well as flint, quartz and diorite pounders.[1]

Ahmed Fakhry's idea dates to before tool mark classifications were established by period, and probably arises from his recognition of the need for a method for shaping blocks in pyramid complexes. But it defies the archaeological record, and so is no longer acceptable to Egyptological standards. The Pyramid Age Egyptians had no more than natural meteoric iron, which would provide a vastly insufficient supply to meet stone cutting needs.

Ahmed Fakhry very likely observed that a minority of blocks in the pyramid complexes exhibit chisel marks. Some of the tool marks found on pyramid blocks are now known to date to long after the Pyramid Age. In the Middle Ages, some pyramid blocks were hacked at and partially cut up with iron tools by treasure hunters and builders. Earlier, during the 19th Dynasty, when iron was smelted on a small scale, pyramids were restored.

A few blocks at Giza exhibit rectangular wedge holes, made to accept iron wedges. These match the wedge holes in the Aswan granite quarries dating to after 500 B.C. So, the same feature at Giza suggests abandoned attempts to cut up pyramid blocks in the Iron Age. There was Greek and Roman stoneworking activity at Giza. A considerable village dating to Greco-Roman times has been known since the early days of Egyptology. This village was reported by both W.M.F. Petrie and Howard Vyse.

Although tool-mark classifications have been established for quarries, no comprehensive study has dated the various tool marks on pyramid blocks. The overwhelming majority of pyramid blocks exhibit no tool marks. When the standard paradigm of pyramid construction is applied, one of the mysteries of Egyptology is why masons would erase all traces of tool marks on the overwhelming majority of blocks. These core, packing and backing blocks were supposed to remain forever hidden from view by multiton casing blocks. A myriad of blocks directly behind the casing and deeper into the interior are custom-fit and highly irregular. So, we must ask why masons would leave these blocks roughly-shaped and yet rid them of tool marks.

Although iron chisels are not suitable for cutting mosaic basalt (diabase) paving slabs (or the plunge cuts in them observed by Robert Moores), or for sculpting monolithic quartzite columns or statues, the use of iron seemed to some Egyptologists to be the best way around the problem of making pyramid blocks.

In 1837, Col. Howard Vyse found a fragment of sheet iron wedged between two blocks at the south air channel of the Great Pyramid's King's Chamber.[2] The piece of iron had been there for a long time. This was obvious by rust on it in the shape of a nummulite fossil shell. Egyptologists pondered the question of the Arabs having left the iron centuries ago. Treasure hunters looking for secret entrances repeatedly pried at blocks over the ages, presumably on both the interior and exterior of the Great Pyramid.

5. Casing blocks on a lower portion of Khufu's Great Pyramid. Some casing blocks are slightly displaced from earthquake damage. These blocks were originally very smooth and unblemished, and many acres of casing hid the rough masonry behind them.

The Great Pyramid's interior was penetrated by the Caliph Ma'moun in the ninth century.[3] A related account states that an expedition of men encountered a chamber containing a sarcophagus. Treasure hunters scoured the Great Pyramid's interior in Abd el-Latif's time (A.D. 1162–1231), when travelers were allowed to go into and out of the monument.[4] An account by Murtada ibn al Khafif, an Arabian writer thought to have lived in the 13th century, collected stories for his *A History of the Marvelous Things in Egypt.*[5] One account tells of a troop of 20 men who entered the Great Pyramid carrying provisions for two months. They had with them iron plates and bars. There is no telling how much tampering with the masonry might have taken place over the centuries.

In the 19th Dynasty, when iron was available, the administration of Pharaoh Ramses II restored several pyramids. This is known from inscriptions left on restored pyramids. Egyptologists suspect that the inscriptions on the Great Pyramid read to Herodotus might have been among those left by Ramses' restoration crews. The plate of iron found by Howard Vyse could be a remnant of a restoration project. Even if the sheet iron were original to the construction of the Great Pyramid, then the idea that iron tools were used to cut the blocks still does not hold. Excavators have found no iron tools inside of other Old or Middle Kingdom tombs. If iron was available from meteorites, it was extremely rare. Dieter Arnold offered some clarification:

> The question of the date when iron came into general use in Egypt is much disputed. Specimens of early iron are reported from predynastic dates on. Fragments supposedly of chisels from Saqqara are said to belong to the Fifth Dynasty, and pieces of a pickax found at Abusir and broken tools from Dahshur are said to be of the Sixth Dynasty. Since the circumstances of these finds are extremely vague, the dating of

the tools may be questioned, and they could as well have been used by stonecutters of a much later period. A later date for these tools is also suggested by the fact that iron objects from the [18th Dynasty] tomb of Tutankhamun were of poor quality and were considered to be so valuable that they were set in gold.[6]

No paintings or papyri support the use of iron during the Old Kingdom's Pyramid Age or earlier times in Egypt. Sealed tombs of these periods have yielded only wood, copper and stone tools. However, it is possible that the iron found by Vyse, which exhibited traces of gold, was a rare object made from a meteorite.

Today, the world's largest iron meteorite weighs 60 tons. But even if larger meteorites were found in ancient times and pounded into tools, the iron yield would be statistically insignificant. The amount of iron required for cutting millions of pyramid blocks would be enormous. Iron-bearing meteorites could not have met the demand—and if the pyramids were built this way we would have ample archaeological evidence.

Given all of the stonework, abundant archaeological evidence would furnish proof of mining, smelting, crafts, tools, or language (or any combination of these) if the Egyptians produced iron on even a modest scale in early times. With the archaeological evidence lacking, Vyse's discovery does not support the idea that pyramid builders shaped blocks with iron tools or that meteorites supplied substantial iron.[7]

The metals available since early times—gold, lead, copper and silver—are found in the native state in the mountain and river channel environs. Iron probably came into use late because of the difficulties of smelting the ore and reducing it to a state of malleability. Iron is not easily fused. It must undergo two laborious heating processes to gain strength. Only from the end of the 18th Dynasty does a gradual increase of iron objects become apparent.

By the 26th Dynasty (664–525 B.C.) iron was in common use in Egypt. During the 26th Dynasty, workers conducted restoration and other activities at Giza and elsewhere. These activities may account for the iron fragment found on the inside of the Great Pyramid and around the outside of other old sites that Arnold mentioned.

No trace of steel has been found, and there is no evidence that steel was known. Egyptologists have accounted for all of the ancient Egyptian words for metals, and none of the words can mean steel.

Ancient literature mentions the difficulties of cutting hard stones with metal tools. In *De Lapidibus*, the Greek philosopher and natural scientist Theophrastus (c. 372–278 B.C.) briefly mentioned stones too firm to be cut with iron.[8] Diorite, basalt, and quartzite are examples.

Even modern and ultramodern tools cannot duplicate the features of some ancient stone artifacts. It bears repeating that drilling into a solid bed of quartzite is quite a task with a tungsten carbide bit, with 950 pounds of pressure on the drill bit and a drill strength of 5,000 to 10,000 pounds per square inch. Heavy-duty, high-strength steel hammer peens and picks are ruined when used to hammer diorite.

No combination of ancient tools can solve the problem. Iron, steel, and hard abrasive powders (the latter used in combination with stone drills) are not adequate for making many examples of Egyptian stonework. Among many dramatic examples, Egyptologist John G. Wilkinson was astonished by crisp, detailed two-inch and deeper hieroglyphic intaglio in granite obelisks.[9]

Comparably, during the 1997 PBS Nova film *Secrets of Lost Empires: Obelisk*, stonemason Roger Hopkins remarked as follows about hieroglyphs on an obelisk of Ramses II:

Even with modern tools and...diamond wheels and all that, we would have...a tough time getting it [the hieroglyphs] to this kind of perfection.

The Nova film did not reproduce such hieroglyphs.

A granite sarcophagus greatly impressed Wilkinson. The pharaoh's image is raised to about nine inches above the lid's surface. In other words, Wilkinson was astonished by the idea of a sculptor's successfully cutting away nine inches of granite across the lid so that he could then sculpt the raised image of the pharaoh.

The sarcophagus found in Menkaura's burial chamber (and later lost at sea), in the Third Pyramid of Giza, is listed as basalt in Egyptological literature. The etchings on the sarcophagus were recorded before the object was lost in the Mediterranean en route to England. Deep etchings form a beautifully decorated palace facade style that covers the sarcophagus. Other examples that defy explanation are the large colossi, temple columns, sarcophagi, corridor plug blocks, and pavement slabs all made of quartzite. Trials using quartzite show that the material defies primitive stone-working techniques. Egyptology offers no satisfactory explanation for the production of these and a myriad of other hard-stone objects.

With regard to iron, Mark Lehner, in his *The Complete Pyramids* (1997), bases his pyramid-building estimate on modern work done with so-called iron tools. His premise is, therefore, invalid. Here is his estimate of the time it took to perform ancient quarry work:

> To build the Great Pyramid in 23 years...322 cu. m (11,371 cu. ft) of stone had to be quarried daily. How many quarrymen would this require? Our Nova pyramid-building experiment provided a useful comparison: 12 Nova quarrymen produced 186 stones in 22 days' work, or 8.5 stones per day. But though they worked barefoot and without power tools, they had the advantage of a winch with an iron cable to pull the stones away from the quarry face. An additional 20-man team might have been needed for the task in Khufu's day.[10]

Lehner added that his "figure can be expanded further to compensate for other advantages of iron tools." In other words, with this last statement, he admits, in a very subdued manner, that his estimate is not based on the use of Pyramid Age tools at all. Studies have shown stone axes and copper chisels to be incapable of quarrying limestone suitable for construction. No number of additional men working with copper and stone tools will compensate for the advantage afforded by iron or the modern steel tools Nova's crew used to cut the softest limestone at Tura. The use of pounding balls will produce cracks in limestone, and can even crack granite.

In addition, Lehner's *The Complete Pyramids* (1997) repeatedly states that the Nova team used iron tools to quarry and cut Tura limestone. Joseph Davidovits witnessed the construction of Nova's miniature pyramid in Egypt and photographed the operation. Joseph Davidovits insists that the tools were made of steel, which is logical: Steel tools are the type used these days and are sold in stores (Nova had to purchase steel tools when their replicated copper tools proved to be useless). Steel was being used in Egypt at Tura when Somers Clarke and Reginald Engelbach studied the quarries in the early 1900s and before. Delivering heavy blows (such as those delivered during Nova's stone quarrying operation) is very hard on tools compared to dressing blocks.

Steel is iron that contains up to about 1.7 percent carbon, which is essential to form the alloy. Lehner's use of the word iron may sound more ancient, but steel cannot accurately be referred to as iron. Steel is tougher than iron and has greater overall strength, making it much better than iron for stone quarrying. Joseph Davidovits' photographs of the Nova pyramid project show the use of heavy modern tools, and modern tools are made of hardened steel. These same tools appear in the Nova film.

Here is a summary of the Egyptological dilemma: Attempts at cutting limestone comparable to the blocks of the Great Pyramid immediately ruin copper chisels. Large quantities of iron were not available when the Great Pyramid was built, and iron will not cut basalt, and certainly did not produce the plunge cuts Robert Moores observed in basalt paving slabs in the flooring next to the Great Pyramid. Iron is not the solution to the rapid cuts in Khufu's sarcophagus, or the smaller artifacts that Petrie used to prove signs of rapid cutting, or many others like them. The Egyptians used thousands of tons of basalt in Old Kingdom monuments, mostly to make paving slabs for temples in pyramid complexes. Basalt was sometimes used to make walls and incorporated into causeways.

The Egyptians could not have cut the pyramid blocks with copper tools because the metal is too soft. Even if copper tools could be made to work, the huge amount of copper needed for trimming and dressing the 12 million blocks produced in the Pyramid Age was not available (according to surveys by Beno Rothenberg and others). Most copper implements found in ancient Egyptian tombs are made of typical copper, not special, hardened copper. The few instances of harder copper known are inadequate.

Hard bronze, which is suitable for cutting pyramid blocks, was not available until about 800 years after the Great Pyramid was built. Iron smelting came even later. The idea that iron can gradually cut a diorite (which is harder than iron) vase does not hold. Features on the vases and other objects prove rapid cutting—and achieving this requires the complete paradigm shift we will be exploring below.

Stone tools cannot achieve the refinement incorporated into the pyramid complexes. The problem is not solved by the softer consistency of freshly quarried limestone, because limestone blocks will dry out and harden by the time they can be transported and shaped to fit with existing masonry. The overwhelming majority of blocks in the pyramid complexes exhibit no signs of tool marks. How were these pyramid blocks prepared? Although many Egyptologists assume that the methods used to construct the Great Pyramid are sufficiently understood, in reality Egyptology is faced with a real mystery.

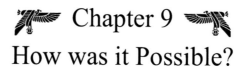

Chapter 9
How was it Possible?

Researchers have tackled both limestone and much hardest rocks with replicas of ancient Egyptian tools. The same bronze tools that Antoine Zuber used to cut limestone blocks had no effect on granite.[1] A Nova experiment showed the same results. Michael Barnes, producer of Nova's *This Old Pyramid*, wrote the following in private correspondence dated April 25, 1995:

> ...our limited financing did not allow us to make enough bronze tools to work the stones. However, we demonstrated that bronze chisels are effective at cutting limestone (but bronze is not hard enough to cut granite).

The distinguished Sir John G. Wilkinson, an early pioneering scholar of Egyptology, found a 9-inch-long bronze chisel in southern Egypt at Thebes.[2] It dated to hundreds of years after the Pyramid Age. The chisel was in an excellent state of preservation. Its cutting edge measures 7/10 of an inch at its greatest width, and the metal contains 5.9 parts tin per 100. When Wilkinson tested it, he found it altogether incapable of cutting granite.

Unlike limestone, granite is very hard within the bedrock. Freshly quarried granite will harden even more after being exposed to the air. Even freshly exposed in the quarry — when it is at its softest, most moist state — a steel tool is required to cut granite. The steel tools, however, will be so badly damaged that the method is not practical. Diamond drills are typically used today to cut granite.

After very long exposure to the atmosphere, granite and other igneous rocks begin to soften from weathering. But the weathering process affects the rocks only after periods ranging from thousands of years to hundreds of thousands of years (depending upon the climate). So, there was no taking advantage of softer bedrock to gain a cutting advantage. Nonetheless, Joseph Roder estimated that during the 450-year-long Old Kingdom, a little less than 1.6 million cubic feet of granite was consumed for incorporation into monuments. Given the tremendous effort required to quarry granite, such statistics invite us to consider the existence of a special, highly-efficient technology during those early times.

Tests show how poorly bronze chisels perform when used against hard rocks. In the 1980s, Denys Stocks produced bronze chisels of different grades of hardness by using ancient casting methods. He tested his chisels on nine different types of stone, ranging from soft sandstone to hard granodiorite (an intermediate between granite and quartz-containing diorite). Stocks found that he could easily cut soft sandstone with bronze chisels. He cut soft limestone with infrequent sharpening of his bronze chisels. He cut hard alabaster with frequent sharpening. Hard limestone and the other hard rocks immediately ruined his bronze tools. Stocks wrote:

> All the copper and bronze chisels suffered expected severe damage against both granites and grano-diorites. The granular structure of rose granite and diorite literally tore away the cutting edges of the chisels...I will mention the test use of a modern engineer's chisel, manufactured of hardened and tempered steel, upon a smoothed surface of grano-diorite. A groove 0.5 mm deep and 1.3 cm long was cut into the surface by utilizing both corners of the chisel edge. It sustained such severe damage,

caused by pieces of steel being torn away, that only considerable sharpening would allow any further cutting.[3]

Stocks concluded that hard stones must have been dressed with stone tools and abrasives. But, as I have already explained, stone tools and abrasives cannot account for quarrying and cutting all of the masonry that has gone into creating the grandiose scale and design complexities of the Great Pyramid and other Old Kingdom monuments. The special features of small artifacts made with diorite and other stones present their own special set of problems.

A brief description of ancient tools makes it clear that they are inadequate for producing the impressive hard-stone artifacts experts have pondered. Museums exhibit many stone tools from ancient Egypt. All the tools are very rudimentary. Flint knife blades date from the middle of the 1st Dynasty, as do wooden sickles with flint cutting edges. Flint is as hard as quartz, and flint will fracture so as to produce sharp edges. But flint is very brittle. Flint tools easily break when struck with a wooden mallet. Pointed flint is useful for hunting and domestic chores, and flint was abundant in ancient Egypt. But flint is useless for detaching and shaping massive granite, quartzite, basalt or limestone blocks.

Ancient Egyptian stone tools fall into four main groups: grinding stones, picks, pounders, and rammers. Actual tools and weapons, and ancient drawings of them, demonstrate the level of implement making before, during, and long after the Pyramid Age. Limestone ax heads dating from the 18th Dynasty (c. 1550–1070 B.C.)—1,000 years after the Great Pyramid was built—are crude slablike chunks of stone. Stone pickaxes were made of granite, chert, basalt, quartzite or hard limestone. The ax heads were tied to wooden handles with leather strips.[4] They cannot endure hard use without the ax heads separating from their handles.

A drawing of a stone hammer from the 5th Dynasty tomb of Ti depicts an egg-shaped rock.[5] A quartzite ax was found with its original handle, which consists of two sticks and banding chord for affixing the ax head. This ax dates between the 22nd and 26th Dynasties, more than 1,500 years after the Great Pyramid was built.[6] A diorite ax head found at Pharaoh Amenemhet I's pyramid at el-Lisht, in Middle Egypt, is believed to date to either the Middle or New Kingdom. Egyptology has established that it was left at the el-Lisht work site at least 500 years after the construction of the Great Pyramid.[7] This ax is like the one replicated and used by Mark Lehner for his futile stone-cutting efforts behind the scenes of the Nova presentation (witnessed by Joseph Davidovits). Ancient Egyptian axes look like the sort we envision being carried by cavemen.

How can we believe that primitive tools, combined with no other technology, produced the features of the Great Pyramid? These include its level, 13-acre platform-foundation; more than 200 tiers made of blocks that conform to the shape of blocks above and below them, and sometimes to all surfaces they touch; the accuracy of the 73 remaining tier heights (making up 200 tiers) to within 1/2 centimeter; the near-perfect planes of the rough core masonry; its four carefully bowed faces and the other masonry patterns we have explored, including precise right angles on a massive scale; the estimated 115,000 outer, form-fitted casing blocks that fit as closely as 1/500 inch or in perfect contact; the angle of casing blocks, which produced its four flat sloping faces each covering five acres of surface area, and which met perfectly at a point at the top; and its magnificent interior features, including giant, beautifully corbelled walls, and exquisitely rendered granite walls and ceilings.

Antoine Zuber conducted a demanding experiment with stone tools.[8] It took him 12 days just to cut six crude holes in a granite quarry so he could detach a small chunk of granite with wooden wedges. He was testing the now-abandoned assumption that rough granite blocks were quarried with wooden wedges.[9] A wedge is tapered to produce a thin edge, which can be used for splitting certain kinds of rocks. The abandoned theory holds that water was poured onto the wedges, causing them to swell and produce enough pressure to split the bedrock along a seam.

Egyptologists long debated the lengthy chains of cavities in the Aswan granite quarries of southern Egypt. Most experts believed that water-swollen wooden wedges were incapable of breaking out granite.[10] But Zuber did manage to break out his granite chunk with sycamore wedges after constant wetting for one day and one night.[11] Given the difficulties Zuber encountered, one might assume that relatively little granite would appear in construction work. But Joseph Roder estimated that during the 450-year-long Old Kingdom, a little less than 1.6 million cubic feet of granite was removed from the Aswan quarries.[12]

Other than limestone, granite is the most common rock found in Old Kingdom architecture. Its use in construction work started during the 1st Dynasty. Evidence from tombs, including paintings and papyri, does not show that Egyptians quarried granite with wedges. Joseph Roder studied the open quarries at Aswan and showed that no wedge holes date before the 26th Dynasty (c. 500 B.C.).[13]

So, Egyptologists had to abandon the wedge theory. Egyptology now holds that, throughout ancient Egyptian history, workers bashed out granite blocks and tall obelisks with pounding balls. With long, hard effort, these tools can be used to bash deep trenches in the quarry floor until blocks and obelisks are formed.[14] A tremendous amount of labor can produce results. To get an idea of the labor involved, consider that Lehner reports spending five hours hammering the quarry floor at Aswan. During those five hours, he produced an approximately 12 by 12 inch patch that was four-fifths of an inch deep.[15]

In the 1920s, Reginald Engelbach produced similar results. Even without further trials, there is ample proof that stone pounding balls were used at Aswan, at least in the New Kingdom or later. In 1921–22, Reginald Engelbach cleared the granite quarry at Aswan, where a huge, unfinished granite obelisk still rests. Deep trenches appear around it, and the distinct, rough impressions of pounding balls are pronounced on the obelisk itself. But the obelisk cracked a number of times while it was being pounded. Each time, its design was reduced. Finally, the obelisk was abandoned when a huge crack split down its interior. Although this failed example shows that granite can be quarried by breaking up the bedrock with stone pounding balls, the pyramid block puzzle is not solved by this method.

As already discussed, if crude pounding balls, alone or in combination with stone pickaxes, were used to extract pyramid blocks, then the Giza quarries should be much larger.[16] There should also be millions of cracked and broken waste blocks at Giza. There should be evidence (bruising, cracking and downstrokes) showing the use of pounding balls on some blocks, and in the large quarries associated with the Great Pyramid. But these quarries, and other Old and Middle Kingdom quarries, exhibit an entirely different kind of tool mark: The quarry walls everywhere show the marks of pointed picks. These tool marks add to the overall enigma because of the problems of producing blocks with picks.

If pyramid blocks were made with pounding balls, the blocks should show considerable bruising, chipping and cracking, There should be pounding-ball channels on rough pyramid stones (such as we see on the sides of the obelisk at Aswan) and on the Giza quarry walls. Pounding-ball marks on the Aswan obelisk are very distinctive channels made by continuous heavy downstrokes. The overall perfection I described for the Great Pyramid cannot be the product of pounding balls.

More than an ability to bash out trenches is required to explain the construction of the pyramids and inscriptions in granite that are of better quality than can be achieved with today's diamond drills. A different ancient technology is required to produce them and the many thousands of superb artifacts made with very hard rock. The problems are very challenging to experts.

A team led by Denys Stocks expended a great deal of effort to cut a round core out of Aswan granite with a bow drill and abrasive sand. As would be expected, the core exhibits striations all merged together that do not match ancient cores. A good example is granite core #7 found at Giza by W.M.F. Petrie. It exhibits a very clean helical cut. The cut is a continuous helix with some interruptions that were continued along the same average helical path. Machinists who worked with Petrie, and in recent years expert machinist Christopher Dunn, deliberated this core long and hard. Their training tells them that the cut is amazing and significant. We can understand why Petrie said that modern cores made with diamond drills look like smudged work compared with the ancient cores.

On a far larger scale, there are huge cores in the crypts in Zoser's Step Pyramid at Saqqara. The crypts of the main and southern tombs feature ceiling beams made with granite. They have round holes in them. These holes were sealed with matching round granite plugs that are up to six feet long and weigh three tons each. But the ancient texts show nothing that would indicate a giant bow drill of the size needed to cut these large cores. There is no direct evidence of the existence of a bow drill during the Old Kingdom. Besides, a bow drill will not produce the cleanly-cut cores that puzzled Petrie and the aforementioned machinists. A much more sophisticated method than using stone pounding balls and bow drills with abrasives is required.

There are a great many more examples. Some monuments incorporate a large amount of granite, and some examples are particularly exquisite. Blocks made with granite case the exterior of some pyramids. Six pyramids have one or more exterior courses of granite casing blocks.[17] The unfinished 4th Dynasty Pyramid of Djedefra, at abu Roash (about five miles north of the Great Pyramid) was all or mostly splendidly cased on its exterior with blocks made of granite.[18] These casing blocks were carefully produced to conform to the pyramid's slope, producing beautifully-made planes for this superstructure.

Another beautiful example appears in Khafra's pyramid complex. The interiors of the Valley and Mortuary Temples in Khafra's complex were made with limestone. But they are cased with form-fitted ashlars (dressing blocks) made with granite. Khafra's Valley Temple measures 147 feet from east to west and similarly from north to south. It rises to 43 feet and is faced both inside and outside with the beautifully-made ashlars. Its exquisite, flat interior walls are made of courses of these ashlars, which interlock at various angles. Some merging joints deeply interlock. Spectacular blocks curve right around the corners of walls before interlocking with neighboring blocks. Massive, square columns made with granite are exquisite features of this building.[19]

Within the Mastabat el-Fara'un at Saqqara, an arched ceiling was made with granite. It covers the burial crypt of Shepsekaf, the last pharaoh of the 4th Dynasty.[20] Another one arches over the crypt in the 3rd Pyramid at Giza, built for Pharaoh Menkaura of the 4th Dynasty.[21] In the 5th Dynasty reign of Sahure, enormous halls in Mortuary Temples (about 17 feet wide by 69 feet long) were constructed with arched roofing made of enormous blocks produced from granite. There is also an arched roof above one of the queens' crypts of Pharaoh Senworset III's 12th Dynasty pyramid at Dahshur. Dieter Arnold mentioned some examples of crypts with spectacular arched roofs:

6. *Interior walls in the Valley Temple incorporated into Khafra's Great Pyramid complex at Giza. The walls are constructed of enormous ashlars made from pink granite. Some of the ashlars curve around the wall corners, a rare architectural style.*

Good examples [of burial chambers with arched roofing] are also the vaults of the crypts of Senwosret III and Amenemhet III at Dahshur (with sixteen more rooms vaulted this way). In the princesses' gallery of the pyramid of Senworset III and in the pyramid of Amenemhet III at Dashur, we also find examples of elaborate methods of joining the two sloping beams at the top. Here the joints are not straight but run in

7. Precision jointing in Khafra's Valley Temple runs throughout the building. The Valley Temple measures 147 feet from east to west and similarly from north to south. It rises to 43 feet. It is appreciated as an engineering wonder. The floor is made with alabaster. Note the oddly-shaped ashlars in the interior, which all fit snugly.

a zigzag line, with correspondent mortises and tenons on each block. The direction of the zigzag joint alternates from one block to the next. The system has prevented the saddle roof in the chambers of Amenemhet III from being pushed in, despite the heavy pressure from above.[22]

8. The Valley Temple features large, squared beams that support squared lintels, all made with pink granite. Most of the roof is missing.

Dieter Arnold thinks that workers made these ceilings by first bashing out granite beams, and then leaning them against one another at their tops. Finally, masons cut away at their undersides. Dieter Arnold assumes that the ancient workers achieved this astonishing feat with nothing more than primitive tools. As mentioned, Arnold also proposed that the Great

Pyramid, with all of its grandiose features, was made with pounding balls (and other stone tools)—although he cannot account for the actual features of the monuments with the use of these implements: We recall that Arnold asserted that even soft stones were dressed and quarried mainly with stone tools until the New Kingdom and perhaps later. He thinks metal chisels were occasionally used for special purposes.

Good scholarship requires careful examination and analyses. But Egyptologists often cite the monuments themselves as proof of method.[23] The monuments exist, the ancient tools are known, and so Egyptology draws the conclusion that a myriad of examples of masonry that cannot be duplicated with the best modern tools must have been made by pounding away at bedrock with nothing more than primitive tools. I have stressed throughout these pages that something is drastically wrong with this picture.

Ancient Egyptian drawings show finishing touches being put onto statues. So, Egyptology is left to speculate about how ancient sculptors beautifully and routinely captured the subtle contours of the human body in complex statuary made with granite, diorite, quartzite, and other hard rock varieties. Given the inadequacies of metal tools, some theorists propose that even the most extraordinary masonry work was carried out with abrasives combined with stone drills or copper saws. Recent experiments, which we next explore, show that these instruments fail to replicate complex features of artifacts. So, the mysteries grow ever deeper.

Chapter 10
Standard Masonry Theory Disproved

A larger-than-life-sized statue of Pharaoh Khafra in the Cairo Museum is very exquisitely detailed. It is one of the most famous ancient statues. It is appreciated as a great world masterpiece. What particularly astounds curators and geologists is that it is diorite. It is a particular type often called "Chephren diorite." The statue was found at Giza and dates to the 4th Dynasty.

Excavations at Giza have unearthed a myriad of fragments of hard-stone objects dating from the Pyramid Age. They include great numbers of fragments of finely-executed diorite objects.

Egyptology has long advocated that hard stone statues and other objects were fashioned with sharp pieces of broken flint and combinations of implements like copper saws and abrasive sand. But tests with the types of implements available to the ancient Egyptians have not reproduced the complex features of artifacts made with diorite or other hard stones.

Fairly recent experiments dispute a long-held theory about how certain features might be made with abrasives and simple tools. These experiments were inspired by the long debates between W.M.F Petrie and Alfred Lucas. For some 35 years, Petrie and Lucas debated enigmatic objects made of hard stones. Knowing that the metal tools available in ancient Egypt cannot produce the features of these objects (such as those made with granite, schist, basalt, diorite, and quartzite), Lucas argued that quartz sand was used as an abrasive in conjunction with a copper tool. Lucas proposed that the action of rubbing forced the sand into the copper, making the embedded sand behave like small cutting teeth.

Petrie responded by arguing that only drills with fixed teeth, made of diamond, corundum, or emery (an impure variety of corundum) gems could possibly make the cuts in artifacts he collected. Petrie showed artifacts to machinists, who agreed that nothing but fixed points could have produced their features. Here is Petrie's retort to Lucas' idea about quartz sand behaving as cutting teeth:

> …It seems physically impossible that any particle of a loose powder could become so embedded in a soft metal by the mere accidents of rubbing that it could bear the immense strain needed to plough out a groove of any considerable depth in such a hard material as quartz…Modern diamond drill cores are clumsy and smudged work when compared to the Egyptian cores.[1]

Lucas responded by pointing out that cutting gemstones into teeth and then setting those teeth in copper, so they can endure the strain of hard use, is totally unrealistic and unworkable. Diamond, the hardest substance known, has a hardness of ten on the Mohs' scale.* Corundum and emery have a hardness of nine. Lucas pointed out that the idea of the ancient Egyptians having shaped these hard gems into cutting teeth produces more problems than it solves.

Furthermore, industrial quantities of gemstones would have been required. But Egyptologists do not believe that the gemstone particles useful as abrasives existed in ancient Egypt. There are no ancient Egyptian drawings or written descriptions of cutting

---

* The Mohs' Scale of Relative Mineral Hardness (which is strictly a relative rather than a precise scale) is named for German mineralogist Friedrich Mohs (1773–1839). He devised

teeth made of gems. Ancient Egyptian jewelry is made with semi-precious stones, like turquoise and carnelian, as are other stone-encrusted objects. These factors, and the inability of ancient Egyptians to shape the gems, rule out the existence of jewel-tipped saws. Besides, gemstone teeth fracture under the great pressure Petrie proposed was needed to force them through granite or other hard rock.

The Egyptians converted many thousands of tons of hard rock into a myriad of form-fitting blocks, and engraved and finely-sculpted obelisks, columns, colossi, sarcophagi, statuary, stone dishes, and other items. Surviving artifacts, including building ruins, are a small fraction of the masonry work produced in ancient Egypt.

Numerous Predynastic dishes and other vessels are made of some of the hardest varieties of rock on the planet. They date from a time when it was even more unlikely that gemstone abrasives were imported. The Egyptians had to overcome the natural, protective barriers of their land before the importation of materials became viable. Dangerous, deafening cataracts border Egypt in the south. The parched Libyan Desert stretches out west of Egypt. The formidable Mediterranean Sea is situated to the north, and the vast, barren Sinai Desert borders Egypt to the east. In early times these geographic features isolated and protected Egypt. But these same barriers prevented the mass importation of goods.

According to Petrie and other experts, artifacts exhibit detail more crisp than artisans can achieve with modern diamond drills. Petrie was amazed by Khufu's granite sarcophagus, which still rests in the King's Chamber of the Great Pyramid.[2] A groove cut along the sides of the top of the sarcophagus accommodated a sliding lid, which was long ago removed from the pyramid. Dowel holes allowed pins to affix the lid. Petrie admired a 90-inch cut, and thought that 9-foot-long saws were used. But what really astonished Petrie was the cutting lines he examined on the north end of the sarcophagus.

These lines show that when the sarcophagus was being made, the saw blade ran askew, slanting into the side of the sarcophagus. The artisan backed his saw out so that he could rectify his cutting angle. His second cut ran askew two inches lower. The workmanship shows that the mason again backed his saw out. Petrie also saw the mistaken tube drill cut, made when workers tilted their drill into the side by not working it vertically. They left the side of the hole three inches long and 1.3 inches wide. These mistaken cuts particularly astounded Petrie because they clearly prove that the mason sliced through the granite at an extraordinarily rapid rate. These cuts make it appear as though a saw was casually withdrawn and reset, and then the granite was cut as easily as if it were a block of cheddar cheese.

Petrie recognized that no one could make these kinds of mistakes when slowly grinding away at granite with a copper saw and an abrasive. Copper is 3.5 to 4 on the Mohs' hardness scale; Aswan granite is 6-8. Pouring on a constant supply of sharp sand will not produce a rapid wayward cut, given the amount of time and grinding (and continual renewing of sharp sand grains) required. Drilling experiments show that it requires roughly 10 hours of sawing

---

the following linear hardness scale, utilizing ten minerals arranged in order of increasing hardness. The minerals are each assigned a number: 1) talc, 2) gypsum, 3) calcite, 4) fluorite, 5) apatite, 6) orthoclase (feldspar), 7) quartz, 8) topaz, 9) corundum, and 10) diamond. Each classification will scratch the one preceding it, e.g., diamond will scratch corundum. So, the relative hardness of any particular mineral is determined by which mineral will scratch a specimen. Galena, for instance, with a hardness of 2.5, scratches gypsum and will be scratched by calcite. There is a much greater gap between the hardness of diamond and corundum than between any other of the two minerals listed. Diamond is four times harder than corundum and six times harder than topaz.

to cut a quarter of an inch into Aswan granite. So, the cuts in Khufu's sarcophagus drastically grate against the assumptions of Lucas—which are today accepted by Egyptology.

We can get a sense of Petrie's amazement by comparing the exhaustive work of Denys Stocks' and his team at Aswan in 2001. They used a bow drill to laboriously cut a granite core.[3] Using a copper saw and sand, it required Stocks and his team about 25 hours of drilling to penetrate one inch into the rose granite bedrock. The hard red granite at Aswan is even harder than the rose granite. So, the time expended can depend on what variety of granite is drilled. The blocks and beams making up the King's Chamber in the Great Pyramid are generally classified as hard, red Aswan granite (granodiorite).

Stocks also did an experiment in 1999 involving sarcophagus manufacture.[4] Using tube drills and a great deal of sand, he producing drill holes with considerable effort. Although Stocks advocates that this kind of operation was the means used to make Khufu's sarcophagus, this slow-grinding system does not explain the rapid cutting lines Petrie observed.

In the 1950s, it required 12 days for Antoine Zuber to cut six crude holes in granite bedrock so he could detach a small chunk with wooden wedges.[5] Reginald Engelbach tried pounding the quarry floor at Aswan for hours. His effort resulted in a small amount of granite debris. Mark Lehner tried the same experiment and produced the same results.

We can also gain an appreciation of Petrie's point of view by considering an eleventh century report by Theophilus concerning how a crystal was cut with an iron lapidary saw:

> If you wish to cut crystal, fix four wooden pins on a bench, with the crystal lying firmly between them. These pins are so arranged that they are joined together in pairs, above and below, so closely that the saw can hardly be drawn between them and can nowhere be deflected. Insert the iron saw and, throwing on sharp sand mixed with water, have two stand by to draw it and to throw on the sand and water without stopping. This is continued until the crystal is cut into two parts.[6]

Petrie thought that jewelled teeth must have made the three-inch-long cut he saw on the interior of the east side of Khufu's sarcophagus. Petrie collected stunning artifacts that show signs of rapid cutting, and he showed and discussed them with machinists and fellow Egyptologists. The artifacts have various features made with sharp, pointed tools that showed no sign of dulling during cutting. Petrie marveled at etchings with fine cross sections, measuring a mere 1/100 inch. The feature shows that the tool that created these etchings rapidly ploughed through the objects in a single pass.

At Giza and elsewhere, Petrie found cores left over from the drilling of hard stone. Some cores are the leftovers of helical cuts. Petrie was amazed by the amount of pressure he reckoned must have been applied to the drills to cut through rock so rapidly:

> The great pressure needed to force the drills and saws so rapidly through the hard stones is very surprising; probably a load of at least a ton or two was placed on the 4-inch drills cutting in granite. On the granite core, No. 7 [Petrie Museum Core UC16036], the spiral of the cut sinks 1 inch in the circumference of 6 inches, or 1 in 60, a rate of ploughing out of the quartz and feldspar which is astonishing.[7]

In his discussion of Khufu's sarcophagus, Petrie proposed the use of jewel-tipped saws several feet long to make a clean slice 90 inches long though granite. In recent years, machinist Chris Dunn calculated that much more pressure was needed to force a drill through Khufu's granite sarcophagus.[8] Dunn also asserts that much more advanced machinery must have existed—of the type just now beginning to be developed.

Dunn and the machinists with whom he consulted find no other way to account for many ancient Egyptian items. They prefer their method for making Petrie's granite core No. 7, from Khafra's Valley Temple. Notwithstanding the severe historical problems associated with Dunn's proposal, we will consider his work in the next chapter.

Alfred Lucas argued relentlessly for abrasion methods. He asserted that sand must have been used to grind down rock. He reckoned that the Egyptians used sand in conjunction with small hand-held pieces of softer materials (like copper, wood, horn or rope), which were frequently replaced because of wear and tear. Lucas speculated that the repeated grinding of rock surfaces would wear them away until cuts were made.

Lucas' *Ancient Egyptian Materials and Industries* (revised by J.R. Harris) is an Egyptological standard. So, Lucas' proposed method became more popular than those Petrie proposed. Besides, Lucas' methods are more acceptable to Egyptology. Lucas' methods suit the primitive technological level and materials of ancient Egypt. Gemstones are unknown for ancient Egypt. Only semi-precious stones are known. Cutting hard gemstones into teeth is outside of the technological capabilities of ancient Egypt. Besides, even diamond teeth will crumble under the great force Petrie proposed.

But Petrie collected many examples that defy the use of abrasives. The diorite bowls he collected at Giza are examples. They bear 4th Dynasty inscriptions made by sharp, pointed instruments:

> These hieroglyphs are incised, with a very free-cutting point; they are not scraped nor ground out, but are ploughed through the diorite, with rough edges to the line. As the lines are only 1/150 inch wide…it is evident that the cutting point must have been much harder than quartz; and tough enough not to splinter when so fine an edge was being employed, probably only 1/200 inch wide. Parallel lines are graved only 1/10 inch apart from centre to centre.[9]

Diorite is one of the most difficult types of rocks to cut. It is extremely hard and incredibly tough. The most common variety of diorite used for bowls of the type Petrie described contains feldspar and black hornblende, such that large quantities of corundum (which is similar in hardness to tungsten carbide) are needed just to scratch it. But Lucas did not believe that the Egyptians of the Pyramid Age or before imported corundum.

There is also the seemingly impossible clean, helical cut on Petrie's granite core No. 7, which he described as follows:

> On the granite core, broken from a drill-hole (No. 7), other features appear, which also can only be explained by the use of fixed jewel points. Firstly, the grooves which run around it form a regular spiral, with no more interruption or waviness than is necessarily produced by the variations in the component crystals; this spiral is truly symmetrical with the axis of the core.
>
> In one part a groove can be traced with scarcely an interruption, for a length of four turns. Secondly, the grooves are as deep in the quartz as in the adjacent feldspar, and even rather deeper. If these were in any way produced by loose powder, they would be shallower in the harder substance — quartz;…and further, inasmuch as the quartz stands out slightly beyond the feldspar (owing to the latter being worn by general rubbing), the groove was thus left even less in depth on the feldspar than on the quartz. Thus, even if specimens with similarly deep grooves could be produced by a loose powder, the special features of this core would still show that fixed cutting points were the means here employed.[10]

Core No. 7 is approximately two inches in diameter, and is a waste product of an ancient Egyptian tubular drill hole. A clean spiral groove winds around the core in unbroken turns. Petrie was astonished by his observation that an ancient mason cut through granite with tremendous ease. Petrie recognized that the feature could not result from a slow grinding process that employed a grit. The spiral groove is relatively deeply incised into the rock surface. The abrasion method produces a great many random scratch marks all over a core made by many hours of grinding. This creates the appearance of a dense mass of scratch marks, rather than a clean spiral groove.

To try to replicate this artifact, the team led by Denys Stocks operated a bow drill and used abrasive sand to very gradually cut a core from Aswan granite. The results do not match the features of Petrie's core No. 7, which shows a groove running a few rotations around the core — equaling three feet of cutting with no wear on the tool. It is to be expected that a team laboriously operating a bow drill and continuously applying a large amount of quartz sand will not produce a helical grove that looks like it was cut with a few clean turns of a drill.

While it is evident that the abrasive grinding process cannot reproduce the clean spiral around Petrie's core, Stocks' bow drill test is touted by some as evidence that his system actually reproduces the enigmatic features of ancient Egyptian granite cores. The reason is that ancient artifacts like this have become a hotbed of debate. Argumentation rages between conservatives who protect the status quo and those who advocate highly-advanced technology to explain the artifacts.

Quartz is an essential component of granite. Quartz sand and/or sharp quartz shards can be used to gradually abrade quartz. A pointed quartz shard can be used to sheer across a piece of quartzite to gradually wear away the quartzite. A problem with the system is that the worn quartz shard quickly gets dull, and so must be constantly replaced. Another problem is that quartz must be crushed to obtain sharp shards. But crushing produces microfractures that will cause many of the shards to break during the scribing process. Opaque quartz consists of a multitude of small air cavities and moisture that produce this appearance. Petrie may have considered these structural weaknesses because he did not include quartz on his list of potential cutting points. Besides, quartz shards will not reproduce the features on artifacts that Petrie collected to prove the rapid advancement of a pointed tool. None of the proposed methods are practical for producing 50-foot-high monolithic statues and tall, monolithic temple columns with quartzite.

To be effective, cutting teeth must be far harder than the material being cut — and remain sharp. The Egyptians possessed flint, which is harder than quartz. But, in 1956, Antoine Zuber showed the problems with using flint shards. They are so brittle that they break when hard blows are applied. Cutting with flint shards also leaves raised ridges when the shards chip. Flint shards do not produce clean tool sweeps, like those on artifacts. A striking example is a bowl made with diorite. Its interior has round cutting lines many feet long. The lines show no evidence of the tool chipping or becoming dull.

Petrie collected a number of fragments of artifacts exhibiting distinct saw cuts. His collection includes fragments from the aforementioned large platform, made with basalt, east of the Great Pyramid. Petrie collected a slice of diorite exhibiting equidistant and regular grooves running in circular arcs that are parallel to one another. In other words, masons rapidly cut this sample with a circular saw. Petrie found crisp, deeply cut hieroglyphic inscriptions that far exceed the results obtained with the best sintered (metal bond) diamond drills and saws of his day.

One of Petrie's impressive specimens is part of a drill hole, in diorite, that is 14 inches in circumference. Seventeen equidistant grooves show successive rotations of the same cutting point. So, what looks like a single cut through diorite is 20 feet in length. Clarke and Engelbach attended a lecture Petrie delivered in 1883 at the Anthropological Institute. They described three of his most impressive artifacts. They described this particular 20-foot, clean cut:

> The second specimen is part of a drill-hole in diorite. The hole has been [cut] 4 inches in diameter, or 14 inches in circumference. As seventeen equidistant grooves appear to be due to successive rotations of the same cutting-point, a single cut is thus 20 feet in length.[11]

Here is how Clarke and Engelbach described another striking artifact:

> The third specimen — a piece of diorite — shows a series of grooves, each ploughed out to a depth of 1/100 inch at a single cut without any irregularity of or 'starting' of the tool.[12]

They also contemplated Petrie's granite core No. 7, and had this to say: "…in one part a single groove may be traced around the core for a length…equal to three feet." Petrie showed them that there is no difference in quality in the whole area of cut, as there would be if the cutting point had started to get dull or fail. Saw marks also typically sweep across the backs of Old Kingdom statues made with different hard stones.

Petrie and Lucas debated the manufacture of these and others features in hard rock over their long careers. The result is that, in general, Egyptology accepts Lucas' abrasion method for cutting the artifacts even though it defies common sense. Many Egyptologists have grown accustomed to accepting that many artifacts just remain unexplained.

Some other Egyptologists try to explain away the artifacts — even though the items defy replication with any known tooling method. Others take the scientific approach of remaining neutral, because they lack appropriate technical training to make a determination.

To try to solve problems, Denys Stocks created some stone objects with simple tools. He created a limestone vessel. So have many a modern Egyptian, after laborious toil. But no one has made a diorite vase. This material presents a whole different set of difficult problems than limestone. So, diorite vases are the real test. They typically exhibit uniformly thick walls that astound experts. Sanding diorite to make vases with uniformly thick walls is not practical with any kind of ancient grinding equipment.

Drilling experiments were designed to test Lucas' proposal about grinding with abrasive sand.[13] Experiments by L. Gorelick and J. Gwinnett showed that flint drills and quartz sand do not reproduce clean, concentric cutting lines (a series of circular lines that are all parallel with a common center). The interiors of shallow bowls in museums exhibit such clean, concentric cutting lines. These bowls were made with a variety of hard stones, including diorite. The crisp, circular cuts represent places where the angle of the cutting tips changed as the items were turned during production.

Gorelick and Gwinnett tested a variety of abrasives to establish which are capable of making clean, concentric lines in granite. Some sarcophagi have a hole at each end, presumably used to attach lids. Gorelick and Gwinnett made casts of concentric cutting lines on the holes in the two-ton lid of an Old Kingdom sarcophagus in the Brooklyn Museum (thought to have belonged to a prince named Akhet-Hotep). They used a slab of similar red granite for their drilling experiment.

They tested with and without lubricants, using a copper rod and a copper tube along with abrasives. The abrasives they tested were beach sand and a variety of crushed materials, including quartz, silicon carbide, garnet, emery, corundum, and diamond.

Their drill operated at a constant rotation speed of 1,000 r.p.m. They also did some drilling with a brace and bit, moving in an oscillating manner. Similar to the experiments by Denys Stocks, Gorelick and Gwinnett tested with a bow drill, too. The use of a bow drill is important because it relates back to the impossibility of making Petrie's core No. 7 with grinding methods.

In all of their tests, the abrasives known in ancient Egypt failed on the hard granite Gorelick and Gwinnett used. Quartz sand did not produce clean, concentric cutting lines, when used wet or dry. Lucas' idea that sand will attach to copper and behave as set teeth did not hold up in their experiments. Chipped flint, fashioned sandstone and quartzite failed to produce clean, concentric lines when used both wet and dry. Their experiments showed that the extent of cutting was negligible when the drills were made with sandstone and quartzite, although quartzite is very hard rock. A flint drill was also ineffective on granite.

The only abrasives that produced comparable concentric cutting lines in the granite were powders of emery, corundum, and diamond. Egyptologists do not believe that these materials were available in ancient Egypt. Not even diamond would explain Petrie's examples of crisp, rapid etching, or the plunge cuts, or the bowl showing that a tool stroke swept through 20 feet of diorite without the tool dulling.

Egyptologists do not think that opal, ruby, or sapphire were available, either. Emery (corundum) occurs in Nubia and on the Grecian Islands. But Alfred Lucas always opted for quartz sand as an effective abrasive because he did not think that emery/corundum was imported early on. He indicated:

> Although it is often stated that emery was employed in ancient Egypt as an abrasive with drills and saws for working hard stones and, although some abrasive powder must have been used, it has never been proved that the material was emery, which in my opinion was most improbable.[14]

No word for emery appeared in the Egyptian vocabulary until Ptolemaic times (the ancient Greek word for emery was "smeris"). Emery is indigenous to the Grecian Cycladic islands in the Aegean Sea. It mostly came from the island of Naxos. But no emery from Naxos or anywhere else has ever been found in the ruins of ancient Egypt. Also, the amount of emery that would have had to be imported would have been tremendous. Such an enormous quantity would be conspicuous in the ancient Egyptian culture.

Lucas was right to think that quartz sand will abrade granite. Denys Stocks showed that long, hard labor can produce some results with sand used in conjunction with tube drills. But producing results that can be shown to match the special features of artifacts made with granite and harder stones is an entirely different matter. Petrie's words again come to mind: "Modern diamond drill cores are clumsy and smudged work when compared with the Egyptian cores."

Egyptology documents granite beams with zigzag joints, granite statuary, granite colossi capturing the subtle curvatures of the human body and weighing over 1,000 tons, granite obelisks with crisp intaglio of better quality than can be achieved with diamond drills, arched granite ceilings over crypts, tall, round, monolithic temple columns made with hard rock, and hard-stone vessels with walls of uniform thickness or that taper to a paper-thin edge. All of these artifacts and many more beckon us to consider a more sophisticated technology — and one that fits with Late Stone Age capabilities and can be proven.

The experiments by Gorelick and Gwinnett and those by Denys Stocks help illuminate this masonry quandary. Gorelick and Gwinnett showed the problems of re-creating a feature that is much easier to achieve than many that Petrie collected, and many thousands of others. Denys Stocks' crew drilled long and hard into granite in an attempt to show how ancient Egyptians made sarcophagi and cores. But the features produced do not match the striking examples of artifacts — like the rapid cuts through granite Petrie observed in Khufu's sarcophagus or the cores he and machinists have pondered. The paradox is clear and unanswered by experiments conducted with standard rock-cutting methods.

We have seen that the methods Lucas proposed have failed. But Egyptologists fall back on Petrie's proposed tools when Lucas' methods do not hold up. Petrie reasoned that a gem such as sapphire, which registers as Mohs 9, can cut granite, which is orders of magnitude softer at Mohs 7. But while it has long been established that sapphire can abrade granite, using sapphire as cutting teeth presents an entirely different set of problems. There is the problem of creating the teeth. There is the problem of cementing the teeth into a saw (using ancient glue) so that they are not torn out during sawing. There is the problem of how well the jewels will hold up during cutting. Concerning the latter problem, I consulted with Michel Barsoum, a Materials Scientist in the Department of Materials Science and Engineering at Drexel University.

Michel Barsoum read my unpublished manuscript of this book, and it inspired him to devote over five years of research and organize an international team devoted to the solution presented later in these pages. His project was followed by experiments at MIT, conducted by a team of professors and their students. Concerning the problem of gems acting as cutting teeth, Michel Barsoum informed me that they will simply flake off within minutes of drilling granite. This is because of internal microfractures that weaken all gems. They cannot withstand the pressure needed to rapidly force them through granite. This is even true of diamond. So, Petrie's idea that ancient Egyptians set their tubular drills with fixed jewel points is unworkable. It does not provide the answer to the enigmatic artifacts. The answers lie in an altogether different discipline.

Chapter 11
Artifacts Defy Modern Reproduction

We can gain a deeper understanding by looking at the work of those who used drastically different experimentation methods. In the 1980s, Denys Stocks performed experiments showing that both ancient and modern metal chisels are unsuitable for working certain types of hard stone.[1] With this in mind, Stocks theorized that the ancient Egyptians must have used stone tools to dress hard rocks. He proposes that the ancient masons used tubular copper drills with large amounts of abrasive sand and a tremendous amount of labor to hollow out granite sarcophagi.

Stocks experimented with rose-granite sarcophagus manufacture. He theorized that the sarcophagus in the Great Pyramid was made with the kinds of tools he used. But the abrasive method is extremely slow. The method Stocks used fails to address the cutting lines on Khufu's sarcophagus, which astonished Petrie because the granite was cut through extremely rapidly. A great many other artifacts show the same kind of crisp, rapid cutting.

The cutting lines on Khufu's sarcophagus, and etchings and other cutting lines that Petrie showed were made with sharp points, demonstrate that Old Kingdom Egyptians did not use the slow grinding methods employed by Stocks. Instead, the highly efficient Late Stone Age method used affords rapid cutting. It stands to reason that the rapid cutting was possible only because of the recovered ancient technology I explain later in this book. When all of the facts are considered, nothing else makes any sense.

Stocks' masonry methods and theories are drastically different than those of machinist Christopher Dunn.[2] Stocks has considerable experience working with simple tools and abrasives. Dunn has long experience in advanced manufacturing methods, including laser processing and electrical-discharge machining. In 1995, Dunn examined a number of Egyptian sarcophagi dating from the Old and New Kingdoms. His cursory examination left him stunned and unshakably convinced of the existence of advanced machining in ancient Egypt.

Arriving at Giza, Dunn set to work, but the King's Chamber of the Great Pyramid was too crowded for him to examine Khufu's sarcophagus. Undaunted, he went to Khafra's pyramid nearby. It attracts less tourist traffic. Dunn was able to enter its sarcophagus. He had with him a flashlight and a parallel, a tool used to test the flatness of a surface. It is a piece of steel ground extremely flat, measuring roughly a quarter of an inch thick and six inches long. Inside Khafra's sarcophagus, Dunn was amazed. He describes what he found at his web site:

> The first object I inspected was the sarcophagus inside the second (Khafra's) pyramid on the Giza Plateau. I climbed inside the box and, with a flashlight and the parallel, was astounded to find the surface on the inside of the box perfectly smooth and perfectly flat. Placing the edge of the parallel against the surface I shone my flashlight behind it. No light came through the interface. No matter where I moved the parallel, vertically, horizontally, sliding it along as one would a gage on a precision surface plate I couldn't detect any deviation from a perfectly flat surface.

Although Dunn would not be able to determine whether or not the surfaces he was measuring are bowed, he says that the several internal and external areas he measured exhibited extreme flatness to within .0002 inch. Dunn recognized that it would not be possible to perform this masonry work by hand on hard granite. The task would be complex and difficult even with modern machinery. This sarcophagus is not the product of the techniques used by Denys Stocks. Stocks would not likely be able to achieve flatness of .0002 inch over a radius of more than a few inches.

Dunn was more wonderstruck by a sarcophagus he measured in the Serapeum, at Saqqara. The Serapeum is a remarkable subterranean tomb that was enlarged during the New Kingdom by the administration of Pharaoh Ramses the Great. Geologists classify a few of its many large sarcophagi as limestone, and the rest as either granite or granodiorite (an intermediate rock type between granite and quartz-containing diorite). These sarcophagi once contained the funerary remains of Apis bulls, the male counterparts of the sacred Isis cows. These great stone sarcophagi weigh at least 65 tons each. The added weight of their lids brings the total to about 100 tons per sarcophagus. They each stand about 11 feet high, 13 feet long, and 7 feet wide.

When French Egyptologist Auguste Mariette (1821–1881) discovered and excavated the Serapeum, he recorded 24 sarcophagi still in position.[3] The heaviest weighs about 70 tons. Each sarcophagus sits in its own sunken rock-cut niche, and these niches form rows along the bedrock walls.

Christopher Dunn reported that he was able to measure the surfaces of some of the sarcophagi. Those he examined are extremely flat. He moved his parallel in many positions against their surfaces. When he shined a flashlight against his parallel, no light came through to its other side. So, again he found flatness to .0002 inch over huge surfaces. He says that he found this all the more intriguing because ancient Egyptians are not thought to have been able to measure this degree of flatness, let alone achieve it.

Dunn was able to make a careful comparison between a sarcophagus and its lid. He found both to be perfectly flat. With its heavy lid in place, the air between the two dense surfaces was pushed out, producing a very effective seal. Dunn's mind was staggered as he reckoned the technical difficulties of producing both a hard stone lid and sarcophagus to fit in this ultraprecise, conforming way. The tight fit brings to mind the huge blocks making up the King's Chamber of the Great Pyramid and many other examples.

Dunn reckoned that making a fitted lid is vastly more difficult than producing the surfaces of the monolithic sarcophagus itself. With an appreciation that can come only come from a long career in advanced machining, Dunn was amazed as he examined a number of ancient Egyptian ruins and artifacts during his trip. These artifacts are taken for granted by Egyptologists these days. Dunn found several that defy the conventional explanations of their manufacture.

After returning home, Dunn conferred with four different U.S. manufacturers that precision-cut granite. None possessed equipment capable of producing a monolithic sarcophagus. They could not make a custom-fitted lid with a comparably tight fit, either. The best the companies could offer was granite slabs bolted together to form a box. The sarcophagi are examples of artifacts that defy modern replication with the best cutting tools—just as are the Colossi of Memnon and the 1,000-ton and heavier statues of Ramses II, and long, clean sweeps that run up to 20 feet long through artifacts with no sign of dulling of the tool used.

Dunn interested some of his peers in the machining industry in contemplating the enigmas posed by Petrie's granite helical-cut core sample No. 7, described above in Petrie's own words. After considerable pondering, Dunn and his peers concluded that highly-advanced machining must have existed in ancient Egypt. Petrie's granite core No. 7 mystified these machinists, particularly because of the great speed at which the drill had to have penetrated the granite.

Donald Rahn, of Rahn Granite Surface Plate Company, in Dayton, Ohio, who works with diamond drills, offered some information. He advised Dunn that diamond drills rotating at 900 r.p.m. penetrate granite at a rate of one inch in five minutes. With this information, Dunn calculated that the ancient Egyptian masons drilled Petrie's granite core sample No. 7 at a feed rate that is 500 times greater.

After much contemplation, Dunn came up with a machining system he thought could explain the enigmatic features of Petrie's granite core No. 7 from Khafra's Valley Temple. Knowing that Egyptologists frown upon ideas that defy the established history of ancient Egypt, Dunn hoped to gain supporting opinions from his peers. Dunn continually challenged them with aspects of the problem.

Finally, one of them suggested the same method Dunn had in mind for producing the features of Petrie's core No. 7. The method they envisioned was ultrasonic machining, which did not exist in Petrie's day. They reckoned that only an ultrasonic toolbit can tear away at granite rapidly enough. The ultrasonic toolbit vibrates at 19,000 to 25,000 cycles per second, and its use satisfies this anomaly of Petrie's sample.

Dunn subsequently engaged in a debate with an opponent named Ralph Ellis. Afterwards, Dunn suspended his assertion that *only* ultrasonic machining could have produced Petrie's core No. 7. But Dunn still favors ultrasonic machining over any other method. He also recognizes that there are a great many artifacts, like the sarcophagus in the Serapeum with the airtight lid, that are far more difficult to explain than Petrie's core No. 7. Petrie's words merit repeating: "Modern diamond drill cores are clumsy and smudged work when compared with the Egyptian cores."

Although Dunn's theories defy ancient Egyptian history as carefully established by Egyptology, we cannot ignore the rapid rate of descent of the tubular drill that cut core No. 7 (it was calculated by measuring the pitch of points on a descending straight line that intersects the helical groove on the core at 1/10 inch per revolution). Dunn calculated that an Egyptian artisan cut through the granite at a feed rate 500 times greater than is possible with today's best diamond drills.

Despite the attempts by detractors to explain away Petrie's core No. 7, Dunn maintains that the helical groove cut into it is significant and amazing. Dunn set up an appointment at the Petrie Museum in London and carefully examined the core firsthand. He observed that the cut is indeed a continuous helix with some interruptions that were continued along the same average helical path.

The surfaces Dunn measured on interior and exterior sarcophagi walls, flat to .0002 inch, also pose a real challenge to the simple methods Egyptology relies on. The instruments the ancient Egyptians possessed could test flatness only to .01 inch. I interviewed a number of stone cutters about the problem. They all advised me that producing a flatness of .0002 inch along a few inches can be achieved with a great deal of work. But because of their appreciation of the problem, they were all astonished when I explained to them that Dunn reports large areas of wall surface on granite sarcophagi to exhibit the extreme flatness of .0002 inch.

Although primitive tools—in combination with no other special technology—are inadequate for building the Great Pyramids and creating a myriad of smaller artifacts, the real means of production negates the need for advanced machining in ancient Egypt. In short, we need not defy the technological level established by Egyptology to explain the remarkable artifacts described in these pages. So, assuming Dunn's calculation of the rapid rate of granite cutting is correct, the ancient Egyptians possessed a simple means of making their impressive artifacts that is 500 times more efficient than cutting hard granite with today's granite cutting technology. Assuming Dunn's flatness measurements are correct, the Egyptians were also producing a degree of extreme flatness over large surface areas that far surpasses today's industrial standard. We have already established that the construction rate at which the Great Pyramid was built was also extraordinarily rapid.

A myriad of artifacts dating to the Archaic Period (c. 3000–2649 B.C.) exhibit features that challenge modern stone-cutting methods. Egyptologist Walter B. Emery presented stunning pieces in his *Archaic Egypt: Culture and Civilizations in Egypt Five Thousand Years Ago*. Among them was a leaf-shaped schist dish dating to the middle of the 1st Dynasty. An inscribed schist statue belonging to the 2nd Dynasty Pharaoh Kha-sekhem is from Hieraconopolis. Kha-sekhem was rendered seated on his throne wearing his ceremonial robe and the crown of Upper Egypt. Its base depicts rows of slain enemies. Among other examples, a cup made of schist, with a pink limestone base, is from the 1st Dynasty tomb of Queen Her-nit at Saqqara. A finely-crafted diorite spoon dates to the middle of the 1st Dynasty.

Fragments of a leaf-shaped schist dish date to the middle of the 1st Dynasty. This wonderful dish is incised in relief, exhibiting the delicate raised pattern of the veins of a leaf. An exquisite schist dish shaped as a reed basket dates from the 2nd Dynasty. Although

9. Rahotep's beautiful statue features extraordinary inlaid eyes. The lenses have been determined to be made of transparent rock crystal, and the whites of the eyes of opaque quartz.

10. The statue of Nofret, wife of Rahotep, was found in the same 4th Dynasty location. Her eyes have the same marvelous construction. The art of making such eyes was lost.

hard, schist is brittle and will easily break along its foliations into thin, flaky plates. But the intricate dish is marvelously detailed. All the symmetric details of a reed basket appear in high relief. It has perfectly formed, delicate carrying handles.[4]

Finely-made diorite pieces are the most perplexing because the rock is so hard and tough to penetrate even with modern means that apply tremendous brute force. But the Petrie Museum in London exhibits a sawed fragment of a diorite palette with a beveled edge and engraved line. The piece (Museum number UC2529) dates to the Neolithic Period and was found in the Faiyum. This and other artifacts give us the strong sense that the special technology that is the focal point of this book was known that far back in the Stone Age in Egypt. This is very exciting because modern scientific testing of very tiny fragments of artifacts can determine if this is so. In later pages, I describe the work at MIT and Drexel on behalf of this special lost technology that is back and being used again today.

The Petrie Museum exhibits an engraved diorite fragment (number UC6560), perhaps part of a 12th Dynasty statue, found at Lahun, a town located at the entrance of the Faiyum. A small black diorite statue of a Theban priest of Amun dates to the end of the 25th Dynasty. Less than 20 inches high, it is now in the Boston Museum of Fine Arts. In the Paris Louvre Museum, a statue of the god Amun and Pharaoh Tutankhamun (now better known as King Tut) dates to about 1347–1337 B.C. This statue is seven feet tall and made of diorite. These and many other artifacts suggest that the special technology survived the decline of pyramid construction.

Another diorite piece (Petrie Museum number UC6539) dates to the Dynastic Period and exhibits a hieroglyphic etching. A diorite fragment from a bowl is inscribed with the name "Khufu" (Petrie Museum number UC11758).

In the Cairo Museum, stone (carnelian and lapis) beads dating to the Middle Kingdom (c. 2040–1640 B.C.) have remarkably small threading holes.[5] Some stone beads measure as small as 0.023 inch in diameter, with smaller threading holes. The smallest bead holes produced by Denys Stocks are much larger, measuring 1 mm. I corresponded with a beadmaker at the top of his field. Although he does not want to be named or involved in the controversy over enigmatic artifacts (because so many wild claims have been made), he felt confident that he could reproduce the .023 beads with smaller holes if he could use modern means. But he was not willing to take up the challenge using only ancient methods.

The best ancient Egyptian beadmaking drill was flint. It is feasible to drill some beads with flint drills. But certain examples, like those tiny beads mentioned above, suggest the use of a special technology. Any drill used to cut into rock like carnelian or lapis must be tough enough at the tiny hole size (less than .023 inch) not to splinter or fracture.

Certain Old Kingdom statues exhibit remarkable examples of eyes so realistic and ingeniously crafted that they give the impression that they follow the eye movements of the onlooker. Striking examples are the eyes of the 4th Dynasty statues of Prince Rahotep and his wife Princess Nofret (c. 2600–2575 B.C.), found in their twin mastabas near the Meidum pyramid.

Like most others with this extraordinary form of eyes, they are *ka* statues (the *ka* having been considered the body double that lingered on in tomb statuary or otherwise inhabited the tomb). An analysis was conducted on a number of such uncanny eyes by optical specialist Jay Enoch, of the School of Optometry at U.C. Berkeley. He consulted with several other specialists for his research project. The specimens investigated include the masterpiece eyes of the famous 4th or 5th Dynasty seated scribe (E-3023) in the Louvre. The lenses appear to be either alpha silica or fused silica. All of the finest examples are beautifully constructed and demonstrate very good knowledge of the anatomy of the human eye. Jay Enoch was astonished by the complex technological achievement dating to such early history. The unique schematic eyes capable of the "following movement" are unprecedented in all of ancient and modern history.

🔯 Chapter 12 🔯
A Technological Riddle

During the Pyramid Age, before hard metal tools were introduced in Egypt, grandiose structures abounded—mostly all made of massive medium-hard to hard blocks. But as the centuries passed, and as better tools were introduced, art and architecture fell into a serious decline that worsened as time passed.

There are impressive exceptions, like the 50-foot-high Colossi of Memnon, built with quartzite during the 18th Dynasty. But the exceptions are relatively few in number. Egyptologists cannot explain this paradoxical architectural peak and decline.

The overview I present here illustrates the scope of this riddle. When only primitive stone tools and abrasives were available, the most ancient masons made great quantities of superb objects. In some cases, as I have explained, the best modern tools will not enable their replication when cutting into hard rocks. In Predynastic times, artisans used extremely hard rock types to fashion many thousands of the most perfect vessels in history.[1]

In the 1st Dynasty, the first stone pavement appeared in the tomb of Pharaoh Den at Abydos, in northern Upper Egypt.[2] It was made with granite. Each slab is a little more than eight feet long and only about five inches thick. After the 2nd Dynasty, numerous pavements were made with hard limestone, basalt, granite, or quartzite. Pavements made from granite are fairly common in Old Kingdom buildings.[3]

At the apex of Egyptian architecture, master pyramid builders of the 4th Dynasty used medium-hard and hard rock on an unprecedented scale. They built the only remaining wonder of the world—the Great Pyramid.

After the Pyramid Age, pyramids were built increasingly smaller. This is a mystery of Egyptology because Egypt was very prosperous in the 5th Dynasty. Egypt's economy remained stable until the end of the 6th Dynasty.[4]

Pyramid construction mysteriously went into steady decline. The last Egyptian pyramids were built in the 12th Dynasty. They were made with mud-brick rather than stone. Most are mounds of rubble today.[5]

By 800 years after the Great Pyramid was built, a hard form of bronze finally became available in Egypt. Even with bronze tools, the monuments of this period pale in comparison with the Great Pyramids. Egyptology has no explanation.

Architecture prospered during the New Kingdom, especially during the 18th and 19th Dynasties. But most constructions were built of relatively small, soft sandstone blocks. Masons also made some temples by hollowing out very soft sandstone cliffs. This eliminated the need to move large building blocks. Some large statues were made in situ by sculpting soft sandstone cliffs, so that the large statues did not have to be moved at all.

The severe architectural decline that set in long before, after the Pyramid Age, was steadily worsening. As mentioned, the Colossi of Memnon made during the New Kingdom with quartzite are exceptions to this trend. So are the 1,000-ton and heavier statues of Ramses II. Engineers have not determined how heavy weights like these could be hauled or erected or correctly aligned onto pedestals in ancient times.

Egyptology has no explanation for the continuing architectural decline. The Egyptians obtained not just bronze, but also eventually iron. But with few exceptions, the Theban monuments do not compare to the fabulous monuments built a millennium earlier.

We arrive at a dramatic statistic when we compare the volume of stone consumed by the Old and New Kingdoms. Pyramid Age workers used millions of massive blocks in a single monument. Khufu's Great Pyramid, consisting of about 2.3 million blocks, was followed by that of Khafra—the Second Great Pyramid at Giza. Khafra's pyramid incorporates about two million blocks and is about 50 feet shorter than the Great Pyramid. Pharaoh Snofru was the most ambitious builder of all, using more stone for his two pyramids collectively than are incorporated into Khufu's Great Pyramid. The pyramid complexes were also equipped with long causeways, temples, and huge retaining walls.

Compare the collective volume of these pyramids with New Kingdom constructions: Pharaoh Ramses II's grandiose architectural presence appears at about half of ancient Egypt's habitation sites. For his great many architectural accomplishments—works intended to renew Egypt's splendor—he was one of the few pharaohs deified during his lifetime.[6] But the total amount of rock used during Ramses' ambitious 65-year reign pales in comparison with the amount incorporated into the Great Pyramid in under 25 years.

During the 18th Dynasty, Pharaoh Amenhotep III glorified Thebes, giving it the monumental beauty of a great capital city. He, too, was deified during his lifetime for this accomplishment.[7] Some other pharaohs also have impressive building records. But all of the Theban architecture built from the New Kingdom down to the start of the Roman occupation of Egypt—an expanse of about 1,500 years—incorporated less stone than the Great Pyramids.

By contrast, the four greatest pyramids were built in only about 60 years. They include the Great Pyramids of Khufu, Khafra and two built for Snofru. Rainer Stadelmann, Director of the German Archaeological Institute in Cairo, estimated that 4th Dynasty workers consumed almost 318 million cubic feet of limestone to build pyramids.[8]

Compare this figure with the approximate volume of stone in Theban constructions. According to geologist Francoise Michel de Roziere of the Napoleonic Egyptian Expedition, the total volume of Theban constructions built over 1,500 years amounts to about 141 million cubic feet of sandstone.[9]

His estimate includes buildings and their foundations, floors and external architectural features, as well as roads, piers and watercourses. He excluded the extensive Nubian structures south of Thebes and demolished Theban constructions, because blocks of the latter group were likely recycled. All of the Theban sandstone constructions of the New Kingdom, Late Period, and Ptolemaic Period—together spanning 1,500 years—do not equal half the amount of stone used during the 80-year Pyramid Age (during which all of the greater and lesser Great Pyramids arose).

The rapid construction of the Great Pyramids alerts us to a highly efficient technology that was gradually lost. The dramatic paradox comes into sharper focus when we consider the materials and structural designs of New Kingdom Theban and later work.

Middle and New Kingdom workers mostly used smaller building blocks than did their illustrious predecessors, with few exceptions. For instance, Ramses II added to the extensive Theban Temple at Luxor. The first pylon at Luxor he built is about 88 feet high, and its towers are 98 feet wide. But these structures are built of relatively small blocks. The bulk of the temple, and all of its external features, are made with interlocking sandstone blocks that are small compared with the blocks of the Great Pyramid.

The Temple of Karnak, the most important in ancient Thebes, is adorned with 122 temple columns that tower 70 feet. These giant columns, like the bulk of the temple itself, are made of relatively small interlocking sandstone blocks. The core masonry of pylons II, III, and IX of the Karnak Temple was built with blocks taken from earlier structures.

Rather than quarrying stone, New Kingdom workers often demolished Middle Kingdom temples to get blocks for building new temples. Builders even expropriated and recycled more ancient statues.

In later Ptolemaic times, the Greek pharaoh Ptolemy XI (c. 112–51 B.C.) began constructing the imposing Hathor Temple at Dendera. The Roman Emperor Augustus Caesar later completed it. The Temple is almost 300 feet long and about 135 feet at its widest point. Its enormous portico is supported by 24 columns, each 50 feet high and more than 22 feet in circumference. But the structures are made of soft sandstone blocks that cannot compare in size to the large blocks in Old Kingdom superstructures.[10]

New Kingdom and later masons and artisans built mostly with the soft sandstone of Egypt's southern quarries. The most commonly used variety, which is abundant in the Theban region, is soft enough to abrade with one's fingernails (which are 2.2 on the Mohs' hardness scale). The famous Abu Simbel Temple of Ramses II is a good example of this kind of soft rock.

Ramses II's masons hollowed the Abu Simbel Temple from a very soft sandstone cliff. Between 1964 and 1966, a United Nations team cut up and moved it to save it from the rising waters of Lake Nasser. Their task was complicated by the tendency of the rock to crumble. Workers had to cut very deeply into the fragile cliff to obtain masses strong enough to tolerate transportation. It was necessary to inject the sandstone with resin to stabilize it so that they could cut the temple blocks into units weighing up to 30 tons each.[11]

Although there are extensive hard limestone mountains at two sites in the Theban area, few limestone buildings were erected in the vicinity. Instead of using this hard, local limestone, the Egyptians of this era transported the softest limestone of Tura — located hundreds of miles to the north. Soft sandstone was the preferred material for construction, although a hard form of bronze was available in the New Kingdom. Even iron was available on a very limited scale.

Limestone casing blocks appear in only a few royal tombs of the early 18th Dynasty.[12] But most New Kingdom tomb interiors were coated with mud plaster instead of stone.[13] Compare interior walls of Old Kingdom tombs. They were mostly made with limestone. They were generally fully or partially lined with blocks and slabs made with granite. This is typical for 4th and 5th Dynasty Mortuary Temples.[14]

A description by Dieter Arnold provides a good idea of the poor quality of most New Kingdom Theban masonry work:

> Close jointing was frequently neglected, however, especially in the huge buildings of the New Kingdom, where the stone broke easily during handling or not enough time was left for more careful work. The results are gaping joints and crevices along the front faces of blocks, which had to be hidden by extensive use of mortar. In buildings of such irregular and neglected joining, one cannot see how the builders could have planned the joint position.[15]

The riddle of Egypt's severe and permanent architectural decline cannot be explained by a shortage of stone. Limestone and granite regions were never exhausted of suitable building stone. As mentioned, New Kingdom artisans did not take advantage of the hard limestone in their nearby Theban mountain ranges.

A labor shortage cannot explain the riddle. Large task forces are known to have existed. They carried out military campaigns and civilian programs during the New Kingdom and later. An example is the huge task force Pharaoh Ramses II organized for his military campaigns. Masses of foreigners crowded into Egypt's northern cities during Ramses II's reign. They were drafted into his armies and large labor forces.[16]

We cannot assume that the answer is that far more men were set to work on pyramids than on later constructions. Densely packing workers produces highly counterproductive conditions, since people cannot work effectively when packed elbow-to-elbow. Teams of densely packed men pulling blocks up slick ramps would result in hazardous conditions. Because of friction and other factors, elevating massive blocks to great heights requires more manpower than building the smaller New Kingdom structures with their relatively small blocks.

A shortage of wealth is not the answer. The 18th Dynasty began with the expulsion of the Hyksos invaders from northern Egypt. During the 18th Dynasty, Egypt evolved from a fractured, occupied nation to become a vast, mighty and exceedingly wealthy empire. Vassal countries paid tribute to Egypt with all kinds of treasures and goods to assure peace and acquire political favors. Nevertheless, soft sandstone monuments—made of relatively small building units—characterize this period of triumph in Egypt's New Kingdom capital city and its environs.

To summarize, the archaeological record clearly shows the problem. Stone Age methods afforded the world's greatest architecture and a myriad of smaller artifacts. Many defy reproduction today when masons tackle granite and harder rocks. As history progressed, Egypt produced increasingly fewer masonry masterpieces. We should expect that architecture would have flourished when stronger metal tools were introduced. But the Bronze and Iron Ages are characterized by architecture made of relatively small, soft sandstone blocks and limestone blocks taken from much earlier structures.

During the 18th Dynasty, artisans produced the Colossi of Memnon and several tall obelisks made with granite. But the amount of hard stone consumed to build these structures is vastly smaller than that of Old Kingdom constructions.

During the 19th Dynasty, a number of pyramids were restored with limestone, and some impressive constructions were built in northern Egypt—perhaps by artisans who inherited the special ancestral knowledge that had given Egypt its architectural splendor in the distant past. But the Theban structures of Egypt's south are characterized by relatively small sandstone blocks. When hard stone was employed, it was usually reserved for smaller objects like sarcophagi and other tomb furnishings.

How can we explain this technological riddle? The reasonable explanation is that some kind of highly-efficient technology was known and gradually declined.

The overall picture is clear in theory: Before Egypt even became a nation, Neolithic people took advantage of this special technology to make vessels with basalt and diorite. Its use gradually increased. So, by the time Egypt became more organized and prosperous, the labor force used it on an industrial scale to build the Great Pyramids. The use of this special technology was gradually lost. This decline is quite apparent. Pyramids were less well built after the 4th Dynasty. They were built increasingly smaller as time went on. The decline continued over the centuries and great masonry works became an exception. Eventually, the technology was lost—and not rediscovered until recent modern times.

Chapter 13
Block Raising Enigmas

To build the Great Pyramid, workers raised more than two million blocks by means of an enormous ramp that rose to nearly 500 feet—so the entrenched theory of pyramid construction holds. The ramp was supposedly made of stone rubble cemented with clay. To ease friction when elevating blocks, workers surfaced their ramps with clay and applied a lubricant. A deeper look into the problem shows why a ramp is unworkable for building the Great Pyramid.

The ramp theory was advanced by architect Somers Clarke and archaeologist Reginald Engelbach in their classic book titled *Ancient Egyptian Masonry* (1930).[1] For more than a half century, this was the most authoritative book on ancient Egyptian building. For lack of a better system that fits with the primitive technological level, ramp theories have been at the forefront of reckoning how the Great Pyramid was built. But the Great Pyramid is a particularly special case because of its heavy weights positioned at great heights, and Clarke and Engelbach were very scientific-minded and understood this. They cautioned that their deductions may require considerable modification.

Engineers have since advanced several problems with ramp theories. These problems have never been resolved. Consequently, some Egyptologists are beginning to recognize that the long-held ramp theories are not workable. Dieter Arnold mentioned some problems:

> ...ramps could not always be used—for example, at the upper parts of pyramids the enormous quantities of materials consumed and the static problems due to such accumulations probably prevented their use.[2]

Arnold rejected all ramps theories proposed for building the Great Pyramid:

> The type of ramp used for the construction of the Cheops Pyramid has been the subject of countless studies. They rarely take into account, however, that we do not have the slightest indication of the kind of ramp or ramp systems used for this pyramid. These studies also forget that traces of such ramps have actually been recorded from other pyramids...For these reasons, we have to dismiss all theoretical systems so far proposed as pure imagination.[3]

In the 1980s, English master builder Peter Hodges successfully argued that the Great Pyramid would not exist if its construction depended on using any kind of ramp. His work has major implications. Hodges evaluated the short, straight ramp style:

> A ramp can be used either as a 'short' or as a 'long' ramp. The 'short' is one where only the load passes up the incline so that the hauliers can either stand or walk on a level area at the top of the slope.

> This is the most efficient method, whereas the 'long' ramp requires the whole train to walk up the slope together thereby wasting much energy in raising the weight of the hauliers themselves, a considerable factor as their combined weight will probably be more than that of the load itself.

> A short ramp may be invaluable in a permanent situation such as an incline out of a quarry, but for building a pyramid shape its use is restricted to the lower levels

because the working platform becomes too small to accommodate the hauliers. No building theory is worth study unless it encompasses the placing of all the stones required and in particular those at the very top.[4]

Hodges also criticized the commonly-held theory of a long, straight ramp:

The long ramp is the one most usually depicted in books on Egyptology, when the drawing shows a pyramid, three-quarters built and serviced by a ramp with a gradient of about 1 in 3. This layout cannot be based on reason because it is a hard task just to walk up such a gradient and it would be impossible for hauliers to manage their work under these circumstances. However, it might be possible for a gradient of 1 in 10 to be used if the friction under the load could be reduced without impairing the foot-hold for the hauliers. No one would use this method for raising stones today so we cannot study the device in use; the nearest I can get to reality is to walk up a slope which exists near my home. The gradient is 1 in 10 and extends for 100 yards (whereas a ramp to the top of the great Pyramid would run for 1,600 yards), but it is a steady pull, and quite enough to confirm my views that the largest pyramids would never have been built if this were the only method available.[5]

Another reason the ramp theories are so persistent is that small ramps remain attached to some of Egypt's small pyramids. But the use of ramps for small pyramids is logical: Most pyramids consist almost entirely of blocks small enough for one or two men to carry up a ramp of low gradation.

Such pyramids include those of the 3rd Dynasty and all of those built after the 4th Dynasty. These structures contain a relatively small number of special features that would pose block lifting (or block lowering) engineering difficulties. It is mostly blocks in the 4th Dynasty Great Pyramids—especially Khufu's Great Pyramid—that pose insurmountable problems on ramps.

Hodges understood the serious danger that an earthen ramp of the size needed for the Great Pyramid would collapse from its own weight. Hodges understood that an earthen ramp cannot be expected to support the transportation of massive blocks like those found in the Great Pyramid, plus the weight of workers. He deduced that any ramp must be as stable as the Great Pyramid itself. He concluded that to have such stability, the ramp must be made of well-fitted, sturdy stones.

If built at the low gradient of 1:10 he deemed workable, then the ramp would have been 4,800 feet long and at least 480 feet high. It would have taken much longer to build than the Great Pyramid itself.[6] This weighs heavily on the rapid construction rate experts have calculated, too.

Even if a ramp made of stone rubble cemented with clay were strong enough, the practical problems of building and maintaining it would be very serious. Clay requires a considerable amount of water to become pliable. Given the size of the Great Pyramid, constructing a clay-rubble ramp would demand that a great many millions of gallons of water be carried up the Giza Plateau from the Nile.

A huge, constant supply of water would also be needed to keep the ramp's surface slick, so that friction would be reduced when moving blocks. A slick clay-surfaced ramp would require constant refurbishing because of the damage block raising inflicts on the ramp's surface. But the main problem is that the ramp would not be strong enough to support the blocks and workers.

There is no evidence that a ramp was used to build the Great Pyramid. Egyptologists found no ramp remains of any kind connected to the base of the Great Pyramid.[7] Only an earthen ramp was found leading from the quarry up to ground level. But it will not support the weight of the massive blocks, either. This ramp simply allowed men to climb in and out of the quarry more easily.

The size of any ramp depends upon its incline. The steeper the incline, the more difficult elevating blocks becomes. The steeper the incline, the more difficult it becomes to get and maintain a foothold when raising massive stones on a slick surface, too. Some engineers have tried to ease the problem by proposing that the ramp extended only part way up the Great Pyramid. In that case, the highest tiers of the Great Pyramid would have to be constructed by some other means. But given that some of the largest blocks in the Great Pyramid were situated at least as high as tier 201, it makes no sense to imagine a ramp design that will not account for placing those blocks.

In 1974, Danish civil engineer P. Garde-Hansen calculated that a ramp built to the top of the Great Pyramid would require 17.5 million cubic yards of material.[8] The amount he calculated is several times the volume of the Great Pyramid itself. Garde-Hansen calculated that it would require 240,000 men to build such a ramp within Khufu's 23 year reign. Additionally, Garde-Hansen calculated that 300,000 men would be required to dismantle the ramp within eight years.

In 1997, Egyptian civil engineer Moustafa Gadalla published a book recognizing that there is only one solution to the problems facing Egyptology: That one solution, of course, is the highly-efficient means explained in these pages and in other writings by Joseph Davidovits and myself. Moustafa Gadalla's book was inspired by our book titled *The Pyramids: An Enigma Solved* (Hippocrene, NY, 1988), and repeats much of it word-for-word.

As a civil engineer, Moustafa Gadalla is qualified to critique certain issues. For example, today it is a challenge to make even small buildings perfectly level. The level foundation and tiers of the Great Pyramid seem wondrous to architects who appreciate the problem. Another factor appreciated as a marvel is the number of blocks set per minute. Moustafa Gadalla wrote:

> Hypothetically, if we agree with Garde-Hansen's theories, try to visualize the staggering figures:...6.67 blocks per minute! Imagine 6.67 blocks every 60 seconds! This rate is impossible to achieve. This is another reason to disregard the validity of the...ramp theories.[9]

Mark Lehner and others adhere to the standard ramp theory, but propose that a helical ramp was used to build the Great Pyramid.[10] Lehner argues that a wraparound ramp would better suit the topography of Giza than a straight-on ramp. He points out that an enormous straight ramp could not have existed on the south side of the Great Pyramid, because it would have covered the quarry area. So, the large open quarries to the south of the Great Pyramid would not exist. The northern area could not accommodate a ramp because of a 120 foot drop in the terrain. Lehner argues that structures to the east and west of the Great Pyramid prohibit the construction of a straight ramp. The monuments he has in mind include three small queens' pyramids situated to the east, and the field of tombs for Khufu's court members to the west. But the problems with this kind of design are very critical. The 1:10 gradient Peter Hodges recognized would be necessary must extend to all surfaces of the ramp. In that case, a wrap-around ramp would require 4,800-foot-long lengths for all of its lifting surfaces—making the problem for accommodating Giza's topography far worse instead of helping it. The ramp would not only cover the sites Lehner mentions, but also extend beyond the Giza Plateau itself.

No helical ramp has been found associated with any pyramid. Dieter Arnold pointed out serious problems with the helical ramp design:

> ...one would even doubt their feasibility. In spite of the ingeniousness of such a device, spiral ramps would have created serious problems. During the whole construction period, the pyramid trunk would have been completely buried under the ramps. The surveyors could therefore not have used the four corners, edges, and foot line of the pyramid for their calculations. Furthermore, at a certain height the sides of the pyramid would no longer be wide enough to provide a ramp from one corner to the next.[11]

As the helical ramp rose, it would increasingly engulf the pyramid, burying its true reference points. The true reference points are the four corner stones at the base of the pyramid, the angle of the sides of the pyramid, and its baseline. Failure to make all measurements from these absolute reference points would introduce errors that would tend to compound as the pyramid rose. Even the slightest measurement error would have compounded as workers took successive measurements from inaccurate reference points. The result would be a structure with irregular sides that would not form a proper pyramid shape.

Neither Arnold nor Hodges could reckon a way around this serious problem. The PBS Nova film *This Old Pyramid* proposed a helical cantilevered ramp winding up the pyramid.[12] The cantilevered design offers one great advantage: It occupies much less space.

Nova displayed a very simplistic, three-dimensional computer-rendered image of a cantilevered ramp wrapping around a pyramid. By definition, a cantilever is a projecting beam or member supported only at one end. Viewed from the side, a cantilevered beam looks like a diving board in that it is supported only at one end. Nova's image showed such a projecting ramp, supported only at the end attached to the pyramid. Nova provided no engineering detail, engineering opinion, or field demonstration to try to establish whether such a ramp design might possibly be workable.

Without a detailed construction design showing exactly how the ramp would be attached to and supported by the pyramid, we are left to speculate about how such a ramp could have been constructed. A cantilevered ramp involves very demanding engineering and construction techniques. Its strength would have to come from thousands of closely-spaced, extremely long, thick, tough, hard-rock support beams. Perhaps these beams would require interlocking joints. The Giza limestone exploited to build the Great Pyramid is not strong enough to provide the needed beams.

Special support beams would have to be built into the pyramid faces to meet complex engineering requirements. For instance, the beams would have to extend far enough into the core masonry to counterbalance the weight of their lengths extending out of the pyramid. Each beam must also have enough counterbalance to safely support the weight of its proportional load of the finished ramp, plus the proportional load of the heaviest anticipated weight moving along the ramp.

If the need for greater strength were anticipated, then engineers would have to stack the beams vertically, as well, in which case the beams would occupy a number of pyramid tiers. Another way to increase counterbalance is to secure the beams to adjacent core blocks with interlocking joints. Piling masonry onto the beams as the pyramid rises also helps with counterbalancing. A ramp must be both strong and strongly-fitted enough in every respect to support the greatest anticipated weight it must bear. Huge girdle blocks, ranging from 12 to 15 feet long, encase large areas of the Ascending Passageway. Beams span the ceiling of the King's Chamber of the Great Pyramid, and measure up to 27 feet long and weigh up to 73 tons. This weight and length estimate comes from William Kingland's survey. He observed that nine beams span not only the ceiling of the King's Chamber, but also extend over its side walls and have an overhang of five feet. He estimated the depth of these 27-foot beams at about 7 feet, and having a cubic capacity up to about 987 feet. Reckoning the weight of granite at 165 pounds per cubic foot, he thereby arrived at a weight of 73 tons for the most massive of these nine beams (see my quote of Kingsland in the endnotes to Chapter 4).

Moving one of these long beams around the corner of a helical ramp would pose incredibly difficult problems. The ramp would have to be extremely wide, at least at the corners that wrap around the pyramid to the level above the King's Chamber. It is not likely that a 27-foot-long beam would have been moved with its long axis vertical: The beam could too easily tip. Nova's ramp design is also entirely too steep to raise a 27-foot-long beam.

Theorists mostly work with an average block size of 2.5 tons. But they would need to factor in the elevation of thousands of enormous cantilevered beams for the ramp itself. These beams would have to be extraordinary—weighing more than the huge weights they must support. Their size at a 1:10 gradient would be stupendous—and it is not reasonable to think that 27-foot-long beams could be raised at a steeper gradient.

The tiers in the Great Pyramid are not tall enough to support the existence of cantilevered support beams of the immense size needed. No one has found evidence of special masonry joints capable of locking in a keyed ramp. No evidence exists for beams that extended into the outer faces of the Great Pyramid—evidence that must be there for this alternative ramp design to be more than wild speculation on Nova's part. Constructing a cantilevered ramp system would be much more demanding than building the Great Pyramid. It creates more problems than it solves.

Nova proposed that after the pyramid tiers were completed, masons lopped off the cantilevered support beams to form the outer faces of a number of pyramid tiers. The cutting operation would have had to achieve the accurate planes that Petrie reported. As mentioned, Petrie found that the mean optical plane that touches the most prominent points of the blocks of the Great Pyramid's rough core faces shows an average variation of only 1.0 inch.

The concave faces would have to be achieved, too. Any beam endings that did not conform to the design features would have to be replaced with blocks made especially to fit into existing masonry. Re-fitting blocks into tiers, so that they meet all specifications, is far more demanding than fitting blocks into tiers in the first place.

How can we believe that such a complex operation was accomplished? How could it be accomplished with primitive tools? Given the overwhelming demands of the cantilevered ramp, it is very surprising that the award-winning science program Nova introduced the idea at all. Since *This Old Pyramid* was released in 1992, it has been used as a teaching aid for school children and also at the college level.

Nova conducted a limited block-pulling experiment on a partially constructed, non-antilevered miniature helical ramp. The Nova crew built the miniature helical ramp to the extent that it allowed a block to pass around one corner of Nova's miniature pyramid. The block-raising operation was aided by a rope and a simple wooden post set up on the ramp's corner. The post was used for turning a 1/2-ton block around the corner of the ramp. This turning post allowed workers pulling a block to exert their force from around the corner of the ramp. They positioned the block slightly beyond the ramp's corner so they could reorient the block and then pull it higher up the ramp. Joseph Davidovits witnessed the operation and gave me this statement:

> The ramp was built around two sides of the pyramid. They took the small block around the first corner, then they used it to experiment with levers to lift it, but they failed.

Nova experiment did not represent the actual problem at all. Because the one block raised up the mini-ramp weighed only 1/2 ton, great liberties were taken the ramp's dimensions. It only had to accommodate the 1/2 block and leave the pyramid accessible to the front-end loader.

The weight of the blocks of the Great Pyramid is averaged at 2.5 tons. But many blocks in the structure weigh much more. For instance, the blocks making up the King's Chamber walls weigh up to 50 tons each. Beams in the ceiling of the King's Chamber weigh up to an estimated 73 tons. The blocks in tier 35 are taller than those in tier two at the base. Blocks in tier 201 (now missing) near the top were taller than those in tier four near the bottom. Because Nova's workers had little problem raising one 1/2-ton block over a short distance, Mark Lehner concluded in *This Old Pyramid* that the Great Pyramid's construction problems were solved.

Lehner concluded that building the Great Pyramid within Khufu's 23 or 24 year reign is feasible based on their experiments. But there are serious problems with this block-raising experiment that Nova did not mention or address.

Given that it is so highly unlikely that a helical ramp was used for the Great Pyramid, the use of a turning post in the 4th Dynasty is suspect. A reason is that a turning post is a primitive precursor to the pulley. According to Dieter Arnold, the oldest true pulley found in Egypt dates possibly to the late 12th Dynasty. But even with a turning post, Nova fell far short of the construction rate theorized for the Great Pyramid.

The Nova film stated its requirement: An average of one block was set in place every three minutes per day for the 23-year reign of Khufu. The problem Nova had meeting this requirement is evident in a letter from the film's producer Michael Barnes, dated April 25, 1995. Barnes responded as follows to a viewer who confronted him about building the Nova miniature pyramid with a front-end loader:

> Our film…is an attempt to demonstrate tools and techniques that the best archaeological evidence suggests were available to the ancient Egyptians. Because of constraints on our budget, we could only afford to have a film crew on location in Egypt for three weeks. Once we began work it quickly became clear we had a choice: if everything was done by ancient means we would probably only finish one or two courses of pyramid stones. Alternatively, if we employed a front-end loader to speed up the repetitive work of placing blocks we had a good chance of building to the top of the pyramid.[13]

If the Nova team could have kept up their planned construction rate, then they should have been able to place the 180 blocks for their miniature pyramid in three weeks without a front-end loader.

There is a basic methodological distortion in drawing conclusions from a miniature experiment: Engineering problems multiply in full-scale operations. The cumulative congestion on a ramp of the size required for the Great Pyramid would be extraordinary. Compare hundreds of blocks set per day, high in the Great Pyramid, with fewer than 200 smaller blocks set in three weeks in Nova's unfinished, 18-foot-high miniature pyramid—almost all with the use of a front-end loader.

The front-end loader placed the heaviest blocks, weighing two tons, on Nova's miniature pyramid. The 1/2-ton block the workers raised manually was put onto the miniature ramp by the front-end loader. No blocks were brought manually from the quarry. Heavy equipment (a flat bed truck and front-end loader) performed all of the heavy work. The front-end loader placed a two-ton block on a concrete road, too. Nova hauled this block on rollers for its roller experiment only after using the heavy equipment to place it on this strong modern surface. Unfortunately for the unsuspecting viewers, the film does not show the heavy construction equipment Nova used. The film never told viewers about it.

It is important to clarify this, because Nova's *This Old Pyramid* has convinced many people that there are no vexing pyramid construction mysteries. The WGBH Educational Foundation sells *This Old Pyramid* as an informal teaching aid to schoolchildren. The film is also used at the high-school and college level. Television station WGBH, in Boston, which produces Nova, is a Public Broadcasting affiliate. For the sake of schoolchildren learning about pyramid construction through this film and its companion book, it is important to distinguish between what *This Old Pyramid* says and shows and how the Nova miniature pyramid was really built behind the scenes.

At the beginning of the film, the narrator clearly states, "They'll [Nova's workers] use the methods and materials available to the Egyptians to build them [the pyramids]." The narration repeats the protocol when stating, "Roger wanted to lower these blocks in place with a fork-lift, but Mark has insisted on ancient methods." The entire film gives the impression that the Nova crew was building the miniature pyramid using strictly ancient means.

But the Nova crew used steel tools to quarry and shape all the blocks. Whereas, Egyptologists insist that the Pyramid Age Egyptians had only relatively soft copper and crude stone tools. A front-end loader placed blocks into the tiers themselves, except for one 1/2-ton block manually raised on a ramp and one levered block. The ramp itself was built only as high as the lowest pyramid tiers—and this is the only clue left in the film that an astute observer could use to deduce that the pyramid was not really built by hand. Nevertheless, the film concluded by claiming that Nova's experiments solved all of the major problems of pyramid construction.

Because Congress oversees public television, I registered complaints with some congressional offices.[14] Consequently, some congressional staff assistants made telephone inquiries to *This Old Pyramid*'s producer Michael Barnes. The congressional office informed me that Barnes verbally promised that he would make a disclaimer or repackage *This Old Pyramid*. His promise disarmed further inquires from congressional offices concerning scientific fraud at taxpayer expense. Barnes' promise appears in writing in a letter to viewer Charles Horton, of Fort Worth, Texas, who learned about Nova's methods from me:

> I am not sure what errors you are referring to as we feel the film was thoroughly researched and represents widely accepted knowledge of Old Kingdom Egypt and their methods of building pyramids…With reference to the discussion with congressional staff I agreed to clarify the narration of the repackaged version of the film so that it clearly states that modern equipment was also used to build the NOVA pyramid…But to avoid possible confusion, we will, when the program is re-broadcast in 1997, as part of a series on ancient engineering, add an additional line of narration to the effect that stonemason Roger Hopkins used a modern loader to help build the pyramid.

The repackaged 60-minute version first aired in February of 1997, as the lead film in Nova's series *Secrets of Lost Empires*. The revised pyramid film does not include the promised disclaimer or in any way admit to the use of modern equipment. Instead, it repeats the same old language, saying that Roger wanted to lower the blocks in place with a forklift, but that Mark Lehner insisted on ancient means. The film contains all of the elements that prompted my original complaints, first to top PBS and WGBH executives, then to Nova sponsor Johnson & Johnson. Only when they all refused to air a disclaimer (after about two years worth of letter exchanges with me), I finally turned to my state congressmen.

The original 90-minute *This Old Pyramid* was repackaged and broadcast by other television programs, too, making them suspect as teaching aids as well. The British Broadcasting Corporation (BBC) aired the Nova film, and the Canadian Broadcasting Corporation (CBC) repackaged it for the science program *The Nature of Things*. CBC advertisements for the October 18, 1993 broadcast unwittingly stated that on the next *The Nature of Things*, viewers would see how the pyramids were built "without a forklift."

The Nature of Things host David Suzuki, in a letter to me dated November 23, 1993, stated:

> I was very surprised to learn from you of the extensive use of machines in the making of the pyramid…it is distressing to realize that the thrust of the show conveyed a totally false impression.[15]

Unfortunately for viewers, I was successful in informing Suzuki of the facts only after the show aired. The CBC ignored my previous attempts to warn against airing the show. After the show aired, Suzuki and top executives at CBC declined to air a disclaimer, despite my persistent requests. WGBH executives, who oversee the Nova show, refused to accept responsibility for CBC's accidental false advertising. Long after the original version of *This Old Pyramid* aired over PBS broadcasting stations, those responsible were still refusing to issue a disclaimer for the Nova film or remove it from the educational market. I finally issued a press release with hope that the educational community would demand a disclaimer if the truth were exposed. There was only one response from the media. When science writer Carlos Byars received my press release and learned of the front-end loader, he confronted Nova producer Michael Barnes.

Byars advised that "the viewer had better beware" in his article in the *Houston Chronicle* (Wrap-up, Saturday, November 13, 1993). The small article reads in part, "Although the use of modern machines is mentioned four times, Barnes said, the emphasis of the piece is on the use of tools and methods available to ancient Egyptians." "That is not quite the way it was," countered Byars, who had watched the film three times before interviewing Barnes. Vague statements about machines in the film, if noticeable at all, lead viewers to assume the use of inconsequential devices. Instruments for checking leveling and vehicles for transporting equipment and people are acceptable for the experiment.

Viewers who noticed the brief references to machines would naturally assume the use of these devices, because the film denies the use of heavy machinery. The film states, "Roger wanted to lower these blocks in place with a forklift, but Mark has insisted on ancient methods." As Byars aptly remarked, "One of the best and most award-winning science programs on television, Nova, has been caught with its front-end loader hanging out."

Some five years after the acceptance of awards and much glorifying praise, and five years after *This Old Pyramid* originally aired, Lehner included a whisper of Nova's use of the front-end loader in *The Complete Pyramid* (1997). His book does not correct the problem, since the very wide, international television audience of Nova will not read it. Worse, Lehner's mention of the front-end loader in his award-winning *The Complete Pyramid*

11. The Nova mini-pyramid. Notice how small the ramp is relative to the size that would be needed to lift the heavy weights incorporated into the Great Pyramid. Notice that the ramp is only built high enough to raise the 1/2-ton block to the lowest tiers.

(1997) (Society for American Archaeology Award, 1999) presents even more misleading information about the front-end loader. Lehner wrote:

> And Roger brought in a front-end loader for shifting and setting the stones of lower courses so that we would have time to test different methods at the top, where restricted space created special difficulties.[16]

With his statement, Lehner implies that the front-end loader only set stones in the lower courses, which is not correct. Joseph Davidovits watched the crew build the entire miniature pyramid in Egypt. He provided a statement for me to include here:

> The front-end loader carried all stones from the quarries and placed them in the miniature pyramid from bottom to top, except for the pyramidion [the capstone], which was very small.[17]

Nova raised its 1/2-ton experimental block up its ramp for the on-camera demonstration—after the block was placed on the ramp by the front-end loader. Joseph Davidovits' above statement agrees with Nova producer Michael Barnes' letter to a viewer:

> Once we began work it quickly became clear we had a choice: if everything was done by ancient means we would probably only finish one or two courses of pyramid stones. Alternatively, if we employed a front-end loader to speed up the repetitive work of placing blocks we had a good chance of building to the top of the pyramid.[18]

But the ramp was only built to reach to the bottom tier, and so it was not designed to raise stones anywhere near the top of the mini-pyramid.

Although they did build to its top with the front-end loader, they left the pyramid unfinished. Even as I finish this book in early 2009, the Nova website still fudges the facts. In an article titled "Who Built the Pyramids?" (copyright 1997 and last updated in December of 2007), Lehner says the following, "So our stones were delivered by a flatbed truck as opposed to barges. You know, we didn't reconstruct the barges that brought the 60-ton granite blocks from Aswan. So basically what we were doing is, as we say in the film and in the accompanying book, that we're setting up the ability to test particular tools, techniques and operations, without testing the entire building project."[19] This avoids telling the whole truth even when challenged to accept responsibility for their cover-up: The truth is that the front-end loader set all of the blocks in the mini-pyramid tiers except for a 1/2-ton block raised manually (after being placed on the ramp by the front-end loader) (and one block was also levered into position), and that raising one 1/2-ton block (cut with hardened steel tools) on a *tafla* ramp does not represent the true engineering problems of building the Great Pyramid. A ramp used to raise the real weights found in the Great Pyramid must be vastly longer (with a low gradient) and much stronger than *tafla*.

With the scientific record necessarily corrected here, we can continue considering Nova's ramp experiment. The Nova crew affixed the 1/2-ton block to a sled. They embedded wooden logs into the miniature ramp's clay surface. The workers poured water onto the timbers to reduce the friction between the ramp and the load. Then they hauled the load over the timbers. To build the Great Pyramid, an average of one block was incorporated every two or three minutes per ten-hour workday (according to the calculations of Rainer Stadelmann). So, the rapid operation requires a steady train of relatively closely-spaced sledges and workers, and the frequent application of water to the ramp's clay surface. But even in Egypt's arid climate, the frequent use of water would quickly cause the clay to become too slick and unstable. It would not be usable.

To avoid hazardous and impossible working conditions, the ramp would have to dry out or be resurfaced before work continued. Nova did not factor this into the speed at which they needed to raise blocks to keep pace with the construction rate for the Great Pyramid.

Raising one 1/2-ton block on Nova's miniature ramp seriously damaged its clay surface. Because of the structural damage, Nova's building supervisor Roger Hopkins remarked that only a strong concrete ramp would be useful for further experimentation. Egyptology assumes that a concrete ramp did not exist. So, the remark by Hopkins fits with Peter Hodges' assertion that any ramp used to raise blocks for the Great Pyramid would have to be solid masonry. As I have already stressed, such a ramp cannot be accounted for. The quarries at Giza are too small to have yielded enough stone for such a ramp, and there are no such ramp remains at Giza. The ramp Nova used was insufficient and inappropriate for raising blocks for the Great Pyramid.

We see that, for many reasons, a huge construction ramp is unworkable for building the Great Pyramid. There is no evidence that a ramp of the size or type required existed. But because no other block raising devices are known from the Late Stone Age, Egyptology adheres to the unworkable ramp method for constructing the Great Pyramid. Analysis shows that Egyptology has not solved one of the most fundamental problems of the construction of the Great Pyramid: Egyptology cannot account for how blocks could be raised to build the Great Pyramid.

Chapter 14
The Block Raising Quagmire Deepens

Egyptology advocates that a 12th Dynasty tomb scene explains the method by which workers hauled blocks for pyramid construction. The scene is from the tomb of a nobleman of Hermopolis named Djehutihotep (1878–1841 B.C.), who lived about 800 years after the Great Pyramid was built.[1]

The tomb scene shows 172 men pulling Djehutihotep's 60-ton colossus on a sledge along a flat surface. A liquid is being poured in front of the giant statue to facilitate its transport along the ground. The worst problem of using this operation to explain the Great Pyramid's construction is that raising blocks up an incline poses a whole different set of difficulties. Before delving into them, we first need to recognize that this tomb scene does not even address how Egypt's truly large objects could be carried along a flat surface.

Some ancient Egyptian monoliths are so large that they are far too challenging for experimentation today. The 19th Dynasty Pharaoh Ramses II had a statue weighing about 1,000 tons built at his Ramesseum at Thebes.[2] In the ruins of Tanis, in northeast Egypt, fragments of either three or four colossi were uncovered that suggest that even heavier statues were built for this pharaoh.[3] They were made with granite, which is more dense that limestone. W.M.F. Petrie estimated one of them to have towered ninety-two feet from head to toe, and totaling 125 feet high with its pedestal. Petrie calculated the weight at 1,200 tons. It is the largest colossus known.

Some experts suggest that 1,000 men or 200 oxen could move a sledge carrying a 1,000-ton colossus on a slick, flat surface.[4] This is a very low manpower estimate compared to others. But even with this low estimate, engineers have not shown how such enormous numbers of men, or combinations of men and animals, could have worked in coordination in such a complicated operation.[5] It has not even been shown how such a weight could be put on a barge or a hauling track, or what kind of track or barge would support the weight during transport.

It is entirely possible to move monoliths weighing 1,000 tons and more along flat ground. But using New Kingdom Egyptian technology makes all of the difference. The machines of those days consisted of chariots with flimsy wheels. Hauling tracks were made of wood. The remains of sufficiently long, flat tracks are unknown in Egypt. The ancient Egyptians producing tracks that could bear such loads would be an amazing accomplishment all by itself.

Erecting a 1,200-ton, 92-foot-high statue presents a greater challenge than has been undertaken with modern stonework. To further complicate matters, the 1,000-ton and heavier colossi rested on pedestals. We see that the scene showing the transport of the colossi of Djehutihotep does not put to rest—or, in reality, even begin to approach—the matter of how the ancient Egyptians put their heaviest obelisks and colossi in place, or how millions of massive pyramid blocks could be raised on an incline to 480 feet and higher.

We can get some idea of how many men would be required to raise Ramses' 1,000 ton and heavier colossi by comparing a calculation by Reginald Engelbach. He studied the problems associated with the famous unfinished obelisk at Aswan. Had this obelisk been completed, it would have weighed an estimated 1,168 tons. Engelbach indicated:

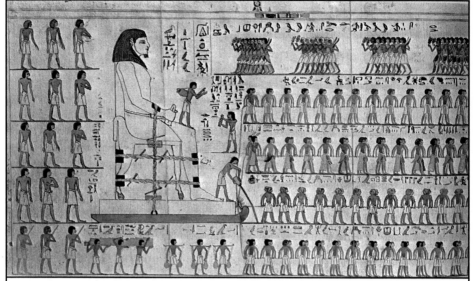

11. The scene is from the 12th Dynasty tomb of Djehutihotep. The scene shows liquid being poured to ease friction as the colossus is transported on a sled over a flat surface.

It may be mentioned here that to pull the obelisk over, on a level surface, would require some 13,000 men, which I am convinced could not be put on ropes in the constricted area of the quarry.[6]

Erecting Ramses II's colossi so that they would be oriented upright on their pedestals would be a far more demanding operation than rolling them over on the ground at the quarry. No modern obelisk-raising operation has moved an obelisk anywhere near the size of Ramses II's colossi that weigh 1,000 tons or more apiece. Engelbach calculated that it would require 2,000 men just to pull the much smaller 227-ton obelisk at Luxor up a ramp.[7]

The ancient Egyptian obelisk called Cleopatra's Needle, now in London, weighs 150 tons. The heaviest obelisk moved in modern times weighs about 330 tons. One of the largest surviving obelisks in the world weighs between 445 and 510 tons. It was moved to Rome in the time of Emperor Constantius (A.D. 317–361), the son of Constantine the Great. The obelisk was presumably brought to Rome and erected in one piece (in the 16th century it was excavated and found in three pieces). A fallen, broken obelisk was found at Axum, Ethiopia, that stood about 110 feet tall.

Raising enormous statues within the confined spaces of already existing building complexes presents another conundrum. Engelbach pointed out that an obelisk built for the 18th Dynasty Pharaoh-Queen Hatshepsut was positioned inside a preexisting court. The problem is that the walls of the court measure less than the length of the obelisk. Curious about this, Engelbach carefully examined these court walls. His inspection convinced him that workers had not torn the wall down or rebuilt it in any way to bring in the obelisk.[8] So, the manner in which this obelisk was brought into this court is unknown to Egyptology. The thought of lifting it over the wall to situate it would be even more puzzling. The obelisk alerts us to the use of a special technology that simplified the task.

For monuments weighing 1,000 tons or more, and for tall obelisks in confined spaces within preexisting walls, calculations involving time and labor do not satisfy the questions.

12. The scene shows Pharaoh Ramses II in a war chariot, fighting in the battle of Kadesh. The wheel shown is very much like those found on the chariots discovered in the tomb of the 18th Dynasty Pharaoh Tutankhamen. Wheels like these are too weak to be useful for hoisting truly massive blocks.

These examples are so extraordinary that they alert us to the existence of some kind of special technology that has nothing to do with the method used to move the 60-ton colossus of Djehutihotep.

Although most building units of the Great Pyramid weigh much less than Djehutihotep's colossus, the stele cannot legitimately be used to address the problems of raising pyramid blocks. French Egyptologist Henri Chevrier performed an experiment during his work at the Karnak Temple, in southern Egypt. His team pulled a sledge bearing a block weighing five to six tons along a lubricated track (the lubrication having greatly reduced friction).[9] He found that each man could pull 330 pounds on a lubricated, flat surface. Based on this figure, it would take 400 men, rather than 172, to pull the 60-ton colossus along the ground. So, the Stele of Djehutihotep was probably not meant to be taken literally in terms of its number of workers. Instead, it was simply intended to convey the means of transport used for this particular project.

Based on Chevrier's experiment, hauling a typical six-ton block for the Great Pyramid along the ground requires 40 men. But on a ramp, the number would be much higher. It would increase in proportion to the angle of the ramp's gradient. The force of gravity works strongly against a team transporting a multiton block on a slick, inclined surface. Some kind of strong mechanisms must be in place to keep blocks from sliding down, and allowing huge numbers of workmen to keep their foothold on an incline in slippery mud.

The noted French Egyptologist Jean-Philippe Lauer studied the problems of pyramid construction for 50 years. He suggested that workers used steep inclines of 3:1 and 4:1 when building the Great Pyramid. We recall master builder Peter Hodges' more recent calculation. He remarked that slopes of 3:1 or 4:1 are entirely unrealistic. Hodges asserted a more workable low gradient of 1:10. In that case, any ramp would have to be 4,800 feet long and over 480 feet high and made of squared stones—a scenario that puts an intolerable strain on the ramp theory (regardless of the shape of the ramp).

If we momentarily pretend that the gradients Lauer suggested are workable, then elevating one six-ton block would have required 140 to 200 men.[10] But even this produces an impossible scenario because of the rapid construction rate. To build the Great Pyramid during the 23 or 24 year reign of Khufu, hundreds of blocks had to be set daily. To meet this rapid rate, thousands of workers would have been required to maneuver the block-bearing sleds to great heights on the slick ramp. This requires too many men working on a slick ramp at once.

Mark Lehner falls far short of recognizing fundamental problems. Here is his calculation for the number of men needed to build the Great Pyramid from his award-winning *The Complete Pyramids* (1997):

> ...the famous scene from the tomb of Djehutihotep...depicts the moving of a large colossus...the statue would have weighed c. 58 tons...there are 172 men shown, each therefore pulling c. 1/3 ton. Modern trials confirm that this is possible on a fairly friction-free surface. By the same ratio (1/3 ton per hauler) a 2.5 ton block on a lubricated, level surface could be pulled by 7.5 men. If we assume that a division (20 men) moved 10 stones per day - allowing one hour to move the stone to the pyramid and return with an empty sledge - then 340 stones could be moved daily from quarry to pyramid by 34 divisions. There are points to note on both sides of this equation. More divisions work simultaneously in the lower levels, when there may have been many ramps, and therefore a higher hauling rate. Far fewer could work nearer the top, where there was less space and ramp gradients were steeper. Also, the stones of Khufu's pyramid are not all 2.5 tons - this estimate of the average block size is frequently quoted, but needs more study. Many stones, particularly near the apex, are smaller, while those of the core are by no means all neat, 2.5 ton cubes, and near the base many blocks exceed 2.5 tons. Perhaps one hour per stone is too demanding...[11]

In his final estimate, Lehner allows for what he calls a "more realistic estimate of 1,360 haulers." His ridiculously low figure arises from fundamental flaws in his calculation. First, he inappropriately uses a calculation for moving blocks on level ground to calculate the number needed to elevate blocks on an incline.

His error allows him to reduce the number of men by many thousands. Then, he rids the calculation of a great many thousands of men by mostly calculating with an averaged block weight of 2.5 tons. By doing this, he fails to acknowledge the real problems posed by raising massive blocks situated at many levels of the Great Pyramid. He says that the sizes need more study. But there are many size estimates, and tier heights have long been confirmed and published. It has been recorded since the time of Napoleon Bonaparte that blocks in tier 201 were taller than those in tier four, and that tier 35 is taller than tier two and so on.

Lehner also calculated the number of men required to haul stones from the Giza quarry to the Great Pyramid:

> Let us assume that the stone haulers could move 1 km (0.62 miles) per hour en route from the quarry to the pyramid. The return journey was done with an empty sledge and so was much faster. The distance from Khufu's quarry to the pyramid, at c. 6° slope, could probably be covered in 19 minutes by 20 men pulling a 2.5 ton block. Certainly, this was well within the capacities of the NOVA team...[12]

13. Owing to their great heights, enormous, very strong ramps are required to manually raise massive blocks of the sizes found in the Great Pyramids of Giza. Khufu's Great Pyramid (seen in the background) is the tallest of Egypt's pyramids, and the careful measurements taken by Napoleon's archeological expedition showed that some of its tallest blocks were incorporated into tier 201 near its peak.

Again, Lehner used averaged weights of 2.5 tons. He did not address the sharp fluctuations in height increase in the pyramid tiers (including 127 cm. at tier 35, 100 cm. at 36, 106 cm. at tier 44, 100 cm. at tier 98, and 112 cm. at tier 201). In the masonry of the Great Pyramid, tier heights suddenly increase and diminish in nineteen sharp fluctuations. Among the samples of heavy interior units, wall blocks in the King's Chamber, nearly half way up the Pyramid, weigh about 50 tons each. Ceiling beams weigh up to 73 tons. Enormous girdle blocks, 12 to 15 feet long, encase the Ascending Passageway. Both Herodotus and Abd el-Latif reported seeing a myriad of outer casing blocks 30 feet long.

To top off his argument, Lehner insinuates that the experiment of Nova validates his calculations. But the Nova team did not haul a single block from the quarry to the miniature pyramid. A flatbed truck hauled all blocks from the quarry, including the 1/2-ton block raised manually for Nova's on-camera demonstration. A front-end loader put the 1/2-ton block onto the miniature ramp, too.

Petrie calculated that 100,000 men per year were needed to build the Great Pyramid during Khufu's reign.[13] This figure produces counterproductive congestion on a ramp. Just one stone sliding out of position would create chaos. Lehner abandoned such large figures because of the small size of Egyptian cities and lack of accommodations for so many workers at Giza or anywhere in the area. So, the problems just go in circles rather than finding resolution.

In 1997, in Tokyo, Japanese engineers tested an elevation method conceived of by Cambridge University engineer Dick Parry.[14] He rejected the theory that pyramid builders moved blocks up ramps on sledges. He recognized that the number of men required would be too great.

Innovating upon the so-called rockers theorized by Clarke and Engelbach, Parry proposed that four rockers be arranged around a block to form a cylinder. Builders coiled a long rope around the cylinder to move it uphill. When workers pulled on the rope from the top of the ramp, the rope uncoiled. This caused the cylinder to roll up the ramp. Parry's ingenious operation reduces the amount of force needed to elevate blocks.

Parry's method was tested on 2.5 ton blocks. To push a 2.5 ton block on a level surface required only three men. To pull a block up a ramp with a 1:4 gradient required only 16 to 20 men. Workers pulled the 2.5 ton block up a 49-foot slope in only one minute. So, the beauties of his system are that it allows for a more rapid construction rate and a steeper ramp than the 1:10 needed for raising sledges. But even Parry's clever system fails when it comes to constructing the Great Pyramid.

A ramp's slope will depend on real weights, and we know of beams weighing up to 73 tons situated 160 feet high in the Great Pyramid's interior. So, Parry's system calls for a very demanding ramp. The ramp must be either very wide or extremely strong.

Imagine a 73-ton beam measuring 27 feet long rolling up a ramp. A beam is most stable when positioned with its length perfectly horizontal. With any ramp design, the ramp would have to be extremely strong, and most likely it would have to be keyed into the Great Pyramid's masonry with long, enormous support beams made of extremely dense rock. If the beams are hauled (while horizontal) to a height of about 160 feet on a wrap-around ramp, then the ramp would have to be constructed with extremely wide corners — wide enough to accommodate the huge beams being turned around them.

Moving the beams while keeping them upright would not require such wide ramp corners for the beams themselves. But the ramp would have to accommodate a tremendous number of workers to keep a beam from tipping over, and so the corners must still be very wide. The ramp would have to be extremely strong. When moving a beam in a vertical orientation, its weight is distributed over a smaller surface area of the ramp. The ramp must also be strong enough to support the weight of the over 2,500 workmen needed to raise the beam (this is an extremely conservative manpower estimate). So, the ramp must be strong enough at every point going at least up to 160 feet high, the level of the ceiling of the King's Chamber. The beams in the relieving chambers are smaller, but they are situated even higher.

If the cylinders up to 27-feet-long were moved up a straight on ramp in a horizontal orientation, then this ramp, too, would have to be equally strong and solidly constructed so as not to come apart under the weight of the men and beam. That weight would include about 70 tons per beam and roughly 150 pounds per worker. The ramp would require far more effort to build and tear down than is needed to build the Great Pyramid itself. So, there are two main problems with Parry's system. It will serve only a limited range of block sizes (especially if a 1:4 gradient is used), and it relies on a ramp that is entirely unworkable.

If Parry's method existed in the 4th Dynasty, then we would expect that the Egyptians would have used the wheel for transportation from that point forward. But the wheel did not come into use for transportation until much later, and known Egyptian wheels were not made to endure hard use. They were very flimsy throughout ancient Egyptian history.

Peter Hodges commented on mistaken ideas about ramps. He found systemic errors in logic throughout accepted Egyptological literature. He recognized that the errors could be corrected only by someone with a lifetime of experience in the building trade:

> An archaeologist has the talent of re-creating history from evidence left by another civilization but his background is one of scholarship rather than craftsmanship. It is not reasonable to expect an archaeologist to be an experienced manual worker in all

the basic trades of living, from farming, building, husbandry, etc., through to embalming…We send an archaeologist to search for history but for practical problems we really need an investigator who could, if need be, carry through the solutions himself on the basis of his practical experiences.[15]

Having recognized the irreconcilable problems with ramps and the proposed block-raising schemes, Hodges devised a levering system to eliminate the need for a ramp. In his book *How the Great Pyramids Were Built* (1989), Hodges proposed the use of his own specially designed levers.

Although they did not use Hodges' instrument, Nova's *This Old Pyramid* tested the levering system. The Nova crew levered a block into place in its miniature pyramid under the supervision of pyramid theorist Martin Isler. Workers pried the block up one end at a time, inserting wooden planks under it. They performed this process repeatedly until the block was slowly and tediously inched up to the desired height.

Workers placed each wooden plank under the edges of the block with great difficulty and trepidation. As the block rose, the wooden stack under it became unstable and difficult to manage, despite the even, planed surfaces of the planks.

Once the block reached the desired elevation, the workers moved it carefully sideways onto the pyramid without disturbing the wooden stack. Otherwise, the block would have crashed to the ground. The workers had problems keeping the stacked planks stable, but they did manage to move the block safely.

It took five hours to raise the block onto the tiny Nova pyramid tier. Levering is too slow and hazardous to be practical on the scale of the Great Pyramid. Based on Peter Hodges' own trials with his special prying levers, he estimated that it would require about two days to maneuver the average block into place in the Great Pyramid. A 2.5 ton block might take about a day. Compare the rate of production established by Egyptology: An average of one block was raised and set in place every two or three minutes per work day for the length of Khufu's 24-year reign. Besides, levering is not practical for raising real weights, like the girdle blocks or the 27-foot-long beams weighing up to 73 tons.

Engineer Edward A. Murphy devised Murphy's Law, which says, "If something can go wrong, it will." With any levering system raising two million blocks, the odds are that some blocks would have gone crashing down. Just one block tumbling from a course high in the pyramid would cause terrible damage to the masonry below. Workers would have to raise new blocks to replace broken ones. Replacing blocks would have been especially difficult because of the problems of fitting them into existing tiers. Peter Hodges understood that fitting pyramid blocks is at least as demanding as raising them.

The tiers of the pyramid substitute for a ramp with Hodges' system. The tiers would suffer from the wear and tear of block raising. Fixing all of the damage raises the average number of blocks that had to be set per day. We see that the levering system is much too slow and dangerous to be viable for building the Great Pyramid.

Hodges' six-foot-long levers were fitted with angled ends like those of a pry bar. The design produces a lever equipped with its own fulcrum. His first trial used a lever of this design that had no metal reinforcement. It broke at the bend. His later model sandwiched the angled wooden pry ends between copper reinforcement fastened by rods. The design prevented its short end from tearing off when he pried blocks. It is not logical to think that his reinforcements would tolerate the weight of the larger monoliths. Some monoliths in pyramid complexes weigh hundreds of tons.

Notwithstanding his remarks about Egyptologists not being properly qualified to solve building problems, Hodges' own system is at odds with what Egyptologists understand about ancient technology. Although Hodges' copper-reinforced levers are simple devices, they are far in advanced of Old Kingdom tools.

To explain why archaeologists have never found such lever tips, Hodges proposed that they were so highly treasured that they must have been stolen or deeply buried. But this would not have prevented drawings or written descriptions of them from being made, or continued reproduction of the devices in later times. Excavators have frequently found highly treasured items in tombs, like gold and jewelry. Evidence of tremendous numbers of copper-reinforced lever tips would have to have vanished from history without a trace—even though many sealed tombs have been found.

Reginald Engelbach commented on the use of simple levers of a size useful for prying large pieces of stone:

> The occurrence of levers is so rare that it has been doubted whether the Egyptians knew of them.[16]

Depictions of levers are unknown for the Old Kingdom. Engineers and machinists have suggested devices to address the Great Pyramid's building enigmas. But Egyptologists understand the very limited technological frame of reference within which they must remain. They are very familiar with the tools and the toolmaking capabilities of the ancient Egyptians. For this reason, Egyptologists do not invent new tools or simple machines to solve the mystery of the construction of the Great Pyramid. Besides, any device proposed must be able to withstand the hardest tests—like situating the heaviest weights found in the pyramid complexes. These include monolithic, 36-foot-high temple columns, 73-ton beams located 160 feet high, and blocks weighing hundreds of tons.

The dilemma is clear. With their understanding of the lifting devices and tools and materials available in the Pyramid Age, Egyptologists are highly reluctant to abandon the ramp theories altogether. But Hodges and other engineers have shown that ramps are not at all workable for building the Great Pyramid. Experiments show that levering systems are too slow, dangerous and cumbersome to be workable on an enormous scale. To be feasible, the system would have to be able to lever 27-foot-long beams up 160-feet high, and do so with the number of men required working in the available space. A combination of the two systems, ramps for lower tiers and levers for higher tiers, would be beset with the same problems already covered. Even a ramp built to the level of the King's Chamber (160 feet high) would be too demanding. The special features of the Great Pyramid are what make it so vexing for all of the engineering systems proposed. Other pyramid complexes feature fabulous architecture, too, like monolithic temple columns up to 36 feet high and blocks weighing hundreds of tons each.

There is a dire need for a cross-disciplinary approach to the masonry and engineering mysteries. Only when Egyptological knowledge is combined with the correct scientific approach can the real solution finally be accepted.

Chapter 15
The Mystery of Obelisks

Experts have not explained how the Egyptians could possibly situate colossi weighing over 1,000 tons on pedestals or erect tall obelisks in confined spaces. An obelisk is a four-sided tapering shaft that terminates in a pyramid-shaped top. Ancient Egyptian documents indicate that obelisks were built during the Old Kingdom, but the surviving obelisks date to later times. There are more than 50 remaining Egyptian obelisks greater than 30 feet high.

The 18th and 19th Dynasty workers produced the most magnificent examples known. The 19th Dynasty Pharaoh Ramses II ordered 14 obelisks for Tanis, in northern Egypt. Workers constructed at least 13 tall obelisks in ancient Thebes (now called Karnak), in southern Egypt. Pharaoh Seti I recorded building several in Heliopolis (the city called *On* in the Bible; Egyptian: *Annu*), in northern Egypt. In the 12th century, Abd el-Latif reported grandiose obelisks with gilded pyramidions in Heliopolis. He indicated that they were surrounded by large and small obelisks too numerous for him to describe individually. Today, only one obelisk remains in Heliopolis.

The operation that transported the 150-ton obelisk called Cleopatra's Needle to New York showed that there is nothing to prevent a massive obelisk from swaying out of control as workers pull it upright. When Cleopatra's Needle began to sway, the ropes tied to its upper portion could not control its motion.[1]

Reginald Engelbach, who served as Chief Inspector of Antiquities of Upper Egypt early in the 20th century, studied the theories of the production and erection of obelisks. Egyptologists still consider his studies authoritative. An obelisk placed within the confined spaces of a preexisting building complex presents critical problems. Engelbach commented:

> The Egyptians could introduce obelisks inside courts whose walls were shorter than the length of the obelisk. Queen Hatshepsowet put hers between her father's pylons where there is no evidence at all that any of the walls had been removed or rebuilt; in fact I am certain that they were not.[2]

Modern engineers have not explained how the ancient Egyptians could possibly have brought this obelisk in and erected it.

With regard to other obelisks, one theory proposes the use of enormous levers. Engelbach pointed out a very serious problem with the idea of prying up obelisks with levers:

> Some obelisks are so close to their pylons that there would hardly be room for the huge levers which would have had to be used.[3]

There is also the question of the strength of wooden levers when dealing with the largest weights of obelisks and colossi. Engelbach reminds us that no large levers or depictions of them have been found:

> The occurrence of levers is so rare that it has been doubted whether the Egyptians knew of them.[4]

One theory Engelbach studied holds that ancient engineers would position obelisks as high as possible on an enormous embankment. The process involves moving an obelisk up a long, sloping embankment until it hangs over the edge. Workers would have to orient the obelisk with its trunk supported well above its balancing point, to prevent it from falling over the embankment's edge.

Workers would then cause the obelisk to slowly descend into a huge, sand-filled, funnel-shaped brick construction. They would carefully remove the sand, while men pull the obelisk upright from the opposite direction with ropes. So, they remove the earthen embankment from below until the obelisk is lowered down to the edge of its pedestal. All the while, workers pull ropes until the obelisk is upright. Engelbach showed this theory to be unworkable:

> a) It would be extremely risky business to cut earth from below an overhanging obelisk of 500 tons and upwards. Anyone who has seen earth undercut below a large stone in excavating work or elsewhere knows that the earth has a partiality for slipping sideways in any direction but the expected—preferably on to the heads of one's workmen.

> b) To make an obelisk settle down from a height on to a small pedestal by under-cutting would be an impossibility. Whatever method the Egyptians used, it was certain.

> c) After pulling the obelisk upright there is nothing to stop it from rocking about and getting out of control.[5]

Archaeological evidence supporting the use of this method is also lacking. Archaeologists found no traces of such brick constructions.

Modern projects that moved heavy obelisks from Egypt and erected them in various cities of the world would not have been able to deal with ancient Egypt's heaviest monoliths—like the 1,000-ton colossi of Ramses. Consider Engelbach's remarks:

> Although the removal of obelisks from Egypt in recent times gives us very little information which might help us to understand the methods of the ancients, a brief account of them is of interest if only to the contrast; it makes us appreciate the work of the Egyptians the more, especially when we bear in mind that every method used in modern days for the lowering and erection of an obelisk—which has never exceeded 331 tons in weight—always taxed the strength of the tackle to the utmost; in each case it was only just strong enough. Every modern removal has been a nine days' wonder, and a ponderous tome has appeared about it, yet the Egyptians, we know for a fact, set up obelisks of over 550 tons, and—if we are to believe their records—of more than 800 tons, without troubling to put on record how they did it.[6]

There is no reason to doubt the ancient record of an 800-ton obelisk, given the 1,000-ton and heavier colossi of Ramses II. They were even situated on pedestals. Imagine hauling enormous granite weights from Aswan to Tanis on a flat track or by river barge. The distance is about 600 miles.

The Roman naturalist Pliny the Elder reported a means of transporting an obelisk.[7] His report complicates matters even more. He wrote of a 120-foot-high obelisk that was moved to Alexandria during the time of the Greek Pharaoh Ptolemy II Philadelphus (285–246 B.C.). Pliny recorded that workers dug a canal from the Nile to the spot where the obelisk rested. By this means, they situated the obelisk so that each of its ends was supported by a river bank.

To get it afloat, workers put two large barges in the water beneath it. The barges were loaded with heavy rocks to get them to partially sink. Then workers unloaded the rocks until the barges floated up high enough in the water to receive the obelisk. Archaeological evidence suggests that the more ancient Egyptians did not use this method. According to Reginald Engelbach, there is no trace of a canal near the Aswan granite quarries, and no canal leading to the Nile has been discovered since his time.[8] The area is well exposed and traces of a large canal would be evident if one existed.

As for how the surfaces of obelisks were finished and engraved, Engelbach reiterated the commonly held ideas about the use of abrasives and stone tools. A true scholar, he was reluctant to accept unproved ideas, and so he qualified his remarks:

> I had intended to devote a chapter to the polishing and engraving of obelisks after they were set up, but our knowledge of the engraving of the hard rocks is so vague that it can be summed up in a paragraph. The details of the process, as given in the various works on the subject, are not clear to me—perhaps owing to my reprehensible habit of making experiments.[9]

Engelbach never tried to fuzz the facts. He simply could not account for how the Egyptians engraved obelisks so exquisitely and said so. We recall the statement by stonemason Roger Hopkins in the PBS Nova film titled *Secrets of Lost Empires*. His remarks concern an obelisk of Pharaoh Ramses II:

> Even with modern tools and…diamond wheels and all that, we would have…a tough time getting it [the hieroglyphs] to this kind of perfection.

The unresolved problems of engraving and raising obelisks and 1,000-ton and heavier monolithic colossi—particularly when they are placed in confined spaces among preexisting building complexes—beckons us to consider the existence of some kind of special technology that was gradually lost.

🗟 Chapter 16 🗟
Proof from Ancient Texts

Along with the tomb painting of Djehutihotep, ancient literature offers a number of documents that Egyptologists interpret to try to explain how the Great Pyramid was built. But all of these documents postdate the Pyramid Age. None provides evidence for determining the construction method.

To explain how huge casing blocks were transported from Tura, some Egyptologists rely on a post-Pyramid Age bas-relief on the causeway of the 5th Dynasty pyramid of Pharaoh Unas (c. 2356–2323 B.C.), at Saqqara.[1] Causeways are long masonry structures that connect pyramids with their Valley Temples. The Unas causeway does not depict blocks being quarried or shaped, but it shows temple columns being moved along the Nile by barge. What is wrong with this scenario as it relates to building the Great Pyramids of the earlier Pyramid Age? A closer look reveals the answer.

Dieter Arnold indicated that workers probably completed temple columns, including these, in the quarries before transporting them:

> That the production was carried out in the quarries can be gathered from reliefs showing the transport of finished columns from Aswan to Saqqara…Thus the columns and cornices for the temple of Unas were sent in their final shape, if we may trust the wall reliefs in the Unas causeway.[2]

For a number of reasons, we cannot take the reliefs on the Unas causeway as an explanation of how Khufu's Great Pyramid was built. One reason is that some temple columns remain at the Unas' pyramid site today. Joseph Davidovits inspected them, and found columns composed of 1/2-ton units fit together by tongue-and-groove joints.[3] So, these columns were not completed as whole columns at Aswan. It is fairly easy to haul 1/2-ton units by river barge, especially when compared to transporting monolithic columns some 36 feet high.

Another reason is that Pharaoh Unas' workers removed building units from the pyramid complex of his predecessor Pharaoh Djedkara-Isesi, located two miles away. Egyptology is very familiar with the way pharaohs of the 5th Dynasty and later expropriated blocks from the monuments of their predecessors. Within the context of the theory presented in these pages, pharaohs exploiting previous pyramid complexes to acquire building material is a consequence of a technology that was experiencing severe decline. The Pyramid Age had passed, and the Egyptians were constructing only small, economically-built pyramids. These structures were made largely of sand and rubble fill — and of expropriated blocks.

Given the 1/2-ton units, Unas' scribes may have rendered the columns as monoliths in the causeway reliefs as a matter of protocol. In this situation, the reliefs were not meant to be taken literally. Instead, they clearly document what was made from the transported units.

For these reasons, it is inappropriate to use the Unas' causeway relief to make a sweeping generalization about the water transportation of great numbers of truly heavy blocks for the Great Pyramid. At Giza, it is not even established that a sufficiently steep harbor existed for importing blocks. Besides, ancient Egyptians made colossi from Aswan granite that confound today's experts. They do not even know how these colossi could have been loaded onto a barge.

So, some objects are too large to have been made in finished form at quarries and then transported hundreds of miles from Aswan. Examples are the 1,200-ton colossi of Ramses II in Tanis and others of nearly the same size. The chances are too great that a colossus would chip or crack during transport and erection. A special technology was required to produce and situate such objects. This special technology—explained in this book—was also used to make casing and other blocks for the Great Pyramids.

Another document Egyptologists use to explain pyramid construction is the Tura Stele. It was engraved into a limestone wall at the Tura quarries.[4] The stele was destroyed during the early days of Egyptology. Only copies remain. The Tura Stele depicted oxen dragging blocks from the quarries to the edge of the river. In his *The Pyramids* (1969 ed.), Ahmed Fakhry presented a drawing of the Tura Stele and related it to pyramid construction, He added:

> There is a scene showing the transport of blocks of stone from the quarries of Tura, in which we see the oxen dragging the sledges. This was not unusual.[5]

The problems of relating the Tura Stele to pyramid construction include its late date. The Tura Stele was engraved almost 1,000 years after the Great Pyramid was constructed, at a time when the special technology used to build the Great Pyramid was in severe decline. Besides, the oxen are shown dragging the block on a horizontal surface. So, the stele cannot be used to explain the hardest problems of raising millions of pyramid blocks on an incline. Clearly, the Tura Stele does not hold the key to the mystery of pyramid construction.

The wheel was in use by the time scribes engraved the Tura Stele in the 18th Dynasty. But the Tura Stele suggests that the wheel was still not being used to haul blocks 1,000 years after the Great Pyramid was built. This is most likely because wheels were still not strong enough.

Many years ago, Hermann Junker performed experiments to test the idea that the dolerite balls found at ancient construction sites served as rollers for heavy stones.[6] Many problems make this cumbersome method unworkable for heavy weights, and sturdy, smooth roads are required to facilitate it. The construction and maintenance of numerous strong, level roads would have demanded much more masonry work—adding greatly to the already overburdened quarry size and construction rate estimated for the Great Pyramid.

Although the wooden roller is a precursor of the wheel, Egyptologists have largely abandoned the old idea that pyramid builders hauled blocks on wooden rollers. Conveying large blocks from the quarries would have required strong, level, smooth roads because wooden rollers cannot function in sand.

One would expect wheeled carts to have developed from such an operation. Engelbach summarized the development of the wheel for transportation in Egypt:

> As far as is known, the wheel played a very small part in the life of the ancient Egyptian; the word for it is almost certainly of foreign origin, and it is not found applied to chariots or wagons until the New Kingdom, though this may well be because horses do not appear in Egypt much before that date. The wheels of the known Egyptian chariots are extremely flimsy affairs, and it is doubtful if any wheel built on lines similar to those which have come down to us would take any load or endure hard wear…all known evidence of the methods of transport for building materials used by the Egyptians indicates that the sled alone was used.[7]

Most roads from quarries to the Nile are very uneven and unpaved — and this should be appreciated for the huge mystery of Egyptology that it is. It begs the question of how monoliths weighing up to a 1,000 tons and more could be transported from quarries. One paved quarry road (which we will explore below), used during the Old Kingdom, shows absolutely no sign of wear and tear or other evidence of block transport.

Early Egyptologists assumed that paintings from the 18th Dynasty tomb of Rekhmira might explain the tools used to shape pyramid blocks.[8] These scenes, dating 1,300 years after the Great Pyramid was built, show workers carving blocks with chisels. But during Rekhmira's time, bronze chisels were in common use. Egyptologists recognize that a hard form of bronze, needed to cut the medium-hard to hard blocks of the Great Pyramid, was not available until about 800 years after the Great Pyramid was completed.

The location of Rekhmira's tomb, in southern Egypt, suggests that the blocks depicted were sandstone. Sandstone soft enough for us to abrade with our fingernails was abundant in the south. Most New Kingdom structures built in the south are made of this soft material. Scenes that most likely show soft blocks (even limestone can be as soft as a sugar cube) being shaped with either bronze or copper chisels do not explain how more ancient Egyptians, with only copper and stone tools, shaped over 12 million medium-hard to hard pyramid blocks. It requires a special technology to produce the many acres of perfectly-angled casing blocks, and a myriad of fancy, custom-fit blocks, and huge pyramid tiers that are accurate to 1/2 centimeter.

The overwhelming majority of pyramid blocks do not exhibit tool marks. Some of the tool marks found on the minority of blocks are known to date to later attempts to cut the blocks up or pry at them in search of hidden entrances to the pyramids. We recall that Dieter Arnold abandoned the idea that copper tools were extensively used for pyramid construction — because of the insufficient copper supply for carrying out such monumental construction works.

Besides, Dieter Arnold is aware of the study conducted on layers of granite debris near the pyramid of Senwosret I. As mentioned, he reported that, "In these layers, no traces of greenish discoloration from copper could be detected." Copper residue from tool use can be found on artifacts after thousands of years. We can expect that copper would have been preserved in these layers if it had been used. This evidence weighs against theories that propose the use of copper saws and tube drills with abrasives to very gradually cut hard granite into blocks and statues. Considering the close, corresponding fit characteristic of pyramid blocks made from granite, we must question how these blocks were perfected without copper combined with an abrasive — which is Egyptology's only option for shaping granite other than pounding balls.

We see that none of the documents or methods Egyptologists have considered explains the construction of the Great Pyramid. We now analyze the archaeological evidence from Giza itself.

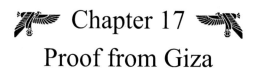

Chapter 17
Proof from Giza

Egyptologists offer archaeological evidence from Giza to explain how workers built the Great Pyramid. A block still sits on a small ramp connected to a small queens' pyramid in the Third Pyramid complex at Giza. The complex was built during the 4th Dynasty for Pharaoh Menkaura (c. 2490–2472 B.C.). In the 1992 Nova film *This Old Pyramid*, Mark Lehner asserted that this block proves that builders raised all pyramid blocks on ramps. He referred to this block as a "frozen moment in pyramid construction."[1] In other words, he uses this block to make the sweeping generalization that the Great Pyramid was built by means of an enormous construction ramp.

But all pyramids of the 3rd Dynasty, all 4th Dynasty queens' pyramids, and all pyramids built after the 4th Dynasty exhibit core and casing blocks small enough to be carried up ramps. One or two men are required to lift a block of the size found in the masonry of these pyramids. For these and later pyramids, only features such as enormous monolithic crypts, beams, plug-blocks, and portcullises present weights that pose engineering problems. As I explained above, the Great Pyramids (especially Khufu's pyramid) categorically defy the use of ramps.

The block Lehner had in mind may just as well represent a "frozen moment" in pyramid demolition or restoration, as carried out in ancient or modern times. There are a number of instances that may account for the block on the ramp. For example, the 19th Dynasty administration of Pharaoh Ramses II partially dismantled some pyramids and restored several others.[2] The ambitious restoration project was undertaken by his son Prince Kha-em-waset, the High Priest of Memphis, who exercised jurisdiction over the entire pyramid necropolis.

From the Old Kingdom's 5th Dynasty (c. 2465–2323 B.C.) forward, blocks were expropriated from older pyramids—until Kha-em-waset's major reconstruction program marked the end of a millennium of pilfering and neglect. Stonemasons' inscriptions suggest that his restoration work started on the 3rd Dynasty pyramid complex of Zoser on the tenth day of the third month of summer, in the 36th year of Ramses II's reign (c. 1243 B.C.). Also known to have benefited were the 4th Dynasty rectangular cenotaph of Pharaoh Shepseskaf, the 5th Dynasty pyramids of both Sahure and Unas, and a Sun temple of Neuserre.

Egyptologists suggest that Kha-em-waset's operation may have also contributed to the restoration of Khufu's Great Pyramid. During Herodotus' 5th century B.C. trip to Egypt, he reported seeing inscriptions on the Great Pyramid.[3] His report cannot be verified because almost all casing blocks are now gone. But Kha-em-waset prominently inscribed large, conspicuous hieroglyphic characters on the outer casing blocks of one face of each pyramid he restored. So, the inscriptions Herodotus saw may have been those of Kha-em-waset.

Kha-em-waset's writings still appear on a number of pyramids. The inscriptions of Ramses II and those of Kha-em-waset's architect Mey are still visible in a quarry at the foot of Khafra's Great Pyramid. Some Egyptologists attribute unfinished granite blocks on Giza's Third Pyramid to the work of Ramses II's administration. So, the several phases of activity at Giza over long ages makes it impossible to use a single small block on a small ramp to draw sweeping conclusions about how the Great Pyramid was built. The demolition and restoration works carried out under Ramses II's administration, and other phases of deconstruction and reconstruction, can more logically explain the block Lehner deemed a "frozen moment" in original construction work that also explains the construction of the Great Pyramid.

A demolition account recorded by Abd el-Latif (A.D. 1161–1231) pertains to the very pyramid complex Lehner used to make his sweeping generalization.[4] El-Latif described an ill-fated government-ordered operation that set out to demolish Menkaura's pyramid. El-Latif described the tremendous toil and expense involved when stripping off a great many pyramid blocks and dumping them nearby.

But the project proved so demanding that it had to be abandoned. After all the work, only a small part of the pyramid had been defaced. Pyramids were also routinely robbed of ready-made blocks by 5th and 6th Dynasty pharaohs and by modern operations, too. In the hope of finding an intact burial site, a crew of Napoleon's men attempted to demolish the westernmost queen's pyramid in this complex.

After tearing down its upper north quarter, they abandoned the project.[5] Treasure hunters over many centuries have pried and moved blocks at Giza. So, Giza has experienced post-19th Dynasty Egyptian, Greek, Roman, Middle Ages and modern reconstruction activity.[6] In their quests for artifacts, early Egyptologists dismantled parts of pyramids, frequently using boring rods, gunpowder, and dynamite. Tradition holds that Egyptian Arabs removed many blocks from the Giza monuments for constructions in Cairo. Petrie witnessed the removal of blocks from a number of structures during his seasons of work in Egypt.

We see that the "frozen moment" Lehner perceived as original construction work can easily date to a subsequent period. In other words, rather than an abandoned block left during construction, the block remaining on the ramp could have been abandoned after being torn off of the pyramid. In any case, we have already considered why a giant ramp of the size needed to raise blocks for the Great Pyramid is unworkable. For reasons we have already considered, it is not logical to assume that small blocks carried up earthen ramps translate into a scenario in which enormous blocks for the Great Pyramid were transported up a giant earthen ramp.

To explain how the pyramid builders quarried blocks, Lehner pointed out a hole in a Giza quarry made by the removal of a block. He insisted that this hole proves that all core blocks for the Great Pyramid were quarried at Giza. His sweeping generalization protested claims by Petrie, and more recently by geologists from Waseda University (who support Petrie's claim), that pyramid builders hauled core blocks from a distant quarry. For Lehner, this quarry hole represented another "frozen moment" in pyramid construction. Let us look at exactly what is so very wrong with Lehner's remark.

Lehner's assertion ignores established facts: First, anyone can see the one area at Giza where trenches were made and rectangular stumps remain. This is a limestone quarry, and it shows very clear evidence suggesting the removal of many blocks. The problem is that it is vastly too small to account for pyramid construction. This is one reason Petrie insisted that blocks must have been hauled from elsewhere.

Second, anyone can compare this area (located next to Khafra's pyramid), with the huge "quarries" (excavated pits) associated with the Great Pyramid. These huge pits do not show massive signs of block removal. They show a few holes, but are instead characterized by the marks of pointed picks all over their walls. We will now look more closely at this problem because it very seriously opposes the standard theory of pyramid construction altogether.

As mentioned, Mark Lehner estimated the volume of the quarry associated with the Great Pyramid as roughly equal to the monument itself. In 2002, I asked Systems Engineer Mike Carrell to add precision to Petrie's observation about the quarried area (next to Khafa's

15. The one quarry at Giza showing signs of the massive removal of blocks with trench-style quarrying is found next to Khafra's Great Pyramid. But it only equals about three percent of the volume of Khafra's Great Pyramid. W.M.F. Petrie was the first to observe that Giza lacks the signs of quarrying needed to account for the Great Pyramids. He searched for miles around Giza to try to learn where blocks could have been quarried.

pyramid) at Giza being too small to account for pyramid construction. So, Mike Carrell studied surveys and maps of Giza to provide an estimate for publication here.

Based on his estimate of the height of its walls and other dimensions, Mike Carrell calculated its volume at only two percent of the volume of Khufu's pyramid. If it were to provide blocks for Khafra's pyramid, Mike Carrell estimated that it equals roughly three percent of the volume of Khafra's pyramid. So, there is, as Petrie insisted, vastly too little evidence of block quarrying at Giza to account for the Great Pyramid.

Dietrich Klemm and Rosemary Klemm were the first to make a survey demonstrating that 4th Dynasty quarrying is not characterized by holes, like the one Lehner pointed out during the Nova film. The Klemms did long and careful work to establish that Old and Middle Kingdom quarry walls are instead covered with the marks of pointed picks. So, Lehner's assertion ignores the long history of rock extraction technique at Giza. Before going further into the ramifications of this, we will take a brief look at how extensive the research is in this area.

Geochemist Dietrich Klemm, of the University of Munich, in Germany, and his wife Egyptologist Rosemarie Klemm, carefully studied quarrying techniques by historical period.[7] These researchers exhaustively identified and classified the quarrying techniques used from the Pyramid Age to the Roman occupation of Egypt in A.D. 30.

By comparing tool marks and considering inscriptions, and by dating pottery shards, the Klemms produced a chronology of the quarrying techniques used in the sandstone quarries at Silsila and in the limestone quarries. In other words, they used the type of tool marks found in the quarries to date the Egyptian quarries to specific historical periods.

The Klemms observed evidence of the crudest quarrying method, which involved insert-ing wooden poles into holes made in the bedrock (like the hole Lehner pointed out). Ancient workers then saturated these large dowel rods with water. The water-swollen poles afforded enough pressure to cause the limestone bedrock to split along a single plane. Quarrymen repeated the operation at 90-degree angles until they isolated a rough block. Workers then undercut the block to extract it. Until the study by the Klemms, Egyptologists thought that this method was the oldest, because it is the most crude. In other words, Egyptologists thought it dates to the Pyramid Age. But the Klemms showed that this was the Roman method. So, this method was used in Egypt 2,500 years after the Great Pyramid was built.

There is little evidence of this method at Giza, assuring that it was not used to obtain millions of blocks for the Great Pyramid. So, in Nova's *This Old Pyramid* film, Mark Lehner incorrectly used Roman-made holes at Giza to draw a sweeping conclusion about how blocks were made during the Pyramid Age.

Another method was to bash out long, straight trenches in the bedrock at right angles until a block was isolated on four sides. Quarrymen crouched in these trenches and bashed out more rock from below to separate the blocks from the quarry floor. The Klemms showed that this technique does not match Pyramid Age quarrying, either.

As startling as it may seem, Egyptology has no true picture of the quarrying process used for building the Great Pyramid. Acknowledging the study by the Klemms, Dieter Arnold admitted:

> The question as to what kind of tools were used to cut the separation trenches and to lift the blocks from their beds has not been answered satisfactorily because of the contradiction between the tool marks left on the quarry walls and the tools actually found in ancient Egypt.[8]

Arnold's observation takes us straight to the heart of a huge problem: No one can explain how blocks can be made with primitive pickaxes. We are being asked to believe that workers made blocks with something like weakly-constructed, crude awls. Such tools are totally inefficient for making blocks. Yet, the marks of these crude pickaxes appear all over the walls of the quarry (excavation pit) associated with the Great Pyramid. The same is true for all Old and Middle Kingdom quarries.

We see that Egyptologists cannot reconcile these crude tool marks—which actually characterize Old and Middle Kingdom quarrying—with making trenches to produce blocks. This is a very important point because Arnold's admission shows that Egyptology really has not determined how workers made blocks for the Great Pyramids. So, this presents yet another serious weakness in the accepted construction theory.

In these pages, I have shown three fundamental, fatal flaws in the accepted theory of how the Great Pyramid was constructed. First, the Egyptological literature itself shows that Egyptology has not determined how the Great Pyramid's blocks could have been raised: Studies show that huge ramps are unworkable and no other ancient lifting device was feasible.

Second, Egyptology has not determined how millions of limestone and harder stone blocks could have been shaped. We have seen that the Pyramid Age Egyptians did not have adequate supplies of appropriate metal tools for creating the masonry work. Pounding balls, Egyptology's last option for shaping pyramid blocks, cannot produce the special features existing on the scale of the giant pyramids, a fact admitted by Dieter Arnold (quoted earlier in these pages). Rubbing blocks with sand or another abrasive is not a practical means of producing giant pyramids, and we a have seen that abrasives cannot explain many of the special features found on Pyramid Age artifacts. Features on pyramid complex paving slabs and various other artifacts show that they were cut through very rapidly.

Third, Egyptology has not determined how even crudely-shaped limestone blocks could have been quarried at Giza during the Pyramid Age on such a massive scale. Clearly, there is a dire need for an entirely new and different pyramid-construction theory that can solve such fundamental problems.

I stress all of this because we cannot appreciate the solution until we appreciate the problem. So, we will press on with this process of putting the facts in order so that we can see the solution come into view.

We must keep in mind the major geological differences between the Giza limestone bedrock and the pyramid blocks—differences observed by a number of geologists. As mentioned, fossiliferous pyramid and temple blocks exhibit jumbled seashells. In contrast, the bedrock at Giza contains the same types of shells, but it is characterized by normal sedimentary layering (wherein the fossils lie flat).

The evidence above shows how important it is to sort out the different periods of quarry work at Giza and at other quarries—so that we can get a true picture of ancient construction methods. Whereas, most books and articles on pyramid construction show the stumps north of Khafra's pyramid, and assert that they explain the method of producing blocks for pyramid construction. The quarried area consists of rows of what appear to be stumps left over from the removal of blocks. But this relatively small grid is associated with Khafra's pyramid; therefore, it is not thought to have existed when the Great Pyramid was built. For that reason, this small quarry is not involved in Mark Lehner's reconstruction (The Giza Mapping Project) of the source of stone for Khufu's Great Pyramid.

Before the study by the Klemms, Egyptologists assumed that these so-called stumps proved how blocks were quarried for the Great Pyramid. This assumption, of course, ignores Petrie's important observation that the quarried area is vastly too small to account for the Great Pyramids (an observation that can easily be confirmed now that Giza has been carefully mapped).

Comments asserting that pyramid blocks were quarried with copper tools appear in the most popular book of all on the pyramids. It is titled *The Pyramids of Egypt* (1985 edition), and was written by former keeper of Egyptian antiquities at the British Museum, I.E.S. Edwards:

> Limestone…presented the pyramid builders with no serious difficulties of its quarrying. A discovery by W.B. Emery in the early dynastic cemetery of Saqqara has shown that even in the 1st Dynasty the Egyptians possessed excellent copper tools, including saws and chisels, which were capable of cutting any kind of limestone…Chisels and wedges were, however, the tools most favoured for quarrying limestone, the former for cutting the blocks away from the rock on every side except the bottom and the latter for detaching the blocks at the base.[9]

As I have pointed out, Egyptology has now made too much progress for statements like this to be considered valid or believable. Although the body of the Sphinx and some blocks in the Giza complexes are soft enough to be cut with copper, Edwards' remarks are out-of-date and erroneous. This is proven by extensive trials with copper tools, by the dearth of copper supplies compared to the amount required, and by the extensive study by the Klemms we have already explored. Many Egyptology books that contain much valuable information are simply out-of-date as it regards issues of cutting, quarrying and lifting pyramid blocks.

Given that the most up-to-date Egyptological findings show that the flat-topped stumps near Khafra's pyramid are uncharacteristic of Pyramid Age quarrying, they should no longer be used to explain how blocks were made for the Great Pyramids. Unfortunately, Dieter Arnold's *Building in Egypt*, which will long remain the new standard on ancient Egyptian masonry, fails to specifically mention that this grid is characteristic of post-Pyramid Age quarrying. Arnold also failed to point out that the grid is vastly too small to have supplied blocks for the Great Pyramids. Although it could date later than the New Kingdom, the grid of stumps may represent the restorations of Ramses II's reign because inscriptions of his administration appear in this quarry.

The long history of intermittent building activity at Giza spans thousands of years and includes several phases. After the original pyramid construction work was completed, maintenance cults preserved the Giza pyramid estates. These cults disintegrated over time, and Egyptians of later times eventually used the pyramids and temples as sources of ready-made blocks. Later still, Ramses' son Kha-em-waset restored the pyramids and reestablished their maintenance cults. The endowment estates were large, and priests of Snofru, Khufu, and other pharaohs were still officiating in Greek Ptolemaic times (after 332 B.C.).[10]

Building activity at Giza was also conducted during the Saite Period, in the 26th Dynasty (664–525 B.C.).[11] The work was so extensive that some Egyptologists suggest that the sarcophagus lid found in the Third Pyramid at Giza, built for Pharaoh Menkaura, was replaced during Saite times.[12] When clearing a chamber in this pyramid, John S. Perring found a fragment of a lid with Menkaura's name on it. But its style is identified as dating to the 26th Dynasty.

There was also Greek activity at Giza, as evidenced by the large number of Greek Sphinxes discovered in 1994. As mentioned, a Greco-Roman village of considerable size at Giza was first reported by Howard Vyse.

Evidence of Roman restoration appears near the Sphinx, where there are inscriptions belonging to the Roman emperors Marcus Aurelius Antoninus (A.D. 161–180) and Septimus Severus (A.D. 193–211). Both restored the court of the Sphinx. The Roman Emperors Antonius Pius (A.D. 138–161) and Lucius Versus (A.D. 161–169) had the Sphinx's retaining walls restored. A number of the early Roman emperors were adherents of the Egyptian religion, most especially as devotees to Isis, and so they involved themselves with Egyptian architecture.

All of this history bears on different phases of historical evidence at Giza. It helps us to sort later quarrying and tool marks from the original, special means of constructing the Great Pyramids—the real technology that is the ultimate focus of this book. To get to this real technology, we must first recognize that when we see tool marks in quarries or on pyramid blocks, we have to consider what period they may date to. As strange as it may seem, only a minority of pyramid blocks exhibit tool marks—even when blocks are very crudely shaped.

Egyptologists assume that workers ground off the tool marks on most pyramid and temple blocks. But Egyptologists offer no explanation for why Egyptians would grind off tool marks on the blocks, which are sometimes highly-irregular in shape and not meant to look perfect, and were supposed to remain forever hidden behind giant, beautifully-made casing blocks. Egyptology offers no demonstration of how workers could have ground tool marks from huge form-fitted blocks, some demonstrating hairline joints as close as 1/500 inch or in perfect contact. The same problem exists for the huge paving slabs with undersides that conform to the bedrock below.

The archaeological record vies against Lehner's assertion that all blocks original to the Great Pyramid were quarried as he supposes. As mentioned above, Arnold admitted that the evidence associated with block extraction is very puzzling. Moreover, Petrie was correct to assert that there is a dearth of evidence for the extraction of whole blocks at Giza—no matter what the quarry method employed—to account for the construction of the Great Pyramid.

In the Nova film *This Old Pyramid*, Lehner also attempted to explain how the ancient workers shaped pyramid blocks. Lehner pointed out stone debris strewn around the floor of the crudely-made subterranean chamber of the Great Pyramid. He said that this debris proves that the ancient builders cut all limestone blocks for the Great Pyramid with primitive tools. His assertion is illogical for the following reasons.

Stone picks and pounding balls are suitable for breaking up limestone to tunnel crude shafts and bash out rough subterranean rooms — like the one in which Lehner was standing. The work mainly involved removing tons of rubble. The main challenge for the workers was avoiding the hazards of the bedrock caving in when they encountered softer strata of desert conglomerate and cracks in the bedrock.

But it is illogical to use the crudely-bashed-out room to argue for producing the overall masonry perfection of the Great Pyramid itself. Limestone is more moist and easier to cut when it is underground. No special masonry features appear in this unfinished, roughly-cut chamber. Whereas, the Great Pyramid features its giant form-fitting casing blocks that fit as closely as 1/500 an inch (and the angle they produced up the sides of the giant pyramid shape), its 13 acre level foundation, its more than 200 corresponding tiers made in about 73 tier heights (covering a great many acres) accurate in height to within a 1/2 centimeter, its four amazingly subtly-bowed faces, and the near perfect planes of these vast sloping faces (behind the level of the casing). All require a vastly more sophisticated technology than the ability to bash and hack rock to produce unfinished underground chambers.

In these pages I have shown that the accepted theories of pyramid construction are not supported by hard evidence. They are supported only by the sheer weight of assumption and very entrenched ideas that are gradually being displaced by the most up-to-date Egyptological findings.

In sum, the small block on a small ramp at Giza cannot legitimately be used to explain the method of building the Great Pyramid. Small ramps attached to small pyramids do not translate into workers using a huge ramp to elevate blocks for the Great Pyramid. Engineering studies we have already considered show that construction ramps are unworkable for building the Great Pyramid.

There is too little evidence of block quarrying at Giza to account for the construction of the Great Pyramid. This shows that something is fundamentally wrong with the accepted pyramid construction paradigm.

Evidence of block quarrying at Giza is characteristic of much later building activity. Arnold admits that Old Kingdom quarrying is very puzzling to him. The crude tool marks, made with pointed picks in the huge quarries associated with the Great Pyramids, do not offer him a clue about how pyramid blocks could have been quarried.

All this evidence may seem very strange, given the existence of enormous pyramids at Giza. But it is a mistake to use the monuments themselves as proof of method. The true method of pyramid construction, which I explain in these pages, causes all of these seemingly overwhelming problems to vanish.

Chapter 18
The Resistance to New Knowledge

In response to the wild speculation of occultists and poorly-researched books, the trend in Egyptology these days is to dismiss or downplay unresolved masonry and engineering enigmas.[1] Consider Dieter Arnold's remarks in *Building in Egypt* (1991):

> The discussion of how the pyramids could have been built seems, however, to be never-ending and continues to produce fantasies. In this respect, Egyptology shares the fate of other archaeological fields that deal with monumental architecture. But although Egyptian builders accomplished great feats in moving and lifting enormous weights, everything was achieved with the relatively simple building methods that are well attested for Pharaonic Egypt. The Egyptian builders used three basic methods to lift a weight: by pulling it up an inclined plane; by lifting it with ropes and primitive devices; and by levering.[2]

These remarks imply that pyramid builders overcame the impossible task of elevating millions of massive building units on a mud-brick ramp much more massive than the Great Pyramid itself. While Arnold himself acknowledged unresolved problems with ramps, he nevertheless makes light of unsolved engineering puzzles:

> The laying of blocks of extraordinary size seems to have presented no real problems for the Egyptian builders. Also, the lifting of core and casing blocks of the pyramids to great heights seems to have been routine work for them.[3]

Arnold implies that because the Great Pyramid exists, raising enormous weights to great heights did not present a problem. But Egyptologists have an intellectual obligation to go beyond such perfunctory observations, which anyone untrained in the principles of valid reasoning and argumentation can make. The construction problems are too compelling to be brushed aside and ignored. Egyptologists have the obligation of explaining how millions of enormous building units could be quarried, cut and elevated on such a grand scale. Egyptologists have the responsibility of explaining all of the difficult problems we have explored. If an Egyptologist cannot figure them out, then that individual should have the presence of mind to at least recognize that the accepted paradigm is fatally flawed.

Esteemed scholars do a serious disservice to science, and to history and Egyptology, and to the history of science, and to scientific methodology itself, by dismissing enigmas that continue to perplex trained engineers and stone masons, as well as defy common sense. Because great weight is accorded to the opinions of learned scholars, the average reader will be greatly persuaded by dismissive comments. I write this book to appeal to readers who think deeply, and I present sufficient evidence to prove that the Great Pyramid would not exist if its construction were solely dependent on the means proposed by Egyptology.

Remarks by the scientific-minded Reginald Engelbach, Chief Inspector of Antiquities of Upper Egypt early in the 20th century, can serve to summarize the problem.

> While the publication of a new grammatical form or historical point will evoke a perfect frenzy of contradiction in the little world of Egyptology, the most absurd statements on a mechanical problem will be left unquestioned and, what is worse, accepted.[4]

Dieter Arnold has made some progress in the discipline of Egyptology by compiling his new standard, and thereby illustrating that certain premises held in previous books on ancient Egyptian stoneworking are inaccurate. He was not always so willing to dismiss problems. He recognized that building Snofru's two large pyramids involved a total volume of about four million cubic yards of rock. Workers incorporated this huge amount of material during this pharaoh's 24-year reign. The Great Pyramids of Khafra and Khufu each have a volume of about two million cubic yards of material. Arnold calculated that in 80 years, workers built 12 million blocks into the major pyramids.[5]

The number of blocks incorporated per day depended on how long it took to choose, plan and prepare construction sites. We must also factor in the usual delays of getting ambitious projects underway. There was also time off, since the ancient Egyptians enjoyed a number of religious holidays per year. To avoid hazards, workers had to be off the construction sites after daylight hours. Considering the various factors, Arnold deduced that the number of blocks set per day could lead to "astronomical numbers."

He saw no solution other than doubling or tripling the life spans of these pharaohs. His proposal is ultra-conservative compared with that of engineers from Japan's Waseda University who drew from hands-on experience. As mentioned, after building a relatively small model of the Great Pyramid (devoid of the special internal features or fancy joints), they calculated that the monument required a 1,200 year construction period.[6] Given the severity of the problem and the known history of Egypt, this speaks to the existence of a special technology that allowed for super-rapid construction.

Mark Lehner, too, dismisses the construction enigmas of the Great Pyramid. After Nova's *This Old Pyramid* aired, Lehner's remarks were published in the January 1995 issue of *National Geographic*:

> To gauge the extent of that labor [for building the Great Pyramid], Mark Lehner and a team built a 30-foot-high pyramid near Giza out of the same Tura limestone used by the ancient Egyptians. The men who built Khufu's pyramid, hauling and positioning an estimated 2.3 million limestone blocks, most weighing 2.5 tons, would have had to set a block in place every two and a half minutes. Using a helical ramp winding upward around their pyramid, Lehner's team found that just ten to twelve men could slide a block up the ramp, using desert clay and water as a lubricant, and lever it into place. Herodotus declared that 100,000 men were needed to build one of the Pyramids of Giza. Lehner calculates that as few as 10,000 could have pulled off the job. As he puts it, "A pyramid turns out to be a very doable thing."[7]

The *National Geographic* reporter made a number of errors. Nova's miniature pyramid was 18 feet high, not 30. The Tura limestone used by Nova was very soft, unlike the harder core and casing blocks of the Great Pyramid. The sizes of the Great Pyramid's blocks are averaged at 2.5 tons (the point is missed that the much larger blocks at great heights pose the greatest challenges). Nova's ramp did not wind upward around the miniature pyramid, but only as high as the lowest tiers—affording the audience the only clue that the pyramid was not really being built by hand. Scaled up to the size needed to build the Great Pyramid, a spiral ramp would have to be over 4,800 feet long on each slope to create the workable 1:10 slope needed to raise heavy blocks on sleds to over 480 feet high (the original monument was about 500 feet). This makes a spiral ramp far more problematic than a straight ramp.

Since the above-quoted *National Geographic* article was published, Lehner has revised his 10,000-man figure. In *The Complete Pyramids* (1997), he offered revised calculations, concluding that a grand total of 25,000 men was required. But he listed most as logistical workers, including copper-tool sharpeners, cooks, and brewers.[8] Calculating workers irrelevant to the central issue of block-raising sidesteps the real problem of figuring out the number of men required to raise heavy weights to great heights. For the critical work of quarrying, elevating, shaping, and setting stones for the Great Pyramid, Lehner's figure is too low:

> Our calculations suggest that Khufu's pyramid could have been built by two crews of 2,000.[9]

I have already shown above how Mark Lehner came to his low estimate with erroneous calculations. Lehner substitutes the calculation of the number of men needed to haul blocks on a flat surface for the calculation needed for elevating blocks on an incline—which allows him to discard a great many thousands of workers.[10] Lehner also calculates with weight averaging and discards real block sizes by saying they need more study. Sadly, the enigmas of pyramid construction cannot be appreciated as long as people in responsible positions incorrectly report them.

PBS Nova's *This Old Pyramid* ignored the unanswered masonry and engineering questions. Producer Michael Barnes planned and scripted the film based on consultations. Barnes primarily consulted with Evan Hadingham, Science Editor for the PBS series Nova (made by WGBH television in Boston). Hadingham consulted with me, but he did not listen to me very much. He declared that his mind was made up when Lehner showed him the "smoking gun of pyramid construction" firsthand. Hadingham was referring to the small block on a small ramp at a tiny queen's pyramid at Giza. Hadingham insisted that there is no archaeological evidence at Giza to support another pyramid construction method. To settle the question of how diorite vessels could be cut with primitive tools, Hadingham sent me a published paper theorizing how ancient Egyptian stone vessels were made with boring techniques. But the paper did not even mention diorite. Barnes also relied on a number of well-known Egyptologists. In addition to Mark Lehner and Jean-Philippe Lauer, one of them was Dieter Arnold. Arnold's *Building in Egypt*, despite its mixed messages, does point out inadequacies of Pyramid Age tools and some severe problems with ramp theories as it concerns building the Great Pyramid.

Here are the most critical points that Nova ignored to base *This Old Pyramid* on outdated ideas that Egyptology is gradually abandoning:

- Arnold admits that Egyptology does not really know how limestone blocks could have been quarried. Arnold wrote: "The question as to what kind of tools were used to cut the separation trenches and to lift the blocks from their beds has not been answered satisfactorily because of the contradiction between the tool marks left on the quarry walls and the tools actually found in ancient Egypt…"[11]

- Arnold admits that Egyptology does not know how blocks could have been shaped: "We do not know exactly how the masons achieved two corresponding and neatly fitted planes on two neighboring blocks…"[12]

- Arnold rejects all ramp designs for the Great Pyramid because none are workable. Regarding a helical ramp, Arnold writes: "…one would even doubt their feasibility. In spite of the ingeniousness of such a device, spiral ramps would have created serious problems."[13]

- Arnold's remarks can serve to sum up the ramp problems associated with constructing the Great Pyramid: "...the most ingenious and scrupulous system developed on the drawing board is nothing but one more example of unproven speculation..."[14]

In short, Nova ignored the most fundamental problems: Egyptology does not know how the Great Pyramid's blocks could have been quarried, shaped or elevated. This presents major deficiencies, but the film misrepresented the problems and then claimed to have reconciled the method of pyramid construction.

PBS repeated the same old mistakes in a newer film that first aired on February 20, 2001, titled *Secrets of the Pharaohs, Part 2: Lost City of the Pyramids*. The film featured a study of pyramid construction by contractor Craig Smith. Here are excerpts from an online article by Mark Rose, Managing Editor of *Archaeology* magazine (dated February 21, 2001), which summarize the project:

> In an interesting experiment, American contractor Craig Smith is called in. Familiar with managing large-scale construction projects, like airports, Smith is primed with what we know of Old Kingdom construction methods: stone and flint implements from the tombs, copper-working, and quarrying at Giza (partially cut-out blocks and ramps along which stones were hauled), an inscription depicting a colossal statue being dragged using ropes and water (to reduce friction), and results of failed stone-levering experiments inspired by Herodotus' tale of how blocks were moved. Smith gets to work, first determining how the pyramids were built. Computer modeling shows that a ramp built perpendicular to one side of the pyramid's base was most economical for positioning blocks until the structure reached one-third of its height (at which point one-half of the blocks would have been laid). Only then would the ramp be built, more narrowly since the blocks farther up would be smaller, spiraling around the upper part of the pyramid. A ramp spiraling up all the way from the base, explains Smith, would require much more fill and construction time. Having established the most economical way to build a pyramid, he looks at the numbers of people required. Surprisingly, Smith says it could be done in only ten years: two or three for preparation, five for the actual construction, and two to remove the ramp and finish the site. This schedule would require 40,000 workmen during the peak years, four through six. Lehner and Hawass believe more time was used, perhaps 20 years, which would bring the annual labor pool down toward the figure proposed by Hawass.

In other words, we see that Smith was provided terribly incorrect data and information. So, he incorrectly assumes that copper, flint and other stone tools are capable of quarrying and cutting millions of limestone blocks and can achieve the perfection of the Great Pyramid. Smith does not explain where vast supplies of copper could have come from, or consider that copper is softer than most blocks in the Great Pyramid.

Smith does not address the absence of tool marks on the vast majority of blocks or the time it would take to grind them off and still achieve the oblique and complex, wavy joints (which are also devoid of tool marks) with mating protuberances.

Smith supplies no data about the strength of the ramp he proposes. Remember that Master Builder Peter Hodges showed that a ramp as solid as strong stone masonry would be needed. The blocks making up such a ramp would have to be heavy enough not to slide out of place when beams up to 70 tons are raised to 160 feet, the level of the ceiling of the

King's Chamber. The ramp must also support the weight of the thousands of workers required to rapidly raise such weights. It is not reasonable to think that such large units could be raised up the kind of incline Smith supposes. But Smith does not even include these challenging weights in his model.

The ramp masonry would have to be of good quality, so that blocks do not crack or give way beneath the workers. During Nova's pyramid-building experiment, Roger Hopkins confirmed the need for a strong ramp. Hopkins remarked in the film that the surface of their ramp (made of stone rubble cemented with clay) was unsuitable after Nova's tiny block-raising experiment.

Smith proposes a partial ramp design, covering 2/3 of the monument. This design eliminates the ability to measure from true reference points. The upper 2/3 of his ramp completely engulfs the Great Pyramid, and so we can expect a distorted pyramid shape as the outcome because he offered no way around the problem.

Smith did not simulate his design based on actual tier height measurements. We must keep in mind that tier 35 is taller than tier two, and that tier 201 was measured as taller than tier four at the base. So, Smith's ramp design would not accommodate men hauling some of the largest building blocks in the pyramid up to tier 201.

His calculation is also devoid of the time required to prepare, set, and cement (with paper-thin cement) huge, form-fitted casing blocks, a feat that baffled W.M.F. Petrie: "To merely place such stones in exact contact at the sides would be careful work; but to do so with cement in the joint seems almost impossible." The situation he described extends to about 20 acres of casing stones for the Great Pyramid.

When critical data are ignored and computer modeling substitutes for real experiments, it is easy to minimize the construction rate and manpower required. Smith's idea that the actual construction work could be done in only five years arises from the terribly flawed information and data he was "primed with." Computer modeling is only as good as the data input. The common phrase, "garbage in, garbage out" comes to mind.

The very idea that millions of blocks can be cut into 73 tier heights (which heights show an error of 1/2 centimeter or less when measured with precise modern instruments), made up largely of conforming masonry to form evenly bowed faces (which show a mean optical plane touching the most prominent points of the blocks at an average variation of only 1.0 inch), staggers the mind and must be factored into legitimate calculations. The problems go far beyond calculating with 2-1/2-ton block weight averages. Proper study shows that the Great Pyramid, with its unprecedented precision, exceeds even modern capabilities (assuming a construction rate of only about 25 years)—unless one is working with the special technology that is the subject of Part 2 of this book.

Egyptology is slowly abandoning unworkable theories, and there are setbacks. A statement by the famous British author George Orwell (1903–50) appropriately describes the situation:

Progress is not an illusion, it happens, but it is slow and invariably disappointing.[15]

Chapter 19
The Supertech Theories

In 1883, William M. Flinders Petrie's book *The Pyramids and Temples of Gizeh* introduced the world to the grand features of the Great Pyramid—along with some of the perplexing puzzles associated with its construction. The enigmas he identified glare after more than a century of cumulative study, and challenging questions continue to arise. As society has become more technology-minded, a number of popular books have advanced speculative theories based in futuristic technology.

Although they existed earlier, the supertech idea was popularized about 40 years ago by author Erich von Daniken in his best-seller *Chariots of the Gods?* (1969). Von Daniken advocates that space-alien technology is responsible for all ancient monuments exhibiting unexplained engineering or masonry features. There has since been no shortage of variations and elaboration on his theme.

Predictably, Egyptologists react by denouncing these ideas and asserting established theories. But there is no denying the need for a theory that solves the enigmas and anomalies I have presented in the previous pages. In the absence of such a truly convincing explanation, alternative explanations abound. Some are outlandish and others fail to properly address problems.

Some popular books propose exotic power sources for running supertech devices ranging from crystal generators to harmonic or magnetic levitation. But if we think along these lines, then we would have to entertain a tremendous wealth of supertechnology to satisfy all of the features of the Great Pyramid.

Let us look at the slippery slope: Antigravity devices are a favorite for transporting granite beams up to 27 feet long from Aswan, about 500 miles south of Giza. We would need a matter scrambler to jumble up fossil shells for the nummulitic limestone building blocks of the Giza pyramid complexes.[1] A machine that recalibrates time would allow for very rapid construction during Khufu's reign. A supercomputer would be useful for addressing the inventorying, storing, and assorting problems associated with the vast masonry patterns of Khufu's Great Pyramid. Computer-driven power saws would allow for shaping the multitudes of form-fitted blocks, and cut the deep hieroglyphic and decorative reliefs in items made of hard rock. A large, exotic power saw could rapidly cut the lid from Khufu's sarcophagus and make the wayward cuts that astonished Petrie. Because this sarcophagus is too large to fit through the long hallway leading to the King's Chamber, a matter shrinker would be useful for installation. The ultrasonic drill Christopher Dunn envisions might play a role, too. The same devices would be useful for post-Pyramid Age objects that defy conventional explanations.

Such supertechnology would have had to exist alongside of a population living in the most rudimentary mud-brick housing, and workers toiling with crude pickaxes as they left their marks in the Old and Middle Kingdom quarries—an unlikely scenario. Although I reject such fanciful ideas, it is important to recognize that the supertech theories exist, to a significant degree, because orthodox theories have failed.

To make matters worse, orthodox books and articles tend to ignore or gloss over the most difficult enigmas, causing proponents of the supertech theories to suspect a conspiracy of censorship.

Some proponents of an Atlantean origin of the Great Pyramid propose that evidence for advanced technologies must be buried deeper than archaeologists have excavated. But this line of reasoning is invalid, too. The reason is that the technology that afforded extraordinary masonry works appears throughout ancient Egyptian history.

We have considered Neolithic artifacts, including those made with diorite. In much later times, Pharaoh Amenemhet III's huge, spectacular monolithic quartzite sarcophagus (which is unrivaled by modern stonework) was constructed only 600 years before the events that came to be recorded in the Bible as the Hebrew Exodus. Many extraordinary artifacts date from much later than Amenemhet III's quartzite sarcophagus.

The gigantic, monolithic 18th Dynasty Colossi of Memnon immediately come to mind. A quartzite bust of Queen Nefertiti dates to the 18th Dynasty, too. It was made with yellow quartzite, and curators consider the detailed, lifelike bust a masterpiece. As mentioned, a number of sarcophagi were made with such material for 18th Dynasty pharaohs.

Inscriptions on enigmatic vessels, statuary, sarcophagi, and obelisks serve to date these items. Among a great many examples, inscriptions etched into a bowl found at Saqqara date this object to Hotep, the first king of the 2nd Dynasty. It was made with diorite. Another example is the hieroglyphic writings in the vaults above the King's Chamber of the Great Pyramid, dated to the reign of Khufu.

For most of his career as an archaeo-Egyptologist, Mark Lehner promoted the idea that the Great Pyramid is an artifact of Atlantis. In his book *The Egyptian Heritage: Based on the Edgar Cayce Readings* (1974), Lehner suggests that Atlanteans painted Khufu's inscription (Khufu's cartouche dated to year 17 of his reign) in the vault above the King's Chamber. Lehner suggested that the purpose was to confound modern researchers. So, Lehner described Khufu's cartouche as a:

> …'red herring' for modern man until the time was right for the real meaning of this Pyramid to be brought to light. This, of course, would require considerable prophetic skill.[2]

As Mark Lehner has since discovered, it is unnecessary to entertain the notion that Atlanteans—supposedly in about 10,500 B.C.—planted hieroglyphics to confound modern researchers. There is nothing un-Egyptian about the Great Pyramid.[3]

As we have considered in these pages, other examples of stunning ancient Egyptian masonry bear characteristics that are remarkable by modern standards. They range in dates from Neolithic times to the late periods of Egyptian history. So, there is no reason to postulate that technology from the fabled Atlantis afforded the Great Pyramid or that evidence for such technology is buried more deeply than the earliest known ruins.

There is a logical solution to all of the masonry and engineering enigmas. The all-encompassing solution operates upon the technical horizon of the primitive tools, materials and methods known even during the Neolithic Period (c. 7,000 B.C.). It later allowed workers to build each pyramid within a pharaoh's reign. The archaeological evidence, including the features of the pyramids, quarries, and tomb artifacts, supports only the real solution. With all the mysteries explained above, we now have enough background set in place to appreciate the real solution to the construction of the Great Pyramids and other dazzling artifacts. We now begin our exploration of that solution, and we will see exactly how it satisfies each and every one of the mysteries I have explained.

Part Two
The Solution

Chapter 20
The Only Logical Solution

A complete paradigm shift eliminates all puzzles of cutting blocks of any size or hardness and positioning them at any height. Both the orthodox and supertech pyramid construction theories entertain the same incorrect premise: the cutting, hauling, and hoisting of stone. The new model eliminates these requirements—along with 95 percent of the work and all of the seemingly impossible challenges we have considered. It allows for the fabrication of monuments, diorite vessels and other artifacts that cannot be made any other way.

Huge ramps vanish, primitive hand tools become perfectly capable of performing the exquisite masonry work. The size of the Giza quarries suddenly also makes sense. So does the geological mismatch that exists at Giza. As with any puzzle, there are clues leading to the solution.

Important clues come from the archaeological record. So, now we will look at these clues in a new way. One clue is the crude tool marks found all over Old and Middle Kingdom quarry walls. The quarrymen made them with pointed stone picks. Dieter Arnold remarked about them:

> Furthermore, the only known metal chisels suitable for working in stone (the round bar chisels) are not pointed, however, but show a flat, wide cutting edge…In consequence, one would have to assume that pointed stone picks or axes were used during the Old and Middle Kingdoms.[1]

As mentioned, quarrying millions of massive limestone blocks with pointed stone picks or axes is so unthinkable that Dieter Arnold summarized what amounts to a newly -recognized mystery of Egyptology:

> The question as to what kind of tools were used to cut the separation trenches and to lift the blocks from their beds has not been answered satisfactorily because of the contradiction between the tool marks left on the quarry walls and the tools actually found in ancient Egypt.[2]

More precisely, the contradiction is between the tool marks and the tools required to quarry blocks. In Part 1 of this book, I demonstrated very compelling clues that we now consider together:

- **Waste Rock:** Given the amount of waste involved in block quarrying, the quarries associated with the Great Pyramid are too small to have furnished over two million cut blocks.[3] Also, the voluminous solid stone construction ramp that Peter Hodges discussed, made of squared blocks, produces a further tremendous demand on the Giza quarries. Long causeways and high walls surrounding pyramid complexes produce additional demands on the quarry size. There is a dearth of waste blocks left over from construction.

- **Geological Mismatch:** Fossil shells in pyramid and temple blocks at Giza are scrambled. The bedrock at Giza is characterized by normal sedimentation.[4]

- **Whole Block Quarrying:** Evidence of whole block extraction at Giza dates to later times.[5] This is shown by the tool-mark classifications made by Rosemarie and Dietrich Klemm.

- **Lost Quarries Enigma:** Petrie was the first to notice that the only area exhibiting evidence of substantial block quarrying at Giza is too small to have been a major source of pyramid blocks.[6] The quarry, located next to Khafra's Great Pyramid, equals about three percent of the volume of this pyramid. So, despite an abundance of limestone at Giza, Petrie and others asserted that the Egyptians must have hauled blocks from distant quarries. But all of the Egyptian quarries are known, and only one other quarry shows evidence of the removal of nummulitic limestone blocks on a truly massive scale. That quarry is called Zawyet Sultan. It is located near El-Minya, in Middle Egypt, far from Giza. But all evidence at this quarry at Zawyet Sultan points to the removal of blocks through trench-style quarrying. In other words, the quarrying style does not match the crude pick marks characteristic of Old and Middle Kingdom quarry walls. The quarrying style matches the type of work found next to Khafra's Great Pyramid at Giza, work most likely associated with New Kingdom or later repairs. So, there are insufficient signs of block quarrying at Giza.

- **No Block Transport System:** There is no evidence for transport systems at Giza. Evidence of a huge ramp has always been lacking. Only a small ramp leads from the quarry to ground level. There is no evidence of the use of barges at Giza or any other transport system for hauling blocks from afar. The sled is unknown from the Fourth Dynasty. Many depictions in books and films show large sleds and barges hauling stones. But no evidence whatsoever of either transport system has been found at Giza. It has not been established that a harbor at Giza was steep enough to transport large blocks by river.

- **Perfection that Defies Modern Reproduction:** One of the most remarkable features of pyramid and temple blocks is the way so many conform to the shapes of neighboring blocks. This is even true when blocks have oddly shaped joints. The undersides of foundation slabs conform to the uneven bedrock below. The backs of the Giza casing stones conform to the blocks behind them on a massive scale. Some of these blocks, including temple blocks weighing hundreds of tons apiece, are so large that it is unfathomable to think they were constantly shifted and cut and reset until they fit perfectly. Tiers heights covering many acres meet the very exacting standards of 73 heights that are accurate within 1/2 centimeter.

- **Lack of Means and Method:** We have seen that Pyramid Age Egyptians had no way to quarry or shape the blocks, or raise the real block weights found in the Great Pyramid. We have explored challenges that cannot be met today. The ancient Egyptians had a better way.

- **Block Extraction Technique:** Quarrymen attacked the quarries with pointed stone picks, which are inadequate for quarrying blocks.[7] These tools are only suitable for making tons of limestone debris. We see that the tool marks all over Old and Middle Kingdom limestone quarry walls show a quarrying method that produces limestone rubble rather than blocks.[8] These are not quarries from which whole blocks were removed. They are instead excavation pits where stone rubble was removed on a very large scale. What does that tell us?

The above clues allow us to approach the long-lost secret of pyramid construction, which I will now describe.

The Great Pyramid's Secret

The Giza Plateau exhibits distinctly different grades of limestone, and they appear in layers. One grade of bedrock, upon which the Great Pyramid is built, is strong enough to support the massive monument. But the thick layer (the so-called middle layer) of limestone bedrock that was extensively removed for pyramid construction is a poor grade. It is characterized by fossil shells that are loosely bound together to form the rock.[9]

The soft body of the Great Sphinx is made of this weak grade of limestone. The Sphinx could not have survived the centuries were it not buried in sand for much of its existence. The limestone in the Giza quarries (excavation pits) is weakly bound because of a high clay content. Five to 10 hours of soaking in water will cause much of this limestone to come apart.[10] When thoroughly soaked, the limestone releases its kaolin clay, which contains silica and aluminum compounds. The secret of pyramid construction is that to build Great Pyramids of Giza, the Egyptians introduced an essential ingredient into the wet kaolinitic limestone rubble they made with their pickaxes.

The ingredient is caustic soda—and it allows for a very special process.

They made caustic soda by adding their natron (with its key ingredient sodium carbonate) and lime to water. This combination of wet, clay-bearing limestone rubble and caustic soda produces a concrete mixture that is almost indistinguishable from natural limestone when set.

So, the forgotten secret of the Great Pyramid is that its blocks are the product of alchemy. They are high-quality rock-concrete, packed directly in place. They are not blocks that were cut or manually raised at all. They are of such high quality that they can readily fool geologists.

Producing rock-concrete is the only logical answer for producing a pyramid that is roughly the same size as its associated quarry. It is the only logical solution to the puzzle of jumbled shells in the blocks and natural sedimentation in the quarries (excavation pits). When limestone is broken up and turned into concrete, the natural orientation of the shells is disrupted. This unique, novel solution especially makes sense when we consider that the shell types in the blocks match those at Giza. Rock-concrete is the only logical solution when we consider that concrete-grade limestone was excavated from the excavation pits at Giza. That weak grade of limestone, which is unsuitable for making blocks, was transformed into rock-hard limestone concrete of far better quality. The massive amount of geological and archaeological evidence that disproves the accepted paradigm of cutting and raising blocks supports only the rock-concrete paradigm.

Packing this special limestone concrete directly in place eliminated the need for heavy lifting and large ramps. In other words, blocks were packed where they now rest, and so it was not necessary to move them at all. All of those insurmountable logistical and ramp problems suddenly vanish. We understand why the only ramp known at Giza was small, useful for climbing out of the excavation pits with baskets of limestone rubble.

The most rudimentary tools will easily cut through or otherwise shape this rock-concrete before it cures. This explains the instances of rapid cutting we have explored. But most pyramid blocks would not need to be shaped with tools. There can be a few exceptions, which I will describe later in these pages.

Packing the wet rock-concrete down with a rammer drives out excess water and makes the new synthetic stone dense. Only concrete production can produce the form-fitting blocks and paving slabs that characterize the Giza pyramids and temples. Making rock-concrete directly in place eliminates the impossible chore of constantly cutting, shifting and re-setting blocks until a peerless fit was achieved on a super-massive scale—and doing so without the tools needed to accomplish such a task when cutting natural rock.

Once set, this rock-concrete is far stronger than the weakly bound, concrete-grade bedrock that was extensively excavated. The alchemically-made pyramid stone is not theoretical. To clarify this, we momentarily digress from ancient studies to modern advances in cement technology.

Today, this blend of pyramid concrete is classified as a polycondensation* commonly known as a geopolymer.[11]

Even the simple geopolymeric mixture described above produces a highly-sophisticated concrete that is actually manmade rock. In an astonishingly short time and at ambient temperatures, silicoaluminate materials (such as the kaolin[†] clay in the Giza quarries) are transformed into three-dimensional aluminosilicates.[12] A comparable geosynthesis more gradually occurred in nature in great abundance to produce more than 55 percent of the Earth's crust.[13]

In 1972, the internationally recognized cement expert Dr. Joseph Davidovits discovered this chemical reaction and coined the word "geopolymer." The 'geo' in geopolymer stands for rock. The 'polymer' denotes the polycondensation of polymeric minerals (in this case mineral polymers).

Today, Davidovits and his industrial partners use numerous geopolymer patents internationally for a variety of applications. They range from fabricated rock to advanced, heat-tolerant composite materials that will not ignite because they are made purely of minerals.[14]

Like other concrete, the aggregates in geopolymeric concrete will be jumbled—just as fossil shells are in disarray in the pyramid and temple blocks at Giza. The jumbling can be slight because the concrete was packed down, but the shells are still scrambled. Except for its scrambled shells and other odd features, pyramid concrete looks like natural rock.

Normal limestone can also exhibit jumbled shells. So, this feature might not necessarily be enough to alert geologists to the artificial nature of pyramid blocks. Pyramid blocks look like natural limestone because the cement particles (zeolites produced by geopolymerization) binding the limestone are submicroscopic. That means that the binder cannot be seen with an ordinary light microscope. A scanning electron microscope is needed to see the cement particles.[15]

Because of their minute size, geopolymeric cement particles can be readily taken for the natural cement particles that bind natural limestone and some other rock types, like quartzite. Geopolymeric cement particles are submicroscopic, and so geopolymeric concrete made as described above looks much different than the portland cement concrete of which modern buildings are made.

One reason portland cement concrete does not look like rock is that it requires more cement (at least 15 to 25 percent by weight) to bind rock particles. Bonding comes from the cement filling gaps between the rock particles. This produces mechanical strength. Because

---

* Polycondensation is a chemical condensation leading to the formation of a compound of high molecular weight.

[†] Kaolin clay is useful for geopolymerization because it normally contains about 45 percent silica and 40 percent alumina. Both of these minerals are chemically integrated to form geopolymeric products. Kaolin has an open pore structure that is readily attacked by caustic soda.

of its mechanical bond, this type of concrete holds together no longer than 150 years in an ideal outdoor environment.[16]

The portland cement is easily visible between the rock particles in the concrete, making this type of concrete readily distinguishable from natural rock with the naked eye. A few portland cement concrete restoration blocks support overhanging blocks on the Great Pyramid, to keep them from dislodging. Thick cement dominates their appearance, making these blocks easy to distinguish from the ancient pyramid blocks.

In sharp contrast, to make pyramid blocks, the ancient Egyptians added as little as one percent (by combined weight) of lime and natron to kaolinitic limestone from the Giza quarries.[17] The percentage can be that low because the silica and alumina needed for the chemical reaction are already present as indigenous kaolin clay. But because of the very tiny particle size, even when 15 percent (by weight) of geopolymeric binder is added to the rock-making mixture, the resulting artificial limestone still looks like normal limestone under a light microscope. This is because geopolymeric cement looks like the cement that binds natural limestone.

When lime, water, and natron come together, caustic soda forms. Caustic soda acts as an alkali that attacks the silica and alumina in the clay. When this happens, the silica and alumina chemically integrate as the limestone concrete cures. In other words, this integration produces a new silicoaluminate, which is a very simple geopolymer. The very strong bond produced is molecular, one of the strongest types of bonds in the universe.

Geopolymerization produces only a slight chemical alteration in the mineralogy of the Giza limestone. Geopolymerized limestone is such an extremely close match that careful scientific testing is necessary to make a chemical distinction between the limestone concrete and the original limestone.[18] Owing to the geopolymeric binder, pyramid blocks retain the beauty and appearance of natural limestone.

Geologists theorize that violent storms sometimes stirred up sea bottoms millions of years ago, when a limestone bed was still in a soft, muddy state.[19] This could result in fossil shells that are disoriented. So, geologists unfamiliar with geopolymerization have not suspected the artificial nature of the pyramid stones. But the pyramid blocks do not match the sedimentary layering of the Giza bedrock. This dramatic contrast provides compelling evidence of the artificial nature of the pyramid blocks.[20]

It is likely that the bedrock floor at pyramid sites exhibit some areas of spilled concrete that now looks like natural limestone with jumbled shells. Such enormous cement-making operations are bound to have some spillage. But all the quarry walls at Giza examined by sedimentation expert Robert L. Folk in 1990 exhibit normal sedimentary layering.

Davidovits' freshly-made limestone concrete mixture has the consistency of wet sand. Workers probably transported their limestone concrete mixture to the construction sites in small containers that were easy to carry. The baskets called 'zambil' are very familiar to archaeologists (such baskets are made of plaited palm-leaves or other material). The wet limestone concrete compresses easily and stays together when a handful is squeezed.

The Lime Question

Alchemical stonemaking explains the evidence we have explored. Today, waste rock from the top layers of quarries is used by the concrete industry, too. Loose rock debris swept up from Giza while the area was being cleared was also perfectly suitable for stonemaking. So, with the geopolymer theorem, there are no missing Khufu quarries.

We will look at the simple chemical means the Egyptians used to make limestone that can fool top geologists today. Instead of importing blocks to Giza, workers imported basket loads of simple ingredients. One ingredient was natron, a salt combination abundant in Egypt and other parts of Africa. Natron contains sodium carbonate, which was essential. The Egyptians gathered natron from several locations, especially the vast natron lakes of the Wadi el-Natrun northwest of Cairo.

The Egyptians had plenty of experience working with natron. They used natron for other processes and products, including ritual cleansing, mummification, ceramic pastes, glazes and mortar.[21] Later, in the New Kingdom, the Egyptians used natron to make a great deal of glass, which was another attempt at imitating many types of natural stones.

Lime (calcium oxide or another variety of lime) was needed to make geopolymeric cement, too. The lime sources are important to this study because Egyptologists have criticized the geopolymer theory on the basis that they do not know if the Egyptians produced lime.

The use of lime was known by early societies, as is known from 9,000-year-old lime plaster at Jericho, west of the Jordan Valley.[22] Lime can be obtained in a number of ways. Lime can come from calcining limestone or from soils containing finely fragmented shells. It is not necessary to crush chunks of limestone because after it is burned it disintegrates to powder.

Calcisols are the most abundant soil type in Egypt. The Egyptians could have tested for calcisols in the vicinity of Giza. In semi-arid and arid regions, native lime is usually high enough for this soil to have a PH of more than 7.5. Such soil will fizz when acid is applied. Drops of 10% hydrochloric acid (the same dilution as stomach acid) and even vinegar will produce noticeable fizzing. Egyptians could have discovered that soil that fizzes when a mild acid is applied is good for making stone. For the chemistry to work, the lime in a soil must be active. So, such soil would probably have to be heated to produce active lime. But conversion to lime would not require extra fuel because plants growing in the soil serve as the needed fuel.

Natural, native lime does not stay active in nature for long periods. The reason is that active lime gradually absorbs carbon dioxide from the air. So, after enough time, it completely converts back to calcium carbonate. We do not count on the Egyptians having had large sources of active lime without burning.

Another source of lime is wood ash (burning wood produces oxides and hydroxides of calcium and other alkaline compounds). Wood ash is high in calcium hydroxide (lime). This seems to be a practical method of obtaining lime because wood was consumed for cooking anyway. The ash could have been collected and brought to Giza by the basket load on donkey back.

A project team speculated on the large-scale burning of wood during the Pyramid Age. The study was administered by Ancient Egypt Research Associates, Inc., which speculated on the reasons for the radiocarbon date discrepancies of Old Kingdom mortar (relating to the mortar dating project I mentioned above). Team members contemplated the reasons why the pyramid mortar they tested dated to almost 400 years older than accepted dates.

Excerpts from an abstract written by this team describe a theory of major deforestation—the utilization of every possible scrap of wood available from the time of the first pyramid to the construction of the Great Pyramid:

> It may have been premature to dismiss the old wood problem in our 1984 study. Do our radiocarbon dates reflect the Old Kingdom deforestation of Egypt? Did the

pyramid builders devour whatever wood they could harvest or scavenge to roast tons of gypsum for mortar, to forge copper chisels, and to bake tens of thousands of loaves to feed the mass of assembled laborers? The giant stone pyramids in the early Old Kingdom may mark a major consumption of Egypt's wood cover, and therein lies the reason for the wide scatter, increased antiquity, and history-unfriendly radiocarbon dating results from the Old Kingdom, especially from the time of Djoser to Menkaura. In other words, it is the old-wood effect that haunts our dates and creates a kind of shadow chronology to the historical dating of the pyramids. It is the shadow cast by a thousand fires burning old wood.[23]

Deforestation began in Egypt even before King Narmer (also called Menes) unified Upper and Lower Egypt and established the 1st Dynasty (3100–2890 B.C.). By the 4th Dynasty, a great deal of old wood could be useful for burning into lime for pyramid building. The Egyptians could have saved the ashes from routine activities requiring firewood. The Egyptian diet was largely bread, and ashes from breadmaking and cooking fish and other dishes could have been recycled for industrial processes, especially alchemical stonemaking that required lime.

Our critics have tried to invalidate the geopolymer theory by saying that it would consume too much fuel for lime production (from burning appropriate soils or limestone). But making rock-concrete consumes less fuel than the accepted paradigm of pyramid construction. The accepted paradigm requires smelting copper on a massive scale to obtain the needed number of chisels Egyptologists claim cut millions of pyramid blocks. The accepted carve/hoist paradigm requires a tremendous amount of fuel for baking bread to feed the vast number of men required to raise blocks manually, too.

Materials Scientist Michel Barsoum, of Drexel University's Department of Materials Science and Engineering, read the unpublished manuscript of this book. It inspired him to devote the next several years to this body of research. He organized an international team, and his research is still ongoing. One of the problems he studied was lime. Michel Barsoum did not find that wood ash was the source of lime in the samples from the Great Pyramid he chemically analyzed. So, although further tests can show otherwise, utilizing lime collected from scraping lime debris from dolomite or limestone bread ovens (oven cleaning) may be a better solution to the problem than the use of wood ash.

Egyptologists have long thought that the ancient Egyptians did not use lime in their industrial processes. But then Dietrich Klemm studied Old Kingdom mortar and detected lime. Klemm found no lime in mortar from the 6th Dynasty though.[24] Egyptologists then wondered if the lime was deliberately produced, or was formed as a by-product of the materials used to make mortar. But, assuming the geopolymer theory to be correct, the amount of lime required for pyramid construction strongly suggests that lime was deliberately produced.

Fabricating stone requires great water supplies. To build the Great Pyramid, the needed water would equal about 10 to 15 percent of the volume of the monument itself. Some of this water was likely used to make the clay-bearing limestone easier to disaggregate. All the water needed is far less than would be required to facilitate the accepted pyramid construction theory. It requires much more water to build a slick ramp (of stone rubble cemented with clay) more massive than the Great Pyramid itself.

An Evolved Ancient Technology

The beginnings of this technology go far back in history. As far back as 5,600 years ago, Predynastic Egyptians used caustic soda (made by mixing natron and lime with water) to fuse chrysocolla to make blue enamel.[25] People may have combined natron and lime with water more anciently, too. Breadmaking is a prehistoric invention. Scraping the calcined debris from chalky limestone bread ovens provides lime. Breadmaking can involve adding the natron salt for flavor, too (natron contains table salt). High-quality, lime-based cements may have arisen from the ancient art of breadmaking invented in prehistoric times.

In short, dwellers along the Nile had long experience working with caustic soda. It was a natural innovation to add it to earthen materials to make various products.

Rapid Construction

The speed at which the Egyptians built the Great Pyramid has confounded researchers. But this problem disappears, too. Packing concrete blocks directly in place at an average rate of one every minute or so is entirely feasible when many blocks were being worked on at the same time. We can expect that Egyptians started different parts of the giant tiers at once. Fabricating stone blocks is so efficient that the Egyptians could have built the Great Pyramid during the reign of Khufu. They could have completed the King's Chamber by Khufu's 17th year of rule, as is suggested by the cartouche in a vault above this exquisite room.

The accepted carve-hoist theory requires a grossly overcrowded work force of between 50,000 and 100,000 men on site every workday—and this is a very conservative estimate.[26] Such vast numbers cause overcrowding and counterproductively. In contrast, a minimum of 2,000 men on site per day can hand-pack the required number of rock-concrete blocks in place.[27] This assumes that more workers brought rock-making materials directly to the tier in progress, so that rapid construction could be achieved.

The 2,000-man figure can be estimated from the amount of materials workers carried to construct Cambodian dams during the Khmer Rouge revolution of 1976. Each worker carried from four to six tons of earth per day, the equivalent weight of a medium-sized pyramid block. At Giza, donkeys probably assisted workers by carrying in natron, food and other necessities.

There were no horses, camels, or elephants in Egypt during the Pyramid Age. The ancient Egyptians used oxen for hauling, at least in later times. The donkey is intelligent and was domesticated in Predynastic times (by about 3,000 B.C.). When treated kindly and well cared for, the donkey is a hearty, hardworking and cooperative pack animal. Inscriptions from the Sinai Desert mining area indicate that the Egyptians used a team of 284 donkeys in an expedition. Another reports a team of 500.[28] Donkeys can carry water and equipment. Today's donkeys are able to carry 220 pounds over short distances.

In 1881, W.M.F. Petrie excavated two galleries at Giza, which he thought housed the workmen.[29] He reckoned that these galleries could have housed as many as four to five thousand men. Mark Lehner has since been involved in cleaning these galleries. The evidence he found shows that they were craft workshops rather than housing facilities. There is no known housing for the 100,000 men Petrie estimated.[30] With the geopolymer system, there is no need for such extensive facilities.

Making rock-concrete eliminates the unlikely scenario of men quarrying blocks with stone picks. While Egyptologists have long presumed that flint fragments at Giza were used to carve blocks, flint is too brittle.[31] Flint and other hard stone picks are suitable for making rubble of Giza limestone. With geopolymer, the operation is eased if the limestone has been water-soaked. According to physicist Mosalam A. Shaltout, increased solar activity brought about high Nile flooding during the 4th Dynasty. This condition makes it much easier to build truly large pyramids. Disaggregating the limestone is far less labor intensive when it is wet. The relatively high clay in the limestone, and the amount of water rising up the Giza Plateau, also translates into fewer men building very huge pyramids. While the number of men required to raise blocks up the pyramid is often studied, the number of men required to raise huge blocks and beams out of quarries is also a factor. It requires far fewer men to dissagregate Giza limestone and carry baskets of rubble from an excavation pit than to cut and raise huge limestone beams and millions of pyramid blocks.

Making Molds

Some blocks at Giza look as though they are merged together into one mass. This cannot be explained by stone cutting. Whereas, if a block is fashioned against another block that has not sufficiently cured, the two can merge into one mass. A separation device can prevent this. Separation devices can also help speed up construction by allowing for many blocks to be cast in a pyramid tier simultaneously. Kaolinitic clay (Arabic: *tafla*) is suitable for making such separation devices. The small earthen ramps found attached to some small pyramids were made from this material. *Tafla* is lightweight and abundant at Giza.

Gaps between some pyramid blocks today suggest that workers left the *tafla* in place when using it to separate backing blocks (and possibly the core blocks behind the backing blocks). These rough materials were expected to remain forever hidden behind the beautiful outer casing blocks.

Clay placed between blocks would only have degraded after the casing blocks were stripped away in much later history. The disappearance of *tafla* and mortar (useful for cushioning blocks against earthquake stress) may explain the gaps between numerous blocks. Both *tafla* and mortar are useful for keeping uncured blocks from merging during rapid construction.[32]

When Joseph Davidovits led a team that made multiton imitation pyramid blocks, the team packed the rock-making mixture into wooden molds. His team overcame problems of the molds bursting by using concrete that did not contain too much water. He produced close, corresponding joints, too. A video of the operation is available at his website (www.geopolymer.org).

The Paper Thin Cement

The outside of the pyramids had to look perfect. So, workers did not use a thick separation device between the form-fitted casing blocks. Workers allowed setting time for casing blocks before casting against them. This prevents blocks from merging. The durable paper-thin cement between casing blocks—which proves the existence of sophisticated cement technology (as does the durable lime-gypsum mortar)—could have been painted on in order to provide a thin separation.

When there is excess water in a geopolymeric concrete slurry, some cement will flow to the surfaces of blocks. The flow may otherwise explain the durable paper-thin cement between pyramid casing blocks that baffled Petrie and others. But deliberately painting a thin coating of geopolymeric cement between the casing blocks would help make the Great Pyramid watertight.

Only casting a once-pliable stone can explain the many giant form-fitting core and casing blocks for which the Great Pyramids is famous. Alchemical stonemaking explains the otherwise baffling oblique and L-shaped joints, too. The form-fitted pyramid stones provide very powerful evidence of work performed with adobe construction techniques.

16. (above): Khafra's Valley Temple at Giza. See the two merged blocks near the top.
17. (opposite page): Khafra's Valley Temple blocks look like adobe turned to granite.

Early High Strength

The high early strength afforded by geopolymerization made rapid construction possible. Pyramid blocks gained strength rapidly because of the early onset of chemical hardening.

Like other concretes, geopolymers become harder over time. But packed pyramid blocks are strong enough to walk on immediately.

While industrialists have formulated today's geopolymers to set instantly, pyramid blocks cured in days if the Egyptians added *tafla* to their lime. If they did not, the blocks took a month

18. Closeup of selected blocks of Khufu's Great Pyramid at Giza. Notice how blocks in these tiers closely correspond to the irregularities of one another. They look as though the blocks themselves served as partial molds for neighboring blocks. It defies logic to think that these blocks are the product of working with abrasives and/or stone or metal tools.

or so to fully cure. Large tiers would have required that much time to build. By the time the builders started the next tier, the blocks in the finished tier were harder than the excavated bedrock material used. So, the layer of limestone at Giza that was extensively excavated was converted into good-quality limestone concrete blocks. Whereas, that concrete-grade

inr-nn

iri-kat

19. Joseph Davidoits points to a joint between his imitation pyramid blocks, which he named Inr-nn and Iri-kat. His joints have the same kind of corresponding fit as Khufu's casing joints, which can only be achieved with cast stone.	*20. A joint between casing blocks on Khufu's Great Pyramid. In addition to the matching joint formation, Joseph Davidovits' geopolymeric limestone passes for natural limestone and has fooled expert geologists.*

bedrock itself is not suitable for cutting into blocks. That material is like the body of the Sphinx, which constantly flakes off and easily becomes water damaged.

In addition to high early strength, another beauty of the system is that geopolymeric rock-concrete does not expand. Its shrinkage is extremely minute, equivalent to the separations between pyramid casing blocks (as little as 1/500 of an inch or in perfect contact).[33]

Automatic Leveling

A special instrument had to be designed to measure the 13-square-acre level platform extending under the base of the Great Pyramid. To try to explain how this platform was made, some Egyptologists interpreted the ditch around it as a leveling device. In *Building in Egypt* (1991), Dieter Arnold commented:

> Lehner, especially, thought that the flat ditches surrounding the pyramids of Cheops and Chephren were actually leveling installations from the time of the construction of the pyramids. He assumed that tree trunks set into holes in these ditches were sawed down to the level of the water in the trenches so that they could thereafter be used as bench marks. Yet the ditches were too large to be filled with water, which had to be carried up from the valley and would have dried out and disappeared in many crevices of the bedrock. Furthermore, the ditches are so similar to that of the pyramid of el-Lahun, which was certainly used as a drainage channel, that they might have had the same function.[34]

Mark Lehner has come to agree with Arnold, and Egyptology still cannot explain how the ancient Egyptians could have cut a 13-square-acre platform made of level limestone blocks. Lehner writes:

> It was long thought that the bases of pyramids were leveled by channeling water. However, water-lifting technology in the Old Kingdom was limited to simple shoulder-poles with pots slung on either end. For leveling operations for a pyramid like Khufu's with a base area of 5.3 ha (13.1 acres), an impossibly large quantity would need to be carried up to the plateau - to say nothing of the problems of the water evaporating before a levelling trench could be filled to the requisite height...practical hurdles make all theories using water unworkable.[35]

Lehner, Arnold and others fail to address the germane problem, which is not how masons measured how level surfaces are produced with simple wooden instruments and water. The glaring problem is how the level blocks forming this giant, hard foundation could be produced with Pyramid Age tools.

The bedrock beneath the foundation blocks is uneven. The production of geopolymeric rock-concrete is the only logical explanation for the undersides of paving slabs conforming to the irregularities in the bedrock below. When packing a pliable stone mixture against rock or rock-concrete, form fitting is automatic.

The long-held notion that paving blocks and huge casing blocks were repeatedly cut and compared until form-fitting joints were achieved on such a large scale — with all the work carried out with primitive tools — is untenable. The logical explanation is that water seeks its own level. So does a cement slurry. So, the level upper surfaces of paving slabs will be automatic, and the undersides of the slabs will conform with the uneven bedrock.

Casing Blocks with Extra Stock

Some pyramids exhibit unfinished casing blocks that have extra stock on their front faces.[36] Egyptologists assume that this features invalidates the geopolymer theory. But we need to think within the geopolymer paradigm and understand how blocks were built.

Producing rock-concrete casing blocks so that joints fit exactly was the primary task. The edges of blocks can be used as partial forms for new blocks under construction. Once a stonemaker built up a block so that form-fitting joints were made with the blocks underneath, next to, and behind it, his next step was to shape its front surface. Copper tools are perfect for cutting rock-concrete that is still pliable (rods and strings were used for measuring). But if for some reason his block hardened before he could finish it (and create its correct angle), the worker left the extra stock on because of the difficulties of cutting hard stone. So, this can explain why some blocks are found with extra stock on their front faces.

Some workers may have waited too long, and then had to remove extra stock after curing was partially underway. This may explain why chisel marks are visible on a small minority of blocks at Giza.

Making the Great Pyramid of rock-concrete eliminates the impossible scenario of using stone tools and abrasives to make the vast, perfectly inclined pyramid faces formed by the estimated 115,000 casing blocks. Geopolymerizing stone is the only viable way to accomplish the task of readily removing the extra stock so as to form the correct angle. With the carve-hoist theory, every cracked or improperly cut block would have to be torn out, with the placement and close jointing begun anew. Considering these obstacles, the

Waseda University engineers' estimate of a 1,200-year construction period for the Great Pyramid seems conservative.

Rapid Cutting Made Possible

French Egyptologist Jean-Philippe Lauer examined casing blocks on the pyramids of Unas and Senworset I, and on the Mastabat el-Fara'un. The latter is a 4th Dynasty mastaba construction that deviates from the usual pyramid design of the period. Lauer noticed that when making some blocks, once the masons reached the bottom of the joint with their copper tools, they cut slightly into the foundation.[37] Cutting lines run an inch or so right into the foundation.

It is logical to think that these blocks were separated in two before chemical hardening set in. In the process, masons sometimes cut into the foundation, which was also only partially cured. Any natural stone this easily cut cannot withstand the quarrying process. Only rock-concrete with the initial consistency of pliable adobe, able to gain high early strength, could make this possible. Cutting into uncured stone makes the otherwise mysterious examples of rapid cutting possible. Any kind of rock aggregate can be made into solid stone objects. To make objects with diorite, quartzite and other stones, Egyptians gathered powdery rock debris and turned it into concrete and sculpted it with tools before it got too hard.

Using copper tools to shape objects when necessary explains how the relatively small amount of available copper could suffice for constructing the enormous monuments. As mentioned, even in the New Kingdom when copper mining reached its peak, the amount of copper annually collected was only about four tons.

There is ample evidence to show that workers rapidly cut many artifacts with drills and saws. We have already considered the cutting lines in Khufu's sarcophagus. These cutting lines convinced Petrie that granite was cut through very rapidly. We considered Petrie's artifact collection showing long, clean sweeps made with pointed tools, too. These artifacts are explained by the use of geopolymerization.

Mark Lehner, in his *The Complete Pyramids* (1997), mentions the impressions of copper chisel marks:

> Nick Fairplay, the English master carver working with my team [the Nova team], studied the evidence of ancient chisel working. Not only is he able to identify the striations left by the edge of an individual chisel, but also precisely at what point the corners of the chisel curled...[38]

Lehner adds that the chisel edges were only 1/3 inch wide. These small copper chisels, familiar to Egyptology, are not strong enough for shaping good-quality limestone. But they will shape geopolymeric rock-concrete in the uncured stage. Copper sheets can be used to shape broad areas. Wooden boards can be pressed against blocks before they have set. Boards can serve as full molds, too.

The Mystery of Sarcophagi Vanishes

The ability to model pliable stone can explain the otherwise mysterious placement of sarcophagi in tombs with shafts that are too narrow to allow for the removal of these structures.

Cast stone is a logical explanation for sarcophagi situated in tombs from which they cannot be removed intact without tearing out doorways and long hallways. Although other sarcophagi in the Valley of the Kings were found broken up (therefore their sizes cannot be

164 The Great Pyramid Secret by Margaret Morris

determined), granite rock-concrete is the most logical explanation for Ramses III's intact sarcophagus. It is too large to fit through the one entrance road leading to and from the Valley of the Kings. Carrying rock-making ingredients through this narrow pass to fashion the sarcophagus on the spot would be vastly easier than hauling the object up and down steep cliffs.

It is logical to think that workers carried baskets of stonemaking material into burial chambers. There they could readily fashion sarcophagi on the spot.

Ultra-Precision Flatness

Precision on-the-spot casting is a logical explanation for the otherwise baffling examples of sarcophagi with surfaces that are extremely flat over large areas and equipped with form-fitted lids.

Because of the small particle size of the geopolymeric binder, the pure binder (including no rock aggregates) is useful for making flat surfaces for molds. A particle size of five microns (a micron is one millionth of a meter in length) results from geopolymerization. The chemistry can be used to make analcime crystals. These 5-micron particles can be used to produce molds with a surface flatness of .0002 inch. This is the flatness Christopher Dunn measured on large areas of sarcophagi in the Serapeum.

In Appendix 2, I provide the results of my consultations with a precision mold maker. He recognized that geopolymerization holds the potential to produce a new industrial standard in precision mold making. When I consulted with him a few years ago, he was working with state-of-the-art technology requiring temperatures of at least 1,700 degrees Fahrenheit to make molds of small particles like zircon flour. The high heat causes these molds to warp. So, a surface flatness of .0002 inch cannot be expected over more than a few inches with the technology he used.

But ancient people could have added natron, clay and slaked lime to pans of water. Water seeks its own level, and these ingredients will not interfere with the flat upper surface of the water. When the mixture has set into analcime crystals, its upper surfaces will be flat to .0002 inch and useful as mold boards. Because no high heat is involved, the upper surfaces of the mold boards are not warped.

Objects cast into a mold made with such boards take on the surface flatness of the mold. Cast objects can be demolded and refined or cut before they are fully cured. Geopolymeric concrete technology is a very flexible system that can meet many construction demands. Geopolymerization is the logical answer to sarcophagi with large surfaces that are flat to .0002 inch. The extreme flatness argues strongly for synthetic granite and other types of hard rock sarcophagi in ancient Egypt.

More Evidence for Synthetic Granite

Granite rock-concrete may explain obelisks like those in New York and London that exude large amounts of salt. Natural granite does not contain salt, and so it will not exude salt. But ancient geopolymeric concrete was made with natron, which contains three kinds of salt (predominantly sodium chloride). Sodium chloride is not part of the geopolymeric chemical reaction. So, this excess salt can eventually exude from stone made with Egyptian natron. (This is not a problem today because natron is not used to make geopolymers industrially.)

Geopolymerization forms either zeolite or feldspathoid crystals, which have open channels that allow water and large ions like salt to travel in and out. Analcime (which some mineralogists classify as both a zeolite and a feldspathoid) can be made with lime, natron, water, and clay. Analcime will behave as a chemical sieve, allowing salt ions to travel in and out.

It could be argued that the salt entered the obelisks because they each rested with one face in salty sand on the Alexandrian coast before being transported. That explanation may not be correct. Granite is generally impervious to just about everything except abrasive action like sandstorms. Even under such harsh exposures as sandstorms, granite is fairly resistant over moderate periods of time. Salt does not readily permeate granite. Salt might enter granite soaked in salt water or otherwise heavily exposed to salt for hundreds of years.

The salt in the London and New York obelisks might be readily dismissed as cases of environmental exposure, except that other ancient Egyptian artifacts not thought to be exposed to environmental salt also contain high levels of salt. Petrie found thick salt encrustation on Khafra's granite sarcophagus, in the Second Pyramid at Giza. The inner limestone walls of pyramids exude salt. The same is true for the granite King's Chamber of the Great Pyramid. Many quartz diorite statues were found to contain salt, too. Other than a concrete mix involving natron, I know of no other explanation for these granite blocks and Khafra's sarcophagus to give off salt.

Surviving Egyptian obelisks date to New Kingdom times, when the stonemaking technology was in severe decline. Obelisks require careful case-by-case study. At my request, Systems Engineer Mike Carrell carefully photographed the obelisk called Cleopatra's Needle, located in Central Park in New York. Because the obelisk rests on a high pedestal, its grain structure is difficult to study. But Mike Carrell was able to determine that the obelisk exhibits no mineral veins. It is not normal for a natural granite object of such great size to be devoid of veins.

As far as can be determined from photographs, the grain structure of the obelisk looks like that of geopolymeric granite concrete. We do not wish to advocate that it is geopolymeric without comprehensive study. But the obelisk in New York has sufficient indications to warrant in-depth study.

Crystals in the granite walls of the King's Chamber of the Great Pyramid do not exhibit normal orientation. They look as though the crystals were packed down (packing makes the concrete more dense). I showed close-up photographs of the rock matrix to igneous rock geologist Robert G. McKinney. He indicated that the grains in the rock matrix take on a preferred orientation, as though they had been packed down while a concrete mix was still pliable. He cautions that the unusual grain orientation does not constitute conclusive proof. Thorough testing of samples is required to draw conclusions.

Machinist Christopher Dunn examined Khafra's sarcophagus with his machinist's parallel, and indicated that its interior is flat to .0002 inch. So, his measurements support my premise that Khafra's sarcophagus is synthetic granite (Dunn disputes this and advocates that it was made with advanced machining). The salt Petrie found encrusting it weighs in favor of geopolymerized granite. Although Dunn has made a genuine contribution to Egyptology by pointing out problematic masonry features (like the extreme flatness of a number of sarcophagi), modern and ultramodern machining have no legitimate place in pharaonic Egyptian history. Dunn's observations about ancient masonry problems are valuable and should be considered and appreciated separately from his untenable idea that the Great Pyramid is a power plant that powered machine tools.

A tremendous wealth of historical and archaeological information tells us that the machining devices Chris Dunn proposes did not exist, and this explains his inability to show why thousands of years of ancient Egyptian history offer no physical trace of advanced machinery (it is inappropriate for Dunn to use the artifacts themselves as proof of method—especially when geopolymerization, which operates at the level of Stone Age technology, can produce the artifacts in question). There are no drawings of machinery, no literary references, no machinery remains, and no associated infrastructure or industrial pollution.[39] Many examples of artifacts that defy conventional tooling were made after the time Chris Dunn proposes that all traces of machine tools disappeared.

A good example is the monolithic quartzite sepulcher of Pharaoh Amenemhet III of the 12th Dynasty. Petrie reported that, "…the sides are flat and regular, and the inner corners so sharply wrought that—though I looked at them—I never suspected that there was not a joint there until I failed to find any joints in the sides." The Serapeum, where Dunn measured the flatness of sarcophagi to .0002 inch, was designed in the 19th Dynasty—about 1,000 years after the Great Pyramid was built. There is no justification for redating the Serapeum to the Pyramid Age, as Dunn hopes to do based on sarcophagi wall surfaces that measure flat to .0002 inch.

Dunn believes that these flat surfaces take precedence over all of the historical and archaeological findings of Egyptology. But a great deal of documentation concerning the Serapeum exists. In addition to the Serapeum's library holdings, a prominent 19th Dynasty stele stood in front of it for centuries. Inscriptions appear on the installed sarcophagi inside, and those inscriptions serve to date them. Apis bulls were installed in the Serapeum starting in the 19th Dynasty (the oldest sarcophagus found inside dates to the 18th Dynasty, but it is believed to have been installed in the 19th).

Inscriptions show that priestly activity continued until the 2nd century B.C. If an advanced machine tool industry existed in the 19th Dynasty, or from then into later times, there is no chance that the industry would have escaped the attention of Egyptologists. Petrie carefully examined remains at Giza, including ancient piles of rubbish, and found no physical traces of an advanced tooling industry.

Dunn's hypothesis is another example of the severe problems encountered when one assumes that hard, natural rock was used to produce Egyptian artifacts that defy modern tooling technology. Only when the alchemical stonemaking paradigm is taken into account does all of the stunning masonry make sense in both an historical and a technological context.

Dieter Arnold mentioned granite dust and other types of rock debris at a pyramid construction site at el-Lisht, in Middle Egypt:

> …near the pyramid of Senwosret I, layers of stonecutters' debris could be studied, and the presence of granite dust indicated that the material was worked there. In these layers, no traces of greenish discoloration from copper could be detected; however, there was a large amount of broken or chipped dolerite, granite, and flint from the tools. We have to assume that these were the instruments used for dressing hard stones.[40]

The debris is perfect for agglomerating granite blocks.

Granite contains feldspar, which eventually degrades into kaolin clay. Weathered granite debris from Aswan is excellent for making geopolymeric concrete. Egyptologists recognize that debris had to be removed from Aswan before blocks could be extracted. Some granite outcrops contain thousands of tons of weathered granite debris that must be removed before blocks can be quarried.

The Egyptians would have used up most of the supply of loose, weathered granite and other types of hard rock in the early dynasties. After loose debris was exhausted from a quarry, the large Egyptian task force would have had to break up hard rock with stone pounding balls to obtain material suitable for geopolymerization. At some point, they tried pounding out a whole obelisk the hard way. After the decline of alchemical stonemaking was well underway, the unfinished obelisk was quarried (but never detached) at Aswan with pounding balls. Probably during or after the 26th Dynasty, when iron came into common use, the Egyptians began breaking granite blocks loose at Aswan with iron wedges. Thousands of wedge holes appear at Aswan, which Reginald Engelbach observed best fit with the use of iron wedges.

The Descending Passageway and Tunneling

Pounding balls were found at pyramid construction sites. These tools were useful for crushing turquoise nodules for making faience tiles and other objects. The Egyptians crushed a variety of other minerals for making paints for tomb scenes, too. Pounding balls were also needed to bash out tunnels beneath pyramids, most of which are equipped with underground burial chambers.

It stands to reason that the Descending Passageway of the Great Pyramid was bashed out and carefully lined with geopolymeric limestone concrete. The entire 350-foot expanse measures only 1/50 inch off square, a level of accuracy that does not seem possible without the advantage afforded by the ability to finish surfaces with a pliable mixture that turns to solid stone.

Unlike ordinary tunneling operations, workers could reinforce tunnels to prevent cave-ins as needed as they excavated. The possibilities are vast. Many people have speculated about ancient tunneling networks under Giza and Saqqara. Given that geopolymerization enhances the potential to construct tunnels, it will not be surprising if the next generation of Egyptologists finds extensive tunneling under pyramid sites. There are stories of underground tunnels all over the ancient world. The potential for such discoveries makes alchemical stonemaking an extra exciting technology because it beckons us to probe deeper into the possibilities. The system even allows for footprints in stone and for things to be hidden within stone. We are reminded of the footprints of the Buddha at India's Mahabodhi Temple and the Arthurian legend of the sword thrust within stone (in ancient custom, a kernal of truth was often wrapped in a mythical tale).

No Rock Crushing was Necessary

In 1998, imitation basalt was discovered in Mesopotamian temple ruins by a team led by Elizabeth Stone, of the State University of New York's Anthropology Department. This imitation basalt was made with a heating process.[41] Similarly, by the time the Great Pyramid was built, the Egyptians were able to reach about 2,000 degrees Fahrenheit. Blowpipes were used with small, primitive kilns to reach about 2,000 degrees Fahrenheit by around 2,500 B.C. But making basalt does not necessarily require heat. I dedicate a chapter below to Old Kingdom Egyptian-made diabase (agglomerated basalt aggregates), produced in quantities of thousands of tons during the Old Kingdom for pyramid complexes. No rock crushing was ever needed when natural, powdery debris was available (and could be sifted in baskets if necessary).

Given that the clay-bearing limestone of the middle geological layer at Giza comes apart with water soaking, it is not necessary to crush it for making rock-concrete. Whole shells

21. Blocks incorporated into Pharaoh Zoser's Step Pyramid at Saqqara. The blocks look like mud brick turned to stone. They are the size and shape of mud bricks, and look as though they were cast in mud brick molds instead of having been cut from natural limestone.

are visible in pyramid blocks. Powdery limestone debris from Tura is ideal for making the fine-grained casing blocks.[42] An abundance of limestone dust still exists at the foot of the desert hill, presently known as "hib."[43] So, we can expect that workers would not have to crush any rock to make casing blocks for the Great Pyramids.

Tura limestone contains little or no clay. To induce chemical hardening, pyramid builders could have added fine clay, lime, and water (to produce caustic soda, which reacts with the silica and alumina in the clay). Millions of tons of kaolinitic clay were available.[44]

The Technology Proves Its Value

The Egyptians made the earliest pyramids of small blocks. Building Zoser's Step Pyramid (Egypt's first) with agglomerated stone requires adobe construction techniques that were long known and used. We can envision a process in which concrete-limestone bricks are demolded and carried up a small mud-brick ramp, and then stacked to build giant pyramid tiers. The blocks in Zoser's pyramid are the size and shape of mud bricks, as attested to by Dieter Arnold in his *Building in Egypt*:

The blocks were small, and the stones were square and brick-shaped.[45]

The edges of mud bricks are rounded, and it is impractical to cut stones in this shape. Given the good engineering properties of geopolymerized limestone, one can see the possibilities: After Zoser's Step Pyramid was complete, the Egyptians began making larger building units. Finally, blocks too heavy to move proved to help ensure that monuments would not be dismantled in later times. The Great Pyramid represents the height of the pyramid-building industry.

The Logistical Nightmares Vanish

Rather than importing, storing, sorting or inventorying a myriad of massive blocks, workers could make the various masonry patterns (described in Part 1) of the Great Pyramids by fashioning their concrete blocks according to a plan. To make tiers, architects can determine tier heights in advance. Mistakes are correctable, since extra stonemaking mix can be either scraped off or added before chemical hardening sets in. The process is similar to working with adobe, Egypt's oldest building material. The unfathomable task of tooling millions of limestone blocks so that their tops conform to the next highest tier disappears. We can understand how huge tiers can be made so that their heights are accurate to 1/2 centimeter.

Producing the huge, subtle concave faces of the Great Pyramid becomes feasible. It was not possible to perform this feat by shaping quarried blocks with abrasives and stone tools on the scale of the Great Pyramids.

Ramps and Levers Vanish from the Scene

Through the 1920s and 1930s, Selim Hassan cleared great quantities of limestone rubble and kaolinitic clay from the Giza quarries (excavation pits). They contained millions of cubic yards of these materials. Egyptologists assume that all of this material is the remains of a construction ramp that pyramid builders discarded. But this enormous volume of material is too small to constitute a ramp of the size needed to build the Great Pyramid. Even at an unworkable slope of 1:4, a ramp would be many times larger than the volume removed from the quarry. What Hassan cleared away was more likely the remains of the stonemaking operation itself.

Peter Hodges' levering system and Egyptology's enormous ramps all vanish when the alchemically-made stone paradigm is applied. Mark Lehner tosses aside germane problems when suggesting the use of the helical ramp:

> The entire ramp is like an envelope, built up at the same time as the pyramid and almost completely cloaking it…Other theorists disagree with this suggestion because it involves entirely cloaking the pyramid. They believe that the builders depended on having a clear view of the masonry already completed in order to control the rise and run of the pyramid face. However, as we shall see, the Egyptians were already in effect cloaking the pyramid surface by leaving extra stock of stone on every casing stone they set up. Sighting back to already laid masonry cannot have been a significant way of controlling the rising pyramid.[46]

Mark Lehner is alluding to his idea that all casing blocks were dressed from the top of the pyramids down, with masons cutting away extra stock as they descended. This would be the worst way to try to build a pyramid because every casing block that did not perfectly conform to the slope would have to be torn out and replaced, with the fitting perfected on all sides and within a very constrained work space. The huge amount of work of moving and shaping multiton blocks until the backs of the casing blocks fit into the protuberances of the backing stones behind them — and fitting the casing with paper thin cement between their joints — would all have been in vein (not that I am suggesting that this was possible in the first place).

Lehner bases his idea on granite blocks with extra stock at the lower tiers of Menkaura's pyramid. He uses these relatively few blocks to make a sweeping generalization about pyramid construction. He then makes the leap of dismissing the critical need to construct pyramids using true reference points. Whereas, critics stress that an inability to measure from these points will produce slight errors that will seriously compound as the pyramids rose. The result would be distorted pyramids. Lehner offers no alternative means.

George Reisner examined these granite blocks and showed that they bear no traces of metal tool marks other than those of Arab stonecutters of the 12th and 13th centuries.[47] This is an indicator that these blocks could be cast stone that cured before they could be finished. It is reasonable to suggest that some interruption in the work schedule caused them to cure before their faces could be perfected. So, they were left rough because they were too hard to cut to the angle of the pyramid. Despite their oddly-shaped faces, these granite blocks fit tightly.

Egyptologist I.E.S. Edwards suggested that they are 19th Dynasty restoration. Whether natural restoration blocks or granite concrete, they cannot legitimately be used to support the idea that a helical ramp makes sense for building the Great Pyramid. But we can put all the ramp problems to rest. Containers of rock-concrete mix were likely passed up the tiers by workers. This is how modern Egyptians restore the pyramids with portland cement concrete blocks. During antiquity, human chains probably extended from the excavation pits to the pyramids, passing loaded containers along as the pyramid rose.

Systems Engineer Mike Carrell outlined a plan for placing the casing blocks with geopolymeric construction techniques. His plan has most casing applied from the bottom up. This allows for standing room and reach as workers apply the casing. His plan leaves a thin 'staircase' open from the bottom of the pyramid to the top, so that when men have built to the top they can work their way down as they fill that 'staircase' by applying the last casing stones. That way, they always have a solid surface to stand on as they complete the last part of the work from the top down. The casing blocks filling that 'stairway' may be the smallest because of the need for the worker to reach far enough to finish the front surface of each casing block he applies on his way down.

Explaining the Small Quarry Near Khafra's Pyramid

Any theory of block quarrying must account for the source of limestone for all three pyramids. The relatively small patch of stumps near Khafra's Great Pyramid does not. Its volume amounts to about two percent of Khufu's Great Pyramid. It likely dates to the restorations of Pharaoh Ramses II or later. Even Lehner's estimate of the larger area of the southern wadi does not encompass the volume of extracted rock needed for all three pyramids, and their long causeways, large temples and retaining walls. The logical solution is that whole blocks were not quarried at all. Workers instead gathered limestone aggregates and used rock debris swept up while clearing construction sites. Many pyramid blocks contain plenty of sand, and were likely made with desert sand. They were classified as "limy shaly sandstone" by geologist Kenneth O. Emery: "The Great Pyramid of Giza (Egypt) was built of four main varieties of rock – gray, hard, dense limestone; gray soft limestone; gray shaly limestone; and yellow limy shaly sandstone..."[48] In other words, the sandstone blocks contain lime, shale (mud or clay) and sand — the very ingredients needed to agglomerate sand into sandstone. We now consider an overview of the geopolymer paradigm of ancient stoneworking.

Chapter 21
An Overview of the Paradigm Shift

The geopolymer theory holds that Egyptians of the 3rd through the end of the 4th Dynasty built pyramids by combining stone debris with their rock-forming binders.[1] The technology began to decline by the end of the 4th Dynasty, so that later pyramids are smaller and incorporate blocks taken from earlier structures. The decline in the rock-making technology brought the Pyramid Age to a close.

The bedrock of both Giza and Saqqara contain the kaolin clay needed to make stone blocks. We have not studied the bedrock of other pyramid sites. But Egypt had many millions of tons of kaolin, which could have been brought to construction sites.

In the most basic formula, workers added natron, lime, and water to the kaolinitic limestone to produce caustic soda in situ. Caustic soda integrates the clay's silica and alumina, so that a new silicoaluminate forms. With the limestone aggregates included, the result is the equivalent of natural limestone concrete. But its cement is the new silicoaluminate, a simple geopolymer.[2]

At Giza, obtaining fossil-shell rubble for rock-concrete was not difficult because the bedrock layer the workers excavated is weakly bound limestone.[3] It automatically comes apart after soaking in water for between five and ten hours (because of its relatively high noncarbonate silt content).[4] As mentioned, Selim Hassan cleared great quantities of limestone rubble and kaolinitic clay from the Giza quarries. Millions of cubic yards of these materials there were perfect for making geopolymeric rock-concrete.

Joseph Davidovits showed how easily some of the remaining rock from this limestone layer at Giza comes apart. His samples came apart in five to ten hours of soaking in water. Nova's original 1992 version of *This Old Pyramid* showed him holding a sample and proving this point. But his presentation was very brief. His ten-minute demonstration, explaining how to make geopolymeric pyramid blocks with Giza limestone, was cut from the film.

Davidovits agreed to participate in *This Old Pyramid* only after being promised by producer Michael Barnes that all of the facilities needed to fabricate at least one massive block would be available when Davidovits arrived in Egypt. So, he rearranged his industrial schedule to go to Egypt to make blocks from natural Egyptian resources. But when he arrived, the promised materials had never been arranged for at all. Rather than returning home on the next plane, he decided to watch the Nova pyramid being constructed and to participate as best he could. But the film presented the fabricated-stone theory so to make it look like a dead theory.

Although our book, Davidovits, J., Morris, M., *The Pyramids: An Enigma Solved* was the inspiration for *This Old Pyramid* (I sent a copy to Nova, and their producers immediately contacted me and began planning a film), the film promoted the carve-hoist theory and reinforced it with out-of-date and erroneous theories. These included the use of a slick, clay and stone rubble helical ramp, which was used to raise a half-ton block (the rest were placed with a front-end loader, except for the one that was levered into place). Nova used the out-of-date assumption that ancient Egyptians used copper tools to carry out the masonry work on pyramid blocks (although Nova's pyramid blocks were cut with steel tools because copper tools are ineffective). The award-winning *This Old Pyramid* film was very popular and resulted in years of set-back in our research progress because the academic and scientific communities received such a terrible misimpression of the geopolymer theory and the truth about pyramid construction.

Davidovits has since completed the demonstration he had planned with Nova. In September of 2002, he led a team from the Geopolymer Institute that constructed five large imitation pyramid blocks. They were made with the same kind of ingredients available to the ancient Egyptians at Giza 4,500 years ago.

His imitation pyramid blocks were independently monitored for one year for compressive strength and other properties. Thin sections from two samples of his imitation pyramid blocks were investigated in a blind petrography study with the French Bureau de Recherche Géologique et Miniere (the French Geological Survey). His imitation pyramid stone is so close to nature's own limestone that the petrography analysis did not distinguish it from natural limestone. The report issued by the French Bureau de Recherche Géologique et Miniere indicated that both of his samples appear to be natural limestone.

The same thing happened when he took his geopolymeric limestone-concrete to the Geology Department of the Museum of Natural History, in Paris. Geologists investigated thin sections of his samples under a microscope. They mistook his samples for real limestone. Their report lists Davidovits' geopolymeric cement as the natural micritic cement that occurs in real limestone.

The in situ production of caustic soda (made with lime, natron and water) integrated the silica and alumina compounds in the limestone's kaolin clay (which constitutes five to ten percent of the total native rock). So, the addition of caustic soda produces only a subtle change in the chemistry of the limestone. As chemical hardening sets in, the silica and alumina minerals molecularly lock together to form a new silicoaluminate (a very simple geopolymer).

Workers transported the moist rock-concrete mixture in containers from the excavation pits to the construction site. There, they packed concrete to form blocks directly in place. Once the rock-making material was packed down, workers could walk on the blocks immediately. The high early strength afforded by geopolymerization allowed for the production of large blocks that did not collapse under their own weight. So, no limestone blocks had to be elevated or moved at all to build the Great Pyramid.

We estimate that about 95 percent of the blocks of the Great Pyramids are limestone concrete. Granite is the second most abundant material of the pyramids, equalling under five percent. A relatively small percent of diabase (collectively equaling thousands of tons of agglomerated basalt aggregates) are incorporated into the pyramid complexes, too. These are mostly paving slabs in temple flooring. Some temple columns, sarcophagi, corridor plug blocks and pavement slabs were made with quartzite. Davidovits showed that the one published chemical analysis of an ancient Egyptian quartzite colossus supports geopolymerization. The chemical analysis was conducted on one of the much later, gigantic Colossi of Memnon. Not all of the limestone in pyramid complexes can be explained by the formula I described. A higher-quality geopolymeric limestone is required for the largest temple and casing blocks, and for several other items.

In 1998, geologist Donald Lindsley, of the State University of New York, determined that basalt found by archaeologists in Mesopotamian temple ruins is an imitation basalt. It was made with heat. Subsequently, a geologist who wishes to remain unnamed did me the favor of inspecting the basalt in the Mesopotamian collection of the British Museum. He told me that he found several examples of synthetic basalt (an assertion I mention so that others may either challenge or verify).

Joseph Davidovits made comparable material as part of his Geocistem project. He made basalt similar to that found in Mesopotamian temple ruins. First, he melted some alumina and silica minerals. Then he added calcium carbonate. His melt formed synthetic basalt (solidified lava) as it cooled. Fine aluminosilicate crystals formed in his basalt as it cooled, and so this rock is like natural basalt. He pulverized it and used it to produce a geopolymeric binder that sets at room temperature. When ground, the basalt-like material (a type of clinker, the raw material for a type of geopolymeric cement) can be made into statues.

Research has not been conducted to determine if Mesopotamian statues were made in that way. All we know at this point is the result of the above-mentioned preliminary investigation of artifacts in the Mesopotamian collection in the British Museum. Also, the silt at Mashkan-shapir, in Mesopotamia where the synthetic basalt temple slabs were found, contains caliche (a soil rich in calcium carbonate), which works in the stonemaking process when heated.

Davidovits also produced synthetic quartzite comparable to that of ancient Egypt. With the aid of a chemical analysis of the 18th Dynasty Egyptian Colossi of Memnon (made with quartzite), he produced synthetic quartzite without heat. In nature, sandstone converts to quartzite through heat and pressure deep in the earth.

Geopolymerization is the most logical explanation for hard stone vessels that baffle researchers. Starting with weathered, naturally disaggregated diorite or basalt, a potter can skillfully shape stonemaking mixtures using potter's wheels. The process is like turning clay pots or Egyptian faience vessels. One can affix handles and other features before chemical hardening sets in. The method solves the mystery of how a primitive lathe can produce hard stone vessels that look lathe-turned, but have handles that would interfere with lathe turning. The method explains vessels with symmetrical walls and other features that have baffled researchers who have investigated the ancient Egyptian hard stone vessels.

As I explain in a chapter below, independent petrography investigations of Old Kingdom vessels, made with hard varieties of stone, do not match the quarries from which authorities assume they came. Only when we factor in the geopolymeric binder, which gradually crystallizes into a variety of minerals, does the problem vanish.

It is not difficult to carve small objects of soft varieties of stone, like soft limestone and Egyptian alabaster. Only simple tools are needed. A mild acid like vinegar or citric acid can aid the cutting process.[5] But the use of a pliable stone mixture is the logical explanation for hard stone vessels, statues, sarcophagi, colossi, some obelisks and certain other objects I describe in these pages. This is also the logical explanation for the otherwise mysterious tall, monolithic temple columns made in true circles. With geopolymerization, rudimentary tools are suitable for cutting hieroglyphics that modern masons recognize are higher in quality than can be achieved with diamond drills.

The ancient implements used to build the pyramids included baskets, troughs, ladders, builder's squares, plumb lines, levels, and builder's trowels. Egyptologists found these very tools, along with wooden molds, in the 6th Dynasty pyramid Pharaoh Pepi II (ca. 2246-2152 B.C.).

The Technological Decline

It is important to trace the decline in alchemical stonemaking. Critics assume that the geopolymer theory is wrong because many Egyptian sites show evidence of stonecutting. But the Egyptians began to cut stone as the stonemaking technology declined. By 800 years after the Great Pyramid was built, a hard form of bronze came into use in Egypt. It is suitable for cutting soft stone. By the 18th Dynasty, iron was available for stone cutting.

The architectural decline started subtly with Khafra's pyramid, built at Giza after Khufu's Great Pyramid. Here are statistics that show the decline setting in: Khufu's Great Pyramid was originally 756 feet square and over 480 feet high. The angle of the triangular faces is about 51.5 degrees. The square of its height equals the area of each triangular face. The base covers about 13 acres. Whereas, Khafra's Great Pyramid is 50 feet shorter than the Great Pyramid. Khafra's Great Pyramid is smaller at 704 feet square and 471 feet high. The face inclination is 53.2 degrees. But the next Great Pyramid built at Giza, called the Third Pyramid, is dramatically smaller. Menkaura's Great Pyramid is about 345.5 feet square and 216 feet high. The face inclination is 51.3 degrees.

The next structure was built for Pharaoh Shepseskaf, and is called the Mastabat el-Fara'un. It reverts back to the mastaba tomb style that predates the pyramids. It was made over 326 feet long and over 244 feet broad, with a rounded top flanked by two almost vertical walls. Shepseskaf chose to build at Saqqara, perhaps because sufficient kaolinitic limestone was still available there. Subsequent pyramids greatly decrease in solid masonry. Egyptology cannot explain this sudden and permanent architectural decline when applying the accepted carve/hoist paradigm.

It stands to reason that the decline in pyramid construction was caused by a decline in the stone-making technology itself. It makes sense to think that the friable sources of diorite were being used up, as were the sources of weakly-bound limestone and highly-weathered granite and other rock types. The best-quality natron was being depleted (inferior natron makes inferior rock-concrete). An inability to obtain lime may have been a factor.

Egypt was very prosperous in the 5th Dynasty, when the Egyptians were making small, economically-built pyramids. These pyramids were made of a series of supporting walls with a filler of sand and rubble between them. The builders cased their exteriors with blocks they expropriated from older monuments. So, some blocks were being moved manually in the 5th Dynasty. It appears that workers conserved fabricated stone to make crypts with large support systems, some of which are spectacular. Rock-concrete mix can be carried in small containers to make blocks, beams and sarcophagi on the spot.

By the 12th Dynasty (ca. 1937-1759 B.C.), the decline in the stonemaking technology was severe. The Egyptians did not start carving stone to build pyramids though. The principle of agglomeration endured: Pyramids were made of mud brick.

Among these mostly ruined pyramids, the 12th Dynasty mud-brick pyramid of Pharaoh Amenemhet III (ca. 1844-1797 B.C.) is remarkable. Its mud bricks have not decomposed after 3,800 years. Ordinary mud-brick can deteriorate in a few seasons, depending upon the weather. Joseph Davidovits suspects that the mud bricks of Amenemhet III's pyramid were chemically hardened with lime and natron. If natron, lime, water, and kaolin are involved in mud brickmaking, then the geopolymeric combination will be more durable. The process also helps sand adhere to the surfaces of the bricks. In that way, a sand coating will help protect the bricks, too.

By about 1,000 years after the Great Pyramid was built, soft sandstone monuments dotted the New Kingdom capital city of Thebes and its environs. The masons cut relatively small blocks with bronze tools to build these large monuments. The geopolymer theory holds that artisans and builders geopolymerized stone on a limited scale in this period, and that the Colossi of Memnon are synthetic rock. We now look at features of artifacts that strongly suggest that they are agglomerated stone, too.

Chapter 22
Evidence from the Stones

Granite objects exhibiting intaglio (impressions depressed inches below the stone surface to produce raised images) amazed Egyptologist John G. Wilkinson:

> The hieroglyphics on obelisks and other granitic monuments are sculptured with a minuteness and finish which, even if they used steel as highly tempered as our own, cannot fail to surprise the beholder, and to elicit from him the confession that our modern sculptors are unable to vie with them in this branch of the art. Some are cut to the depth of more than two inches, the edges and all of the most minute parts of the intaglio presenting the same sharpness and accuracy; and I have seen the figure of the king in high relief, reposing on the lid of a granite coffin, which was raised to the height of nine inches above the level of the surface.[1]

We are reminded of the remark by Roger Hopkins acknowledging that hieroglyphs on an obelisk of Ramses II would be difficult to produce with modern diamond tools.

Tomb drawings appear to show workers cutting granite in the soft stage of geopolymeric setting. A painting comes from the New Kingdom tomb of Rekhmira. It shows artisans using simple hand tools to cut inscriptions in granite.[2] Egyptologist John G. Wilkinson described the scene as depicting sculptors chiseling and polishing a colossus. According to Wilkinson, a scribe cuts inscriptions on the back of the colossus with a small hand tool. A painter follows the scribe and fills the inscriptions with glaze. Egyptologists are certain that the scene depicts granite, as opposed to another type of softer rock.[3] Based on these factors, this scene is best explained by cutting granite in the uncured stage of geopolymeric hardening.

If a tomb scene shows hard stone statues being carved from natural rock, the sculptors should be striking stone tools with mallets. Instead, most scenes show sculptors working on a finished statue with small hand tools.[4] In at least two instances, the scenes show that the material for colossi is granite.[5]

Dieter Arnold, in *Building in Egypt*, published a drawing showing a simple toothed handsaw cutting though a piece of wood.[6] He cites the depiction as coming from the tombs of Beni Hassan, a site that has tombs dating from the 6th to the 12th Dynasties. Another segment of the same drawing shows the saw cutting a granite sarcophagus to form its lid. The same kind of toothed saw is used. If this latter segment is from a tomb scene from Beni Hassan, it is telling in the extreme.

Arnold accepts the tests by Denys Stocks showing that copper or bronze saws will not cut granite — and will certainly not slice off a sarcophagus lid.[7] The same deduction can be made by consulting Mohs' scale.

The drawing Arnold presents is not an example of using an abrasive with a saw. Small cutting teeth are clearly shown advancing through a block of granite in the drawing he shows. The drawing shows no sand or hint of abrasive. Arnold assumes that simple toothed saws cut through hard rock because, as he notes, Old Kingdom examples of hard stone, including "the famous triads of Mycerinus [Menkaura: 4th Dynasty] made of greywacke, show traces of sawing." The definite saw marks on the backs of statues like this present examples of rapid cutting, and so it is logical to think that the stone would have to be relatively soft when cut. The only other alternative is power tools, and all historical evidence invalidates that. Working with acids on such hard rock is not the answer because etching (such as we see with frosted

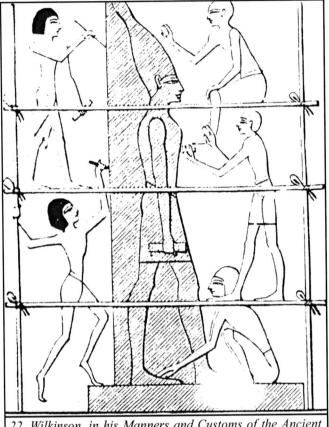

glass) would show up on rock surfaces. Artifacts in museums that show signs of rapid cutting do not exhibit acid etching.

Graywacke is a dense sandstone conglomerate of firmly-cemented fragments of quartz or feldspar. Like many other examples, the back of the famous triad of Menkaura is covered with saw marks, suggesting that a saw swept over the back of the stone unimpeded.

Denys Stocks and others argue that saw marks such as these are the product of long, slow abrasion with loads of sand and a copper saw. But the method does not produce clean cutting lines, such as those found on Petrie core No. 7 and many other examples. The slow grinding system will not produce very fine sharp point etchings or 20-foot-long tool sweeps

22. Wilkinson, in his Manners and Customs of the Ancient Egyptians (p. 311), says the artisans on the left are "painting and sculpting hieroglyphics at the back" of a granite colossus.

in diorite, either. The archaeological record does not support the methods used by Denys Stocks: Egyptian art does not provide a representation of stone being cut with a copper blade along with an abrasive. No evidence of lapidary slabing saws has been found. The ancient Egyptians had toothed copper saw blades (like the one Arnold shows). But they are useful for cutting wood and uncured stone.

Mark Lehner, too, includes a drawing of a copper handsaw cutting through a block of hard stone in *The Complete Pyramids* (1997). Lehner's caption reads:

> Ancient Egyptian masons drilled and sawed hard basalt and granite. Copper blades probably guided the gypsum and sand that did the actual cutting.[8]

No sand shows up in the ancient images. We are left wondering how this system, or any other available to the ancient Egyptians, could produce the definite saw strokes swept across natural hard stone artifacts.

Lehner may inadvertently provide examples of rock cut in the soft stage of geopolymeric setting in *The Complete Pyramids* (1997):

> How ancient builders cut through stone as hard as granite and basalt remains one of the truly perplexing questions of pyramid-age masonry. Drill holes in granite showing

pronounced striations survive in many different 4th and 5th dynasty monuments. Whatever was used to cut it had to be at least as hard as the hardest of the minerals that granite is composed of - quartz.

It is most likely that a copper drill or saw was employed in conjunction with an abrasive slurry of water, gypsum and quartz sand. The copper blade simply acted as a guide while the quartz sand did the actual cutting. I have seen dried remains of this slurry, tinted green from the copper, in deep saw cuts in basalt blocks in Khufu's mortuary temple.[9]

Given that the system Lehner describes is unworkable, what he observed was likely copper residue left over from cutting partially cured basalt (diabase) concrete.

Petrie greatly admired these slabs, which are presumably flooring for Khufu's Mortuary Temple. Petrie calling these slabs "magnificent work" in his classic book *The Pyramids and Temples of Gizeh* (1883). As mentioned, tool expert Robert Moores, of the Black & Decker company, observed plunge cuts on these slabs. He stated that these cuts show the definite action of a saw blade. Moores indicated that the plunge cuts eliminate any possibility that the saw striations are the result of working with abrasives. So, the plausible explanation is that these slabs were cut with a copper saw while in the soft stage of geopolymeric setting.

As mentioned, imitation basalt was found in Mesopotamian ruins in 1998. I dedicate an entire chapter below explaining why the basalt (diabase) incorporated into Old Kingdom monuments — including Khufu's complex — is not natural rock. Besides, the experiments of L. Gorelick and J. Gwinnett (summarized in Part 1) show that the abrasives known in Egypt do not duplicate the clean saw striations they were trying to imitate. These researchers showed both flint and quartzite drills to be inadequate. They also had no success with a bow drill, the instrument used in the experiments

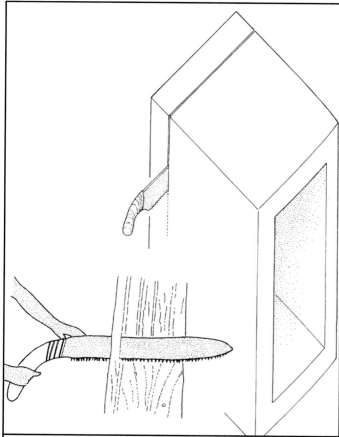

23. *Dieter Arnold shows a toothed saw advancing through wood (bottom). Arnold shows the same kind of toothed saw advancing through granite to cut a lid from a sarcophagus.*

of Denys Stocks. Striations such as those L. Gorelick and J. Gwinnett sought to imitate, and the features Petrie pondered, are easily cut into partially cured geopolymerized rock with simple tools.

Lehner also reports seeing traces of copper on granite in the South Tomb of Zoser's Step Pyramid:

> The granite vault is similar to the one under the pyramid, but it is much smaller, and its interior was covered in green traces of copper.[10]

The copper traces make sense if workers cut extra stock from the faces of granite blocks before they cured. A copper chisel is useless for shaping a block of natural granite. Given Egypt's copper yield, it is difficult to believe that the method Lehner advocates could have been used to cut the approximately one million cubic feet of granite consumed during the Old Kingdom and also supply copper for cutting the approximately 318 million cubic feet of limestone consumed to build the 4th Dynasty's Great Pyramids. As mentioned, even at the peak of copper production in the New Kingdom, the annual copper yield was only about four tons.

Distinctive saw marks appear on an unfinished 4th Dynasty granite sarcophagus in the Egyptian Museum, in Cairo. The sarcophagus belonged to a 4th Dynasty prince named Dedef Hot. To produce its lid, the mason sawed off a thick slice of granite from its upper portion. His sawing produced a large area covered with regular, flat-topped ridges surrounded by grooves. Petrographer Donald Campbell describes these very distinct sawmarks:

> The base of the granite sarcophagus was being cut off to form a lid for the top when the lid broke…The project was left unfinished, although the sides and the interior surfaces appear to be at or near their final form. The interior bottom as well as exterior sides were polished, as was the base from which the top was being sawn. Close inspection of the exterior polished base reveals numerous narrow grooves and shallow, slightly wider plateaus with a spacing of 1 to 2 mm over the entire observable surface, an area of approximately two square meters which is roughly 75 percent of the base area. These are undoubtedly sawmarks in hard granite. What is even more astonishing is that, within the 3 to 4 mm-wide sawcut between the remaining attached lid and base, the saw marks are likewise polished. It seems likely, therefore, that during the sawing operation, the hard Aswan granite was being simultaneously polished. A plot of the leading edge of the sarcophagus sawcut reveals its gentle curvature. Further examination of the sarcophagus base indicates the intersection of two slightly overlapping sawcuts, producing a steplike form and suggesting that the position of the sarcophagus, or the sawmen, changed.[11]

The caption with Campbell's published photograph of these saw marks reads, "This is an incredible technological feat for four millennia ago, but proves that the Egyptians could indeed saw hard rock." This is an example of rapid cutting, and the logical solution is granite concrete cut when semi-cured.

In 1984, the Egyptian Antiquities Organization (EAO) denied us permission to remove pyramid limestone samples. Materials Scientist Michel Barsoum later tested more samples from the Giza monuments and quarries (excavation pits). But the EAO denied Barsoum permission to remove enough samples from the pyramids for full scale testing for geopolymerization. So, we have relied a lot on borrowed samples and independently published data and information. The denial of the EAO is understandable because of all of the damage to the monuments that has taken place over time. An article from *World Review Press*, titled "Puncturing Pyramids" (1989), illustrates the point:

> An Arabic proverb says, "Holes in the Pyramids puncture the honor of Egypt." This saying has prompted national authorities in Egypt to call for strict scientific and antiquarian supervision of all future foreign digs. Beginning in 1977, some "wasteful and useless digs at Egyptian national monuments, including the Pyramids and the Sphinx" carried out by foreign archaeological teams produced only "self-important fanfare and damage to antiquities."[12]

Since the above article was published, holes have been drilled in search of hidden chambers. The potential of geopolymeric rock-concrete and mortars for restoring endangered monuments is tremendous. But this remains unrecognized by the EAO. This may seem surprising given our efforts over several years, and all the scientific data available on geopolymerization. Today, geopolymeric materials can be designed in ways that are optimal. The U.S. Army Corps of Engineers tested the general properties of geopolymers in the 1980s. The excellent engineering properties of geopolymers have since been thoroughly studied. Repairs made with hard geopolymerized rock can be expected to survive even in harsh environments for thousands of years without need of repair. Geopolymerized rock is highly resistant to acid rain and environmental pollution—elements that are rapidly destroying many ancient Egyptian monuments. Geopolymers are only attacked by strong, highly-corrosive hydrochloric acid. Modern geopolymerized rock is routinely shown to endure freeze-thaw cycles in simulated testing.

On behalf of this body of research, in December of 2003, Sanford H. Rose investigated Khafra's Valley Temple, located just southeast of the Sphinx at Giza. Sanford H. Rose also investigated the Double Mastabas of Akhti-Hotep and the Mastaba of Ptah Hotep at Saqqara. Rose is President of Hallco Technologies, and he is particularly qualified for this investigative analyses. He has extensive experience in the design, development, tooling and manufacture of products using a broad range of fabrication methods and materials. He writes:

> Many of the interior Valley Temple building units have rectangular corners, some with angular, precisely-fitted complimentary angles to abutting blocks. They also have notched edges that fit perfectly with the profile of complimentary notched abutting blocks. Some blocks curve right around wall corners to achieve interlocking fits. All blocks interlock much like pieces of a jigsaw, producing design complexities that are unprecedented when judging by modern standards of granite cutting.

> I estimate a weight of over 100 tons for columns and beams incorporated into the Valley Temple. The design features both inverse right angled corners and notched support beams, all of which are likewise notched with right angles to produce a precision fit for beams that are positioned both vertically and horizontally.

> Moving along to Saqqara, I observed immense temple blocks in the Double Mastaba of Akhti-Hotep and in the Mastaba of Ptah Hotep. The blocks have outer surfaces that are flat to tolerances of 0.01 (1/100th) inch of perfectly straight. These units are consistently flat over very broad areas, as measured with a machinists' parallel. These large blocks have right angles on all six sides, and they exhibit a uniform gap between them of 2/100th inch. This slight gap allowed for bonding material to cushion them from stress or for waterproofing.

Based on my expertise, the limitations of tools, handling devices and techniques known to be available to masons and builders of the Pyramid Age calls the conventional, accepted theory of their fabrication into serious doubt. The carve/hoist theory does not satisfy observable facts. Realistically, the profile, size, contour, and uniformity of block patterns of these Saqqara tombs speak for concrete-making processes, which could easily be achieved with primitive devices used for preparing structures built with rammed earth. For highly regular blocks, the properties of the materials employed would have allowed for pouring or packing into reusable forms, relatively fast setting, and a simple mold release.

Whereas, Khafra's Valley Temple at Giza has a sculptured look, as though a pliable adobe has transformed to solid, homogenous granite. This suggests manufacture with a superior concrete mixture dominated by granite aggregate. The sides of finished granite-concrete blocks could have been used as the forms for densely packing new rock-concrete blocks directly in place. The look of stone sculpture can be thus achieved. Upon analysis, given the primitive tools known to exist at this time, no other explanation is plausible. — Sanford H. Rose, 4/29/2004

Ancient Egyptian artifacts present some very strange geological features that do not match the characteristics of normal rock. The following quote by Egyptologist Ali el-Khouli, from his *Egyptian Stone Vessels: Predynastic Period to Dynasty III* (1978), can serve to briefly summarize:

Alabaster and limestone were the most common because they were easily obtained in Egypt. Other types could only be procured after the expenditure of great labor and at the risk of some danger. Other mineralogical terms employed in the fundamental publications by excavators are somewhat harder to identify. Examination of the original vessels probably would give some of the answers, though it must be pointed out that even qualified geologists are hesitant to give identifications in some cases.[13]

In other words, geologists do not even know how to classify some of the more unusual stones. Geopolymerization is a logical explanation for artifacts like these. Sometimes artifacts show characteristics that do not occur in natural rock.[14] But the rock matrix will look like rock, and so geologists do not know what to think of strange features or mixes that sometimes appear.

Magnificent quartzite objects date to early times. But Egyptology has not explained the ancient methods of quarrying quartzite. Dieter Arnold pondered the matter:

Cutting quartzite…must have been a more severe task [than working granite] …The extent to which dolerite balls were used for pounding quartzite is not clear…the walls of the quarry are not as vertical as those of granite quarries but show steps as deep as 1 foot. The front of these steps is banded by many horizontal grooves that consist…of files of punctuated strikes, apparently produced by a pointed stone pick. Engelbach suggested that a trench was cut into the rock by hacking closely set, long files of small holes into the surface, thus producing narrow ridges in between that could be jarred off by heavy blows of a stone hammer. This would explain why the walls were not vertical but quite inclined…It would not explain, however, the foot-high steps.[15]

Some years earlier, Reginald Engelbach found no evidence that pounding balls were used at the quartzite quarries. The evidence at the quarries suggests that pointed picks were used to strike off quartzite fragments useful for agglomeration. Such an operation would be necessary after loose, friable rock was mostly used up.

Researchers of the Napoleonic Expedition and later investigators combed the quartzite ranges to try to determine where the Egyptians quarried chunks of rock large enough to sculpt the seven-story-high Colossi of Memnon.[16] The trenches made when removing such monuments would be enormous. But no one has found any huge trenches.

The quarry of origin has been the subject of considerable debate. Some researchers argue that the colossi must have been transported all the way to Thebes from Gebel el-Ahmar, east of modern Cairo.[17] The locale is some 435 miles from where the Colossi of Memnon stand. Hauling them 435 miles overland to the Theban necropolis presents a formidable task, especially given that strong flat tracks are need all along the way. Floating these weights from Gebel el-Ahmar would be an incredible feat. The Nile flows from south to north, and we must take the sheer force of the current into consideration. Fighting the current while hauling the heavy load would be such a futile task that a demonstration is needed for the scenario to be believable.

Anyone who has rowed against a river current has some understanding of the physics of the problem. We can consider the example of the early Lewis and Clark Expedition (1803–1806). Their boats traversed so slowly against the current of the Missouri River that Lewis and Clark preferred to walk along the shore so they could study plants and animals. Add a 50-foot-high quartzite colossi to a scenario like this: The barge will flow with the Nile's current — and so would never arrive at Thebes. This presumes that a strong enough barge could be constructed with ancient materials and loaded in the first place.

John Wehausen, a specialist in ship hydrodynamics at the University of California at Berkeley, along with some colleagues, theorized a means for building a barge strong enough to float the Colossi along the Nile. Although they worked out the needed size and strength of a suitable barge, Wehausen admits:

> On the other hand, we were aware that we had not broached the problem of how one might load or unload the barge. Although we did have ideas about how one might do that, we never tried to analyze them.[18]

One problem involves loading such giant objects without capsizing the barges. Another outstanding problem is erecting the giant statues on their pedestals. Such a task has not been duplicated in modern times. But all such problems vanish when the geopolymer paradigm is applied. The most logical explanation for the Colossi of Memnon is that the Egyptians hauled baskets of quartzite debris on barges to the Theban plains. Then they fashioned the twin Colossi on the spot.

The Colossi of Memnon were made under the supervision of the illustrious architect Amenhotep-son-of-Hapu. He was born in the north of Egypt, where the pyramids stand. So, it is not unlikely that he mastered the old stonemaking technology known in the north. Whereas, Theban artisans of his time were stonecutters, as we know from many soft sandstone monuments cut with bronze tools to glorify the nation's capital during this era.

In 1984, a team led by H. Bowman chemically analyzed samples of these giant twin statues.[19] Joseph Davidovits examined the study and observed that its chemical charts show an appropriate amount of aluminosilicates. The form they take can be the result of geopolymerization.[20]

Another clue to the method of manufacture comes from inscriptions. Geologists from the Napoleonic Egyptian Expedition examined the inscriptions on the lower sides of the Colossi of Memnon:

> When the tool of the engraver in the middle of a hieroglyphic character hit a flint or agate in the stone, the sketch was never hindered, but instead it continued in all of its purity. Neither the agate fragment nor the stone itself was ever slightly broken by engraving.[21]

In other words, the rock particles yielded to the engraving tool. To achieve this, the masons would have inscribed the quartzite while it was pliable. I am not suggesting that all crystals in all monuments that may be geopolymeric will be pushed aside. Geopolymerization can gradually produce very tiny crystals. Geopolymeric rock undergoes a geological evolution in which one mineral gradually converts to another. Even when made at ambient temperatures, geopolymers undergo secondary crystallization (geopolymeric metamorphism is further discussed in a chapter below). Sometimes clumps of material were cut through (and these crystalized clumps can be mistaken for whole crystals by the casual observer today).

It stands to reason that if the ancient Egyptians knew how to make high-quality rock-concrete, they used that knowledge to avoid unfathomable tasks like erecting the Colossi of Memnon and the 1,000-ton and heavier colossi of Ramses II on pedestals.

Anyone observing the well-known 18th Dynasty depiction of a barge hauling twin obelisks of Pharaoh-Queen Hatshepsut might think that the ancient Egyptians routinely hauled very heavy loads. But Reginald Engelbach called this depiction "impressionistic," and he explained why it cannot be taken literally (see my chapter below on building obelisks).

Using heat and pressure, scientists have produced many kinds of rocks, including various types of jewels. Joseph Davidovits' unique contribution is to make rock (rock-concretes with the properties of real rock) without heat. So, today enormous amounts of rock can be made (with very simple ingredients) for many purposes without high energy input or special equipment. Unprecedented engineering projects can result from this technology.

Some ancient man-made rocks, such as the Mesopotamian imitation basalt, were made with heat (about 2,000 degrees Fahrenheit). Although most of the rocks Davidovits makes are produced at room temperatures, they still undergo secondary crystallization. A statement by Davidovits in the *Geopolymer Tribune* (March 3, 2001) alludes to his creation of rock textures that have only previously been re-created by science with the use of heat and pressure:

> What I am trying to achieve in my lab is to get hard stone features without smelting and solidifying stone mixtures. All mineralogical analysis performed on Egyptian hard stone artifacts (stone vases) dating from the Old Kingdom demonstrate that the hard stone is not a recently (young) recrystallized, slowly solidified matrix. The hard stones are…strongly affected by saussuritization.* This strange term saussuritization is used by geologists and petrographers when describing the alteration of hard stone constituent feldspar to albite, epidote, calcite, sericite and/or zeolite. In other

---

* The geological definition of saussuritization (saus'-su-rit'-i-za'-tion) is mainly the replacement of plagioclase in basalts and gabbros by a fine-grained aggregate. Some minerals that form are zoisite, epidote, albite, calcite, sericite, and zeolites. Geopolymerization produces zeolites and feldspathoids that undergo a metamorphic process that will gradually produce a variety of fine-grained silicoaluminates.

words, this strange geological term suggests geopolymerization, not smelting and slowly cooling. We always get this saussuritization mechanism when, in my lab, we solidify hard stone replicates obtained by the agglomeration of feldspar aggregates and modern geopolymer binder.

The German scholar Kurt Lange was awestruck by the early Egyptian stoneware with features that convinced him they were made on a potter's wheel:

> On examining them attentively, I only became more perplexed. How were they made, the dishes, plates, bowls, and other objects in diorite, which are among the most beautiful of all the fine stone objects? I have no idea…But how could such a hard stone be worked? The Egyptians of that time had at his disposal only stone, copper, and abrasive sand…It is more difficult to imagine the fabrication of hard stone vases with long narrow necks and rounded bellies. This noble and translucent material is of exceptional hardness…of unequaled finesse and elegance of shape, they are of supreme perfection. The internal face is covered with a microscopic, network of tiny grooves so regular that only an ultramodern potter's wheel of precision could have produced them. To see the grooves one needs a magnifying glass and good lighting…Obviously, the equipment used must have been some kind of potter's wheel. But how could such a hard material be worked? …the plates on which earthenware pots were made with such regularity of form had only just been invented, and it is hard to believe that it was this tool, doubtless still extremely primitive, which was used in the fabrication of the hardest and most perfect bowls ever made.[22]

The potter's wheel grooves in diorite show us that this is an example of rapid cutting—done with a primitive potter's wheel. Common sense tells us that the rock-concrete was pliable (like a clay pot) when the vases were being turned.

Sir W.M.F. Petrie's report in *The Pyramids and Temples of Gizeh* (1883) confirms Lange's observations:

> The diorite bowls and vases of the Old Kingdom are frequently met with, and show great technical skill. One piece found at Gizeh, No. 14, shows that the method employed was true turning, and not any process of grinding, since the bowl has been knocked off its centering, recentred imperfectly, and the old turning not quite turned out; thus there are two surfaces belonging to different centerings, and meeting in a cusp. Such an appearance could not be produced by any grinding or rubbing process which pressed on the surface.[23]

The diorite of which Egyptian vessels are made is almost as difficult to cut as quartzite. Natural diorite cannot be fashioned on a potter's wheel or with an ancient lathe. Using sand as an abrasive, Denys Stocks made cusps by rotating stone borers adjacent to one another. But he worked with limestone (which can be as soft as a sugar cube). This is not the same problem as working with natural diorite, which is both very hard and tough.

Some have argued that tooling for a very long period of time is the answer to enigmatic artifacts. Water produced the Grand Canyon over eons. But it did so in a way that is very irregular. Common sense tells us that no amount of cutting with meteoric iron would create these potter's wheel grooves. Iron is softer than diorite. So, if iron were used over a very long period of time to try to wear down diorite, regular potter's wheel grooves would not appear on these vases. The same is true when using gems as cutting teeth. Gems flake off and will not leave grooves. These vases are made to the kind of precision that a potter's wheel affords when using a mixture of pliable stone-concrete.

Long, slow production will not produce the features of rapid cutting found on artifacts. These features include the definite action of a saw blade (plunge cuts and other definite saw marks), crisp sharp-point etchings, and potter's wheel groves in diorite. A 4th Dynasty diorite bowl fragment in the Petrie Museum (UC16042) is labeled, "Rim fragment of diorite bowl, showing evidence for use of lathe."

Found at Giza in the Menkaure Valley Temple in 1910, a thin-walled vessel, made with anorthosite gneiss (which is closely related to diorite) is in the Boston Museum of Fine Arts. The vessel takes the shape of 4th Dynasty carinated pottery bowls, according to its catalogue description. In other words, this vessel was styled like clay pottery. There are severe limitations when cutting this kind of hard, natural rock to these specifications.

The features of these vases can be achieved by fashioning agglomerated rock-making mixture on a potter's wheel. It stands to reason that anyone possessing this technology would not go through the hard labor of grinding. Besides, vases with handles would interfere with lathe turning, and so cannot be explained by ordinary lathe-turning methods. But handles can be affixed to geopolymeric vessels after they are turned on a potter's wheel — making geopolymerization the most logical explanation for such items.

Although soft alabaster can be easily cut with primitive tools, a delicate 2nd Dynasty alabaster bowl from Saqqara exhibits five corners that look as if they were folded over towards the bowl's inner center.[24] While this design would be extremely difficult to carve, it is a natural inclination to press a pliable stone bowl into various configurations.

Denys Stocks is immensely impressed by a circular schist vessel in the Cairo Museum. He refers to it as "...stone working at its highest level." He says that those who see this piece "...will be enchanted and mystified" by its unique shape. The vessel (Catalogue No. JE71295) is from Saqqara and is thought to date to the First Dynasty.

Stocks recognizes that schist cannot be cut with metal tools. He described the design of this vessel as exquisitely executed, and made of three petal-shaped pieces that cause the observer to think the petals were folded forward from the rim. He assumes the vessel was painstakingly chiseled, scraped and ground with flint tools and sandstone rubbers. But this piece is a good candidate for geopolymerization. It could be made very easily by folding its petals while in an uncured state, and otherwise shaping it with simple tools while still soft. Given that its petals look folded, it stands to reason that they probably were.

Denys Stocks also recognizes the great challenges an alabaster bowl in the Cairo Museum pose to the skilled craftsman. The vessel comes from Saqqara and dates to the First or Second Dynasty (Catalogue No. JE6075). Stocks reported that when a candle is placed inside the vessel in a dark room, the vessel will glow with an exquisite luminosity because its uniform walls are so thin. Although the stone is soft (about 3 and 4 on Mohs' hardness scale), the vessel is circular (about 30 centimeters in diameter) and intricately built with three separate circular compartments. Stocks easily recognized that the circularity and intricacy, along with the striations on the vessel, are features of lathe turning. But he also recognized that Old Kingdom tools would not permit this kind of work with Egyptian alabaster.

He pointed out that using a brittle flint shard to cut a rotating Egyptian alabaster vessel is not possible. The flint will immediately break when pressed against the rotating calcite. Any lathe used to form this vessel must be extremely durable and devoid of any shaking during rotation to afford such accurate machining. So, he concluded that the complex vessel must have somehow been masterfully carved with flint chisels, punches, and scrapers, and then finished with stone rubbers and ground sand. Given that the features of this vessel strongly suggest lathe working of partially cured rock, it is an excellent candidate for geopolymerization.

A 1st Dynasty bowl from Saqqara, made of yellow limestone, has extremely thin walls that curve inward to give it a cruciform shape. It appears as though the artisan fashioned a round bowl and then gently pressed in its pliable walls to transform it to a cruciform. He then left the bowl to cure.

Tubular jars have walls .04 inch thick. It is logical to think that their manufacture required a technology that allowed complete control over the material being worked.[25]

Some stone vases are called composites because they are made of more than one kind of stone. Pots made this way are not uncommon from the Early Dynastic Period until the 3rd Dynasty. An example comes from an excavation of an early cemetery in the Eastern Delta, led by German Egyptologist Detrich Wildung in the 1970s. Here is a description by Karla Kroeper:

> The upper part of the vessel is made of graywacke which is well polished on the outside…The lower part of the vase is made of calcite…At the widest part of both pieces the edges fit exactly, one on top of the other and here the two pieces must have been connected with some form of adhesive of which no traces remain.[26]

With geopolymeric cement, a molecular bond forms between the cement and the rock aggregates. Given that the geopolymeric binder bonds aggregates together, nothing resembling glue is detectable. Crystals eventually form from the binder, but anyone not knowing that will mistake them for natural crystals in the rock.

Karla Kroeper mentions that the same method used to unite the composite vases was also used to repair vessels. So, the composite vessels were deliberately united. In other words, they were not made from natural rock chunks composed of two different kinds of stone that formed together in nature. We can expect that the Egyptians would sometimes have mixed two different types of stone, and here we find examples.

Clarke and Engelbach, in *Ancient Egyptian Masonry* (1930), recorded evidence that can be explained by fabricated stone. They wrote that on:

> ….an unfinished schist statuette of Saite date, in the Cairo Museum, the marks of the tool can be clearly seen; each blow has removed a small fragment of the stone without any apparent bruising and a succession of a dozen blows or more can be traced without any evidence of wear on the tool.[27]

A logical explanation is that this is an example of sculpting man-made rock before it has fully cured. Perhaps the artisan later gave up on his statuette because the stone got too hard.

Jean-Philippe Lauer is most famous for spending much of his career restoring Zoser's pyramid complex. He privately recognized that geopolymerization is the only logical solution to the vexing mystery of the hard stone vessels.[28] But he rejected the premise that the pyramids could be synthetic stone.[29] The reason is that for 50 years Lauer relied on the viability of ramps and copper tools—which are only now beginning to be abandoned by Egyptology because they are proven to be unworkable. But his experience with the hard stone vessels found at Zoser's pyramid presented him with examples of stonework that defies any explanation other than geopolymerization.

Chapter 23
Proof from the Basalt Quarries

My study below reveals powerful evidence that thousands of tons of basalt found in Old Kingdom monuments are manmade rock. A quick overview is followed by the details.

Thousands of tons of weathered basalt fragments were excavated at Egypt's only known Old Kingdom basalt outcrop. It is located in Egypt's northern Fayum region at Gebel el-Qatrani. Tool marks are always associated with block quarrying, but the Gebel el-Qatrani outcrop bears no tool marks. Although there is always breakage during block-quarrying, no broken blocks are found at Gebel el-Qatrani.

A seven-mile-long flagstone* road once led from Gebel el-Qatrani to Lake Moeris. The intact areas of the road were studied, and show no sign of the wear that would be caused by heavy block transport. There are no abandoned blocks anywhere along the roadsides, either. Instead, the roadsides are littered with many heaps of basalt debris. This may represent places where baskets of basalt debris accidentally spilled and were abandoned.

Independent testing has long proved to Egyptologists that the mineralogical composition of the Gebel el-Qatrani outcrop matches the Old Kingdom artifacts made with basalt. This testing proved to Egyptologists that all of the Old Kingdom basalt came from Gebel el-Qatrani. But there is a serious problem: The thousands of tons worth of Old Kingdom artifacts do not have the extremely fine-grained texture of basalt. Instead, the artifacts consist of a coarser grade of rock called diabase. This would be expected of agglomerated basalt debris. But it is impossible for quarried basalt blocks from Gebel el-Qatran.

Geologists have determined that medium- to coarse-grained basalt (classified as diabase and also called dolerite) does not occur at all in the Fayum. So, the logical explanation for this otherwise mysterious and unexplainable geological circumstance—occurring on a monumental scale—is that Old Kingdom basalt artifacts are agglomerated stone.

There is no other logical way to account for the excavation of thousands of tons of fine-grained basaltic material that does not match the coarser texture of the Old Kingdom artifacts—when the artifacts are all (or almost entirely) determined to come from this fine-grained basalt outcrop. There is no other explanation for why the thousands of Old Kingdom artifacts would be classified as diabase, a medium- to coarse-grained material not found in the Fayum. Here are the details supporting these strong lines of evidence for the massive production of hard, manmade rock during the Old Kingdom for pyramid complexes.

Basalt is black volcanic rock with a crystal grain size too small to be seen without a microscope. Vessels called basalt (they are more properly called diabase) date as early as Late Predynastic times. Basalt (diabase) later appears in Egypt's Old Kingdom on a massive scale, mostly as mortuary temple flooring slabs, walls blocks, sarcophagi, and in causeways in pyramid complexes.

Basalt outcrops are found at a number of sites in Egypt, but only one was excavated during the Old Kingdom for pyramid complexes. This is the Gebel el-Qatrani outcrop. From a high mountain peak at Gebel el-Qatrani, we can see the pyramids of Giza, Saqqara, and Dahshur on a clear day. Giza is roughly 40 miles across the desert.

---

* A flagstone is a flat stone slab used for paving, or an evenly layered sedimentary rock that can be segmented to form paving slabs.

The world's oldest known 'flagstone' road leads from the Gebel el-Qatrani basalt outcrop to Lake Moeris. The road is estimated to have originally extended a little over seven miles. All of the roadway was originally paved.[1] Within the geopolymer paradigm, no flat, smooth roads are needed for hauling blocks. Instead, this seven-mile-long road served to mark the way to and from these rock extraction sites to the lake.

Although Egyptology long ago determined from microscopic studies that the basalt (diabase) artifacts of Old Kingdom Egypt come from this outcrop at Gebel el-Qatrani, the actual rock extraction sites were long unknown. The reason is that the excavated areas are on higher ground than was searched. Then, in 1992-3, geologists James A. Harrell, of the University of Toledo, Ohio, and Thomas M. Bown, of the U.S. Geological Survey, studied the road and environs of Gebel el-Qatrani. They discovered two large Old Kingdom basalt outcrops that were heavily excavated.

According to these researchers, weathered material from these areas (which they call the east and west quarries) was massively excavated. They indicate:

> Rather than continuing the excavations further downward or backward, where unweathered basalt could be found, the quarrymen preferred to extend them laterally along the outer rim of the escarpment. The reason for this is unclear, but the rim rock may have been more fractured due to its greater exposure and so easier to work. No tool marks were seen in the quarry and this together with the highly fractured nature of the rock suggests that blocks of basalt were simply wedged out of place with levers.[2]

The force of men using wooden levers alone is useless for breaking out truly massive blocks made of such hard stone. Harrell and Bown did not mention observing any actual remains of wooden levers, and there are no signs of trenches showing that blocks were isolated and undercut for removal. So, their remarks quoted above are based on their presumption that natural rock was employed to build the monuments. Even if basalt is conveniently separated by natural cracks, forming basalt blocks the size of those in the pyramid complexes requires quarrying, the remains of which will be visible. But Old Kingdom basalt (diabase) slabs, such as those found at Giza, are massive—far too massive to be pried out with levers. It is not uncommon for the mortuary temple slabs to be over six feet long at pyramid sites. The only way to remove blocks of this size is to quarry around their edges. If blocks were quarried at Gebel el-Qatrani, tool marks and trenches would dominate the appearance of the quarries.

In 1965, Joseph Roder showed that wedges were not used in Egyptian quarrying at Aswan before Ptolemaic times (332–30 B.C.).[3] It is reasonable to think that the same applies to other hard rock excavation projects. Gebel el-Qatrani supplied thousands of tons of basalt for Old Kingdom architecture. So, many thousands of wedge marks should be visible at Gebel el-Qatrani if basalt blocks were quarried there with this method. The lack of any detectable tool marks of any kind and the lack of broken lever remains or wedge slots suggests that only powdery or loose or easily loosened debris was removed from the top of the weathered areas.

The interior of the middle layer, which contains relatively unweathered basalt suitable for making blocks, was never quarried. The hard rock was simply left untouched and remains today. Only the weathered rock was exploited. These factors all support my premise of the massive removal of rock debris for agglomerating this basalt (so that it appears as and is classified as diabase when we examine Mortuary Temple slabs, sarcophagi, etc.).

Harrell and Bown reported two broken diorite mauls in the eastern quarry, and assumed that they were used to quarry blocks.[4] These mauls are typical for the Old Kingdom. They are notched so they can be affixed to wooden handles with leather strips. But we cannot expect a maul held together with leather banding to be useful for quarrying basalt blocks. We must question how such flimsy tool construction could bear repeated hard strikes without failing. But this tool is suitable for loosening and/or gathering aggregates. Besides, if diorite mauls were used to quarry blocks, there would be tool marks all over the quarries and places where whole blocks were removed on a massive scale.

Experiments by Denys Stocks showed that copper and bronze chisels are unsuitable for shaping basalt.[5] Egyptian basalt ranges from 6 to 8 on the Mohs' hardness scale.[6] A tough, modern tool-steel chisel has to be frequently sharpened when used to shape basalt. Shaping and dressing thousands of tons of large temple flooring slabs of natural basalt with Old Kingdom tools presents many unresolved problems. The carve/hoist paradigm is simply unworkable.

Even when weathered rock is available, gathering it depends upon how well it is exposed. Harrell and Bown mentioned that the available evidence about basalt near Saqqara suggests that it is also weathered and of poor quality. But it would be too difficult to obtain because the outcrops are not well exposed.[7] The extreme difficulty of obtaining this basalt debris may explain why it was not excavated despite its closer proximity to the pyramid complexes.

So, at Gebel el-Qatrani an ideal area of weathered basalt was selected. This area lies at the outer rim of the escarpment. The weathered basalt there was either manually disaggregated with mauls, or else a great deal of naturally loose debris was gathered (mostly using mauls to scrape the stone into baskets) and hauled away in baskets.

Earlier expeditions, between 1926 and 1934, were undertaken by archeologist Gertrude Caton-Thompson and geologist Elinor W. Gardner. They found a segment of the quarry road at Gebel el-Qatrani that they suggested originally ended at the scree.[8]* As the road segment there would have served a purpose, it is logical to think that debris was removed from this area, too.

Sarcophagi Made with Basalt

Harrell and Bown recognize that the huge Egyptian basalt sarcophagi could not have been made from blocks quarried at Gebel el-Qatrani. The problem is that the basalt at Gebel el-Qatrani is riddled with closely spaced fractures. So, these quarries can yield blocks no larger than 6.5 feet.

Basalt sarcophagi are reported for the 4th Dynasty Pharaohs Menkaure, and Shepseskaf, and for the 5th Dynasty Pharaohs Userkaf, Unas, and Djedkara Izezi, and for the 6th Dynasty Pharaohs Merenre, Teti, and Pepi I. The Old Kingdom sarcophagi list also includes one for a queen of Pharaoh Pepi II. To account for the fracture-free sarcophagi, Harrell and Bown speculate that other unknown quarries capable of bearing large chunks of high-quality basalt must have been worked.[9] But no such quarries have ever been identified—and experts, including Harrell, otherwise state that all of the hard stone Egyptian quarries are known. Harrell has explored all of them. The one known outcrop, which is Gebel el-Qatrani, yielded suitable aggregates for molding or otherwise fashioning these large sarcophagi.

---

* Scree can mean loose rock debris covering a slope. Scree can also refer to a slope composed of loose rock debris at the base of a steep cliff or incline. Scree areas of the latter type are dangerous to excavate because of the potential for a landslide. The Egyptians would have had to avoid any extensive gathering of basalt debris in such areas. So, inaccessible rubble would remain in such places today.

Sorting out Old Kingdom Basalt Extraction

Like other Egyptian quarries, Gebel el-Qatrani has a long history of rock extraction. Many Old Kingdom pottery shards were found there. Roman pottery shards, dating to the 4th to 6th centuries A.D., were also found.[10] So, just as at Giza, original rock excavation activities must be distinguished from any later work. Statues and sarcophagi called basalt (in published literature) are known to date from the Late Period to Greco-Roman times. They have to be studied on a case-by-case basis to determine if they are products of geo-synthesis or not.

It is important to recognize that different rock extraction techniques were used in different historical periods. An Egyptian temple was dedicated in the general area during the Middle Kingdom. But it was left unfinished. Excavations at Gebel el-Qatrani appear to have stopped at about that time. This is suggested by the dearth of Middle and New Kingdoms basalt (diabase) objects. Pottery shards found at the nearby quarrymen's camp date to the Ptolemaic-Roman period (2nd century B.C. to 2nd century A.D.). Christian monks lived in the area in the 7th to 9th centuries, at the Coptic monastery of Deir Abu Lifa. So, these findings may suggest some very modest rock extraction activity much later than the Old Kingdom. But presently no evidence of block quarrying in the Fayum outcrop has been found.[11] This makes the overall picture easier to analyze because there is no sorting out original rock extraction from many periods of later block quarrying, such as we find at Aswan, Giza and elsewhere.

Most areas at Gebel el-Qatrani exhibit three lava* flows. Of these, the bottom and top flows are extremely weathered. The middle flow is dense, and much of that material is relatively unweathered. Harrell and Bown report that this area is left untouched. Instead, excavations extended over a vast weathered area. This huge area extends to the east quarry along about 1/2 mile around the more weathered rim, and almost 200 feet along the more weathered rim in the west quarry.[12]

Making Diabase with Basalt Debris

Basalt is the most common variety of volcanic rock. It forms from the outpouring of lava. Basalt is largely feldspar, which gradually breaks down into kaolin clay. So, only natron, lime, and water are needed to geopolymerize very weathered basalt debris. Additional kaolin can be added to the basalt-making mix, if necessary.

Basalt debris can be made into solid rock with or without heat. But the texture will differ depending on whether heat is used or not. When weathered basalt debris is agglomerated at room temperature, the grains can be seen with the naked eye in the finished product. So, this medium- to coarse-grained rock is classified as diabase (also called dolerite). The temple slabs and other Old Kingdom artifacts are diabase, and so making the bulk of these objects with basalt debris did not require fuel consumption.

Making fine-grained basalt requires heat. Using heat, Joseph Davidovits created material similar to the imitation basalt slabs found in Mesopotamian temple ruins (he also made synthetic lava).[13] He produced the binder for his basalt objects predominantly with aluminosilicates (like kaolin) and calcium carbonate (which produces lime when heated). He heated the mix to 2,000 degrees Fahrenheit and allowed it to cool.

The way the finished rock looks will depend on how it cools, too. When making basalt by using heat, rapidly cooling the hot rock with water will produce a glassy appearance.

---

* The molten rock from beneath the Earth's surfaces that rises through volcanic vents is called magma. After the magma erupts it is known as lava.

This can also cause fractures, just as sometimes occurs when natural lava cools. Extremely slow cooling, such as occurs in nature, produces a granite texture.

The geological description of the mineralogy of the imitation basalt of Mesopotamia resembles that of the basalt (diabase) paving slabs next to the Great Pyramid.[14] The big difference is that rock particles in the slabs next to Khufu's Great Pyramid are large enough to see with the naked eye (because this rock was made without heat).

The Telling Mineralogy Studies

A number of investigators have studied samples of basalt (diabase) from Egyptian artifacts. The purpose of these analyses was to compare the inclusions* in the artifacts with those in the quarries. This process allows researchers to identify the quarries that artifacts come from.[15] All but one of the studies predate the rediscovery of the chemistry of geopolymerization by Joseph Davidovits.

The one study of basalt (diabase) that dates to after the discovery of geopolymerization was performed on samples from the Mortuary Temple flooring slabs next to Khufu's Great Pyramid. That examination was made by R. Hamilton, of Manville Service Corp., in Denver, Colorado. He was unfamiliar with the chemistry of geopolymerization, and so he would not have known how to detect this geosynthesis.[16]

After Hamilton's study was published, I contacted him in the hope of arranging for the thin sections or microphotographs to be examined by geologists who study ancient geopolymerization. But Hamilton does not own the samples he studied, and was not at liberty to provide anything. So, none of the studies concluding that the basalt (diabase) from the monuments is identical to basalt from the quarries take the issue of geopolymerization into scientific consideration.

Harrell and Bown assert that the Giza temple flooring slabs are identical to the basalt from Gebel el-Qatrani. They wrote:

> It has also been shown that the basalt used for the paving stones in the mortuary temples of Khufu at Giza and Userkaf at Saqqara is identical to that from Gebel el-Qatrani.[17]

To make the above-quoted statement, Harrell and Bown relied on the aforementioned study by R. Hamilton. He performed a petrography examination of two specimens from the slabs in the Mortuary Temple flooring next to Khufu's Great Pyramid: But Hamilton reported these Giza slabs to be:

> Pyroxene diabase — medium grained, hypidiomorphic-granular, sub-ophitic to intergranular...[18]

James Harrell, an expert on Egyptian quarries, is very well aware that diabase does not occur in Egypt's Fayum region at all.

Diabase is only found in Egypt's Eastern Desert.[19] In other words, basalt is very fine-grained rock (like that in the Gebel el-Qatrani basalt outcrop). So, there is a big difference between the diabase in Khufu's slabs and the basalt at Gebel el-Qatrani. That difference is not mineralogy. It is texture.

To geosynthesize basalt that looks like natural basalt, one must melt basalt debris at 2,000 degrees Fahrenheit. Heat processing is feasible when making vessels, and may account for

---

* Inclusions, also called xenoliths, are fragments of older rock caught up in igneous rocks.

the few existing examples of fine-grained Egyptian vessels classified as basalt. But using heat is not practical for making the hundreds of thousands of tons of flooring slabs in Old Kingdom monuments.

Crushing thousands of tons of basalt fragments to fine powder (to obtain a fine texture) would also be too laborious. But without thoroughly melted or extremely fine-grained basalt debris, the agglomerated stone will look like diabase—exactly like the Giza slabs. Simply put, using weathered basalt debris will produce the diabase texture.

To summarize, Hamilton's petrography study inadvertently provides evidence showing that the slabs next to Khufu's Great Pyramid are not natural basalt from Gebel el-Qatrani: The inclusions found in the slabs match those at Gebel el-Qatrani (proving that the material to make the slabs originated there). But the texture of the rock is that of a diabase, which does not occur at Gebel Qatrani or anywhere else in the Fayum. So, the texture of the Giza slabs demonstrates my premise that the slabs near Khufu's Great Pyramid are the result of a geosynthesis. Khufu's Mortuary Temple paving slabs are not an exception.

Remarks by Alfred Lucas quoted below explain that the many basalt objects from Old Kingdom Egypt are this kind of medium- to coarse-grained rock. Lucas' remarks demonstrate that studies of the artifacts show them to have originated from Gebel el-Qatrani, too. Lucas indicated:

> Basalt is a black, heavy, compact rock, often showing tiny glittering particles: it consists of an aggregate of various minerals, which in true basalt are too fine-grained to be distinguished separately, except by means of a microscope, the coarser varieties of rock where the separate minerals can be recognized with the naked eye being dolerite [diabase]…the material so largely employed in ancient Egypt, being relatively coarse-grained, though generally called basalt, is strictly a fine grained dolerite [diabase]…[20]

Lucas continued by identifying the many Old Kingdom objects, mostly paving slabs, that have this coarser texture. So, it becomes obvious that a great percentage of the Old Kingdom artifacts fall into this category and are consistent with synthetic rock:

> Basalt [diabase] was employed largely in the Old kingdom as a material for pavements, thus in the Third Dynasty step pyramid at Saqqara and in the large tomb adjoining a few basalt [diabase] paving slabs were found; the pavement in the Fourth Dynasty pyramid temple of Khufu at Giza (all that now remains of the temple) is of basalt [diabase]; also pavements of a court, causeway, two small chambers and a small offering place of a Fifth Dynasty mortuary temple at Saqqara and pavements, and possibly other parts of the building, in the mortuary temples of two Fifth Dynasty temple-pyramids at Abusir (between Giza and Saqqara).[21]

Lucas continued by explaining that microscopic examinations determined that all of these slabs and the other diabase (dolerite) objects—commonly referred to as basalt in Egyptological literature—came from Gebel el-Qatrani in the Fayum. Lucas indicated:

> The basalt [diabase] employed in such large quantity during the Old Kingdom in the necropolis stretching from Giza to Saqqara was probably local and all of the available evidence points to the Fayum [Gebel el-Qatrani] as the source. Thus, in the Fayum, within easy reach of the necropolis, there is a basalt quarry, approached by a made road, and, therefore, manifestly worked on a large scale and, near the quarry, is a small temple probably of Old Kingdom date and there is no evidence of the ancient

quarrying of basalt near Cairo, except in the Fayum, the present quarry at Abu Za'bal being entirely modern. Moreover, the basalt [diabase] employed in the Old Kingdom is found to be more nearly like that from the Fayum than that from Abu Za'bal.

On this point Miss Caton-Thompson writes 'Microscopical examination of the Fayum [Gebel el-Qatrani] basalt and a specimen from the Fifth Dynasty pavement of Saqqara shows them to be indistinguishable; and although the rock type is a common one, the presence of similar inclusions in both supports their community of origin.'[22]

Given the amount of extensive rock extraction found by Harrell and Bown at Gebel el-Qatrani, it is logical to conclude that the many Old Kingdom Egyptian artifacts should match with regard to mineral content. But these same artifacts do not have the texture of basalt. They have the medium-to coarse-grained texture of diabase (dolerite), which is simply not found at Gebel el-Qatrani or anywhere else in the Faiyum. Despite this major geological discrepancy, Egyptology calls the many artifacts 'basalt' because of the mineralogical match with the basalt of Gebel el-Qatrani.

The entire major and thorny geological discrepancy is immediately resolved once we understand that the medium to coarser grain of the myriad of Old Kingdom slabs is present because powdery fragments from Gebel el-Qatrani were geopolymerized. The mystery of Egyptian basalt, persisting since the early days of Egyptology, is solved by geopolymerization.

The World's Oldest Paved Road

The sandstone road from Gebel el-Qatrani also has a story to tell. Having served pyramid construction efforts more than 4,500 years ago, it is the world's oldest known flagstone road. It is much older than the roadway crossing the island of Crete from Komo to Kronos, which many historians assume it to be the world's oldest flagstone road.

The road from Gebel el-Qatrani is not the only ancient Egyptian paved road. Some shorter paved roads are associated with pyramid complexes. But the road from Gebel el-Qatrani is also distinguished because its seven miles of roadway were fully paved. This is fortunate because its paving allows us to assess damage to the road. This road shows no sign of damage or other evidence of heavy hauling.

For the most part, the road was originally made of close-fitting slabs with no mortar between them. Harrell and Bown provide a description:

> Along its entire length, the road was originally constructed of closely fitting, unmortared fragments of locally available bedrock...[23]

These relatively flat slabs (measuring up to almost eight inches thick and usually less than about 20 inches wide), rest directly on the ground covering this area of the Fayum Desert. Fortunately, Harrell and Bown were able to study preserved portions of the road.

Owing to sand-blowing winds, the ancient road is now very weather-damaged in many places. There are small sand-filled gaps between many intact slabs. These slabs are good candidates for geopolymerization, too. Most of them are sandstone, probably made from local sand. The sandstone of the vicinity was friable and weathered until it degraded into the sand covering the surface of the desert. The slabs are irregularly shaped, instead of squared. Yet, Harrell and Bown report that they observed no tool marks on any of the slabs.[24]

One might argue for natural rock in that sandstone and other sedimentary rocks can be evenly layered and split to form slabs. But Harrell and Bown reported that the preserved road slabs were originally very close-fitting, such that no mortar was ever used between them—and that the slabs show no tool marks. In contrast, the joints of flagstone paths made with natural rock must be shaped with tools to fit together closely. Harrell and Bown reported no evidence of broken slabs. But there would be many when producing this kind of long road with natural sandstone.

Many thousands of tons of basalt were transported along this road. Instead of abandoned basalt blocks, Harrell and Bown encountered many piles of basalt fragments along the roadside.[25] Harrell and Bown proposed that these fragment heaps represent places where basalt blocks spilled and then gradually disintegrated in place.[26] It is surprising that Harrell and Bown draw this conclusion.

Harrell and Bown did not explain how basalt—which must be dense and compact to be suitable for construction—could disintegrate into heaps of rocks while sandstone slabs, which they call "relatively soft and fragile" are intact. Both are found in the same spot, and so were equally exposed to weathering.[27]

A basalt block will weather some in 4,500 years, but it should not simply fall apart. Some forms of diabase (dolerite) weather spherically into small granules. But Harrell and Bown would not have mistaken diabase for basalt—and no diabase is found in the Fayum at all. According to Harrell and others, diabase only occurs in Egypt's Eastern Desert.[28] The fragment heaps Harrell and Bown observed are best explained as places where loads of basalt aggregates being carted from the quarry were spilled and abandoned. The lightest particles have long since blown away.

I stress that we must expect that if relatively soft sandstone slabs held up for 4,500 years, then basalt blocks in the same environment should remain intact, too.

Harrell and Bown were surprised that the southernmost stretch of the road ended at the edge of a cliff. They assume that the main purpose of the road was for hauling blocks. But since there is no evidence that blocks were moved along the road, they postulated that they were dropped over this cliff instead. That seems illogical because the road shows no wear. Besides, blocks will chip and break when dropped from a cliff, and so Harrell and Bown opted to propose that a slope once existed that has somehow disappeared:

> The fifth and southernmost of the quarry road segments lies on the flat below the first break in slope that marks the upper part of the Qasr el-Sagha escarpment. This stretch, which is 300m long, is made from slabs of sandstone and limestone. The road ends at the edge of a vertical, 5m high cliff, the first of many breaks in the 80m high Qasr el-Sagha escarpment. That the road would end where it does is surprising because about 100 m to the east is a convenient pass through the cliff which is, in fact, the only useful route down to the lower levels for several kilometers in both directions. Perhaps the quarrymen dropped the basalt blocks over the cliff and retrieved them at the bottom. This seems unlikely, however, unless there was a thick accumulation of loose sand at the base to absorb the impact of the fall. Otherwise, many blocks would have broken. It seems more likely that an artificial or natural inclined slope (perhaps a sand dune) leading to the lower levels existed at the present cliff edge and has since been eroded away.[29]

We see by Harrell's remarks that this locale is not a logical spot for transporting huge blocks. It is difficult to think that the Egyptians would have risked dropping quarried basalt blocks off a cliff. Besides, lowering multiton blocks on ropes would have been very difficult. If the road ending at the cliff provided a shortcut to Lake Moeris, it is more reasonable to think that baskets or pots of basalt rubble were lowered down from the cliff.

A desert track leads from Gebel el-Qatrani to Dashur. But moving large blocks on sledges overland to the pyramid construction sites would not be possible. This kind of operation is prohibited because of the difficulties of transporting blocks over long distances of sand-covered ground. So, the only way to move whole blocks would have to have been taking them along the paved road. From Lake Moeris, materials can be transported by barge to the construction sites. Harrell and Bown recognized that shipping huge blocks by water from Lake Moeris could only have been done for a couple of months each year.[30]

Barges filled with basalt debris need not present heavy loads. The combined loads of several barges carrying fragmented basalt might equal 20 tons per day. Also, teams of men or donkey trains loaded with filled baskets could have made the desert journey to the pyramid construction sites throughout the year — with return trips bringing supplies for workers excavating rock debris. As mentioned, inscriptions from the Sinai mining area indicate that teams of up to 500 donkeys were used for transporting materials across the desert.[31]

Harrell and Bown examined the best-preserved stretches of the quarry road leading to and from the basalt excavation pits at Gebel el-Qatrani. They were surprised to find that the paving slabs did not exhibit the wear expected from the transportation of massive blocks. The observations of Harrell and Bown make sense if only containers of basalt fragments were carried along the road. Harrell and Bown observed:

> Although weathering may have destroyed some of this evidence, one would still expect to see considerable abrasion, given that the thin slabs of friable sandstone used are relatively soft and fragile. If sledges had been dragged along the pavement, deep grooves would surely have been worn into the slabs by the runners, and many of the slabs would also have been broken. The absence of broken slabs discarded along the roadside indicates that few if any of the original slabs were replaced as part of some regular maintenance.[32]

Another problem with the idea of hauling massive blocks on sledges is that the operation is only practical on slick, flat surfaces where friction can be reduced. But, as Harrell and Bown realize, pouring water on sandstone pavement will not reduce friction.[33] So, the standard sledge system Egyptology advocates for moving all large objects does not work in the Gebel el-Qatrani road setting.

Harrell and Bown had to reject the idea that anything as heavy as the Mortuary Temple slabs were hauled along the road surface. They then pondered the idea that heavy blocks were lifted and carried on biers, or by another means of lifting. They abandoned their ideas for ways of doing this — because the very idea is fundamentally highly impractical. There is no reason to think that crews hauling thousands of tons of blocks over miles of roadway would employ the most difficult method (lifting and carrying blocks instead of pushing and pulling them along the road).

Harrell and Bown suggested methods they think might have prevented visible wear on the roadway. But they offer no evidence from the road to support the actual use of such methods. They suggested embedding closely-spaced wooden beams crosswise in a packed aggregate. Sledges can be pulled over such beams.

Alternatively, flattened beams can be laid across the road in front of block-bearing sledges. The rearmost beam is leapfrogged to the front, once the sledge clears it. Egyptologists found a track system, used on a small scale over a short distance, dating to the 12th Dynasty at el-Lahun. But at el-Lisht, these hauling tracks are as wide as 36 feet. Spaced wooden beams and a fill of limestone and mortar are still evident at the site.[34] But Harrell and Bown provided no physical evidence whatsoever for this method on the road to Gebel el-Qatrani.

Given the thousands of tons of basalt transported over the vast expanse of roadway, an abundance of evidence of broken sledges and worn-out and splintered beams or other evidence would be present if this method had actually been used for hauling multiton units over the road from Gebel el-Qatrani. So, the best explanation is that lightweight baskets of basalt debris (weighing perhaps 20 pounds each), were carried over the road.

The Telling Tool Marks

We have already considered (in Part 1) Black & Decker tool expert Robert Moores' examination of a plunge cut (the definite action of a saw blade) in the basalt (diabase) slabs at Giza. Robert Francis also examined these slabs and described features that prove rapid cutting through the basalt (diabase). In his Internet article, which shows photographs of the tight-fitting slabs, Francis writes:

> Notice how crisp and parallel the edges are. The quality of this work indicates that the blade was held completely steady. Apparently, cutting basalt was not so slow and arduous that extra cuts like these would have been avoided as being an unnecessary waste of time.

> There are several places where overcuts like these can be seen. If you find this spot, look around behind you to the north - there are several more within 30 ft. In one place you can find many vertical parallel saw cuts right next to each other.

> In another place near those, you can see long saw cuts going through this hard rock very quickly. In most cases it can be seen that the cut is straight and clean with smooth, consistently parallel sides - even at the start of the cut. They show no trace of the 'walking' or wobble that might be expected of a long hand pulled blade as it starts into a hard material. That may be because these cuts were made as the blade was coming out of a cut above it and it was held firmly in place by the rock above it...They had lathes that would turn and polish granite, schist, basalt, etc. (in ways we have not duplicated).

The hardest metal available during the Old Kingdom was copper, which cannot be made into saws that will produce a plunge cut (showing the definite action of a saw blade) or the features described by Robert Francis (basalt is Mohs' 6–8). But we must consider the value of Francis' observations of features revealing that the slabs were rapidly sliced through. Rapid cutting would only be possible when the geopolymerized slabs were cut through while in a semicured state. The bottoms of the slabs also correspond exactly to an isolated layer of fine-grained limestone beneath them. This circumstance (fine limestone under Old Kingdom diabase temple slabs) is not unique to Khufu's pyramid complex. The most logical explanation is that ground reinforcement was needed, and so limestone concrete was poured to prepare a good surface for the temple floors.

Fundamental Mysteries of Egyptology Solved

Fundamental problems argued since the inception of Egyptology are solved by alchemical stonemaking. For instance, the decades-long debate between Alfred Lucas and W.M.F. Petrie over how artifacts were made can never be resolved as long as researchers think in terms of cutting hard, natural rock. Petrie argued for the use of jewel-tipped saws, estimating that thousands of tons of pressure were applied to rapidly force cutting teeth into granite. The sawcuts in the sarcophagus in the King's Chamber of the Great Pyramid are examples he pondered. When I consulted with materials scientist Michel Barsoum, he assured me that all gems, including diamond, invariably have microscopic flaws and cracks. Barsoum added that under the concentrated stress Petrie proposed, gems will break. This is what happens in experiments, too.

On one hand, jewel-tipped saws will not work, because jewels will fracture when used in saws. Alfred Lucas pointed out many problems with the idea that toothed gems could be made at all with the technological level of ancient Egypt. On the other hand, Petrie collected artifacts made with sharp points, along with opinions from machinists, to demonstrate that features on certain artifacts cannot be the result of rubbing or grinding with an abrasive. Petrie also collected artifacts, such as those made with diorite, exhibiting many feet of continuous cutting. The entire enigma is solved by geopolymerization.

Pointed flints, tube drills, wood-cutting instruments and other Pyramid Age tools are perfect for cutting into uncured and semicured objects made with hard stone aggregates and a geopolymeric binder. Now that the binder has crystallized, artifacts made of hard rock are wholly crystalline (see below for "geopolymeric metamorphism"). While many people argue that hard stone was somehow cut through rapidly, in reality the evidence shows that material was in a pliable or partially cured state when cut.

Summary

Weathered basalt was excavated on a huge scale at the Gebel el-Qatrani quarries. Harrell and Bown found no tool marks in the quarries at Gebel el-Qatrani. The absence of tool marks suggests that a great deal of loose debris and very weathered rock was removed. In other words, there was no need to strike the rock surfaces with heavy blows that leave tool marks.

Weathered basalt debris is perfect for geosynthesis. Although Old Kingdom paving slabs and other objects match the mineral profile of the Gebel el-Qatrani basalt quarries, these artifacts do not have the extremely fine-grained texture of basalt. The coarser texture of the artifacts demonstrates that the massive amount of weathered, powdery basalt debris excavated at Gebel el-Qatrani was agglomerated to produce temple slabs, large sarcophagi and many construction blocks in Old Kingdom pyramid complexes. There is no other accounting for the extraction of thousands of tons of basalt at Gebel el-Qatrani that does not match the texture of the Old Kingdom artifacts. There is no other logical explanation for why the Old Kingdom artifacts have a medium- to coarse-grained diabase texture, representative of diabase not found in the Fayum at Gebel el-Qatrani.

The road leading from Gebel el-Qatrani to Lake Moeris is largely paved with sandstone slabs, which are probably agglomerated stone. Stretches of preserved roadway are paved with slabs that are excellent for study. The slabs exhibit no tool marks and fit together closely with no mortar between them.

Sandstone slabs can be readily agglomerated with clay, lime, water, natron and local sand. Such slabs can be packed so that they are tight-fitting and relatively flat like the road slabs. The slabs will look like natural sandstone to the naked eye and under an ordinary microscope.

No quarried basalt blocks are strewn along the roadside. Instead, the archaeological record shows heaps of basalt fragments, as would be expected from accidental spills from baskets packed with basalt fragments.

The road surfaces show no wear from the transportation of thousands of tons of massive blocks. The evidence suggests that only the weight of men carrying aggregate-filled baskets, or perhaps donkeys carrying filled pots or baskets, went along the road.

The basalt (diabase) temple slabs associated with the Great Pyramid of Giza exhibit features showing that they were cut through very rapidly—a sure sign that they are the product of alchemical stonemaking.

Altogether, the archaeological evidence at Gebel el-Qatrani, the evidence from its associated quarry road, microscopical examinations comparing Old Kingdom basalt (diabase) artifacts with the Gebel el-Qatrani basalt outcrop, and the evidence for rapid cutting on the temple slabs all demonstrate that basalt debris from Gebel el-Qatrani was synthesized on a massive scale for Old Kingdom pyramid complexes. The archaeological evidence that so strongly opposes the standard carve/hoist construction paradigm serves to prove the large-scale use of artificial rock for pyramid complexes during Egypt's Old Kingdom.

❧ Chapter 24 ❧
More Hard-Rock Proof

Authorities in the Egyptological community take it for granted that the ancient hard rock extraction sites have all been confirmed by geologists. These old places are the sources of hard stone for Old Kingdom vessels, statues, sarcophagi, and temples. But in the last chapter we encountered an ancient, abandoned basalt extraction site that does not serve Egypt today. In the Pyramid Age, 4,500 years ago, it teemed with life as workers gathered its basalt debris to make the kind of exquisite masonry work that awed Petrie and astonishes stone cutters. We encountered a deeper, untold story that Egyptology never knew. We now explore equally intriguing pieces of the overall picture.

In the early 1900s, Alfred Lucas (1867–1945), Chief Chemist of the Research Laboratory of the Egyptian Museum, in Cairo, was involved in documenting quarry sources. His book *Ancient Materials and Industries* (1926) remains an Egyptological standard.

Since Alfred Lucas' time, researchers have much more extensively investigated Egyptian quarries and compared them with stone artifacts. In Egypt and Sudan, 162 ancient quarries have been located. Since 1989, geologist James A. Harrell and petrologist Vernon Max Brown visited at least 122 of them. They used a variety of analytical techniques to examine representative rock samples they selected from over 75 of them. Harrell and Brown visited and sampled all of the quarries that provided hard rock to the ancient Egyptians.

Geochemist Dietrich Klemm also visited about 80 ancient Egyptian rock extraction sites and has taken samples. He also performed analytical investigations on specimens he collected. He and his wife, Egyptologist Rosemarie Klemm, studied inscriptions found at quarries, dated pottery remains, and catalogued the types of tool marks found at rock extraction sites. Their investigations resulted in a chronology that shows the style of rock-excavation techniques used during various historical periods. In some cases, inscriptions serve to identify the reign — sometimes even the year — in which rock extraction took place.

Weathered outcrops with loose, powdery or friable rock debris are of minor interest to investigators as they study the history of block quarrying. They are trying to understand how huge building blocks were quarried for Old Kingdom pyramid complexes and other architecture. But friable rock is sometimes mentioned in their reports. Some even document excavations into the weathered outcrops. So, the studies support the premise that loose rock debris was excavated — and that blocks weighing several tons were not quarried during the Pyramid Age operations at the hard-rock quarries.

Studies also compared the petrography of quarry samples with artifacts of the same rock type. I show below that these investigations are consistent with geopolymerization, too, but not with artifacts that are natural rock. Independently tested artifacts include samples from vessels, statues, and temples.

Geopolymeric Metamorphism

It is important to know that geopolymerized rock undergoes secondary crystallization.[1] This means that tiny crystals of various types gradually form in a geopolymerized rock matrix. A gradual rearrangement of the alumina and silica into ordered structures takes place. Something similar takes place with glass. Solid glass is technically a liquid because it has no crystal structure. But as glass ages, it very slowly crystallizes. Once it has crystallized, it can be mistaken for quartz, which is nature's glass.

Both natural rock and the rock-making geopolymeric binder undergo gradual changes in mineralogy.[2] Over long periods of time, natural rock can alter deep within the Earth's crust because of heat, pressure, or chemical reactions. When natural rock is altered, it has tiny secondary crystals formed between its larger rock grains. The same thing will happen with geopolymeric rock concrete. The geopolymeric binder can crystallize so that tiny secondary crystals form between the larger natural rock particles in the concrete.

To examine the potential, Davidovits made basalt similar to that found in Mesopotamian temple ruins. He melted alumina and silica minerals and then added calcium carbonate. Upon cooling, his material forms synthetic basalt (solidified lava). Fine aluminosilicate crystals form in his basalt as it cools. So, this rock is like natural basalt.

He pulverized this synthetic lava and used it to produce a geopolymeric binder that sets at room temperature. Yet, the rock he made at room temperature is classified as a "vitreous (glassy, amorphous) matrix" by X-ray tests. Thirty-seven microprobe quantitative analyses were carried out by the Bureau de Recherches Géologiques et Minières, in France. The researchers determined the mineralogical profile of his rock.

The electron microprobe analysis showed that his matrix is not homogeneous. It instead contains an internal varying distribution of silica and alumina. This preparation can in time crystallize into minerals including amphibole, plagioclase, and pyroxene.[3] These are all minerals that make rock very hard. Within only twenty years, certain other minerals have formed in rocks that Davidovits made wholly at room temperature, too.

These geopolymers begin to set as soon as he mixes the ingredients. While still fluid, fine aggregates or stone powder can be mixed in, resulting in material with a claylike consistency that can be sculpted with simple tools, shaped on a potter's wheel, or poured into a mold. Once the geopolymer has hardened (at room temperature), the object is wholly stone. It will gradually undergo geopolymeric metamorphism.

Thousands of years later, such objects can be expected to have "altered," meaning that the geopolymeric binder crystallized. So, minerals have been created that do not match the powdered rock aggregates put into the original rock-making mixture.

The other thing we need to know is that in natural plagioclase (feldspar) rock, a similar natural process is called sausseritization. Similarly, Davidovits gets the sausseritization effect when he uses feldspar with his geopolymeric binder at room temperature. Feldspar can alter to different fine-grained minerals (albite, epidote, calcite, sericite and zeolite).

With this information about geopolymeric metamorphism in mind, we are equipped to consider ancient Egyptian artifacts examined by geologists and see how they compare to natural rock from the quarries. Just as with basalt extraction, a lot of information that makes no sense suddenly makes perfect sense when the geoplymer paradigm is factored in.

Altered Rock Artifacts

Stone vessels classified as granodiorite date from Predynastic times to the 3rd Dynasty.[4] In the 1980s, Barbara Aston, a petrographer who specialized in pottery when working with the Theban Mapping Project, examined granodiorite statues and vessels. She found that they were heavily saussuritized. Saussuritization usually imparts a greenish color to the rock.[5] She wrote:

> The heavily saussuritized feldspars indicate that the rock has been altered. It is notable that most of the mineral grains lack developed crystal faces.[6]

The lack of developed crystal faces is important and may indicate crystallization of a geopolymeric binder, rather than true saussuritization as it occurs in nature.

Aston noted that granodiorite in Egyptian outcrops do not show signs of saussuritization. So, she concluded that the source of ancient Egyptian granodiorite artifacts had not been found. She indicated:

> The specific source of this rock is not known.[7]

Granodiorite can be found at from Aswan. But none of the representative samples of granodiorite from Aswan examined by Barbara Aston, James Harrell, and other researchers show any sign of saussuritization.[8]

The mystery disappears when the artifacts are determined to be composites of weathered rock bonded with a geopolymeric binder that has at least partially crystallized. The words of Joseph Davidovits concerning saussuritization in his geopolymerized rocks bear repeating here:

> What I am trying to achieve in my lab is to get hard stone features without smelting and solidifying stone mixtures. All mineralogical analysis performed on Egyptian hard stone artifacts (stone vases) dating from the Old Kingdom demonstrate that the hard stone is not a recently (young) recrystallized, slowly solidified matrix. The hard stones are…strongly affected by saussuritization. This strange term, saussuritization, is used by geologists and petrographers when describing the alteration of hard stone constituent feldspar to albite, epidote, calcite, sericite and/or zeolite. In other words, this strange geological term suggests geopolymerization, not smelting and slowly cooling. We always get this saussuritization mechanism when, in my lab, we solidify hard stone replicates obtained by the agglomeration of feldspar aggregates and modern geopolymer binder.[9]

Barbara Aston examined thin sections (paper-thin slices of rock mounted on glass slides) of vessels and found that those dating from the Old Kingdom and before were predominantly altered rock.[10] She was unable to find matching quarry sources.

Unable to explain the difference between the artifacts and the quarries, she proposed that the Egyptians must have selectively chosen altered rock because of its superior properties. She wrote:

> A high portion of the plutonic* rocks which the Egyptians used for stone vessels, when examined in thin section, turn out to be altered rather than fresh rock. It is possible that the Egyptians selectively chose the more altered rocks, as the secondary intergrowth of crystals during alteration makes them tougher, more cohesive, and less likely to split and fracture under stress than unaltered rocks.[11]

If the earliest Egyptians had actually sought out and quarried hard, altered rock, as Aston proposed, we would find an altogether different scenario in quarries confined to Old Kingdom usage. The Faiyum basalt quarries present a good example. As I explained in the last chapter, all the hard basalt was left untouched and still remains today. In contrast, thousands of tons of basalt debris were removed from the rock extraction sites—enough to serve Old Kingdom usage. The same is true at Giza; the hard limestone was left untouched and the weakly-bound rock was utilized. So, the geopolymer premise holds. Besides, the tiny minerals showing that rock is altered can only be seen with a microscope—and that

---

* Plutonic rocks are those resulting from the solidification of magma. They are thoroughly crystalline.[12]

begs the question of how altered rock could be so thoroughly selectively isolated during antiquity.

Barbara Aston found no quarry match for Old Kingdom artifacts made of gabbro, diorite, marble, or serpentine. She remarked as follows about gabbro (granular igneous rock):

> The source for the gabbro found in stone vessels has not yet been determined.[13]

Aston's analysis of gabbro is consistent with the use of weathered rock cemented with a geopolymeric binder. This results in a granular texture similar to that of natural gabbro (a coarse-grained mineral containing calcium-rich plagioclase). Aston found no matching quarries for marble or serpentine, either:

> Studies of marble and serpentine produced similar negative results. Comparison of thin sections of a marble vessel and samples from the Gebel Rokham quarry north of Wadi Barramiya indicate that the latter was not the ancient source of marble exploited during the Old Kingdom. Likewise, serpentine samples collected from the Wadi Atolla and Gebel Sikhait proved to differ in thin section from the serpentine used for vessels, thus eliminating these locations as likely ancient sources.[14]

We see that although Egyptology takes for granted that all the hard rock extraction sites are accounted for, something is amiss when the quarries are studied in thin section against artifacts. None of the marble and serpentine quarries in the Egyptian environs match the vessels that Barbara Aston examined. Aston could not find a matching quarry for diorite rocks, either:

> Regarding the sources of diorites, thin sections of diorite from stone vessels, and from two quarry sites, indicate that neither the diorite of Mons Claudianus nor of Wadi Semna—both worked by the Romans—was the source of the diorite used by the ancient Egyptians for stone vessels.[15]

In other words, the quarries in the Eastern and Western deserts, and in the Sinai, were worked during the Roman period. She was compelled to check these sites opened in Roman times because she found that Aswan diorite does not match the artifacts.

Experts assume that diorite for Predynastic and Old Kingdom vessels came from somewhere at Aswan (except for the variety called "Chephren diorite").[16] But Barbara Aston found that none of the thin sections of diorite vessels from Egyptian vessels matched Aswan diorite.[17] She concluded:

> …diorite used for stone vessels have not yet been pinpointed.[18]

The diorite outcrop at Aswan is small, and the rock is not suitable for cutting into objects. It fractures very easily. John Ball described Aswan diorite this way:

> …frequently much crushed…the masses break very irregularly owing to numerous cracks, and…even where sound blocks can be extracted, the stone is still very difficult to work, breaking capriciously along lines other than the wedge lines.[19]

Diorite was used for vessels from Predynastic times to the 4th Dynasty. According to Barbara Aston, only one diorite vessel dates to the New Kingdom.

Geopolymer chemistry is important to some of the most fundamental questions of Egyptology. Egyptologists have long been concerned with the roots of Egyptian culture. The issues involve whether the art of making hard stone vessels developed along the Nile or was introduced by invaders.

Theories of Egyptian cultural roots include determining where hard stone like diorite came from. When there is no match between a Predynastic stone vessel and the known rock extraction sites, arguments favoring outside cultural roots are strengthened. But when geopolymerization is factored in, we see that friable diorite from Aswan may have been the source material for diorite vessels—potentially negating this particular argument favoring invasion. Much more can be understood about cultural exchange when this budding technology of ancient geosynthesis has been fully explored cross culturally.

The Rosetta Stone

The Rosetta Stone may hold more secrets than the key to deciphering Egyptian hieroglyphs. There is enough uncertainty about the geology of the Rosetta Stone to warrant a new investigation to determine if it may be geopolymeric. The Rosetta Stone was originally part of a larger stele inscribed with the Memphis Decree issued in 196 B.C. The Rosetta Stone itself was later found in the Egyptian town called Rosetta in 1799 by Napoleon's soldiers. It was later made famous when Jean-François Champollion utilized its inscriptions to decipher ancient Egyptian hieroglyphic writing. A few years ago, it was cleaned of the modern wax and other substances used when making impressions of its inscriptions. This cleaning proved to be a convenient time for a geological study. A team including Andrew Middleton, of the British Museum, and Dietrich Klemm, performed the geological analyses.

I studied their scientific paper and recognized that it shows that the Rosetta Stone has geological features that fit with the anomalies we have been exploring. The study describes it as altered rock (in this case less altered than the best match for the possible quarry of origin). The tiny secondary crystals (that characterize altered rock) in the Rosetta Stone may be gepolymeric binder that has crystallized. Plagioclase is the most abundant mineral in the Rosetta Stone. Microprobe analysis showed that basaltic rock made by Joseph Davidovits can gradually convert to plagioclase (and other minerals found in the Rosetta Stone).

Because of its abundance of tiny crystals, the Rosetta Stone is commonly thought of as basalt (even though some of its mineral grains can be seen with the naked eye). But its chemistry is not that of basalt / diabase. Andrew Middleton and Dietrich Klemm observed that its chemistry is more like that of granodiorite—and so they suggest that it should be classified as granodiorite despite its texture. Like granodiorite, it is high in quartz (which removes it from the basalt / diabase category)—much like the granodiorite of the King's Chamber of the Great Pyramid.

While saussuritization takes place in the natural bedrock, it is also a strong feature of aging geopolymerized rock. The Rosetta Stone is saussuritized.

Andrew Middleton and Dietrich Klemm made a straightforward analysis under the assumption that the Rosetta Stone is natural rock. To try to determine where the rock came from, they examined a great many quarry samples. They finally settled on a quarry south of Aswan as the best match. Middleton and Klemm were very cautious—rather than assertive—about this quarry match. The reason is that there are both commonalities and differences between the Rosetta Stone and the quarry they decided upon.

The Rosetta Stone is anomalous for several reasons: According to Middleton and Klemm, it mostly has the texture of the basalt group, but it has the mineralogy of granodiorite instead. If it is natural granodiorite, some inconclusive process has altered its texture. It has not been matched with a particular quarry with confidence. It is saussuritized and less altered than the quarry decided upon as the closest match. According to Middleton and Klemm, the Rosetta

204 The Great Pyramid Secret by Margaret Morris

Stone is close to tonalite, also called quartz diorite (see below for the very strange case of quartz diorite artifacts of ancient Egypt). To settle the issue of its true nature, close observation can determine if its rock grains were cut through or pushed aside during the inscribing process. Close examination of its inscriptions could determine if the stone was rapidly cut, too. This kind of observation is completely non-destructive. If the Rosetta Stone passes this kind of scrutiny in favor of geopolymerization, then a new study involving scientists who are experts at detecting geopolymerization could study the sample already removed—so that no further destruction need take place. A new study is warranted to determine if the Rosetta Stone presents an example proving the survival of the know-how to geopolymerize stone during Greek times in Egypt.[20]

Granite (Granodiorite)

Barbara Aston found no quarry match for granodiorite. Gigantic objects like the 1,000-ton statue of Ramses II at the Ramesseum, in Thebes, and those weighing 1,000 tons and more that stood in Tanis, should leave considerable archaeological traces of their transport and manufacture—if they were quarried, carved, and hauled. Ramses II's colossus at Thebes stood about 60 feet tall. We would reasonably expect enormous trenches at Aswan and traces of enormous barges or physical traces of long expanses of flat hauling tracks and dry docks.*

One might argue that later quarrying at Aswan erased all traces of enormous trenches. But a late 1800s report by J.A.W. Dawson emphasized the striking difference between Ramses II's gigantic statue at the Ramesseum and Aswan granite:

> The stupendous fragments of this statue confirm the description of Diodorus, who comments in not only for its great size, but for the "excellence of the stone." This is, in fact, not a granite, but a mass taken from a thick bed of gneiss of fine colour and uniform texture, and more dense and imperishable than any true granite.[21]

The density may suggest the use of the rammer, a tool typically used to compact rammed earth. The Geopolymer Institute team used a rammer to compact imitation pyramid blocks made with geopolymeric limestone concrete. This drives out excess water. These stones are strong and dense because of compression. Africa and Mediterranean countries still make structures with rammed earth and compress the material with simple ramming devices. Building with rammed earth dates back to at least 7000 B.C. in Pakistan. Material called mud-brick, adobe, terre crue, pisé, or rammed earth is Egypt's oldest building material, too. Many of the adobe construction techniques carried over to working with agglomerated stone.

J.A.W. Dawson also provided a description of a granite statue of Ramses II in the British Museum:

> One [statue] of Ramses II in the British Museum is a stone from the junction of red granite and diorite, and thus consists of two distinct kinds of rock.[22]

---

* A dry dock is a huge deep water chamber, and it would have to be large enough to accommodate a ship of the size needed to haul statues weighing 1,000 tons and more. Dry docks are constructed with thick masonry floors and walls. They have no roofs. A ship is floated into the structure and locked in by gates. Water is then pumped out of the chamber so that the ship or barge settles onto a cradle for stability. The water stays locked out until workers have finished loading the docked vessel. This whole process is reversed when the ship is ready for launch, so that it can be floated out of its docking

The statue brings to mind the early composite vessels. As mentioned, they were made with more than one type of stone and present excellent evidence for manmade stone.

The King's Chamber of the Great Pyramid is wholly made of granite (granodiorite according to Harrell). Geologist Robert G. McKinney observed close-up photographs of the rock matrix of wall blocks in the King's Chamber. He observed that the crystals take on a preferred orientation, as though they have been packed down in a concrete mix. The wavy, hairline joints between the wall blocks, where protuberances of the blocks mate, are characteristic of molded stones. Without a thin section for analysis, the stone cannot be properly studied.

The Strange Case of Quartz Diorite

In the early 1980s, artifacts made with quartz diorite were examined by Joanna McFarlane and her team of researchers.[23] Those researchers encountered a very strange circumstance.

A beautifully-made quartz diorite statue of the 18th Dynasty Pharaoh Tuthmosis III was excavated in perfect condition from the Deir el-Bahari Temple complex, located in western Thebes. The statue was in such good condition that it still exhibited some of its decorative surface paint. But within a few years, the statue developed deep cracks—despite the nature of quartz diorite. Quartz diorite has the composition of diorite, but also contains large amounts of quartz. The deterioration became so severe that the statue had to be strengthened with ordinary concrete to prevent it from collapsing under its own weight.

Many other statues made of very hard igneous rock also deteriorated after being unearthed. Examples are a torso of Queen Hatschepsut, now in the Louvre, in Paris, some statues in the National Museum, in Cairo, and several diorite figures in the Boston Museum of Fine Art. In sharp contrast, other diorite statues remain in perfect condition, like those of Khafra and Menkure found at Giza.

Joanna McFarlane and her team decided to investigate the cause of the mysterious cases of the deterioration of such hard igneous rock. They gained permission from the president of the Egyptian Antiquities Organization and its Permanent Committee to remove two samples of diorite that had already fallen from Egyptian monuments.

One had fallen from the dioritic doorway of Queen Hatshepsut's chapel, located adjacent to and immediately north of the Main Sanctuary of the Karnak temples. They found another diorite sample near the pyramid in the Temple of Mentuhotep I, located in the Deir el-Bahari complex. The researchers think this sample originated from the adjacent collapsed Temple of Tuthmosis III.

After careful inspection, they determined their sample to be identical in condition and composition to the above-mentioned statue of Tuthmosis III, found near the center of his Temple. In other words, their sample matched his above-mentioned statue found in perfect condition, but which badly deteriorated within a few years of being unearthed.

Taking precautions to avoid contaminating their samples, Joanna McFarlane and her colleagues subjected them to a number of scientific testing procedures. These included X-ray fluorescence, thin-section analyses, atomic absorption, and neutron-activation analyses. Their investigation of thin sections from both samples resulted in the samples being classified as quartz diorite.[24] They looked like normal diorite.

But then something strange happened. During the first water washes of the samples prepared for the atomic-absorption analysis, many of the fragments broke apart. After being stirred overnight in water, the samples disintegrated completely. All that was left of them was a slurry. The researchers reported:

They formed a slurry at the bottom of a suspension of what was suspected to be fine alumino-silicate.[25]

The researchers found nothing on the surface of the rocks that could have caused them to be so structurally weak as to fall apart from overnight stirring in water.

The researchers theorized that salt (sodium chloride) was responsible for the deterioration. Joanna McFarlane and her team found nothing suspicious other than ordinary salt in the matrix of their quartz diorite samples. The researchers theorized that salt weakened the stone from repeated swelling (crystallization) and contraction (dissolving). The sandstone artifacts of the south are prone to damage because of salt introduced into the soil after the construction of the Aswan Dam. The Dam prevents salts from washing out of the soils. But sandstone in Egypt's south is mostly soft rock to begin with.

W.M.F. Petrie found a great deal of crystallized salt thickly encrusted on Khafra's undamaged sarcophagus in the Second Pyramid of Giza. Heavy salt encrustation appears on inner limestone walls of pyramids and must periodically be cleansed. The King's Chamber of the Great Pyramid must be frequently cleansed of salt. These blocks made with granodiorite are in good condition.

So, salt may not be the root cause of the deterioration of the quartz diorite objects that fell apart and turned to a slurry when stirred in water. Joanna McFarlane reported that the quartz diorite altered to clay. The salt-damage theory does not explain the alteration of the quartz diorite to clay (an alteration process that will greatly weaken a stone). Natural quartz diorite does not fall apart or behave this way. It stands to reason that a natural quartz diorite artifact will not fall apart a few years after being unearthed or turn to a slurry overnight in water. A logical explanation is that the quartz diorite statues that are falling apart in museums were made with a New Kingdom rock-making formula that was inferior, and did not withstand the test of time.

The Deir el-Bahari Temple

One of the quartz diorite samples McFarlane and her team investigated came from the Deir el-Bahari Temple complex. It was from the Temple of Pharaoh Tuthmosis III, a nephew of Queen Hatschepsut. Tuthmosis III's Temple is near that of Hatshepsut's at Deir el-Bahari.

Queen Hatschepsut's Deir el-Bahari Temple was investigated by Dietrich Klemm. He performed a geological analysis of its limestone terrace. Klemm wrote:

> Hatschepsut's quarries. Location: approximately 3 km north west from Qurna (western Thebes). Stone type: grey-white porous limestone. In a wadi East of the Valley of the Kings Tombs, there is a large quarry which, according to the local inhabitants, was the place where the stones for the Hatschepsut terrace Temple came from…It is a relatively soft limestone, strikingly very friable, which at first glance would not be suitable for building purposes. Comparative analysis made on this quarry stone shows that it is actually the same material as the limestone of the Hatschepsut Temple at Deir-el-Bahari, confirming that this was evidently Hatschepsut's quarry.[26]

The limestone in this quarry is so friable that it readily disaggregates in water. It is perfect for making limestone concrete. No stone crushing is necessary. This is important because it means that dolomite crystals remain intact when this rock debris is geopolymerized. The intact crystals contribute to its natural appearance. So, it is easily mistaken for natural rock by geologists.

Klemm used a powerful microscope to compare the limestone of the quarry with that of Hatschepsut's Temple. In both, he found intact rhombus-shaped dolomite crystals ranging from about 0.005 to 0.02 mm in length. Klemm remarked:

It is very easy to determine that the samples taken from the Hatschepsut temple were extracted in this quarry.[27]

So, Klemm matched this limestone bed with the limestone of Hatschepsut's Temple. But the limestone of Hatschepsut's Temple is much harder than the bedrock it came from. Klemm also compared how both eroded when subjected to the same climatic conditions. He found that erosion completely destroyed the structure of the limestone from the quarry. The material is so friable and porous that Klemm remarked:

Its properties make it not recommendable at all for any construction purpose.[28]

Klemm observed that the limestone of Hatschepsut's Temple exhibited almost no erosion.[29] But Klemm did not offer an explanation for the dramatic difference between the quarry and temple limestone. It is logical to suspect that, like Giza limestone that was converted into stronger rock by adding a geopolymer cement, the limestone from Hatschepsut's quarry was converted to limestone concrete to build Queen Hatschepsut's Temple. Further testing is warranted.

Khufu's Diorite Quarry

In 1932, Reginald Engelbach was Keeper of the Egyptian Museum, in Cairo. One day, officials of the Egyptian Army came to his office at the Cairo Museum. They had discovered some steles in the Nubian Desert, 40 miles northwest of Abu Simbel. Engelbach examined the steles and found that one bears the name of Djedefra, a son of Khufu. Engelbach realized that the quarry that yielded a particular kind of diorite called "Chephren diorite" may have at last been found.

Khafra's (Greek: Chephren) famous larger than lifesized statue in the Cairo Museum is made from this kind of rock. So are a number of other statues. This kind of diorite is very different than other varieties found in Egypt. But Khafra's statue is heavily sausseritized.

Engelbach made trips to Khafra's quarry area. It looks like an oasis in the middle of the desert from afar. The reason is that rock there contains a mineral called bytownite. It produces an internal blue iridescence when viewed in bright sunlight. Engelbach found banded boulders lying on the ground. The material is much like the rock (classified as a banded diorite gneiss) of which Khafra's statues are made. Joseph Davidovits also makes banded stone objects. He simply combines two different rock-making mixtures together to create bands.

Not all ancient Egyptian objects made with diorite gneiss look like Khafra's statues. Many are vastly different in appearance. Some are translucent or white with black spots or streaks. An example is the thin-walled vessel found in the Menkaure Valley Temple at Giza in 1910 (labeled anorthosite gneiss), now in the Boston Museum of Fine Arts. Another vessel, made of the same material, in this same museum is white with dark streaks. The Petrie Museum contains similar examples, including one that belonged to Khufu. These and many other examples look nothing like the boulders (90% bytownite and 10% hornblende and trace minerals) found at Khufu's quarry in Nubia.

Engelbach found something at Khufu's quarry that made no sense to him:

An interesting point arises in connexion with the diorite outcrop. Although Chephren [Khafra] is known to have had six statues of life size and over made from this material,

Cheops [Khufu] seems not to have had any stone statues at all, and other Old Kingdom kings apparently only used this diorite for statuettes and vases. Boulders are lying in the open amply sufficient for three-quarter-size statues or for any vase which might be required, yet a vast amount of deep digging occurs everywhere.[30]

Large boulders suitable for cutting monumental statues and other objects were left untouched. They are strewn on the surface of the ground. No quarrying was required to obtain them. They could simply be hauled away. But the Egyptians ignored them because they sought a different material. They needed the friable rock found there. Some rocks found there are so friable that you can pick up lumps and easily crush them to dust between your fingers. This material is perfect for agglomerating statues and vessels. Engelbach mentioned friable material, too:

> The north-east quarries proved a disappointment. With our limited personnel we could not do more than follow a quarry-face down for some 2 metres. At that depth we were far from the level for which the ancient quarrymen were seeking, since large quantities of strange, multi-coloured quartz, scattered over the area, which had been thrown away as useless, must have originally lain beneath the friable quartz mixture which we were able to reach.[31]

His search for a layer of high-quality banded diorite proved futile.

A site with suitable hard boulders untouched, and exhibiting a great many excavations into friable material, suggests an operation that harvested rock debris instead of large pieces suitable for carving. These particular diorite gneiss sites mined for Khufu, Khafra, and later by pharaohs of the 12th Dynasty, are not quarries in the traditional sense. There are no protruding rock faces or trenches with tool marks or other evidence of block removal. The land is entirely flat, except for boulders lying on the ground.

The ancient excavators dug into the ground in many spots, with their excavations spanning over miles. The ground exhibits large excavation pits. These areas of ground were easy to excavate. The fact that there are scattered dug-out areas, rather than one large excavation, suggests that the workers identified and attacked the most weathered spots, which were the most easily excavated. This is what took place at Giza, too: The hard stone was left untouched and the soft stone was harvested for rock-making.

Experts who investigated Khafra's quarry assume that the ancient Egyptians harvested huge boulders (which they reckon were either sitting on the ground or dug from the earth) and cut them into statues. But the evidence supports the removal of aggregate for agglomeration.

Engelbach found no abandoned blocks or boulders along the road leading away from these quarries and back to the Nile. He reported that the road was never used after ancient times. He found only small lumps of diorite gneiss strewn along the road.[32]

Engelbach found no ancient wheel tracks or wooden tracks (called sleepers). These would be needed in ancient times for hauling boulders weighing several tons on sleds. Surely, evidence of sleepers would be preserved (as they are at 12th Dynasty construction sites) if a hauling track ever existed. This is evident because Engelbach found hundreds of hoofprints that he determined were made by donkeys (the hoof marks are too narrow and straight to be camel tracks). The hoofprints show that donkey caravans went to and from the rock extraction sites. Given that donkey hoofprints remain, evidence of sleepers or block hauling would remain if it ever existed.

The evidence is consistent with donkeys carrying containers loaded with aggregate. A donkey can easily carry a load of rock debris from the quarry to the Nile for barge shipment. But a donkey cannot carry a boulder weighing several tons. Today, a donkey can carry 200 pounds over short distances. A loaded pot might weigh 20 to 40 pounds.

Engelbach stated that, "By Chephren's time [4th Dynasty], statues weighing several tons had been transported to Giza…"[33] But he found no evidence of the transport of boulders weighing several tons—he found no tracks or other evidence of heavy hauling. He simply wondered why suitable boulders were left on the ground and the Egyptians instead dug out the friable portions of the ground.

A couple of unfinished diorite vessels were found at this site in recent years. They are touted as natural rock simply because they are unfinished. But that does not follow logically. An unfinished geopolymeric object could have been just as easily abandoned as a carved one (assuming the artifact could have been carved in the first place with ancient means). It is possible that vase making was tested at the site with the interesting soil (lateritic or calcrete) there as an ingredient. It is logical to field test rock-making formulas with natural resources. The iron and kaolin in lateritic soils make them ideal for geopolymerizing hard rock vessels. Calcrete (caliche) can be burned to make lime.

Engelbach found an inscribed copper chisel at one of the rock extraction sites. He dated it to the 4th Dynasty based on associated pottery dating. It is much too soft to cut hard diorite.[34]

Starting in 1997, archaeologist Ian Shaw began visiting these lonely old excavation sites of Khufu and Khafra. Shaw's goal was to determine the logistics of harvesting and transporting boulders. Shaw and his team located a crude stone ramp that Engelbach previously examined, and they found another one. The Shaw team questioned the purpose of these isolated structures. They settled on the idea that they must be loading ramps for boulders.

The team deduced that boulders were first rocked onto the lower part of the ramp. Then they were elevated up the ramp to 5.25 feet. The boulders were then lowered down onto some kind of large vehicle. In other words, the Shaw team supposes that the isolated ramp structures accommodated loading a large vehicle. But Engelbach observed years before that the ramp is unnecessarily steep for loading large boulders. He could find no evidence that boulders were ever transported along the road that leads out of the site or hauled at the site itself.

The Shaw team recognized that a wheeled transport system was out of the question. The site has no ancient traces of wheel marks, and wheels were not used for transportation until much later times—and were never sturdy devices suitable for heavy hauling. The Shaw team had to postulate unconventional ways of moving blocks weighing several tons over long distances. They proposed that each boulder was secured onto a huge wooden raft, which was tied with cords and outfitted with inflated animal hides to provide buoyancy. The team suggests that this kind of vehicle, loaded with a boulder weighing several tons, was transported overland for ten miles to the Nile. From there, the loaded vehicle had to traverse the Nile, crossing the First Cataract (the rocky rapids in the area of Aswan) and then sail to northern Egypt.

If this kind of transport vehicle was used, tracks would extend from the ramp—showing that a large, heavy raft was moved along the ground. The tracks should run for miles and be as visible and identifiable as the donkey hoofprints that lead to the Nile. We should also expect a 4th Dynasty canal allowing the rapids at Aswan to have been bypassed. It would be a large shipping canal like the one excavated to bypass the rapids during the 6th Dynasty.

The Shaw team offers conjecture about the use of a raft, but no supporting physical evidence. The evidence at the site shows that nothing was transported except material that donkeys carried.

There are two parallel "tracks" on the original surface of the ground that emanate from the faces of the ramp the Shaw team inspected. But these "tracks" disappear only about ten yards from the faces of the ramp. Besides, the Shaw team recognizes that these "tracks" were dug rather than being the result of abrasion. The sides of the "tracks" do not exhibit the wear that would be caused by the passage of a heavy vehicle.

The ramps are easily ascended. So, rather than having been used for hauling rocks to nowhere, they may have served as lookout posts. This would allow the Egyptians to spot unfriendly people entering the area. The landscape is flat, and so a high point would be useful for that purpose.

The Telling Quarrying Methods

Above we have considered two parts of the quarry picture. First, hard stone artifacts do not match the quarries. This makes sense when we consider that a geopolymeric binder (which can gradually crystallize and produce altered rock) was added to aggregates to make many artifacts. Moreover, the evidence at Old Kingdom quarries shows that heavy chunks of rock were not hauled away. The evidence instead shows that donkeys transported rock debris from the diorite gneiss quarries to the Nile.

Second, different methods were used to extract rocks in different periods. Evidence of the various methods used to extract rock from the hard-stone quarries helps to prove the alchemical rock-making theory. The evidence also helps us trace the rise and decline of this technology.

Aswan has been a source of granite from Old Kingdom times (and probably before) to the present. The evidence at Aswan suggests that most of the ancient signs of block quarrying date from the construction of Alexandria forward. Much of the work may date to Roman times. Thousands of sites at Aswan show the removal of blocks with wedges. Engelbach suspected that iron wedges were used (he was not assertive about this point—probably because iron came along so late in Egyptian history). Since Engelbach's time, investigators have established that the earliest evidence of the use of iron wedges is observed in Greek quarries worked in the 6th century B.C.[35] A Greek colony existed in Naukratis, Egypt, in the Late Period, and Egypt was occupied by the Greeks after 332 B.C. So, Greek quarrying methods were implemented in Egyptian quarries. Until the work of Joseph Roder in 1965, Egyptologists assumed that the massive evidence of wedge quarrying at Aswan was produced by earlier, native Egyptian dynasties.[36]

So, the thousands of wedge holes at Aswan may suggest that a great deal of natural granite was quarried into blocks to build monuments for the capital city of Alexandria, founded by Alexander the Great in 332 B.C. Granite blocks, thought to have been part of the Great Lighthouse, and other granite artifacts, were found off the coast of Alexandria. Wedge holes at Aswan also likely date to Roman times. The city at Aswan (called Syene) prospered during Roman times. During that period, Aswan granite was exported to other parts of the Roman Empire. The granite incorporated into the temples dedicated to Jupiter at Baalbek, Syria, is an example.

Investigators believe that the use of pounding balls predates the use of iron wedges at Aswan. The most famous example of the pounding-ball technique is the giant unfinished granite obelisk at Aswan. It is logical to think that the use of pounding balls for working granite dates to a time when alchemical stonemaking was in very severe decline.

Joseph Davidovits suggests that there was some rivalry between the masons of the north and south. They each tended to worship gods of their own regions, too. Skills were passed from fathers to worthy sons. So, people in the north may not have shared their alchemical knowledge with people in the south. Davidovits suggests that religious philosophies about stone, and how to render it into objects, clashed during the New Kingdom and later, too. Throughout ancient Egyptian history, stone was always considered sacred. It was associated with immortality and the gods. Red stones represented the blood of Isis and so on. The geopolymer theory holds that southerners mostly created inferior stone monuments because they were stonecutters. The northern artisans created great masterpieces with agglomerated stone. Sometimes pharaohs brought these artisans to Thebes to supervise elaborate stoneworks in the south. A case in point is Pharaoh Amenhotep III enlisting Amenhotep-son-of-Hapu of Athribis to supervise the construction of the Colossi of Memnon.

A small number of failed objects remain in the Aswan quarries. Joseph Davidovits suggests that they were pounded out with pounding balls by Theban devotees of the god Amun. Other granite objects of this period may have been successfully executed and transported to temple complexes.

The quartzite quarries at Gebel Ahmar provide evidence supporting the excavation of aggregates for agglomerating stone. Reginald Engelbach found no evidence of pounding ball activity at Gebel Ahmar. Instead, he found lines of holes about two inches deep and made with a pointed tool. He believed they were made by some sort of mason's pick or a pointed tool struck with a mallet. He could not explain the rows of holes in terms of quarrying blocks.[37] Striking pointed picks with a mallet can only be expected to flake off the most weakly bound chunks useful for agglomeration. Researchers have never found enormous trenches showing the extraction of the 50-foot-high quartzite Colossi of Memnon, made during the 18th Dynasty, either.

James A. Harrell and Thomas Bown found two broken diorite mauls in the eastern basalt rock extraction site at Gebel el-Qatrani. They write:

> Prior to the advent of the iron-wedge technology, hardstones were quarried with handheld stone mauls. As can still be seen in the Aswan and other Egyptian quarries, the mauls were used to pulverize the bedrock and in so doing excavate trenches and produce leveled or shaped surfaces.[38]

Diorite mauls are useless for quarrying either basalt, quartzite, diorite or granite blocks. Mauls are stone ax heads tied to sticks by leather strips. They cannot endure hard use. It is logical to think that they were used to scrape up debris to help avoid wear and tear on the workers' hands.

Engelbach reckoned that the use of pounding balls was the first technique used at Aswan. This is fully accepted by Egyptology today. But it is reasonable to think that using mauls to scrape up debris was the first method used, long before pounding balls were needed to bash out obelisks or blocks.

Engelbach alluded to loads of weathered granite debris at Aswan:

> To find a flawless piece of granite of any great size, it was necessary to go down to a considerable depth.[39]

If we are to judge from the amount of granite found in Old Kingdom monuments, much of this surface material was removed before the era of block-bashing began. It is not unusual for granite and quartzite quarries to contain very large amounts of loose, weathered rock debris.

In 1996, Harrell inspected the granite gneiss quarries located at the south end of the Third Cataract. He reported seeing a weathered outer layer.[40] In this case, he found no evidence that mauls were used to harvest rock material. He wrote:

> The distinctive traces left by such activity [the use of mauls] are not seen on the bedrock outcrops at Tombos and Daygah. This suggests that the earliest quarrying at these sites, during the 18th and 25th dynasties, was done on loose boulders where such activity would only leave piles of chippings and dust. The more difficult to work bedrock outcrops would not have been exploited until iron tools became available.[41]

When experts find piles of dust and loose chips, and "pulverized basalt"with no evidence of block quarrying, we have an indicator of dynastic activity that sought debris for agglomerating stone. Great amounts of loose debris suggested to Harrell some kind of quarrying operation. But the granite gneiss area shows no signs of wedges or other means of block extraction.[42]

Other areas of the granite gneiss sites were worked after the introduction of iron. Harrell found holes cut to accept iron wedges. These were hammered into the rock to cause it to split. This feature dates this work in these areas to Greek or later times.

Conclusion

Hard stone quarries confined to Old Kingdom usage support only one scenario: alchemical stonemaking. Sites with histories that range over thousands of years, like the Aswan quarries and Giza, exhibit a number of rock-extraction techniques. It is a job of archaeologists and historians to understand history, and the history of science, in terms of periods. But stoneworking is treated by Egyptology in aggregate, as though nothing changed much over thousands of years except for tool mark styles. Tool marks took on a herringbone pattern or random strokes during different periods. Only when iron was introduced was there a better way of block extraction. But we have seen that the story runs much deeper.

Rock aggregates cemented with geopolymeric binder produces hard rock that looks like real rock under an ordinary microscope — with no block quarrying necessary. The geopolymeric binder is rock-forming (zeolitic). This level of quality presents a problem for scientifically establishing that hard-rock artifacts are composites instead of natural stone. The problem is almost as severe as trying to use petrography to distinguish a synthetic zeolite from its natural analog. A mineralogist will see no tell-tale signs that the synthetic zeolite was manufactured outside of the natural geological environment (unless it is a type of zeolite that does not occur in nature).

When Michel Barsoum used his expertise as a materials scientist to examine pyramid stone, he thought he would be able to distinguish a geopolymer from a natural rock very quickly. He set to work after reading this book (at the unpublished, manuscript stage). Instead of instantly detecting synthetic rock, he devoted over four years, organized an international team, and performed a great deal of research before publishing his first paper on the topic. His work has been ongoing for over five years as I write this.

My own approach to overcoming the problems is to show that the accepted theory of pyramid construction is entirely unworkable. The same evidence that disproves the carve/hoist theory proves the geopolymer theory. This book shows how massive the evidence is. Independent investigations of samples and quarries support the case for the ancient Egyptian stonemaking processes. For example, the literature supports the premise that artifacts are altered rock, such that they no longer match the quarries where the rock debris was excavated. Egypt's rock extraction sites show that weathered material was available and removed. This is true for basalt, diorite, granite gneiss, granodiorite, limestone, quartzite and other rock varieties. The transport of huge boulders is not supported for the Old Kingdom quarries in Nubia or the Faiyum or Giza.

New Kingdom and later objects must be studied on a case-by-case basis to determine whether they are natural or geopolymeric. Many New Kingdom artifacts can be expected to be products of alchemical stonemaking. Alchemical stonemaking was still alive and well, but its use was steadily declining.

Chapter 25
Simplifying Obelisks and Colossi

Despite the decline in stonemaking, items of agglomerated stone date well beyond the Old Kingdom. In these pages, we will consider artifacts that were once thought to be natural rock until curators learned that they are synthetic. There are many other candidates. Middle Kingdom beads in the Cairo Museum measuring 0.023 inch in diameter, with smaller threading holes, are examples. As mentioned, reproducing these beads would be a challenge even with modern drilling and grinding tools.[1]

To agglomerate such beads, a stonemaking mixture can be fashioned around a coated or oiled fiber so that the mix will not adhere to the fiber. The fiber with the strung beads is then suspended between two points, by securing each end of the fiber to a surface. Once the beads have sufficiently hardened, pulling the fiber out will expose the tiny threading holes. Some tiny beads in the Cairo Museum have flat bottoms, a feature suggesting that they were instead left to harden on a flat surface.[2]

It is logical to suggest that large examples of manmade stone include the monolithic quartzite sarcophagus of Pharaoh Amenemhet III and other stone objects that modern means of stone cutting cannot reproduce. The 1,000-ton and heavier colossi of Ramses II are certainly candidates. Other candidates are sarcophagi situated in niches from which they cannot be removed intact without tearing out associated doors and hallways, or without hauling a sarcophagus over a steep mountain cliff. Sarcophagi with form-fitted lids, and those with large surfaces that are extremely flat to .0002 inch are all candidates. It is logical to think that the twin seven-story-high Colossi of Memnon at Thebes are examples of geopolymerization.

Even the tomb scene documenting the transport of the colossus of Djehutihotep might be more carefully studied.[3] The operation is curious because the tomb depiction shows men pulling the colossi in an upright position. Transporting a colossus from a quarry in a recumbent position would make it much less likely to tip over. Its upright position may suggest that it was already standing when workers pulled it a short distance to a more elaborate or otherwise more suitable tomb. It was common for nobles and royalty to move the location of their tombs if they were awarded a higher social status and given a more esteemed location. Unless something proves otherwise, the tomb scene showing men hauling the colossus may have nothing to do with how it was made.

Concerning the transport of this colossus, I found insufficient evidence in the Egyptological literature of the remains of the necessary long, flat tracks from the Eastern Desert to the Nile across from el-Bersha. There is an ancient road from Hatnub. It undulates and leads to the Nile in the general region. The colossus of Djehutihotep is thought to have been transported to el-Bersha, in Middle Egypt (on the east bank of the Nile), from the Hatnub quarries in the Eastern Desert. The distance from Hatnub to el-Bersha is roughly ten and 1/2 miles. Tugging a 60-ton statue for miles presents severe problems with the system shown in Djehutihotep's tomb painting. The Hatnub quarry and its environs are very rough terrain. The quarry itself is still characterized by loose rock debris. Inscriptions there show a history of rock extraction from Khufu's time down to Roman times. The late activity makes it difficult to sort out cutting and hauling work. But this instance of hauling a 60-ton colossus from the quarry to an Egyptian town, by the method shown in the stele, is called into serious doubt.

Egyptian craftsmen of the 18th and 19th Dynasties produced numerous colossi and huge obelisks. Moving and erecting obelisks was a real technical challenge for engineers from Roman times to the 19th century. Teams managed to transport Egyptian obelisks and set them up in Constantinople, Paris, London, New York, and Rome.[4]

Although engineers ingeniously executed each operation, and their efforts shed light on the engineering problems, these projects and numerous other studies have not determined how the ancient Egyptians raised their tallest obelisks.[5] According to Reginald Engelbach's calculations, 2,000 men were required to pull the 227 ton obelisk at Luxor up a ramp.[6] Reginald Engelbach contemplated the theory that engineers led obelisks as high as possible before allowing them to slowly descend within funnel-like brick constructions filled with sand. The method involves removing the sand as workers pull an obelisk into position from the opposite direction with ropes attached to its upper portion. Reginald Engelbach dismissed the theory as unworkable, and Egyptologists have found no such brick constructions or traces of sufficiently long ramps.[7] The ramp needed would be too long to fit into temple enclosures, which were already densely covered with religious buildings and other monuments.

A shorter ramp presents its own problems. Engineers have not figured out how the Egyptians could have calculated the centers of gravity of obelisks. That is, they do not know how workers could have figured out how obelisks would descend into their exact positions on pedestals. The problem is one of controlling movement, to guide an obelisk so that its corners line up exactly with those of its pedestal.[8]

In 1997, the Nova science series titled *Secrets of Lost Empires* experimented with concrete obelisks weighing 40 tons. These units were too small to properly address the problem. Compare these 40 ton weights to a 455 ton obelisk built for Pharaoh Tuthmosis III—or the 1,000-ton and heavier colossi of Pharaoh Ramses II. They stood on pedestals.

The Nova crew had considerable difficulties raising the 40 ton obelisks. One was successfully raised. The other was stuck in a partially raised position at the close of the televised obelisk-raising experiment.

Experts do not know how ancient Egyptians could have transported the largest standing monoliths overland for long distances to the edge of the desert or through fields to the construction sites—a far different problem than hauling weights along a relatively short, flat track. Formidable problems include loading huge objects onto large barges so they can be floated along the Nile. Serious problems apply to granite obelisks because there is no canal at Aswan leading to the Nile, and no evidence of a drydock.

Determining how the obelisks could have been erected is even more challenging.[9] For Ramses II's colossi located in Tanis—some weighing more than 1,000 tons—granite would have to be transported about 600 miles from Aswan. It is logical to suggest that the builders transported baskets of granite debris on barges from Aswan to Tanis, in northern Egypt. They then used the debris to fabricate colossi on the spot within Ramses' temple complexes.

An ancient text mentions a pair of 172-foot-tall obelisks built for the 18th Dynasty Pharaoh-Queen Hatshepsut. Dieter Arnold dismissed them as a "fairy tale." He considers it impossible to move and erect an obelisk taller than the obelisk of Pharaoh Tuthmosis III weighing 445 to 550 tons.[10]

But the ability to fashion a 172-foot-tall obelisk directly in place with agglomerated rock suggests that Hatshepsut's text was no mere fairy tale. Besides, Pliny the Elder witnessed and reported even taller obelisks built for Pharaoh Ramses II. Pliny indicated that one was 230 feet high. He said that Ramses also had one that was 200 feet high—and that each of its sides was 17 feet wide.[11]

Reginald Engelbach contemplated inscriptions concerning twin obelisks, each 186 feet high, recorded in the Theban tomb of Djutiy. Engelbach recognized that unless these obelisks were vastly thicker than all others known, they would break apart under their own weight during transport. Fabricating the stone on the spot would eliminate the problem.

Dieter Arnold commented on inscriptions engraved on the bases of a pair of 98-foot-high obelisks built for Pharaoh-Queen Hatshepsut in front of Pylon V at Karnak. The inscriptions state that it took only seven months to place her obelisks. Arnold wrote:

> Quarrying hard stones with stone tools was a difficult and time consuming activity, but one that apparently did not create real problems. We are told in the inscriptions of the base of the obelisk of Hatshepsut that quarrying and moving the pair of 30 meter high obelisks in front of Pylon V of Karnak took only 7 months.[12]

Modern comparative experiments are lacking, so we cannot readily determine whether or not it is feasible to carry out all the tasks in seven months. It may be possible to extract obelisks of this size in seven months by bashing out quarries with pounding balls. But the more difficult problem would be transporting them from Aswan. There is no canal there, and the surface is not flat, and there is no evidence of a drydock. The remains of a drydock would be enormous and conspicuous.

Although larger weights have been moved along flat surfaces in modern times, no modern project has raised a 1,000-ton (comparable to the statues of Ramses II) object onto a pedestal. An 18th century project ordered by the Russian Empress Catherine the Great employed 400 men to move a granite boulder weighing about 1,500 tons. It was transported about four miles over land. Having served as a base for a bronze equestrian statue of Peter the Great, the boulder did not require raising or setting on a pedestal.

Her crew spent less than six months hauling the granite boulder (called the Thunder Stone) to St. Petersburg. The men utilized a windlass hauling machine to move the boulder on a road that was specially cut through a forest. The haulers worked with large friction balls that were alternatively placed and removed within grooves affixed on each side of this road. After moving the boulder about four miles, they pushed it onto a great barge. It was then taken by water about another four miles to land near its present location. The boulder is 17 feet high, 42 feet long at the base, 36 feet long on top, and 21 feet wide.

But erecting even 320 ton obelisks on pedestals presents an entirely different set of problems than moving weights along flat surfaces or on barges. Hatshepsut's inscriptions, mentioned above, may alert us to the existence of a special technology that simplified the tasks. We have already considered evidence favoring an agglomeration process for statues dating from her reign and for the terrace of her Deir el-Bahari Temple. So, it is reasonable to question the nature of her obelisks, too.

Making Obelisks

In theory, to make obelisks, workers swept up fine granite particles and transported them in containers overland or by river barge to the construction sites. After the pedestals were built, the tall sides of obelisks would be built from the pedestals up. This eliminates the problems of aligning obelisks on pedestals.

Workers packed the stone mix to make it very dense and release excess water. With the core constructed, the workers could refine and inscribe the obelisk surface as they worked their way down. All the while, they would tear down any ramp or scaffolding they were standing on. Workers inscribed the obelisk surfaces before the stone became too hard. If necessary, to produce the outer surface, a coating of granite-making mix could be plastered over the granite before it got too hard. Then the inscriptions were made before the granite coating cured.

For the small obelisks of the Old Kingdom, light wooden scaffolding was suitable. For the taller New Kingdom obelisks, earthen ramps could be short and fan out around the obelisks. Egyptologists found small ramps in this configuration in association with an obelisk.[13] But these small ramps are useless for raising obelisks the hard way.

Anyone who wants to try this experimentally should remember that Joseph Davidovits' own imitation limestone pyramid block project showed the importance of working in a dry environment, like Egypt, when making stone with the very simple geopolymer formula described in this book. His team had to overcome considerable problems when making blocks on humid and rainy days in France. The simple formula given in this book would most likely only endure over the long-term in warm, dry environments, too. A higher quality, modern formula is needed for long term endurance in climates that seasonally fluctuate between warm and freezing. Davidovits' team had to work with unrefined kaolin, too. The scientists working in this area of research have not discovered the formula Egyptians may have used for granite, or determined that granite was geopolymerized at all.

My contention that granite was agglomerated is based on the surface features of some granite wall blocks (their wavy, interlocking hairline joints characteristic of agglomerated stone), and signs of rapid cutting, merged blocks in Khafra's Valley Temple, sarcophagi and cores that cannot be replicated when tooling natural granite, colossi too large to transport or set on pedestals, and the otherwise puzzling way certain obelisks and sarcophagi are situated, and the lack of a canal or drydock at Aswan needed to facilitate the transportation of the largest granite monoliths. More research on granite is warranted. It is also hard to imagine that anyone who could geopolymerize stone would cut, haul or raise granite in ways that are impossible today with brute force.

Testing Granite

The Egyptians did eventually quarry large pieces of granite. The pounding ball marks on the failed obelisk at Aswan provide an example. The many iron-wedge marks at Aswan made after 500 B.C. are examples. A number of tests can help identify synthetic granite. One way is to measure entrance and exit ways of underground tombs to determine if they will allow for the passage of sarcophagi or not.

One test determines iron orientation. When magnetic grains like iron settle in water, they do so under the influence of the Earth's magnetic field. In natural granite, iron will orient to the Earth's field. But in a granite concrete made at room temperature, the grains will be disturbed. So, the overall iron orientation will be disturbed.

Other criteria are the veins commonly found in natural granite, bruising from pounding balls, and the quality of inscriptions. To inscribe natural granite, workers might have used abrasive sand and/or chert, a very hard rock. The results with chert will be somewhat crude. There will be a noticeable difference between such inscriptions and those more crisp than can be made with a modern diamond drill. Signs of rapid cutting are important, too.

Iron can be used to strike freshly quarried rose granite (syenite). A mason can tear crystals off by striking them with pointed tools hit with wooden mallets (to absorb shock). Some granites are easier to fashion than the hard red granite from Aswan. Some granites are riddled with black mica, which has a hardness of 2.5 on Mohs' scale—the same hardness as plaster. Mica crystals are weak points in the rock, which masons can strike with a pointed instrument (hit with a mallet) to tear into this rock. Sometimes soft black mica crystals are mistaken for amphiboles, which requires a tempered steel tool to penetrate.

Pink and gray granite called syenite (from Aswan) contains mica. Egyptians used pink syenite during the New Kingdom. Because of the decline of the alchemical stonemaking technology, it is to be expected that many objects of post-Old and Middle Kingdom times are natural, carved syenite granite.

By toiling long and hard, Denys Stocks made a single hieroglyphic incision in rose granite when using only flint and abrasives.[14] His results are also useful for comparing with the crisp hieroglyphs and sharp-point etchings in diorite and granite objects of ancient Egypt. As mentioned, Roger Hopkins remarked that hieroglyphic inscriptions on certain obelisks would be difficult to achieve with modern diamond tools.

The Failed Aswan Obelisk

During the New Kingdom and later, Theban masons probably tried to compete with the Memphite artisans who mastered the art of alchemical stonemaking and produced unprecedented work. The famous undated, unfinished granite obelisk lying in the Aswan quarry could represent an attempt to parallel the 1,000-ton and heavier colossi of Ramses the Great (the Roman naturalist Pliny reported giant obelisks for this pharaoh). The Aswan obelisk is 137 feet long.[15] If completed, it would have been one of the largest monoliths surviving from antiquity, weighing some 1,168 tons.

Most Egyptologists assume the unfinished obelisk dates to about the time of the 18th Dynasty Pharaoh Tuthmosis III (c. 1479–1425 B.C.) because this was when Egyptians made the largest obelisks still in existence. But it could date to a much later period. Inscriptions appear in different languages near the obelisk, and accompany the various quarrying techniques used in different historical periods.

There are traces of hieratic writing on the upper quarry face of the obelisk site at Aswan. This language was used from the 1st Dynasty until the 7th century B.C. These are likely associated with the original work phase, carried out sometime before Egypt's 26th Dynasty (when iron was introduced into Egyptian quarries and pounding ball use may have been coming to a close). A later inscription at the obelisk site preserves writings from Greco-Roman times. Another faint group of signs is very hard to distinguish. But the writing is not Egyptian hieroglyphics.

Quarry marks demonstrate both ancient and modern activity. Engelbach found many dolerite pounding balls around the obelisk. Rough hammer dressing is very pronounced on the obelisk itself, particularly on its pyramidion. Engelbach found modern chisel dressing and evidence of what he thought to be a more advanced method of using the wedge than is typical for Aswan quarrying.

He determined that the entrance to the trench (in which the obelisk rests), to be modern work. That means that the Egyptians gave up on ever trying to detach or move it. The modern chisel work is characterized by fine, modern chisel marks. Engelbach even found a block there with a hole made by a gunpowder blast. His findings suggest that a modern effort was designed to detach the obelisk and move it out of its enclosure. But the project was again abandoned.

Egyptologists assume that, during all periods of pharaonic Egypt, quarrymen made obelisks by pounding away the ground beneath their feet with stone balls. The theory holds that workers bashed out trenches wide enough to accommodate them as they isolated an obelisk on four sides. Their next step was the dangerous and awkward task of undercutting.

Workers crouched in the trenches as they banged away from beneath an obelisk until only stumps held it in place. They made the overall shape by pounding in a well-coordinated effort to produce correct longitudinal lines.

To move an obelisk, stonemasons pounded away a large area of the bedrock in front of it. The structure was broken from its stumps and levered out of its enclosure. Workers then pushed it out and rolled it down over its long sides to a transport ramp. They then somehow transported the obelisk to its final destination.

Masons finally polished it with sandstone and inscribed it with flint tools. The engineers somehow erected it so that it aligned with the corners of the pedestal upon which it rested. The unfinished obelisk at Aswan inspired this theory. The problem is that engineers have not determined how this obelisk could have been moved or erected at all.

Egyptologists believe that workers abandoned the Aswan obelisk because a large crack appeared in its top surface during the pounding operation. The obelisk has a number of fissures. Theorists think that each time a crack appeared, the masons scaled down the size of the obelisk. Every time they scaled the obelisk down to start anew, a new crack appeared. Finally, the huge crack that appeared near the very center of the obelisk forced an end to the project. But given a finished weight of 1,168 tons and the problems of pounding granite so as to prevent cracking, the workers probably abandoned the project because it was too ambitious of an undertaking.

As mentioned, Engelbach reported that he did not believe the 13,000 men needed to pull the obelisk from its bed could have worked in the constricted area. He found no trace of a canal or drydock at Aswan for transporting the obelisk to the Nile. There is also the problem of using ancient Egyptian means to build a barge strong enough to carry the load — and the problems of loading the barge.

Abdel Aleem acted as Chief Foreman for the Nova team that erected a 40-ton obelisk. At that time, Aleem had 48 years of experience in Egypt, where he moved objects weighing up to 400 tons using steel rollers. When asked by Nova if he could move the unfinished obelisk, Aleem replied with this statement (published at the Nova web site) offering considerable insights:

> I could use a modern technique to move it. To lift from the ground 1,200 tons with the ancient methods would be very difficult. But using new methods and new technology, I could lift it. There are giant cranes that can hold 350 tons. I could use three of these in order to lift it. I would have to coordinate so that the three cranes lift every millimeter at the same time.

For those people who are content to study problems superficially, this undated, unfinished obelisk makes the geopolymer theory seem incorrect and unnecessary.

The Baalbek Trilithon

A similar scenario appears to have taken place in Baalbek (City of the Sun-god Baal), Syria, at the great Temple of the Sun.[16] The largest blocks known in ancient architecture are positioned within the confines of an exterior wall at the west end of the Temple. The three great monoliths together command their own name: the Trilithon. One of them measures 64 feet long and 14 feet square. It weighs an estimated 1,200 tons.

All three blocks, made with limestone, are situated about 20 feet above ground level. The blocks are so perfectly fitted that when William M. Thomson (1806–1894) measured them he thought they were a single block. He provides a description in his book titled *The*

Land and the Book (1912). At first he mistook the precision fit of two blocks. He thought he was looking at one 120-foot-long block. Because of the smoothness and very exact fit, he actually had to search for the joint between the two blocks. Their joints are like a myriad of pyramid blocks with hairline separations (they can look like very fine cracks). The feature is a sign of alchemical stonemaking. So, the Trilithon stones at Baalbek warrant further investigation.

In a quarry about a quarter mile away, there is an enormous partially-quarried block. It leads researchers to assume that the Trilithon are also quarried blocks. But the Sun Temple features reconstructions made after the original temple was built. These include temples dedicated to the Roman god Jupiter. There is Christian architecture at the site. It may be that Roman builders attempted to imitate the Trilithon, but the fruits of their toil remain unmoved in the quarry.

The Trilithon blocks are assumed to be Roman work. But the reason is that the much earlier Phoenician people of Baalbek are not thought to have had the mechanical means to raise stones of this weight. Given the potential for alchemical stonemaking, I know of no solid evidence for dating the Trilithon to Roman times.

Historical records provide abundant proof that in Roman times obelisks were laboriously moved from Egypt rather than agglomerated. Examples are the obelisks Augustus Caesar moved from Egypt to Rome after his defeat of Mark Anthony and Cleopartra. So, the partially quarried block resting a quarter of a mile from Baalbek could be an example of the way the Romans treated stone. The Trilithon blocks may very well be agglomerated stone dating to far more ancient Phoenician times.

Technology transfer from Egypt to Phoenicia is not at all unlikely. The two countries had close religious and political ties. Besides, we know from the 1998 findings of the team led by Elizabeth Stone, of the State University of New York's Anthropology Department, that the production of agglomerated rock was not confined to Egypt. I am referring to the aforementioned imitation basalt slabs found in Mesopotamian temple ruins.

Aswan and Queen Hatshepsut's Lighter

If all of Egypt's granite blocks, beams, sarcophagi, statuary and obelisks were cut and hauled, there should be thousands of failed attempts strewn all over the quarries and along the roadsides. Aswan would likely still exhibit a myriad of broken Old Kingdom objects and the large trenches from which later colossi weighing over 1,000 tons were removed. Although the Aswan quarries do exhibit thousands of wedge marks, associated with places where rock was removed, Reginald Engelbach believed that these marks were made with iron wedges. The use of iron dates to a period when making geopolymeric rock-concrete was in severe decline. Engelbach indicates:

> They [the wedge marks] can be seen in thousands all over the quarries. It has been asserted that the wedges themselves were made of wood and made to expand by wetting them. Without wishing to deny that the Egyptians knew and used this method, I will merely observe that the taper of the slots seems so great, and the two sides of the slots so smooth, that there would be a great tendency for the wedges to jump out after wetting rather than exert their pressure; another point is that it would be a somewhat difficult matter to wet a horizontal wedge, and still more difficult to do so from below. I am inclined to think that the normal method was to use metal—perhaps iron—wedges with thin metal plates between the wedge and the stone which are now known as "feathers."[17]

Reginald Engelbach's keen observations are right. More than 40 years later, in 1965, Joseph Roder showed that wedges were not used in Egyptian quarrying before Ptolemaic times (332–30 B.C.). By that time, iron was in common use.

In Pharaoh-Queen Hatshepsut's temple at Deir el-Bahari, a bas-relief shows the transport of a pair of twin obelisks, which together weighed about 700 tons. They are shown loaded end-to-end on the same barge. This barge is often referred to as Queen Hatshepsut's Lighter, and it is shown being towed by rowboats. Reginald Engelbach demonstrated that we cannot take this temple scene literally:

> Several of the details appear to be wrong. Thus he [the scribe] slurs over the manner in which the baulks of timber at the top of the obelisk were attached to those on the sled…The position of the hauling rope in the centre of the obelisk must also be surely wrong, as that would be the worst position for pulling the obelisk…It seems likely too that the obelisk was really on the sled the reverse way around…In the view of the great barge…the obelisks are placed high up on her deck. This is probably a trick by the artist so that they may be visible.[18]

Another problem is that when Bjorn Landstrom, author of *Ships of the Pharaohs: 4000 years of Egyptian Shipbuilding* (1970), calculated the size of Queen Hatshepsut's Lighter (based on the height and weight of her obelisks), he had to increase the dimensions by 1.5 times those recorded in the tomb of Ineni. The architect Ineni was in charge of Hatshepsut's constructions at Karnak, and Ineni's inscriptions are often associated with Hatshepsut's Lighter by Egyptologists. A problem is that a pair of 330-ton obelisks loaded end-to-end requires a ship about 300 feet long by 100 feet wide.

We are probably witnesses to a matter of scribal protocol. Had Queen Hatshepsut's scribe depicted a barge loaded with baskets of granite debris, viewers would not know what the finished object was.

Queen Hatshepsut had two pairs of twin obelisks erected. It will not be surprising if her obelisks prove to be agglomerated stone: Their positioning strongly suggests that they are. We recall Reginald Engelbach's comments:

> The Egyptians could introduce obelisks inside courts whose walls were shorter than the length of the obelisk. Queen Hatshepsowet put hers between her father's pylons where there is no evidence at all that any of the walls had been removed or rebuilt; in fact I am certain that they were not.[19]

These factors are compelling and warrant careful study of Hatshepsut's obelisks. We now turn to ancient historical sources that document alchemical stonemaking.

Chapter 26
Ancient Literary Testimony

A number of ancient accounts support the existence of the stonemaking technology. Other ancient texts will lead anyone willing to consider problems superficially to assume that there was no need for such technology. There is no doubt that large teams of men dragged heavy weights after the art of stonemaking declined. Some accounts, however, claiming that men dragged truly gigantic objects over hundreds of miles contain elements revealing a legendary character. So, they should not be taken literally.

For instance, the Roman naturalist Pliny the Elder (A.D. 23–79) assumed that 20,000 workers raised a 99-foot-high obelisk for Pharaoh Ramses the Great.[1] The legend he reported said that, fearing that the engineer might not take enough care to calibrate the power of his machinery to the weight of the obelisk, Ramses ordered his own son to be bound to its apex. The account is simply unbelievable when taken literally.

The story is typical of ancient accounts that blend myth or legend with historical elements. It is more logical to think that Ramses II possessed the technology to agglomerate stone to build his obelisks, and 1,000-ton and heavier colossi. His son Kha-em-waset was probably vaguely remembered in the legend Pliny preserved. Kha-em-waset was responsible for supervising the construction of the statuary of his royal father. Kha-em-waset was also deified, and so he could have been associated with the solar deity who lights upon the tip of the obelisk (all deities were considered an aspect of the solar deity).

Pliny also described the transport of an obelisk to Alexandria for the Greek Pharaoh Ptolemy II Philadelphus (285–246 B.C.):

> A canal was dug from the river Nile to the spot where the obelisk lay; and two broad vessels, loaded with blocks of similar stone a foot square — the cargo of each amounting to double the size and consequently double the weight of the obelisk — were put beneath it; the extremities of the obelisk remaining supported by the opposite sides of the canal. The blocks of stone were removed and the vessel, being thus gradually lightened, received their burden.[2]

The account may very well be true. Sometimes kings needed to order objects moved from their original locations. A number of rulers in Egyptian history improved their burial conditions, abandoning original tombs for better constructions. Doing so necessitated the relocation of sacred objects. But if we are to apply the method Pliny recorded for Aswan obelisks, a canal is absolutely required. As mentioned, there are no traces of an ancient canal leading from the Aswan quarries to the Nile. There are no traces of a drydock, either. So, the hauling methods used by the Greek pharaohs do not necessarily apply to earlier Egyptian dynasties.

We must exercise caution when accepting numbers provided by ancient texts. We recall that Herodotus' account of 30-foot-long casing blocks on the Great Pyramid matches measurements provided by Abd el-Latif many centuries later. So, we can tend to trust other figures given by Herodotus. His account of Egypt's largest known monolith deserves analysis because it shows the enormity of the problems of hauling such a weight.

In the Delta city of Buto, Herodotus measured what may be the heaviest recorded man-made monolith of all antiquity (excluding those cut into cliffs, which did not require any kind of transport). Herodotus recorded:

> The name of the city, as I have before observed, is Buto; and in it are two other temples also, one of Apollo and one of Diana. Latona's temple, which contains the oracle, is a spacious building with a gateway ten fathoms in height. The most wonderful thing that was actually to be seen about this temple was a chapel in the enclosure made of a single stone, the length and height of which were the same, each wall being forty cubits square, and the whole a single block! Another block of stone formed the roof and projected at the eaves to the extent of four cubits.[3]

Measuring a cubit as equal to 18 inches, Sir John G. Wilkinson was amazed as he roughly estimated the weight of the monolithic walls of this structure:

> ...but when we calculate the solid contents of the temple of Latona at Buto, our astonishment is unbounded; and we are perplexed to account for the means employed to move a mass which, supposing the walls to have been only 6 feet thick—for Herodotus merely gives the external measurements of forty cubits, or 60 feet in height, breadth and thickness—must have weighed upwards of 5,000 tons.[4]

Wilkinson added:

> This is supposing it to be granite, as these monolithic temples were.[5]

John Wilkinson's rough estimate of its weight can be refined for our analysis: The volume of a solid quarried cube measuring 60 feet x 60 feet x 60 feet is 216,000 cubic feet. This volume multiplied by the weight density of granite (averaging 172.5 pounds per cubic foot) means a quarried block weighing 18,630 tons.

We will assume that anyone attempting such a task would hollow out the block before raising it from the quarry to avoid maneuvering such a staggering weight. So, the block to be removed will be much closer to the weight of the finished structure. It would be heavier because of extra stock left on to help protect the monolith from cracking if dropped and when struck with pounding balls.

Given that Herodotus gives no information about the interior of the temple, he was apparently unable to go inside to see the floor or other features. So, we will leave the great weight of a floor out of the equation (such a floor would add over 1,000 tons). Herodotus thought that the overhanging roof was a separate unit, which would have weighed well over 1,000 tons if monolithic. To calculate the weight of the monolithic walls of the Buto temple, we subtract the volume of the material to be removed (48 feet x 48 feet x 60 feet = 138,240 cubic feet) from the solid cube quarried (about 18,630 tons). Assuming the same weight density of granite (172.5 pounds per cubic foot), the resulting hollowed out monolith (with no floor or roof) would weigh 6,706.8 tons.

The historical record gives us no reasonable expectation that the ancient Egyptians had the technology (construction materials and technique) to move such a massive structure either by land or water.

If this monument were quarried, an Egyptian granite quarry should, but does not, exhibit traces of such a monumental operation. Quarrying the monolith would have produced huge trenches well over 60 feet square going down to a depth of well over 60 feet.

Removing such a mass would have produced traces of a very long, gradual slope for raising the structure out of the bedrock. The operation would also have required a distinctive, huge loading area and an extremely strong hauling sledge. No direct evidence for the existence of either exists.

A canal would be used to transport a massive block by water from the quarry to the Nile. An example is the canal dug by order of Pharaoh Ptolemy II Philadelphus to move an obelisk he expropriated. For the Buto monolith, any canal would be enormous and conspicuous. Such a canal does not exist.

The only known canal in the Aswan area is near the island of Sehel. It was build during the Old Kingdom and reopened and enlarged during the Middle Kingdom by the 12th Dynasty Pharaoh Senusret III. His purpose was to facilitate his military campaigns against the Nubians. The canal allowed boats to bypass the rapids, but it only measured 225 feet long by 30 feet by 22.5 feet.

No granite quarries are found in the Delta, and so there would be no ability to avoid transport from the south of Egypt to the Delta city of Buto. Worse, there would be no ability to avoid an extraordinarily complex operation of water transport because Buto is on a landmass surrounded by Nile streams. Moving such a weight by water is vastly more risky and problematic than overland transport.

A major problem is producing a barge with the strength to carry over 6,500 tons. Surviving records are rich with information about ancient Egyptian shipbuilding. The reason is that the Nile served as an intercity highway. The Egyptians traversed the Nile instead of building roads to connect cities. The longest known ancient Egyptian water transport vehicle from before Herodotus' time was 206 feet long with a 69-foot beam.

It was built for the New Kingdom Pharaoh Tuthmosis I during the 18th Dynasty. Hundreds of years after Herodotus' time, the Greek Pharaoh Ptolemy Philadelphus is said to have built the largest ship of any king. The ship was an impressive 300 feet long. By comparison, the monolithic Buto temple walls would require a transport vehicle a great many times larger.

John Wehausen estimated that to haul one colossus of the Memnon pair (720 tons without its pedestal) would require a barge with an area of about 4,462 square feet.[6] By comparison, the Buto monolith weighed over 6,500 tons.

We cannot arrive at a length and width for the needed barge because these figures may vary considerably. The barge must be designed with loading, unloading and navigation considerations in mind. But we can get a sense of how enormous such a vessel must be.

To be able to carry the Buto monolith, a craft would have had to be equal in strength to today's steel hulled ships. But the boat-building materials of ancient Egypt were cedar or acacia planks or logs tied together with ropes and caulked with papyrus reed bundles.

Egypt's shipbuilding methods steadily improved. In the 18th Dynasty, Queen Hatshepsut sent a fleet of five ships along the Red Sea to Somalia to obtain myrrh for the Amun Temple. By then, shipbuilding had developed such that the hull was stronger, true cables were used, and the ships were designed for speed and equipped with large sails and great steering paddles. Some cargo could be carried on the deck and in the hold. By the 20th Dynasty, Egyptian ships improved even more as builders imitated more advanced models innovated in other cultures. But no direct literary or archaeological evidence supports a barge capable of hauling a weight equal to the Buto monolith.

As a transport model for heavy loads, Egyptologists rely on the depiction of Hatshepsut's Lighter, which appears on the walls of the Temple of Deir el-Bahari. As mentioned, the scene shows two obelisks loaded end-to-end on a ship being towed by smaller boats along the Nile. They presumably traveled from the granite quarries at Aswan to Luxor. Somers Clarke and Reginald Engelbach describe some technical problems with the scene:

In attempting to glean information from this sculpture several points must be appreciated; first, it must be remembered that the artist cannot have done his drawing on the walls from the actual ship, but probably did it from rough sketches which he had made when he attended the arrival of the obelisks in his official capacity. It does not follow that he must have been an expert in the details of ships; indeed, from his representation of the tackle, it seems he was not. Secondly, it must be borne in mind that an Egyptian, when he wished to represent an object in another, or behind another, often drew what was inside or further away above that which was nearer. The drawing of the barge gives the impression of top-heaviness with the two obelisks standing high on its deck, and it may be that they were really inside…While waiting for further information the student is completely in the dark regarding the internal structure of these barges; the patchwork method of boat-building seems hopelessly inadequate to resist the strain that the skin of the barge would have to endure even if it were externally stiffened with a series of queen tresses. It is extremely likely that the great barges were solid rafts made of tree-trunks, the whole raft being, if necessary, designed to give it the appearance of a true ship. Their draught would admittedly be great, but not too great to prevent them from passing down the Nile during flood time…Such is the unsatisfactory state of our knowledge of great weight-carrying ships.[7]

In other words, the details show impractical methods, and that the ship itself is inadequate as drawn. The scene shows us the level of shipbuilding in ancient Egypt, and it is not realistic for carrying the load. Whole logs would be needed to provide greater strength to the design. A realistic way of looking at this whole matter is to consider that the scribe had no concept of the strength needed or of the technical problems that would be encountered in carrying the load—because the Egyptians never actually had to deal with these tasks. We may really be dealing with a matter of scribal protocol: The scene was drawn to show the object that was agglomerated from the mission sent to bring back Aswan granite. But even if Hatshepsut's obelisks prove to be natural granite, and an enormous ship able to carry two 330-ton obelisks really did exist in 18th Dynasty Egypt, it would certainly not present a model for carrying the Buto temple monolith.

John Wehausen, an expert in ship hydrodynamics at the University of California, estimated that a strong raft could have been designed using acacia wood and the other shipbuilding materials used in Egypt. He estimated that an enormous, sturdy raft could actually carry both of the Memnon colossi. He proposed that such a raft be built and tested. No direct evidence indicates that such a barge existed. According to John Wehausen's calculations, a vessel able to carry the Memnon colossi would have to cover an area of about 6,069 square feet.[8]

Today, hauling loads the weight of the Buto temple walls is accomplished by extremely large, strong ships with engines affording incredible horsepower and built with steel hulls and superstructures. They are equipped with hydraulic jacks and cranes.

For instance, in the year 2000, the 505-foot-long U.S.S. Cole, a guided-missile-armed destroyer, was attacked and had to be hauled. It was taken aboard the 712-foot-long M/V Blue Marlin, a Norwegian heavy-transport drydock ship. It maneuvered under the U.S.S. Cole off the coast of Aden, Yemen. The M/V Blue Marlin then hauled the U.S.S. Cole to the Gulf of Mexico.

Navigating a ship carrying the weight of the Buto monument poses an enormous problem. Buto is hundreds of miles from the granite quarries at Aswan and Elephantine. Although it is the longest river in the world, the Nile is not a wide river. It is not uniformly wide as it runs through Egypt, and its depth is not uniform, either. In the area of the granite quarries at Aswan, the width of the Nile is about 1,640 feet, which is narrower than in certain other areas with only modest allowance for ships today.

We must assume greater allowance during antiquity, especially during the floods, when the riverbanks swelled to maximum capacity. But the Nile also has many small bends and islands that can present navigational obstacles for large craft. For instance, Elephantine Island occupies a large area in the middle of the Nile adjacent to the granite quarries at Aswan. A large craft must be able to be steer around visible and underwater islands that can cause it to go aground.

Al-Ahram Weekly (July 16–22, 1998) provided some idea of the number of islands along the Nile in Egypt today:

> …144 so-called "permanent" islands covering 137,000 feddans and 95 other islands totaling 32,344 feddans will be designated protected areas. There are an estimated 19 islands in the Damietta branch and 30 in the Rosetta branch in addition to 216 islands which at times are submerged under the water.

North of Cairo, the Nile breaks up into branches and smaller streams to form the Delta. The Delta was originally cut by seven major tributaries. Buto is near the east bank of the above-mentioned Rosetta branch, which is now dotted with many islands that can present obstacles for navigation.

The unloading dock would have to have been at a stream near the Rosetta branch (which is a major tributary leading near Buto). Today, the Rosetta branch has an average width of 590 feet and a depth varying between 6 and 13 feet.[9] Its width and depth in ancient times are unknown, but we must assume it was much wider during the floods. It would have had to be vastly wider for our theoretical craft to get through—and much deeper, or our theoretical craft would have gone aground.

We cannot recover knowledge of the bends, visible and underwater islands or depth or width of the actual stream leading to Buto. But this stream to Buto was much smaller than the Rosetta branch.

The final result is that John Wehausen calculated that one of the Memnon statues (weighing 720 tons) would require a barge of about 4,462 square feet; so, a craft ferrying a monolith weighing over 6,000 tons to Buto would be too large to make the trip.

All of the problems of navigation, load-carrying capacity by water, the lack of loading docks or the remains of strong, flat tracks, and the lack of direct archaeological evidence of quarrying and moving the massive Buto temple vanish when we apply the geopolymer theory. So do the terrible problems of loading and unloading a barge.

Some would be tempted to solve the problem by discounting Herodotus' report about the Buto temple. But reports of extremely large weights are not unique to Herodotus' writings. In Book 36 of his *Natural History*, Pliny the Elder reported a 230-foot-high obelisk built for Pharaoh Ramses II. Pliny provided measurements for another one of Ramses' obelisks at 200 feet high, with each of its sides 17 feet wide.[10] Given that obelisks taper and that granites vary in density, and that the obelisk has not survived, we can only estimate the weight of the 200-foot-high obelisk at about 4,500 tons (using a weight density of 172.5 x 200 x 17 x 17).

We do not know the cubic dimensions of the taller 230-foot-high obelisk. If its walls were as thick as the 200-foot-high obelisk, it would have weighed about 5,000 tons.

We have considered the major problems of river transport for heavy weights, and we can get a sense of the magnitude of the problems of using ancient means to transport monoliths weighing 4,500 tons and more overland. An award-winning modern engineering feat gives us more insight into what is required for land transport. Some engineers warned that it would be impossible. But in 1999, the 208-foot-high Cape Hatteras Lighthouse, in Buxton, North Carolina, had to be moved to protect it from the encroaching waters of the Atlantic Ocean. The Cape Hatteras Lighthouse is the tallest in the U.S., and weighs 4,830 tons—about the weight of the obelisks of Ramses that Pliny described.

Attempts to protect the Cape Hatteras Lighthouse from the ocean failed. So, transporting it was the last rescue hope. After more than 10 years of extensive evaluation, engineers determined that it was impractical to disassemble the structure for transport. They also determined that using cranes would be impractical for moving it.

So, they devised and carried out a highly-complex engineering project to move the lighthouse half a mile further inland. Their system involved undercutting the structure to remove more than 800 tons of its granite base. This mass of stone was replaced with steel support towers equipped with hydraulic jacks. The jacks were used to raise the lighthouse six feet, so that steel support beams could be installed to provide the very strong foundation needed to support the lighthouse during its relocation.

A sturdy, flat road was made with crushed stone and sand. It was reinforced on top with steel mats. The smooth road was sufficient to support the enormous weight and reduce friction, so that the lighthouse could be moved as freely as possible. One hundred hydraulic jacks, used in combination with steel rollers, were set up to enable the lighthouse to be moved over the road while being kept level.

With these devices in place, powerful hydraulic push jacks moved the lighthouse five inches at a time over the road. The entire hauling operation required 23 days, during which the lighthouse was moved 2,899.57 feet. Once the relocation was complete, the lighthouse was mechanically lowered with great care to its final resting place. The steel foundation was replaced with bricks instead of granite.

Moving a 208-foot-high erect lighthouse that must be kept from toppling produces problems that would not be encountered when hauling an obelisk on its side. Those differences aside, moving both structures would require lifting, transport, and extremely strong, flat tracks. The hauling tracks known from ancient Egypt are not extensive, and consist of wooden beams packed with earth. So, they cannot be expected to tolerate the great weights discussed here.

Besides, hauling Ramses' 4,500-ton obelisk would require river transport, given that the granite came from Egypt's south. Such an operation would surely leave major unmistakable traces at the granite quarries. Somewhere there would be evidence of strong flat tracks able to support the weight, or evidence that the ancient Egyptians could build and load the kind of incredible barge required to conduct the hauling operation.

As with the Buto monolith and the others I have mentioned, no direct archaeological evidence of such an operation exists. There is also the problem of erecting and aligning the obelisk on its pedestal. We recall that Dieter Arnold thinks that the ancient account of the much smaller 172 foot tall obelisks for the 18th Dynasty Pharaoh Queen Hatshepsut represents a "fairy tale"—because he does not think erecting such obelisks was possible.

Successfully transporting a 4,500-ton obelisk would be an incredible engineering feat with primitive means, requiring loading, balancing, successfully floating, navigating, and unloading and erecting the weight. So, I consulted with Senior Engineer George Gardiner of the International Chimney Corporation, in Williamsville, New York. The company headed the Cape Hatteras Lighthouse Relocation Project. George Gardiner's experience also includes using a crane to erect a 500-ton monument that fell over at Arlington National Cemetery, in Virginia. He advised me that river transport presents by far the most difficult transport problem when hauling a 4,500 ton monolith.

A loaded barge carrying a 4,500 ton monolith would displace roughly 20 to 30 feet of water, and so the barge would have to be extremely large and incredibly strong. If smaller barges were tied together, there would be even more serious problems distributing the enormous weight of the monolith on the barges.

Many other formidable factors must be considered, especially those involving loading and unloading a barge or connecting barges. Given the array of very difficult problems, George Gardiner concluded that he seriously doubted that the necessary technology existed to haul a 4,500 ton or heavier monolith by water. He also provided the following statement:

> I am of the opinion that a 5,000 ton monolith could be moved using primitive tools and basic principles of physics. These tools and methods, used on a large scale, could do the job. I am not qualified to comment on the water move, however I see significant problems loading and unloading the structure. The barge design and ballast calculations would require an extensive shipbuilding technology.[11]

His statement is not meant to assume that sufficiently strong flat tracks extended from a quarry for hundreds of miles to a monolith's final destination, because that would not be realistic. We know that no such shipbuilding technology existed during Egyptian antiquity. So, those who insist that there was no rock-concrete pyramid construction technology and refuse to look at the evidence do a disservice. They inadvertently advocate the existence of high technology that did not exist. They open the door to notions of power tools and other high technology and the many rampant distortions of ancient history that are so prevalent today.

If we wish to solve these major problems for the carve/hoist paradigm by doubting the reports of both Herodotus and Pliny, then a modern eyewitness report by Thomas Witlam Atkinson shows that ancient people certainly created truly large monoliths approaching the weight of the obelisks Pliny reported. In the 1800s, Thomas Witlam Atkinson traveled through Russia and China. He recorded his journeys in books, including his *Travels in the Regions of the Upper and Lower Amoor* (1860). He found great pillars near the Kora River in Turkestan, Siberia.

Five standing pillars are sunk several feet into the ground to keep them stationary. The largest pillar observed is estimated to weigh about 3,800 tons. Here is Thomas Witlam Atkinson's eyewitness report:

> Having travelled onward several miles, I arrived at a part of the valley where the Kora makes a bend toward the cliffs on the north, leaving, a space of about 200 yards in width, between the base of the rocks and the river. As I approached this spot, I was almost induced to believe that the works of the Giants were before me, for five enormous stones were standing isolated and on end, the first sight of which gave me the idea that their disposition was not accidental, and that a master mind had superintended the erection,—the group being in perfect keeping with the scene around. One of these blocks would have made a tower large enough for a church, its height being 76 feet above the ground, and it measured 24 feet on one side and 19 feet on the other.
>
> It stood 73 paces from the base of the cliffs, and was about 8 feet out of the perpendicular, inclining towards the river. The remaining four blocks varied from 45 to 50 feet in height, one being 15 feet square and the rest somewhat less. Two of these

stood upright, the others were leaning in different directions, one of them so far that it had nearly lost its equilibrium.

A sixth mass of still larger dimensions was lying half buried in the ground; on this, some young pieta trees had taken root and were growing luxuriantly. About two hundred yards to the eastward, three other blocks were lying, and beneath one was a cavity many a family in Kopal would have considered a splendid dwelling. Not far from these stood a pile of stones undoubtedly the work of man, as a great quantity of quartz blocks had been used, with other materials, in its construction. It was circular, 42 feet in diameter and 28 feet high, shaped like a dome: a circle of quartz blocks had been formed on the ground, enclosing a space ten feet wide all round the tomb. Finding such a tumulus in this valley surprised me greatly; it could not have been the grave of a chief of the present race, but was as ancient as those I had found on the steppe.[12]

Ancient technology transfer between Egypt and other nations is not unlikely in this case. Cultural exchange is proven by bottles with Chinese writing on them found in sealed dynastic Egyptian tombs of Thebes. Moreover, Chinese rulers buried themselves in flat-topped, stepped pyramidal tombs, similar in overall design to Egypt's step pyramids and Babylonian mud-brick ziggurats. About 100 such earthen burial mounds are known in China. In addition, like the Egyptians, Chinese astronomers considered the Pole Star the pivot point around which the visible arc of the heavens endlessly turns. In ancient Chinese texts, the word T'ai Chi, denoting the "Cosmic Mountain" (pyramid structures re-create the Cosmic Mountain of mythology, the traditional place of heavenly ascension for the king) is variously translated as "the Axis of the Universe," "the Pole Star," and "the Wheel of the Universe." So, we can see that similar concepts were held.

Finally, an ancient text recorded the twin 172-foot-tall obelisks built for Hatshepsut in the 18th Dynasty. In this case, we are dealing with primary text, eliminating the problem of a misreporting of the height because of a scribal re-copying error in later history. If we calculate assuming walls 14 feet wide (sufficient for the monument to be stable) and use a granite weight density of only 166.5 pounds per cubic inch, we arrive at two obelisks each weighing about 2,400 tons.

When we consider the great weights of certain ancient monolithic structures in conjunction with alchemical stonemaking, it follows that we no longer need to accept unfathomable engineering feats as the work of brute force just because they are unquestioned in seemingly authoritative books published by prestigious academic publishers.

Some ancient records paint a sober, realistic picture of the river transport of stones in ancient Egypt. Excavations at the construction office of Ramses II's Ramesseum, at Thebes, revealed records accounting the transport of building blocks for this enormous temple.[13] The accounts indicate that ten boats moved blocks from the sandstone quarries at Gebel Silsila to the construction site. The records suggest that each of the ten boats carried from five to seven sandstone blocks, and delivered 64 stones per day. The combined weight of all the daily loads was 15 to 20 tons.

Telling Ancient Texts

Let us now turn to ancient accounts that document fabricated stone. The Old Testament clearly indicates that a technique other than carving was used to prepare stone for altar construction. The law for making altar stones appears directly after the Ten Commandments (Exodus 20:25). It is the 11th of the Commandments:

> If you will make me an altar of stone, do not build it of dressed stones; for if you use a chisel on it, you will profane it.[14]

The passage forbidding dressed stones has led to scholarly speculation that fieldstones were so carefully selected that they fit together perfectly. But regular, tight-fitting blocks are found in ancient altar design. An example was excavated from a level of Megiddo dating from the 10th century B.C. The altar is thought to have been built by King Solomon, who would have followed Mosaic Law. Nature does not supply rocks with flat, level surfaces and squared edges, made at right angles, and other tight-fitting decorative shapes.

A Greek version of the Old Testament, called the Septuagint (Version of Seventy), was translated from a Hebrew version older than the earliest extant Hebrew Old Testament. According to the Apocrypha, rabbis translated the Septuagint in Egypt under the decree of a Ptolemaic pharaoh, probably Ptolemy II Philadelphus. In the Septuagint, the word for altar is "bomos." This word "bomos" compares closely with the Ionic Greek word Herodotus used for the pyramid blocks, "bomidas." Herodotus wrote:

> This pyramid [the Great Pyramid] was built thus: in the form of steps, which some call crosae, and others call bomidas.[15]

The word intimates a linguistic link between the altar ("bomos") stones, which by Mosaic Law (Ex.20:25) must not be carved, and the pyramid blocks ("bomidas") that were not carved, either.

The root word also appears as the Greek "bema," meaning a stone step or raised platform. The bema appears in synagogues as the place from which the Torah and Pentateuch are read. The bema also became standard in Christian basilicas. We can see this rooted in pyramid construction. The Coptic Christian Monastery of Saint Jeremias is located near Egypt's first pyramid, which was built for Pharaoh Zoser. Scholars recognize that the architectural design of Saint Jeremias Monastery's pulpit resembles the stairs and shrines of the court (called by the Egyptians the *Heb Sed*) of the funerary complex of Zoser's pyramid. The architectural design feature from the first pyramid court carried forward as the sanctuary (bema) area of churches. We can expect that Zoser's pyramid is made with the once-sacred alchemical stonemaking process.

Compare pyramid blocks with the original blocks in Solomon's Temple. The Jewish historian Josephus (ca. A.D. 37–c. 100) described Solomon's stones:

> All things having been prepared, King Solomon began to build the Temple during the fourth year of his reign…The foundation of the Temple was made very deep in order to resist the deterioration that age would cause, and for support to prevent the shaking of the huge mass which would be put upon them. The stones which filled the foundations were enormous. All of the stones which were used, from the foundation up to the roof, were very white. The entire structure of this beautiful building was made with stones that were so polished and closely joined together than no joints between the stones were noticeable. It seems that nature had formed them in such a way, in a single piece, without using any of the skill or tools usually used by the workers and carvers to embellish their works.[16]

As mentioned, the blocks of Solomon's Temple were some 16 and 17 feet long (I Kings 7:10). The biblical description of constructing Solomon's Temple may be telling (1 Kings 6:7), too:

> ...there was neither hammer nor ax nor any tool of iron heard in the house, while it was in building.[17]

We see that neither pounding nor cutting of stone was allowed within the sacred structure. The description brings to mind Mosaic Law (Ex.20:25), which forbade dressing an altar block (bomos). The Jerusalem Temple had a hall of hewn stone ("lishkat ha-gazit"), where the Sanhedrin held its meetings. This hall took on its special name, which may distinguish it from the rest of the Temple.

We must be cautious of biblical verses that refer to the blocks in Solomon's Temple itself as hewn stone (or natural field stones) — because it is not uncommon for the meaning of truly ancient words in the Old Testament to be lost. Translators found it necessary to replace archaic words (the meaning of which had been lost) with more recent terms. These more recent terms may not express the original meaning of the texts.

There are several differences between the various translations of the Bible with regard to stone in general, because early translators were not usually trained in mineralogy. To recognize the striking variations between different translations, consider the conflicting translations regarding the stones of Aaron's breastplate (Ex.28:15–20) listed in my endnote.[18]

Another work we must approach with caution is the Latin translation of the Greco-Egyptian High Priest of Heliopolis Manetho's (3rd century B.C.) text.[19] The Church father Eusebius (c. A.D. 300–359) and the Christian chronographer Sextus Julius Africanus (c. A.D. 150–232) preserved Manetho's work. But there was linguistic corruption.

Eusebius and Africanus, or perhaps those who preserved their texts, misreported Manetho's passage on Imhotep. He was the priest-architect credited with building Egypt's first pyramid for Pharaoh Zoser. They have it reading, "Imhotep was the inventor of the art of building with hewn stone."

Joseph Davidovits studied the words used to indicate pyramid stone: *xestos* (*xeston*) *lithon*. He explains that they did not mean hewn stone.[20] Today, these words are translated as "polished stone," as opposed to cut stone. *Xestos lithon* aptly described pyramid casing stone, the predominant material visible in ancient times. Pyramid casing blocks are so fine-grained and smooth that they look polished.

Casing blocks at the tip of Khafra's pyramid still reflect moonlight. Early European travelers often mistook pyramid casing blocks for marble. Today, very fine-grained natural limestone, resembling pyramid casing blocks, is called lithographic limestone. It can be made smooth enough to capture images in the lithographic process. Translators assumed that pyramid blocks were carved, leading them to misunderstand the distinction between the so-called polished stone and hewn stone.

As they are presently translated, some ancient texts appear to defy the idea that ancient people fabricated limestone by using rock aggregates, water, lime, clay and natron. The natron salt central to stonemaking was itself highly sacred. It was used in ancient Egyptian purification rites. Natron was also mixed with castor oil to produce clean, sootless fuel for lamps inside of temples. For the Hebrews, natron was the salt of the covenant. Leviticus 2:13 reads:

And every oblation of thy meat offering shalt thou season with salt neither shalt thou suffer the salt of the covenant of thy God to be lacking from thy meat offering: with all thine offerings thou shalt offer salt.[21]

The salt alluded to was not table salt (sodium chloride) or potassium nitrate (saltpeter). Proverbs 25:20 shows that it was natron:

As he that taketh away a garment in cold weather, and as vinegar upon nitre [salt], so is he that singeth songs to a heavy heart.[22]

The verse implies that vinegar produced an adverse effect on the salt. When vinegar is applied to sodium chloride or potassium nitrate, these salts do not dissolve or disintegrate. But vinegar dissolves natron, leaving an acetate solution.

In the 1st century B.C., Diodorus Siculus mentioned that mounds of salt were dissolved by Nile waters to build the Great Pyramid. Although Diodorus had no idea of the alchemical process used so many centuries before to build the Great Pyramid, his report does carry a vital element of it:

The entire construction is of hard stone, which is difficult to work but lasts fore ever; for though no fewer than a thousand years have elapsed...the stones remain to this day still preserving their original position and the entire structure undecayed. It is said that the stone was conveyed over a great distance from Arabia and that the construction was effected by means of mounds, since cranes had not yet been invented at that time; and the most remarkable thing in the account is that, though the constructions were on such a great scale and the country round about them consists of nothing but sand, not a trace remains either of any mounds or of the dressing of the stones, so that they do not have the appearance of being the slow handiwork of men but look like a sudden creation, as though they had been made by some god and set down bodily in the surrounding sand. Certain Egyptians would make a marvel out of these things, saying that, inasmuch as the mounds were built of salt and saltpeter, when the river was let in it melted them down and completely effaced them without the intervention of man's hand.[23]

Diodorus' account helped to inspire the unworkable theories of huge construction ramps for building the Great Pyramid. But the tradition Diodorus preserved clearly indicates that dissolved natron (salt and saltpeter were both loosely called natron in ancient times) was involved in pyramid construction. The pyramids would not exist without this vital substance. Heaps of natron and lime, placed on concrete-grade kaolinitic limestone, will convert to rock-making cement when Giza is flooded by a high Nile.

An ancient Egyptian document dating long before scribes penned the Old Testament may testify to the existence of the sacred Egyptian-made stone. The reference appears in the Contendings of Horus and Seth, a mythicized decree. The decree gave the god Horus the right to inherit Egypt's throne after the god Osiris, his father, was murdered and passed into the netherworld. Seth, Osiris' brother and lead conspirator in the murder, tried to claim the throne. But Horus avenged his father's death and claimed the throne by defeating Seth in combat. The relevant passage reads:

Seth challenged Horus to a combat in boats. First, Horus made a boat of cedar and plastered it on the outside. Its appearance deceived Seth, who thought it was made of stone.[24]

The storyline appears to imply that Seth was ignorant of the alchemical sciences. Thinking that Horus' boat was solid, natural rock, Seth carved a stone boat, which sank.

Alchemically made stone applied to a boat hull is appropriate for such a contest. Thousands of years later, in 1989, an annual race took place involving only concrete boats. A participant was a leading institution specializing in concrete, the civil engineering school of Purdue University, in West Lafayette, Indiana. Professor Menashi D. Cohen, head of the Civil Engineering Materials Area, and his students, built a concrete canoe. It required several weeks to harden and gain full strength. Only three days before the race, the team discovered that their canoe was too heavy to compete. There was not enough time to make a new boat. The team needed an immediate solution.

Professor Cohen suggested a new cement that sets in hours instead of weeks. The team contacted Lone Star Industries, Inc., and requested some bags of Pyrament. The product was portland cement enhanced with Joseph Davidovits' geopolymeric cement. The team made a lightweight canoe of Pyrament and fiber reinforcements. It gained strength overnight. The Purdue team, having had no chance at all to practice in the canoe, entered the race and took second place. The following year, they used Pyrament with a different boat design and won the regional championship.

Experts who translated the ancient documents assumed that the Egyptians carved stone to build monuments. The mindset can dramatically affect the final wording of translations. But sometimes translators cannot reconcile information at all. A case in point is the Famine Stele, inscribed on a large rock on Sehel, an island in southernmost Egypt. Written by priests of Khnum (one of Egypt's oldest gods) in about 190 B.C., it was translated by a number of Egyptologists.

The priests of Khnum indicated that they derived the account they inscribed on the Famine Stele from an Old Kingdom land deed they looked up at the Hermopolis library. The stele focuses on three intriguing figures: Imhotep, Pharaoh Zoser, and the god Khnum. The account records that Pharaoh Zoser, for whom Imhotep built the first pyramid, drew up a decree providing certain sovereign rights in perpetuity for Khnum's temples. Under the Greek administration in power in Egypt in 190 B.C., it became necessary for Khnum's priests on Sehel to assert their sovereign rights.

A portion of the Famine Stele describes a dream attributed to Pharaoh Zoser, in which the god Khnum appeared before him and gave him different kinds of minerals. Joseph Davidovits considers these minerals relevant to building Zoser's pyramid complex. Of about 2,600 hieroglyphs making up the Famine Stele's inscriptions, about one-third pertain to minerals and ores. In Zoser's dream, Khnum instructed him to draw on the rich mineral deposits of Sehel and the nearby island of Elephantine. Egyptologists have not been able to decipher all of the minerals and ores listed, partly because the Egyptians did not systematically name stones for their color or appearance.

The Latin and Greek words for stones, which were named for color and appearance, do not offer reference points. So, Joseph Davidovits took a new approach to deciphering some words in the Famine Stele.[25]

He employed determinative mineralogy—a simple means of determining various properties of minerals. In prehistoric times, the forebears of the Egyptians heated minerals to produce enamel. This made the dwellers along the Nile long familiar with the properties of heated minerals. When heated, some minerals melt and give the flame a color, such as violet when potassium is heated and yellow when sodium is heated. Some types of minerals decompose when exposed to heat, while others swell and emit bubbles. Some heated minerals produce irritating fumes. The irritating fumes may correlate with a hieroglyphic word for a stone inscribed on the Famine Stele, which Egyptologists avoid translating because it seems completely out of context.

The word for the stone matches the word for onion. Joseph Davidovits points out that heating minerals containing arsenic (such as the olivenite and scorodite from the Sinai mines) will give off a strong odor resembling that of onion or garlic. Arsenic minerals also produce rapid setting, useful for very large geopolymerized stone blocks and beams.

Arsenic minerals may be relevant to the inscriptions on the casing of the Great Pyramid read to Herodotus by Egyptian guides when he visited Giza. Here is Herodotus' account:

> On the pyramid is shown an inscription in Egyptian characters of how much was spent on radishes, onions, and garlic for the workmen. The person interpreting the inscriptions, as I remember well, told me this amounted to 1,600 talents of silver [over 100 million dollars in U.S. currency].[26]

Not having considered determinative mineralogy, Egyptologists assume that this account pertains to food for the workers. The Egyptians primarily ate bread, and their diet contained fish, small game, and a variety of vegetables and fruits. That onion, garlic, and radishes were singled out and consumed in great quantities is seen as an oddity. So, Egyptologists assume that Herodotus was given an inaccurate reading. Although the terms could have been code words of another nature, the key to the enigmatic inscription may be arsenic minerals useful for making enormous beams and casing blocks—those so large that they had to be made to set very rapidly. Remember that Herodotus reported seeing a myriad of casing blocks 30 feet long on the Great Pyramid, and that Abd el-Latif reported the same in the Middle Ages. In 2003, Guy Demortier, of the University of Notre-Dame de la Paix, in Namur, Belgium, analyzed casing stone from the Great Pyramid on behalf of this body of research. He found arsenic in the casing stone.

Until the emergence of modern chemistry within the past 200 years, the practices of working with minerals, including copper smelting and glassmaking, were considered part of the alchemical arts. The High Priest and architect Imhotep, who built the first pyramid, is remembered in a Renaissance drawing as "The Alchemist."[27] The drawing preserves Imhotep's legacy. Between A.D. 250 and 300, the alchemist Zosimus wrote a book called Imouth (Imhotep), which shows that Imhotep was strongly remembered in association with alchemy.

In the first half of the tenth century, the noted Arab alchemist Ibn Umayl reported a visit to a temple dedicated to Imhotep not far from Zoser's pyramid, in the village now called Abusir.[28] Within the temple, Umayl encountered inscriptions on a stone tablet in the lap of a stone statue of Imhotep posed as a seated scribe. During this era, Arab scholars studied these inscriptions as an essential source of alchemical learning.

Great alchemical works were ascribed to the biblical Moses, who is credited with Mosaic Law—including the law of the altar stone that must not be dressed (Ex.20:25). Great alchemical works were ascribed to Pharaoh Khufu, for whom the Great Pyramid was built.[29] The Greek historian Diodorus recorded Khufu's name as Chemmis, a rendering that may relate to the word "alchemy" (Greek: chemmy or chemmis).[30]

Chemmis may be a language corruption of the name Khnum. In ancient languages, "m" and "n" were not as distinct as they are in modern languages.

Khufu's name appears in the Great Pyramid as "Khnumu-Khufu," which means "may the god Khnum protect me, Khufu."[31] Alchemy, from which our modern word chemistry is derived, is thought by some etymologists to mean to pour or cast materials. Compare a depiction of the god Khnum, called the Divine Potter, fashioning a pharaoh and his spiritual double on his potter's wheel. The Egyptians revered Khnum as the god who individually created each person by this method (presumably from the earth of Egypt called *kmt*). As mentioned, hard-stone vessels show signs of lathe turning and potter's wheel grooves, suggesting that they were once pliable stone turned on potter's wheels.

As such, these objects were associated with Khnum, whose hieroglyphic symbol is a vase with a handle and a small pouring spout. The manufacture of vessels made with hard stones flourished during the main era of Khnum worship.

Khnum, revered by Pharaoh Khufu, appears to have been closely associated with the very ancient science of alchemical stonemaking. According to Heinrich Brugsch (1844–1926), one of the most prominent scholars of early Egyptology, the four rams' heads signifying Khnum in ancient Egyptian art symbolized the four alchemical elements air, water, fire, and earth. So, we can consider that Khufu having been remembered as "Chemmis" and "Chemististes" may preserve an alchemical relationship to Khnum (cf. Khnumu-Khufu).

It is interesting that the priest-alchemist Zosimus, the first to use the word "chemistry," was keenly interested in written materials concerning both Imhotep and Khufu.

Classical Greek literature retains a wide array of alchemical linkages, including reverence for Imhotep.[32] He was a High Priest of Heliopolis (Egyptian: *Iwnw*, the biblical city of On), near Memphis. For thousands of years, the Heliopolitan priests were considered Egypt's traditional wise men. This preeminent priesthood was always closely associated with royal power, and the priests exerted great influence on pyramid design.

In Greek times, the alchemical writer and physical scientist Empedocles (490-430 B.C.) proposed that matter was made of four elements: air, earth, fire, and water. Long before Empedocles' time, alchemical learning was associated with the primeval Egyptian Heliopolitan creator-gods. So, again, we see Imhotep, a High Priest of Heliopolis, in connection with alchemical traditions.

According to their biographers, a number of important Greek thinkers, including Plato, Pythagoras, Thales of Milet, and Homer, were influenced by the priests of Heliopolis.[33] In addition, two thousand years after Imhotep's death, the Greeks identified him with their god of medicine Asclepius.[34] A triad of gods, including the father Ptah, the mother Sekhet, and the son Imhotep headed the Memphite ennead, worshipped near Heliopolis.[35] This gives us a sense of how important Imhotep was. Today, he is best remembered as the architect responsible for the first pyramid. But now his alchemical traditions make sense in relation to that legacy.

For a long time, Egyptology knew Imhotep only through inscriptions that characterized him as a deified sage. No artifact proved that Imhotep was more than legendary until Egyptologists excavated a statue base from Zoser's Step Pyramid. It bears Imhotep's name along with that of Pharaoh Zoser. The base lists Imhotep's titles, some of which include "High Priest of *Iwnw* (Heliopolis)," "Chief Architect of Pharaoh Zoser," "Sculptor," and "Maker of Stone Vessels." All of these titles are relevant to pyramid building and alchemical stonemaking.[36]

Before Imhotep's time, stone shows up in a limited way in architecture. It primarily appears as vessels, statuary, plug blocks, portcullises, and doorjambs in the mud-brick mastaba tombs that preceded the pyramids. Making early synthetic stone was probably a costly and time-consuming process. Joseph Davidovits thinks it was necessary for the earliest alchemical stonemakers to obtain and crush *mafkat* (the ancient Egyptian word for turquoise, chrysocolla, and other blue and blue-green minerals from the Sinai).

24. A Renaissance drawing. The great ancient Egyptian cultural hero Imhotep was long remembered as The Quintessential Alchemist, as shown in this Renaissance artwork.

The Egyptians combined the crushed turquoise (which contains the needed hydrated* aluminum) and chrysocolla (which contains a useful hydrous silica) with lime, water, and natron (the latter three ingredients needed to produce caustic soda). This combination produces a simple geopolymeric binder. *Mafkat* minerals were mined in the blazing-hot, barren Sinai Desert. The minerals had to be transported to the construction sites, altogether an expensive process.

The geopolymer theory holds that Imhotep added lime, natron, and water to Saqqara's bed of kaolinitic limestone and found that it reacted. The result was a revolution in construction.

* Hydrated material contains water in the molecule, making it more easily attacked by an alkali such as caustic soda.

The discovery eliminated the great cost of making stone, and it allowed for tremendous amounts of agglomerated limestone to be packed into mud-brick molds.

The innovative building material proved excellent. But the Egyptians did not yet recognize its full potential. Only upon the completion of Zoser's giant mastaba did they really appreciate the new stonemaking process. They then expanded the mastaba's tiers six times before the 200-foot-high Step Pyramid finally emerged.

They then converted the surroundings of the pyramid into a building complex, consisting of a square-mile city that included cult-related buildings, shrines, altars and statuary. Finally, they enclosed the complex with synthetic limestone walls 30 feet high. Zoser's Step Pyramid was the first great architectural jewel of Egypt, the world's first entirely man-made stone superstructure—and its existence is credited to Imhotep.

The clean architectural lines of Zoser's temples and walls, which depict the theogonic theme of the "First Time" event in creation mythology, provided inspiration for modern architecture some 4,500 year later. European architects visiting Saqqara early in the 20th century were inspired by these pure geometric lines that dramatically contrast with ornate Victorian architecture.

Proponents of an Atlantean or space-alien origin for the Great Pyramid question how the Egyptian culture emerged fully formed out of a Neolithic cultural complex about 2,700 B.C.[37] They propose outside intervention. But archaeological discoveries have shown that all of the needed elements were within the early Egyptian culture itself. Egyptology has shown that writing was a much earlier art in Egypt than had been assumed. Simple crafts began to flourish in an organized way after the unification of Upper and Lower Egypt. But Imhotep's innovation produced a sudden architectural flowering. The masterful masonry works that followed Zoser's Step Pyramid owe their triumph to the innovative mind of the High Priest Imhotep.

The archaeological record offers no document even remotely suggesting that the Egyptians built the Great Pyramids by quarrying, carving, and hoisting blocks. But this method was deeply entrenched in the earliest Egyptological thinking even before Egyptology became an independent discipline.

In other words, the carve/hoist concept was entrenched before portland cement was invented in 1824. For this reason, the idea that the pyramids could be made of concrete was not a consideration. George Zeoga (1755–1809) published a treatise on obelisks in 1797, in which he assumed that ancient builders hauled and manually hoisted their obelisks.

Napoleon's *Description de l'Egypte*, published between 1809 and 1830, was the first extensive study on the pyramids. The work set the stage for later thinking, and it carried the presumption that Egyptians carved, hauled, and hoisted the pyramid blocks.

After the invention of portland cement in 1824, some early Egyptologists recognized that the pyramid blocks must be concrete. The form-fitting blocks, and blocks that merge into one mass, are obvious clues. They simply cannot be made any other way.

An ancient Egyptian drawing showing a worker climbing a pyramid with a basket on his back also inspired them. The drawing is said to have been in either the Museum of Dresden or in Berlin, two cities that suffered extensive bomb damage in World War II. Because I am unable to locate the document or find any other confirmation of this drawing, I can only rely on a description in an old book dating to 1875:

> In the Egyptian section of the Dresden, or Berlin Museum, we forget which, is a drawing which represents a workman ascending an unfinished pyramid, with a basket of sand on his back. This has suggested to certain Egyptologists the idea that

the blocks of the pyramids were chemically manufactured in loco. Some modern engineers believe that Portland cement, a double silicate of lime and alumina, is the imperishable cement of the ancients. But, on the other hand, Professor Carpenter asserts that the pyramids, with the exception of their granite casing, is formed of what "geologists call nummulitic limestone. This is newer than the old chalk, and is made of the shells of animals called nummulites—like little pieces of money about the size of a shilling."[38]

Despite its merit, the idea was abandoned after experts of the time insisted that the pyramid blocks are natural limestone. More recent geologists, in response to the geopolymer theory, tried to prove that pyramid stone is natural limestone. But Joseph Davidovits' discovery of the chemistry of geopolymerization has prevented them from arguing successfully.[39] Appendix Two below summarizes my published debates with these geologists in the *Journal of Geological Education*.

A well-known scene from the New Kingdom tomb of Rekhmira gives us an idea of the first pyramid's stone block making operation.[40] Mud bricks are shown being produced in mud-brick molds. They are the size and shape of the building units of Zoser's pyramid.

Building units became larger for later pyramids. Synthetic stones became more irregular, too. The stones in these later pyramids are slablike, and some are bun-shaped. Finally, pyramid builders began to model massive blocks directly in place. Some of these blocks are irregular, yet fit very tightly with neighboring blocks. Some are very neatly shaped and form-fitted. Some blocks appear to merge with others, and some have very tight, hairline separations. Notice the photograph (provided by Sanford Rose) in this book, in which two granite blocks in the Valley Temple at Giza adhere.

The Roman naturalist Pliny mentions the use of natron for hardening minerals in Book 31 of his encyclopedic *Natural History*:

> The soda-beds of Egypt used to be confined to the regions around Naucratis and Memphis, the beds around Memphis being inferior. For the soda becomes stone-like in heaps there, and many of the soda piles there are for the same reason quite rocky. From these they make vessels, and frequently by baking melted soda with sulfur.[41]

We cannot be sure from this translation if the vessels were stone or another material. But Pliny also described exquisite, translucent-stone vessels called murrhine.[42] They were imported to Rome during his time, from Parthia (an ancient country in Southwest Asia) and Carmania (a region of southeastern Iran). Dedicated to the god Jupiter, god-supreme of the time, these gorgeous items were extremely prized. One murrhine urn preserved remains of Alexander the Great. Pliny mentioned a murrhine vessel belonging to the Roman Emperor Nero (A.D. 54–68) that cost the equivalent of more than a $1.5 million today.[43]

In 1883, the French Academy of Sciences translated Pliny's Latin encyclopedia into French.[44] The academy members devoted particular attention to Pliny's description of the murrhine vessels. After much pondering and debate, they deduced that the murrhine vessels must be carved fluorite, an exquisitely beautiful type of rock when it is of gem quality. Fluorite can be translucent with a glassy luster. It exhibits a range of colors, including yellow, blue, purple, green, rose, and brown. Fluorite can even be fluorescent. The academy members decided that only fluorite correlates with Pliny's description of murrhine's glistening, swirling veins that merge and range in color from fiery pink to milky white shades.

But Pliny described murrhine vessels as exhibiting bubbles and being made of a material that hardened upon heating. He recorded that the vessels had a characteristic scent, too. The puzzled scientists of the French Academy did not believe Pliny. They especially doubted his claim that heat caused murrhine to harden during manufacture. Thermosetting materials were unknown in the 19th century. Today, we can recognize that Pliny's descriptions appear to refer to a particularly beautiful type of gem-quality fabricated rock, the manufacture of which requires heat to harden.

Today, people assume that vessels in museums labeled murrhine are natural fluorite. Only proper scientific analyses can determine the nature of these items. There is currently inadequate knowledge of murrhine. For several reasons, curators need to take advantage of the new body of knowledge pioneered by Joseph Davidovits. For example, researchers know very little about the varieties of limestone used for sculpture and about their geological origin. The lack of knowledge presents problems for curators dealing with objects of unknown origin. Archaeologists know little about the limestone sources used to build many monuments. Testing for geopolymerization can help museums detect forgeries, verify authenticity, determine political geographies, date objects, and properly label and protect some museum pieces.[45]

In various countries, people have reported finding objects embedded in solid stone that presumably formed eons ago.[46] A nail was found in sandstone that is dated from 360 to 408 million years old. A gold thread was found embedded in rock assumed to be between 320 and 360 million years old. A uniformly-shaped, hexagonal coin-like object was found in rock dated to between 200,000 and 400,000 years old. Some theorists consider these objects evidence for redating high culture. But before we rethink the social evolution of humankind based on isolated finds, we need to consider that rock-forming minerals can naturally come together and bond relatively quickly compared to usual rock formation. Such natural concretes are not necessarily geopolymeric (zeolite-forming), because many mineralogical systems are possible. For the sake of correct historical knowledge, I hope archaeologists and geochemists will take full advantage of this budding area of mineralogy.

Continuing with the literary references to alchemical stonemaking, an account comes from early Christian literature. To prove that pagan idols are the product of mere human hands, the Church father Clement of Alexandria (c. A.D. 150–215) preserved a description of the manufacture of the giant stone colossus of the Greco-Egyptian god Serapis. Clement reported legends about its place of origin, and he included a description of how an artist made the Serapis colossus — not with stonecutting, but with alchemy and in a mold:

> But Athenodorns the son of Sandon, while wishing to make out the Serapis to be ancient, has somehow slipped into the mistake of proving it to be an image fashioned by human hands. He says that Sesostris the Egyptian king, having subjugated the most of the Hellenic races, on his return to Egypt brought a number of craftsmen with him. Accordingly he ordered a statue of Osiris, his ancestor, to be executed in sumptuous style; and the work was done by the artist Bryaxis, not the Athenian, but another of the same name, who employed in its execution a mixture of various materials. For he had filings of gold, and silver, and lead, and in addition, tin; and of Egyptian stones not one was wanting, and there were fragments of sapphire, and hematite, and emerald, and topaz. Having ground down and mixed together all these ingredients, he gave to the composition a blue colour, whence the darkish hue of the image; and having mixed the whole with the colouring matter that was left over from the funeral of Osiris and Apis, moulded the Serapis, the name of which points to its connection with sepulture and its construction from funeral materials, compounded as it is of Osiris and Apis, which together make Osirapis.[47]

Pharaoh Ptolemy I introduced Serapis to merge the Greek and Egyptian religions. At that time, a crew moved the Serapis colossus to Alexandria, on Egypt's Mediterranean coast. It was said to come from Sinope, which some scholars accept was the sacred hill in the Memphite region associated with the Serapeum at Saqqara.[48] The site is a short distance from the Pyramid of Zoser.

We see that Clement's report presents clear evidence of alchemical stonemaking in the time of Sesostris, a king some Egyptologists think represents Ramses II. Byraxis' ingredients were alchemically relevant. He amalgamated into Serapis a number of mineral elements that represented the gods. The ancient Egyptians considered rocks and minerals the dense, earthly equivalents of the higher cosmic essences of the gods, who, in turn, represented natural or cosmic forces. Red stones, such as carnelian, represented the blood of Isis.[49] Blue or green malachite (a *mafkat* mineral) was associated with sky goddesses like Isis-Hathor, patroness of the Eastern Sinai Desert. Tradition held that the gods had bones made of silver. The metal represented the moon and, therefore, Isis, wife of the Sun-god Osiris. Byraxis employed gold, too, which represented the imperishable flesh of the Sun god.

Laboratories that analyzed pyramid limestone on behalf of this body of research, including the Pennsylvania State University Materials Research Laboratory, found a fleck of embedded gold.[50] This sample came from a wall of the Ascending Passageway of the Great Pyramid. The piece is called the Lauer sample, because Jean-Philippe Lauer (1902–2001), a prominent figure of Egyptology, provided it to Joseph Davidovits for testing.

Blue *mafkat* minerals were Byraxis' main ingredients, used liberally enough to produce Serapis' pigmentation. As mentioned, turquoise *mafkat* is a good source of hydrated aluminum for making high-quality geopolymeric stonemaking formulations. Blue-green chrysocolla is a good source of hydrated silicate.

The mummified remains of the Apis bull that Byraxis added included the animal's bones. Comparably, brushite (an organic calcium phosphate found in bones) is part of the chemical makeup of the Lauer sample from the Ascending Passageway. The presence of brushite helps to demonstrate that the Lauer sample is not natural limestone. Organic calcium phosphate is rarely present in natural limestone, but brushite is found in bones and guanos.

Geopolymerization produces zeolites, which can be any of a variety of hydrous silicates that are analogous in composition to the feldspars. A synthetic zeolite, made during geopolymerization, is called ZK-20. It occurs when natron is reacted with organic ammonium. The latter can come from urine or collagen from flesh or bone. The very word ammonia (Latin: *sal ammoniacus*) is terminology rooted in ancient alchemy. Ammonia was named after the Egyptian god Amun. The zeolite ZK-20, produced with natron and animal remains, is present in the Lauer sample from the Great Pyramid. Natural zeolites are rare in limestone. But ZK-20 is a synthetic zeolite not found in natural limestone. This is one of several lines of evidence showing that the Lauer sample from the Ascending Passageway of the Great Pyramid is synthetic limestone. The evidence above may shed new light on the ancient practice of animal sacrifice. The Egyptians, Hebrews, Greeks, Romans, and other ancient peoples burned animals on altars of sacrifice. In ancient Egypt, the funerary remains of the Apis bull were immortalized during the manufacture of Serapis, a god who mainly represented the dead Apis bull. We now continue exploring the Lauer sample, a specimen from the Great Pyramid that may also immortalize sacred remains, and tests of other samples, too.

Chapter 27
Analysis of Specimens

Joseph Davidovits was the first modern scientist to make room-temperature-setting synthetic stone equivalent to natural rock, and then apply his discovery to the enigmas of pyramid construction. He also applied his chemical discoveries to the manufacture of a number of durable ancient mortars, and thereby re-created mortars that are expected to stay intact for thousands of years. He also reproduced the world's oldest known ceramic, which was made with only the heat of a wood fire many thousands of years before the first ceramic kiln was invented.

Egypt's Oldest Artificial Stone – 5,500 Years Ago

A previous French scientist named Henri Le Chatelier (1850-1935) was the first to demonstrate that the Egyptians made synthetic stone.[1] Henri Le Chatelier is best known for contributing to the knowledge of thermodynamics, and for formulating something called Le Chatelier's Principle (the direction in which chemical equilibrium shifts can be determined with his general principle). In Le Chatelier's day, Egyptologists thought that the sandstone agglomerate today called Egyptian faience was natural sandstone.

After Le Chatelier's discovery of its synthetic nature, this exquisite self-glazing product had to be renamed. But the name it acquired (Egyptian faience) is not sufficiently descriptive. Egyptian faience has little in common with ordinary faience, which is fired clay coated with enamel. Egyptian faience contains no clay, and is surfaced with a glassy bright blue-green luster. As with later glass making, the ancient production of Egyptian faience was an attempt to imitate natural stone. Egyptian faience resembles the blue semi-precious stones from which its glaze was made.

Le Chatelier's discovery was made possible by what were then new analytical methods. Most especially, he used the then newly-developed glass slides to observe very thin slices of material suitable for microscopic observation. Using thin sections, he viewed Egyptian faience materials as they had never been seen before.

He observed that minerals had migrated from the inner portion of his samples of Egyptian faience to their outer surfaces. So, he could see the remnants of the self-glazing action that produced the outer coating of blue enamel. Before Le Chatelier's discovery, Egyptologists believed that the enamel coating was painted on. But the observation of the self-glazing process proved that Egyptian faience is not natural sandstone.

Le Chatelier also saw spherical air bubbles in the sandstone itself. These unequivocally proved Egyptian faience to be artificially agglomerated sandstone: Bubbles do not occur in natural sandstone.

Today, it is taken for granted that the manufacture of Egyptian faience is well understood.[2] The accepted theory of Egyptian faience production was advanced by Alfred Lucas (1867–1945). It is considered one of his greatest achievements. But there is a fundamental flaw in his theory of its manufacture: It does not hold true for the earliest faience, and so it does not account for the invention of Egyptian faience. The problem is that the Predynastic people who first made Egyptian faience are not thought to have been able to achieve the temperatures that Lucas' system requires.

Lucas' method requires a minimum firing temperature of 1,500 degrees Fahrenheit. Geopolymerization solves the problem. It requires only 500 degrees Fahrenheit or less to make Egyptian faience. This temperature was easily reached by Predynastic people 5,500 years ago, using only a wood fire. With the geopolymeric system, sand is not melted to form the glassy binder or the glaze. To achieve what is mistaken for high heat fusing (to produce a glassy binder), a hydrated silica was used to prepare the faience body paste. Hydrated silicas are readily attacked by caustic soda at only 500 degrees Fahrenheit. Over the course of ancient Egyptian history, the use of the geopolymer system over the accepted system is apparent because the internal sand particles of Egyptian faience only appear fused to each other where they touch. Whereas, high heat would create the different appearance of true melting and fusing. Geopolymeric faience is an altogether different system than the accepted system (the latter has more in common with modern glass making) and produces a type of artificial sandstone (natural sandstone is sedimentary rock) at a modest temperature of 500 degrees Fahrenheit or less.

Le Chatelier observed angular grains of sand in the body of fired Egyptian faience. These grains are angular because they were never melted — and, as mentioned, this is characteristic of Egyptian faience. Le Chatelier also performed a bulk chemical analysis of blue Egyptian faience tiles from the subterranean compartments of Zoser's Pyramid at Saqqara. The tiles form patterns depicting the mythical primeval marsh from which the Benben (Cosmic or Primordial Mountain) first emerged. Le Chatelier's analysis shows that Zoser's tiles contain the necessary materials for geopolymerization (the chemical integration of silica and alumina by means of an alkali).[3] The tiles are composed of 92.5 percent silica, 1.2 percent alumina, and 2.5 percent soda (no clay is present). Le Chatelier's analysis serves to show that these examples of Egyptian faience comply with the chemistry of geopolymerization. Joseph Davidovits produces Egyptian faience with a geopolymeric formula that chemically matches the Egyptian faience tiles in the substructure of Zoser's pyramid.

The moderate temperature geopolymeric faience system may explain the production of pieces of exquisite glass art that provoked a fury that makes the battles over geopolymerized pyramid stone pale by comparison. Even after hundreds of pieces of exquisite glass art were brought from Egypt to museums in the early days of Egyptology, experts refused to believe that the ancient Egyptians produced glass that rivals examples of modern glass making. Even with the gorgeous ancient pieces before their eyes, the Egyptian pieces were deemed impossible because experts thought in terms of modern glass making methods (especially melting sand at high temperatures and all that goes into shaping very hot, molten glass to perfection). While today's glass making requires very high heat and modern technology for handling hot molten glass, the ancient means of vitrification did not suffer this disadvantage. Egyptian faience making evolved into glass making by the 18th Dynasty. A couple of much earlier faience beads are argued to be accidental examples of pure glass formation. As mentioned. the exquisite eyes in the Old Kingdom statues of Rahotep and Nofret may be "fused silica." If so, we can expect that the Egyptians made ultralow expansion, high purity synthetic amorphous silicon dioxide at moderate temperature.

We can appreciate the value of perfecting this technology today. One of the most impressive ancient pieces is a seven-layer cameo glass of the god Dionysos. It is difficult to make a three-layer cameo glass sculpture with today's technology because of heat-induced warping between layers. The Egyptians made gem-quality glass and thereby imitated gemstones. Emerald was a favorite — and this brings to mind the ancient accounts of multiton emeralds held by Alexander the Great and other kings. The 60-foot-high emerald obelisk in the Temple of Jupiter in ancient Rome also comes to mind. It is said to have been made of four pieces of emerald, each 15-feet high. Its broken pieces are said to have been inherited by the Church (and, if so, it is logical to suspect that some may have wound up in royal crowns of Europe and other gem-studded treasures).

Today, the largest piece of glass is probably the 20-ton telescope reflector disc at Mount Palomar, in California. It took months to cool and years to grind. The largest surviving piece of ancient glass is the Beth She'arim block, which has posed a stunning mystery since its discovery in a cave in Galilee in 1963. There is a lot of speculative discussion over its manufacture 1600 years ago— all based on modern glass making methods. The Beth She'arim block measures 6-1/2 x 11 feet and weighs about 9 tons. When discovered, it was the third largest piece of glass in the world. The production of glass of this size seemed so impossible that before the chemical analysis proving it to be glass was made, one expert on the test team said that if it was glass he would eat it.

Other reports of ancient glass making may be related. The Koran preserves precious information in its Surah Al-Naml. It says that when the Queen of Sheba entered King Solomon's palace court, she picked up her skirt to avoid getting it wet because she thought she had approached an ornamental lake. But she was told that, "This is not water you see before you; it is a palace paved with clear glass." Another translation reads, "This is a palace constructed with glass." Given its enormous size, it stands to reason that the opaque Beth She'arim block is a product of moderate-temperature glass making. We are also left to wonder about the material nature of the enigmatic Black Stone at Mecca, which is deemed too sacred to study. Some consider it to be a very rare (because of its enormous size) tektite, which is natural glass made by meteoric impact. It is reputed to give off a magnificent scent.

Casting Stone Statues

Although some Egyptian faience objects were made on potter's wheels and others were entirely built up by hand, the Egyptians also made molds for casting and firing Egyptian faience. Objects can be cast into molds to form their overall shapes. Then the figurines and other objects can be demolded, and their details refined with simple tools while the new stone is still relatively soft. Molded faience objects show that the Egyptians possessed the molds and techniques that would prove useful for casting fabricated stone statuary at either ambient or higher temperatures.

Several thousand examples of molds, most made of red pottery, have been found in ancient Egyptian ruins. Most date to the New Kingdom or later. Although fewer molds date back to the Old Kingdom, this is generally true for all artifacts because of the destruction of the great cities of Memphis and Heliopolis.

A very large gypsum-plaster mold used to cast a hippopotamus head was found in Memphis. This mold shows that the Egyptians were skilled at making the kind of large molds needed for life-sized agglomerated stone statuary.

The molds for casting Egyptian faience are so-called open molds. They were shaped so that only the front and sides of an object were cast. The back portion of the objects came out flat. The artisans produced their flat backs by scraping off excess material after they packed the mold. Many statues of ancient Egypt, made with different types of stone, exhibit saw marks swept cleanly along their flat backsides. This simple process can explain those otherwise mysterious examples of rapid cutting.

Gypsum plaster is useful for casting stone statues. The reason is that the plaster can be broken away without harming the cured or partially cured stone object inside. The strength of gypsum plaster made it possible to mold large objects. If some plaster stuck to the stone, some clean-up of the final product was required. Details could be applied to freshly demolded statues with simple tools before the stone fully cured. This may explain the Egyptian scenes of stone statues being touched up with simple tools.

Gypsum plaster was used for covering the bodies of the deceased in the Old Kingdom, and also for casting facial images. So, some of these examples of gypsum plaster casts may not be recognized by Egyptology for what they are: They could be molds for casting stone statues of the deceased.[4]

The First Scientific Battle Over Egypt's Synthetic Stone

In the early 1950s—before the modern rediscovery of the chemistry of geopolymerization—experts argued over a collection of artifacts called the Mansoor Collection. It dates from the 18th Dynasty Pharaoh Akhenaton's capital city of el-Amarna. Like certain other examples in museums, pieces in this collection are oddly colored. The stones are pink, dull red, yellow, and pale grayish yellow. Most of the burning scientific debate over the Mansoor Collection concerned whether or not the artifacts are synthetic or natural rock. In those days, if the pieces were synthetic, they were considered worthless fakes. Now we know better.

The two largest heads in the collection were examined by William J. Young. He was then Director of the Boston Museum Fine Arts Laboratory. He wrote:

> The larger of the two heads was examined from a minute fragment and appears not to be a natural material. It shows all the indications of being a made stone...[5]

Zaki Iskander, at the time the Chief Chemist of the Egyptian Department of Antiquities, examined 66 of the objects in the Mansoor Collection for the Cairo Museum. He argued that the collection is natural rock.

For several years, a number of experts were involved in the searing debate over whether the items are natural or synthetic. Alfred Mansoor, the owner of the collection, hired a number of geologists in an effort to prove that his collection is natural stone—so as to prove that his collection is genuine.

Geological studies indicated that the patina on artifacts investigated showed all the signs of an ancient, genuine desert varnish. This is a feature consistent with great antiquity, and so the patina was very valuable to the argument that the collection is genuine.

Robert E. Arnal, a geologist of San Jose State University, examined three of the statuettes. He commented on some artificial-looking white patches in the stone itself. Although he admitted that they look artificial, he assumed the samples are natural. The reason is that he observed fractures filled with material he interpreted to be calcite. In natural limestone, the calcite would have filled these fractures millions of years ago. That would make the stone natural. But with a geopolymeric agglomeration, fracture fill (called self-healing) can occur when uncured stone cracks before it has cured. Some of the geopolymeric binder will flow into the crack and fill it. The cured stone will look as though it is filled with natural calcite. So, it will also be interpreted as natural stone that formed millions of years ago. This can explain why these three statuettes have artificial-looking white patches, but can still fool a geologist.

Leon T. Silver, of the Geochemistry Laboratory at the Division of Geological Sciences, at the California Institute of Technology, in Pasadena, examined three of the pieces of the Mansoor collection. He indicated that there were indeed small quantities of surface deposits that appeared "secondary and perhaps artificial." But when he did not detect any artificial paste (the rock matrix itself looks natural), he discounted these surface materials in the rock. But these deposits would not be present in natural limestone.

When thin sections of Joseph Davidovits' limestone samples are viewed by geologists under an ordinary microscope, the results are the same. Some kind of particle that does not occur in natural limestone must fall into the mix, or bubbles must appear, for a geologist to see that there is something unnatural about the rock matrix. Davidovits' thin sections were investigated in a blind petrography study with the French Bureau de Recherche Géologique et Miniere in 2002. The report issued by the French Bureau de Recherche Géologique et Miniere indicates that both of his samples appeared to be natural limestone. Geologists working on behalf of this body of research have to use more sophisticated microscope testing to detect a geopolymer. These include the SEM (scanning electron microscope) and TEM (transmission electron microscope). But sometimes the artificial nature of the ancient Egyptian-made limestone can be detected at 200x—because of particles or other features that would not be found in natural limestone.

We can understand how geologists like Leon Silver and Robert E. Arnal—who performed their analyses before the modern rediscovery of the chemistry of geopolymerization—would naturally assume that they were examining natural rock. They would naturally try to justify any unnatural-looking features within the rock matrix. Richard L. Hay, Professor of Geology at the University of California, Berkeley, made a thin section of a sample from the Mansoor Collection. He wrote:

> The aim of this study was to determine the nature of the material of which these figures were made, with the particular object of proving whether or not it is a man-made material (artificial stone)…I have gone farther than necessary in documenting what is really a simple matter. The intact nature of the delicate foram tests (shells) together with the euhedral shapes (rhombus-shaped) dolomite crystals shows that this limestone could not have been made by cementing crushed limestone;…It can perhaps be conjectured that a technology might exist (say beings from another planet technologically much more highly advanced than Homo sapiens) for artificially duplicating the several geological processes required.[6]

As it turns out, duplicating the several geological processes required to make this kind of limestone is a very simple geopolymeric process—with no beings from another planet required. In other words, using quarry material so friable that no crushing is required will produce rock-concrete with intact crystals. More importantly, the man-made cement will look like nature's own. Geopolymerization produces the near-equivalent of the natural cements that bind certain types of rock in nature—rock such as limestone.

A similar report, claiming that an ancient limestone object could only have been made using space-alien technology, appeared in an article in the November 14, 2002, issue of the Russian newspaper *Pravda*. The article excerpted below carries the title: "Sensation: Apostle Jacob's Coffin Made by Aliens." The coffin itself appeared in news headlines after its owner discovered that it exhibits Aramaic writing that reads "James, son of Joseph." This led some to suspect that the inscriptions alluded to James, called "Brother of the Lord." The *Pravda* report summarized the unnatural qualities of the limestone coffin.

> Hardly had the controversy settled down when another sensation happened. Andre Lemer said after a certain period of study that it was impossible to determine the composition of the stone. The professor stated that the coffin was made of a material that does not exist on planet Earth. "Hundreds of such coffins have been found in Jerusalem during archeological excavations. The research has showed that they were made in the first century A.D. That is why, the first thought that I had in my

head when I saw Jacob's [James'] coffin was there is something wrong with it. The stone differed from all other stones that I saw before. It had very small pores that could hardly be seen. At the same time, it was incredibly solid. After the tests that we conducted in the lab, I can assure you that our planet does not know this material," said the professor. However, the professor did not answer where the stone could have come from.

Much doubt has been cast on the authenticity of this object. But I know from years of personal experience that solid research can be falsely discredited because people can jump to conclusions and rely on misinformation, rather than try to understand the facts. Experts must be chosen very wisely. I have included the above report just in case ancient stone-making could be involved—and because artifacts can be misunderstood by people who do not understand the ancient stonemaking technology. After the reports on this artifact were released in the news, some have jumped to all kinds of wild conclusions about an alien agenda surrounding Christ. All of this is totally unnecessary.

More Egyptian Synthetic Stone

Even the famous Portland Vase of Augustus Caesar—thought to have been made by an Egyptian craftsman in Alexandria, Egypt—was originally thought to be natural agate by curators. Now that it is known to be artificial, it is classified as 'cameo glass.' This example shows that high-quality alchemical stonemaking still flourished in Alexandria during the early Roman Period.

A remark by Egyptologist Ali el-Khouli, in his work on hard-stone vessels, can serve to summarize the encounters by geologists with artifacts that exhibit unnatural features:

> Alabaster and limestone were the most common because they were easily obtained in Egypt. Other types could only be procured after the expenditure of great labor and at the risk of some danger. Other mineralogical terms employed in the fundamental publications by excavators are somewhat harder to identify. Examination of the original vessels probably would give some of the answers, though it must be pointed out that even qualified geologists are hesitant to give identifications in some cases.[7]

Egyptologist John G. Wilkinson provided a summary showing the remarkable skills of the ancient Egyptians at imitating natural stones:

> The green emerald, the purple amethyst, and other expensive gems were successfully imitated; a necklace of false stones could be purchased at a Theban jeweller's to please the wearer or deceive a stranger, by the appearance of reality; and the feelings of envy might be partially allayed, and the love of show be gratified, by these specious substitutes for real jewels.

> Pliny says that the emerald was more easily counterfeited than any other gem, and considers the art of imitating precious stones a far more lucrative piece of deceit than any devised by the ingenuity of man; Egypt was, as usual, the country most noted for its skill in this manufacture. And Strabo says than an earth found there was the only kind which would answer for certain rich and variegated compositions. The emeralds mentioned by Apion and Theophrastus, which, as before observed, are supposed to have been of glass, might also be cited to show that the art was known in the Pharaonic age, if we had not abundant and far more satisfactory proofs from specimens found in the ruins of Thebes; and we can readily believe the assertion of

Pliny, that in his time they succeeded so completely in the imitation as to render it 'difficult to distinguish false from real stones.'[8]

Egyptologists have been throwing rocks at the geopolymer theory for more than 25 years. The misinformation generated has made it hard for scientists to publish test results and findings, and gain research funding and samples. Journal editors do not take the submissions seriously because they are already swayed by so much misinformation that makes the premise seem absurd. Even Materials Scientist Linn W. Hobbs at MIT had trouble getting funding with so many rocks being thrown—notwithstanding the many constructive uses the material can serve. The idea is so controversial that "you can't get research funding, and it's difficult to get a paper through peer review," says Linn W. Hobbs.

But given all of the documented examples of synthetic rocks and other blatant evidence, we would think that learned Egyptologists would recognize that the theory rings true. We would think Egyptologists would welcome a theory that does away with unwarranted new age ideas about Atlantean and space alien technology and the like.

According to a recipe found in the Stockholm Papyrus, written in the early Christian era, even pearls were fabricated such that, "if managed properly it [the pearl being made] will excel the natural." The Stockholm Papyrus has, in the words of translator Earl R. Caley, "…some seventy recipes treating of the art of imitating precious stones and of improving the appearance of genuine ones."

Some of the words in the recipes in the Stockholm Papyrus have not been translated. But the recipes call for all sorts of organic and inorganic materials, like specific oils, pigeon blood, horse hair, dyes, bile (of tortoise, steer or calf), milk, gums, wax, hen and goose eggs, mercury, sulfur, vinegar, turpentine, talc, honey, human excrement, and many other substances.[9] It appears that the Egyptians experimented with anything and everything they could find, and succeeded in imitating stones through the long, slow process of trial and error. The possibilities are so vast that we cannot recover the means by which all of the fabricated stones of ancient times were created or all of the means by which natural rocks were enhanced.

8000-Year-Old Geopolymer

In 1981, Joseph Davidovits performed his first analysis of ancient samples of geopolymeric material. His work was a collaborative effort with Liliane Courtois, of the Center for Archaeological Research, in Paris. They carried out X-ray chemical analyses to determine the makeup of lime vessels from Tel-Ramad, Syria. The vessels date to 6000 B.C. These 8,000-year-old vessels are not stone, but consist of a white, stony lime material. They are mostly lime. Davidovits and Courtois made their presentation at the Twenty-First International Symposium on Archaeometry, held in 1981 at the Brookhaven National Laboratory, in New York.[10]

They reported that the samples contained up to 41 percent of analcime (analcite), a zeolite (or feldspathoid) easily made by mixing natron, lime, water, and clay. This high amount of analcime zeolite is not in the raw material from which the vases are made. So, the vessels can only be the product of geopolymerization. Davidovits and Courtois thereby proved that a simple geopolymer, made using a chemical reaction that produces synthetic zeolites, was produced 8,000 years ago in the Eastern Mediterranean. In modern times, synthetic zeolites were first made in the 1950s, by an English scientist named Richard Maling Barrer.[11]

The analysis of the Tel-Ramad vessels may have profound implications. Vessels of this type might help explain the spread of culture during remote antiquity. Norwegian anthropologist Thor Hyerdahl and others tried to demonstrate that people could cross the ocean much earlier than is advocated by mainstream archaeology. Hyerdahl demonstrated that a replicated ancient Egyptian boat is capable of ocean travel.[12] But detractors argue that ocean voyage was not possible because ancient people had no way of obtaining fresh water at sea on a highly-dependable basis.

But the 8,000-year-old geopolymeric Tel-Ramad pots are capable of converting seawater into fresh water. Desalination takes place through ion exchange.* When the pots are tightly corked and immersed in seawater, fresh water passes through the porous walls of the lime vessels. Minerals in seawater, including salt (sodium chloride), exchange for the zeolite in the walls of the pots. Consequently, only salt-free water enters the pots. Ion exchange using zeolite is also the basis of modern water softening.

A Roman historical account alludes to such desalination. The Roman naturalist Pliny the Elder wrote an account in his *Natural History*, a 37-volume encyclopedia of natural science. His article titled "Remedying Unfit Water" describes special water pots. Seafarers tightly corked the pots and submerged them into the sea in nets during ocean voyages.[13] According to Pliny, the pots automatically filled with fresh water. We may, therefore, postulate the use of desalination pots from at least 6000 B.C. to the early Christian era. The very long usage suggests the existence of an essential invention that is completely unknown to mainstream archaeology.

It is reasonable to propose that prehistoric people used desalination pots during travel along seacoasts. The pots would ease a descent into Egypt from lands to the north. Cross-culturization is apparent from fundamental parallels at the heart of the Babylonian and Egyptian religions. For instance, the sky religion of Heliopolis, in northern Egypt, has distinct parallels with Babylonian doctrine. Sumer, Egypt, and numerous other lands embraced the mythical concept of the Primordial Mountain, the symbolic foundation from which the world formed.[14] Rulers expressed the mound in architecture as ziggurats, pyramids, and burial mounds.

The more difficult question pursued by Thor Hyerdahl and others regards the Americas. In Mexico, the Pyramid of Quetzalcoatl at Cholula, Teotihuacan, is the largest single pre-Columbian structure.[15] It is larger than the Pyramid of the Sun at Teotihuacan. Although their building units are not as massive as those of Egypt's Great Pyramids, both of these American pyramids are larger than any of ancient Egypt in area and volume.

Mound architecture is also prevalent from a broad range of dates in the regions of East, South, and Southwest Asia and in the Mediterranean world.[16] Was there influence on the Americas by any of these mound-building cultures? The discovery of the function of the Tel-Ramad pots certainly helps us reckon the feasibility of broad cultural exchange in very ancient times.

Analyses of Synthetic Pyramid Stone

In 1982, Joseph Davidovits obtained more samples of geopolymeric material when he visited the Paris office of the eminent French Egyptologist Jean-Philippe Lauer. He provided Joseph Davidovits with two samples of pyramid limestone. Lauer added that he "defied any mineralogist to prove that they are not natural stone." The smallest sample was from the outer casing of the 6th Dynasty pyramid of Pharaoh Teti (ca. 2323–2291 B.C.). It was too small to have been viable for X-ray chemical analysis of trace elements with available

---

* Ion exchange is an interchange between an ion (an electrically charged atom or group of atoms) in an insoluble solid (like the zeolites in the pots) with an ion of like charge in a solution (like sodium chloride dissolved in seawater).

methods at that time. The larger sample came from the fine-grained limestone casing the interior Ascending Passageway of Khufu's Great Pyramid.

Davidovits took this sample to two independent European laboratories, in France and Belgium, for X-ray chemical analysis. Involving two different laboratories allowed for cross-verification of test results. The resulting charts and lists of minerals and their concentrations show that these samples of pyramid stone include minerals that can result from geopolymerization.[17] The sample even contains a type of zeolite (ZK-20) that does not occur in nature.

The chemical charts for the Lauer sample show trace minerals that are extremely rare in natural limestone. Because these trace minerals can be the result of a geopolymeric chemical reaction, Davidovits decided to make a comparison. So, he made samples of geopolymeric limestone concrete and submitted them for chemical analysis, too. His samples were devoid of animal remains (the pyramid stone contains brushite, which suggests material from animal sacrifice), so an exact match was not expected. The resulting chemical charts of his own geopolymeric samples show the same type of mineralogical pattern as the Lauer sample's charts.

Similar results came from a study by a team from Waseda University, led by Sakuji Yoshimira. He conducted chemical analysis on a random sample of limestone from the Great Pyramid. His results clearly show the chemical profile of geopolymerization. The main ingredients of the sample are calcite, zeolite (analcime), calcium silicoaluminate hydrate, and calcium silicoaluminate. The presence of these minerals results from the geopolymerization of kaolin clay, lime, and natron. Yoshimira's analysis represents independent data (the team was not testing for geopolymerization and is not affiliated with us).[18]

For purposes of further comparison, Joseph Davidovits analyzed several limestone samples from the Tura quarries, Egypt's primary source of fine-grained limestone. Their chemical charts show that they are pure calcite, although some contain traces of dolomite. The quarry samples tested do not have the unusual mineralogy of the Lauer sample or of the sample tested by Sakuji Yoshimira.

There is a much more definitive and important finding. The Lauer sample from the Great Pyramid is particularly interesting because it has a white coating on it that is topped by reddish-brown paint. Every geologist who has examined this white coating agrees that it is synthetic. They may argue with one another as to whether or not this white coating is stone or some kind of hard plaster, but they all agree that it is man-made. In the *Journal of Geological Education,* limestone geologist Robert L. Folk considers the white coating to be limestone and had this to say about it:

> It does indeed seem to represent an Egyptian-made replacement of the mother limestone by phosphate, as the structure of the limestone goes right through the coating.[19]

Importantly, chemical analyses of this white coating show the same unusual mineralogy as the bulk of the Lauer sample itself (these minerals include apatite, brushite, a volcanic form of silica, and a very small amount of the synthetic zeolite ZK-20). This combination of minerals is not water soluble. In other words, the minerals could not have migrated from the white coating to the body of the sample or vice versa. So, migration cannot account for this strange situation. The odds against the bulk of the Lauer sample having a naturally-occurring mineralogy that matches the mineralogy of the synthetic white coating are astronomically high. It is more logical to conclude that both the synthetic white coating and the limestone (which each contain minerals typical of a geopolymeric chemical reaction) are geopolymeric products.

Drexel University – Michel Barsoum's Team

Materials Scientist Michel Barsoum of Drexel University, in Philadelphia, read my unpublished draft of this book. He recognized the exciting scientific ramifications, and decided to undertake an intensive research project to test the geopolymer theory of pyramid construction. His study has continued for years. Barsoum and his international team of experts produced over 1000 individual microphotographs. Some scanning electron microscope measurements were made for the project at Oak Ridge National Laboratory, in Tennessee. Michel Barsoum and his team also made elemental maps, and performed local chemical analyses and other highly-advanced testing procedures.

They analyzed the microstructure of native rock from the relevant limestone beds and samples of pyramid casing stone from Giza. They compared the pyramid samples to the quarry samples. They studied the Lauer sample, too. Through their very extensive and thorough means of close investigation, the team determined Giza pyramid samples to be synthetic rock.

Barsoum's results were partially summarized in the prestigious science journal *Nature* (December 2006) as follows:

> Some of the massive blocks making up the great pyramids of Giza in Egypt are not limestone, but a synthetic mix like concrete, argue materials scientists. The paper by Michel Barsoum of Drexel University in Philadelphia, Pennsylvania, and his colleagues is the latest entry in a decades-long argument. Most Egyptologists reject the idea, put forth in the mid-1980s, that the pyramids contain concrete. Barsoum's team took a fresh look at 15 samples using scanning- and transmission-electron microscopes. The samples contain ratios of elements, such as calcium and magnesium, that do not exist in nearby limestone.

> The imaging also revealed regions of amorphous structure. Both observations suggest that other substances were added to make a concrete mix, say the authors. Michel Barsoum and his team found four different rockmaking chemistries evident in their analyses of masonry samples from the Giza monuments. In their paper published in the *Journal of the American Ceramic Society* (December 2006), Michel Barsoum and his co-authors remarked about the very impressive high level of sophistication in the synthetic rock chemistry they found: The sophistication and endurance of this ancient concrete technology is simply astounding.

MIT Investigations

I also provided my unpublished manuscript of this book to Professor Linn W. Hobbs, a Professor of Materials Science and Engineering, and Professor of Nuclear Science and Engineering, at MIT. As I write this, the latest tests of the geopolymer system are being conducted at MIT by Linn W. Hobbs and continue at Drexel University by Michel Barsoum.

MIT Professor Linn W. Hobbs co-instructed a class beginning in the spring of 2008. The MIT class, called Materials in Human Experience, tested to help identify ancient concrete pyramid blocks. The professors and class also built a small pyramid using both cast and cut stone. They used microscopic studies and chemical analysis to investigate ways of distinguishing the difference between natural rocks and the high-quality geopolymeric rock-concrete that can pass for real rock.

After working with geopolymer in preparation for the project, Linn W. Hobbs noted the difference between the wet consistency of geopolymer compared to modern portland cement.

Linn W. Hobbs said, "It's like something between mortar and Jell-O. When you try to pack it, it kind of ripples." "It's rather like Silly Putty," he added. After working with the unusual geopolymer material, Hobbs and his associates recognize a significant advantage: It did not shrink when cured. "With most cements, you worry about shrinkage," Hobbs said.

The MIT class experimented with different proportions and variations in the geopolymer formula to study the strongest, most durable and natural-looking results. A *Boston Globe* article dated to April 22, 2008 tells the story:

> CAMBRIDGE, Massachusetts: It is a theory that gives indigestion to mainstream archaeologists. Namely, that some of the immense blocks of the Great Pyramids of Egypt might have been cast from synthetic material - the world's first concrete - not just carved whole from quarries and lugged into place by armies of toilers.

> Such an innovation would have saved millions of man-hours of grunting and heaving in construction of the enigmatic edifices on the Giza Plateau.

> "It could be they used less sweat and more smarts," said Linn Hobbs, professor of materials science at the Massachusetts Institute of Technology.

> "Maybe the ancient Egyptians didn't just leave us mysterious monuments and mummies. Maybe they invented concrete 2,000 years before the Romans started using it in their structures."

> That is a notion that would dramatically change engineering history.

> It has long been believed that the Romans were the first to employ structural concrete in a big way, although the technology may have come from the Greeks.

> A handful of determined materials scientists are carrying out experiments with crushed limestone and natural binding chemicals - materials that would have been readily available to ancient Egyptians - designed to show that blocks on the upper reaches of the pyramids may have been cast in place from a slurry poured into wooden molds.

> These researchers at labs in Cambridge, Philadelphia and St. Quentin, France, are trying to demonstrate that Egyptians of about 2,500 B.C. could have been the true inventors of the poured substance that is humanity's most common building material.

> At MIT, Hobbs and two colleagues teach a course called Materials in Human Experience. Over the years, undergraduates in the program have recreated from scratch such artifacts as samurai swords, tinkling Meso-American bells and even a swaying 60-foot, or 20-meter, plant-fiber suspension bridge like those built by the Incas.

> Now a scale-model pyramid is rising in Hobbs's sixth-floor lab, a construction made of quarried limestone as well as concrete-like blocks cast from crushed limestone sludge fortified with dollops of kaolinite clay, silica and natural desert salts - called natron - like those used by ancient Egyptians to mummify corpses.

> The MIT pyramid will contain only about 280 blocks, compared with 2.3 million in the grandest of the Great Pyramids. And no whips cracked overhead last week as Myat-Noe-Zin Myint, Rachel Martin and three other undergraduates stuffed quivering, just-mixed "Egyptian" concrete into cobblestone-sized wooden molds marked "King Tut Plywood Co."

> "It feels like Jell-O but will turn rock-hard," Myint said of the sharp-smelling concoction.

The aim of the class is to teach engineering innovation, but the project may also prove that ancients, at least in theory, could have cast pyramid blocks from similar materials, which would have been available from dried river beds, desert sands and quarries.

Hobbs described himself as "agnostic" on the issue but said he believed mainstream archaeologists had been too contemptuous of work by other scientists suggesting the possibility of concrete.

"The degree of hostility aimed at experimentation is disturbing," he said. "Too many big egos and too many published works may be riding on the idea that every pyramid block was carved, not cast."

Archaeologists, however, say there is simply no evidence that the pyramids are built of anything other than huge limestone blocks. Any synthetic material showing up in tests - as it has occasionally, even in work not trying to prove a concrete connection - is probably just slop from "modern" repairs done over the centuries, they say.

"The blocks were quarried locally and dragged to the site on sleds," said Kathryn Bard, an Egyptologist at Boston University and author of a new book, "An Introduction to the Archaeology of Ancient Egypt."

"There is just no evidence for making concrete, and there is no evidence that ancient Egyptians used the stuff," she said.

The idea that some pyramid blocks were cast of concrete-like material was aggressively advanced in the 1980s by the French chemical engineer Joseph Davidovits, who argued that the Giza builders had pulverized soft limestone and mixed it with water, hardening the material with natural binders that the Egyptians are known to have used for their famous blue-glaze ornamental statues.

Such blocks, Davidovits said, would have been poured in place by workers hustling sacks of wet cement up the pyramids - a decidedly less spectacular image than the ones popularized by Hollywood epics like "The Ten Commandments," with thousands of near-naked toilers straining with ropes and rollers to move mammoth carved stones.

"That's the problem, the big archaeologists - and Egypt's tourist industry - want to preserve romantic ideas," said Davidovits, who researches ancient building materials at the Geopolymer Institute in St. Quentin.

In 2006, research by Michel Barsoum at Drexel University in Philadelphia found that samples of stone from parts of the Khufu Pyramid were "microstructurally" different from limestone blocks.

Barsoum, a professor of materials engineering, said microscope, X-ray and chemical analysis of scraps of stone from the pyramids "suggest a small but significant percentage of blocks on the higher portions of the pyramids were cast" from concrete.

He stressed that he believes that most of the blocks in the Khufu Pyramid were carved in the manner long suggested by archaeologists. "But 10 or 20 percent were probably cast in areas where it would have been highly difficult to position blocks," he said.

Barsoum, a native of Egypt, said he was unprepared for the onslaught of angry criticism that greeted peer-reviewed research published two years ago by himself and his fellow scientists, Adrish Ganguly of Drexel and Gilles Hug of the National Center for Scientific Research in France.

"You would have thought I claimed the pyramids were carved by lasers," Barsoum said.

Ancient drawings and hieroglyphics are cryptic on the subject of pyramid construction. Theories as to how the Egyptians might have built the huge monuments to dead pharaohs depend heavily on conjecture based on remnants of rubble ramps, as well as evidence that nearby limestone quarries contained roughly as much stone as is present in the pyramids.

Zahi Hawass, head of the Supreme Council of Antiquities in Egypt, minced no words in assailing the concrete idea. "It's highly stupid," he said via a spokesman. "The pyramids are made from solid blocks of quarried limestone. To suggest otherwise is idiotic and insulting."

Hobbs and his students are undismayed by the controversy.

"It's fascinating to think that ancient Egyptians may have been great materials scientists, not just great civil engineers," Hobbs said.

"None of this lessens the accomplishments of the ancient Egyptians, although I suppose pouring concrete is less mysterious than moving giant blocks. But it really just suggests these people accomplished more than anyone ever imagined."

The reporter has made a few mistakes. Davidovits suggests naturally disaggregated material rather than pulverizing. Barsoum's idea that most blocks were carved and hoisted does not fit with the archaeological evidence I have presented in these pages. Michel maintains his opinion because he has not determined where the needed lime came from. His tests do not show that it came from burning wood. More testing could show otherwise. So far, our best solution is that collecting scrapings from limestone bread ovens spared Egyptians from the routine of deliberately burning materials for the sake of creating lime. Even if lime was produced by burning, it would require no more fuel consumption than the accepted paradigm of pyramid construction, as I have already explained. Geologists stress that a thin section is required to determine the nature of blocks that are presumed to have been carved.

The *Boston Globe* article gives readers a sense of the battle for intellectual progress. The most fundamental principle of scientific methodology is to understand a theory before criticizing it. Any archaeologist who thinks geopolymers can be confused with portland cement proves to know nothing about the subject, and argues for the sake of argumentation. All Egyptologists should be aware of Egypt's sophisticated cement technology because of the high-quality cement found between pyramid casing blocks. This highly-sophisticated cement was documented at the beginning of Egyptology and long before. Egyptological literature also documents cement in the 18th Dynasty city of el-Amarna. So, it is well-established that Egyptian cement-making predates the Greek and Roman cultures. It stands to reason that anyone who possesses cement of this type can add limestone aggregates and produce high-quality limestone concrete. Although Kathryn Bard says there is "simply no evidence that the pyramids are built of anything other than huge limestone blocks," given the abundance of evidence and proof between the covers of this book, it is natural to expect that something in the careers of learned Egyptologists and archaeologists would give them a strong hint that this theory rings true.

We have yet to understand why Zahi Hawass finds the geopolymer theory "insulting." But his comment may reflect his statements published in various media sources (responding to the publication of Michel Barsoum's research), which show that Hawass does not understand the difference between geopolymeric concrete and portland cement concrete. The production of high-quality rock concrete that can pass for real rock, and even fool modern researchers, is a great credit to the ancient Egyptians. We continue now with the investigations of scientists in the important field of geophysics and other key areas of geology.

Chapter 28

More Supporting Data and Opinions

Limestone geologist Robert L. Folk advises that only a few geologists are qualified to determine whether the Giza pyramid stone is natural or geopolymeric based on its physical characteristics. Geopolymeric limestone is so close to nature's own limestone that the distinction is not easy to make — unless some obvious telltale signs show up in the samples. Adding natron, lime, and water to the kaolinitic Giza limestone induced only a subtle change in the chemistry of the limestone.

I have shown the Lauer sample to highly-qualified experts for microscopic study. One of them was Edward J. Zeller, then the Director of the Radiation Physics Laboratory at the University of Kansas, in Lawrence. His expertise included limestone geology, carbonate micropaleontology, geochemistry, and geophysics. He is known to archaeologists for having helped develop the thermoluminescence and electron-spin-resonance dating methods frequently used in archaeological research. Zeller's experience included 15 years of working with the micropaleontology and petrology of carbonate rocks.

Following his microscopical examination of the Lauer sample, Zeller issued a statement to me, which I published in the *Journal of Geological Education*. It is excerpted below and asserts the artificial nature of the Lauer sample:

> I examined this sample with a Zeiss stereomicroscope with a magnification range from 6X to 8OX. As a result of this examination, I was able to determine that the Lauer sample is not a natural piece of limestone…I was unable to make a chemical analysis of the sample, but I have no doubt that it is an example of a synthetic stone…In my opinion, it presents a particularly strong justification for an expanded research program in this interesting aspect of Egyptology…there is no doubt in my mind that the existence of a sample of high-quality synthetic stone produced by the pyramid builders does establish the fact that the technology existed at the time the pyramids were built.[1]

Rather than investigating its submicroscopic cement, Zeller focused on minute features that nature does not produce in limestone. His experience as a micropaleontologist made him particularly well qualified for this area of study.

I also provided Edward J. Zeller with some published microphotographs of the Giza quarries made by German geochemist Dietrich Klemm.[2] In one of them, Zeller detected what appear to be needle-shaped zeolite crystals. Zeller pointed out that it is highly unlikely that zeolites would have formed during the natural geological formation of limestone. It is much more likely that the zeolite crystals are the result of a subsequent chemical reaction — geopolymerization.

The evidence suggests that pyramid builders mixed zeolite-forming geopolymeric concrete directly in the quarries (excavation pits), where some hardened on the bedrock floor and remains intact today. Given the several million blocks produced at Giza for pyramids, causeways, retaining walls and other structures, we would expect the bedrock floor to show evidence of spilled cement.

Every type of concrete should contain some chemically bound water. This is water that is locked into the chemical structure of the concrete. Chemically bound water is not the

25. *The Lauer sample, as it appeared after geologist Robert G. McKinney removed a wedge so he could make a thin section for microscopic investigation.*

same as so-called free water (like rain), which soaks into pores of the concrete. Free water comes out of concrete in warm climates. But much higher heat is required to release water that is chemically bound.

Edward Zeller took a geophysical approach to demonstrating chemically bound water in the overall pyramid masonry. I provided him with all of the data from electromagnetic sounding experiments at Giza. There were three main experiments, conducted by three different teams. All three experiments failed because the pyramid blocks are so full of moisture.[3] So, the question is whether the water is free or chemically bound.

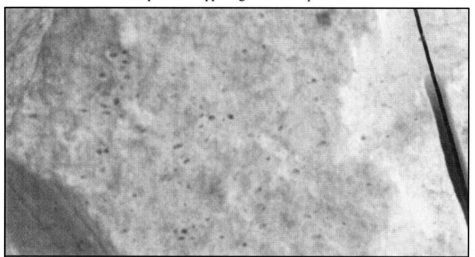

26. A surface of the Lauer sample near Robert G. McKinney's cut. Notice the oval-shaped bubbles. They are an unnatural feature. They are stress bubbles that formed when this rock was being manipulated before it cured.

The best known of these experiments was conducted in the 1970s, and headed by physicist Lambert Dolphin, from Stanford Research International (SRI). The team's goal was to find hidden chambers inside the pyramids.[4] Their test protocol operated on the concept that electromagnetic waves aimed at the pyramids will reflect. By measuring reflection, the team expected to detect hollow spots (such as hidden chambers) inside of the pyramids.

They found the Giza bedrock to be dry. So, the SRI team expected the pyramid core masonry to be dry, too. But there was so much moisture in the pyramid masonry that the electromagnetic waves were absorbed. The research project failed because of the unexpectedly high moisture content in the pyramid stone.

The results of this and the other sounding experiments suggest that the pyramid blocks contain permanent chemically bound water. To be sure, Edward J. Zeller studied the problem. On August 23, 1995, Edward Zeller provided me with his statement on the data produced by Dolphin and others:

> Only an onslaught of rain, at least six inches falling a month or so before Dolphin's experiment, could produce the amount of free water needed to cause the pyramid blocks to absorb the electromagnetic waves.

Rainfall typically measures in fractions of an inch per month in the Cairo area during the winter months. Typically, there is no measurable rainfall at all for four, five, or six months in a row during the warmest months. For more than a year before Dolphin and his team conducted their sounding experiments, there was only the typical dearth of rain in the Cairo area.

A record of the rainfall is retained in the detailed monthly precipitation records of the U.S. National Oceanic & Atmospheric Administration.[5] So, equipped with all the monthly records showing almost no precipitation, Zeller's statement continues:

> In short, it looks unlikely to me that free water could account for the microwave absorption that was reported.[6]

So, the premise of chemically-bound water—and, consequently, limestone concrete—holds up for the overall masonry of both the Great Pyramids of Khufu and Khafra.

Zeller also suggested another way of testing the blocks: He proposed evaluating the amount of salt and water in the pyramid blocks compared with Egyptian limestone. When made with natron and water, synthetic pyramid stone can be expected to contain more salt and water than does natural Egyptian limestone.

Experts have long noticed a seemingly strange phenomenon within the pyramids. A number of inner walls exhibit an encrustation of sodium chloride (common table salt). Inside the Great Pyramid, salt appears on the walls of rooms and hallways. The best known and most dramatic example of efflorescence (crystallized salt deposition on surfaces due to water) in the Egyptian pyramids is the 1/2-inch-thick encrustation of sodium chloride that formed on the walls of the Queen's Chamber.

While a source of water is absolutely necessary for salt to escape from stone or concrete, the Queen's Chamber is located at the 25th course of the Great Pyramid. So, a wicking of groundwater cannot be the source of the water needed to cause the salt solution to escape from the pyramid blocks and crystallize on the outer surfaces. Besides, according to Edward Zeller, joints between blocks will prevent the wicking process that occurs in natural hills.

The crystalline salt deposits within the pyramids are assumed by Egyptologists to have resulted from millions of tourists giving off small amounts of water vapor while breathing within enclosed, poorly-ventilated areas. But, while any water source will encourage efflorescence, salt also deposits on inner pyramid walls where no tourist traffic is allowed. For instance, in 1997, the Pyramid of Menkaura at Giza was closed to remove salt that crystallized on the walls and ceiling of its burial chamber. So, water vapor (breathing and perspiration evaporate water and not salt) from tourists cannot be the cause of the salt deposits.

When the Caliph Al Ma'mun broke into the Great Pyramid in A.D. 820, it was reported that the Queen's Chamber was covered with encrusted salt as much as 1/2 inch thick. In Caliph Al Ma'mun's time, the casing blocks still covered the Great Pyramid and protected it from rain. The tight-fitting joints filled with hard, paper-thin cement also helped protect it from rain. The pyramidal design itself allows for water to run off immediately. This means that heavy rainfall is not a likely source for the water needed to cause the salt deposits.

Al-Ahram Weekly (issue 542, 2001) reported salt cleansed from the walls of the King's Chamber during a conservation project at Giza:

> ...Cracks caused by the accumulation of salt have been filled, the walls of the pyramid's passageways and the king's chamber were cleaned of salt residue..."

In his *The Pyramids and Temples of Gizeh* (1883), W.M.F. Petrie reported finding the granite sarcophagus in Khafra's burial chamber thickly encrusted with salt. Natural granite does not contain salt. I consulted with igneous rock geologist Robert G. McKinney about the problem. He advised me that granite must be immersed in salt water for hundreds of years to absorb salt.

When limestone aggregates are mixed with a geopolymeric binder made with natron, the resulting rock-concrete contains a higher percentage of salt than the natural aggregate. The reason is that Egyptian natron is typically over 50 percent sodium chloride. This can explain the salt encrustation on walls of inner pyramid chambers and passageways.

In contrast, James A. Harrell's analysis of natural Tura and Masara limestone showed no sodium chloride.[7] W.F. Hume, in a monograph titled *The Building Stones of Cairo*

Neighbourhood and Upper Egypt (1910), mentioned an analysis of 32 samples from Tura and Masara. The mean percentages by weight of soluble salt (mostly sodium chloride) were only 0.33 and 1.21 percent for Tura and Masara, respectively. So, the relatively high amount of salt that continues to come out of the pyramid blocks for centuries must come from somewhere. It stands to reason that it comes from the natron and water the pyramid builders added to the limestone aggregates.

Efflorescence will not occur without water. So, the water content of blocks is also a critically important factor. Geopolymeric concrete is hydraulic concrete (it is made with hydraulic lime and will harden under water). Geopolymeric blocks will typically vary in water content. When the Geopolymer Institute team, led by Joseph Davidovits, produced multiton imitation pyramid blocks in 2002, blocks with higher water content had the smoothest surfaces. Because blocks were made on cooler, more damp days than those typical for Egypt, they held more water.

The rock-making mixture made on humid days was less evaporated than the mixtures made on warm days. The Geopolymer Institute team compressed their rock-making batches with a rammer (the sort of tool used for making rammed earth), so that the cured stones would be very dense and contain less water. Nonetheless, the wetter batches contain more water and had the smoothest surfaces. It makes sense to think that when making very smooth, seemingly polished surfaces, like those of the walls of the Queen's Chamber, the Egyptians added extra water to the rock-making mixture. Excess water in hydraulic concrete will result in more efflorescence. So, this can explain the 1/2-inch-thick salt encrustation found on the very smooth walls of the Queen's Chamber.

Even with concrete made from portland cement (which is hydraulic cement), water in the hardened concrete will dissolve soluble salts. As with pyramid concrete, the result is that a salt-water solution migrates to the surface because of either evaporation or hydraulic pressure.

In short, too much salt and water in synthetic pyramid stone, which is a hydraulic form of concrete, results in efflorescence on the inner walls of pyramids. The efflorescence itself strongly supports the case for geopolymerized pyramid stone.

If the blocks were natural limestone, the water source needed to cause the efflorescence would be unaccounted for. The relatively high amount of salt required to produce such dramatic and prolonged instances of salt encrustation is unaccounted for with natural rock. So, the water and salt in the pyramid stone strongly suggests that it is a type of hydraulic concrete. According to Edward J. Zeller, this phenomenon of salt formation presents an extremely strong case showing that the masonry of the pyramids is fundamentally different than quarry sources.

The next geologist to examine the Lauer sample was highly recommended by Edward J. Zeller. He is petrographer Robert G. McKinney, an igneous-rock geologist, geophysicist, and geochemist who at the time had more than 40 years of experience working with nummulitic limestone for the oil industry. This type of limestone is often associated with oil. Robert McKinney produced a thin section from the Lauer sample for microscopic observation. He took dozens of microphotographs of areas of the thin section. Nontechnical portions of his statement read:

This is a very strange rock indeed, and does not exhibit properties which one normally sees together in a sedimentary rock...The rock underneath the coating exhibits a texture that is definitely wood grain.[8]

27. A limestone block on Khafra's pyramid shows a rock within a rock, called an inclusion. Robert G. McKinney writes: "The inclusion couldn't be there any other way than to be immersed in the slurry. Limestone is usually a low energy sediment, and one solitary cobble of that sort would not appear (unless it is a sandstone accretion, and it doesn't look like that)." Robert L Folk, a limestone geologist at the top of his field, could not account for this block within the formation of natural limestone, either.

Wood grain should not appear on natural limestone. But wooden boards are useful for shaping and flattening a pliable stonemaking mixture. So, Robert McKinney may have observed evidence of their use.

His observation could tie in with the reddish-brown paint covering the white coating on the Lauer sample. The red paint also appears on various other parts of the Ascending Passageway of the Great Pyramid.[9] Also, in the Third Pyramid at Giza, the name of Menkaura appears in red paint on the roof of his burial chamber. The head of the Sphinx used to exhibit a great deal of red paint.

Dieter Arnold, in *Building in Egypt*, suggests that the flatness of surfaces was tested by touching a stone surface with a true surface—a freshly painted wooden board.[10] The wet paint would stick to protruding areas, showing that they need more shaping. Arnold's explanation is plausible, and we can consider it in combination with the wood-grain impression left on the Lauer sample. A good explanation for the wood-grain impression is that it was made by pressing a board against uncured man-made stone.

During our investigations of Giza and Saqqara, geologist Robert L. Folk noticed an unusually high amount of wood fragments embedded in surfaces of pyramid blocks. He frequently stopped to inspect blocks close up with his 50x pocket microscope. Repeatedly, he observed small pieces of embedded wood. He finally remarked that he was seeing an unusually high number of wood fragments. In response to Folk's observation, geologist Robert McKinney provided the following statement:

As to wood pieces in the stone, this I think is highly significant. Wood certainly would not be common in Eocene limestone.[11]

The small blocks of the first pyramids are shaped like mud-bricks, which suggests that the workers cast them in small wooden molds. Bits of wood from the molds may have sometimes stuck to the stone, accounting for the wood fragments Folk observed. We can expect that Zoser's workers generally removed the stone bricks from the wooden molds before the wood adhered to the stone. But sometimes bits of wood adhered, and some remain today.

Robert L. Folk, who is highly qualified, examined microphotographs of the Lauer sample. He is also very hostile to the geopolymer theory (see our debates in Appendix 2). But he inadvertently confirmed the artificial nature of the Lauer sample in published geological literature. In short, he observed a microphotograph published in *The Pyramids: An Enigma Solved* (Davidovits and Morris, 1988) and recognized that it is not natural limestone.

Assuming the geopolymer theory to be wrong, Folk asserted in published literature (without ever having seen the sample itself) that it must be plaster—based on its artificial appearance. To prove to him that the sample is limestone instead, I published another microphotograph. It was taken at higher magnification, so that Folk could better see its grain structure. I published the microphoto in my article in *Concrete International* magazine. Folk responded by saying that it looks like normal limestone. Folk has never reconciled his contradiction.

At one magnification, he recognized that the material must be artificial. At a higher magnification, he recognized that the Lauer sample as limestone (rather than plaster). McKinney and I later engaged Robert Folk in a blind study, during which we gave Folk 12 microphotographs of the Lauer sample without him knowing what he was looking at.

Folk designated five out of 12 of the microphotographs of the Lauer sample as artificial stone. In other words, the Lauer sample looks so much like natural limestone under a microscope that only five out of 12 spots on the thin section exhibit telltale artificial features.

Robert McKinney later sent Folk the limestone stub left over from cutting the thin section from the Lauer sample. So, there is no question that Robert Folk knows full well that the Lauer sample is not the piece of plaster he initially (and unscientifically) reported it to be after looking at our microphotograph in *The Pyramids: An Enigma Solved* (1988). Folk has never reconciled his contradictions. But he has inadvertently confirmed the artificial nature of the Lauer sample from the Ascending Passageway of the Great Pyramid.

See Appendix 2 for *The Great Pyramid Debates*, which fully explains the argumentation of our critics and the evidence we (Joseph Davidovits, Robert McKinney, Edward Zeller, and I) produced to prove them wrong.

Robert G. McKinney also examined the features of some pyramid blocks. For publication here, he made the following statement about Figure 27. It shows a large chunk (inclusion) in a limestone block from Khafra's Great Pyramid:

The inclusion couldn't be there any other way than to be immersed in the slurry. Limestone is usually a low energy sediment, and one solitary cobble of that sort would not appear (unless it is a sandstone accretion, and it doesn't look like that).

Robert L Folk, a limestone geologist at the top of his field, could not account for this block within the formation of natural limestone, either.

Before his retirement, physicist Guy Demortier was Head of the Laboratory for the Analysis of Nuclear Reactions at the University Notre Dame de la Paix, in Namur, Belgium.

He studies archaeologic materials and technologies, and analyzed stone from the Great Pyramid on behalf of this body of research. In 2004, he presented his findings in a lecture, titled "Construction of the Cheops Pyramid at Gizeh – An Enigma Solved," at the National Gallery of Slovenia (organized by J. Stefan Institute and the National Museum of Slovenia). Demortier showed slides that produce evidence of molded stone, and reported his tests demonstrating arsenic in pyramid casing stone. As mentioned, arsenic minerals from the Sinai allow for rapid setting of very large blocks.

We continue by looking at the evidence showing that there is no justification for re-dating any of the architecture at Giza. So, no extra construction time need be allocated that would alter the rapid rate Egyptology has established for building the Great Pyramid.

⫷ Chapter 29 ⫸
Return to the Pyramid Mystique

I f the Great Pyramid could be shown to have been built much earlier than 4th Dynasty
Egypt, the time it took to build it would become an open question. I show here that
there is every reason to believe that the Great Pyramid dates to the 4th Dynasty.
Some popular books are convincing a growing number of people that both the Great Pyramid
and the Sphinx are either prehistoric or at least Predynastic monuments. Consequently, with
increasing frequency, people ask me if geopolymeric concrete was Atlantean technology. I
address the controversy here.

The meaning, purpose, and origins of the pyramids clear to the Egyptologist range from
clouded to highly distorted in much popular literature. Popular books interpret the Great
Pyramid as everything from a UFO receptor, to a so-called "stargate," to a power station
that holds the Earth itself in balance.

We can expect myths and fantasy to revolve around anything so ancient, famous, fabulous, and enchanting as the pyramids. But modern notions have taken a toll on the popular
perception of the Great Pyramid's symbolic, cosmogonic meaning and place in history.
Since the inception of Egyptology, untenable notions have grown up around the fringes of
this discipline. As long as untenable ideas are not challenged and dispelled, many people
will continue to be influenced by wrong-headed hypotheses that push the historical context
of the pyramids further into obscurity.

Pyramid Lore through the Ages

Ancient and modern myths and legends differ in nuance depending upon their era of
origin. In the 1st century B.C., historian Diodorus Siculus visited Giza. He reported that
the Great Pyramid was in perfect condition at that time. He witnessed no construction ramp
remains or heaps of broken blocks. Diodorus reported that the Great Pyramid seemed as
though it had been left behind by the hands of a deity. The Egyptians of his day considered
the monument to be the result of a miracle.[1] This fits the definition "object of wonder" and
the Great Pyramid was proclaimed the First Wonder of the World.

The pyramids are associated with biblical lore. According to a supposedly authentic
account, French Egyptologist Gaston Maspero (1846–1916) searched for the cup of King
Solomon. Legend holds that it is buried beneath the Great Sphinx.[2] The large cup was reput-
edly made of onyx and possessed oracular properties. Legend held that liquid poured into
the cup would begin to swirl, and that good omen portended from a spin from right to left
and the opposite direction foretold calamity.

Jewish extrabiblical tradition tells that the Israelites built the pyramids while in captiv-
ity in Egypt.[3] The Great Pyramids were built some 500 to 1,000 years before Abraham's
descent into Egypt. Although the date could be off considerably, mainstream scholarship
places Abraham in about the 16th century B.C.[4]

But the tradition that Israelite labor built the pyramids may preserve a genuine folk
memory. The 19th Dynasty administration of Ramses II restored several pyramids.[5] Most
scholars believe that the Exodus occurred during this time—because the northern city of
Pi-Raamses is mentioned in Exodus 1:12. Pi-Raamses means the "City of Ramses," and
refers to a northern city that Ramses II enlarged and renamed after himself.[6] During Ramses

II's reign, numerous Semitic people from Palestine were concentrated in northern Egypt, in Pi-Raamses and other Delta cities.[7] It is not improbable that Ramses II set masses of these foreigners to work clearing and restoring the pyramids. This may account for the tradition that Israelites built them.[8] But some of the smaller pyramids were built at about the time many historians think Abraham was in Egypt. It is entirely possible that Semitic labor was involved.

In the 5th century B.C., Herodotus recorded a folktale that held that the Egyptians were badly governed by Pharaoh Cheops (Egyptian: Khufu).[9] Herodotus' report was the inspiration for the grandiose 1955 William Faulkner Hollywood epic *Land of the Pharaohs*—with its seeming cast of millions constructing Khufu's giant pyramid tomb. Gigantic stone blocks float along the Nile on barges to Giza. Extrabiblical Jewish legend saying that Hebrews built the pyramids influenced Cecil B. DeMille's *The Ten Commandments*. A famous scene shows Hebrew slaves dragging huge blocks. Egyptologists now believe that a large civilian task force built the Great Pyramid, rather than whip-driven slaves.

Taking biblical lore to the extreme, in his best-selling book *The Sign and the Seal* (1993), author Graham Hancock proposed that the Ark of the Covenant was the product of a lost science secretly handed down through a line of priests from Atlantis. Hancock suggested that this lost science afforded "unprecedented mastery over the physical world." He associates the Ark of the Covenant—which he thinks was a portable power machine equipped with "power packs"—with pyramid construction. Hancock also thinks that the Ark of the Covenant raised obelisks.[10] But the Ark of the Covenant was produced over 1,000 years after the Great Pyramid was already built.

Pyramidologists have tried unsuccessfully to show that the Great Pyramid encodes a map of history and biblical prophecy. Based on such notions, David Davidson, in his book *The Great Pyramid: Its Divine Message* (1940), predicted that the world would end in August of 1953.[11]

In the late 1800s and early 1900s, Scottish royal astronomer Charles Piazzi Smyth studied the Great Pyramid. Heavily influenced by the English writer John Taylor (1781-1864), Smyth used the dimensions of the Great Pyramid to deduce that the Second Coming of Christ would take place between 1892 and 1911, and no later than 1960.[12] In the 1950s, Adam Rutherford made a failed attempt by calculating that the event would occur by 1977. Popular literature has a history of failed biblical doomsday predictions.

Arabic-Egyptian and Roman legends remember the pyramids as the storehouses of Joseph, the Hebrew Patriarch. The pyramids are Joseph's granaries in a mosaic from the church of San Mark's in Venice.[13] The scene is preserved from a tradition found in the cosmography of the 4th or 5th century Roman orator Julius Honorius.[14] Medieval Egyptian tradition calls the pyramid at el-Lahun, in the Faiyum region of Middle Egypt, the Pyramid of Joseph.[15]

An extrabiblical Jewish tradition reports that the grain Joseph stored—unlike other stored grain—did not rot.[16] Egyptologists have found grain in tombs that is thousands of years old. The grain is so well preserved that researchers attempted germination.[17] Whereas, wheat stored in modern silos usually becomes unfit for human consumption after only a few seasons of storage. Because of fungus and insect infestation, grain usually keeps no longer than four years without a preservative.

The preservation of organic material in pyramids has received no shortage of attention in popular books. In the 1930s, a Frenchman named Antoine Bovis observed that a dead cat in the Great Pyramid did not decompose. The animal apparently wandered into the King's Chamber and perished before finding an exit route. The cat's body dried out, even though the air in the King's Chamber is always humid. Constant moisture is also present in above ground chambers in other pyramids in which no tourists are allowed. The moisture in these other pyramids invalidates the commonly-held belief that the many tourists breathing in the enclosed area of the King's Chamber create its high humidity.

Bovis' observation gave rise to the idea of pyramid power, which holds that the dimensions of the Great Pyramid preserve organic matter. Advocates of pyramid power include a French radiologist named Jean Martial, an engineer from Prague named Karl Drbal, author and biologist Lyall Watson, and maverick physicist Patrick Flannagan.[18]

Small models made not of stone, but of paper, wood, or other materials have been tested for desiccating organic matter and sharpening razor blades. Independent tests have not consistently demonstrated pyramid models to be capable of preserving organic matter. Today, so many foods are filled with preservatives that this is a consideration during testing, too.

The phenomenon of preservation may be due to microclimate, the climate within a structure. The importance of microclimate seems apparent from the remarkable examples of food preservation in Egyptian tombs that do not involve a pyramid.

At Saqqara, Egyptologists excavated a 2nd Dynasty tomb of a woman of lesser nobility.[19] Her tomb dates to before the pyramids were built. In accordance with funerary customs, an elaborate meal was set out on pottery platters, and alabaster and diorite plates and bowls. The state of preservation was so excellent that Egyptologists easily recognized all of the foods in the entire meal—even though this meal was almost 5,000 years old. The ritual meal consisted of porridge, quail, kidneys, pigeon, fish, beef ribs, triangular loaves of bread, circular cakes, and fruits.

The popularity of the idea of pyramid power, combined with claims by popular writers that only ultramodern technology can account for the construction of the Great Pyramid, generates increasingly imaginative speculation. New ideas abound concerning the symbolic meanings, purposes, and origins of the Great Pyramid.

No Solid Evidence for Redating Giza Architecture

Early in the 20th century, tourists typically left Egypt convinced that the ancient builders must have possessed engines, and were able to manipulate natural forces in ways unknown in modern times. In recent years, the idea of a link between the Great Pyramid and the fabled lost continent of Atlantis has gained popularity.

Plato mentioned Atlantis in two dialogues, *Critias* and *Timaeus*. Ancient people thought that the legendary sunken island continent was located somewhere west of Gibraltar, at the southern extremity of Spain.[20] Proponents of a pre-Egyptian dating for the Great Pyramid assert that survivors of Atlantis built this monument long before the rise of Egyptian culture. They theorize that Pharaoh Khufu later expropriated the Great Pyramid.

But it seems likely that Atlantean survivors possessing superior technology would also have introduced the wheel as a means of transportation. The wheel is such a fundamental invention. But all known evidence suggests that wheel usage was extremely minimal in the Pyramid Age (one instance from a tomb scene shows wheels attached to a ladder). Only flimsy wheels are known for all of ancient Egyptian history—and they are unable to tolerate heavy loads. The wheeled chariot is only known from the much later Hyksos takeover (c. 1640 B.C.), and there is no evidence that wheeled carts were used before that time.

After theosophist Helena Petrovna Blavatsky (1831–1891) popularized the notion that Atlantis possessed high technology, the reputed psychic Edgar Cayce (1877–1945) popularized a link between Atlantis and Giza in the early decades of the 20th century. In a so-called sleep state, he said that the Great Pyramid was built during the time of a priest named Ra Ta, in 10,500 B.C. Cayce indicated that an Atlantean Hall of Records would be found beneath the Sphinx. The tradition of a subterranean chamber beneath the Sphinx is very old, and Egyptian temples are typically equipped with underground chambers. As far back as the Ptolemaic period, tradition held that a sacred chamber or tomb exists under the Sphinx.

More recently, Mark Lehner, of the University of Chicago's Oriental Institute and an associate of the Harvard Semitic Museum, championed Edgar Cayce's claims. Lehner expounded Edgar Cayce's material in a book titled *The Egyptian Heritage: Based on the Edgar Cayce Readings* (1974).[21] In his book, Lehner speculated that followers of Ra Ta inscribed the cartouches above the King's Chamber as a feat of prophetic skill. In his book, Lehner described Khufu's cartouche as a:

> ...'red herring' for modern man until the time was right for the real meaning of this Pyramid to be brought to light. This, of course, would require considerable prophetic skill.[22]

The untenable notion is put forth even though Khufu was born some 8,000 years after the alleged priest Ra Ta—and the modern investigators some 12,500 years after the supposed priest. Lehner's more recent projects, including his participation in the PBS Nova film *This Old Pyramid*, are listed as accomplishments of the Foundation of the Archaeological Record (FAR), founded in 1992 by members of the Edgar Cayce organization called the Association For Research and Enlightenment.[23] Their stated goal is to seek archives from Atlantis under Giza's sands.

Before anyone is willing to entertain the notion of Atlantean origins for any monument of Egypt, I hope that he or she will take a closer look at the Cayce doctrine itself. Lehner includes some of it in his book *The Egyptian Heritage: Based on the Edgar Cayce Readings* (1974). In its pages, Mark Lehner promised to "attempt to demonstrate good reasons for believing that the Ra Ta story is rooted in truth."[24]

Mark Lehner went on to cite portions of the Ra Ta story, which include an alternative theory of human evolution—in which humankind forcibly pushed itself from the spiritual realm into the physical world. Consequently, Mark Lehner purported the notion that many individuals of 10,500 B.C. were grotesque hybrid beings. Mark Lehner purported that some had horse heads and human bodies. Mark Lehner went on to explain that others were sphinxes (human-headed lions). Mark Lehner professed that most people had tails, and that native Egyptians had feathers on their legs. Mark Lehner also wrote that a physical cleansing in the Egyptian temple services caused many to lose their leg feathers. Mark Lehner went on to say that many tails fell away, and claws transformed into hands.[25]

Anyone willing to buy into this line of thinking can readily accept Edgar Cayce's purported lighter-than-air machines and Atlantean dominance of our planet for hundreds of thousands of years.[26] According to Lehner, one of the few archaeologists positioned to excavate the Giza Plateau, "The final confirmation of the Ra Ta story lies beneath the paws of the Sphinx of Giza."[27]

The fossil records of Egypt and the rest of the world do not support the existence of hybrid human beings, as Lehner himself now apparently knows. Lehner has more recently adapted his thinking and states that he thinks the Cayce 'readings' reflect reality in a Jungian sense.

Plato described the fabled Atlantis as a prosperous land of abundance. But nothing in his language suggests high technology or knowledge unknown to the rest of the ancient world. The idea that Atlantis possessed advanced technology is a modern notion. It has been advocated since the late 19th century, when Helena Blavatsky and the theosophists imagined that Atlanteans invented airplanes and harvested an extraterrestrial form of wheat.

Now that we understand how the Great Pyramid was built with agglomerated stone, we can easily see that Edgar Cayce was not at all accurate. When asked how the Great Pyramid was built, Cayce gave the following incorrect answer. It is recorded in Reading 5748–6 of the Cayce Library:

> By the use of those forces in nature as make for iron to swim. Stone floats in the air in the same manner. This will be discovered in '58.

Authors Graham Hancock and Robert Bauval are also attempting to redate Giza architecture. In the *Message of the Sphinx* (1996), they wrote:

> When we say that the Sphinx, the three Great Pyramids, the causeways and other associated monuments of the Giza necropolis form a huge astronomical diagram we are simply reporting a fact. When we say that this diagram depicts the skies above Giza in 10,500 B.C. we are reporting a fact. When we say that the Sphinx bears erosion marks which indicate that it was carved before the Sahara became a desert we are reporting a fact.[28]

Let us examine these so-called facts to see how well they stand up to scrutiny. In *The Orion Mystery* (1994), Robert Bauval purported that the Great Pyramid dates to 4th Dynasty Egypt.[29] Subsequently, in the *Message of the Sphinx*, he proposed that the Giza site had been actually planned much earlier—in 10,500 B.C.[30] His assertion would allow for a construction period of several thousand years.

To develop his hypothesis in *The Orion Mystery*, Bauval drew heavily on research performed in the 1960s by Alexander Badawi and his associate Virginia Trimble.[31] Badawi and Trimble were able to persuade some Egyptologists that two shafts in the King's Chamber (which extend to the exterior of the outer core masonry), point to stars. Badawi and Trimble argued that one pointed toward Orion's Belt and the other toward Thuban (Alpha Draconis), the pole star during 4th Dynasty Egypt.[32] The idea put forth by Badawi and Trimble appears in the most widely read book on the pyramids *The Pyramids of Egypt*, by British Museum curator I.E.S. Edwards. From there, the theory became more generally accepted.[33]

The shaft alignments fit with the usual interpretation that a pyramid was a device for ritually transporting the deceased pharaoh's soul to its proper place among the stars. Egyptian religious texts indicate that the pharaoh's soul would ascend to the "Imperishable Ones" (the circumpolar stars). Ancient people considered celestial bodies as deities, and religious custom held that at death the pharaohs joined the gods to rule from heaven.[34]

Extrapolating on the theory of Badawi and Trimble, Bauval proposed that the Giza pyramids corresponded to the three brightest stars in Orion's Belt.[35] Astronomer Edwin C. Krupp, Director of the Griffith Observatory, in Los Angeles, California, is particularly qualified to address Bauval's remarks pertaining to astronomy. Krupp is one of the few astronomers whose training extensively extends to ancient monuments and their relationship to the celestial bodies. For publication here, Edwin Krupp provided me with the following comments about Bauval's idea that the Great Pyramid was planned in 10,500 B.C.:

> Although Hancock and Bauval assert the equinox sunrise configuration of Leo and Orion in 10,500 B.C. explains the disposition of the Sphinx and the primary pyramids on the Giza plateau, astronomy actually contradicts the Orion Mystery and the

"message" of the Sphinx. In the sky, Orion is separated from Leo by the Milky Way, the "celestial Nile," but the real Nile is east of both the pyramids and the Sphinx. Twelve and a half thousand years of precession can shift the vernal equinox sun back among the stars of Leo the Lion, but the Sphinx is still on the wrong side of the river for matching heaven to earth.

Also, zodiac constellations are not Egyptian, and there is no evidence that Leo was recognized as a lion by anyone, least of all Egyptians, 12,500 years ago. The Egyptian astronomical system was completely different from the Mesopotamian scheme that eventually gave us the zodiac. The oldest Egyptian representations of a lion constellation are New Kingdom, and there is good evidence that the Lion is not Leo. The zodiac we know was not introduced into Egypt until the Ptolemaic period, and it is a Graeco-Roman transplant.

If the star-aligned shafts in the Great Pyramid tell us the Egyptians wanted the north sides of their pyramids to face the northern sky, and south sides of their pyramids to face the southern sky, why would they arrange Giza with the southernmost pyramid matching the most northern star of the Belt and vice-versa? If the Egyptians intended the Giza pyramids and the Sphinx to reflect the arrangement of the sky in 10,500 B.C., why is the Sphinx on the wrong side of the Nile? In fact, Bauval and Gilbert had to turn a map of Egypt upside-down to get the Giza pyramids to match the stars in the Orion Belt.[36]

Bauval and Hancock also claim to be reporting a proven fact when they say that the Sphinx exhibits erosion showing it to date before the Sahara became a desert. To make this assertion, Bauval and Hancock rely on the work of author John Anthony West and Boston University geologist Robert M. Schoch.[37] Let us explore their claim to see if it can be called a proven fact.

The Sphinx: As a proponent of the Atlantean theory, John A. West fostered a project to examine the severe erosion on the 240-foot-long body of the Great Sphinx and the bedrock walls enclosing it. He interested geologist Robert Schoch, of Boston University, in the project. Because Robert Schoch and some other geologists believe water caused the erosion, West purported that the Sphinx is a remnant of the fabled Atlantis.

Although Schoch does not promote the Atlantean theory, he does believe that the water damage must have occurred when the region was subjected to a relatively moist, rainy climatic phase. In other words, he thinks the water damage on the Sphinx must have taken place toward the end of the glacial melts of the last Ice Age—thousands of years before Egypt became a nation. Schoch thinks the Sphinx could be at least 7,000 years old.

In sharp contrast, Egyptology assigns the Sphinx to the 4th Dynasty reign of Khafra (c. 2520–2494 B.C.), about 4,500 years ago. Robert Schoch thinks only the current face, headdress, paws, and rump date to historical times.[38] Schoch theorizes that the main body of the Sphinx may have been carved in about 5000 B.C. or before. According to a century of anthropological study, at the time Schoch suggests the Sphinx was carved, people were still in the hunter-gatherer stage. Egyptology asserts that another 2,000 years would pass before enormous stone masonry construction projects began.

One of the reasons Egyptologists believe the Sphinx cannot date to Neolithic times is that constructing it involved much more than sculpting a large monument. The Sphinx sits in an excavation pit used to obtain limestone for pyramid and temple construction. In that case, constructing the Sphinx involved an enormous pyramid-building project that removed about 66 feet of bedrock. A new ground surface was created, a protrusion of which is the rock mass from which the Sphinx was shaped.

Many proponents of an Atlantean origin for the Sphinx do not see this as a problem. They think that the nearby Great Pyramid is also pre-Egyptian, and so they question the age of Giza architecture in general. So, they accept that the Sphinx ditch could have very well provided for pyramid construction. This is because they believe that the readings of the reputed psychic Edgar Cayce are true—so they have faith in his readings concerning the Great Pyramid being Atlantean. We have already considered the serious problems with that line of thinking.

Water Damage on the Sphinx: Early Egyptologists theorized that Nile runoff (occurring in historical times), produced the water damage on the Sphinx.[39] Schoch argues that erosion is severe on the upper portions of the Sphinx, whereas Nile flooding should have undercut the monument only around the base. The erosion is characteristic of water cascading over the sides of the Sphinx and its surrounding enclosure pit.

The theories of Schoch and West depend on a dearth of water in the Cairo region since 5000 B.C. Egyptian geologist W.F. Hume, in his *Geology of Egypt* (1965), gives an excellent account of pounding rains in modern times that caused much damage to the Cairo area. In one instance, Cairo looked like Venice, with people navigating the city in boats because of severe flooding. Whole villages were destroyed.[40] There is no reason to think that such rains did not occur in ancient Egyptian history. While this kind of hard rain does no appreciable harm to the Great Pyramids, the Sphinx is much more fragile because it is mostly made of concrete-grade limestone.

The Critical Difference Between the Pyramids and Sphinx: Schoch does not believe that periodic violent rains or high Niles could have caused the erosion on the Sphinx. He points out that surrounding tombs are unaffected by water erosion. But Schoch's assumption, that Giza masonry and the body of the Sphinx largely weather to the same extent, is not valid. The fact is that the Sphinx is of a different quality than most of the limestone blocks at Giza. While the head of the Sphinx is weather-resistant limestone, the body was carved from the softer marly strata below.

The body of the Sphinx is much softer than most of the pyramid and temple blocks. The body of the Sphinx endures weathering so badly that it is in danger of collapsing. Emergency measures were put in place. Despite the rescue efforts, some predict it will collapse within 20 years. In sharp contrast, geologist Kenneth O. Emery studied the rate at which the Great Pyramid weathers. He estimated that it could remain standing for 100,000 years.[41] The extreme difference in quality between the Sphinx and the masonry at Giza is evident.

The soft limestone of the Sphinx was also determined by K. Lal Gauri, an expert on the Sphinx who conducted tests that show how weakly-bound the limestone is.[42] The degradation of the Sphinx's body (resulting from erosion) shows seven sequences of projected and recessed layers. Gauri measured the quantity and content of water-soluble salts and noncarbonate clastic materials (clays, silt, and sand) in those strata.

Salts and clastics are readily affected by water. The salts dissolve. The clays and silt expand in water. The amount of clastic material is very high. So, the body of the Sphinx will easily erode when soaked with water. But this is not the case with most of the temple and pyramid blocks.

Joseph Davidovits pointed out that a test used by civil engineers (ASTM D4843 Code) could be used to estimate the durability of the Sphinx's body. The ASTM test applies water, heat, and drying cycles to test the durability of building materials. The code requires soaking material (such as stone or concrete) in water for 24 hours and then letting it dry at 140 degrees Fahrenheit for 23 hours. The material is then allowed to sit for one hour at room temperature. If the material being tested remains intact, it undergoes more cycles until it disintegrates. The test roughly compares to what happens to stone in nature. Nature produces wet and dry cycles, and the temperature of 140 degrees Fahrenheit used in the test compares to the direct heat of the Sun on stone during the summer in Egypt.

Based on existing data, Joseph Davidovits estimates that the body of the Sphinx could endure from one to three cycles of testing by the ASTM D4843 Code specifications. This is less than what medium-quality limestone can endure. The Sphinx would not have survived the centuries had it not remained mostly dry and buried in sand through much of history.

The stone removed from the Sphinx's ditch is not medium-hard to hard limestone like the pyramid blocks. The pyramid blocks are medium-hard to hard because they have been geopolymerized. This is why the Sphinx weathers differently than the masonry at Giza. There are a few exceptions in the Giza masonry, and they can be accounted for by nonuniformity in making batches of rock-forming cement.

Before Gauri's study of the Sphinx, Thomas Aigner studied the Giza bedrock. He documented that the rock extraction sites consist of limestone containing a high amount of clay.[43] As mentioned, this clay makes the fossil shells separate from their (clay-bearing) matrix relatively easily when they are soaked in water. Today, anyone can go to Giza and pick up chunks of hard rock from the Sphinx area. Most of the limestone suitable for pyramid construction was heavily excavated during the Old Kingdom. The hard rock was left untouched. The quarry was also cleared of stone rubble during modern times.

In 1992, Joseph Davidovits demonstrated in Nova's *This Old Pyramid* film that limestone can still be found in the Sphinx excavation ditch that will quickly come apart in water. The day before Davidovits appeared on-camera, he selected limestone from the weakly-bound layer that was extensively excavated in ancient times. He placed a sample in a plastic bag containing water. He let the limestone soak overnight. He showed the results of soaking on-camera: The clay had separated from the nummulitic fossil shells in a matter of hours, so that the material was perfect for making geopolymeric concrete. We begin to see why the Sphinx is so easily damaged by violent rain.

Consequently, we see why Robert Schoch's idea does not hold: The masonry at Giza should not be expected to exhibit the same kind of weathering as the body of the Sphinx.

Temple Blocks: Schoch assumes that the temple blocks associated with the Sphinx are made of carved blocks from the ditch where the Sphinx is situated. For this idea to hold, Schoch must show temple blocks with natural sedimentary layering. In other words, Schoch must prove that what Davidovits believes are lift lines (construction separations) in geopolymeric concrete blocks are instead natural strata. Schoch assumes that they are natural strata because they look like natural strata.

But Davidovits and Egyptian geologist Hisham Gaber measured these so-called strata in these temple blocks. They demonstrated that they do not compare to strata in the Giza bedrock.[44] So rather than strata, the separations in the temple blocks associated with the Sphinx are actually lift lines that form in large concrete blocks.

Lift lines are areas of separation that form because huge blocks must be built in stages. The first stage begins to cure before the next stage is cast, and so on. This produces separations that look like natural strata. In short, the temple blocks did not come from the Sphinx ditch as whole blocks. If they did, they would have strata that matches Giza's strata.

To test the findings of Davidovits and Gaber on strata versus lift lines, geologist Robert G. McKinney and carbonate expert Richard McLeod examined a number of lift lines in concrete blocks made with modern portland cement. They went to large parking garages in Houston, Texas, to look at lift lines in huge blocks. They agree that lift lines in concrete do indeed look like natural strata in limestone.

In short, Robert Schoch has improperly dismissed the geopolymer theory without due consideration. In that case, without testing the material of which the strata in the temple blocks are composed (to look for silicas and trace minerals involved with geopolymerization), Schoch cannot properly proclaim that the temple blocks contain natural strata. Consequently, Schoch has failed to factor in important data that can make all the difference in the way the age of the Sphinx is interpreted.

Sphinx Exposure Time: One of the issues debated in the Schoch / West Predynastic Sphinx hypothesis is how long the Sphinx was exposed while nearby tombs were protected by sand. If the Sphinx was unburied for extended periods of time, then it could have been subjected to high Niles and to the kind of pounding torrents that have ruined villages in modern times around the Cairo area. Egyptological literature shows that the Sphinx was indeed exposed for extended periods.

After the 4th Dynasty Giza pyramid complexes were completed, priestly cults maintained them and their estates.[45] Egyptologists presume that the Giza priesthoods replaced fallen pyramid and temple blocks as needed. The maintenance cults presumably protected both the above- and below-ground tombs of royal dignitaries surrounding the pyramids, and kept the Sphinx clear of sand.

The richly-endowed pyramid estates were expected to last throughout history. But with the fall of the Old Kingdom, these cults would have had fewer incoming resources. At some point in history, the pyramid cults disbanded, and structures other than tall pyramids were buried by the ever-blowing sands.

The Sphinx is known to have been cleared of sand again during the 18th Dynasty by Pharaoh Tuthmosis IV (ca. 1401–1391 B.C.), who erected a stele in front of it. The stele bears an inscription linking the Sphinx to Pharaoh Khafra of the 4th Dynasty.

The Sphinx was also cleared during the 19th Dynasty (c. 1254–1224 B.C.) reign of Ramses II.[46] Two stelae, now in the Louvre Museum, attest to the work and stood in front of the stele of Tuthmosis IV. Ramses II's administration reestablished the pyramid maintenance cults, too. Starting in the 19th Dynasty reign of Ramses II's, Memphis enjoyed a renewed era of prestige. Once again, the heir apparents were required to be crowned pharaoh in Memphis. This level of renewed wealth and prestige increases the chances that the Sphinx was maintained.

Twenty-sixth Dynasty tombs exist at the Sphinx site, too. Memphis enjoyed its renewed status until at least the time of Alexander the Great, who was crowned pharaoh there in 332 B.C. His successors restored the Sphinx, as is known from the durable Ptolemaic mortar repairs.

Later inscriptions at Giza attest to Roman restoration of the Sphinx. It was, therefore, clear of sand at least during the period of approximately A.D. 138–211. Other ancient periods in which the Sphinx may have been unburied are not so clearly attested. It is possible that the Sphinx was clear of sand from the 19th Dynasty until the first few centuries of Christianity, a period of about 1,000 years.

The millennia-long age of the Sphinx increases the chances of it being subjected to damaging rainfall and high Niles. As mentioned, given that the Cairo area has experienced pounding, damaging torrents in modern times, there is no reason to think that the same kind of events did not happen during Egyptian antiquity.

A Difference of Opinion: Schoch stands by an earlier date for the Sphinx because he believes the erosion required thousands of years to form on the Sphinx. Schoch does not think that occasional heavy violent bursts of rain or high Niles could have caused the erosion even under the most generous amount of time that the Sphinx could have been exposed. But he is basing this opinion, at least in part, on the way Giza masonry weathers.

During work at Giza in 1990, I was accompanied by geologist Robert L. Folk, who is among the world's foremost limestone experts. I asked him how long it would take rain to damage the Sphinx. Folk disagrees with Schoch's assessment of the amount of time required for rain to produce such erosion. Folk stated that with this kind of fragile limestone, the damage could take place in a relatively short time. But Folk indicated to me that he did not want to get involved in the controversy. He became heavily involved with research on nanobacteria as it regards Martian rock. So, he has been in no position to publish papers and engage in debates.[47] But Robert L. Folk's opinion is highly regarded on matters of this type.

Given all of the above, it is unscientific for Schoch to conclude that the Sphinx should not have been harmed by hard rains just because the pyramids and other masonry remain largely undamaged by water.

Face of the Sphinx: Other arguments by West and Schoch must be taken into account For instance, West argues for an earlier date for the Sphinx based on its profile.[48] The face of the Sphinx does not closely resemble the famous diorite statue of Pharaoh Khafra in the Cairo Museum. West enlisted a police artist named Detective Sgt. Frank Domingo to demonstrate this point.

By producing reference points for comparing the two profiles, Sgt. Domingo showed the lack of resemblance very precisely. But the faces of Egyptian statues in museums invalidate West's argument. It is common for portrait statues of the same pharaoh to vary significantly in their resemblance to one another. The same is true for statues of members of the royal court.

Libyan palette: Schoch calls the "Libyan palette" in the Cairo Museum (dating from about 3100 B.C.) a "tantalizing piece of evidence." The late Predynastic palette commemorates the founding of fortified cities in the Western Delta. The Libyan palette shows large structures surrounded by walls. But Egyptologists insist that all field evidence shows that buildings and fortifications built in Egypt before the 3rd Dynasty were made of mud-brick.

The 3rd Dynasty Step Pyramid at Saqqara is the world's first known large building complex made entirely of stone—that is, geopolymerized stone. At this point in time, there is no evidence to demonstrate that the structures depicted in the "Libyan palette" were anything other than mud-brick.

Restoration Blocks: West and Schoch question restoration blocks applied to the body of the Sphinx anciently. Mark Lehner studied the restorations of the Sphinx, and dated the earliest repairs to the New Kingdom.[49] The New Kingdom repair blocks are Old Kingdom-style masonry. So, West and Schoch propose that Old Kingdom-style repairs suggest that the Sphinx was already old during the time of the Old Kingdom, when it needed and received repair.

But the 19th Dynasty is known for harking back to Old Kingdom style architecture. So, there is an explanation for these Old Kingdom-style blocks that fits with conventional Egyptology: The pyramids were in a dilapidated state when the New Kingdom administration of Ramses II repaired them. Ramses' administration restored several pyramid complexes to their former grandeur. His administration had the monuments carefully inscribed with the names of the pharaohs for whom they were built. We can still see the large hieroglyphic restoration documentation banners on some pyramids. Ramses' administration is well known to Egyptology for avid archaizing—and for the reintroduction of Old Kingdom building style.

For instance, Ramses' administration emulated the architectural style and designs that adorned the 3rd Dynasty pyramid complex of Pharaoh Zoser (c. 2630–2611 B.C.) at Saqqara—Egypt's first pyramid complex.[50] The temple columns represent the symbolic ambiance of the "First Time" (the Primeval Time in Egyptian creation mythology). Ramses' administration harked back to Old Kingdom-style masonry for columns and other restorations. The 19th Dynasty crews cleared and restored the Sphinx, too. This work during the New Kingdom can explain the Old Kingdom-style repair blocks that John Anthony West proposes date from the Old Kingdom.

Khafra's Valley Temple: Schoch studied limestone blocks in Khafra's Valley Temple.[51] These limestone wall blocks have uneven front surfaces, which Schoch attributes to erosion. These rough-faced blocks were covered with form-fitting granite ashlar tiles. But those who have studied geopolymerization are very familiar with these kinds of rough faces. We do not attribute them to erosion. We interpret them as a characteristic of the adobe construction techniques used to build the pyramids. The backs of all of the casing blocks at Giza have this kind of rough surface. But these rough surfaces fit perfectly with the rough surfaces they connect to on all sides. The surfaces lock together on all contact surfaces, and help to secure blocks snugly in place. This is the kind of custom-fitting that adobe construction techniques allow for when agglomerating stone.

Robert Schoch and John West interpret the appearance of the aforementioned blocks in the Valley Temple to mean that the walls eroded long before the 4th Dynasty, and that Khafra repaired them in the 4th Dynasty by surfacing them with form-fitting blocks.

If these surfaces could be proven to be the result of erosion (instead of construction technique when working with geopolymers), we would still have to consider the much later restorations of the 19th Dynasty: Ramses' administration may have added the granite ashlar tiles to restore the Valley Temple. In that case, the Valley Temple blocks could just as well date to the 4th Dynasty.

The blocks in Khafra's Valley Temple bear inscriptions that suggest an association with Khafra, too. Ramses' administration is known to have applied inscriptions to monuments they restored so as to identify them with the original builders. So, these inscriptions could have been added to attribute the structure to Khafra. This scenario would allow over 1,000 years for erosion to have occurred—if we operate on the premise that the uneven surfaces are the result of erosion.

Given the considerations I have explained above, there is no solid basis for interpreting these temples as Predynastic. The evidence presented by Schoch and West can be interpreted in favor of historical dates for the Sphinx and all associated architecture.

Inventory Stele: One piece of evidence does favor an older date for the Sphinx. The document is a 26th Dynasty (c. 1500 B.C.) text called the Inventory Stele. It was found at Giza in 1857 by Auguste Mariette. The Inventory Stele indicates that Khufu had the headdress of the Sphinx restored after it was damaged by lightning. The implication is that the Sphinx predates the time of Khufu. But the Inventory Stele contrasts the two earlier inscriptions mentioned above, associating the Sphinx with Khafra. So, the Inventory Stele cannot be depended upon.

Scientific Testing Methods: Robert Schoch and John West have put a great amount of effort into their hypothesis for an older Sphinx date. It should be tested to see if they could be right. Schoch agrees that the age of the Sphinx is tied to the ages of its associated temples. He assumes that the blocks used to build these temples were quarried from the bedrock at the foot of the Sphinx. I already mentioned the lift lines versus strata issue. Giza rock extraction sites show relatively little evidence that blocks were ever quarried there—because the pyramid and temple blocks came from those quarries as rubble that was formed into blocks. The evidence of whole block quarrying at Giza is minor and dates to later reconstruction phases.

Nonetheless, to try to settle the issue of the age of the temple blocks associated with the Sphinx, the following scientific testing could be performed: Natural limestone dates in the millions of years. Geopolymeric concrete can be dated to the approximate time geopolymeric setting took place. So, it is possible to test the severely-eroded temple blocks that Schoch uses to support an older construction date for the Sphinx.

The first step in such testing could involve using nondestructive electromagnetic sounding waves. All hydraulic concrete contains chemically bound water, and the amount of water in the pyramid masonry is sufficient to absorb the waves. Electromagnetic sounding experiments performed on the masonry of Khufu and Khafra failed because the waves were indeed absorbed.[52] I have explained that all the independent electromagnetic sounding data for Giza was evaluated by geophysicist Edward J. Zeller, who was at that time the Director of the former Radiation Physics Laboratory at the Space Technology Center of the University of Kansas, in Lawrence. Zeller concluded that the electromagnetic sounding and other data from Giza shows that blocks of Khufu and Khafra are indeed hydraulic concrete.

Assuming the temple blocks associated with the Sphinx also prove to be rock-concrete through such testing, the next test phase could be done with an age-dating analysis. A relatively new variant of thermoluminescence is suitable for testing buildings made with limestone. The method was used in 1997 to date two Greek pyramids, one located at Hellenikon and the other at Peloponnese, in Greece.

It might even be possible to date the Sphinx itself, depending upon how it was made. It is possible that the head is man-made stone: The head of the Sphinx is assumed to be the remnant of a hard geological layer that was all quarried away. But if the head is natural rock, it exhibits some unusual features.

I studied its features and here present something very odd that anyone can easily see. The headdress belongs to the hard limestone portion (which is a darker color than the body). But the headdress reaches well into the soft strata forming the body (see photos 28, 29, and 30). If the head and headdress are natural rock, we would expect the lower part of the headdress to be soft rock, too. Instead, the hard-rock headdress merges into the soft bedrock in the very shape of a headdress. Did nature provide this convenient hard-stone headdress shape?

The subtle curve of the chin line also separates hard and soft rock (see the color variants of the two distinctly different types of rock). Did nature provide this convenient chin-line shape, too? How could the Egyptians standing on the original ground surface know that they could quarry in this exact spot and find, several feet below their feet, a large headdress-shaped area of rock perfect for sculpting a huge royal Sphinx?

It could be that the giant head of the Sphinx was built up of geopolymerized stone, rather like when one builds a sandcastle. As a result, lift lines (such as appear in other types of concrete and look like natural strata) formed such that they are oriented according to the way the work was carried out in stages. In short, if geopolymeric construction was used to

28. The Great Sphinx. Notice how the headdress (made of hard rock that is darker in color than the softer rock below) reaches into the soft rock to complete the bottom portion of the headdress. It does this on both sides. and is fairly even across the back. Did nature form this convenient headdress outline? Could this be the origin of the riddle of the Sphinx, made famous from legends of the Theban Greek Sphinx in ancient Greek times?

make the head, the Sphinx could be dated by the same means I mentioned above for the temple blocks.

But it is also possible that the head was made from a natural feature that inspired its design. The geological layer constituting the head is depicted in maps of the Giza Plateau as having been flat. But it is possible that the head area was instead a knoll resembling a head, and that the Egyptian sculptors helped the shape along.

Although John A. West recognizes that isotopic analysis may not work, it is still a test worth trying. He attempted to organize an effort to use the method to date the third chamber in the Red Pyramid at Dahshur. Egyptology dates this pyramid to the 4th Dynasty. Because of the deteriorated state of the blocks in the corbelled third chamber, West proposes that the chamber was built of reused stones from a Predynastic monument, or that the pyramid itself was built around an earlier structure.

West suggests the use of isotopic analysis because when bedrock is first exposed to air, it is bombarded by cosmic rays. These rays gradually change the isotopic content of certain trace elements in the stone, allowing for analysis if appropriate quarry samples can be obtained for comparison. This method may be feasible for dating the Sphinx, too (regardless of how the head was made).

29. The Great Sphinx at Giza. A side view showing the bottom outline of the darker-colored headdress, as it merges with the lighter, softer stone below. Electromagnetic sounding could be used to test the head to see if it contains more water than the natural limestone below. Electromagnetic sounding is a non-destructive testing method that could be used to determine if the head it natural or manmade stone. If it is man-made rock, it presents an excellent example of very high-quality synthetic limestone.

The close, corresponding fit of blocks in the Red Pyramid characterize geopolymerized rock. The chamber has an adobe-construction-turned-to-stone look. This close fit is evident in the third chamber of the Red Pyramid and in other parts of the interior of this pyramid. So, the same tests I mentioned above could be applied to the Red Pyramid, with or without isotopic analysis.

Comparing the Sphinx with Neolithic Sites

John Anthony West asserts that the Sphinx dates long before the known prehistoric megalithic sites that dot various parts of the world. More than a thousand Neolithic sites are found in the British Isles. In the Egyptian environs, the Nabta stone circle in the Nubian Desert (west of Egypt's traditional border), has been dated to about 6,000 years old. The Nabta site measures about 12 feet in diameter and consists of four sets of flat, upright stones made of sandstone.

The Nabta stone circle, discovered by a team led by Southern Methodist University, is thought to be the oldest astronomically aligned megalithic site in the world. According to astronomer J. McKim Malville, of the University of Colorado at Boulder, the Nabta stone circle dates to about a millennium earlier than the sites in England, Brittany, and Europe. West advocates that the Sphinx is an even older astronomical symbol, a 36,000-year-old Leo marker.

30. View of the Giza Sphinx from the front. It is possible that the Sphinx's head started as a knoll instead of a layer of limestone that had to be excavated. It is possible that workers studied the knoll and realized a fortunate 'headdress' configuration that inspired their Sphinx design. In that case, the head would be an example of very hard natural rock that does not match the rest of the Giza bedrock.

A logical question arises: Why not directly associate the Nabta stone circle with the Sphinx, given that they are both megalithic structures in Africa? After all, the Sphinx is believed to be a solar monument, too. A survey utilizing a global-positioning satellite confirmed the alignment of the Nabta stones to north-south, east-west, and to the summer solstice Sun as viewed about 6,000 years ago. The finding brings to mind Egypt's Predynastic solar calendar, and Egyptologists accept a Nubian influence on the early Egyptian civilization. Moreover, bovine bones were found buried at the Nabta site, suggesting that Late Neolithic people may have conducted rituals with cattle. Similarly, the later Egyptians sacrificed cattle, and revered the Isis cow and the Osirian bull of Memphis. The Nabta stone circle also dates to the era of the earliest diorite vessels. Similar vessels were abundantly made in early times in Egypt.

Despite these circumstances, evidence strongly argues against a Neolithic date for the Sphinx. As mentioned, the Sphinx is the remnant of a large construction project, during which about 60 feet of limestone were removed to produce masonry for buildings at Giza. If the Sphinx is Predynastic, those buildings would also have to date much earlier. But all evidence for an earlier date for the Giza masonry blocks is argued against by a great deal of historical and archaeological evidence established by Egyptology—although the dating question should be settled scientifically by age-testing the blocks. The Giza monuments also mark a vastly more organized, and far superior and advanced level of construction work than is known for prehistoric megalithic sites.

I think a logical scenario is this: Solar structures influenced the Benben held sacred in Egypt's city of Annu (called On in the Bible and Heliopolis by the Greeks), which Egyptology has established had prehistoric beginnings. The Benben is depicted in Egyptian art as conical or pyramidal in shape and situated on top of a large pillar. Egyptologists think that the earliest buildings in the city of Annu were made of mud brick. The Benben, like the Nabta circle, was useful for tracking the solar cycle. Upright stones either cast or fail to cast shadows, depending upon the position of the Sun. These shadows are useful for marking off the Sun's path across the sky. The early Egyptian cultural blend is also believed to have included influence from Mesopotamia, where astronomy reached a high art.

As Egypt organized over time, the Benben, of mythological significance and a solar symbol, was reproduced in architecture as obelisks and pyramids. This is a logical progression of events. But based on the evidence so far brought to bear on the question of the age of the Sphinx, a 36,000 B.C. date for the Sphinx remains highly speculative and unfounded. So does a 7,000 B.C. date.

Nonetheless, unless an astronomer will step in and show otherwise, a remark by the erudite Richard Hinckley Allen, in his *Star Names: Their Lore and Meaning* (1899) compels one to investigate the idea that skywatchers were civilized enough to chart the heavens well before the earliest known cities of Mesopotamia and Egypt. Here are Hinckley's startling remarks about the charting of Sirius:

> Its risings and settings were regularly tabulated in Chaldaea about 300 B.C., and Oppert [the German Assyriologist Jules Oppert] is reported to have recently said that the Babylonian astronomers could not have known certain astronomical periods, which as a matter of fact they did know, if they had not observed Sirius from the island of Zylos in the Persian Gulf on Thursday, the 29th of April, 11542 B.C.![53]

We know that human civilization was making ceramics 25,000 years ago elsewhere in the world. But so far no evidence shows that the Predynastic civilization along the Nile reached the brilliant heights of construction that we see at Giza. Marine archaeologists are steadily engaged in investigating and dating submerged structures, and their efforts can be expected to help clarify prehistory. Some underwater sites, such as the mysterious geological structures off of Okinawa, Japan, are under debate. Featuring enormous, flat terraces, walls, block with right angles, steps, and hexagonal pillars, geologists question whether these giant megaliths are natural or sculpted with tools. It is logical to also question whether or not they are man-made stone — and how far back in history megalithic stonemaking appeared and the maximum rock strength achieved.

The Real Pyramid Mystique

We can get back in touch with the real meaning and purpose of the pyramids, and also get a sense of how widespread its fundamental concept is. Egyptian priests adept in Egyptian theogony understood the "First Time" event of creation as "the day of the elevation of the Earth." So it is documented in *The Egyptian Book of the Dead*, 1:19. The elevation of the Earth refers to a mythical hill, called the Cosmic Mountain (in ancient Egyptian, the Benben).[54] The doctrine holds that in the beginning, this Primordial Mountain emerged from the firmament. Life came into being — every kind of vegetation, creeping and swift-running creatures, and eventually humans. The mythical Cosmic Mountain is symbolically re-created in every pyramid.[55]

Henry Breasted (1886–1935) was the first to recognize the pyramids as re-creations of the mythical Cosmic Mountain. In both the Egyptian and Mesopotamian mythologies, the Cosmic Mountain was the first place to emerge from the waters of chaos originally covering the Earth. As time went on, the pyramid-building era passed in Egypt, and temples became the remaining representations of the Cosmic Mountain (otherwise called the Creation Hillock). Although they were not necessarily funerary monuments, temples still represented places of direct contact with the divine realm. Ancient religion revolved around the great temples, sites of the annual nature festival that re-created the mythical, primeval cosmic drama.[56] The purpose of the festival was to ensure the renewal of nature's bounty each year. At the heart of the annual celebration was the triumph of the solar deity's victory over death.

The tradition survived for many centuries. In Baalbek, Syria, the great Temple of the Sun sits on an artificial mound denoting the Primordial Mountain. The spectacular Brahman Kailasa Temple at Ellora, in central India, built in A.D. 785, represents a Cosmic Mountain. The place is the celestial mountain palace of the Hindu god Siva, whose contact point with the earth is considered to be a peak of Mt. Kailasa in the Himalayas. The stupas of ancient India denote the same tradition. The temple of Angkor Vat, completed about A.D. 1150 in Cambodia, is an exceedingly ornate representation of the Cosmic Mountain. The temple of Angkor Vat exhibits in its dimensions the fundamental cosmological concepts of Veddic and Hindu creation mythology.[57]

The Great Pyramid incorporates principles of Egyptian theogany (the systematic gene-alogy of the gods), which was heavily steeped in cosmology and cosmogonic myth (the cycle of birth, life, death, and rebirth on the cosmic level, with the life phases of the pharaoh mirroring the cycles of the cosmos). The Great Pyramid is in near perfect alignment with the Earth's four cardinal directions. Its square base represents the theogonic "Four Corners of the Earth," the cardinal points of north, east, south, and west. Cosmological beliefs are also arguably built into the King's Chamber's diagonal shafts extending to the exterior of the pyramid. Some Egyptologists accept the theory that the northern shaft is aligned directly with Alpha Draconis, the pole star in the 4th Dynasty.

If a pole-star alignment was intended, it may be the key to determining the construction date of the Great Pyramid.[58] Several ancient cultures considered the pole star the pivot point around which the visible arc of the heavens endlessly turns. In ancient Chinese texts, the word for "Cosmic Mountain" (T'ai Chi) is variously translated as "the Axis of the Universe," "the Pole Star," and "the Wheel of the Universe." A Chinese example of the Cosmic Mountain is the massive earthen burial mound of the Chin Dynasty's Emperor Shin Huang Ti, built about 210 B.C. in the northeastern province of Shanxi, China.[59]

Ancient people considered their kingdoms the analog to the perfect divine heavenly kingdom, and they believed that their king was cyclically sent to the mortal world to carry out divine will. Pyramids and burial mounds were the media by which a king's soul would return to heaven to take its place among the stars.

Because of a lack of mummies found in pyramids and a wealth of speculation about high technology at Giza, there is a great deal of popular resistance to Egyptology's insistence that the Egyptian pyramids are funerary monuments. It is true that the remains of mummies found in pyramids are of uncertain date. For instance, a mummy was discovered in the pyramid of Pharaoh Merenre I, at Saqqara, by Gaston Maspero in 1881. Because the mummy was discovered in a black granite sarcophagus within the pyramid itself, Egyptologists tentatively identified the body with Merenre I. But Australian anatomist G. Elliot-Smith examined the royal mummy and suggested that the body could date to the much later 18th Dynasty.

The pyramid of Merenre I, like so many others, was raided and looted. Khufu's sarcophagus was broken into at an unknown date. Many mummies were used as fuel over the centuries because of the scarcity of wood in Egypt. So, relatively few mummies exist today. But Egyptologists believe that the pyramids are funerary monuments because they were built in the vast desert necropolis (city of the dead), they were equipped with sarcophagi (coffins), they were surrounded by royal tombs, and they were considered contact points with the heavenly realm. All evidence suggests that the pyramids replicate Cosmic Mountains, the places where the kings ritually ascended to the stars at death. Upon coronation, the pharaohs represented the newborn Sun who would perpetually die and return to an earthly life, analogous to the rising and setting Sun.

In keeping with the mythical context of the Great Pyramid, the Greek historian Herodotus may have preserved elements of the Cosmic Mountain myth. Herototus reported that the mound on which the Great Pyramid sits was surrounded by water, brought from the Nile by an artificial canal to convert the site into an island. He reported that the waters of the Nile surrounded subterranean vaults under the Great Pyramid itself.[60] The report is consistent with the belief that the Cosmic Mountain rose from the waters of chaos. Issues of water, such as the Nile and Euphrates, were considered the sacred effusions of the primordial expanse of water banished to the edges of creation in the beginning. Ancient Egyptian tradition held that the Nile was a continuous terrestrial upwelling of this cosmic flow.

Within the context of pyramid-temple mythology, this upwelling from beneath the pyramids and temples watered garden paradises. The orchards and gardens imitated the mythical original earthly paradise, believed to mirror the heavenly paradise itself. There is much evidence that courtyards and terraces of ancient Near Eastern temples were cultivated as exotic plantations.[61] Temple precincts re-created the creation motif, cultivating animals and trees in garden settings representing paradise.

Summary and Conclusions

The pyramids are conceptual interpretations of divine or natural laws rendered in stone, thought of as an eternal material. The design of the pyramids reflects a civilization that built its regal architecture according to its doctrine of divine principles. These included the turning of the heavens, the rise of the Primeval Hill from the waters of chaos, and the perpetual cycle of the ascent and descent of the god-king from heaven.

There is every reason to think that the Great Pyramid is a product of known Egyptian history. The monument fits perfectly with the mythological designs of known history. Its splendor is not out of place for the 4th Dynasty, and there is no legitimate evidence that would date the Great Pyramid to Predynastic history. Egyptians produced marvelous masonry products, ranging from the minute to the gigantic, during all periods of ancient history.

The Great Pyramid is characteristic of ancient Egyptian alchemical stonemaking abilities. It is history's most conspicuous example. It is so famous, revered, and ancient that through the ages popular myths have detracted from its real legacy. Only in modern times has its forgotten ancient character been recovered by Egyptology.

I have shown above that the body of evidence amassed so far can be interpreted to support the standard 4th Dynasty construction date for the Great Pyramids and the Sphinx at Giza. The Sphinx is in danger of collapsing within a few generations. This, I believe, is the most important issue concerning the Sphinx. *This monument needs rescue efforts more than ever.*

🦅 Chapter 30 🦅
Geopolymers: Past, Present and Future

T he oldest piece of ceramic known to mankind dates to 25,000 B.C. The Palaeolithic figurine comes from Dolní Vestonice in what is now the Czech Republic. Here, in his own words, is the story of Joseph Davidovits' encounter with this astonishingly ancient artifact:

Organized within the framework of my meetings with the scientific institutions of the Czech Republic, this visit to the Brno Anthropology Museum will certainly mark a date in my studies on the technological knowledge of prehistoric mankind. Dr. Martin Oliva, paleontologist, presented to me the collection of Paleolithic artifacts – engraved bones – discovered in Moravia, in particular at Dolni Vestonice. Then, in the presence of the journalist of the local national daily and a photographer of Czech Press Agency, he unveiled the queen of his collection, the Venus. I still had [before] my eyes the image of the yellow limestone Venus displayed at the Vienna Museum, Austria, to be very surprised by this one. It was not worked in soft stone, but manufactured out of terra cotta. Thus, I was looking at the oldest ceramic manufactured by Homo Sapiens 25,000 years ago.

We have been taught that the terra cotta pottery was not invented before the Neolithic Age, 15,000 years later. And yet, I had in front of me an artifact resulting from the use of fire, at a time when, logically, the prehistoric men did not master this technique, according to the teaching of Prehistory. Like all other Paleolithic Venus', it is only 11 cm high. It is of brown-black color, a color that immediately reminded me of our previous study carried out on Etruscan ceramics...I thus knew how it had been produced: in an open wood fire (a garden fire), at a temperature of 300-400 °C maximum, but with a clay containing natural chemical ingredients, such as alkaline soluble salts, generating a geopolymeric reaction, which I call in my technical jargon, the L.T.G.S. (Low Temperature Geopolymeric Setting of ceramic; see the Geopolymer Institute internet page on that subject).

To obtain this terra cotta, one starts with a clay that contains natural salts such as natron, sodium carbonate CO_3Na_2. This type of clay is very often found in the countries of the Middle-East. It should have been naturally occurring in the area of Dolni Vestonice. A second possibility was the addition to any clay type of an other alkaline soluble salt, the salt kali, potassium carbonate CO_3K_2, found in ashes of certain plants, like the fern. Then, lime was added to the clay, a type of ash-lime extracted from wood ashes (like the oak). Thanks to these ingredients, the clay will be "fired" at a low temperature of 300 °C, in a simple garden open wood fire, burning dry plants or small tree branches. This is an ultra simple technology, that only works in association with a type of clay and natural chemical ingredients. One obtains a solid terra cotta, of brown color. The contact with the smoke of the wood fire will produce the black shades, by carbon deposition in the pores of the terra cotta. This technique is explained in a scientific publication that I presented with my son Frederic at the 2nd International Conference on Geopolymers, in 1999. See on the site of the Geopolymer Institute, the paper on The making of brown-black ceramic in Prehistory and Antiquity.

Davidovits announced his successful re-creation of this artifact — with its simple, highly-efficient chemistry — at the Geopolymer 2008 Conference.

Lime production is one of the oldest industrial processes of civilized humanity.[1] The ruins of Jericho, a city made famous by the Bible, exhibits 9,000-year-old lime-plaster. Some of this plaster is still in good condition.[2]

During Egypt's Neolithic Period, artisans were already making vases with basalt.[3] Some of the earliest mace heads of this era were made with either diorite or granite. A fragment that Egyptologists think was part of a diorite palette also dates to the Neolithic Period.[4] The stonemaking technology blossomed in the 3rd Dynasty, with the construction of the first pyramid. The technology began to wane in the 4th Dynasty, especially after Khafra's Great Pyramid was built.

We have yet to determine when the technology was finally completely lost and forgotten for making small works of precious art. Alchemists in Alexandria were still making artificial pearls from a mica paste and treating stones to imitate gems in the 3rd or 4th century A.D., as we know from the Stockholm Papyrus.

In 1998, Elizabeth C. Stone led a team of archaeologists that found imitation basalt in Iraq dating from Mesopotamian times. Their findings, published in the journal *Science* (July 1998), inadvertently offer independent proof from the mainstream archaeological community of our long-held premise—that ancient people agglomerated rock.[5] Using very simple chemistry, Joseph Davidovits makes basalt similar to these slabs found in Mesopotamian ruins. Like Egyptian faience (which early Egyptologists thought was natural sandstone), the imitation basalt from Mesopotamia required modest heat to produce.

Davidovits began presenting the ancient Egyptian stonemaking chemistries to international Egyptological symposia in the 1970s. He suggests that the ability to make fired brick made a difference between how architecture developed in Egypt and Mesopotamia. The builders of Mesopotamian ziggurats used fired brick because this construction system fit best with their natural resources. But Nile silt is not good for firing into brick. To best utilize their natural resources, Egypt took the different path of alchemically making stone at ambient temperatures—and developed a tremendous legacy as a master building civilization.

Other non-Egyptian artifacts may one day prove to be man-made rock, as well. The famous black basalt-diorite "Stele of Hammurabi," commemorating the greatest ruler of the 1st Babylonian Dynasty, stands seven feet high and dates to about 1792–1750 B.C. This exquisite pillar, an item of major importance in France's Louvre Museum, is made in relief and shows the king before the Sun-god Shamash on the sacred Cosmic Mountain.

Another possible candidate is the most intact Assyrian obelisk known. Made of black basalt at about 850 B.C., it was found in Iraq, south of Mosul, at the site of ancient Kalhu (modern Nimrud). Now in the British Museum, the obelisk stands six feet high and is decorated with inscriptions and reliefs. The Moabite stone found near Dibon, Jordan, dates to the same period. The block of black basalt bears an inscription in the Moabite language. All of these artifacts should be investigated to determine if they are agglomerated rock.

Moving forward in history, on the Greek island of Rhodes, concrete walls of the cistern at Kameiros date from 500 B.C. The Romans are more well known for durable lime-cements. The Roman architect and engineer Marcus Vitruvius Pollio (ca. 70–25 B.C.) described Roman cement.[6] A number of ancient Roman structures exhibit concrete and mortar that is unaffected by severely corrosive conditions, including hot flowing water and salt-laden air. The Colosseum, built around A.D. 75–80, and the Pantheon built by Admiral Marcus Agrippa in 27 B.C., are examples. By comparison, modern portland cement concrete survives no longer than 150 years under ideal environmental conditions. Portland-cement concrete buildings, in close proximity to ancient Roman structures and subjected to the same conditions, are severely weathered. In some cases, the corrosive conditions deteriorated the modern buildings in as little as ten years.[7]

High-quality Roman cement is intact after being underwater at Italy's Port Pozzuoli for more than 2,000 years.[8] Archaeologists found concrete blocks underwater at Caesarea, the harbor city built by King Herod the Great to honor Augustus Caesar in Roman Palestine.[9] Roman baths in Israel, built over flowing hot mineral springs, have withstood hydrothermal conditions for two millennia. They were damaged by human hands, along with other traces of Roman occupation. Modern repairs of the baths with portland cement concrete have not endured.[10] Portland cement cannot endure hydrothermal conditions.

Joseph Davidovits re-created a type of Roman mortar (Latin: *Opus Signinum*) made around 200 B.C. and later.[11] Rather than a simple product made with lime, *Opus Signinum* is a high-strength mortar based on complex geopolymeric hardening. To reproduce it, Joseph Davidovits analyzed ancient samples and used a linguistic study made by his son Frederic Davidovits. Frederic investigated the description of Roman mortar by Marcus Vitruvius Pollio, who wrote ten books on architecture titled *De Architectura*.[12]

Joseph Davidovits' replication sheds new light on the fabrication of Rome's best cement, required for the most complex building designs that require high early strength. Because this material was also made during Greek antiquity (ca. 300 B.C.), it may be comparable to the excellent mortar used in Egypt to repair the Sphinx during Ptolemaic times.

Aside from what may be a few isolated examples of good cement, the knowledge required to make superior concretes was lost to the world after the fall of the Roman Empire. It was not until the 19th century that the cement used in modern construction was invented. In 1824, the English bricklayer Joseph Aspdin (1799-1855) created cement that looks similar to building stone on the Isle of Portland, off the British coast.[13] The name portland cement arose from this comparison. The rediscovery of geopolymerization by Joseph Davidovits was the first major innovation in the cement industry since Aspdin's discovery.

Joseph Davidovits discovered the geopolymeric chemical reaction in 1972, when he was attempting to create a fireproof construction material.[14] At that time, he was an organic chemist who recognized that he must incorporate the inorganic chemistry of the mineral kingdom to succeed. His research led to a formula that hardened into synthetic rock over-night in a petri dish.

Thinking that others must have known about the simple chemistry he discovered, he searched the patent literature. He could hardly believe it when his search determined that no one had discovered this chemical reaction before. With much further research, he came to understand that this chemistry is the basis of long-surviving ancient cements. He began investigating pyramid stone in association with the chemical reaction after re-creating the durable pink mortar incorporated into the masonry of the Great Pyramids and other Old Kingdom monuments. He knew that a minor variation in the mortar formula would afford geopolymeric limestone concrete at ambient temperatures.

Until Joseph Davidovits' contributions, the modern cement industry had no precise understanding of the chemistry of the most durable cements of antiquity, such as those of Egypt and Greece, and the best Roman mortar. His geopolymeric mortars are the modern counterparts. Egypt's large rock-concrete industry is probably not an isolated example for the ancient world. Continuing research on ancient megalithic structures may identify examples that have endured very harsh environmental extremes.

Unlike modern materials, geopolymeric cements, mortars and, concretes will not damage ancient monuments.[15] The modern gypsum mortar used to restore ancient Egyptian monuments has badly damaged them.[16] In contrast, original mortar in the Great Pyramids and other Old Kingdom monuments has survived for 4,500 years without causing damage.

Salt released from modern mortar used to repair the Sphinx caused decay to its fragile limestone body.[17] In recent years, aggressive monitoring and restoration plans had to be enacted on an emergency basis — because the Sphinx is not expected to survive another 100 years. Some think it is in danger of collapsing within 20 years. In the 1980s, after stones fell off of a hind paw, stone and cement repairs broadened the back of the Sphinx's body by up to nine feet. Its original contour was ruined in the process. Worse, salt moved from the modern cement repair into the body of the Sphinx. The Egyptians have already had to replace some large repair slabs placed in the 1980s.

Other damage occurred when a large chunk of stone fell from a shoulder of the Sphinx. A 30-foot crack appeared in the Sphinx's back, and its chest suffered damaged.

But repairs to the Sphinx made more than 3,500 years ago prevented damage by forming a protective surface duricrust.[18] The most recent repair operation used quarried limestone blocks and mortar made with sand and lime. But for permanent Sphinx restoration, Joseph Davidovits' proven mortars would be a wise choice. The high-quality ancient cements demonstrate an ability to survive thousands of years of exposure to the elements. Joseph Davidovits' modern counterparts (which contain no sodium chloride) have been subjected to rigorous simulated testing.[19]

Joseph Davidovits and I previously published the following formula for making good mortar for Sphinx restoration. It is worthwhile to reiterate it here:

> ...ancient Egyptian lime-gypsum mortar does not have the same chemical makeup as modern gypsum mortar. The modern material consists exclusively of hydrated calcium silicate, whereas the ancient mortar is based on a silicoaluminate, a result of geopolymerization...At Saqqara and Giza I [Joseph Davidovits] found geological layers of well-crystallized gypsum sandwiched between layers of limestone and aluminous clay. When a combination of these three materials [limestone, gypsum, and aluminous clay] is combined with natron [sodium carbonate should be substituted], a geopolymeric lime-gypsum cement results, which sets rapidly and resists erosion.[20]

Davidovits has put this and some other formulas in the public domain. This mortar is useful for Third World people living in dry environments. Mainstream Egyptology assumes that the ancient Egyptians may not have intentionally used lime to make cements. In his *Building in Egypt*, Dieter Arnold indicated:

> In stone construction, gypsum mortar was used at least since the Second Dynasty. It consisted of burned gypsum and sand and very often chipped limestone. But we still do not know if the Egyptians of Pharaonic times knew the use of lime or if lime found in mortar was of natural origin, as impurities derived from the raw material.[21]

The amount of lime needed to cast stone for pyramid construction speaks for itself to resolve the question. Ancient Egyptian lime-gypsum mortar is as good as the highest-quality Roman mortar. Davidovits makes the ancient Egyptian mortar in a one-step process.[22] He adds water, gypsum, and natron [or sodium carbonate] to aluminous clay and chalky limestone debris. He fires these materials at 1,500 to 1,600 degrees Fahrenheit to produce the kind of lime-gypsum mortar found on the Great Pyramid.

Despite its long-term durability, ancient Egyptian lime-gypsum mortar is improperly classified in Egyptological literature as ordinary gypsum mortar.[23] Ordinary gypsum mortar, made at 250 degrees Fahrenheit, simply does not withstand erosion — as the many deteriorated examples of modern gypsum mortar on Egyptian monuments clearly demonstrate.

This is an important point, because, like the Sphinx, numerous structures throughout Egypt are in grave jeopardy — deteriorating at an alarming rate.[24] *The Independent* (March 18, 2001), in an article headlined "New riddle over Sphinx's future," informs us that the Sphinx is still in grave danger, and it could collapse without drastic action:

> The Great Sphinx at Giza…Why, after the Egyptian government spent 10 years and millions of dollars on its restoration, is it now in imminent danger of crumbling into the desert? A British team of Egyptologists believes that the huge 4,500-year-old man-headed lion in the shadow of the pyramids, one of the world's greatest tourist attractions, could collapse within 25 years as a direct result of the techniques intended to save it.
>
> …The bill soared as restorers used 12,000 limestone blocks to shore up the statue's stomach, legs and paws. British Egyptologist Ahmad Osman and Dr. Ali el-Kholy, former head of Egyptian Board of Antiquities, fear the chemicals used by the restorers, shoddy workmanship and the failure to close the site to visitors could prove fatal. "…the Sphinx, which has been guarding the Giza necropolis for thousands of years, seems to be approaching the end of its life," said Mr. Osman." Unless revolutionary steps are taken it will disintegrate in 25 years."

Like the Sphinx, some pyramids are restored with corrosive modern material. Damage is particularly extensive at Zoser's Step Pyramid, build by Imhotep. Egyptologist J.P. Lauer used portland-cement concrete blocks in his extensive restoration at Zoser's pyramid complex. The portland blocks cracked within only 30 years and had to be replaced with natural limestone.

Without immediate attention, many structures will not exist in the coming century.[25] Because of the construction of the Aswan Dam, the Nile no longer annually washes salts from the soil. Salts are moving up from the ground, and they are rapidly damaging Theban monuments. They gravely need underground barriers to protect them. A geopolymeric slurry can be injected into the ground to form man-made rock barriers. Some ancient Egyptian monuments need to be protected from flash floods. Some tombs need fortification to prevent water from seeping in from the bedrock below. In the Valley of the Kings, temples are absorbing water and then collapsing under their own weight. The ground under the Theban Luxor Temple is permanently wet.

The superior properties of geopolymers are well documented in the scientific literature. Geopolymers are sorely needed in Egypt today for a wide range of applications. Even our opponents Donald H. Campbell and Robert L. Folk have recognized this, and stressed their concerns regarding this important matter in *Concrete International* (August 1991):

> …the application of geopolymeric (zeolitic) substances…should be considered most seriously with rigorous testing to restore the environmental good health that once existed over most of our planet. And, by all means, a geopolymeric concrete may be an ideal material for pyramid repair.[26]

To preserve the monuments, industrial quantities of waterproof, high-quality materials proven capable of offering strength, as well as resistance to attack by salts and industrial pollutants, are needed. The materials must also be durable over the long term.[27] These materials should maintain the beauty of the tombs and landscape and be affordable. These are the qualities of geopolymerized rock. I hope that alerting readers unaware of this crisis will help draw new energy into efforts to save endangered monuments, so that our cultural heritage can be properly preserved.

Many ancient sites around the world beckon us to investigate the spread of this technology during antiquity. Enticing structures range from many around the world that are assumed to be normal, natural rock-cut structures to those that present vexing engineering or geological anomalies. Some are even submerged under water, and may date to very remote antiquity. The magic of geochemistry, materials science and archaeology brought together can serve to age-date sites that may prove to be manmade rock, so as to better understand the history of our ancient past.

As for the modern history of geopolymerization, Joseph Davidovits also pioneered its industrial development. He coordinates international technological-development programs with major institutions and universities in various parts of the world, including Europe, the U.S., Brazil, Japan, and Australia. Geopolymerization provides green chemistry and sustainable development solutions. It is a very important mission to industrialize this emerging green technology so that it can meet its great potential for solving many of the most fundamental problems the modern world faces.

A project with the Fire Research Section of the U.S. Federal Aviation Administration (FAA) involves fire-resistant geopolymeric composites.[28] Among its many uses, passenger jets can become much safer. In an airplane crash, passengers may have only a few seconds to escape the cabin before being overcome by toxic fumes and fire. The FAA flammability requirement for testing new materials is that the materials must withstand a fully-developed aviation-fuel fire that has penetrated the cabin, but without the cabin being on fire. When tested, the only material shown to withstand this arduous test was a geopolymer composite.

Because they are made purely of minerals, geopolymers tolerate high heat. The carbon-fiber-reinforced geopolymeric composite tested by the FAA does not ignite, burn, or release any smoke—even after extended heat-flux exposure.[29] No toxic fumes are released.

Many lives and tremendous sums of revenue could be saved by protecting buildings from fire hazards with geopolymeric composites and stone structuring. The average building fire burns as hot as 1650 degrees Fahrenheit. At the critically higher temperature of 1800 degrees Fahrenheit, steel begins to weaken, glass begins to melt and portland cement blocks are prone to exploding. Geopolymerized stone and composites can tolerate 2,000 degrees Fahrenheit, at which point they start degrading.

The general properties of modern geopolymers were tested by the U.S. Army Corps of Engineers in the 1980s. Geopolymers are routinely shown to withstand all the freeze-thaw cycles the samples are subjected to without deteriorating. Tremendous sums of money could be saved by constructing roads and infrastructure built to last. The material is ideal for bridges, underground pipes and other infrastructure. In Third World countries, geopolymeric bricks made with local soils, and that require no firing, can provide for good housing, schools, public buildings, dams and roads. Geopolymerized soil approximates fired bricks.

Because it sets at ambient temperatures and requires no special equipment, geopolymerization can afford tailor-made geology. Areas devastated by strip mining could be backfilled so that land can be recovered. If polar ice continues to melt and cause a rise in sea levels, strong, permanent dams need to be built to protect coastal cities. In Venice, Italy, 40% of the city's historic buildings have already been affected by floodwaters. In 2008, some parts of the city were neck deep in water. People constantly fight back mold and have largely abandoned ground floors in buildings and homes. In 2008, extreme inland flooding caused tremendous economic damage in Europe. A rise in the sea level threatens China's coastal cities of Shanghai and Tianjin. The rate at which the Arctic coast of Alaska erodes has doubled in the past 50 years. Environmental geologists are enormously concerned about flood damage in the U.S., and stress the need to protect coastlines and fortify cities while there is still time and before costs rise too high. Strong, permanent, massive protective structures that require little or no maintenance can be achieved with tailor-made geology.

A green geopolymeric project that has been in place for years is the mitigation of carbon dioxide emissions, carried out in cooperation with the European Commission in Brussels, Belgium.[30] Making portland cement requires large amounts of fuel, usually natural gas or coal. This burning generates significant amounts of pollutants, including carbon dioxide, carbon monoxide, sulfur dioxide, nitrogen oxides, particulates and volatile organic compounds.

Emissions of carbon dioxide from the manufacture of portland cement are increasing at a much more rapid rate than those from all other industrial sources. In the year 2000, an estimated nearly 10 percent of all global greenhouse gases came from new construction with portland cement concrete. By the year 2015, global carbon dioxide emissions from the manufacture of portland cement are expected to reach more than 3,500 million tons annually.

Depending upon how it is made, manufacturing geopolymeric cement generates one-fifth the amount of carbon dioxide as does manufacturing portland cement. Joseph Davidovits has even achieved a 90 percent reduction. Clearly, these figures show the dramatic benefits that could be realized if all countries were to convert to geopolymeric concrete.

Another project is the rehabilitation of radioactive wastes. An example is the rehabilitation of uranium-mining sites for the German Government's WISMUT program. Mixing mineral wastes with geopolymeric concrete will permanently trap the waste into the molecular structure of the rock-concrete once the blend cures. Even liquid radioactive wastes can become much less of a threat because they are solidified in a geopolymeric rock matrix. In essence, the wastes are converted into an ore that cannot be mined because the wastes are more strongly locked in than in natural ore. Battelle Institute, in Germany, tested geopolymerization for the European high-level nuclear waste classification and determined the material to be a "valuable alternative" to present-day technologies.[31]

The Chernobyl nuclear reactor that exploded in 1986 continuously leaks radioactive materials into the ground. Radioactive materials are pulled into local trees through their root systems. The Chernobyl reactor containment system must be frequently repaired because it is built of inadequate materials. All nuclear reactors must ultimately be either dismantled (a very expensive and dangerous process) or safely entombed after they reach the end of their service lives—and the repair system must have the integrity to tolerate freeze thaw cycles and the hydrothermal conditions created when groundwater from rain, snow or floodwaters reaches the reactors. Permanent, on-the-spot entombment of wastes generated at nuclear power plants can also prevent barrels of radioactive wastes from being carried through city highways on their way to remediation dumps. Green geopolymeric applications are very important endeavors because they can address some of the most serious problems we face.

Gigantic man-made stone barriers can protect nuclear plants, and monoliths can cover radioactive waste burial sites. When radioactive waste itself is geopolymerized, it is well dispersed inside rock-concrete blocks and molecularly locked in to avoid leakage. Given the amount of waste that requires remediation, a myriad of rock-concrete blocks could result—enough to build truly Great Pyramids. The old rock-concrete technology has come full circle.

To conclude these pages, I mention a project inspired by the honor we pay to the late Dr. Edward J. Zeller (1925-1996), a former long-term Director of the Radiation Physics Laboratory of the Space Technology Center, a focal point of federal agencies funding, including NASA-sponsored research, at the University of Kansas. Edward J. Zeller always generously gave freely of his time and expertise to the body of research covered in this book. NASA is contemplating a Moon Base that will support continuous operations on the Moon. Building a highly-functional Moon Base that includes massive, virtually permanent, sturdy structures becomes feasible much sooner than is currently anticipated. Many advocate a 'Mars first' strategy, and the same system is perfectly suitable for Mars.

A massive, permanent Moon Base can be accomplished without ferrying huge cranes, forklifts or other heavy construction equipment to the Moon. The first architectural phase could be a permanent megalith built on the lunar surface with the readily-abundant regolith (moon dust), water and manageable bags of rock-forming geopolymeric cement. Details of construction, feasibility, economy and high-level functionality, when combined with an array of instruments that withstand the space environment, are described in my forthcoming book *Moon Base and Beyond* (Scribal Arts, 2010).

Moon regolith is high in iron, plagioclase and contains pyroxene, all of which give geopolymeric rock extra strength. The regolith ground cover, made of inorganic pulverized rock, is extraordinarily plentiful. A Moon Monolith made this way requires 1/10 or more of its weight in water ferried to the Moon. The project can begin as an Earth prototype, so that every step of a lunar operation is conducted in a simulated environment.

To afford great functionality, the prototype Moon Monolith's surface is embedded with diamond microcircuitry* (creating computing and electrical circuits made with single crystal diamond film).[32] Diamond microcircuitry was invented by physicist Dr. Gisela A. Dreschhoff, who served as Director of the former Radiation Physics Laboratory at the Space Technology Center for about a decade, and geophysicist Edward J. Zeller. Diamond microcircuitry film (DMF) provides for both ultra-advanced electronics and space computing. The characteristics of diamond microcircuitry render today's electronics and space-enabled computing obsolete. It can provide for advanced electronics and space computing with far better ability to tolerate cosmic ray bombardment. When equipped with a power supply (like diamond film solar panels) and an array of equipment, it can continually collect and transmit data from its local environment and digital images of the Earth and deep space. Given the highly-superior electronics and outer space computing capabilities of diamond microcircuitry, and its ability to withstand the space environment, humankind can achieve the first permanent, orbiting super-computer monitoring our solar system.

A successful manmade rock Moon Monolith on the lunar surface will prove humankind's ability to construct virtually permanent architecture there. DMF-equipped rock architecture can be designed so that it is highly automated, able to monitor temperature, radiation levels and many other conditions. The GEO-DMF Moon Monolith can be the forerunner of a permanent colony on the Moon—all built at a fraction of the cost and effort of working with huge pieces of natural rock and using heavy construction equipment and power tools on the

---

*This combination of geopolymer and diamond microcircuitry film (the GEO-DMF System) is patent-pending, an endeavor by the author under the advisement of the co-inventor

Moon to achieve permanent, functional structures. Eventually, this system helps to enable the creation of underground manufacturing and other facilities because every foot of tunneling into the lunar surface can be immediately reinforced with rapid-setting geopolymeric rock-concrete. This will prevent cave-ins, and geopolymerized regolith can be used to form thick, structurally solid support structures and wall surfaces. Geopolymer molecularly binds with silicate rock, such as the lunar crust. The electronics and computing abilities of DMF will be an advantage to the complex task of underground construction work on the Moon.

As explained at length in *Moon Base and Beyond*, the GEO-DMF System (geopolymer diamond microcircuitry film system) can also aid substantially with the very complex effort of mining platinum and other precious metals from asteroids. Platinum-rich asteroids are crumbly, and this can make it difficult to land and dock a large spacecraft. But crumbly ground can be geopolymerized so as to allow for landing and docking. DMF can afford great functionality to robotics, and mining and testing equipment. Experts estimate that there is enough platinum in asteroids near the Earth to support everyone on our planet under magnificent conditions. Space manufacturing and asteroid mining are viewed by many experts as critical to building robust global economies.

The serious potential to build megalithic superstructures with synthetic rock on the Earth and beyond excites the imagination—and helps to shape our vision of a future marked by tremendously fabulous and protective architecture. Inscriptions on the title page of *Uber das Gedachtnis* (1885) summarize the goal ahead:

De subjecto vetustissimo novissiman promovemus scientiam, "From the most ancient subject we shall produce the newest science."

---

of diamond microcircuitry, physicist Dr. Gisela A. Dreschhoff. New diamond film solar panels can provide a dependable power source within the GEO-DMF System. Diamond solar panels can help to make the Moon Base permanent because diamond is more tolerant of the space environment than gallium arsenide solar panels. Once powered with solar panels, all manner of sensors and other instruments can be incorporated into this architectural system. The property of diamond's high thermal conductivity will be an advantage in providing for temperature stability. DMF electronics are made by using a proton beam to etch single-crystal diamond film, so that zones of electrically-conducting graphite are created in any desired configuration (including as whole circuit boards)—all protected by diamond so as to withstand the extreme stresses of the lunar and other space environments. Instruments can be connected by graphite ports instead of metal wires. Diamond microcircuitry film can also eventually provide for untethered, computerized machines and industrial robots that are built with fixed and moving parts that are electrically-conducting throughout—made of and fastened with parts constructed of layers of DMF. Assuming the machine and robotic phase of the technology is perfected in the future, computerized, powered robots made with etched diamond film can be ferried to the Moon or Mars to perform construction and other work. They can operate through commands from an Earth base. DMF is becoming more economical and is ideal for the new generation of miniature spacecraft, too.

The GEO-DMF System is enabled by the brilliant inventions of Joseph Davidovits, Gisela A. Dreschhoff, and Edward J. Zeller.

Appendix 1
Tier Heights of The Great Pyramid

The following tier heights of the Great Pyramid are the measurements, in centimeters, made by Egyptologist Georges Goyon and published in 1978.[1] Goyon rounded off the tier height measurements to 1/2 centimeter. So, the margin of error of the tier heights is 1/2 centimeter or less. In general, the Great Pyramid incorporates blocks made with 73 different heights (rounded to less than 1/2 centimeter). By the time Goyon made his measurements, tier 201 was missing. He lists the measurement of the Napoleonic Expedition for that tier.

Increases in tier heights can be observed at tiers 35, 98 and several other tiers high in the Great Pyramid, including the missing tier 201. Tier 35 is taller than tier two, and tier 201 was taller than tier four. Although the monument exhibits a general decrease in tier height as it rises, tall tiers high in the masonry present engineering problems because of the difficulties of lifting thousands of massive blocks to great heights.

Table 1: Tier Heights (in Centimeters) of the Great Pyramid

Tier No.	Cm	Tier No.	Cm	Tier No.	Cm	Tier No.	Cm	Tier No.	Cm	Tier No.	Cm	Tier No.	Cm	Tier No.	Cm
1	150	29	65	57	62	85	57.5	113	60	141	56	169	53.5	197	56.5
2	124	30	64	58	68.5	86	67	114	58	142	56.5	170	54	198	55
3	120	31	73	59	75	87	66	115	57.5	143	74	171	53	199	57.5
4	102	32	72	60	70	88	58	116	67.5	144	68.5	172	52	200	56.5
5	99	33	54	61	67.5	89	61	117	58	145	60	173	49.5	201*	112
6	90	34	66	62	63.5	90	97	118	90.5	146	59	174	53		
7	100	35	127	63	65.5	91	90.5	119	83	147	56	175	53		
8	97	36	100	64	67.5	92	83.5	120	75	148	56	176	52.5		
9	93	37	97	65	66	93	77.5	121	74.5	149	70	177	53		
10	91.5	38	95	66	60.5	94	68	122	67	150	63.5	178	53		
11	86.5	39	84	67	86	95	63	123	66	151	59.5	179	67.5		
12	76	40	84	68	83.5	96	60.5	124	63	152	59	180	63.5		
13	76	41	83	69	78	97	61	125	58	153	55	181	60		
14	75	42	72	70	64	98	100	126	60.5	154	55	182	58		
15	75	43	83	71	71	99	99.5	127	59.5	155	54	183	56		
16	73.5	44	106	72	67.5	100	90.5	128	59	156	54.5	184	54.5		
17	75	45	97	73	66	101	85	129	70	157	54.5	185	53		
18	83	46	73	74	80	102	74	130	65	158	54.5	186	52		
19	95	47	90	75	76	103	76	131	60.5	159	54.5	187	52.5		
20	62	48	90.5	76	62	104	68	132	56.5	160	54.5	188	52		
21	58	49	86	77	64	105	67.5	133	55.5	161	60	189	52.5		
22	87	50	70	78	60	106	64	134	54.5	162	59	190	54		
23	89	51	72.5	79	59.5	107	63.5	135	61	163	64.5	191	51.5		
24	83	52	61	80	62.5	108	75.5	136	58	164	54	192	52		
25	80	53	68	81	60	109	68	137	68	165	54.5	193	52		
26	74	54	63	82	60	110	59	138	65	166	54	194	52		
27	78	55	69	83	60	111	60.5	139	57	167	54.5	195	58.5		
28	69	56	55	84	67	112	59.5	140	56	168	52.5	196	60.5		

* Missing tier number documented by the Napoleonic measurements.

🏛 Appendix 2 🏛
The Great Pyramid Debates

O ne of the best ways to invite a lot of knee-jerk reactionary criticism is to introduce an idea that goes sharply against the grain of orthodoxy. A statement by the English philosopher John Locke (1632–1704) is no less true today:

New opinions are always suspected, and usually opposed, without any other reason but because they are not already common.[1]

The geopolymer theory has met with fierce opposition for a number of reasons. The idea that the pyramids are made of great blocks of stone that were quarried, cut and manually raised is very entrenched. The geopolymer theory requires an entirely new way of considering evidence. Since the inception of Egyptology, all the evidence in books and other information sources has been interpreted from the carve-hoist perspective. Many people have a difficult time thinking outside of that very entrenched framework. In addition, the Egyptian landscape exhibits a great many marks of stoneworking with primitive tools, dating from those later periods when stonecutting methods prevailed. Sorting out these work phases and layers of history is imperative.

All unorthodox theories about the Great Pyramid are highly suspect and unwelcome to orthodoxy, to say the least. The finding of large slabs of synthetic basalt in Mesopotamian ruins met with no opposition whatsoever. It was published in the journal *Science*. But what if the same team would have found synthetic stone at the Great Pyramid? The same journal, *Science*, declined to publish Michel Barsoum's first paper describing his analyses of geopolymeric pyramid stone. When Michel Barsoum's first paper on geopolymeric pyramids was published, he told me about immediately receiving a threatening email from our hostile opponent James A. Harrell. This is just one incident among many vehement reactions against the cast-stone theory of pyramid construction.

Another problem is that, as I have shown in these pages, it is not easy for readers to get a true picture of many of the unresolved masonry and engineering problems by reading authoritative books. Information quickly becomes outdated as knowledge advances, and we see a giant whitewash along with genuine attempts at solving problems. Many unresolved problems have been played down by authorities in recent decades. So, readers would have to go to greater lengths to uncover, collect, and evaluate problems to gain an appreciation of the magnitude of problems that remain unresolved by the carve/hoist theory.

Another problem is that geopolymerization produces real rock. Critics who look at the pyramid blocks with the naked eye or a pocket microscope do not see concrete as they know it. When they do not see something akin to portland cement-based concrete, they assume that the limestone pyramid blocks cannot be concrete. Their thinking is locked into the portland cement paradigm. Even though Egyptology could greatly benefit from geopolymer technology, people in authoritative positions have a long track record of denouncing it rather than trying to understand it and its potential.

The best I can do is present the available evidence so that intelligent readers will be equipped to evaluate the legitimacy of any criticism. Even Robert L. Folk, a limestone geologist with 45 years of experience when he visited Egypt with me in 1990, could not tell the difference between geopolymerized rock and real rock. On the way home from Egypt in 1990, Folk visited the Geopolymer Institute, in France. He examined all of the statues in Joseph Davidovits' front office. Each of these statues is made from a different type of rock aggregate. Folk could not distinguish any of these statues from natural stone with the naked eye or with his 50x pocket microscope. In Egypt, we encountered the same problem. Here we will delve into the debates with Robert Folk and others.

With the benefit of scientific consultation with Edward J. Zeller, Robert G. McKinney, Joseph Davidovits, and others, I debated the geopolymer theory of pyramid construction in detail with aggressive opponents, including Robert Folk. Our debates, mostly published in scientific and technical journals, show that opponents have no successful arguments.

Folk and Campbell vs Morris

The first opposing team consisted of Robert L. Folk, of the University of Texas, in Austin, and Donald H. Campbell, principal petrographer at Construction Technologies, Inc., in Skokie, Illinois. Their arguments were based on our field investigations at Giza and Saqqara. Folk also microscopically examined both a thin section of the Lauer sample and an industrially-made piece of modern geopolymeric limestone produced by Joseph Davidovits. Below is a summary of our debates published in *The Journal of Geological Education*.[2]

When we arrived at the Great Pyramid of Giza, Folk made up his mind within one minute that the geopolymer theory is wrong. The reason is that he expected the pyramids to resemble ordinary concrete if they are geopolymeric. His unscientific approach appears in writing in the following quote:

> Within the first minute at the Khufu (Cheops) pyramid, we knew that all other Egyptologists and geologists were correct and that the pyramids are built of real limestone blocks, and not concrete.[3]

Folk based his snap decision on his knowledge of portland cement technology. If the pyramid limestone is concrete, Folk reasoned, he must see its cement with his 50x pocket microscope.[4] But Folk failed to examine the modern samples of geopolymerized limestone sent to his laboratory before our trip.[5]

Had he looked at them, as he was expected to as a prerequisite for our field study, he would have known that he would not be able to detect geopolymeric cement with a 50x pocket microscope.

When Robert Folk later returned to his laboratory and examined Joseph Davidovits' modern limestone specimens, he required a scanning electron microscope to see the geopolymeric cement between the rock grains.[6]

In other words, the particles in geopolymeric cement are comparable in size to those in the natural micritic cement that binds natural limestone.[7] As little as 1 percent by combined weight of lime and natron activates naturally-occurring minerals in the clay inherent to Giza limestone. The chemical reaction affords limestone concrete that is very close in composition to natural limestone.[8]

While we were in Egypt and later, despite the numerous U.S. and international patents issued for geopolymers and my attempts to explain the chemistry to him (and the description of it in our book—which he carried with him and had supposedly read), Folk insisted that geopolymeric chemistry cannot exist. He claimed that geopolymeric cement "goes against the laws of physical packing."[9] Folk insisted that "every concrete must show at least 25 percent of cement between its rock particles."[10]

He simply could not erase portland cement technology from his mind. So, he instantly pronounced the geopolymer theory of pyramid construction wrong—within the first moment at Giza—because he refused to consider anything new.[11]

His refusal to understand the cement chemistry of pyramid stone set the stage for his further activities in Egypt. So, within the first minute at Giza—having taken one look at pyramid stone with his pocket microscope—Folk and Campbell abandoned our agreed-upon work plan. It consisted of a systematic comparison of pyramid and temple blocks with the strata of Giza's excavation pits (commonly called quarries in reference to block quarrying).[12] This kind of study became unimportant to them once they made up their minds that the theory is wrong. Instead, they aggressively went in search of evidence that could bolster their point of view.

Thousands of pyramid and temple blocks are in plain view at Giza. Folk searched in vein for fossil shells that are not jumbled in pyramid and temple blocks.[13] The large excavation pits are easy to walk through, and we inspected their vast walls. Folk observed that their walls are characterized by natural sedimentary layering.[14] In contrast, the fossiliferous pyramid blocks exhibit jumbled shells, as they must if the blocks are concrete. Often, the shells are slightly jumbled because the blocks were packed down during production. But their disarray is still very evident.

Folk spotted an area of the Great Pyramid that Egyptology believes is a natural bedrock protrusion incorporated into the monument. Folk recognized features in the rock that he believes prove that it is natural limestone. He photographed this area so he could use it against the geopolymer theory. He wrote:

> …within a few minutes at Khufu, we found, at the pyramid base, similarly jumbled nummulites in undoubted Eocene bedrock cut by tectonic fractures and unmoved by man. These jumbled fossils are attributed by Aigner* (1983) to storm deposition, a straightforward sedimentary interpretation.[15]

But in a letter to Joseph Davidovits dated February 19, 1992, Folk privately conceded his mistake:

> I was impressed by your reasonable and interesting letter in *Concrete International*, Feb. 1992…Your argument that the lower two courses of Khufu (Kheops), on the east face, are in place bedrock is intriguing and I must admit was a new thought to me. This morning, thanks to your citation, I went over and read Lehner (1983) on Khufu (Kheops) and he does indeed show the NE corner of Khufu to be bedrock in his sketch. Our photo was of that corner. So I concede that, on the North-East corner, you are correct as the bedrock idea had not entered my head at the time we were there.

Although the Great Pyramid is built upon a relatively level plateau, Mark Lehner (based on W.M.F. Petrie's observation) determined that Khufu's builders incorporated part of the bedrock at the northeast corner of Khufu. Although this area cannot legitimately be used to support the contentions of Folk and Campbell, they contended that, "These fractures generally are only about 1 mm wide, and run in a more or less straight path all across a single block. These are obvious tectonic fractures formed when the block was flexed millions of years ago,

---

* Thomas Aigner, whom Folk mentioned in his above quote, studied Giza bedrock for his master's degree in the 1980s.[16] To account for the jumbled shells, Aigner assumed that they resulted from violent storms that stirred up the ocean bottom millions of years ago. At that time, the components of the limestone were still in a muddy state.

and demonstrate that the pyramid core stones were quarried blocks, not poured geopolymer." Folk had every opportunity to correct his mistake in print, but he failed to do so.

Consequently, his mistaken evidence is still cited by opponents of the geopolymer theory as proof that it is wrong. Moreover, he exercised no caution about using calcite-filled fractures as a criterion. Freshly-made blocks of geopolymerized limestone will also fill in if they crack. The fill in the crack will, of course, be geopolymeric binder. But once it has set, the difference between the binder and calcite is not apparent to the naked eye or when examined with a 50x pocket microscope. One of the ideal properties of geopolymeric concrete is "self-healing"—the ability for a freshly-made block to fill in a crack automatically if one forms because of stress. Given that McKinney and Zeller advised me that features Folk argued as natural can be argued either way, it would probably be best to take a fresh look at the northeast corner of Khufu's Great Pyramid to see if it is real bedrock or merged geopolymer.

Objective researchers would test before declaring any material at Giza to be natural based on fractures. The reason is that we are dealing with an enormous rock-concrete-making operation, and so geopolymeric concrete can appear anywhere at Giza—on the ground as reinforcement, as slabs, and spilled onto the quarry floor and walls in a hardened state. It is unscientific for Folk to claim that any rock at Giza is natural without at least knowing what geopolymeric concrete actually looks like, and without at least accepting that unless he can perform a definitive test he must remain cautious about assertions.

It was unscientific for Folk to assert that jumbled shells necessarily come from ancient storms that stirred up ocean bottoms when our original mission was to make a detailed comparison between the quarries and blocks. If jumbled shells in the blocks result from ancient storm activity, then the quarries should be made up of jumbled shells, too. But that is not the case.

Although Folk and Campbell could not find any jumbled shells in the excavation pits, the feature may exist there as spilled concrete mix. As mentioned, Edward Zeller detected needle-shaped crystals in microphotographs taken by Klemm in the excavation pit floor. Zeller recognized that it is very unlikely that zeolites would form during the natural geological formation of limestone. Zeolite crystals are much more likely to result from a subsequent chemical reaction—geopolymerization.

Folk and Campbell also used the aforementioned *bedrock* area of the Great Pyramid to argue for other features that would disprove the geopolymer theory. For instance, they used this area to argue for burrows and tubes formed by sea animals when the sediment had a muddy consistency on the Eocene sea floor millions of years ago. These features would not exist in geopolymeric concrete because they would be broken up during disaggregation. But these holes have been otherwise interpreted as the results of desert wind blasting. Folk and Campbell also used this same area to show examples of natural geological stratification in pyramid blocks. Natural strata would be broken up during disaggregation. But Folk and Campbell produced no evidence to overturn the aforementioned measurements of strata Davidovits and Gaber made for Giza bedrock. In other words, Folk and Campbell did not show that the so-called strata they pointed out matches that of Giza. I have already explained that lift lines in concrete look like strata.

In 1984, Joseph Davidovits and Hisham Gaber compared pyramid and temple blocks with the Giza quarries (excavation pits).[17] Davidovits undertook this study to verify the observation by geologist de Roziere, of the Napoleonic Expedition, that the fossiliferous pyramid blocks are composed of jumbled shells.[18] Davidovits would never have introduced his geopolymer theory if the main pyramid blocks exhibited normal sedimentary layering. The outcome of these various observations is that, although Folk abused the evidence, he is a highly-qualified sedimentation expert who inadvertently confirmed something of importance. That is, the pyramid and temple blocks exhibit jumbled shells, while the quarry walls are characterized by natural sedimentary layering. So, his observation, which confirms previous studies, is a critical point of evidence favoring the geopolymer theory.[19] In other words, although anyone can observe these features, now they are inadvertently confirmed by a top sedimentation expert.

To try to make their case for the carve-hoist paradigm, Folk and Campbell had to ignore these overwhelming features and point out features on pitifully few blocks.[20] In other words, they ignored overall features in favor of their interpretations of a statistically insignificant number of blocks at an area that Petrie and Lehner documented as a natural bedrock protrusion.

Folk and Campbell refused to hear my citations of the several documented phases of ancient and modern repair on the monuments. Once they made up their minds in a snap judgement after one look with a 50x hand lens, my remarks about the tool mark classifications of the Klemms, the extensive 19th and 26th Dynasty restorations, and the Greek, Roman, modern and other repair work was of no interest to them.[21] Given that the Egyptian Antiquities Organization uses cut stone for repair whenever possible, it would not be surprising if Folk and Campbell spotted natural stones. Folk and Campbell always tried to make their case by pointing out "one stone," "a few stones," or "some stones." These are statistically insignificant numbers when considering that there are thousands of blocks in close, unobstructed view at Giza.[22]

Having tossed aside our work plan, Folk and Campbell failed to address another critically important feature we went to Egypt to study: The transition point between the blocks in Khafra's pyramid and the partial natural bedrock tiers of this pyramid shows the distinct difference between the bedrock and the pyramid blocks.[23]

When building Khafra's pyramid, workers took advantage of part of the natural bedrock. They used the natural bedrock area to shape five tiers in situ. Shaping these solid bedrock tier areas does not pose the same difficulties as cutting vast corresponding tiers made of quarried blocks, which must be individually cut to close specifications.

The transition between these bedrock tiers and the adjoining blocks appears near the middle of the north and south sides of the base of Khafra's pyramid. The area is critically important for study because it clearly shows how the natural bedrock (exhibiting normal sedimentary layering) differs from the adjoining pyramid blocks (made of jumbled shells). Rather than properly considering this feature, which strongly favors geopolymerized stone, Folk and Campbell ignored it. They always ignored the issue when confronted with it later, too.

Folk and Campbell resorted to trying to support their premise with archaeological evidence. In doing this, they showed their complete lack of understanding of the history and archaeology of Giza and Saqqara. First, they pointed out the unfinished granite casing blocks on Menkaura's pyramid, the third and smallest of Giza's Great Pyramids.[24] As mentioned, these unfinished blocks, with extra stock on their front faces, contrast sharply with the other blocks in the Great Pyramid complexes.

Folk and Campbell assumed these blocks to be carved granite. Some Egyptologists interpret them to be repair blocks, perhaps the work of Ramses II's administration.[25] But

George Reisner examined them and demonstrated that they show no traces of metal tool marks aside from those of Arab stonecutters of the 12th and 13th centuries. But for Folk and Campbell, tool marks are definite indicators of natural stone. Folk and Campbell were insensitive to Reisner's report. They showed no willingness to consider when these tool marks were made. As mentioned, Campbell even interpreted the rapid saw marks on a sarcophagus lid in the Cairo Museum as an indicator of natural stone. As a geologist, we would expect him to recognize that producing these tool marks on granite would be impossible unless the granite was soft while being cut.

So, if these blocks are natural, their method of manufacture has not been determined. These tight-fitting blocks may be original units that cured (because of a work stoppage) before workers could complete them. But only scientific testing can say for sure.

In any case, it is unscientific for Folk and Campbell to declare these blocks to be natural because they are unfinished, and to use these exceptions to the norm to make a sweeping generalization about pyramid construction.

Folk and Campbell spotted the famous grid of stumps from block quarrying near Khafra's pyramid. Folk and Campbell insisted that this grid proves that the geopolymer theory is wrong—and that the pyramid blocks were quarried, carved, and hoisted. As mentioned, anyone can easily refer to a map of Giza to compare this grid to the large excavation pits associated with the Great Pyramid. At a glance, anyone will see that the grid is very small by comparison. As mentioned, Mike Carrell measured and determined this quarry grid to equal about two percent of the masonry of the Great Pyramid. Besides, this grid is associated with Khafra's pyramid and is not thought to have existed when the Great Pyramid was built.

Petrie was the first to inspect this grid and recognize that there is vastly insufficient evidence of block quarrying at Giza to account for the Great Pyramid. Joseph Davidovits and I quoted Petrie's remarks concerning the dearth of block quarrying at Giza in our book *The Pyramids: An Enigma Solved* (1988). Folk carried a copy of our book with him at Giza for purposes of reference, but refused to consider this information by Petrie. My attempts to explain and defend the geopolymer theory were futile during our entire field trip.

Folk and Campbell had seen enough, and claimed they could not register so much information. Their first moment at Giza convinced them. They saw no cement between the rock grains in pyramid blocks, they saw "undoubted" (based on filled fractures and holes) natural rock, and they even saw a quarry showing the removal of whole blocks. Then Campbell spotted a crack that greatly impressed him.

Campbell was struck by a series of pyramid blocks with a horizontal crack running from one to the next in perfect alignment.[26] The crack appears as a fine line. To make pyramid concrete, workers used limestone debris, and cracks cannot survive a disaggregation process. So, Campbell upheld these cracked blocks as proof that the geopolymer theory is wrong.

But cracks cannot survive the ancient quarrying process, either. Campbell's concept of ancient quarrying has no basis in reality. This is proven by his comments in *Concrete International* magazine:

> The Egyptians must have transported carefully sawn blocks from the quarry and placed them in…exactly matching order…It is almost as if the masterful ancient Egyptian engineers and quarrymen purposefully placed the blocks in their original geologic orientation to mimic the order of nature and, perhaps not to offend the gods.[27]

Let us try to imagine a fine crack surviving ancient quarrying methods. According to the masonry theory held by Egyptology, workers created trenches large enough to crouch in to isolate blocks in the quarries. They then bashed out the bedrock from beneath so that they could break blocks from the quarry floor. Some theorize that workers used wooden levers to break out blocks. For Campbell's idea to hold, the ancient Egyptians would have had to have highly advanced quarrying technology that generated absolutely no waste: Campbell claimed that the Egyptians cut the blocks from the bedrock with a fine copper wire. But copper is too soft to cut pyramid limestone. Compare the heavy steel tools the Nova crew used on the softest limestone of Tura when copper chisels failed them. Mark Lehner's on camera test of a copper chisel shows that the tool was badly blunted after only a few blows against a pre-shaped block of soft Tura limestone. A copper wire is useless.

Even modern quarrying generates a great deal of waste. Today, after a crew exposes a quarry, the workers use power saws to cut through its limestone faces to section it into blocks. If ancient workers really carved the pyramid blocks, it is extremely unlikely that they could have perfectly aligned a fine crack ranging across two blocks. Even if this operation were possible, which is doubtful, why would anyone go to all of the trouble? Cracks are undesirable weak points.

The crack Campbell found does not prove his point or negate observations favoring the geopolymer theory.[28] It is more likely that the crack is simply a stress fracture that formed after blocks were in place. As mentioned, J.P. Lauer examined casing blocks on the pyramids of Unas and Senworset I, and on the Mastabat el-Fara'un. He noticed that when some blocks were separated in two, workers cut an inch or so into the foundation. His observation suggests that the stone was separated in two while still pliable. So, it is conceivable that if cracking occurred during this kind of process (before the stone cured), it would not be surprising to see a crack spanning more than one block. A stress fracture running through concrete blocks produced this way is more likely than the scenario proposed by Campbell.

Having studied for one week at Giza and Saqqara collectively, Campbell boldly declared that geopolymerization was not an industrial-scale process of antiquity. When I challenged him with the Tel-Ramad lime vases, Campbell dismissed them as a mere accidental occurrence of geopolymerization. When making his sweeping generalization, Campbell—a portland cement expert—refused to consider the geopolymeric lime-gypsum mortar that cushions some pyramid and huge temple blocks.

Some of the lime-gypsum mortar is 4,500 years old and intact. It sharply contrasts with modern gypsum mortar, which degrades in only a few generations.[29] Despite the longevity of the pyramid mortar, Campbell refused to consider the ramifications of its longevity or its geopolymeric makeup. The mortar is described in *The Pyramids: An Enigma Solved* (1988). If Campbell had properly considered pyramid mortar, he would have realized that geopolymerization was used on an industrial scale during antiquity.

In that case, the geopolymeric nature of the pyramid blocks would have been within his intellectual grasp. But Folk and Campbell could not have had such a revelation because they revealed that they did not understand the chemistry of geopolymerization. This lack of understanding was a big surprise to me, because for years I provided Campbell with every one of Joseph Davidovits' industrial papers.

Campbell wanted to closely follow Joseph Davidovits' research. Campbell was attempting to influence the company he worked for to utilize geopolymerization. Infrastructure made with geopolymerized rock can be expected to be devoid of the weaknesses that plague today's concrete infrastructure. As a portland cement petrologist, Campbell is acutely aware of the alarming frequency of bridge and other infrastructure failures.

After we left Egypt, Folk and Campbell published articles in which they argued that if the Egyptians wanted to agglomerate stone, they would not have gone to the trouble of disaggregating limestone. Folk and Campbell reasoned that, instead, pyramid builders would have used sand to obtain the necessary silica needed for geopolymerization.[30] Their assertion proves that they failed to understand the most basic principle of geopolymerization: The silica in sand is crystalline. A high temperature is required to chemically integrate the crystalline form of silica with alumina so that a new silicoaluminate (a simple geopolymer) forms. The pyramids are far too massive, and fuel was too precious, for the geopolymerization of sand to be practical on such an enormous scale. But the limestone of Giza and Saqqara contains kaolin clay, which provides a form of silica that is easily attacked by caustic soda without heat.

Besides, I have already mentioned that in 1960, in the *Journal of Sedimentary Research*, geologist Kenneth O. Emery reported his inspection of the Great Pyramid. He found that one of the four main rock types incorporated into the Great Pyramid is "yellow limy shaly sandstone." This kind of rock can be made by mixing water, kaolin clay, sand, and caustic soda (natron, lime and water), and packing the material down. But this is the weakest of the four main stone types incorporated into the Great Pyramid, according to Kenneth O. Emery. The sandstone may have been made at times when workers had trouble keeping up the pace of supplying limestone debris. It could have been made with materials left over from clearing Giza for construction. But Folk and Campbell argued on the basis of obtaining silica for the needed chemical reaction (rather than using sand as an aggregate filler), and their argument is not valid because of the heat requirement I already explained.

Soon after our return from Egypt, Folk set to work analyzing Joseph Davidovits' modern geopolymerized limestone samples. Folk required a scanning electron microscope to see the geopolymeric cement between its rock particles.[31] Folk was not discouraged though. He had already embarked upon a mission to stamp out what he saw as the next pseudo-science frenzy:

> We feel it is the duty of professional geologists and other scientists to expose this egregiously absurd theory before it becomes part of entrenched pseudoscience like that of the Von-Daniken or Velikovskian cults. Poorly founded theories of wide popular appeal like this give all scientists a bad reputation and de-value valid scientific methodology.[32]

Folk's self-contradictory thinking is apparent in his writings. On the one hand, he admitted to requiring a scanning electron microscope (with 400x and much higher magnifications), to observe the geopolymeric cement between the limestone particles of Joseph Davidovits' modern samples. In the same paper, Folk makes the contradictory declaration that geopolymeric chemistry cannot exist. He wrote that geopolymerization "goes against the laws of physical packing" and that "every concrete must show at least 25 percent of cement between the rock particles."[33] The approach and arguments of Folk and Campbell reflect hostility and a zeal to trample a theory they refused to try to understand.

Folk and Campbell misused data generated by Dietrich and Rosemarie Klemm, too. The Klemms made chemical analyses of Giza and Tura excavation pits to compare to pyramid stone. Folk and Campbell commented on this study:

> Recently, we have obtained a copy of Klemm and Klemm (1981), which gives a very thorough analysis of pyramid stone and demonstrates clearly that most pyramid core stones chemically match the rocks from adjoining quarries, and the casing stones chemically match Tura limestone from quarries near Helwan.[34]

Folk and Campbell failed to understand that the Klemms made only bulk chemical analyses—which cannot detect zeolites. To detect zeolites, the calcite in a limestone sample must be dissolved so that only trace minerals remain for analysis. Studies of pyramid stone performed this way (including one by the British Museum, those made for Joseph Davidovits, and the one made by Waseda University), detected trace minerals typical of geopolymerization.

The Klemms' study also included photographic evidence of zeolites (needle-shaped crystals), which Folk failed to appreciate.[35] As mentioned above, the independent chemical analysis made by Waseda University also showed zeolites in a sample from the Great Pyramid. In other words, photographic evidence in the Klemms' study inadvertently revealed what their bulk chemical analysis could not—evidence of geopolymeric concrete on the floor of an excavation pit at Giza.

Folk went so far as to reinvent the Lauer sample by arbitrarily declaring it to be plaster.[36] He had observed some of its characteristics in a microphotograph published in the book I wrote with Joseph Davidovits, *The Pyramids: An Enigma Solved* (1988).[37] Folk immediately recognized an unnatural feature in the microphotograph. He was particularly struck by its oval-shaped bubbles. These clearly demonstrated the synthetic nature of the material to him. The oval-shaped bubbles are air bubbles that underwent stress when the stone mixture was still pliable.

But because Folk assumes that the geopolymerized-stone theory is spurious, he decided that the Lauer sample could not be made of limestone. He actually announced to the scientific community that it is plaster after reading a description, in J.P. Lepre's book, of gypsum mortar in the Grand Gallery of the Great Pyramid.[38] Folk then proceeded by making telephone calls to every geologist and Egyptologist who would listen to him, thereby generating misinformation that helped turn the Egyptological community against the geopolymer theory.

Knowing that PBS Nova was considering a film on the geopolymer theory after I submitted a copy of *The Pyramids: An Enigma Solved*, Folk wrote letters to Nova producer Michael Barnes. Folk's letters vehemently denounced the geopolymer theory. The Nova film *This Old Pyramid* makes the geopolymer theory look like a dead issue. When I learned of the new attitude of the Nova staff, I immediately contacted Rustum Roy, who was then Head of the Materials Research Institute at Pennsylvania State University. I also contacted Edward J. Zeller, then Head of the Radiation Physics Lab at the University of Kansas. I contacted Robert G. McKinney, too. But no amount of calls or letters to PBS from these scientists could turn back the tide.

Because of Folk's efforts, rumors were spreading by word of mouth. The gossip found its way back to me in the form of angry letters from Egyptologists to our publisher. Folk's misinformation was published, too. For instance, Campbell and Folk wrote an article published in *Concrete International* stating that the Lauer sample probably comes from the Grand Gallery and is plaster. In other words, Folk and Campbell totally reinvented the location from which the Lauer sample came and the material of which it is made. Campbell has never seen the Lauer sample itself. He simply bullied the evidence and tortured scientific methodology.

In this way, Folk made it very difficult for us to present our case in debates in scientific journals and elsewhere. Editors to whom he submitted his article assumed that the geopolymer theory is absurd because of the distorted way he presented it. I had to pursue James Shea, Editor of the *Journal of Geological Education*, for months before he would consider reading my rebuttal to Folk and Campbell. James Shea assured me that I would not be able to argue against Folk, who at that time had 45 years of experience in limestone geology. James

Shae and others told me that it is futile for anyone to try to debate Folk. Other geologists turn to Folk's classifications and his other writings when it comes to pondering difficult questions about limestone. When James Shea finally read the rebuttal I submitted to him, he was shocked and exclaimed, "My God, you have the stronger paper!"

After seeing our point of view, Dr. James Shea turned out to be the only objective and fair science editor I have ever encountered in my years of trying to set the record straight by submitting articles to journals. Michel Barsoum later had nearly the same experience. It took him a long time and many rejections to finally get his first paper published. Despite his remarkable scientific credentials, one curator laughed in Michel Barsoum's face when he asked if he could examine fragments of museum samples.

To prove that the Lauer sample is not plaster, I published microphotographs in *Concrete International* magazine. These photographs of the Lauer sample were taken at much higher magnification (200x plane polarized and taken by geologist Robert G. McKinney).[39] Folk responded to them by claiming that they are nothing other than natural limestone.[40] Folk has never reconciled his contradicting claims: At a magnification that shows surface features (such as stressed air bubbles), Folk recognizes the Lauer sample as synthetic material. At much higher magnification, he asserts that the same sample is natural stone.

Putting Folk's hostility and bias aside, his findings are consistent with the physical characteristics of geopolymerized stone. We can deduce from all of this that Folk inadvertently recognized the Lauer sample as man-made stone. Despite the comedy of errors in his methodology, Folk is highly qualified, having microscopically examined a great deal of limestone in his long career.[41] So, hoping to benefit from Folk's expertise, McKinney and I devised a plan.

I asked Folk to engage in a blind study, knowing that a blind study would eliminate any problem of bias. Folk consented. So, I sent him a dozen microphotographs of a thin section of the Lauer sample. These microphotos were taken by Robert G. McKinney.

Without knowing what he was looking at, Folk's task was to mark the back of each photograph (all show the rock matrix as it looks under a microscope). He was to indicate which photographs look like natural limestone and which ones represent synthetic limestone. Folk returned the 12 photographs to me with five marked as synthetic and seven marked as looking just like natural limestone. His observations show that most parts of the Lauer sample thin section look natural. But telltale spots show up in five microphotographs — revealing the man-made nature of the rock.

Folk's findings were so encouraging that McKinney and I decided to send him the Lauer sample thin section itself. This time, we let him know what the specimen was. He studied the thin section and published his observations. But he listed only the reasons to believe that the sample is natural limestone — and totally omitted any mention of the unnatural spots in the thin section.[42]

McKinney countered Folk's arguments in my part of this debate.[43] Given that Folk failed to inform readers that he designated five out of 12 microphotographs of the same Lauer sample thin section as synthetic stone, I quoted his written remarks to me from the blind study in my portion of our debate:

> They [the microphotographs] are quite strange and do not look like any normal common rock…I would suggest that these are in fact artificial material…synthetic stone if you wish.[44]

31 and 32, on opposite page: Microphotographs of the Lauer Sample, designated as synthetic rock by Robert L. Folk.

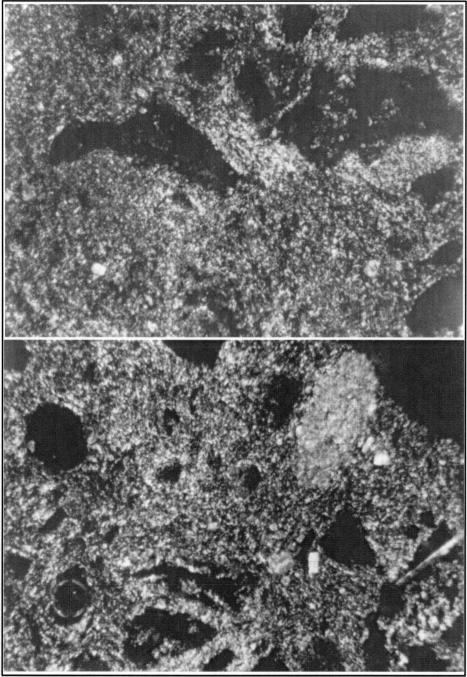

It is surprising that Folk left himself wide open to this public embarrassment. He has not engaged in a public debate with me on the topic since then.

But knowing that the Lauer sample is not plaster, Folk never retracted his remarks that mischaracterize the material, either. Folk subsequently delivered a number of university lectures in which he asserted his own poorly-understood version of the geopolymerized stone

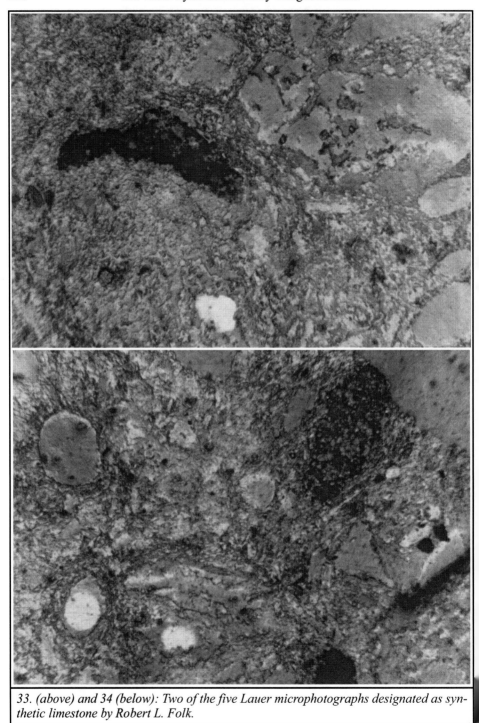

33. (above) and 34 (below): Two of the five Lauer microphotographs designated as synthetic limestone by Robert L. Folk.

theory, which makes it seem absurd. He denounces and distorts it with the same tortured logic found in his portion of our debates.

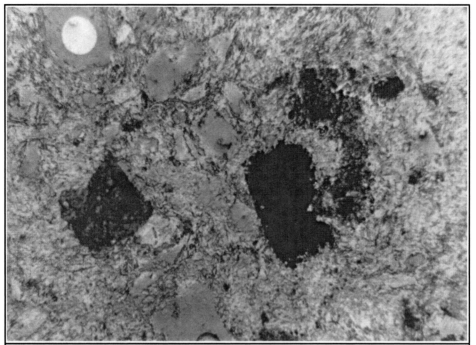

35. This image shows another place on the thin section from the Ascending Passageway of the Great Pyramid that limestone geologist Robert L. Folk designated as synthetic limestone. The original microphotographs are in color. They were taken by Robert G. McKinney and provided to Folk in a blind study. Five out of 12 microphotographs reveal the synthetic nature of the rock.

For example, at a university lecture in Sacramento, California, delivered in April 1995, Folk showed his usual slides. One shows a close-up of saw cuts on the unfinished granite sarcophagus of Prince Dedef Hot in Cairo's Egyptian Museum.[45] Folk touts these saw cuts as evidence proving that the geopolymerized-stone theory is specious.

I talked to him after his lecture and asked him how he could prove that the Egyptians did not saw the sarcophagus while in an uncured state. Folk was silent for a moment. Then he admitted to being stumped. I then asked him how 4th Dynasty Egyptians could possibly make rapid cuts through granite and other hard rock, such as is evidenced by Petrie's collection (showing clean sweeps many feet long through diorite). Folk answered me, "This problem should be left in the hands of Egyptology."

Harrell vs Morris

The next team of challengers consisted of James A. Harrell, Chairman of the Geology Department at the University of Toledo, Ohio, and Bret E. Penrod, of the Libbey-Owens-Ford Company, also in Toledo.[46] Harrell has extensive experience in analyzing Egyptian quarries.[47] So, I approached him after my debates with Folk and Campbell were published. Harrell had read our debates and suggested a new chemical analysis.

I agreed when Harrell assured me that his tests would require material no larger than the size of a sugar cube. I supplied Harrell with the Lauer sample and the pertinent scientific literature describing the proper protocol for testing. I also gave him a copy of the chemical analyses made for Joseph Davidovits by two laboratories in Europe.[48]

Harrell also proposed another type of test that measures chemically bound water, which is water locked molecularly into all types of concrete. Detecting chemically bound water would prove that the Lauer sample is hydraulic concrete.

Harrell's chemical analysis showed no sign of geopolymerization.[49] The reason is that he failed to follow standard testing protocol. He conducted a bulk chemical analysis, instead of first dissolving away the sample's calcite so that only trace minerals were left. To detect zeolites, one must analyze only trace minerals. Properly conducted tests do show the unusual (for limestone) trace minerals that result from geopolymerization. As mentioned, these include the original, properly conducted chemical analyses of the Lauer sample made for Joseph Davidovits, a British Museum chemical analysis of casing stone from the Great Pyramid, and an analysis by Waseda University of a sample from the Great Pyramid (Michel Barsoum's tests had not yet been conducted).[50]

Michael S. Tite, Head of the Laboratory of London's British Museum, made his test in 1984. At that time, he was also the coordinator of the Archaeometry '84 Symposium, held that year at the Smithsonian Institution, in Washington, D.C. With access to all of the papers submitted, he was privy to Joseph Davidovits' testing of the Lauer sample soon to be presented at the symposium. Tite took the opportunity to chemically analyze a sample of casing stone from the Great Pyramid in the British Museum's laboratory collection. Because Tite used proper testing protocol, his charts reveal the unusual mineralogical characteristics of the Lauer sample.[51]

After Davidovits delivered his paper at the symposium, Michael S. Tite rose from the audience and asserted that the odd mineralogy could be natural. But there are fundamental problems with Tite's methodology. First, he did not show the same chemistry in any natural limestone. He did not compare Tura limestone samples. He did not show consideration of the chemistry of geopolymerization, either. Instead, Tite's approach was to treat minerals in the Lauer sample separately—arguing that this or that element can occur in natural limestone. But he could not find the totality of the chemical profile in any particular natural limestone. Zeolites are very rare in natural limestone. The zeolite ZK-20 found in the Lauer sample is a synthetic compound that forms when natron reacts with organic ammonium—and this is not the sort of reaction that would occur during the formation of natural limestone. Tite made his assertions even though the synthetic zeolite Zk-20 is unheard of in natural limestone (or even in nature).

Tite's approach is also unreasonable because geopolymerization is rock-forming chemistry. So, many of the elements it produces are found in natural rock. Tite also ignored the telling mineralogy in the manmade white coating on the Lauer sample. As mentioned, the bulk of the Lauer sample has the same unusual mineralogical characteristics as does its synthetic white coating.[52] These minerals are not water soluble and cannot migrate from the coating to the body of the sample or vice versa. The odds against the bulk of the Lauer sample's having a naturally-occurring mineralogy unknown in natural limestone—which matches the mineralogy of its synthetic white coating—are astronomically high.

Geologists can argue endlessly over whether the unusual trace minerals in pyramid blocks result from some freak of nature or from geopolymerization. But the other method Harrell tried, testing for chemically bound water, is a decisive test when properly conducted.

Water that is chemically bound is not moisture that simply soaks into the pores and cracks in rock. Water that is not chemically bound is called free water. Free water from rain and/or other sources evaporates from limestone in warm climates soon after soaking in. But chemically bound water is molecularly tied up in the material itself. Chemically bound water is normally permanent. Releasing it requires a far higher temperature than needed to evaporate free water from a sample.

Harrell's testing of a tiny subsample of the Lauer sample did not detect chemically bound water.[53] Based on my consultations with Edward Zeller, Robert McKinney, and Joseph Davidovits, I cannot explain exactly why James Harrell did not detect chemically bound water. Joseph Davidovits suspects that Harrell overheated the sample. We did not have the advantage of consulting directly with Harrell to try to figure out the problem. The reason is that once the first portion of my debate with Harrell was published, he openly revealed a concealed vehement hostility toward the geopolymer theory. His rage is blatant in his part of our published debate. His arguments degenerate from scientific debate to unprofessional, unfounded, libelous personal attacks.[54]

Despite his promise to remove material only about the size of a sugar cube, James A. Harrell greatly reduced the size of the Lauer sample in his failed attempt at testing it.[55] When he returned it to me, there was not much left. Important features were destroyed. Joseph Davidovits suspects that James Harrell's serious damage to the Lauer sample occurred because of destructive testing in an attempt to find a natural-looking portion that could be used to support his argumentation. As mentioned, the unnatural features of the Lauer sample were clear to Folk even in a microphotograph.

Harrell's findings are not consistent with other studies that detected a high moisture content in Giza blocks. As mentioned, Edward J. Zeller detected chemically bound water in pyramid masonry by studying the various electromagnetic-sounding experiments at Giza. They were conducted independently by different teams. All electromagnetic-sounding attempts failed because the pyramid stone is so full of moisture.[56]

In the 1970s, physicist Lambert Dolphin and his team from Stanford Research International (SRI) conducted the most widely-known of the electromagnetic-sounding experiments. Their goal was to detect hidden chambers in the pyramids.[57] These experiments operated on the concept that electromagnetic waves directed at the pyramids would reflect. So, by measuring what bounces back, researchers could detect hollow spots in the pyramids. But because the Giza bedrock was dry, the SRI researchers expected that the pyramid core masonry would be dry, too.

Instead, there was so much moisture in the pyramid masonry that the electromagnetic waves were absorbed. The project, designed to detect hidden rooms, failed because of the unexpected moisture in the pyramid stone.

The results of this and the other sounding experiments imply the presence of permanent chemically bound water within the pyramid blocks. To be certain, Edward J. Zeller studied the problem. Zeller offered the following opinion:

> Only an onslaught of rain, a minimum of six inches falling a month or so before Dolphin's tests, could produce the amount of free water needed to cause the pyramid core masonry to absorb the electromagnetic waves.

Rainfall is typically measured in fractions of an inch per month in the Cairo area during the winter months. There will typically be no measurable rainfall at all for four, five, or six months in a row during the warmest months. For more than a year before Dolphin and his team conducted their tests, there was only the typical dearth of rain in the Cairo area. The monthly precipitation records for Egypt are recorded at the U.S. National Oceanic & Atmospheric Administration.[58]

According to Zeller, the data strongly support the premise that the water in the pyramid stone is chemically bound. That is consistent with concrete containing chemically bound water. In a statement issued to me on August 23, 1995, Zeller commented on the data produced by Dolphin and others:

> In short, it looks unlikely to me that free water could account for the microwave absorption that was reported.[59]

Like Folk and Campbell, Harrell and Penrod have not sought to debate the geopolymer theorem again. Harrell has denounced it in settings in which we have very limited or no ability to counter his attacks. This situation has left even more misinformation in the published scientific record.

The Ingram Tests

The last in the geological community to seriously challenge the geopolymer theory was a team that included Kevin Ingram, at the time a graduate student at the University of North Texas. He designed his project to put the presumably specious geopolymer-stone theory to the ultimate test. Under the direction of his Ph.D. supervisor Kenneth Daugherty and others, a series of tests was performed on limestone samples they obtained from the Giza pyramids of Khafra and Menkaura.

These researchers published an article in the *Journal of Archaeological Science* (December 1993) stating that their tests showed no evidence supporting the geopolymerized-stone theory. They advanced the typical arguments that tool marks appear on some blocks, that there is mortar between some joints, and that ramps are found at some pyramid sites. They asserted that these observations disprove the geopolymer theory. With their minds made up based on these superficial observations (which have all been accounted for in these pages), they performed their tests and obtained the results explained below.

After consulting with Joseph Davidovits, Zeller, and McKinney, I wrote our rebuttal and submitted it to the *Journal of Archaeological Science*. The editor declined to publish it. My paper was accompanied by reviews urging publication by geologists and by materials scientist Rustum Roy, then Head of the Materials Research Institute at Pennsylvania State University. Given that our rebuttal was repeatedly rejected and never published, I necessarily correct the scientific record here.

Ingram et al. used inductively coupled plasmography (ICP) to determine the molecular composition of the samples. When Ingram et al. found the needed aluminum, they considered it to be consistent with natural stone. Proper interpretation of the analyses requires consideration of the chemistry produced by geopolymerization: The amount of aluminum–203 detected by Ingram et al. is inconsistent with their conclusion that the sample appears to be natural limestone. The noncarbonate ratio is high (at 8%), and this can be assigned to aluninosilicates.

The high amount of aluminum detected by Ingram et al. is highly significant, since aluminum–203 is only in the 1% range in analyses performed on Mokattam limestones. The information published by Harrell et al. points out that, "the chemistry for limestones in Table 1 [from Gebel Mokattam] (1.48%), Tura (0.68%), and Massara (0.0%) is typical of those from the Mokattam."[60]

What is more important is that Ingram et al.'s samples lost over 60% of their mass during decarboxylation at 900 C. Assuming that the amounts given in Ingram's Table 1 are accurate, 91.5% calcite would yield a 40.26% weight loss during decarboxylation, and 1.4%

dolomite would yield a 0.74% weight loss. This totals a weight loss of 41%. This 41% loss can be expected for calcite. The difference between the measured loss and the calculated loss for the calcite fraction is 19%. This 19% would have been in the form of chemically bound water.

In other words, their ratios support the other tests showing that the pyramid stone contains chemically bound water, which is a characteristic of hydraulic concrete and of zeolitic materials. I have already explained Edward J. Zeller's study of the chemically bound water based on electromagnetic-sounding experiments conducted on the Great Pyramids of Khufu and Khafra.[61] Suggesting that the moisture in the pyramid stone is free water (from rainwater or ground water) would defy physics — given the absence of a source of sufficient free water from rainfall (as measured over many months and even years prior to the tests) or other possible water sources from the environment.

The studies Edward Zeller considered include the one that was partially funded by *National Geographic* and conducted in 1988. The project, when attempting to determine the thickness of blocks weighing ten to fifteen tons covering a funerary boat pit associated with the Great Pyramid, obtained, "no unusual reflections…owing to the moisture trapped in the stone."[62]

In another study, a Waseda University team, using ground penetrating radar, compared large samples from the Great Pyramid against Japanese limestone and found that the two have distinctly different physical properties.[63] To obtain results, the Japanese scientists calibrated their equipment to overcome the problems of moisture content in the pyramid masonry.

Not counting the Ingram study, at least three studies encountered the moisture in the pyramid blocks.[64] In short, Ingram's data inadvertently support these studies indicating the presence of chemically bound water in the blocks of the pyramids of Khufu and Khafra.

To summarize, Ingram's Table I shows that the pyramid material lost 60 percent of its mass during decarboxylation when powdered and heated at 900 degrees centigrade. Assuming that the figures in Ingram's Table 1 are correct, there was a 19 percent weight loss that is attributable to chemically bound water. This water loss is indicative of the presence of either clay (kaolin is 13 percent chemically bound water by weight, and the amount of kaolin in the Giza bedrock is too small to produce Ingram's results) or zeolite material (geopolymerization produces zeolites), the latter of which is also suggested by Ingram's infrared data showing a shoulder on a peak for a Menkaura sample at 1030 cm–1.[65] This figure is within the zeolitic vibrational range. Ingram did not recognize the implications of his data, i.e., that zeolite is present as a result of geopolymerization.

The team also used infrared spectroscopy. Ingram indicates that "the shoulder on the peak at 1030 cm–1 is stronger in the sample from Menkaure…" This must be considered with regard to the infrared spectra of zeolitic materials. The strongest vibrations in zeolites are found at 950–1250 cm–1. Ingram's shoulder at 1030 cm–1 is within the infrared spectra for zeolites. Because the zeolitic material is diluted with calcite, the intensity of the spectra for these materials is weaker than would be expected for pure zeolites. The presence of zeolitic materials aligns with the high weight loss due to chemically bound water.

The shoulder for Khafra is not as strong as for Menkaura. A new comparative study reanalyzing the spectra over the range of 1000 cm–1 could also show zeolitic material for Khafra. We proposed that the Ingram team work with members of our team on a new study. But our request was declined.

Another test by Ingram et al. utilized electron-diffraction Xrays (EDX). As it regards Ingram's EDX detection of aluminum, when its value is deducted from the aluminum contamination that occurred from the polishing compound, a figure of 8 to 10 percent for aluminum is obtained for molecular composition. The value of 3.9 percent, provided in Table 1, is normal for pyramid stone and consistent with geopolymerization.

A chemical analysis of pyramid limestone by Waseda University shows the zeolite analcime* among its primary constituents.[66] Although it would be very strange for analcime to form in natural limestone, geopolymerization produces zeolites and feldspathoids (including analcime).

A chemical analysis was conducted on two very small samples of casing from the Great Pyramid in 1975 by Gordon Brown, of Stanford University. Aluminosilicate minerals associated with geopolymerization are present.[67] These findings are consistent with those of Joseph Davidovits. As mentioned, he was provided a fist-sized sample of fine-grained limestone from the Ascending Passageway of the Great Pyramid by Egyptologist J.P. Lauer. Davidovits took this sample to two independent European laboratories, in France and Belgium, for X-ray chemical analysis. Involving two different laboratories allowed for cross-verification of test results. The resulting charts, which list the minerals found and their concentrations, show minerals that result from geopolymerization.

The chemical charts for the Lauer sample show trace minerals that are extremely rare in natural limestone. He even found the synthetic zeolite ZK-20, which does not occur in nature. Davidovits performed a comparative study. He made samples of geopolymeric limestone concrete and submitted them for chemical analysis, too. His samples were devoid of animal remains (the pyramid stone contains brushite, which suggests material from animal sacrifice). So, an exact match was not expected. The resulting chemical charts of his own geopolymerized limestone samples show the same type of mineralogical pattern as that of the Lauer sample's charts.

For purposes of further comparison, Davidovits analyzed several limestone samples from the Tura quarries, Egypt's primary source of fine-grained limestone. Their chemical charts show that they are pure calcite, although some contain a trace of dolomite. The several quarry samples tested do not have the unusual mineralogy of the Lauer sample.

There is a much more definitive and important finding. The Lauer sample from the Great Pyramid is particularly interesting because it has a white coating on it that is topped by reddish-brown paint. Every geologist who has examined this white coating agrees that it is synthetic. They may argue with one another as to whether or not this white coating is stone or some kind of hard plaster, but they all agree that it is man-made.

Importantly, chemical analyses of this white coating show the same unusual mineralogy as the bulk of the Lauer sample. These minerals include apatite, brushite, a volcanic form of silica, and a very small amount of the synthetic zeolite ZK-20, which is not present in natural limestone.

These minerals could not have migrated from the white coating to the body of the sample or vice versa because they are not water soluble. The odds against the bulk of the Lauer sample having a naturally-occurring mineralogy that matches the mineralogy of the synthetic white coating are astronomically high. It is logical to conclude that both the synthetic white

---

* The mineral analcime is sometimes classified as a feldspathoid because its chemistry is similar, but it has the typical open framework of a zeolite. Some mineralogists classify it as both a zeolite and a feldspathoid. With prolonged high-temperature heating and dehydration, the structure of analcime will eventually collapse. In contrast, true zeolites maintain their structures upon high-temperature heating, even when they are dehydrated.

coating and the limestone (which each contain minerals typical of a geopolymeric chemical reaction) are geopolymeric products.[68]

Michel Barsoum vs Donald H. Campbell

After Michel Barsoum's first paper on his test results of pyramid and quarry samples were published, he attended a panel discussion of the International Cement Microscopy Association, held in May of 2007. It was also attended by Donald H. Campbell, who came to re-assert the Folk/Campbell claim that, "It is not easy to give a geological education to a brilliant and determined chemist [Davidovits]." Barsoum provides the following report at his web blog:

I just returned from International Cement Microscopy Association (ICMA, www.cemmicro.org) that was held in Quebec City. Yesterday afternoon, I participated in a panel public discussion on the evidence for/against cast-in-place origin of the Egyptian pyramid blocks. Drs. Donald Campbell and Dipayan Jana made the case for carving; they talked first and I closed. At the end of my talk, when asked if anybody had any questions, nobody, including the two aforementioned gentlemen, had any question, comments or objections. I assumed, by their silence, that they were convinced that at least some of the blocks were indeed cast.

Robert L. Folk did not participate and remained silent. Months later, he did contact me saying that he read the newspaper headlines announcing Michel Barsoum's findings.

Mark Lehner's Objections

Mark Lehner also challenged the geopolymerized theory in a minor way. He took issue with thick mortar between some core blocks of the Great Pyramid.[69] But Alfred Lucas, in *Ancient Egyptian Materials and Industries*, observed that the pyramid blocks are much too large for mortar to have any adhesive power.[70] Lucas pointed out that the Egyptians applied mortar to cushion blocks against stress. Mortar appears even between temple blocks at Giza weighing 200 tons.[71] In other words, the presence of the mortar is irrelevant to the question of how the Egyptians made the pyramid blocks.

Lehner also questioned gaps between some pyramid blocks. The now-vanished *tafla* (used to separate some blocks so that they would not merge into one mass during rapid construction) can account for gaps, as I explained above. We can expect that some of the thick, pink lime-gypsum mortar used to cushion blocks has disappeared, too, leaving gaps.

In his Letter to the Editor, published in *Harvard Magazine* (September - October 2003), Lehner made a sweeping generalization about geopolymerization by taking issue with tool marks he observed on pyramid blocks. But in reality, tool marks work against the accepted carving theory: The overwhelming majority of blocks are devoid of tool marks of any kind. Within the context of the carving hypothesis, one must ask how and why masons would erase a myriad of tool marks from the bulk of the masonry—which is largely extremely rough and highly irregular and was meant to remain forever hidden behind the beautifully-formed casing blocks. Even mating protuberances between blocks are free of tool marks. The other tool marks he mentioned are counterproductive. Picks make gouge marks and hammers bruise and crack rock and encourage structural weakness. So, the tool marks mentioned by Lehner logically fit better with destructive hacking at the pyramid masonry centuries after its construction.

Only cutting rock-concrete during the uncured stage of geopolymeric setting can explain the many stunning examples of tool marks that sweep across surfaces with no sign of dulling of the tool. Artifacts of this description, made with extremely hard rock types, were found at Giza by W.M.F. Petrie and are now in the Petrie Museum, in London. He found clean, unbroken tool strokes up to 20 feet long on artifacts made with extremely hard, tough rock like diorite. Petrie collected examples with no sign of dulling of the tool. So, in reality, tool marks work strongly in favor of the geopolymer theory.

Although Lehner wrote in his Letter to the Editor that "few of the blocks have a single flat face," in actuality twenty acres of flat, carefully-angled casing blocks originally covered the Great Pyramid—according to measurements and reports from ancient witnesses who saw its vast, smooth triangular surfaces. Another major example of a flat surface that Lehner fails to acknowledge is the 13-square-acre foundation upon which the Great Pyramid rests. It was measured by the Egyptian government in 1925 and found to be very flat, off only 7/8 of an inch from the northwest to the southwest corner. The Egyptian government report suggests that the slight deviation may be due to settling.

Tier heights were measured by Georges Goyon and others, and the measurements show that the 200 (previously 201) tiers of the Great Pyramid consist of only about 73 different course heights (some top tiers are missing) that are all off in height by 1/2 centimeter or less.

Questions about the techniques used to build the pyramids with man-made stone are bound to arise. Architects and others with specialized expertise are now in a position to rethink the techniques used for pyramid construction. But hostile opponents often defy scientific protocol, and hurl questions as weapons and then tout their inquiries, valid or not, as proof that the theory is erroneous.

Lehner indirectly refutes the geopolymeric pyramid theory by continuing to assert that he can match places in Giza quarries where blocks were removed to build Khafra's Valley Temple. He writes:

> In a few places, almost detached from the parent rock, blocks remain about the size of those forming the walls of Khafra's Valley Temple. This and the Sphinx ditch were probably the quarries for those temples, which must have been the last element of Khafra's pyramid complex to be built.[72]

Lehner's claim ignores the study by the Klemms that dated quarrying techniques. They showed that the style of channel quarrying apparent at Giza does not date to the Old or Middle Kingdoms. Wedge holes Lehner exemplifies as Pyramid Age masonry work at Giza actually date to the Iron Age, as we know from the exhaustive studies by the Klemms, Joseph Roder, and others.

Like Lehner, Dieter Arnold assumes that separation ditches were made to quarry blocks. But because Arnold recognizes the Klemms' work, he realizes that something is seriously amiss with the whole concept as it pertains to Old and Middle Kingdom quarrying. Arnold wrote:

> The question as to what kind of tools were used to cut the separation trenches and to lift the blocks from their beds has not been answered satisfactorily because of the contradiction between the tool marks left on the quarry walls and the tools actually found in ancient Egypt...[73]

The blocks in Khafra's Valley Temple to which Lehner alludes are enormous. They weigh 200 tons or more. Because of their great size, if they were carved, it is not likely that

4th Dynasty quarrymen would have started more blocks than were needed. Instead, the huge, unfinished blocks in the quarries characterize later work that had to be abandoned. In *The Complete Pyramids* (1997), Lehner provides a photograph of the ditch behind the Sphinx, where he thinks the 4th Dynasty workers quarried blocks to build the Valley Temple.[74] The quarry wall shows a huge, deep rectangular slot. Slots like his were made to accept iron wedges, a technique consistent with Iron Age quarrying methods.

In short, it is improper for Lehner to support the orthodox carve-hoist theory with the limited quarry features at Giza that are characteristic of more advanced quarrying techniques than were available in 4th Dynasty Egypt. By the 26th Dynasty, when iron was in common use, quarrymen were in a much better position to cut notches into the bedrock to facilitate attempts to pry large blocks with iron levers. Egyptology has documented definite 26th Dynasty, Greek, and Roman activity at Giza, too. As mentioned, Joseph Davidovits measured the distances between the lift lines in these temple blocks and showed that they do not match the heights of the natural strata in the Sphinx quarry.

Besides, during our geological study in 1990, Robert Folk and Donald Campbell studied these same 200-ton temple blocks in Khafra's Valley Temple.[75] Folk and Campbell claim that these enormous blocks must be natural because they exhibit strata at the same level from block to block. Folk and Campbell claimed that these blocks must have been set in the Valley Temple exactly as they existed in the bedrock. Their fantasy implies some kind of super technology because it suggests that no quarry waste other than a little powder was generated. As I mentioned above, Campbell even suggested that the ancient quarrying method allowed delicate cracks to be preserved and realigned in the monuments. But according to standard masonry theory, enormous trenches separated quarried blocks.

The standard theory holds that the workers tunnelled into the bedrock so that the blocks could be cracked from the quarry floor (supposedly with wooden levers). Assuming that this method was used, the chances are extremely poor that they would all break free so that their strata would line up. To get strata to align, the gargantuan blocks would have to have been very closely leveled and cut. Folk and Campbell proposed that this was somehow accomplished so that the gods might not be upset with blocks that did not match the bedrock configuration.

As mentioned, it is more logical to think that the strata are not natural features at all. They are typical lift lines in concrete. So-called lift lines occur in gigantic concrete blocks because of the length of time required to produce them. With huge portland cement-based concrete blocks, too, setting starts to get underway before the work can be finished. The lift line is a line of distinction between the area cast first and the subsequent casting. Lift lines all at the same level, as in the huge Valley Temple blocks, suggest that the workers made the blocks simultaneously.

In this scenario, workers carefully built them up all at the same time so that their joints would be perfect. Perhaps the workers build the blocks gradually and simultaneously to be sure that such huge blocks would be strong and not collapse under their own weight before they cured.

In short, Mark Lehner presents no valid evidence for his claim that Valley Temple blocks were quarried and match areas of the Giza bedrock. Matching shell types shows that the rock came from Giza bedrock. But it does not follow that the masonry was quarried at Giza as whole blocks.

Dunn vs Morris

Machinist Christopher Dunn, author of *The Giza Power Plant* (1998), has misreported and challenged the geopolymer theory. As mentioned, Dunn measured some of the surfaces of ancient Egyptian sarcophagi and found them to be extremely flat. He measured areas of Khafra's sarcophagus and two in the Serapeum with a six-inch machinist's parallel ground flat to .0002 inch. When he shined his flashlight against his parallel, he found that no light came through anywhere he checked. So, he was able to show extreme flatness in the areas he measured.

Dunn asserted that it was not possible to cast synthetic stone walls to this level of precision. He assumes that it is not possible to cut pliable or partially cured rock to this level of precision with simple tools. Dunn believes that machining hard rock is the only answer to account for the flatness he measured.

I consulted with experts who precision-cut granite, and posed the problem Dunn raised. They advised me that his method of measurement (using a machinist's parallel) cannot accurately measure the entire surface of a wall even if he inched along slowly with his parallel. In other words, if the wall itself is slightly bowed, it will not be possible to detect the irregularity with a six-inch parallel. It is important to determine actual flatness over the entire expanse of walls because exact measurements set the requirement for precision molding.

I consulted with two precision-molding companies to obtain professional opinions about the specifications for casting sarcophagi to the specifications Dunn measured. Their opinions are based on what is theoretically possible given their own long experience and the properties of geopolymers.

To create a truly flat sarcophagus that is not bowed requires a special mold—a mold made of a pure geopolymeric binder (with no rock aggregates added). Geopolymerization produces zeolites such as analcime crystals, which measure only 5 microns (a unit of length equal to one millionth of a meter). This extremely small particle size is needed if one wishes to produce flat panels for assembling a mold within which to cast a monolithic sarcophagus that will be truly flat to .0002 inch.

I consulted with Gary Mellinger, who at the time had 28 years of precision-casting experience with Spokane Industries, in Spokane, Washington. He became very interested in using a geopolymeric binder for precision-casting techniques because he recognized that the material had the potential to set a new industry standard.

The reasons are (1) the 5-micron analcime crystals allow for a very flat surface, (2) the geopolymeric binder is very strong (with compressive strength of 25,000 psi), such that it will not break during the work processes, and (3) the pure binder requires no high heat to cure (it gives off only a small amount of heat while curing).

Whereas, high heat (up to 1,800 degrees Fahrenheit) causes the molds Gary Mellinger normally worked with to warp, which prevents flat surfaces over large areas. This was typical for the industry. Another important consideration is that geopolymeric rock-concretes will cure in a mold at ambient temperatures. A rock-making slurry cast into a mold made of geopolymeric binder will, of course, take the shape of the mold itself. But the precision flatness of the walls requires rock particles that are sufficiently coated with geopolymeric binder. According to Gary Mellinger, the cast surfaces will be true if the mold is well made, free of debris, and given enough time to fully cure.

Panels for assembling such molds are flat. This is provided for by putting the ingredients for the geopolymeric binder into large pans of water, which automatically creates a level upper surface. Adding the materials for the binder does not interfere with the flat upper surface of the water. So, Dunn's flatness specifications are met with a mold made with a pure geopolymeric binder.

As I write this, such a large sarcophagus has not been reproduced to illustrate this point. Joseph Davidovits has worked with precision casters to make several molds for aeronautical applications. These molds had to be very precise. According to Davidovits, one of the licensees cast geopolymeric toolings for 3D precision computer-assisted measurements as a replacement for machined granite toolings. With the geopolymeric toolings, the precision and dimensional stability outperformed the machined granite tooling.

Mold panels can be affixed with geopolymeric binder. Techniques other than molding, such as tube drilling (without the need for sand), could be used to hollow out semi-cured sarcophagi made with agglomerated stone, too.

General Objections by Egyptology

Some Egyptologists have discounted the geopolymerized pyramid theory by claiming that it is unnecessary. They base their assumptions on erroneous, outdated theories asserting that copper tools are capable of cutting the millions of pyramid blocks. Most incorrectly assume that enormous ramps raised the blocks and beams. In both parts of this book, I have shown that these notions are without basis, and that Egyptology has no real explanation for how the pyramid blocks could have been quarried, carved, or hoisted.

The tortured logic of the carve-hoist paradigm has been met with a backlash of sensational books that attribute the Great Pyramid to space alien, Atlantean, or interdimensional travelers. From there, the extrapolation grows ever more outlandish as time goes on. Some popular authors, encouraged by all of this, are at the point of asserting that humankind, too, is the product of highly advanced technology—and that humankind is still being instructed by those who engendered it with the futuristic technology used to build the Great Pyramid. Some imagine the Great Pyramid to be a machine for generating special powers, time travel, or transporting adepts to the stars or deep into the center of the Earth.

The careless defense of the status quo by mainstream experts has engendered this destructive dumbing down of the general populace. Contrast the simple truth of early dwellers along the Nile mixing earthen materials with lime and water until they developed durable materials fit for their royal monuments. Sheer logic and the full weight of the archaeological and scientific evidence presented in these pages fully support the geopolymer masonry theorem.[76]

Appendix 3
Comments by Geologist James Shelton

G eologist James Shelton tried to account for the behavior of Folk and Campbell, and offered the following explanation in a letter to me.

...a realization occurred that is fundamental to Folk, et. al's position as to why they are so dead set against geopolymer origins of antiquities. It has to do with fundamental geological assumptions which, if you value your geological position, you do not violate. It has nothing to do with the pyramids or how they were constructed; it has to do with cold cryptocrystallization* processes and the times it takes if the right ingredients are present.

Stop and consider Folk's position as a carbonate sedimentologist. All these years of study devoted to saying that these little carbonate cementing organisms take millions of years to lay down massive carbonate sequences via bio-precipitation from seawater according to uniformitarian principles. Little did I realize that in geology, there has been an old debate about the material balances of calcium and calcium carbonate as well as salt in seawater related to the massive carbonate and salt/evaporite[†] deposits found around the world and how there are no corresponding large scale examples of present day fast carbonate and evaporite deposition.

Along comes Joseph and demonstrates that by using a little igneous derived salt and given an ample supply of calcium carbonate he can both dissolve it and reprecipitate it in a matter of hours. What this is demonstrating is not uniformatarianism but worldwide catastrophism leading to massive undersea volcanism and hydrothermal activity oversupplying the oceans with quantities of soluble minerals capable of precipitating vast bathtub like rings of carbonates and evaporites on continental margins replete with corresponding massive marine organism die-offs. When one considers that when seawater altered volcanic ash and carbonates are merged together, you have an instantaneous geopolymer for forming massive carbonates and evaporites in a very short period of time.

---

* The process of cryptocrystallization occurs when calcium carbonate precipitates in small spaces and chambers of coralline algae that contain organic material isolated from the surrounding seawater. Geologists believe that the release of ammonia, as organic material decays, will result in the gradual precipitation of calcium carbonate. Geologists think that this process of calcification takes place over millions of years and plays a role in the formation of the cement that binds coral reef materials.

† Evaporites are rocks that form from minerals that precipitate out of evaporating water. Common examples are calcite, gypsum, anhydrite, and rock salt. In other words, geochemists hold that sedimentary rock like limestone forms from mineral residues as ancient seas and salt lakes evaporate in arid locations. Limestone, dolomite, gypsum, rock salt and other minerals are common constituents of evaporites.

This mechanism has haunted geologists in the past and is a thorn in the side of the geosciences that severely compromises our already shakey-snakey slight of hand radiometric dating methods, which are touted as the backup to the principles of superposition related to dating. Basically, geology's fragile little theories come under scrutiny that they will not be able to bear up to. Geology remains part of the old Newtonian mechanistic paradigm, 100 years behind relativity and quantum mechanics which itself is being superseded. Geochemistry is relegated to using the more than 100-year-old method of performing pressure bomb melts for silicate crystallization research. Along comes some new blood from organic chemistry, demonstrates the likeness of silicates to organic polymers and demonstrates a cold silicate polymerization process unlike ferrocement and 150 years of geochemical arm waving goes up in smoke.

Basically, Folk et al. were not just protecting the concrete industry, they were fighting for their lives and the solvency of their profession. Joseph engineered something here that is much bigger than he anticipated. You have hit geoscience, and consequently, your profession, archaeology, in a vital organ.[1]

James Shelton has spent years investigating the mysterious site called Rockwall, in the town of Rockwall, Texas. An enormous rock wall was discovered in the mid-1850's and partially excavated. It covers an area of up to 20 square miles. Rockwall is still mostly buried. Owing to its features, people have interpreted it as the ruins of an ancient, long lost civilization—conceivably a Pre-Columbian building civilization right here in the United States. Most geologists oppose the idea, and interpret it as a very strange natural geological feature instead. But they cannot account for where the wall's rocks came from and have no theory of its geological formation.

The wall construction has an adobe look, giving it the classical appearance of a manmade stone wall. This look is attributed by most geologists to cracking throughout, to create highly irregular, form-fitted stones. The stone is classified as feldspar granite. James Shelton removed pure cement from the top portion of the wall. I have not examined the wall. But if an early drawing of the portion showing arched windows is accurate, it is hard to believe that Rockwall is a natural formation. It could be an ancient territorial marker and fort. The evidence to date may very well suggest that one of the most precious ancient sites in the United States lacks the full-scale archaeological and scientific attention it deserves. For the most part, experts do not appreciate it as anything but an odd geological formation, and so not likely accompanied by buried artifacts from ancient human activities.

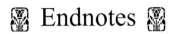 Endnotes

Chapter 1: A Stunning Secret of the Ages Revealed

. For the theory that stone pounding balls were used to build the pyramids, refer to Arnold, D., *Building in Egypt: pharaonic stone masonry,* New York, N.Y., Oxford University Press (1991), 48. On the Mohs' hardness scale, copper and bronze have a hardness of from 3.5 to 4. Good-quality limestone generally ranges between 4 to 5. Up-to-date Egyptological writings, e.g., Dieter *Arnold's Building in Egypt,* recognize that the demand for copper would be too great to produce about 12 million pyramid blocks in about 79 years for the 4th Dynasty pyramids. In general, the pyramid complexes are made of about 5 percent granite, which ranges from 6 to 8 on the Mohs' scale, according to Dieter Arnold. No iron tools have ever been found in a sealed tomb of the Old Kingdom, and rare examples of iron tools found around tomb sites of this era are thought to have been left by later operations to either restore the tombs or to remove ready-made blocks. Arnold lists Mohs' hardness for Egyptian stones in particular: dense limestone 4?; quartzite 6–8; granite 6–8; basalt 6–8; diorite 5–6. Refer to Arnold, D., *Building in Egypt: pharaonic stone masonry,* New York, N.Y., Oxford University Press (1991), 28. These factors lead Egyptologists who are up to date on such issues to believe that stone tools were used. Most of the Egyptological literature (including Mark Lehner's 1997 book titled *The Complete Pyramids*), however, uses out-of-date information stating that copper tools were used to build the Great Pyramids.

. For example, no Late Stone Age potter's wheel can cut into diorite through a turning mechanism, but Petrie referred to diorite bowl fragments he believed were made by turning. See Petrie, W.M.F., *The Pyramids and Temples of Gizeh,* Field, London (1883), 176 and pl. XIV, 14, 15. See many more examples in the present book.

. For the supertech theories and the problems with them, see Chapter 19 of this book.

Chapter 2: The Great Masonry Wonder

. Petrie, W.M.F., *Pyramids and Temples of Gizeh,* Field, London, (1883), 210. The latest figures agree with Petrie's count. Mark Lehner, who has mapped Giza, gives the same figure. Refer to Lehner, M., *The Complete Pyramids: Solving the Ancient Mysteries,* New York, Thames and Hudson (1997), 109. On page 109, the following statement appears: "The Great Pyramid contains about 2,300,000 blocks of stone, often said to weigh an average of 2.5 tons. This might be somewhat exaggerated; the stones certainly get smaller towards the top of the pyramid, and we do not know if the masonry of the inner core is as well-cut and uniform as the stone courses that are now exposed....On the other hand some of the casing stones at the base may weigh as much as 15 tons, and the large granite beams roofing the King's Chamber and the stress-relieving chambers above it have been estimated to weigh from 50 to 80 tons. Such statistics, while repeated frequently, never cease to astound." In the 5th century B.C., when the Great Pyramid was still in perfect condition, Herodotus wrote that he saw many casing blocks 30 feet long, and Abd el-Latif gave the same figure in the 12th century. The tier heights have been measured, and these measurements show massive blocks at levels high in the Great Pyramid (see my Appendix 1). Some blocks in the outer masonry of the Great Pyramid, situated at about the level of the King's Chamber, occupy the height of two tiers.

. Arnold, D., *Building in Egypt: pharaonic stone masonry,* New York, N.Y., Oxford University Press (1991), 165.

. Arnold, D., *Building in Egypt: pharaonic stone masonry,* New York, N.Y., Oxford University Press (1991), 167–8.

. For the study by Goyon, refer to Goyon, G., "Les Rangs D'assises de la Grande Pyramide," *Bulletin de l'Institut Francais d'Archeologie Orientale,* Cairo (1978), Vol. 78, No. 2, 405–413.

5.   Arnold, D., *Building in Egypt: pharaonic stone masonry,* New York, N.Y., Oxford University Press (1991), 165–167.

6.   For the study by Goyon, refer to Goyon, G., "Les Rangs d'assises de la Grande Pyramide, *Bulletin de l'Institut Francais d'Archeologie Orientale,* Cairo (1978), Vol. 78, No. 2, 405–413. Refer also to Vyse, Richard William Howard (1784–1853), *Operations carried on at the pyramids of Gizeh in 1837: with an account of a voyage into Upper Egypt, and an appendix,* London, Pub. J. Fraser (1840-1842).

7.   Davidovits, J., Morris, M., *The Pyramids: An Enigma Solved,* Hippocrene, NY (1988), 109–112.

8.   Davidovits, J., Morris, M., *The Pyramids: An Enigma Solved,* Hippocrene, NY (1988), 109–112.

9.   The feature was photographed in about 1940 by a British Air Force pilot named P. Groves. According to J.P. Lepre, "One very unusual feature of the Great Pyramid is a concavity of the core that makes the monument an eight-sided figure, rather than four-sided...That is to say, that its four sides are hollowed in or indented along their central lines, from base to peak. This concavity divides each of the apparent four sides in half, creating a very special and unusual eight-sided pyramid; and it is executed to such an extraordinary degree of precision as to enter the realm of the uncanny." See Lepre, J.P., *The Egyptian Pyramids: A Comprehensive, Illustrated Reference,* McFarland, Jefferson, N.C. (1990), 65.

10. Petrie, W.M.F., *Pyramids and Temples of Gizeh,* Field, London (1883 reprint 1990), 37.

11. Arnold, D., *Building in Egypt: pharaonic stone masonry,* New York, N.Y., Oxford University Press (1991), 122–123, note 56 on page 203; ibid., 123, Arnold adds, "In pyramid casing, oblique joints are therefore more frequent in granite than in limestone."

12. Owing to their smooth surfaces, casing blocks still intact at the tip of Khafra's Pyramid reflect moonlight. Also, John Greaves (1602–1652), a professor of mathematics and an astronomer at Oxford University, mistook Khufu's granite sarcophagus for marble; refer to his book *Pyramidographia* (1646). Petrie referred to unusually colored limestones as marble.

13. Petrie, W.M.F., *Pyramids and Temples of Gizeh,* Field, London, Histories and Mysteries of Man, Ltd., London (1883 reprint 1990), 13.

14. Petrie, W.M.F., *Pyramids and Temples of Gizeh,* Field, London, Histories and Mysteries of Man, Ltd., London (1883 reprint 1990), 13.

15. Abd al-Latif, *The Eastern key: Kitab al-ifadah wa'l-i'tibar of 'Abd al-Latif al-Baghdadi, Translated in English by Kamal Hafuth Zand, John A. and Ivy E. Videan,* Allen and Unwin London (1964), 117.

16. Herodotus, *The History of Herodotus,* New York, L. MacVeagh, The Dial press, Toronto, Longmans, Green & company (1928), 124–126; Herodotus, Histories 2.124.5 reads, "The pyramid itself was twenty years in the making. Its base is square, each side eight hundred feet long, and its height is the same [Herodotus could not have measured the height, whereas he could have measured some individual blocks and some sides]; the whole is of stone polished and most exactly fitted; there is no block of less than thirty feet in length." To say that all of the blocks were that long, Herodotus must have been generalizing or he examined the Great Pyramid when the smaller casing blocks remaining now at the lower level were covered with sand.

17. The official Egyptian government survey found that the foundation of the Great Pyramid does not exceed 7/8 inch from dead level, and that this variation may be due to subsidence. Refer to Cole, J. H., "Determination of the exact size and orientation of the great pyramid of Giza," Government Press, Cairo (1925), Series: *Egypt. Finance, Ministry of, Survey dept. Survey of Egypt,* paper; no. 39. The paper can be found in 1 ERMM European Register of Microform Masters (Master microform), 2 NYBA The Brooklyn Museum, 3 NYMA Metropolitan Museum of Art Library 4 UKBX British Library (Master microform).

18. Arnold, D., *Building in Egypt: pharaonic stone masonry,* New York, N.Y., Oxford University Press (1991), 147.

19. For explanations of making the foundation, refer to Lepre, J.P., *The Egyptian Pyramids: A Comprehensive, Illustrated Reference*, McFarland, Jefferson, N.C. (1990), 235 and Edwards, I.E.S. (Iorwerth Eiddon Stephen), *The pyramids of Egypt*, Rev. and updated, repr. with minor revisions, Harmondsworth, Middlesex, England; New York, N.Y., Penguin Books (1988), 310 pp.

20. Diodorus witnessed the Great Pyramid when it was intact, see Diodorus, *Library of History*, Book I, 63 (Oldfather translation).

Chapter 3: Incredible Construction Speed

1. Arnold, D.,"Ueberlegungen zum Problem des Pyramidenbaus," *Mitteilungen des Deutschen Archäologischen Instituts Kairo* (1981), 37, 15–28.

2. Ashley, M., *Seven Wonders of the World*, Ashley Pub., London (1980), 288 pp. New York Times, March 12, 1978, Section IV, p. 7, col. 5. The project was led by Sakuji Yoshimura, formerly of Waseda University, and sponsored and filmed by Nippon TV.

3. Kitchen, K.A., *Pharaoh Triumphant: the life and times of Ramesses II, King of Egypt* (edition: third corr. impression), Warminster, Wiltshire, England: Aris & Phillips; Mississauga, Ont., Canada: Benben (1985, c. 1982), 107.

4. Kitchen, K.A. *Pharaoh Triumphant: the life and times of Ramesses II, King of Egypt* (edition: third corr. impression), Warminster, Wiltshire, England: Aris & Phillips; Mississauga, Ont., Canada: Benben (1985, c. 1982), 107. For Giza's cults dedicated to guarding and maintaining the sepulchres of dead pharaohs, refer to Zivie, C.M., *Giza au deuxieme millenaire*, Cairo (1976), 185 ff; for Teti's cult, refer to Yoyotte, J., "A Propos De La Parente Feminine Du Roi Teti (VI Dynastie)," *Bulletin de l'institut d'archeologie orientale* 57 (1958), 96, n. 4; for Sahure, Martin, G.T., "The tomb of Hetepka and other reliefs and inscriptions from the Sacred Animal Necropolis, North Saqqâra 1964–73," *Egypt Exploration Society*, London (1979), pl. 55.

5. Stadelmann, R., "Snofru und die Pyramiden von Meidum und Dahschur," *Mitteilungen des Deutschen Archäologischen Instituts Kairo*, 36 (1980), 438–439; Arnold, D., *Building in Egypt: pharaonic stone masonry*, New York, N.Y., Oxford University Press (1991), 61, which reads: "...the pyramids of the Fourth Dynasty would have consumed at least 9 million cubic meters of limestone, mortar, and sand, which had to be delivered quickly in small quantities." More precisely, convert cubic meters to cubic feet – multiply by 35.31, and the figure equals 317,790,000 cubic feet or 9,000,000 cubic meters. Add to this amount hundreds of thousands of tons of granite and basalt.

6. Lehner, M., *The Egyptian Heritage: Based on the Edgar Cayce Readings*, Virginia Beach, Va., A.R.E. Press (1974), 135 pp.

7. For the mortar dating tests, refer to Haas, H., et al., "Radiocarbon Chronology and the Historical Calendar in Egypt," *British Archaeological Report, International Series*, Archaeological Series, No. 3, Chronologies in the Near East, pp. 585–606; Lehner M., "Radiocarbon Dating the Pyramids," *Venture Inward* (1985), 40–45. An analysis of mortar in two boat pits on the south side of the Great Pyramid was made. Refer to Nour, M.Z., Iskander, Z., Osman, M.S., and Moustafa, A.Y., *The Cheops Boats*, Cairo (1960), 31: "The mortar...is coarse and pinkish white. Chemical analysis showed that it is mostly composed of calcium sulfate and contains some silica, iron and aluminum oxides, calcium carbonate, sodium chloride and magnesium carbonate." Although the charcoal and reeds in the mortar underwent acid leaching to remove carbon contamination before the dating process, there was no pretreatment that could remove contamination due to a concentrated alkaline solution of sodium or potassium carbonate. The scientific literature provides examples of errors dating aquatic plants that grew in hard-water lakes similar to the Egyptian lakes where natron was gathered. Refer to Aitken, M.J., *Physics and Archaeology*, Clarendon Press, Oxford (1974), 42; Shotton, F.W., "An example of hard-water error in radiocarbon dating of vegetable matter," *Nature* (1972), 460–61; Deevey, E.S., Gross, M.S., Hutchinson, G.E., and Kraybill, H.L., "The natural C14 contents of materials from hard-water lakes," *Proceedings of the National Academy of Science*, Washington, 40 (1954), 285–88. Trees and reeds taken from

natron lakes and burned will typically date older. Cellulose fibers chemically react with sodium carbonate. Because of its high porosity, charcoal absorbs a great deal of natron solution and also carbon dioxide, which results from the decomposition of natron. There is also speculation that burning old wood produced the date discrepancies; see Part 2 of this book.

8. For the issue of carbon pollution, refer to Davidovits, J., Morris, M., *The Pyramids: An Enigma Solved*, Hippocrene, NY (1988), 232. In addition, consider that carbon-14 dating of a mortar sample removed by Lehner from between two blocks in the Sphinx Temple resulted in two different dates from two different laboratories. One laboratory produced a date of 2086 B.C. and the other of 2746 B.C.

9. For a description of how the ancient Egyptians made gypsum (lime-gypsum) mortar, refer to Davidovits, J., Morris, M., *The Pyramids: An Enigma Solved*, Hippocrene, NY (1988), 107–108 or see Chapter 30 below. The geopolymeric (silicoaluminate) mortar corresponds to chemical analysis. Refer to Nour, M.Z., Iskander, Z., Osman, M.S., and Moustafa, A.Y., *The Cheops Boats* Cairo (1960), 31, which reads, "The mortar…is coarse and pinkish white. Chemical analysis showed that it is mostly composed of calcium sulfate [gypsum] and contains some silica, iron and aluminum oxides, calcium carbonate, sodium chloride and magnesium carbonate."

10. For the odd results of the mortar-dating study, refer to Lehner et al.'s results in the Nov./Dec 1985 *Venture Inward* and a follow-up article in 1986 titled "The Great Pyramid Reveals Her Age," published by the Association for Research and Enlightenment (A.R.E.). The A.R.E. is the international headquarters of the proponents of Edgar Cayce.

11. For the mortar-dating tests, refer to Haas, H., Devine, J., Wenke, R., Lehner, M., Wolfli, W. Bonani, G., "Radiocarbon Chronology and the Historical Calendar in Egypt, Chronologies in the Near East," Aurenche O., Evin J. and Hours P. eds., *British Archaeological Report, International Series* No. 379, Part II (1987), 585–606. Page 592 illustrates this point, "…Table 4 illustrates the range and average of dates for the Khufu Pyramid. An attempt has been made to determine the spread of age dates from samples from the lower levels of the monuments, as compared with samples from the apex. The spread is nearly 100 years, but the trend is reversed, the youngest dates are from the bottom samples…" Also refer to Lehner M., "Radiocarbon Dating the Pyramids," *Venture Inward* (1985), 40–45.

12. Lehner, M., *The Egyptian Heritage: Based on the Edgar Cayce Readings*, Virginia Beach, Va. A.R.E. Press (1974), 136 pp.

13. Arnold, D., *Building in Egypt: pharaonic stone masonry*, New York, N.Y., Oxford University Press (1991), 186.

14. *Newsweek*, Feb. 13, 1978, p. 55; Ashley, M., *Seven Wonders of the World*, Ashley Pub., London (1980), 288 pp.; *New York Times*, March 12, 1978, Section IV, p. 7, col. 5.

15. Joseph Davidovits, founder of the Geopolymer Institute, in France, was invited to Egypt by Nova producer Michael Barnes. Dr. Joseph Davidovits witnessed the entire pyramid building operation. I initially had the impression that Nova raised three or four one-ton stones (and published that information), but Davidovits later clarified, telling me that the Nova team raised only one block manually, and that he estimated its weight at 1/2 ton.

16. For Tura limestone, refer to Klemm, R., Klemm, D., *Steine und Stein-Burche im Alten Agypten*, Springer-Verlag, Berlin (1993), 60–71; Harrell, J. A., "An Inventory of Ancient Egyptian Quarries," *Newsletter of the American Research Center in Egypt*, 146 (1989), pp. 1-7. Davidovits also tested the limestone Nova used and found it to be very soft compared to the Great Pyramid's blocks.

17. Arnold, D., *Building in Egypt: pharaonic stone masonry*, New York, N.Y., Oxford University Press (1991), 72.

Chapter 4: Enigmatic Interior Features

1. For a theory about the plug blocks, refer to Lepre, J. P., *The Egyptian Pyramids: A Comprehensive, Illustrated Reference*, Jefferson, N.C.: McFarland (1990 reprint), 235, and Edwards, I.E.S., *The pyramids of Egypt*, Rev. and updated, repr. with minor revisions, Harmondsworth, Middlesex, England; New York, N.Y., Penguin Books (1988), 75–86. An entire chapter is devoted to the

theories of the plug blocks in Tompkins, P., *Secrets of the Great Pyramid. With an appendix by Livio Catullo Stecchini* (1st ed.) New York, Harper & Row (1971), Ch. XIX titled "Why were the Pyramid Passages Plugged? When? and How?" pp. 236–255 (diagrams included).

2. For the measurements of the plug blocks in the Ascending Passageway, refer to Kingsland, W., *The Great Pyramid in Fact and Theory*, Mokelumne Hill, Calif., Health Research (1923–72), Part I, 50, 64–66, 74. Edwards, I.E.S., *The pyramids of Egypt*, Rev. and updated, repr. with minor revisions Harmondsworth, Middlesex, England; New York, N.Y., Penguin Books (1988), 102, 106–110, 264; Petrie, W.M.F., *Pyramids and Temples of Gizeh*, Field, London (1883), 102, 106–110, 264.

3. Kingsland, W., *The Great Pyramid in Fact and Theory*, Mokelumne Hill, Calif., Health Research (1923–72), Part I, 65.

4. Kingsland, W., *The Great Pyramid in Fact and Theory*, Mokelumne Hill, Calif., Health Research (1923–72), Part I, 50, 64–66, 74, or Edwards, I.E.S., *The pyramids of Egypt*, Rev. and updated, repr. with minor revisions Harmondsworth, Middlesex, England; New York, N.Y., Penguin Books (1985), 109–110; Lehner, M., *The Complete Pyramids: Solving the Ancient Mysteries*, New York, Thames and Hudson (1997), 40, which presents a drawing showing how close the correspondence is between the ceiling and the plug blocks.

5. Kingsland, W., *The Great Pyramid in Fact and Theory*, Mokelumne Hill, Calif., Health Research (1923–72), Part I, 65; Petrie, W.M.F., *Pyramids and Temples of Gizeh*, Field, London (1883), 65.

6. Arnold, D., *Building in Egypt: pharaonic stone masonry,* New York, N.Y., Oxford University Press (1991), 79.

7. For the Ascending Passageway running through the girdle stones, which range from 12 to 15 feet long, Edwards indicated, "Borchardt considered the presence of the 'girdle-stones' in the Ascending Corridor as proof that the Great Pyramid followed the standard pattern, each 'girdle-stone' being part of an internal casing, but two equally eminent authors, Somers Clarke and R. Engelbach, refused to accept Borchardt's arguments." Edwards, I.E.S., *The pyramids of Egypt*, 275–276, 111; Edwards gives no specific pages for the Borchardt reference, but the reference itself is Borchardt, L., "Einiges zur dritten Bauperiode der grossen Pyramide bei Gise, mit einer Bemerkung zur zweiten Bauperiode det dritten Pyramide," von Herbert Ricke, Berlin, Verlag von Julius Springer (1932). Series: *Beitrage zur agyptischen Bauforschung und Altertumskunde*, Hft. 1. Refer also to Clarke, S., Engelbach, R., *Ancient Egyptian Masonry: The Building Craft*, London, Oxford University Press, Milford (1930), 242 p. Edwards' footnote to Clarke and Engelbach refers to pages 123–4. Refer also to Kingsland, W., *The Great Pyramid in Fact and Theory*, Mokelumne Hill, Calif., Health Research (1923–72), Part I, 66–68, 70. Petrie also discussed the girdle stones, "Several of the roof-blocks are girdle-blocks, being all in one piece with the walls, either wholly round the passage, or partially so. These vertical girdle-blocks are a most curious feature of this passage (first observed and measured by Mr. Waynman Dixon, C.E.), and occur at intervals of 10 cubits (206.3 to 208.9 inches) in the passage, measuring along the slope. All the stones that can be examined round the plugs are partial girdle-blocks, evidently to prevent the plugs forcing the masonry apart, by being wedged into the contracted passage." Refer to Petrie, W.M.F., *Pyramids and Temples of Gizeh*, Histories and Mysteries of Man, Ltd., London (1990 reprint), 21 (Note that this quote differs from the original version of *The Pyramids and Temples of Giza*, as the 1990 new and revised edition has been abbreviated).

8. The Grand Gallery is discussed by Edwards. Refer to I.E.S., *The pyramids of Egypt*, Rev. and updated, repr. with minor revisions Harmondsworth, Middlesex, England; New York, N.Y., Penguin Books (1985), 103, 107–9.

9. For a description of the King's Chamber and the compartments above, refer to Edwards, I.E.S., *The pyramids of Egypt*, Rev. and updated, repr. with minor revisions Harmondsworth, Middlesex, England; New York, N.Y., Penguin Books (1985), 103, 105–6, 264.

10. The problems of cutting granite with simple tools are raised in Edwards, I.E.S., *The pyramids of Egypt* (1985), 240; Lucas, A., *Ancient Egyptian Materials and Industries*, 82–83. While granite

can be cut with long, hard work by using abrasives, features found in ancient Egyptian artifacts have not been replicated. These include subtle and complex curves, such as those found in portrait statues, examples of rapid cutting (the latter of which Petrie determined for the sarcophagus in Khufu's Great Pyramid and hard stone artifacts featuring crisp etchings made with sharp points), surfaces as flat as .0002 inch (according to machinist Christopher Dunn, who measured large areas of three sarcophagi). Compare that with .01 flatness Denys Stocks can account for when working with replicas of ancient Egyptian tools.

11. Kingsland, W., *The Great Pyramid in Fact and Theory*, Mokelumne Hill, Calif., Health Research (1923–72), 95.

12. Stocks, D.A., "Stone Sarcophagus Manufacture in Ancient Egypt," *Antiquity* 73, 918–922. Stocks cut granite with a bow drill and sand. He believes that all of the work was done slowly but surely. However, it is impossible to believe that the ancient workers used the slow-cutting method employed by Stocks only to achieve the mistakes Petrie described for their effort. Surely, these stray cuts are signs of rapid cutting. Machinist Christopher Dunn discusses some instances of rapid cutting in his *The Giza Power Plant, The Technologies of Ancient Egypt*, Bear & Company, Sante Fe (1998), NM, 70–93. Although Dunn's ideas about advanced machining in ancient Egypt and the notion that the Great Pyramid functioned as a power plant are untenable, Dunn is an expert machinist with long experience. His observations about cutting rates are compelling and should be given full consideration. Refer to a review by Systems Engineer Mike Carrell in *Infinite Energy* magazine, Issue 32 (July/August 2000). Mike Carrell's review does not go into detail about the many problems with Dunn's power plant system, but Mike Carrell corresponded with Dunn and sent me a list of extensive explanations describing why the King's Chamber of the Great Pyramid will not support maser activity. Dunn still contends that the Great Pyramid is a power plant and has not presented arguments contesting the problems Mike Carrell raised, although years have passed.

13. Lepre, J.P., *The Egyptian Pyramids: A Comprehensive Illustrated Reference*, McFarland & Co., Inc., Jefferson, NC and London (1990), 110.

14. For a study asserting that only solid masonry could provide the necessary strength needed for ramps, refer to Peter Hodges, *How the Great Pyramids Were Built*, Element Books, Wilshire (1989). The PBS Nova film, *This Old Pyramid* (1992), confirmed Hodges' assertions. Stonemason Roger Hopkins observed that the Nova miniature ramp quickly became unsuitable.

15. Kingsland, W., *The Great Pyramid in Fact and Theory*, Mokelumne Hill, Calif., Health Research (1923–72), Part I, 89, 97.

16. Kingsland, W., *The Great Pyramid in Fact and Theory*, Mokelumne Hill, Calif., Health Research (1923–72), Part I, 89. Kingsland wrote, "The roof of the Chamber consists of nine granite beams, varying in width from 44.8 to 62.7 inches (refer to Plates XXXVI and XXXVII). They extend about 5 feet beyond the side walls, and are therefore about 27 feet long. The 62.7 inch stone has a depth of about 7 feet, and therefore a cubic capacity of approximately 987 cubic feet. Reckoning 165 pounds per cubic foot, it will weigh about 73 tons, or about the weight of a modern locomotive. How did the builders raise this enormous weight to a height of 160 feet, and up the steep angle of the Pyramid?" Arnold reckoned these beams to weigh 50–60 tons. Refer to Arnold, D., *Building in Egypt: pharaonic stone masonry*, New York, N.Y., Oxford University Press (1991), 60. Lehner alludes to estimates up to 80 tons, see Lehner, M., *The Complete Pyramids: Solving the Ancient Mysteries*, New York, Thames and Hudson (1997), 109.

17. Arnold, D., *Building in Egypt: pharaonic stone masonry*, New York, N.Y., Oxford University Press (1991), 61.

18. Lepre, J.P., *The Egyptian Pyramids: A Comprehensive, Illustrated Reference*, McFarland, Jefferson, N.C. (1990), 95–97.

Chapter 5: Egyptology Has no Explanation

1. Lehner, M.,"Development of the Giza Necropolis: The Khufu Project, "*Mitteilungen des Deutschen Archäologischen Instituts Kairo* (1985), 109–143.

2. Davidovits, J., Morris, M., *The Pyramids: An Enigma Solved*, Hippocrene, NY (1988), 106.

3. Lehner, M., *The Complete Pyramids: Solving the Ancient Mysteries*, New York, Thames and Hudson (1997), 206.

4. For pyramid blocks as hard as the head of the Sphinx, refer to Klemm, R, and Klemm, D.D., *Steine und Steinbrüche im Alten Ägypten*, Springer-Verlag, Berlin (1993), 193–194, Figures 213 and 214.

5. Arnold, D., *Building in Egypt: pharaonic stone masonry*, New York, N.Y., Oxford University Press (1991), 31, 34, Fig. 2.7.

6. Arnold, D., *Building in Egypt: pharaonic stone masonry*, New York, N.Y., Oxford University Press (1991), 261, Fig. 6.14.

7. Petrie, W.M.F., *Pyramids and Temples of Gizeh*, Field, London (1883), 209. Yoshimira, S., *Studies in Egyptian Culture, No. 6, non-destructive pyramid investigation (1) by Electromagnetic Wave Method*, Waseda University Press, Tokyo, 2 Vols; Davidovits, J., Gaber, H., in Davidovits, J., Morris, M., *The Pyramids: An Enigma Solved*, Hippocrene, NY (1988), 97–108, 89. A drawing of the jumbled shells that characterize Giza pyramid and temple blocks appears in Jomard, E.F. (ed.), *Description de l'Egypte, ou, Recueil des observations et des recherches qui ont été faites en Egypte pendant l'expédition de l'armee française*, Paris, Pub. Imprimerie Imperiale (1809-1828) and is reproduced in Davidovits, J., Morris, M., *The Pyramids: An Enigma Solved*, Hippocrene, NY (1988), Fig. 14; Kingsland, W., *The Great Pyramid in Fact and Theory*, Mokelumne Hill, Calif., Health Research (1923–72), Part I, 25. Aigner, T., *"Facies and Origin of Nummulitic Buildups: An Example from the Giza Pyramids Plateau (Middle Eocene, Egypt)," Neues Jahrbuch für Geologie und Paläontologie, Abhandlung, V. 166 (1983)*, 347–368. *Mark Lehner commented on Aigner's study as follows: "…*According to Aigner's model, the Pyramids Plateau began as a bank of nummulites seen to exceed 30 m in thickness in the northern escarpment. A shoal and reefal facies was laid over the southern slope of the nummulites bank. A "back bank" facies was, in turn, laid over the shoal reef, forming a series of limestone/marl beds which 'lens out' over the shoal reef to the N. In practical terms, this left the very hard and brittle limestone of the nummulites bank to the NNW part of the Pyramids Plateau, and the softer thickly bedded layers to the lower SSE area of the plateau…" Refer to Lehner, M., "The Development of the Giza Necropolis: The Khufu Project," *Mitteilungen des Deutschen Archäologischen Instituts Kairo*, 41 (1985), 113–114. Also on page 118, Lehner wrote: "…According to Aigner's depositional model of the plateau, the pyramid was based on the harder, more massive nummulites bank which swells up along the N–NW part of the formation…" Joseph Davidovits showed in the 1992 Nova film *This Old Pyramid* that limestone from the Sphinx quarry is so high in kaolin clay content that it comes apart within hours of soaking in water. In short, the limestone from the Giza quarries does not match the better-quality blocks that characterize the Giza pyramids and temples.

8. Jomard, E.F. (ed.), *Description de l'Egypte, ou, Recueil des observations et des recherches qui ont été faites en Egypte pendant l'expédition de l'armee française*, Paris, Pub. Imprimerie Imperiale (1809-1828), 23 v.

9. Petrie, W.M.F., *Pyramids and Temples of Gizeh*, Field, London (1883), 209.

10. Kingsland, W., *The Great Pyramid in Fact and Theory*, Mokelumne Hill, Calif., Health Research (1923–72), 25.

11. Yoshimira, S., *Studies in Egyptian Culture, no. 6, non-destructive pyramid investigation (1) by Electromagnetic Wave Method*, Waseda University Press, Tokyo, 2 vols., 4–5.

12. Davidovits, J., Morris, M., *The Pyramids: An Enigma Solved*, Hippocrene, NY (1988), 97–104.

13. For the quote by Diodorus Siculus, refer to Diodorus of Sicily, *Library of History*, Book I, Ch. 63, lines 6–7. The translation is by Oldfather, the Loeb Classical Library edition, William Heinemann Ltd., London, and G.P. Putnam's Sons, New York (1933), Vol. I, 217.

14. Strabo, *The Geography of Strabo* 17.1.34, which reads, "One of the marvelous things I saw at the pyramids should not be omitted: there are heaps of stone-chips lying in front of the pyramid; and among these are found chips that are like lentils both in form and size; and under some of

the heaps lie winnowings, as it were, as of half-peeled grains. They say that what was left of the food of the workmen has petrified; and this is not improbable." For this translation, refer to *The geography of Strabo with an English translation by Horace Leonard Jones; Based in part upon the unfinished version of John Robert Sitlington Sterrett*, W. Heinemann, G. P. Putnam's sons, London; New York (1917–33). Contributors, Jones, Horace Leonard, Vol. 8, 95.

Chapter 6: Egyptian Masonry Marvels

1. Emery, W.B., *Archaic Egypt: Culture and Civilizations in Egypt Five Thousand Years Ago*, Penguin Books, Baltimore (1961 edition), 214–215. Also refer to Hoffman for the primitive level of technology used to produce hard diorite and basalt vases at the Nagada II ritual complex at Hierakonpolis, Hoffman, M.A., "The Predynastic of Hierakonpolis: An Interim Report," *Egyptian Studies Association*, Publication No. 1, Cairo, 130. This primitive technological level mystifies geologists who recognize the difficulties of drilling tough diorite. Diorite is almost as difficult to drill as quartzite, the drilling of which is difficult with the best modern tools equipped with tungsten carbide drill bits and thousands of pounds of pressure applied to the bits. Also refer to el-Khouli, A., *Egyptian Stone Vessels: Predynastic Period to Dynasty III typology and analysis*, von Zabern, Mainz/Rhein (1978). In Vol. II titled *Manufacture of Stone Vessels - Ancient and Modern*, page 797, el-Khouli summarizes, and his summary shows that the method for making hard-stone vessels is not really known. So, it is not described in detail by Egyptologists. He wrote, "Hundreds of thousands of stone vessels have been discovered in the pyramids and tombs of Egypt. The making of stone vessels must have been, therefore, a very common industry...Many Egyptologists (e.g. von Bissing, Petrie, Quibell, Bonnet, Emery, Reisner, Balcz, Lucas, Baumagartel, Hartenberg and Schmidt) have discussed the method of production of stone vessels, using the evidence of the Old Kingdom tomb-scenes and materials excavated in the field (especially partially worked stone vessels). Much of the discussion was somewhat brief."

2. Emery, W.B., *Archaic Egypt: Culture and Civilizations in Egypt Five Thousand Years Ago*, Penguin Books, Baltimore (1961 rev.), 11.

3. Lange, K., *Des Pyramides, des Sphinx, des Pharaons, Ed. Plon*, Paris, 169–174.

4. Refer also to remarks by A. el-Khouli, *Egyptian Stone Vessels: Predynastic Period to Dynasty III typology and analysis*, von Zabern, Mainz/Rhein (1978). In Vol. II, titled *Manufacture of Stone Vessels - Ancient and Modern*, page 789, Rl-Khouli wrote, "No other country, before or since, has achieved such perfection in this skilled industry in its efforts to produce not only objects of utility but also of beauty. A high level of achievement in this respect was reached in the Predynastic Period and during the first three Dynasties." On page 801 el-Khouli wrote, "Stone vessel craftsman soon showed his mastery over the material by producing vessels of floral and leaf shapes, and in the shapes of fish, animal, birds, etc." On page 789, "No stone was too hard or intractable for the ancient craftsman."

5. Petrie referred to diorite bowl fragments he believed were made by turning, see Petrie, W.M.F., *The Pyramids and Temples of Gizeh*, Field, London (1883), 176 and pl. XIV, 14, 15.

6. Maspero, G., *Manual of Egyptian archaeology and guide to the study of antiquities in Egypt*. For the use of students and travellers, 6th ed., rev. and enl. London, H. Grevel and co. (1914): Article on stone vessels, pp. 281–282.

7. For the quote by l'Hote, refer to Perrot G, Chipiez, C., *Histoire de l'Art dans l'Antiquité*, Vol. 1, Paris (1882), 676.

8. Arnold, D., *Building in Egypt: pharaonic stone masonry*, New York, N.Y., Oxford University Press (1991), 174. Refer also to Emery, W.B., *Archaic Egypt: Culture and Civilizations in Egypt Five Thousand Years Ago*, Penguin Books, Baltimore (1961), 182. Large granite blocks first appeared in the 2nd Dynasty. Refer to Petrie, W.M.F., *The Royal Tombs of the Earliest Dynasties* (1900–1901), II, pl. 31 (The stelae of Peribsen); Fischer, H.G., "An Egyptian Royal Stela of the Second Dynasty," *Artibus Asiae*, 24 (1961), 45 ff.

9. Arnold, D., *Building in Egypt: pharaonic stone masonry*, New York, N.Y., Oxford University Press (1991), 174.

Endnotes   329

10. Garstang, J., *Mahâsna and Bêt Khallâf (With a chapter by Kurt Sethe)*, B. Quaritch, London (1903), 9, 11, pls. 7, 17, 18.
11. For the splendid Valley Temple, refer to Hoelscher, U., *Das Grabdenkmal des Konigs Chephren*, Veroflentlichungen der Ernst von Sieglin Expedition in Agypten, Vol. 1, Leipzig (1912).
12. Two industrial cranes exist with the necessary capacity. The K-10000 tower crane by Kroll Giant Towercranes, in Denmark, is the world's largest tower crane as of this writing. The capacity of the standard 269-foot crane is 132 tons. A diagram showing the hook radius and crane capacity appears at this company's Web site: http://www.towercrane.com.
13. Perrot G, Chipiez, C., *Histoire de l'Art dans l'Antiquité*, Vol. I, Hachette et Cie, Paris (1882), 775.
14. Arnold, D., *Building in Egypt: pharaonic stone masonry*, New York, N.Y., Oxford University Press (1991), 184–189.
15. Petrie, W.M.F., *Pyramids and Temples of Gizeh*, Field, London (1883), 168. Strabo, *Geography* 17. 1. 33. Strabo visited Egypt in 24 B.C. and wrote an extensive history that has not survived. His surviving geographical appendix indicates that the swivel door in the Great Pyramid allowed access to a square passage descending 374 feet to a pit. Greek and Roman initials made with torches appear on the ceiling of the pit, showing that the Descending Passageway and pit were explored during those eras.
16. Petrie, W.M.F., *Pyramids and Temples of Gizeh*, Field, London (1883), 168. Any remains of such a door would have disappeared when the casing blocks were stripped away. Refer to Edwards, I.E.S., *The Pyramids of Egypt*, 130 ff; Tompkins, P., *Secrets of the Great Pyramid*, Harper & Row, New York (1971), 3, which mentions an attempt to reconstruct a pivoting door.
17. Arnold, D., *Building in Egypt: pharaonic stone masonry*, New York, N.Y., Oxford University Press (1991), 192, Fig. 4.130. ibid. 61, "Blocks of huge dimensions, weighing up to 90 tons, were also found in the gable-roof constructions of the pyramids of the Fifth and Sixth Dynasties."
18. Arnold, D., *Building in Egypt: pharaonic stone masonry*, New York, N.Y., Oxford University Press (1991), 120, Fig. 4.129.
19. Arnold, D., *Building in Egypt: pharaonic stone masonry*, New York, N.Y., Oxford University Press (1991), 40.
20. For Lucas' general remarks, see Lucas, A., *Ancient Egyptian Materials and Industries*, Dover Publications, Mineola, N.Y. (1999 1962), 70–4. For quarrying quartzite, Arnold remarked that the methods were not clear. He wrote, "The extent to which dolerite balls were used for pounding quartzite is not clear…There seems to be no clear indication for the pounding method, and we must assume that chiseling was employed. This work could have been achieved only by experienced laborers, who probably were not numerous enough to produce huge quantities of quartzite. Still, the sepulchral chamber of Amenemhat III at Hawara and the statues of Memnon were made of that stone, and their production certainly required a sizable number of such people." Arnold, D., *Building in Egypt: pharaonic stone masonry*, New York, N.Y., Oxford University Press, (1991), 40. In other words, Egyptologists have no idea whatsoever how large quartzite items could have been quarried. The Colossi of Memnon were originally monolithic and stand (including the statues mounted on separate pedestals), 63 feet high. No one has found an extraction site showing dug-out trenches of this great size in the quartzite quarries. Arnold cannot and does not try to explain what kind of chisels could possibly have been used to quarry the huge monoliths of quartzite. In short, there is no evidence of pounding balls at the quartzite ranges and no ancient chisel would be adequate for quarrying quartzite blocks. The best that could be done is to strike off aggregates by hitting tools with mallets. We can detect a fundamental flaw in the accepted paradigm.
21. The first undoubted reference to diamond appears in the writings of the Roman poet Manilius (A.D. 16): "The diamond [Latin: adamas, meaning unconquerable or invincible] a stone no bigger than a dot, is the most precious of substances in the world." Pliny (A.D. 100) also described six types of diamonds. Refer to Pliny, *Natural History*, Book 37, page 15, line 55 (Wormington 1972).

330   The Great Pyramid Secret by Margaret Morris

22. Petrie, W.M.F., *Kahun, Gurob, and Hawara* (London, 1890); Petrie, W.M.F., *Hawara, Biahmu and Arsinoe*, London (1889). Arnold reported the weight of the sepulcher at 110 tons (he assumed that it was made from a block of this size) and he indicated that it had come from the quarries at Gebel el-Ahmar. See Arnold, D., *Building in Egypt: pharaonic stone masonry*, New York, N.Y., Oxford University Press (1991), 61.

23. For the Labyrinth, see Lloyd, A.B., "The Egyptian Labyrinth," *Journal of Egyptian Archaeology*, 56 (1970), 81–100; Arnold, D., "Das Labyrinth und Seine Vorbilder," *Mitteilungen des Deutschen Archäologischen Instituts Kairo*, 35 (1979), 1–9; Uphill, E.P., *Pharaoh's Gateway to Eternity, The Hawara Labyrinth of King Amenemhat III*, Keagan and Paul, London (2000). Wainwright, G.A., and Mackay, E., *The Labyrinth, Gerzeh and Mazghuneh, British School of Archaeology in Egypt and Egyptian Research Account, 18th Year*, Bernard Quaritch, London (1912). Arnold, D., "Labyrinth," *Lexikon der Ägyptologie*, Band III (1980), 905–908.

24. Herodotus, 2.148.1; Strabo, *The geography of Strabo with an English translation by Horace Leonard Jones; based in part upon the unfinished version of John Robert Sitlington Sterrett*. W. Heinemann; G. P. Putnam's sons, London; New York (1917–33), Contributors: Jones, Horace Leonard, Vol. 8, 103–105.

25. A well-known example is the French Gothic Chartres Cathedral, built around 1230, which incorporated a labyrinth design into its floor plan. The labyrinth is forty feet across, set with blue and white stones into the floor of the nave of the church. Other French Gothic cathedrals with labyrinths are Amiens, Rheims, Sens, Arras, and Auxerre.

26. The heights of the figures are about 51 feet and the pedestals (on which the feet rest) are about 13 feet high. The original heights of the total structures may have reached 69 feet with their crowns, which are now destroyed. The legs (from the soles of the feet to the knees) each measure 19½ feet. Pliny mentioned the hardness of the stone, which he called basalt (to denote a stone harder than iron). Pliny, *Natural History*, Volume 36, Chapter XI reads: "…The Egyptians have found a stone in Ethiopia that has the color and hardness of iron, and consequently, it was called basalt. It is said that there exists at Thebes, in the Temple of Serapis, a statue which was made with this same stone. It represents Memnon, and makes a sound all during the day when touched by sunbeams…" Jollois and Devilliers of the Napoleonic Egyptian Expedition also described the hardness of the stone. Jollois and Devilliers, *Description de l'Egypte*, Edition Panckoucke, Paris (1809-828), Vol. II, Chap. IX, Section II, page 153 reads, "…The Colossi are facing the southeast, and are standing parallel to the Nile. They are known in this country by the names of Tama and Chama. Chama is the southern Colossus, and Tama is the northern Colossus. Both are alike in many ways. They show differences in their dimensions that we will indicate step by step: both are made from a variety of conglomerate consisting of a mass of agatized flint, bound together by a cement of exceptional hardness. This material is very dense, and has a highly heterogeneous structure which is much more difficult to sculpt than granite. What we have witnessed shows that the Egyptian sculptors have mastered their task with the greatest success." For more on the colossi, refer to R.F. Heizer, F. Stross, T.R. Hester, A. Albee, I. Perlman, F., Asaro, H. Bowman. 1973. "The Colossi of Memnon revisited" *Science*, 182, 1219–25. Bowman, H., et al., "The Northern Colossus of Memnon: New Slants," *Archaeometry* (1984), Vol. 26, 218–229.

27. Petrie, W.M.F., *A History of Egypt During the XVIIth and XVIIIth Dynasties*, London, Metheun & co. ltd. (1904), 192; Breasted, J.H., *Ancient Records of Egypt; historical documents from the earliest times to the Persian conquest, collected, edited, and translated with commentary*, New York, Russell & Russell (1962), Vol. II, 355–356.

28. The statue was found in 1820 and the Egyptian ruler Mohammed Ali donated it to the British Museum.

29. The Egyptian *Hikuptah* ("The Palace of Ptah") was corrupted into *Aigyptos* in Homeric Greek, coming to our time as "Egypt." The word Coptic is a later corruption, as well. Refer to Baines, J., Malek, J., *Atlas of Ancient Egypt*, Facts on File Publications, NY (1985), 134.

30. The remarks of Stuart M. Edelson are quoted from West, J., *The Traveler's Key to Ancient Egypt: A Guide to the Sacred Places of Ancient Egypt*, Knopf, New York (1985), 193–194.

31. For the stele of Djehutihotep, refer to Baines, J., Malek, J., *Atlas of Ancient Egypt*, Facts on File Publications, NY (1980), 126–127. Arnold, D., *Building in Egypt: pharaonic stone masonry*, New York, N.Y., Oxford University Press (1991), 61.

32. For theories on lowering stones, refer to Arnold, D., *Building in Egypt: pharaonic stone masonry*, New York, N.Y., Oxford University Press (1991), 73–79.

33. Jomard, E.F. (ed.), *Description de l'Egypte*, Volume III, Section XI, Panckoucke Ed., Paris (1809-1828), 181.

34. Jomard, E.F. (ed.), *Description de l'Egypte*, Vol. III, Section XI, Panckoucke Ed., Paris (1809–1828), 181.

Chapter 7: It Staggers the Imagination

1.   Arnold, D., *Building in Egypt: pharaonic stone masonry*, New York, N.Y., Oxford University Press (1991), 41. Stocks, D., "Tools of the ancient craftsman," *Popular Archaeology*, 7 (1986), 24–29. Stocks, D., "Tools of the ancient craftsman," *Popular Archaeology*, 7 (1986), 24–29.

2.   Arnold, D., *Building in Egypt: pharaonic stone masonry*, New York, N.Y., Oxford University Press (1991), 48.

3.   Yoshimira, S., *Studies in Egyptian Culture, No. 6, non-destructive pyramid investigation (1) by Electromagnetic Wave Method*, Waseda University Press, Tokyo, 2 vols. 4–5.

4.   Zuber, A., "Techniques Der Travail Des Pierres Dures Daus L'Ancienne Egypt," *Techniques et Civilizations 30*, Vol. 5, No. 5 (1956), 161–178.

5.   Baines, J., Malek, J., *Atlas of Ancient Egypt*, Facts on File Publications, N.Y. (1980), 19.

6.   Arnold, D., *Building in Egypt: pharaonic stone masonry*, New York, N.Y., Oxford University Press (1991), 33–34, 50.

7.   Arnold, D., *Building in Egypt: pharaonic stone masonry*, New York, N.Y., Oxford University Press (1991), 48.

8.   Refer to Roder, J., "Zur steinbruchgeschichte des rosengranits von Assuan," *Archalogischer Anzeiger* 3, Jahrbuch des Deutschen Archaeologischen Instituts (1965), 523.

9.   Lehner, M., *The Complete Pyramids: Solving the Ancient Mysteries*, New York, Thames and Hudson (1997), 211.

10. Arnold, D., *Building in Egypt: pharaonic stone masonry*, New York, N.Y., Oxford University Press (1991), 43.

11. Petrie, W.M.F., *Pyramids and Temples of Gizeh*, Field, London (1883 reprint 1990), 37.

12. Arnold, D., *Building in Egypt: pharaonic stone masonry*, New York, N.Y., Oxford University Press (1991), 48.

13. Arnold, D., *Building in Egypt: pharaonic stone masonry*, New York, N.Y., Oxford University Press (1991), 122. On page 42, Arnold wrote, "...toolmarks left on numerous unfinished or unsmoothed limestone blocks from the Old and Middle Kingdoms show such a distinctive rectangular shape with very sharp inner corners that it is difficult to believe that they were produced by stone tools (fig. 2.21)." With regard to shaping rock, Arnold wrote, "But again for reasons of metal consumption, the sawing of stone was restricted to rare and special cases." Ibid. 50.

14. For the rockers and an illustration, refer to Clarke, S., Engelbach, R., *Ancient Egyptian Construction and Architecture*, Dover pub., N.Y. (1990) (a reprint of *Ancient Egyptian Masonry*), 102–4, Figs. 89, 109.

15. Arnold, D., *Building in Egypt: pharaonic stone masonry*, New York, N.Y., Oxford University Press (1991), 72.

16. Moores, R., "Evidence for Use of a Stone-Cutting Drag Saw for the Fourth Dynasty Egyptians," *Journal of the American Research Center in Egypt* XVIII (1991), 141 Fig. 3, 4. Also refer to Petrie, W.M.F., *Pyramids and Temples of Gizeh*, Field, London (1885), 14 and 75; Clarke, S., Engelbach, R., *Ancient Egyptian Masonry*, London (1930), 204; Lucas, A., *Ancient Egyptian Materials and Industries*, 4th Edition, Mineola, N.Y., Dover Publications (1962), 69–72.

17. Moores, R., "Evidence for Use of a Stone-Cutting Drag Saw for the Fourth Dynasty Egyptians," *Journal of the American Research Center in Egypt*, XVIII (1991), 142–3, Fig. 5. Moores also

suggested that the basalt slabs were hammer-dressed on top. Hammering tends to break basalt along its internal fractures. It makes no sense to use this crude method in conjunction with the method that allowed workers to produce plunge cuts in basalt. It seems more likely that the signs Moores interpreted as hammer dressing resulted from later activity on the basalt slabs, such as the dismantling operation W.M.F. Petrie witnessed.

18. Arnold, D., *Building in Egypt: pharaonic stone masonry*, New York, N.Y., Oxford University Press (1991), 251–268. For more information, refer to Petrie, W.M.F., *Tools and Weapons: illustrated by the Egyptian Collection in University college, London and 2,000 outlines from other sources*, British School of Archaeology in Egypt and Egyptian Research Account, London (1917), 71 p.

19. De Garis Davies, N., *The Tomb of Rekh-mi-Re' at Thebes*. Publications of the Metropolitan Museum of Art Expedition 11, New York (1943), pls. 52–55. Arnold, D., *Building in Egypt: pharaonic stone masonry*, New York, N.Y., Oxford University Press (1991), 258.

20. The blocks above the King's Chamber are among the examples of large, form-fitted masonry units. Such blocks hug one another very closely along their whole joints, although the joints deviate from being purely straight. Much of the core masonry fits this way, while many core blocks have gaps between them where mortar or tafla cushioning has disappeared.

21. Mendelssohn, K., *The Riddle of the Pyramids*, Praeger (1974), New York, Illustration 18. The caption reads, "The slabs forming the corbelled roof of the tomb chamber in the Meidum pyramid are perfectly fitted but remain undressed." More precisely, they are highly irregular and snugly fit with form-fitting irregularities.

22. Arnold, D., *Building in Egypt: pharaonic stone masonry*, New York, N.Y., Oxford University Press (1991), 168–169. Arnold also commented with regard to granite (which was used to partially case some of the pyramids). Arnold wrote as follows on ibid. pages 47–48, "The dressing of hard stones, which were used abundantly in the Egyptian building industry, was certainly a problem for the ancient masons, and the work in granite quarries was used as a punishment for criminals. Because of this difficulty, Egyptian masons avoided working in hard stones as much as possible and restricted the dressing of such material to an absolute minimum and to visible parts of the blocks only. The underside and the rear of blocks, which came into contact with bedrock, were often left rough, and the bedrock was cut accordingly to take into account the protuberances of the granite." Contrasting Arnold's remarks, Joseph Roder estimated that during the 450-year-long Old Kingdom, a little less than 1.6 million cubic feet of granite was removed from the Aswan quarries to incorporate into monuments. Joseph Roder, "Zur steinbruchgeschichte des rosengranits von Assuan," *Archalogischer Anzeiger* 3, Jahrbuch des Deutschen Archaeologischen Instituts (1965), 461–551. Granite casing blocks covered the first course of Khafra's pyramid, the first sixteen courses of Menkaura, the first course of Menkaura IIIa, the first course of Shepseskaf, the first course or more of Neferirkara, and possibly covered the whole of the pyramid of Djedefra (refer to ibid., 169). Moreover, Arnold's statement does not take into consideration the difficulties of cutting granite blocks so that they would conform to one another. An example is the King's Chamber of the Great Pyramid, where all of the blocks made with granite fit together with conforming hairline joints. Conforming basalt slabs characterize Old Kingdom temple flooring.

23. Arnold, D., *Building in Egypt: pharaonic stone masonry*, New York, N.Y., Oxford University Press (1991), 168–169.

24. Arnold, D., *Building in Egypt: pharaonic stone masonry*, New York, N.Y., Oxford University Press (1991), 147.

25. Arnold, D., *Building in Egypt: pharaonic stone masonry*, New York, N.Y., Oxford University Press (1991), 47.

26. Arnold, D., *Building in Egypt: pharaonic stone masonry*, New York, N.Y., Oxford University Press (1991), 46–47.

Chapter 8: Iron is not the Solution

1. Fakhry, A., *The Pyramids*, University of Chicago Press, Chicago; London (1969 ed.), 9.
2. British Museum # 2433.

3. Caliph Al-Ma'moun (A.D. 813–833). Tourists enter the Great Pyramid today through the rough passage cut by Al-Ma'moun.

4. Abd al-Latif, *The Eastern key: Kitab al-ifadah wa 'l-i'tibar of 'Abd al-Latif al-Baghdadi. Translated in English by Kamal Hafuth Zand, John A. and Ivy E. Videan.* London, Allen and Unwin (1965), 286.

5. *The Egyptian History of Murtada ibn al-Khafif.* Also see *Land of Enchanters: Egyptian Short Stories from the Earliest Times to the Present Day*, edited by Bernard Lewis, Stanley M. Burstein, and Stanley Burstein. Markus Wiener, Princeton, NJ, 183 pp. The book includes the "Miraculous Stories of the Pyramids Of Queen Charoba of Egypt and Gebirus the Metapheguian."

6. Arnold, D., *Building in Egypt: pharaonic stone masonry*, New York, N.Y., Oxford University Press (1991), 257.

7. For Vyse's discovery of the iron plate, refer to Vyse, R.W.H., *Operations Carried On at the Pyramids of Gizeh in 1837: with an account of a voyage into Upper Egypt, and an appendix*, Pub. J. Fraser, London (1840 1842), vol. I, 275–276.

8. Theophrastus, *De lapidibus*, edited, with introduction, translation and commentary, by D. E. Eichholz, Oxford, Clarendon Press (1965), 73. Engelbach indicated, "I have spent hours trying to cut granite with iron, copper, and even dolerite chisels, and though granite can be cut—in a manner of speaking—with all of them I am convinced that the Egyptians used a much harder tool." Engelbach, R., *The Problem of the Obelisks, From a Study of the Unfinished Obelisk at Aswan*, T.F. Unwin, limited, London (1923), 40. The problem is that the Egyptians did not have harder tools. Refer also to el-Khouli, A., *Egyptian Stone Vessels: Predynastic Period to Dynasty III typology and analysis*, von Zabern, Mainz/Rhein (1978). In Vol. II titled *Manufacture of Stone Vessels - Ancient and Modern*, page 789, Alexander el-Khouli wrote, "To my knowledge, until a few years ago villagers in some parts of Middle and Upper Egypt were still manufacturing mortars of limestone in a rather simple fashion, boring out the interiors of the vessels…or manufacturing spindles from such horns using a very small chisel of iron. They spent a long time even on one stone vessel, and the finished product, it must be admitted, was hardly commensurate with the labour and trouble expended."

9. Wilkinson, J.G., *The Manners and Customs of the Ancient Egyptians*, New ed. rev. and corrected by Samuel Birch, London, J. Murray (1879). 252–253.

10. Lehner, M., *The Complete Pyramids: Solving the Ancient Mysteries*, New York, Thames and Hudson (1997), 206.

Chapter 9: How was it Possible?

1. Zuber, A., "Techniques Der Travail Des Pierres Dures Daus L'Ancienne Egypt," *Techniques et Civilizations* 29, Vol. 5, no. 5 (1956), 170.

2. Wilkinson, J.G., *The Manners and Customs of the Ancient Egyptians*, New ed. rev. and corrected by Samuel Birch, London, J. Murray (1879), 255.

3. Stocks, D., "Tools of the ancient craftsman," *Popular Archaeology*, 7 (1986), 24–29.

4. Arnold, D., *Building in Egypt: pharaonic stone masonry*, New York, N.Y., Oxford University Press (1991), 261, Fig. 6.14.

5. Arnold, D., *Building in Egypt: pharaonic stone masonry*, New York, N.Y., Oxford University Press (1991), 261, Fig. 6.13.

6. Arnold, D., *Building in Egypt: pharaonic stone masonry*, New York, N.Y., Oxford University Press (1991), 261, Fig. 6.14.

7. Arnold, D., *Building in Egypt: pharaonic stone masonry*, New York, N.Y., Oxford University Press (1991), 261, Fig. 6.14.

8. Zuber, A., "Techniques Der Travail Des Pierres Dures Daus L'Ancienne Egypt," *Techniques et Civilizations* 29, Vol. 5, no. 5 (1956), 201–202.

9. Antoine Zuber, "Techniques Der Travail Des Pierres Dures Daus L'Ancienne Egypt," *Techniques et Civilizations* 29, Vol. 5, no. 5 (1956), 161–178.

10.   Edwards, I.E.S., *The pyramids of Egypt*, Rev. and updated, repr. with minor revisions Harmondsworth, Middlesex, England; New York, N.Y., Penguin Books (1988), 249. The topic was long debated and Edwards, referring to Lucas, indicated, "The methods employed in the Pyramid Age for quarrying granite and other hard stones are still a subject of controversy. One authority even expressed the opinion that hard-stone quarrying was not attempted until the Middle Kingdom, before that time, the amount needed could have been obtained from large boulders lying loose or the surface of the ground." Lucas, A., *Ancient Egyptian Materials and Industries* (1948), 82–83. Arnold, D., *Building in Egypt: pharaonic stone masonry*, New York, N.Y., Oxford University Press (1991), 39, wrote, "For a long time, Egyptologists believed that granite was quarried with the help of wooden wedges inserted into wedge holes (made with copper chisels), since long chains of wedge holes could still be seen in the quarries of Aswan. This theory was abandoned for two reasons. First, Roder showed that no such wedge holes could be dated before 500 B.C. Second, most specialists seem to agree that wooden wedges, after being watered, would not be able to break granite. This new finding contradicts the remarks of Petrie, who described what he interpreted as wedge marks on the floor of the fourth construction chamber of the Cheops Pyramid." Besides, copper chisels are too soft to produce wedge slots in granite.

11.   Zuber, A. "Techniques Der Travail Des Pierres Dures Daus L'Ancienne Egypt," *Techniques et Civilizations 29*, Vol. 5, no. 5 (1956), 161–178.

12.   Roder, J., "Zur steinbruchgeschichte des rosengranits von Assuan," *Archalogischer Anzeiger 3*, Jahrbuch des Deutschen Archaeologischen Instituts (1965), 461–551.

13.   For Roder's study showing that wedge holes date to after 500 B.C., refer to Roder, J., "Zur steinbruchgeschichte des rosengranits von Assuan," *Archalogischer Anzeiger 3*, Jahrbuch des Deutschen Archaeologischen Instituts (1965), 523.

14.   The method was used during the New Kingdom and later at Aswan. Refer to Engelbach, R., *The Problem of the Obelisks, From a Study of the Unfinished Obelisk at Aswan*, T.F. Unwin, limited London (1923), 42–43.

15.   For Lehner's test, refer to Lehner, M., *The Complete Pyramids: Solving the Ancient Mysteries*, New York, Thames and Hudson (1997), 207. In addition, Lehner recalled (at the Nova Web site) that after pounding the surface at a granite quarry for several hours he could hardly type on his computer. He said that after 20 minutes of pounding all he had to show for his effort was a baby's palmful of granite dust, and that the granite bedrock looked no different from when he started. For Engelbach's study of Aswan, refer to *The Aswan Obelisk, with Some Remarks on the Ancient Engineering*, Cairo (1922). Refer also to Engelbach, R., *The Problem of the Obelisks, From a Study of the Unfinished Obelisk at Aswan*, T.F. Unwin, limited, London (1923), 40. Refer also to Labib Habachi, *The Obelisks of Egypt: Skyscrapers of the Past*, The American University in Cairo Press, Cairo (1985), 203 pp.

16.   See Chapter 5 above. The large number of blocks that should have broken and be strewn around must be considered relative to the size of the Great Pyramid. For the size, refer to Cole, J.H., "The Determination of the Exact Size and Orientation of the Great Pyramid of Giza," *Survey of Egypt*, Paper No. 39, Cairo (1925).

17.   Pyramids with granite casing are Khafra's first course; the first sixteen courses of Menkaura; the first course of Menkaura IIIa; the first course of Shepseskaf; at least the first course of Neferirkara, and possibly the entire casing of the pyramid of Djedefra.

18.   For the pyramid of Djedefra at abu Roash, refer to Lehner, M., *The Complete Pyramids: Solving the Ancient Mysteries*, New York, Thames and Hudson (1997), 120. For this and other pyramids, refer to Arnold, D., *Building in Egypt: pharaonic stone masonry*, New York, N.Y., Oxford University Press (1991), 168.

19.   For the Valley Temple, refer to Hoelscher, U., *Das Grabdenkmal des Konigs Chephren*, Veroflentlichungen der Ernst von Sieglin Expedition in Agypten, Vol. 1, Leipzig (1912), 120 pp.

20.   Fakhry, A., *The Pyramids*, University of Chicago Press, Chicago and London (1969 ed.) 151–53.

21. Arnold, D., *Building in Egypt: pharaonic stone masonry*, New York, N.Y., Oxford University Press (1991), 197.

22. Arnold, D., *Building in Egypt: pharaonic stone masonry*, New York, N.Y., Oxford University Press (1991), 199.

23. Arnold, D., *Building in Egypt: pharaonic stone masonry*, New York, N.Y., Oxford University Press (1991), 66. Here is a translation (by Joseph Davidovits) of Jean Paul Adams, *L'Archeologie devant I'mposture*, Ed. Robert Laffont, Paris (1975), 135. "Nowadays, it is difficult to imagine workers attacking a rocky cliff with stone axes. It is, however, in this way that numerous megaliths were detached and squared." Edwards, I.E.S., *The pyramids of Egypt, Rev. and updated, repr. with minor revisions*, Harmondsworth, Middlesex, England; New York, N.Y., Penguin Books (1988), 249.

Chapter 10: Standard Masonry Theory Disproved

1. Petrie, W.M.F., *Journal Royal Anthropology Institute*, 13 (1884), 90–1.

2. Petrie, W.M.F., *Pyramids and Temples of Gizeh*, Field, London, Histories and Mysteries of Man, Ltd., London (1883 reprint 1990), 29. Petrie wrote, "On the outer sides the lines of sawing may be plainly seen: horizontal on the N., a small patch horizontal on the E., vertical on the S., and nearly horizontal on the W.; showing that the masons did not hesitate at cutting a slice of granite 90 inches long, and that the jeweled bronze [copper] saw must have been probably about 9 feet long. On the N. end is a place, near the W. side, where the saw was run too deep into the granite, and was backed out again by the masons; but this fresh start they made was still too deep, and two inches lower they backed out a second time, having altogether cut out more than 1/10 inch deeper than they intended. On the E. inside is a portion of a tube drill hole remaining, where they tilted the drill over into the side by not working it vertically. They tried hard to polish away all that part, and took off about 1/10 inch thickness all round it; but still they had to leave the side of the hole 1/10 deep, 3 long, and 1.3 wide; the bottom of it is 8 or 9 below the original top of the coffer. They made a similar error on the N. inside, but of a much less extent."

3. Stocks, D.A., *Testing Ancient Egyptian Granite-Working Methods in Aswan. Upper Egypt, Antiquity* (2001), 75, 89-94.

4. Stocks, D.A., "Stone sarcophagus manufacture in ancient Egypt," *Antiquity* (1999) 73, 918-22. For more on tools and crystal cutting, see Long, F.W., *The Creative Lapidary: Materials, Tools, Techniques, Design*, Van Nostrand Reinhold, New York (1976), 136 p.; Petrie, W.M.F., *Tools and Weapons: illustrated by the Egyptian Collection in University College London and 2,000 outlines from other sources*, British School of Archaeology in Egypt and Egyptian Research Account, London (1917), 71 p; Sinkankas, J., *Gem Cutting: A Lapidary's Manual*, Van Nostrand Reinhold, New York (1984), 365 p.; Stocks, D.A., *Industrial technology at Kahun and Gurob: experimental manufacture and test of replica and reconstructed tools with indicated uses and effects upon artifact production*. Unpublished Masters thesis (1988), University of Manchester; Wainwright J., *Discovery of Lapidary Work*, Mills & Boon, London (1971), 216 p.

5. Antoine Zuber, "Techniques Der Travail Des Pierres Dures Daus L'Ancienne Egypt," *Techniques et Civilizations* 29, Vol. 5, no. 5 (1956), 161–178.

6. Naum, G., *Of Divers Arts*, Pantheon Books, New York (1962), 170.

7. Petrie, W.M.F., *Pyramids and Temples of Gizeh*, Field, London, Histories and Mysteries of Man, Ltd., London (1883 reprint 1990), 78.

8. Dunn, C., *The Giza Power Plant, The Technologies of Ancient Egypt*, Bear & Company (1998), Sante Fe, N.M., 67–106.

9. Petrie, W.M.F., *Pyramids and Temples of Gizeh*, Field, London (1883), 173–4. Lucas argued that the cutting was done with quartz sand. Refer to Lucas, A., *Ancient Egyptian Materials and Industries*, Mineola, N.Y., Dover Publications (1999 1962), 71.

10. Petrie, W.M.F., *Pyramids and Temples of Gizeh*, Field, London, Histories and Mysteries of Man, Ltd., London (1883 reprint 1990), 75.

11. Clarke, S., Engelbach, R., *Ancient Egyptian Construction and Architecture*, Dover pub., N.Y. (1990) (a reprint of *Ancient Egyptian Masonry*), 202. Petrie's lecture is titled "On the Mechanical Methods of the Ancient Egyptians," *Journal of the Anthropological Institute of Great Britain and Ireland* (August 1883).

12. Clarke, S., Engelbach, R., *Ancient Egyptian Construction and Architecture*, Dover pub., N.Y. (1990) (a reprint of *Ancient Egyptian Masonry*), 202.

13. Gorelick, L., Gwinnett, J., "Ancient Egyptian Stone Drilling: An Experimental Perspective on a Scholarly Disagreement," *Expedition* (Spring 1983) 40–46.

14. For Lucas' general discussion of emery, refer to Lucas, A., *Ancient Egyptian Materials and Industries*, Dover Publications, Mineola, N.Y. (1999 1962), 70–4.

Chapter 11: Artifacts Defy Modern Reproduction

1. Stocks, D., "Tools of the ancient craftsman," *Popular Archaeology*, 7 (1986), 24–29.

2. Dunn, C., *The Giza Power Plant, The Technologies of Ancient Egypt*, Bear & Company (1998), Sante Fe, NM, 281 pp.

3. For Mariette's discovery of the Serapeum, refer to Mariette, A., *Le Sérapeum de Memphis*, F. Vieweg, Paris (1882).

4. For all of these objects, refer to Emery, W.B., *Archaic Egypt: Culture and Civilizations in Egypt Five Thousand Years Ago*, Penguin Books, Baltimore (1961), 38–39.

5. For the tiny beads, refer to Lucas, A., *Ancient Egyptian Materials and Industries*, Dover Publications, Mineola, N.Y. (1999 1962), 44.

Chapter 12: A Technological Riddle

1. Lange, K., *Des Pyramides, des Sphinx, des Pharaons, Ed. Plon*, Paris, 169–174. Lucas, A., "Egyptian Prehistoric Stone Vessels," *Journal of Egyptian Archaeology*, XVI (1930), 210, n.9. Alexander el-Khouli, author of *Egyptian Stone Vessels: Predynastic Period to Dynasty III typology and analysis*, von Zabern, Mainz/Rhein (1978). In Vol. II titled *Manufacture of Stone Vessels - Ancient and Modern*, 796.

2. Arnold, D., *Building in Egypt: pharaonic stone masonry*, New York, N.Y., Oxford University Press (1991), 141.

3. Arnold, D., *Building in Egypt: pharaonic stone masonry*, New York, N.Y., Oxford University Press (1991), 147.

4. Aldred, C., *The Egyptians*, Thames and Hudson, London; New York (1984), 120–122.

5. Most 5th and 6th Dynasty pyramids are little more than mounds of rubble. They were built of loose stone rubble and sand sandwiched between stone walls. Once the casing blocks were removed, the structures degraded.

6. Wildung, D., *Egyptian Saints: Deification in Pharaonic Egypt*, New York University Press, New York (1977), 8–28, Fig. 6, 7.

7. Wildung, D., *Egyptian Saints: Deification in Pharaonic Egypt*, New York University Press, New York (1977), 8, Fig. 4.

8. Arnold, D., *Building in Egypt: pharaonic stone masonry*, New York, N.Y., Oxford University Press (1991), 61, which reads: "...the pyramids of the Fourth Dynasty would have consumed at least 9 million cubic meters of limestone, mortar, and sand, which had to be delivered quickly in small quantities." Arnold cites Stadelmann, R., *Mitteilungen des Deutschen Archäologischen Instituts Kairo*, 36 (1980), 438–439.

9. Jomard, E.F. (ed.), *Description de l'Egypte*, Panckoucke Ed., Paris (1809–1828), Vol. I, 245.

10. Badawy, A., *A History of Egyptian Architecture*, Giza, Studio Misr (1954). Refer to his Vol. 1 for the Old Kingdom and Vol. 3 for New Kingdom architecture.

11. *Temples and Tombs of Ancient Nubia: The International Rescue Campaign at Abu Simbel, Philae, and Other Sites*, general editor, Torgny Säve-Söderbergh, New York, N.Y. Thames and Hudson; Paris, France: UNESCO (1987). Between 1964 and 1966, the United Nations Educational, Scientific and Cultural Organization (UNESCO) and the Egyptian government reinforced with

resin, cut up, and moved two temples, one dedicated to Hathor and the other to Ra-Harakhte, and reconstructed them on a cliff 200 feet above the site.

12. Arnold, D., *Building in Egypt: pharaonic stone masonry*, New York, N.Y., Oxford University Press (1991), 174–175.

13. Arnold, D., *Building in Egypt: pharaonic stone masonry*, New York, N.Y., Oxford University Press (1991), 175.

14. Arnold, D., *Building in Egypt: pharaonic stone masonry*, New York, N.Y., Oxford University Press (1991), 175; Arnold wrote, "In general, either the limestone core walls were completely cased with granite or at least the lower parts received a casing of orthostats made of granite or, as in the case of Niuserra, of basalt." For granite, examples include the mortuary temples of Khafra and Menkaura at Giza. For the granite orthostats, refer to Borchardt, L., *Das Grabdenkmal des Konigs Sahu-Re*, Vol. 1, Der Bau. Ausgrabungen der Deutschen Orient-Gesellschaft in Abusir (1902–08), No. 6. Leipzig, (1910), 12, 16, 22, 33, and 40. For basalt, ibid. 24, Fig. 20, and Borchardt, L., Das Grabdenkmal des Konigs Ne-user-Re. Ausgrabungen der Deutschen Orient-Gesellschaft in Abusir (1902–04), No. 1. Leipzig, (1907), 56.

15. Arnold, D., *Building in Egypt: pharaonic stone masonry*, New York, N.Y., Oxford University Press (1991), 124.

16. Kitchen, K.A. (ed. and trans.), *Ramesside Inscriptions. Translated and Annotated*, Blackwell, Oxford, UK; Cambridge, MA (1993–2000).

Chapter 13: Block Raising Enigmas

1. Clarke, S., Engelbach, R., *Ancient Egyptian Construction and Architecture*, Dover pub., N.Y. (1990) (a reprint of *Ancient Egyptian Masonry*); Wilkinson observed, "Diodorus tells us (Diodorus i., 63), that machines were not invented at that early period [for raising pyramid blocks] and that the stone was raised by mounds of inclined planes; but we may be excused for doubting his assertion, and thus be relieved from the effort of imagining an inclined plane five hundred feet in perpendicular height, with a proportionate base." Wilkinson, J.G., *The Manners and Customs of the Ancient Egyptians*, New ed. rev. and corrected by Samuel Birch, London, J. Murray (1879). 309. Besides, Diodorus indicated that the mounds were made of salt, which would not be suitable for hauling blocks. A mud-brick ramp associated with the Great Pyramid is situated in the quarry. It was useful for climbing in and out of the quarry, but is not strong enough for raising the pyramid blocks out of the quarry. Dieter Arnold remarks, Arnold, D., *Building in Egypt: pharaonic stone masonry*, New York, N.Y., Oxford University Press (1991), 83, "It was probably used for the delivery of stones to the plateau, probably not for the pyramids but for one of the mastabas of later Fourth Dynasty." In other words, it was not strong enough for raising a great many massive stone pyramid blocks. This begs the question of how large blocks could be raised from the quarries, which show no evidence of strong stone ramps.

2. Arnold, D., *Building in Egypt: pharaonic stone masonry*, New York, N.Y., Oxford University Press (1991), 67.

3. Arnold, D., *Building in Egypt: pharaonic stone masonry*, New York, N.Y., Oxford University Press (1991), 98–99.

4. Hodges, P., *How the Great Pyramids Were Built*, Element Books, Wilshire (1989), 11.

5. Hodges, P., *How the Great Pyramids Were Built*, Element Books, Wilshire (1989), 11.

6. For ramp studies, Hodges, P., *How the Great Pyramids Were Built*, Element Books, Wilshire (1989); Isler, M., "Ancient Egyptian Methods of Raising Weights," *Journal of the American Research Center In Egypt*, 13 (1976), 31–41; Isler, M., "On Pyramid Building," *Journal of the American Research Center In Egypt* 24 (1987), 95–112; Dunham, D., "Building An Egyptian Pyramid," *Archaeology* 9, no. 3 (1956), 159–165; Fitchen, J., "Building Cheops' Pyramid," *Journal of the Society of Architectural Historians*, 37 (1968), 3–12. A report by Georges Legrain shows that 52 tons can be pulled on a ramp. Refer to Legrain, G., *Les Temples de Karnak*, Brussels (1929), 166–171, Figs. 102–7. However, hauling one block is feasible, whereas hauling many will cause a ramp to quickly degrade. Legrain's report is sometimes misused to justify the theory that the

ramp system can be used to place millions of huge pyramid blocks in about twenty-three years. Also refer to Arnold, D., *Building in Egypt: pharaonic stone masonry*, New York, N.Y., Oxford University Press (1991), 79–101.

7.   Arnold, D., *Building in Egypt: pharaonic stone masonry*, New York, N.Y., Oxford University Press (1991), 84.

8.   Garde-Hansen, P., *On the Building of the Cheops Pyramid*, Dansk ingeniørforening, Copenhagen, (1974), 36 p. Garde-Hansen's study is commented on by Egyptian engineer Moustafa Gadalla, *Pyramid Illusions: A Journey to the Truth*, Bastet Publishing, Erie, PA (1997), 98–99. "There are many problems with the existence of such a ramp. If such a ramp existed, how could so much material disappear?" Because the figures are so staggering, Garde-Hansen theorized that some kind of additional lifting device would have been involved. Garde-Hansen's theories amount to a building rate of 6.67 blocks per minute.

9.   Gadalla, M., *Pyramid Illusions: A Journey to the Truth*, Bastet Publishing, Erie, PA (1997), 98–99.

10. Hamblin, D.J., "A Unique Approach to Unraveling the Secrets of the Great Pyramid," *Smithsonian*, April (1986), 88–89, and all of Lehner's subsequent published remarks on the topic to date.

11. Arnold, D., *Building in Egypt: pharaonic stone masonry*, New York, N.Y., Oxford University Press (1991), 100. Also, Arnold notes that "The oldest true pulley in Egypt possibly dates to the late Twelfth Dynasty and was probably not used to gain mechanical advantage..." ibid., 71.

12. For Arnold's criticism of the helical ramp design, refer to Arnold, D., *Building in Egypt: pharaonic stone masonry*, New York, N.Y., Oxford University Press (1991), 100. For the Nova film, refer to *This Old Pyramid*, South Burlington, VT: Pub. WGBH Video (1992), Audiovisual, 1 videocassette (VHS) (57 min.): sd., col.; ½ in.

13. The viewer was my mother, who kindly wrote a letter because Barnes does not respond to my letters that explain fundamental problems with the film and show the need for a disclaimer.

14. The congressional staff people included Alison Pascal from Michigan Senator Carl Levin's Washington office. She called me on 9/15/94 in response to my letter of August 1994 regarding Michael Barnes' disclaimer. Tom Hestor of Michigan Senator Donald Riegle's office called Nova producer Michael Barnes in August of 1994, during which conversation Barnes promised that the revised film would include a disclaimer.

15. I sent David Suzuki copies of all of my correspondence that attempted to correct the problem, until he wrote to me indicating that he refused to consider any more information or attempts to correct the problem. So, he left his own viewers with no knowledge about the truth of the matter, and there was no disclaimer for his own program.

16. Lehner, M., *The Complete Pyramids: Solving the Ancient Mysteries*, New York, Thames and Hudson (1997), 209.

17. Joseph Davidovits was invited by Nova to participate in the film. Here is a description of Joseph Davidovits' career profile: Dr. Joseph Davidovits is an internationally recognized, award-winning materials scientist who holds numerous patents for his products and processes. He is involved in major international technology development programs, for which he coordinates research and development projects that are carried out at major institutions and/or universities, including some in Europe, the U.S.A., Brazil, Japan, and Australia. These research programs include, 1) the development of fire-resistant composites for the Fire Research Section of the U.S. Federal Aviation Administration, 2) the rehabilitation of uranium-mining sites for the German Government's WISMUT program, and 3) the mitigation of global warming for the European Commission in Brussels, Belgium. Dr. Joseph Davidovits has published many scientific papers and participated in scientific committees and held university posts in the U.S.A, including the position of Visiting Professor of Solid State Science at Pennsylvania State University (a primary hub of materials science in the U.S.). He is the founder and president of the Geopolymer Institute, a nonprofit organization based in Saint-Quentin, France. In 1994 he received a Gold Ribbon award from the National Association for Science, Technology, and Society (NASTS), in Washington, D.C., U.S.A. The NASTS issued Gold Ribbon awards for "the most significant real advances in mate-

rials research of the last decade." He is the founder of the chemistry of geopolymerization. See his Web site for much more: www.geopolymer.org

8. The viewer was my mother, who wrote to Barnes on my behalf, because he does not respond to my appeals for a public disclaimer.

9. See: http://www.pbs.org/wgbh/nova/pyramid/explore/builders.html. If the web page goes down, see the entry in the Wayback Machine archive (as I write this, the Nova page was last updated on December 18, 2007).

Chapter 14: The Block Raising Quagmire Deepens

1. For the stele of Djehutihotep, refer to Baines, J., Malek, J., *Atlas of Ancient Egypt*, Facts on File Publications, N.Y. (1980), 126–127. Arnold, D., *Building in Egypt: pharaonic stone masonry*, New York, N.Y., Oxford University Press (1991), 61.

2. For the 1,000-ton statue at the Ramesseum, refer to Leblanc, Ch., "Les sources grecques et les colosses de Ramsès Rê-en-hekaou et de Touy, au Ramesseum," *Memnonia*, IV-V, Cairo (1994), 71–101 and Pls. XVI–XX, and Leblanc, Ch., "Diodore, le tombeau d'Osymandyas et la statuaire du Ramesseum," *Mélanges Gamal Eddin Mokhtar*, B d'E XCVII/2, Cairo (1985), 69–82 and Pls. I–VI.

3. For Ramses II's 1,000-ton statues in Tanis, refer to Uphill, E.P., *The Temples of Per Ramesses*, Aris & Phillips, Warminister, England (1984), 129–132. Arnold, D., *Building in Egypt: pharaonic stone masonry*, New York, N.Y., Oxford University Press (1991), 62, which reads, "At Tanis, fragments of up to four granite colossi were found that could even have surpassed the size of that in the Ramesseum and certainly weighed about 1,000 tons."

4. For Arnold's estimate of oxen and men, refer to Arnold, D., *Building in Egypt: pharaonic stone masonry*, New York, N.Y., Oxford University Press (1991), 64. Arnold's estimate also requires a slick, flat surface all of the way from Aswan to Tanis, a distance of hundreds of miles. No evidence that such a long, flat surface existed has been found, and such a surface is not realistic. The idea of barges strong enough to float this kind of weight along the Nile is highly speculative and does not correlate with the strength of the known ship building capabilities. We would also expect to find the remains of a suitable, gigantic loading dock at Aswan if the weight was floated, but no such feature is known.

5. Arnold, D., *Building in Egypt: pharaonic stone masonry*, New York, N.Y., Oxford University Press (1991), 64.

6. Engelbach, R., *The Problem of the Obelisks, From a Study of the Unfinished Obelisk at Aswan*, T.F. Unwin, limited, London (1923), 53.

7. Engelbach, R., refer to *The Aswan Obelisk, with Some Remarks on the Ancient Engineering*, Cairo (1922), 36–43; Engelbach, R., *The Problem of the Obelisks, From a Study of the Unfinished Obelisk at Aswan*, T.F. Unwin, limited, London (1923), 66–84. For Ramses II's 1,000-ton statues in Tanis, refer to Uphill, E.P., *The Temples of Per Ramesses*, Aris & Phillips, Warminister, England (1984), 129–132. For the 1,000-ton statue at the Ramesseum, refer to Leblanc, Ch., "Les sources grecques et les colosses de Ramsès Rê-en-hekaou et de Touy, au Ramesseum," *Memnonia*, IV–V, Cairo (1994), 71–101 and Pls. XVI–XX and Leblanc, Ch., "Diodore, le tombeau d'Osymandyas et la statuaire du Ramesseum," *Mélanges Gamal Eddin Mokhtar*, Cairo (1985), 69–82 and Pls. I–VI.

8. Engelbach, R., *The Problem of the Obelisks, From a Study of the Unfinished Obelisk at Aswan*, T.F. Unwin, limited, London (1923), 67.

9. Chevrier, H., *Revue d Egyptologie*, 22, Paris (1970), 20–21. Chevrier, H., *Le temple reposoir de Ramsès III à Karnak*, Impr. de l'Institut français d'archéologie orientale, Cairo (1933), 21 p.

10. The account of Herodotus stating that 2,000 men were needed to haul the "green naos" of Nectanebos II, weighing 580 tons, corresponds with Chevrier's findings of each man being able to pull about 1/3 ton. Refer to Herodotus, *History*, II, 175. Refer also to Chevrier, H., *Revue d Egyptologie* 22, Paris (1970), 20–21. Lauer, J.-P., "Comment furent construites les pyramides," *Historia*, 86 (1954), 57–66.

11. Lehner, M., *The Complete Pyramids: Solving the Ancient Mysteries*, New York, Thames and Hudson (1997), 224–225.

12. Lehner, M., *The Complete Pyramids: Solving the Ancient Mysteries*, New York, Thames and Hudson (1997), 224.

13. Petrie, W.M.F., *Pyramids and Temples of Gizeh*, Field, London (1885), 210. Edwards repeat Petrie's gross oversimplification of the problem, but notes that "In the face of so many unknown or unconfirmed factors, speculations regarding the number of men required for building one of the larger pyramids and the time needed for the work may perhaps appear vain." Refer to Edwards I.E.S., *The pyramids of Egypt*, Rev. and updated, repr. with minor revisions, Harmondsworth Middlesex, England; New York, Penguin Books (1988), 270.

14. Parry, R.H.G., "On the Construction of the Great Pyramid at Giza," *Cambridge University Engineering Department Report* No. DUED - Struct/TRI53 (1995). For the rockers that inspired Dick Parry, refer to Clarke, S., Engelbach, R., *Ancient Egyptian Construction and Architecture* Dover pub., N.Y. (1990) (a reprint of *Ancient Egyptian Masonry*), 102–4, Figs. 89, 109. Arnold D., *Building in Egypt: pharaonic stone masonry*, New York, N.Y., Oxford University Press (1991) 271–2, Figs. 6.29, 6.30.

15. Hodges, P., *How the Great Pyramids Were Built*, Element Books, Wilshire (1989), 8.

16. For the quote, refer to Engelbach, R., *The Problem of the Obelisks, From a Study of the Unfinished Obelisk at Aswan*, T.F. Unwin, limited, London (1923), 56.

Chapter 15: The Mystery of Obelisks

1. Engelbach, R., *The Problem of the Obelisks, From a Study of the Unfinished Obelisk at Aswan* T.F. Unwin, limited, London (1923), 67. Also refer to Noakes, A., *Cleopatra's Needles*, H.F. & G. Witherby, London (1962), 128 pp.

2. Engelbach, R., *The Problem of the Obelisks, From a Study of the Unfinished Obelisk at Aswan* T.F. Unwin, limited, London (1923), 67.

3. Engelbach, R., *The Problem of the Obelisks, From a Study of the Unfinished Obelisk at Aswan* T.F. Unwin, limited, London (1923), 67.

4. Engelbach, R., *The Problem of the Obelisks, From a Study of the Unfinished Obelisk at Aswan* T.F. Unwin, limited, London (1923), 56.

5. Engelbach, R., *The Problem of the Obelisks, From a Study of the Unfinished Obelisk at Aswan* T.F. Unwin, limited, London (1923), 67, 118.

6. Engelbach, R., *The Problem of the Obelisks, From a Study of the Unfinished Obelisk at Aswan* T.F. Unwin, limited, London (1923), 134 pp.

7. Pliny the Elder, *Natural History*, Book 36, Ch. 14.

8. Engelbach, R., *The Problem of the Obelisks, From a Study of the Unfinished Obelisk at Aswan* T.F. Unwin, limited, London (1923), 88–89. Excerpts from a Nova on-line article titled "Gifts of the River," by Peter Tyson, dated March 19, 1999, read: "Herodotus, the father of history said famously that Egypt was the 'Gift of the River.' The same could be said of obelisks, that they are a gift of the Nile, for without the river, the task of shuttling these massive pillars of stone hundreds of miles from quarry to temple would have been orders of magnitude more challenging." As mentioned, however, Engelbach found no evidence of a canal at Aswan when he cleared the quarries, and the ship designs known from ancient Egypt will not tolerate hauling the heaviest surviving colossi or obelisks reported in ancient literature. Herodotus measured a much heavier monolithic temple in the Delta that would have weighed about 5,000 tons. Studies that calculate the strength requirements and speculate on a suitable craft (made of known ancient building materials) for the Memnon Colossi do not correlate with actual ancient Egyptians ships The archaeological information on ship and barge building from ancient Egypt is abundant and it allows for a good understanding of the technological level and strength of the river and sea crafts. For a more detailed analysis of the problems, see Part 2 of the present book.

9. Engelbach, R., *The Problem of the Obelisks, From a Study of the Unfinished Obelisk at Aswan* T.F. Unwin, limited, London (1923), 80.

Chapter 16: Proof from Ancient Texts

1. For Unas' causeway, refer to Raslan, M.A.M., "The Causeway of Ounas Pyramid," in *Annals du Service des Antiquites de l'Egypt*, LXI (1973), 151–60.

2. Arnold, D., *Building in Egypt: pharaonic stone masonry*, New York, N.Y., Oxford University Press (1991), 52; ibid. 2. Arnold wrote, "The transport scenes from the causeway of Unas and the temple of Hatshepsut indicate that columns, architraves, and obelisks were dressed to their final shape in the quarry—" ibid. 39. Engelbach showed that the transport scene at Hatshepsut's temple is impressionistic. Engelbach, R., *The Problem of the Obelisks, From a Study of the Unfinished Obelisk at Aswan*, T.F. Unwin, limited, London (1923), 57.

3. Joseph Davidovits investigated the site and inspected the temple column units. Davidovits, J., Morris, M., *The Pyramids: An Enigma Solved*, Hippocrene, N.Y. (1988), 62–63.

4. Davidovits, J., Morris, M., *The Pyramids: An Enigma Solved*, Hippocrene, N.Y. (1988), 60.

5. Fakhry, A., *The Pyramids*, University of Chicago Press, Chicago and London (1969 ed.), 12.

6. Junker, H., *Gîza. Bericht über die von der Akademie der Wissenschaften in Wien auf gemeinsame Kosten mit Dr. Wilhelm Pelizaeus unternommenen Grabungen auf dem Friedhof des Alten Reiches bei den Pyramiden von Gîza*, Wien, Leipzig Hölder-Pichler-Tempsky A.G., (1929–55), Vol. x, 16; Arnold, D., *Building in Egypt: pharaonic stone masonry*, New York, N.Y., Oxford University Press (1991), 262.

7. For Engelbach's quote concerning the wheel, refer to Clarke, S., Engelbach R., *Ancient Egyptian Construction and Architecture*, Dover pub., N.Y. (1990) (a reprint of *Ancient Egyptian Masonry*), 87–88. Refer to ibid. Fig 83 for a small ladder mounted on wheels from the 5th Dynasty. The invention does not appear to have flourished, however, perhaps because wheels do not function well in the sand. All known further development of the wheel dates to much later times. Ancient Egyptian wheels were not strong enough to endure heavy lifting.

8. Newberry, P.E., *The Life of Rekhmara*, Constable, London (1900), 39 pp.

Chapter 17: Proof from Giza

1. Lehner made this statement in the 1992 WGBH Nova film titled *This Old Pyramid*, South Burlington, VT: Pub. WGBH Video (1992), Audiovisual, 1 videocassette (VHS) (57 min.): sd., col.; ½ in.

2. Kitchen, K.A., *Pharaoh Triumphant: the life and times of Ramesses II, King of Egypt* (edition: third corr. impression), Aris & Phillips, Warminster, Wiltshire, England; Mississauga, Ont., Canada: Benben (1985, c. 1982), 107.

3. Refer to Herodotus, *The History of Herodotus*. New York, L. MacVeagh, The Dial press; Toronto, Longmans, Green & company (1928), 124–6.

4. Abd al-Latif, *The Eastern key: Kitab al-ifadah wa 'l-i 'tibar of 'Abd al-Latif al-Baghdadi, Translated in English by Kamal Hafuth Zand, John A., and Ivy E. Videa*, Allen and Unwin, London (1964), 119–123.

5. Lehner, M., *The Complete Pyramids: Solving the Ancient Mysteries*, Thames and Hudson, New York, (1997), 47, which reads: "In 1801 Coutelle and Lepere began to dismantle Pyramid GIII-c, the westernmost queen's pyramid of Menkaure, in the hope of finding an undisturbed burial. They abandoned their efforts after removing the upper north quarter of the pyramid."

6. For the extensive 19th Dynasty repairs, refer to Kitchen, K.A., *Pharaoh Triumphant: the life and times of Ramesses II, King of The Egypt* (edition: third corr. impression), Warminster, Wiltshire, England: Aris & Phillips; Mississauga, Ont., Canada: Benben (1985, c. 1982), 107. In 1853 Auguste Mariette found the Inventory Stela (also called the Stela of Khufu's Daughter) dated to the 26th Dynasty (c. 500 B.C.) Saite Period. The stela indicates that the Sphinx was repaired in the Saite Period. Zahi Hawass found a number of Greek Sphinxes at Giza in 1994. Roman restorations incorporated a protective layer of small brick-sized stones to the paws and two sides of the Sphinx. The floor of the Sphinx sanctuary was also paved in the Roman period. Modern activity at Giza is apparent from portland-cement-based concrete blocks on the pyramids, placed

to keep some blocks from falling. In a letter from the Egyptian Antiquities Organization, I was told that natural stone blocks were also used whenever possible.

7. A study by Klemm, D., and Klemm, R., show that quarrying methods that have been associated with pyramid building at Giza match Roman-style quarrying techniques. This evidence is, therefore, to be associated with Roman activity at Giza. The Klemms presented their study at the Second International Congress of Egyptologists in 1979. Here is the abstract of their paper describing Roman-style quarrying, as the quarrying appears at the sandstone quarries of Gebel el-Silsila: "Most quarries were dated to well-defined historical periods with the aid of chisel marks, block technique, inscriptions, and pottery shards. The most anciently quarried areas are at the northern edges of Gebel el-Silsila. These were quarried prior to the New Kingdom, perhaps in the Middle Kingdom. The chisel marks of this period are irregularly oriented (Fig. 7). The northern part of Gebel el-Silsila was exploited during the New Kingdom, in about the Eighteenth Dynasty, and chisel marks form a herringbone pattern. In the Nineteenth Dynasty, Ramses II introduced a fine parallel pattern that still prevailed when the Ptolemies exploited large quarries at the site. At the southern end of Gebel el-Silsila are the Roman quarry sites. No chisel marks of the previous types are found, but only wedge marks made by wooden dowels." The Klemms subsequently studied the limestone quarries, including those at Giza. Fourth Dynasty rock excavation was carried out with pointed stone tools. Refer to Klemm, R. and Klemm, D. D., *Steine und steinbrüche im alten Ägypten: Spring-Verlag*, Berlin (1993); Arnold, D., *Building in Egypt: pharaonic stone masonry* New York, N.Y., Oxford University Press (1991), 33.

8. Arnold, D., *Building in Egypt: pharaonic stone masonry*, New York, N.Y., Oxford University Press (1991), 33.

9. Edwards, I.E.S., *The pyramids of Egypt, Rev. and updated, repr. with minor revisions*, Penguin Books, Harmondsworth, Middlesex, England; New York, N.Y. (1988), 248.

10. For Giza's cults dedicated to guarding and maintaining the sepulchres of dead pharaohs, refer to Zivie, C., "Giza au deuxième millénaire," Bibliothèque d'étude, *Fouilles de l'Institut francais d'Archaeologie oriental*, Cairo (1976), 185 ff; for Teti's cult, refer to Yoyotte, J., "A Propos De La Parente Feminine Du Roi Teti (VI Dynastie)," *Bulletin de l'institut d'archeologie orientale* 57 (1958), 96, n. 4; for Sahure, refer to Martin, G.T., *The tomb of Hetepka and Other Reliefs and Inscriptions from the Sacred Animal Necropolis, North Saqqâra, 1964–73* (with chapters by Alan B. Lloyd and J.J. Wilkes, and a contribution by R.V. Nicholls), Egypt Exploration Society London (1979), pl. 55. Fakhry, A., *The Pyramids*, University of Chicago Press, Chicago and London (1969 ed.), 18–19. Fakhry cites Junker, H., Giza, VI (*Gîza. Bericht über die von der Akademie der Wissenschaften in Wien auf gemeinsame Kosten mit Dr. Wilhelm Pelizaeus unternommenen Grabungen auf dem Friedhof des Alten Reiches bei den Pyramiden von Gîza*, Wien. Leipzig Hölder-Pichler-Tempsky A.G., [1929–55]), 6–25 for a study of priests and officials of the pyramid cult.

11. Fakhry, A., *The Pyramids*, University of Chicago Press, Chicago and London (1969 ed.), 164 Arnold, D., *Building in Egypt: pharaonic stone masonry*, New York, N.Y., Oxford University Press (1991), 173. In Arnold's caption for Fig. 4.104, he says, "Granite casing blocks of the Chephren Pyramid, with medieval wedge holes for splitting." In other words, his photo shows an abandoned attempt to cut apart an existing granite casing block. In 1853 Auguste Mariette found the Inventory Stela (called the Stela of Khufu's Daughter) dated to the 26th Dynasty (c. 500 B.C.) Saite Period. The stela indicates that the Sphinx was repaired in the Saite Period.

12. Edwards, I.E.S., *The pyramids of Egypt*, Rev. and updated, repr. with minor revisions, Penguin Books, Harmondsworth, Middlesex, England; New York, N.Y. (1988), 141.

Chapter 18: The Resistance to New Knowledge

1. Arnold, D., *Building in Egypt: pharaonic stone masonry*, New York, N.Y., Oxford University Press (1991), 66. Here is a translation (by Joseph Davidovits) of Jean Paul Adams, *L'Archeologie devant I'mposture*, Ed. Robert Laffont, Paris (1975), 135. "Nowadays, it is difficult to imagine workers attacking a rocky cliff with stone axes. It is, however, in this way that numerous mega-

liths were detached and squared." Refer also to Edwards, I.E.S., *The pyramids of Egypt*, Rev. and updated, repr. with minor revisions, Penguin Books, Harmondsworth, Middlesex, England; New York, N.Y. (1988), 249; Arnold, D., *Building in Egypt: pharaonic stone masonry*, New York, N.Y., Oxford University Press (1991), 62, 66.

2. Arnold, D., *Building in Egypt: pharaonic stone masonry*, New York, N.Y., Oxford University Press (1991), 66. One of the purposes of Arnold's book is to protest alternative theories. He wrote, "This book also tries to combat speculative literature on how the ancient Egyptians solved certain technical problems. Such studies, often filled with unproven theories, obscure our outlook." Ibid., 5. With regard to levering, Arnold had in mind an experiment that used 200 men to raise a 32-ton block up steps almost 20 inches high using three large levering beams. He cites Mohen, J.-P., *Les Dessiers d'Archeologie*, 46 (1980), 66. The rapid construction speed, the enormous scale, the weakness of a clay and stone rubble ramp, congestion, and the potential for damaging masonry when blocks go crashing down prohibit this method for building the Great Pyramid.

3. Arnold, D., *Building in Egypt: pharaonic stone masonry*, New York, N.Y., Oxford University Press (1991), 120.

4. Engelbach, R., *The Problem of the Obelisks, From a Study of the Unfinished Obelisk at Aswan*, T.F. Unwin, limited, London (1923), 22.

5. Arnold, D.,"Ueberlegungen zum Problem des Pyramidenbaus, "*Mitteilungen des Deutschen Archäologischen Instituts Kairo* (1981), 37, 15–28.

6. Ashley, M., *Seven Wonders of the World*, Ashley Pub., London (1980), 288 pp. New York Times, March 12, 1978, Section IV, p. 7, col. 5. The project was led by Sakuji Yoshimura, formerly of Waseda University and sponsored and filmed by Nippon TV.

7. Roberts, D., "Age of Pyramids: Egypt's Old Kingdom," *National Geographic Magazine*, National Geographic Society (January 1995), Vol. 187, 31, 31 ff.

8. Lehner, M., *The Complete Pyramids: Solving the Ancient Mysteries*, New York, Thames and Hudson (1997), 225.

9. Lehner, M., *The Complete Pyramids: Solving the Ancient Mysteries*, New York, Thames and Hudson (1997), 225.

10. See chapters 13 and 14 of the present book.

11. Arnold, D., *Building in Egypt: pharaonic stone masonry*, New York, N.Y., Oxford University Press (1991), 33.

12. Arnold, D., *Building in Egypt: pharaonic stone masonry*, New York, N.Y., Oxford University Press (1991), 122.

13. Arnold, D., *Building in Egypt: pharaonic stone masonry*, New York, N.Y., Oxford University Press (1991), 72.

14. Arnold, D., *Building in Egypt: pharaonic stone masonry*, New York, N.Y., Oxford University Press (1991), 100.

15. Orwell, G., *Dickens, Dali & Others*, Reynal & Hitchcock, N.Y. (1946).

Chapter 19: The Supertech Theories

1. Dr. Volodymyr Krasnoholovets of the Institute of Physics, in Kyiv, in the Ukraine, proposed the use of a matter scrambler. Krasnoholovets, a physicist, actually proposed that Dunn's Giza Power plant caused the large nummulitic fossil shells (which are coin-shaped and about as big around as a quarter) to twist around in the rock matrix. Krasnoholovets has not demonstrated the process by which this amazing feat could actually happen, and Dunn has not demonstrated his Giza Power in action. Krasnoholovets does not explain how large nummulitic shells can scramble in a solid matrix without causing the pyramid blocks to become misshapen (affecting the level tiers and the contact points between backing and casing stones, etc.). He does not explain how the large nummulitic shells could twist around without causing the blocks to crack or otherwise degrade. Even normal stresses, like salt repeatedly dissolving and recrystallizing in the pores of limestone, will cause rock to degrade. Krasnoholovets' proposal amounts to sheer science fantasy.

His surprising proposal has not been published to my knowledge, and only appears in private email correspondence that attempts to argue my point of view.

2   Lehner. M., *The Egyptian Heritage: Based on the Edgar Cayce Readings*, Virginia Beach, Va., A.R.E. Press (1974), 132.

3.   Lehner has retracted certain notions, explaining that he no longer believes in the Cayce idea the same way as he did back in the 1970s. Speaking of his more recent talks before the Cayce group he wrote, "In these talks I began to suggest to the Cayce community that they look at the Egypt/Atlantis story as a myth in the sense that Joseph Campbell popularized, or that Carl Jung drew upon in his psychology of archetypes. Although the myth is not literally true, it may in some way be literally true. The Cayce 'readings' themselves say, in their own way, that the inner world of symbols and archetypes is more 'real' than the particulars of the physical world." Refer to these and other comments by Lehner renouncing his old beliefs in Hancock, G., Bauval, R., *The Message of the Sphinx: a Quest for the Hidden Legacy of Mankind*, Crown Publishing, Inc., New York (c.1996), 290–95.

Chapter 20: The Only Logical Solution

1.   Arnold, D., *Building in Egypt: pharaonic stone masonry*, New York, N.Y., Oxford University Press (1991), 33.

2.   Arnold, D., *Building in Egypt: pharaonic stone masonry*, New York, N.Y., Oxford University Press (1991), 33.

3.   For the discussion concerning the quarries associated with the Great Pyramid being too small, see Chapter 5.

4.   For the scrambled fossil shells in pyramid and temple blocks at Giza, which contrast with the normal sedimentation at the site, refer to Aigner, T., "Facies and Origin of Nummulitic Buildups: An Example from the Giza Pyramids Plateau (Middle Eocene, Egypt)," *Neues Jahrbuch für Geologie und Paläontologie, Abhandlung*, V. 166 (1983), 347–368. A drawing of the jumbled shells that characterize pyramid and temple blocks at Giza appears in Jomard, M. (Edme–François), *Description de l'Egypte*, ou, Recueil des observations et des recherches qui ont été faites en Egypte pendant l'expédition de l'armee française, Paris, Pub. Imprimerie Imperiale (1809 1828) and is reproduced in Davidovits, J., Morris, M., *The Pyramids: An Enigma Solved*, Hippocrene, N.Y. (1988) Fig. 14.

5.   A study by Klemm, D., and Klemm, R., show that quarry methods that have been associated with pyramid building at Giza match Roman–style quarrying techniques. They are, therefore, to be associated with Roman activity at Giza. The Klemms presented a study at the Second International Congress of Egyptologists in 1979. Fourth Dynasty quarrying was carried out with pointed stone tools, refer to Arnold, D., *Building in Egypt: pharaonic stone masonry*, New York, N.Y., Oxford University Press (1991), 33.

6.   See my above Chapter 5.

7.   For the evidence that the quarries were worked with pointed stone picks, which are inadequate for quarrying blocks, refer to Arnold, D., *Building in Egypt: pharaonic stone masonry*, New York, N.Y., Oxford University Press (1991). On pages 33–26, Arnold wrote, "The question as to what kind of tools were used to cut the separation trenches and to lift the blocks from their beds has not been answered satisfactorily because of the contradiction between the tool marks left on the quarry walls and the tools actually found in ancient Egypt.…In consequence, one would have to assume that pointed stone picks or axes were used during the Old and Middle Kingdoms. The type of tool used from the New Kingdom on, however, has still to be found.… These observations would again be in accord with the assumption that even 'soft' stones were not only dressed but also quarried mainly with stone tools, an assumption that would not deny, of course, that metal chisels existed and were occasionally used for special purposes."

8.   Arnold, D., *Building in Egypt: pharaonic stone masonry*, New York, N.Y., Oxford University Press (1991), 33.

9. The poor grade of limestone is apparent in the study of the Great Sphinx at Giza, made of this material. Refer to Chikaosa, T., Kiyoshi, K., Onuma, E., Kunio, M. "The Salinization and Slaking of Egyptian Mokattam Limestone," *Journal of the Society of Materials Science*, Japan, v 44 n 502 (July 1995), 862–868.

10. Joseph Davidovits showed how easily the limestone comes apart after soaking in water in the 1992 version of the WGBH Nova film *This Old Pyramid*. Refer to South Burlington, VT, Pub. WGBH Video (1992), Audiovisual, 1 videocassette (VHS) (57 min.): sd., col.; 1/2 in. Joseph Davidovits' demonstration was cut from the later 60-minute version of *This Old Pyramid* included in the series *Secrets of Lost Empires*.

11. The Geopolymer Institute Internet Web site (http://www.geopolymer.org) library provides several downloadable papers on the industrial applications of geopolymerization.

12. These reactions are of the poly(sialate), poly(sialate–siloxo/ disiloxo) types. Geopolymerization involves a chemical reaction between various aluminosilicate oxides (Al^{3+} in IV–V fold co-ordination) with silicates, yielding polymeric $Si–O–Al–O$ sialate bonds like the following: $2(Si_2O_5,Al_2O_2)+K_2(H_3SiO_4)_2+Ca(H_3SiO_4)_2$ —> $(K_2O,CaO)(8SiO_2,2Al_2O_3,nH_2O)$. Refer to Davidovits, J., *GEOPOLYMERS: Inorganic polymeric new materials*, presentation at "Real Advances in Materials" Symposium, Washington, D.C., Sept. 26, 1994, pub. *Journal of Materials Education*, Vol. 16 (2,3) (1994), 91–138.

13. In the Earth's solid outer crust almost all the mass contains eight elements, the most abundant of which is oxygen (47%). Silicon is the second most abundant (28%) and combines with oxygen and other atoms to form hundreds of silicate compounds. The third most common element is aluminum, not free but in compounds (8%). The remaining mass contains iron (5%), calcium (almost 4%), sodium (less than 3%), potassium (less than 3%), magnesium (just under 2%), the other 84 naturally occurring elements (1.4%).

14. Lyon, R, "Fire Response of Geopolymer Structural Composites," REPORT DOT/FAA/AR–TN95/22, Federal Aviation Administration (January 1996); Foden, A, Balaguru, P.N., Lyon, R, Davidovits, J., "High Temperature Inorganic Resin For Use in Fiber Reinforced Composites," ICCI'96, Fiber Composites in Infrastructure, Tucson, Arizona (1996), 166–177; Lyon, R, Sorathia, U., Balaguru, P.N., Foden, A., Davidovics, M., Davidovits, J., "Fire Response of Geopolymer Structural Composites," J., ICCI'96, Fiber Composites in Infrastructure, Tucson, Arizona (1996), 972–981. For more recent developments reported in 2009, see: http://www.physorg.com/news167306601.html

15. For Folk's use of a scanning electron microscope, refer to Morris, M., "Geopolymeric Pyramids: A Rebuttal to R.L. Folk and D.H. Campbell," *Journal of Geological Education*, The National Association of Geology Teachers, Madison, WI, Vol. 40, No. 1 (January 1992), 38. Folk, R.L., Campbell, D.H., "Are the Pyramids built of poured concrete blocks?" *Journal of Geological Education*, The National Association of Geology Teachers, Madison, WI (1992), Vol. 40, No. 1, 29.

16. Davidovits, J., "Ancient and Modern Concretes: What is the Real Difference?," *Concrete International: Design and Construction*, American Concrete Institute, Detroit, Michigan, Vol. 9, No. 12 (December 1987), 23–28.

17. By adding 1 percent (by combined weight) lime and natron to the Giza quarries, building the Great Pyramid would require between 50,000 and 60,000 tons of natron and lime. Compare Diodorus' account of mounds of salt that were dissolved by the Nile waters to build the Great Pyramid, Diodorus, *Library of History*, Book I.63.

18. Normally, when geologists investigate rock samples they consider the bulk of the crystalline materials. A geologist unfamiliar with geolpolymerization will classify the 5–10% by weight (the geopolymeric binder) as impurities. Chemical analyses conducted so that trace elements are analyzed will detect the minerals present because of geopolymerization. Certain types of rock, like the kaolinitic limestone of Giza and Saqqara, already contain the aluminum and silicon needed for geopolymerization. So, only an alkali additive is needed to cause the reaction. Weathered basalt, too, is largely feldspar, which breaks down into kaolin clay. Only the addition of natron, lime, and water is needed, making the binder about the same as in natural rock.

19. Aigner, T., "Facies and Origin of Nummulitic Buildups: An Example from the Giza Pyramids Plateau (Middle Eocene, Egypt)," *Neues Jahrbuch für Geologie und Paläontologie, Abhandlung*, V. 166 (1983), 347–368.

20. Also see the information in this book about Hatschepsut's limestone quarry compared to her temple terrace.

21. In addition to industrial uses, natron had a sacred value. The Pyramid Texts, inscribed on the walls of the burial chamber of the 5th Dynasty pyramid of Unas, preserve the use of natron for ritual purification. In the Talmud, natron symbolized the Torah (the Law). Also refer to Leviticus 2:13 in combination with Proverbs 25:20.

22. The production of lime (calcium oxide) is one of the oldest chemical processes, and its use pre-dates recorded history. Most ancient languages have a word for lime. In Latin, the word is *calx*, from which the word calcium derived. The word is lim in Old English, the origin of the modern commercial name for lime. Limestone in very abundant in the Earth's crust and can be easily transformed into calcium oxide or active lime soils can be used. Plastered floors and walls, which required lime to produce, were found in or near the houses of ancient Jericho. These were discovered during the excavations by John Garstang in the early 1930s. These floors and their construction are described in Garstang, J., and Garstang, J.B.E., *The Story of Jericho*, Marshall, Morgan and Scott, Ltd., London and Edinburgh (New Edition, Revised, 1948), 58–59, 67–68. The plastering appears to have been applied to preserve mud bricks that were not durable in damp conditions. To make the floors, a bed of limestone chips was applied to a depth of two or three inches, with the finest material at the top. The material tended to fuse into a hard mass. Both walls and floors were finished with a smooth lime surface. The floors have survived and are quite durable. Refer to *The Oxford Companion to Archaeology*, Brian M. Fagan, Editor in Chief, Oxford University Press, Oxford, New York (1996), 364 (refer to the article about "Jericho," by Ian Kuijt, which states that in the period 9300–8000 B.C., villagers in Jericho "lived in rectangular thirteen-by-twenty-six-foot (4 by 8 m) houses with painted red and white lime plaster floors."

23. The quote is from an abstract of the David Koch Pyramids Radiocarbon Project, which is a collaborative effort of Shawki Nakhla and Zahi Hawass, the Egyptian Supreme Council of Antiquities; Georges Bonani and Willy Wölfli, Institüt für Mittelenergiephysik, Eidgenossische Technische Hochschule; Herbert Haas, Desert Research Institute; Mark Lehner, The Oriental Institute and the Harvard Semitic Museum; Robert Wenke, University of Washington; John Nolan, University of Chicago; and Wilma Wetterstrom, Harvard Botanical Museum. The Ancient Egypt Research Associates, Inc. administered the project. Katherine Kershen, after reading a prepublication draft of my book, calculated the minimum amount of wood that would be needed for making Khufu's pyramid blocks: If the Great Pyramid is one percent lime, 170,000 tons of wood would have had to be burned to make blocks. This assumes that lime came from wood burning, which remains an unanswered question.

24. Klemm, D., Klemm, R, "Mortar Evolution in the Old Kingdom of Egypt," *Archaeometry '90*, Birkhäuser Verlag, Basel, Switzerland (1990), 445–454. In the same report, Klemm opposed the geopolymer theory based on his study of lime. According to Joseph Davidovits, Klemm's objection is invalid because the amount of lime in pyramid blocks is much lower than Klemm could detect. According to Joseph Davidovits, although the mortar Klemm studied contained about 30-40 percent by weight recarbonated lime, the blocks would at most contain only 3-4 percent. This smaller amount would not be easy to detect by the method Klemm developed. Klemm also chemically analyzed samples of pyramid stones, and he objected to the geopolymer theory based on his analyses. But Klemm carried out only bulk chemical analyses, methodology insufficient for detecting geopolymerization.

25. For the production of blue enamel, refer to Davidovits, J., Morris, M., *The Pyramids: An Enigma Solved*, Hippocrene, N.Y. (1988), 245–246.

26. Hodges, P., *How the Great Pyramids Were Built*, Element Books, Wilshire (1989), 5. Hodges wrote, "A man can lift 80 lb. The largest pyramid of all needed the equivalent of 200 million man-loads, a total of about 6,500,000 tons." On page 4, Hodges reminded us that "The Great Pyramid

weight probably exceeds all of the buildings within the square mile of the City of London put together." On page 6, "The average stone in the Great Pyramid is cut in chunky proportions and stands about waist high. The courses are always level but are of differing thicknesses, although each individual course maintains the same thickness throughout."

27. Davidovits, J., "No More Than 1,500 Workers to Build the Pyramid of Kheops with Agglomerated Man–Made Stone," presented at the International Congress of Egyptology, Toronto, Canada, 40, held September 5-11, 1982; Arnold notes that "We have reports, however, that Asian porters were able to carry up to 150 kilograms as far as 10 kilometers a day over terrible roads." Refer to Arnold, D., *Building in Egypt: pharaonic stone masonry*, New York, N.Y., Oxford University Press (1991), 57. Arnold cited Konigsberger, O., *Annals du Service des Antiquites de l'Egypte* 40. Cairo (1990), 247–255.

28. Cerny, J., Gardiner, A., Peet, T.E., *The Inscriptions of Sinai I, II*, London and Oxford (1952 1955), nos. 110, 114. Or refer to Arnold, D., *Building in Egypt: pharaonic stone masonry,* New York, N.Y., Oxford University Press (1991), 58, which says, "And the sign of these animals packed with a heavy basket full of soil was certainly as familiar to the ancient Egyptian builders as it is to us. Horses and camels were not used for carrying in Pharaonic Egypt, and cattle were only used for pulling."

29. Petrie, W.M.F., Sir, *Pyramids and Temple of Gizeh*, Field, London (1885), 213. Petrie found buildings to the west of Khafra's pyramid that he thought could have housed 4,000 men.

30. Lehner, M., *The Complete Pyramids: Solving the Ancient Mysteries*, New York, Thames and Hudson (1997), 238–239.

31. A variety of chert, flint is a brittle, hard, and compact mineral. It is brown, black, gray and is found as nodules in limestone or shale deposits. It is made up of cryptocrystalline grains (too small to be visible under a light microscope), silica (SiO) that usually occurs as quartz. Although flint is very hard, it fractures into sharp flakes.

32. Tafla rubble from the Al-Ma'mun breach of the Great Pyramid was cleared at the beginning of the 20th century. In the 19th century, this breach was unknown to the Napoleonic expedition or to Lepsius. I do not have sufficient information concerning how much tafla rubble was cleared from the interior of the pyramids.

33. Petrie, W.M.F., Sir, *Pyramids and Temple of Gizeh*, Histories and Mysteries of Man, Ltd., London (1990 reprint), 13.

34. Arnold, D., *Building in Egypt: pharaonic stone masonry*, New York, N.Y., Oxford University Press (1991), 14.

35. Lehner, M., *The Complete Pyramids: Solving the Ancient Mysteries*, New York, Thames and Hudson (1997), 214, 210.

36. Arnold wrote, "Normally, building stones were set with extra stock on their front faces." Refer to Arnold, D., *Building in Egypt: pharaonic stone masonry*, New York, N.Y., Oxford University Press (1991), 13.

37. Arnold, D., *Building in Egypt: pharaonic stone masonry*, New York, N.Y., Oxford University Press (1991), 266.

38. Lehner, M., *The Complete Pyramids: Solving the Ancient Mysteries*, New York, Thames and Hudson (1997), 211.

39. Engineer Mike Carrell's review of *The Giza Power Plant* demonstrates that the Giza Power plant Dunn envisioned would not function. Refer to Carrell's review in *Infinite Energy* magazine, Issue 32 (July/August 2000). Mike Carrell has subsequently pointed out (in personal correspondence addressed to Dunn and me) that the high moisture content in the masonry of the Great Pyramid also would have prevented the maser activity Dunn claims took place.

40. Arnold, D., *Building in Egypt: pharaonic stone masonry*, New York, N.Y., Oxford University Press (1991), 48.

41. For the information on imitation basalt, refer to Stone, E.C., Lindsley, D.H., Pigott, V., Harbottle, G. Ford, M.T., "From Shifting Silt to Solid Stone: The Manufacture of Synthetic Basalt in Ancient Mesopotamia," *Science* (June 1998), Vol. 280, no 5372, 2091–93. Here are the geologi-

cal descriptions of Egyptian basalt (diabase) from the paving east of the Great Pyramid) and the fabricated Mesopotamian basalt: Donald Lindsley, the geologist who discovered that the Mesopotamian basalt is synthetic, wrote as follows (in private correspondence to me) about the synthetic Mesopotamian basalt: "I'll just note that the Mashkan-shapir samples do show characteristics of high temperatures. Not only do they contain interstitial silicate glass, but the abundant pyroxenes are high-temperature phases, and their textures are strongly characteristic of nonequilibrium crystallization from a relatively rapidly cooled melt." Here is a description of basalt from the flooring of a destroyed temple in the Great Pyramid complex at Giza: "The two samples of paving stones were examined by a combination of optical microscopy and X-ray diffraction. The two samples were very similar except as noted and are part of the same rock unit. A scientific description of the rock is: Pyroxene diabase—medium grained, hypidiomor-phic-granular, subophitic to intergranular, 65% plagioclase feldspar (labradorite in composition), 30% augite, 5% ilmenite. Five to 30% of the intergranular material originally consisted of glass which has now been altered to a mixture of clays and iron oxides. The brown color is due to the chemical alteration of the volcanic glass which originally occurred between the grains. The glass has reacted with water and oxygen to form a mixture of iron oxides and clays. The browner of the two samples contains more altered glass than the blacker one. The alteration could be produced either soon after formation of the diabase or as a result of weathering near the surface over a long period of time. The alteration is a very slow process and was not produced after the quarrying of the rock. Despite their difference in color the two samples came from the same rock unit." These are excerpts from an analysis by R. Hamilton, Senior Research Physicist, Manville Service Corp., Denver, Colorado, June 1989, published in Moores, R., "Evidence for Use of a Stone-Cutting Drag Saw for the Fourth Dynasty Egyptians," *Journal of the American Research Center in Egypt* XVIII (1991), p. 139. When geologist Robert G. McKinney read Dr. Lindsay's description (above) of the synthetic basalt from Mesopotamia, he remarked that the description was similar to the Egyptian basalt (diabase) described above. McKinney wrote: "They sure sound similar. The [amorphous silica-based] glass may be the binder in the synthetic rock. Other components are typical of diabase and may have been added in a decomposed state. No note of weathering though." McKinney adds, "It seems like your postulation that [amorphous silica-based] glass (or something resembling glass) was used as a binder is compelling. Sometimes it helps to look at nature in reverse. This from Williams, Turner & Gilbert entitled 'Petrography': 'When tholeiitic basalts are weathered under conditions of poor drainage and in the presence of alkaline solutions, yellow and green nontronite (iron-rich clay mineral) is formed at the expense of the original glass and mafic minerals. Under conditions of better drainage and where the ground waters are neutral or slightly acid, nontronite is accompanied by kaolinite and halloysite, formed at the expense of the feldspars. In thermal regions such as Iceland, hot acid waters remove virtually all of the cations in basalts, leaving little but silica; neutral waters tend to form more or less ferruginous clays; and alkaline waters cause little chemical change but develop new minerals, such as zeolites, chlorite, and calcite.' Put this in reverse and you have your synthetic basalt." In other words, as McKinney explains, "Weathering is an exothermic reaction. Application of heat and a catalyst should reverse the reaction and produce something like the basalt you started with."

42. Klemm, D., Klemm, R., *Steine und Steinbrüche im Alten Ägypten*, Springer-Verlag, Berlin (1993), 60–71.

43. Arnold, D., *Building in Egypt: pharaonic stone masonry*, New York, N.Y., Oxford University Press (1991).

44. Kaolin clay forms as a result of the decomposition of aluminosilicate minerals, especially the feldspars. Kaolin is available in the area of the Aswan granite quarries. Refer to Szamalek, K. Badania, *izotopowe pizolitowych kaolinow z okolic asuanu* (Egipt). Przeglad Geologiczny, 39(9) (1991), 420–422. For other clays in the Cairo region, refer to Helck, W., *Lexikon der Aegyptologie*, Vol. 6 (S-Z) under pottery (clay). Today, Egypt exports great quantities of kaolin.

45. Arnold, D., *Building in Egypt: pharaonic stone masonry*, New York, N.Y., Oxford University Press (1991). Arnold summarizes the beginning of stone architecture relative to brick construc-

tion, "The construction methods of brick building were applied at first to building in stone. Small, regular blocks were set in a pattern of brick bonding, frequently in rows that inclined inward and were joined with a lot of mortar. Just a few generations after King Djoser, in the reigns of Snofru, Cheops, and Chephren, pyramids and pyramid temples of gigantic dimensions were erected with blocks weighing up to 200 tons; ibid., 3. The method of making inclined faces was practiced since the First Dynasty, ibid., 11–12. Also refer to Scharff, A., "On the Statuary of the Old Kingdom," *Journal of Egyptian Archaeology*, Vol. XXVI, 43, which says, "Looking at a well-founded reconstruction of a building belonging to King Djeser's [Zoser] temple-complex, we are struck by the smallness of the stones, which seem to be petrified bricks. . . ." Also refer to Emery, W.B., *Great Tombs of the First Dynasty*, Cairo and London (1949–58) [3 volumes].

46. Lehner, M., *The Complete Pyramids: Solving the Ancient Mysteries*, New York, Thames and Hudson (1997), 216.

47. Reisner, G.A., *Mycerinus, The Temples of the Third Pyramid at Giza*, Cambridge, MA (1931), 71. With regard to the granite blocks on the Third Pyramid at Giza, Petrie wrote (*Pyramids and Temples of Giza*, 1990 reprint, page 37), "The Third Pyramid has never been quite finished. Its granite casing blocks are left in probably the same condition that they were sent from Assonan, with their outer faces in the rough, but smoothly dressed down on the joint surfaces. One writer has described them as 'rusticated,' as if the roughness was a prepared feature; and another has attributed all the rounded irregularity of the stones to their weathering away since they were built. To say nothing, however, of innumerable cut holes in the outer surface, left for lifting the blocks, no weathering would add to a stone a part above its original face...." Petrie mentioned holes in some of the blocks, which he interpreted as there to assist handling. But the blocks do not all have holes in them, which they should if this were the means needed to lift these blocks, and workers would not have positioned quarried blocks with holes facing the exterior of the pyramid. Casing blocks were meant to create a smooth, perfect surface. These holes could be either (a) later work (as mentioned by Reisner), or (b) places where the workers meant to attach another structure. For instance, causeways were connected to pyramids, and to make a strong connection, sockets are desirable. This can explain so–called handling bosses, areas of stone that protrude out like the male end of a socket. In short, the granite blocks on the Third Pyramid exhibit features that can be interpreted more reasonably within the paradigm of fabricated stone, especially the glaring feature of well–fitted blocks with no original tool marks on them. A study of their geological features (or iron orientation) could settle the issue one way or the other.

48. K. O. Emery, "Weathering of the Great Pyramid," *Journal of Sedimentary Research*, Volume 30 (1960), 140-143. See the abstract, "The Great Pyramid of Giza, Egypt, was built of limestones and limy sandstones of varying resistances to weathering."

Chapter 21: An Overview of the Paradigm Shift

1. See Chapter 20.

2. Natural cements are found in clastic rock (rocks formed from fragments of other rocks). For instance, sandstone can form as particles of sand become cemented together from mineral-laden water soaking through the sand particles. Over long periods of time, the process leaves behind natural cements that bind the sand particles into sandstone. The quality of natural cements within the sandstone can make the difference between soft rock or an incredibly dense, hard sandstone matrix. Natural cements can contain minerals such as calcium carbonate, silica, and iron oxide.

3. The diagram of the geological layers of Giza appears in the revised version (with Frederic Davidovits) of Davidovits, J., Morris, M., *The Pyramids: An Enigma Solved*, Hippocrene, N.Y. (1988), 360.

4. In the 1992 PBS Nova film *This Old Pyramid*, Joseph Davidovits showed how easily limestone still remaining in the extensively quarried middle layer will come apart within hours of soaking.

5. Davidovits, J., Bonett, A., Mariotte, A.M., "The disaggregation of stone materials with organic acids from plant extracts, an ancient and universal technique" presented at the 22nd Symposium

on Archaeometry, University of Bradford, U.K. (1982), published in the Proceedings, pp. 205–12. El–Khouli, A., *Egyptian Stone Vessels: Predynastic Period to Dynasty III* typology and analysis, Von Zabern, Mainz/Rhein (1978). In Vol. II titled *Manufacture of Stone Vessels – Ancient and Modern*, page 973. Alexander el–Khouli wrote, "Alabaster and limestone were the most common because they were easily obtained in Egypt. Other types could only be procured after the expenditure of great labor and at the risk of some danger." W.M.F. Petrie, J.E. Quibell, W.B., Emery, G.A. Reisner, A. Lucas and others discussed the manufacture of stone vessels based on evidence from Old Kingdom tomb scenes. Tomb scenes depict large stone vessels being hollowed out, but the methods shown would only apply to the softer rock varieties or to semicured rock concrete.

Chapter 22: Evidence from the Stones

1. Wilkinson, J.G., *The Manners and Customs of the Ancient Egyptians*, New ed. rev. and corrected by Samuel Birch, J. Murray, London (1879), 252-253.

2. Newberry, P.E., *The Life of Rekhmara*, Constable, London (1900). The scene appears in Wilkinson, J.G., *The Manners and Customs of the Ancient Egyptians*, New ed. rev. and was corrected by Samuel Birch, J. Murray, London (1879), 311. On page 255 Wilkinson wrote, "Another remarkable feature in their bronze is the resistance it offers to the effect of the atmosphere; some continuing smooth and bright, though buried for ages and since exposed to the damp of European climates, and some presenting the appearance of previous oxidation purposely induced." We would expect to find this kind of preservation with geopolymer. The geopolymeric binder could have seeped into the pores of the chisels used to inscribe and otherwise sculpt uncured geopolymerized stone.

3. Wilkinson, J.G., *The Manners and Customs of the Ancient Egyptians*, New ed. rev. and corrected by Samuel Birch, J. Murray, London (1879), 308–311.

4. Wilkinson, J.G., *The Manners and Customs of the Ancient Egyptians*, New ed. rev. and corrected by Samuel Birch, J. Murray, London (1879), 311.

5. Wilkinson wrote about the tomb scenes, "…two instances occur of large granite colossi, surrounded by scaffolding [woodcut N. 931], on which men are engaged in chiseling and polishing the stone; the painter following the sculptor to colour the hieroglyphs he has engraved at the back of the statue," Wilkinson, J.G., *The Manners and Customs of the Ancient Egyptians*, New ed. rev. and corrected by Samuel Birch, J. Murray, London (1879). 309. If the scene is to be taken literally, it suggests cutting with small, simple tools. It is logical to think that the material depicted was semicured concrete made with granite aggregates.

6. Arnold, D., *Building in Egypt: pharaonic stone masonry*, New York, N.Y., Oxford University Press (1991), 268. Also on page 50, Arnold wrote, "We know from some examples that the lid of a sarcophagus was occasionally sawed from the same block as the bottom part of the sarcophagus with tools up to 2.40 meters long." In other words, Arnold assumes the existence of toothed metal saws capable of slicing a lid from a block from which a sarcophagus was to be made. The very idea defies the archaeological record and all of the careful study of the known metals and tools. The most logical solution is that the stone was cut before it cured. I wrote to Dieter Arnold asking him if the scene showing a lid being sawed off of a granite sarcophagus with a toothed metal saw was his conceptualization or if it is taken from a tomb scene. I received a reply from an assistant who indicated that he would answer my letter. But I have no reply from Arnold on the matter.

7. For the conflicting ideas, refer to Arnold, D., *Building in Egypt: pharaonic stone masonry*, New York, N.Y., Oxford University Press (1991), 41. D. Stocks, *Popular Archaeology* (July 1986), 25-28.

8. Lehner, M., *The Complete Pyramids: Solving the Ancient Mysteries*, New York, Thames and Hudson (1997), 210.

9. Lehner, M., *The Complete Pyramids: Solving the Ancient Mysteries*, New York, Thames and Hudson (1997), 210.

0. Lehner, M., *The Complete Pyramids: Solving the Ancient Mysteries*, New York, Thames and Hudson (1997), 92.

1. Campbell, D.H., and Folk R.L., "The Ancient Pyramids - Concrete or Rock?," *Concrete International: Design and Construction*, Vol. 13, No. 8, American Concrete Institute, Detroit, Michigan (1991), 34 and Fig. 8 on page 33.

2. Sterett Pope, "Puncturing Pyramids," *World Press Review*, Vol. 36, No. 1 (January 1989), 43.

3. El-Khouli, A., *Egyptian Stone Vessels: Predynastic Period to Dynasty III typology and analysis*, von Zabern, Mainz/Rhein (1978), Vol. II, titled *Manufacture of Stone Vessels - Ancient and Modern*, 796.

4. For example, the Lauer sample exhibits air bubbles. Also see the geological descriptions of the Mansoor Collection for unnatural features.

5. For the quote, refer to Arnold, D., *Building in Egypt: pharaonic stone masonry*, New York, N.Y., Oxford University Press (1991), 40.

6. Not only is the place of extraction unknown, but researchers do not know how stones large enough to make into objects could have been extracted. Jollois and Devilliers, *Description de l'Egypte*, Edition Panckoucke, Paris (1822–1828), Vol. II, Ch. IX, Sec II, 153. Here is a translation made by Dr. Joseph Davidovits: "None of the quartzite hills or quarries show tool [wedge] marks, as are so common in the sandstone and granite quarries. We have to conclude that a material so hard and unworkable by sharp tools must have been exploited by a process other than that generally used for sandstone, or even granite....We do not know anything about the process used by the Egyptians to square this stone, to trim the surfaces, or to impart the beautiful polish that we see today on some parts of the statues. Even if we have not determined the means used, we are forced to admire the results....When the tool of the engraver in the middle of a hieroglyphic character hit a flint or agate in the stone, the sketch was never hindered, but instead it continued in all its purity. Neither the agate fragment nor the stone itself was even slightly broken by engraving." Arnold's remarks are much the same. The quarrying methods are not clear to him. He wrote, "The extent to which dolerite balls were used for pounding quartzite is not clear....there seems to be no clear indication for the pounding method, and we must assume that chiseling was employed. This work could have been achieved only by experienced laborers, who probably were not numerous enough to produce huge quantities of quartzite. Still, the sepulchral chamber of Amenemhat III at Hawara and the statues of Memnon were made of that stone, and their manufacture certainly required a sizable number of such people." Refer to Arnold, D., *Building in Egypt: pharaonic stone masonry*, New York, N.Y., Oxford University Press (1991), 40. In other words, Egyptologists have no idea whatsoever how quartzite items could have been quarried. The Colossi of Memnon are gigantic monolithic statues, and no researcher has ever found the extraction site. Arnold cannot and does not try to explain what kind of chisels could possibly have been used to quarry the huge monoliths of quartzite.

7. Based on petrographic analysis, in 1913, M.G. Doressy and G. Steindorff proposed that the Colossi of Memnon was transported from Edfu or Aswan to Thebes. In 1965, L. Habachi, of the Cairo Institute, agreed. Based on a geochemical study, in 1973 a Berkeley, California, team proposed that the statues were quarried at Gebel el-Ahmar, near Cairo. Refer to Heizer, R.F., Stross, F., Hester, T.R., Albee, A., Perlman, I., Asaro F., Bowman, H, "The Colossi of Memnon Revisited, *Science* 182 (1973), 1219–25. Bowman, H., et al., "The Northern Colossus of Memnon: New Slants," *Archaeometry,* Vol. 26, (1984), 218–229.

8. Wehausen, J.V., "The Colossi of Memnon and Egyptian Barges," *International Journal of Nautical Archaeology and Underwater Exploration* (1988), v. 17, no. 4., 295–310.

9. Heizer, R.F., Stross, F., Hester, T.R., Albee, A., Perlman, I., Asaro F., Bowman, H, "The Colossi of Memnon Revisited, *Science* 182 (1973), 1219–25. Bowman, H., et al., "The Northern Colossus of Memnon: New Slants," *Archaeometry,* Vol. 26 (1984), 218–229.

0. For the chemical analysis of the quartzite, refer to Bowman, H., et al., "The Northern Colossus of Memnon: New Slants," *Archaeometry,* Vol. 26, (1984), 218–229.

21. Jollois and Devilliers, *Description de l'Egypte*, Volume II, Chap. IX, Section II, page 153, Panckouke Ed., Paris 1822–1828.
22. Lange, K., *Des Pyramides, des Sphinx, des Pharaons, Ed. Plon*, Paris, 169–174.
23. Petrie, W.M.F., *The Pyramids and Temples of Gizeh* (1883), 176 and pl. XIV, 14, 15.
24. For an image of this type, see Davidovits, J., *They Built the Pyramids*, Geopolymer Institute publication, Saint Quentin (2008), Fig. 1.2 on page 6 (the dark specks are crystal clusters).
25. Emery, W.B., *Archaic Egypt: Culture and Civilizations in Egypt Five Thousand Years Ago*, Penguin Books, Baltimore (1987 edition), 215.
26. Kroeper, K., "Some Stone Vessels from Minshat Abu Omar – Eastern Delta," *Varia Aegyptiaca 1. San Antonio, TX* (1985), 52. Kroeper mentioned three vessels made of two different types of stone from the Eastern Delta and two or more from Saqqara, p. 54. The published evidence of jars made of different stones is small, 54. "The work methods used to produce composite or segmented vessels were the same used in repair of stone objects broken during manufacture. A schist bowl from Minshat Abu Omar is, most likely, an example of such repair work." p. 54. Barbara Aston mentioned a pot in the British Museum that had a body made of siltstone and a rim of serpentine. Refer to the Ph.D thesis of Barbara Greene (married name Barbara G. Aston), *Ancient Egyptian stone vessels: materials and forms*. Heidelberg: Heidelberger Orientverlag (1994), xix, Studien zur Archaologie und Geschichte Altagyptens 5), p 42.
27. Clarke, S., Engelbach, R., *Ancient Egyptian Construction and Architecture*, Dover Pub., N.Y. (1990 edition), a (reprint of *Ancient Egyptian Masonry*), 24–25.
28. During the Second International Congress of Egyptologists, Grenoble, France in 1979 Joseph Davidovits pointed out that Le Chatelier's work demonstrated that science had already proven that the ancient Egyptians produced manmade stone. Acknowledging that, the Egyptologists present were still unwilling to consider that the pyramid stones might also be manmade.
29. Lauer's remarks were made in private correspondence and in conversations with Joseph Davidovits. They are unpublished. Lauer has never denied them when asked. For instance, when producer Michael Barnes was researching the Nova film *This Old Pyramid*, he visited Jean-Philippe Lauer in Paris. At that time, geologist Robert L. Folk, of the University of Texas at Austin, had already made his claim, purely of his own invention, that the Lauer sample was a piece of plaster. Folk decided this purely because he read a book stating that plaster is present in the Grand Gallery. The statement prompted Folk to reinvent the location from which Lauer had removed the limestone sample, and the material of which it is made. Folk had never seen or held the Lauer sample itself. The reason Folk reinvented the Lauer sample is that he recognized that the published photograph of its features in *The Pyramids: An Enigma Solved*, Hippocrene N.Y. (1988) reveal it to be some kind of synthetic material. So, Folk called everyone he thought would listen to him with his claim that the Lauer sample is plaster. He also advocated this in print and wrote to Nova. With this behavior, Folk managed to successfully send his falsehood throughout the Egyptology community. We have a sense of how far and fast the rumor spread because our publisher, Hippocrene Books soon received a letter protesting our book. The letter was from an Egyptologist who learned of Folk's claim while having lunch with a colleague in the British Museum. So, Nova producer Michael Barnes interviewed Lauer in Paris. But despite Folk's remarks, Jean-Philippe Lauer asserted that the sample is limestone from the Ascending Passageway of the Great Pyramid.

Chapter 23: Proof from the Basalt Quarries

1. Harrell, J.A., and Bown, T.M., "An Old Kingdom Basalt Quarry at Widan el-Faras and the Quarry Road to Lake Moeris," *Journal of the American Research Center in Egypt*, Vol. 32 (1995), 78.
3. Harrell, J.A., and Bown, T.M., "An Old Kingdom Basalt Quarry at Widan el-Faras and the Quarry Road to Lake Moeris," *Journal of the American Research Center in Egypt*, Vol. 32 (1995), 74.
3. Roder, J., "Zur steinbruchgeschichte des rosengranits von Assuan," *Archalogischer Anzeiger 3* Jahrbuch des Deutschen Archäologischen Instituts (1965), 523.

4. Harrell, J.A., and Bown, T.M., "An Old Kingdom Basalt Quarry at Widan el-Faras and the Quarry Road to Lake Moeris," *Journal of the American Research Center in Egypt*, Vol. 32 (1995), 75.

5. Stocks, D., *Popular Archaeology* (July 1986): 25–28. Arnold, D., *Building in Egypt: pharaonic stone masonry*, New York, N.Y., Oxford University Press (1991), 41.

6. Arnold, D., (citing Harrell) *Building in Egypt: pharaonic stone masonry*, New York, N.Y., Oxford University Press (1991), 28.

7. Harrell, J.A., and Bown, T.M., "An Old Kingdom Basalt Quarry at Widan el–Faras and the Quarry Road to Lake Moeris," *Journal of the American Research Center in Egypt*, Vol. 32 (1995), 77.

8. Caton–Thompson, G., "Explorations in the Northern Fayum," *Antiquity* (September, 1927), op. cit., 338–339, pl. 8; Caton–Thompson, G., Gardner, E.W., *The Desert Fayum*, Vol. 1, Royal Anthropological Institute, London (1934), op. cit., 136, pl. 77.

9. Harrell, J.A., and Bown, T.M., "An Old Kingdom Basalt Quarry at Widan el–Faras and the Quarry Road to Lake Moeris," *Journal of the American Research Center in Egypt*, Vol. 32 (1995), 71.

10. For the shards found from various periods, refer to the Appendix by Michael Jones, in Harrell, J.A., and Bown, T.M., "An Old Kingdom Basalt Quarry at Widan el–Faras and the Quarry Road to Lake Moeris," *Journal of the American Research Center in Egypt*, Vol. 32 (1995), 90–91.

11. A nearby camp exhibits circular concentrations of basalt fragments. Instead of large boulders, the fragments are mostly only of sizes that would be useful as tent weights. Harrell and Bown interpret these stone circles as shelters. There are few large fragments, and no large broken blocks. Harrell, J.A., and Bown, T.M., "An Old Kingdom Basalt Quarry at Widan el–Faras and the Quarry Road to Lake Moeris," *Journal of the American Research Center in Egypt*, Vol. 32 (1995), 77.

12. Harrell, J.A., and Bown, T.M., "An Old Kingdom Basalt Quarry at Widan el–Faras and the Quarry Road to Lake Moeris," *Journal of the American Research Center in Egypt*, Vol. 32 (1995), 74–6.

13. GEOCISTEM, published in proceedings available online at the Geopolymer Institute's Web site.

14. For the synthetic basalt, refer to Stone, E.C., Lindsley, D.H., Pigott, V., Harbottle, G., Ford, M.T., "From Shifting Silt to Solid Stone: The Manufacture of Synthetic Basalt in Ancient Mesopotamia," *Science* (June 1998), Vol. 280, no 5372, 2091–93. For the Giza paving slabs, refer to R. Hamilton, Senior Research Physicist, Manville Service Corp., Denver, Colorado, June 1989, published in Moores, R., "Evidence for Use of a Stone–Cutting Drag Saw for the Fourth Dynasty Egyptians," *Journal of the American Research Center in Egypt*, XVIII (1991), 139.

15. For the studies, refer to Lucas, A., *Ancient Egyptian Materials and Industries*, Mineola, N.Y., Dover Publications (1999 1962), 62; Blanchkenhorn, M., in Hume, W.F., *Geology of Egypt*, 3,2, Egyptian Geological Survey, Cairo (1965), 719–20. For the paving slabs next to the Great Pyramid, refer to Adams, F.D., 270–271 in Dawson, J.A.W., "Notes on Useful and Ornamental Stones in Ancient Egypt," *Journal of the Transactions of the Victoria Institute*, London (1884), 265–83; Hamilton, R., published in Moores, R., "Evidence for Use of a Stone–Cutting Drag Saw for the Fourth Dynasty Egyptians," *Journal of the American Research Center in Egypt*, XL (1991), 139.

16. Hamilton, R., published in Moores, R., "Evidence for Use of a Stone–Cutting Drag Saw for the Fourth Dynasty Egyptians," *Journal of the American Research Center in Egypt*, XVIII (1991), 139.

17. Harrell, J.A., and Bown, T.M., "An Old Kingdom Basalt Quarry at Widan el–Faras and the Quarry Road to Lake Moeris," *Journal of the American Research Center in Egypt*, Vol. 32 (1995), 76.

18. Hamilton, R., published in Moores, R., "Evidence for Use of a Stone–Cutting Drag Saw for the Fourth Dynasty Egyptians," *Journal of the American Research Center in Egypt*, XVIII (1991), 139.

19. Aston, B.G., Harrell, J.A., and Shaw, I, "Stones" (Chap. 2), in Nicholson, P.T., and Shaw, I. (eds.), *Ancient Egyptian Materials and Technology*, University of Cambridge Press, Cambridge (2000), 5–77.

20. Lucas, A., *Ancient Egyptian Materials and Industries*, Mineola, N.Y., Dover Publications (1999 1962), 61.
21. Lucas, A., *Ancient Egyptian Materials and Industries*, Mineola, N.Y., Dover Publications (1999 1962), 61.
22. Lucas, A., *Ancient Egyptian Materials and Industries*, Mineola, N.Y., Dover Publications (1999 1962), 61–62.
23. Harrell, J.A., and Bown, T.M., "An Old Kingdom Basalt Quarry at Widan el–Faras and the Quarry Road to Lake Moeris," *Journal of the American Research Center in Egypt*, Vol. 32 (1995), 78.
24. Harrell, J.A., and Bown, T.M., "An Old Kingdom Basalt Quarry at Widan el–Faras and the Quarry Road to Lake Moeris," *Journal of the American Research Center in Egypt*, Vol. 32 (1995), 79.
25. Harrell, J.A., and Bown, T.M., "An Old Kingdom Basalt Quarry at Widan el–Faras and the Quarry Road to Lake Moeris," *Journal of the American Research Center in Egypt*, Vol. 32 (1995), 79.
26. Harrell, J.A., and Bown, T.M., "An Old Kingdom Basalt Quarry at Widan el–Faras and the Quarry Road to Lake Moeris," *Journal of the American Research Center in Egypt*, Vol. 32 (1995), 79.
27. Harrell, J.A., and Bown, T.M., "An Old Kingdom Basalt Quarry at Widan el–Faras and the Quarry Road to Lake Moeris," *Journal of the American Research Center in Egypt*, Vol. 32 (1995), 82.
28. Aston, B.G., Harrell, J.A., and Shaw, I, "Stones" (Chap. 2), in Nicholson, P.T., and Shaw, I. (eds.), *Ancient Egyptian Materials and Technology*, University of Cambridge Press, Cambridge (2000), 5–77.
29. Harrell, J.A., and Bown, T.M., "An Old Kingdom Basalt Quarry at Widan el–Faras and the Quarry Road to Lake Moeris," *Journal of the American Research Center in Egypt*, Vol. 32 (1995), 81.
30. Shipping could only be accomplished between late August and early October, according to Harrell J.A., and Bown, T.M., "An Old Kingdom Basalt Quarry at Widan el–Faras and the Quarry Road to Lake Moeris," *Journal of the American Research Center in Egypt*, Vol. 32 (1995), 83–85.
31. Cerny, J., Gardiner, A., Peet, T.E., *The Inscriptions of Sinai I, II*, London and Oxford (1952 1955) nos. 110, 114. Or refer to Arnold, D., *Building in Egypt: pharaonic stone masonry*, New York N.Y., Oxford University Press (1991), 58, in which he states, "And the sign of these animals packed with a heavy basket full of soil was certainly as familiar to the ancient Egyptian builders as it is to us. Horses and camels were not used for carrying in Pharaonic Egypt, and cattle were only used for pulling."
32. The largest actual chunk in the area that can be interpreted as a block (rather than a boulder weighs over three tons. It appears in the area interpreted as the quay at Lake Moeris itself. For a photograph of the unit, refer to Harrell, J.A., and Bown, T.M., "An Old Kingdom Basalt Quarry at Widan el–Faras and the Quarry Road to Lake Moeris," *Journal of the American Research Center in Egypt*, Vol. 32 (1995), 82, fig. 16. The abandoned chunk or block may fit with Roman activity because, as mentioned, if massive units were extensively quarried during the Old Kingdom there should be hundreds of thousands of prominent tool marks in the quarries. There should be evidence that large boulders were moved along the ground, but no such evidence exists. The surface of the quay is, according to Harrell and Bown, "strewn with smaller basalt fragments that, like those along the roadside, appear to have been derived from larger blocks that disintegrated in place." Ibid., 86. For the Roman quarrying in the area, refer to ibid., 86.
33. Harrell, J.A., and Bown, T.M., "An Old Kingdom Basalt Quarry at Widan el–Faras and the Quarry Road to Lake Moeris," *Journal of the American Research Center in Egypt*, Vol. 32 (1995), 82.
34. For the evidence, including timber, at el–Lahun, refer to Arnold, D., *Building in Egypt: pharaonic stone masonry*, New York, N.Y., Oxford University Press (1991), 86–90. Compare Harrell, J.A. and Bown, T.M., "An Old Kingdom Basalt Quarry at Widan el–Faras and the Quarry Road to Lake Moeris," *Journal of the American Research Center in Egypt*, Vol. 32 (1995), 82–83. For the tracks at el–Lisht, refer to Lehner, M., *The Complete Pyramids, Solving the Ancient Mysteries*, Thames and Hudson (1997), 202–203.

Chapter 24: More Hard-Rock Proof

1. Metamorphism in a geological sense implies considerable heat, pressure, and time. The process and conditions in geopolymerization are distinct from this general usage.

2. Geopolymer, whether used as a pure binder or with an aggregate, will result in stone that is an amorphous zeolitic rock, containing alumina and silica, but initially without any internal form or order. A rearrangement of the alumina and silica into ordered crystal structures has been observed by Joseph Davidovits to occur in his geopolymers within 20 years. The result is analogous to the natural geological process called sausseritization, a change in the mineral structure of plagioclase feldspars. Feldspar is a large class of aluminosilicate minerals containing sodium, potassium, calcium, and quartz. Depending on the proportion, minerals in this group have different characteristics and are given different names. Plagioclase is a subset containing sodium or calcium.

3   The following is from an unpublished paper by Joseph Davidovits concerning his synthetic basalt and lava: "...synthetic lava-based Geocistem binders set at ambient temperature (in Egypt up to 65°C) or at temperature below 100°C. The resulting modern matrix is X-ray amorphous and is coined 'vitreous matrix' by geologists...The characterization is uncertain because very little is known about how 4,000-year archaeological aging infers on the mineralogical evolution of the vitreous matrix. However, electron microprobe quantitative analysis shows that the vitreous matrix is not homogeneous in composition, but is instead constituted of various aluminosilicate rock-forming candidates ranging from chain, branched (sheet) and network aluminosilicates. Thirty-seven microprobe quantitative analyses were carried out by the Bureau de Recherches Géologiques et Minières (research project GEOCISTEM). The atomic Si:Al ratio in the vitreous matrix range between 1.5 and 5.05 corresponding to tecto-alumino-silicate, branched and chain silicate gels. Because of the hydrated nature of the vitreous matrix, archaeological aging might induce the crystallization of amphiboles and plagioclases. Thus, with a technology inspired from the one developed for the making of Thinite and Nagadian statuettes at 600–900°C, it is theoretically possible to let the vitreous matrix crystallize into hard stone constituents (amphibole, plagioclase) such as those found in Egyptian diorite gneiss stone artifacts...X–ray powder diagrams confirmed the amorphous structure of the quenched Geocistem lava, which was further characterized with solid state MAS–NMR spectrometry (Fig. 3)....The interpretation of the corresponding 29Si and 27Al MAS–NMR spectrometry for Geocistem lavas suggests a structure containing glassy ferro–amphibole (for example ferropargasite with low MgO content) or glassy alkali pyroxene (augite–jadeite series), embedded in a glassy alumino–silicate matrix..."

4. Aston, B.G. (Barbara Greene), *Ancient Egyptian stone vessels: materials and forms*, Heidelberg: Heidelberger Orientverlag (1994), xix, [196 pages] (Studien zur Archaologie und Geschichte Altagyptens), 32–33.

5. Chlorite is often green but can be white, yellow, red, lavender or black. Both mica and chlorite result from saussuritization, which involves the replacement of plagioclase by epidote–zoisite–clinozoisite. These secondary minerals give the rock a greenish color. The granodiorite samples examined by Harrell do not show saussuritization.

6. Aston, B.G. (Barbara Greene), *Ancient Egyptian stone vessels: materials and forms*, Heidelberg: Heidelberger Orientverlag (1994), xix, [196 pages] (Studien zur Archaologie und Geschichte Altagyptens 5), 33.

7. Aston, B.G. (Barbara Greene), *Ancient Egyptian stone vessels: materials and forms,* Heidelberg: Heidelberger Orientverlag (1994), xix, [196 pages] (Studien zur Archaologie und Geschichte Altagyptens 5), 31. Aston describes artifact granodiorite as follows on pages 32–33: "To be even more precise, this rock would be called hornblende granodiorite....This is a fine–grained black and white speckled rock where the small size of the grains (> 2 mm) gives the overall rock a grey appearance, it is composed primarily of plagioclase (45%) and hornblende (30%), but also contains 15–20% quartz and 5% potassium feldspar. Micro accessory minerals include 3% opaque oxides, sphene, and apatite. The heavily saussuritized feldspars indicate that the rock has been altered. It is notable that most of the mineral grains lack developed crystal faces. In identifying this rock without a thin section, the grey color and black and white speckled appearance might

suggest that it should be classed as a diorite; however, the high percentage of quartz actually puts it with the granites. The thin section reveals that it has a composition between diorite and granite and falls into the category of granodiorite in the detailed classification of Streeckeisen I (see Figure 4)."

8.   The sarcophagi in the Serapeum, dating from the 19th Dynasty, are commonly called basalt in Egyptological literature. But, according to geologist James A. Harrell, most of the sarcophagi are granodiorite.

9.   Refer to the quote by Joseph Davidovits in his *Geopolymer Tribune* at his Web site: http://www.geopolymer.org/cgi/doc/dcforum/forum/archeo/10.html

10. Aston, B.G. (Barbara Greene), *Ancient Egyptian stone vessels: materials and forms*, Heidelberg: Heidelberger Orientverlag (1994), xix, [196 pages] (Studien zur Archaologie und Geschichte Altagyptens), 23.

11. Aston, B.G. (Barbara Greene), *Ancient Egyptian stone vessels: materials and forms*, Heidelberg: Heidelberger Orientverlag (1994), xix, [196 pages] (Studien zur Archaologie und Geschichte Altagyptens), 23.

12. The crystal size in plutonic rocks will range between fine–grained (below 1 mm), medium–grained (1–5 mm), coarse–grained (3–30 mm), or very coarse (above 3 cm). In composites cemented with a geopolymeric binder, a combination of these crystal-size ranges will be present depending upon the rock debris used. The geopolymer cement itself can be expected to crystallize over time, thereby altering the mineralogical classification of the artifact rock.

13. Aston, B.G. (Barbara Greene), *Ancient Egyptian stone vessels: materials and forms*, Heidelberg: Heidelberger Orientverlag (1994), xix, [196 pages] (Studien zur Archaologie und Geschichte Altagyptens), 25. According to Aston, "Gabbro occurs in the Precambrian rocks of the Red Sea Hills at Wadi Sodmein (north of Wadi Hammamat) and in Wadi Barramiya, but not at Aswan. The two stone vessel samples I have identified as gabbro are both fragments of vessels from the Mycerinus Valley Temple where gabbro comprises a small percentage of the black and white plutonic rocks present, the majority of which are hornblende diorite. Thus, on the present evidence, the use of gabbro for vessels is restricted to the Fourth Dynasty, and is probably connected with the extensive exploitation of the similar appearing hornblende diorite (of Type A) at that time." Ibid., 25

14. Aston, B.G. (Barbara Greene), *Ancient Egyptian stone vessels: materials and forms,* Heidelberg: Heidelberger Orientverlag (1994), xix, [196 pages] (Studien zur Archaologie und Geschichte Altagyptens), 408.

15. Aston, B.G. (Barbara Greene), *Ancient Egyptian stone vessels: materials and forms*, Heidelberg: Heidelberger Orientverlag (1994), xix, [196 pages] (Studien zur Archaologie und Geschichte Altagyptens), 408.

16. While Alfred Lucas did not try to identify the sources for all diorites, he suggested that the coarse black and white speckled diorite came from Aswan. Refer to Lucas, A., *Ancient Egyptian Materials and Industries*, 4th Edition, Mineola, N.Y., Dover Publications (1962), 409.

17. Aston, B.G. (Barbara Greene), *Ancient Egyptian stone vessels: materials and forms,* Heidelberg: Heidelberger Orientverlag (1994), xix, [196 pages] (Studien zur Archaologie und Geschichte Altagyptens), 31.

18. Aston, B.G. (Barbara Greene), *Ancient Egyptian stone vessels: materials and forms*, Heidelberg: Heidelberger Orientverlag (1994), xix, [196 pages] (Studien zur Archaologie und Geschichte Altagyptens), 32.

19. Ball, J., *A Description of the First or Aswan Cataract of the Nile*, Cairo, National Print Dept. (1907), 80.

20. Middleton, A. and Klemm, D., "The geology of the Rosetta stone," *Journal of Egyptian archaeology* (2003), Vol. 89, pp. 207-216.

21. Dawson, J.A.W., "Notes on Useful and Ornamental Stones in Ancient Egypt," *Journal of the Transactions of the Victoria Institute*, London (1884), 268.

Endnotes 357

22. Dawson, J.A.W., "Notes on Useful and Ornamental Stones in Ancient Egypt," *Journal of the Transactions of the Victoria Institute*, London (1884), 270.
23. McFarlane, Joanna (Univ. Toronto, ON, Canada), Wilson-Yang, Kristine M., Joseph, Sidney, Frey, Carla, Burns, George, "The mechanisms of the physicochemical reactions in diorite used in the construction of ancient royal Egyptian statues," *Canadian Journal of Chemistry*, 61 (4), p. 718–723, illus. incl. 3 anal., 19 refs (1983), 718–723.
24. The description of the quartz diorite samples analyzed by J. McFarlane, et al. reads: "The thin sections revealed that the rocks under investigation were quartz diorites, as there was 10 to 15% quartz in the KG-1 sample and 30% quartz present in the Deir el-Bahri rocks. The plagioclase, a sodium-calcium aluminosilicate, of the Deir el-Bahri rocks had been altered to clay minerals to a greater extent than the Karnak plagioclase, which also contained some muscovite. More biotite, but less apatite, was observed in the KG-1 thin section than in those of DG-1 and DG-2. Large crystals of magnetite and 1 grain of calcite were seen in all the samples. The KG-1 rocks also contained hematite, and very small amounts of feldspar and zircon. Approximately 10% hornblend was noticed in the Deir el-Bahri rocks." Refer to McFarlane, Joanna (Univ. Toronto, ON, Canada), Wilson-Yang, Kristine M., Joseph, Sidney, Frey, Carla, Burns, George, "The mechanisms of the physicochemical reactions in diorite used in the construction of ancient royal Egyptian statues," *Canadian Journal of Chemistry*, 61 (4) (1983), 720. I do not have a detailed description of quarry samples for comparison. Harrell described his sample of the quarry rock as "Quartz diorite: speckled white, pale green and dark green, fine- to medium-grained [Precambrian basement]….Location: in Wadi Qattar near Gebel Umm Disi—not a true quarry but rather an exploratory prospect [27d 4.75m N, 33d 14.15m E] (R: unknown ca. AD)….Two varieties of quartz diorite [Precambrian basement]: (a) Yellowish-white to light gray and spotted with large, isolated blocky to ovoid greenish-black crystals, medium- to mainly coarse-grained (from the lower quarry workings). (b) Light gray with irregular, interconnected patches of greenish-black grains, medium- to coarse-grained (from the upper quarry workings)." Harrell was referring to Roman quarrying. The information from Harrell comes from his Web site, where there are also photographs of his samples:
http://www.eeescience.utoledo.edu/faculty/harrell/egypt/Quarries/Hardst_Quar.html
25. McFarlane, J., Wilson-Yang, Kristine, M., Joseph, S., Frey, C., Burns, G., "The mechanisms of the physicochemical reactions in diorite used in the construction of ancient royal Egyptian statues," *Canadian Journal of Chemistry*, 61 (4), 718–723, illus. incl. 3 anal., 19 refs (1983), 720.
26. Klemm D., and Klemm R., *Steine und Steinbrüche im Alten Ägypten*, Springer-Verlag, Berlin (1993), 183–185. The translation of the quote from German to English is by Joseph Davidovits.
27. Klemm D., and Klemm R., *Steine und Steinbrüche im Alten Ägypten*, Springer-Verlag, Berlin (1993), 183–185. The translation of the quote from German to English is by Joseph Davidovits.
28. Klemm D., and Klemm R., *Steine und Steinbrüche im Alten Ägypten*, Springer-Verlag, Berlin (1993), 183–185. The translation of the quote from German to English is by Joseph Davidovits.
29. D Klemm D., and Klemm R., *Steine und Steinbrüche im Alten Ägypten*, Springer-Verlag, Berlin (1993), 183–185. The translation of the quote from German to English is by Joseph Davidovits.
30. Engelbach, R., "The quarries of the Western Nubian Desert and the ancient road to Tushka," *Annales du Service des Antiquités de l'Egypte* 38 (1938), 372.
31. Engelbach, R., "The quarries of the Western Nubian Desert and the ancient road to Tushka," *Annales du Service des Antiquités de l'Egypte* 38 (1938), 372.
32. At the quarry sites, many ceramic pieces were found dating from the Old Kingdom to the Middle Kingdom, including a set of 22 intact flat-bottomed storage jars dating to the 12th Dynasty. The latter were found at the settlement called Quartz Ridge. This type of jar was used to transport or store dry materials, like grain. The pots would be useful for carrying rock debris. Pot shards were also found from about the time of Khufu, according to the Shaw team. Refer to Shaw, I., "Khafra's quarries in the Sahara," *Egyptian Archaeology: Bulletin of the Egypt Exploration Society* 16 (2000): 29–30.

33. Engelbach, R., "The quarries of the Western Nubian Desert and the ancient road to Tushka," *Annales du Service des Antiquités de l'Egypte*, 38 (1938), 389.

34. If we assume that the 1-meter-high stele of Khufu found at this location is all natural rock (with no surface coating of geopolymer), copper chisels were not the instruments used to inscribe it. Engelbach describes Khufu's stela as black granite, which also ranges from 5 to 6 on Mohs scale. Refer to Engelbach, R., "The quarries of the Western Nubian Desert and the ancient road to Tushka," *Annales du Service des Antiquités de l'Egypte*, 38 (1938), 371, pl. LV). A sharp crystal made of the precious gem topaz (Mohs' 8), quartz (Mohs' 7) or possibly agate (Mohs' 6.5–7) would be required to scratch the rock. I have not seen the quality of Khufu's inscriptions on his desert stela.

35. Waelkens, M., De Paepe, P., Moens, L. "The Quarrying Techniques of the Greek World," *Marbl – Art Historical and Scientific Perspectives on Ancient Sculpture*, J. Paul Getty Museum, Malib (1990), 62–63.

36. Refer to Roder, J., "Zur steinbruchgeschichte des rosengranits von Assuan," *Archalogische Anzeiger* 3, Jahrbuch des Deutschen Archaeologischen Instituts (1965), 467–552.

37. Clarke, S., Engelbach, R., *Ancient Egyptian Masonry: The Building Craft*, London, Oxford University Press, Milford (1930) 31.

38. Harrell, J.A., "Ancient stone quarries at the Third and Fourth Nile Cataracts, northern Sudan," *Sudan and Nubia* (1999), n. 3, 27.

39. Clarke, S., Engelbach, R., *Ancient Egyptian Masonry: The Building Craft*, London, Oxford University Press, Milford (1930), 27.

40. Harrell, J.A., "Ancient stone quarries at the Third and Fourth Nile Cataracts, northern Sudan," *Sudan and Nubia* (1999), n. 3, 25.

41. Harrell, J.A., "Ancient stone quarries at the Third and Fourth Nile Cataracts, northern Sudan," *Sudan and Nubia* (1999), n. 3, 27.

42. Harrell, J.A., "Ancient stone quarries at the Third and Fourth Nile Cataracts, northern Sudan," *Sudan and Nubia* (1999), n. 3, 26.

Chapter 25: Simplifying Obelisks and Colossi

1. Lasers have been suggested for cutting stone by proponents of ancient high technology. This creates irreconcilable historical problems. In addition, a laser beam melts stone, creating a glassy texture. The stone is vaporized rather than cut. Laser cutting is successful when materials being cut have melting and boiling points that are very close. So, a laser can mark stone, but it does not drill or cut it cleanly.

2. For the tiny stone beads, refer to Lucas, A., *Ancient Egyptian Materials and Industries*, Mineola N.Y., Dover Publications (1999 1962), 44.

3. For a large color depiction of the stele of Djehutihotep, refer to Baines, J., Malek, J., *Atlas of Ancient Egypt*. Facts on File Publications, N.Y. (1980), 126–127.

4. Labib Habachi, *The Obelisks of Egypt: Skyscrapers of the Past*, The American University in Cairo Press, Cairo (1986), 203 pp. For Engelbach's study of Aswan, refer to *The Aswan Obelisk, with Some Remarks on the Ancient Engineering*, Cairo (1922), 57 pp. Also refer to Engelbach, *The Problem of the Obelisks, From a Study of the Unfinished Obelisk at Aswan*, T. F. Unwin, limited London (1923), 134 pp.

5. For Engelbach's study of Aswan, refer to *The Aswan Obelisk, with Some Remarks on the Ancient Engineering*, Cairo (1922). Also refer to Engelbach, *The Problem of the Obelisks, From a Study of the Unfinished Obelisk at Aswan*, T. F. Unwin, limited, London (1923), 134 pp.

6. Engelbach, R., *The Aswan Obelisk, with Some Remarks on the Ancient Engineering*, Cairo (1922) 36–43; Engelbach, R., *The Problem of the Obelisks, From a Study of the Unfinished Obelisk at Aswan*, T. F. Unwin, limited, London (1923), 66–84.

7. Arnold, D., *Building in Egypt: pharaonic stone masonry*, New York, N.Y., Oxford University Press (1991), 68.

8. Arnold, D., *Building in Egypt: pharaonic stone masonry*, New York, N.Y., Oxford University Press (1991), 67–69. Hodges, P., *How the Great Pyramids Were Built*, Element Books, Wilshire (1989), 11.

9. For Engelbach's studies of obelisks, refer to Engelbach, R., *The Aswan Obelisk, with Some Remarks on the Ancient Engineering*, Cairo (1922); Engelbach, R., *The Problem of the Obelisks, From a Study of the Unfinished Obelisk at Aswan*, T. F. Unwin, limited, London (1923), 134 pp.

10. Arnold, D., *Building in Egypt: pharaonic stone masonry*, New York, N.Y., Oxford University Press (1991), 62. "No higher obelisks [than the Lateran obelisk of Tuthmosis III weighing 445 to 500 tons] could be removed from the quarries or transported and erected, and the mention of 100–cubit obelisks (52.5 meters) of Hatshepsut certainly was a fairy tale."

11. Pliny, *Natural History*, XXXVI, 8–9.

12. Arnold, D., *Building in Egypt: pharaonic stone masonry*, New York, N.Y., Oxford University Press (1991), 40.

13. Arnold, D., *Building in Egypt: pharaonic stone masonry*, New York, N.Y., Oxford University Press (1991).

14. For Denys Stocks hieroglyphic incision in rose granite, refer to D. Stocks, *Popular Archaeology* (July 1986), 25–28.

15. For details, refer to Engelbach, R., *The Aswan Obelisk, with Some Remarks on the Ancient Engineering*, Cairo (1922) and Engelbach, R., *The Problem of the Obelisks, From a Study of the Unfinished Obelisk at Aswan*, T. F. Unwin, limited, London (1923). 134 pp.

16. Doumato, L., *The Temple Ruins of Baalbek*, Vance Bibliographies, Monticello, Ill. (1979) [9 pages], Series: Architecture series.

17. Clarke, S., Engelbach, R., *Ancient Egyptian Construction and Architecture*, Dover pub., N.Y. (1990). 242 pp.

18. For the quote, refer to Engelbach, R., *The Problem of the Obelisks, From a Study of the Unfinished Obelisk at Aswan*, T. F. Unwin, limited, London (1923), 57. Another impressionistic document dates to the reign of the Greek Pharaoh Ptolemaios XII Neos Dionysos. The king is shown in superhuman size pulling up two obelisks at once with a rope. The obelisks reach to about the top of his legs in the depiction. Although the scene is impressionistic, the method of using ropes is not unlikely for this late period. The Greeks used iron-wedge quarrying, too. For the depiction, refer to Arnold, D., *Building in Egypt: pharaonic stone masonry*, New York, N.Y., Oxford University Press (1991), 70, Fig. 3.14.

19. For the quote, refer to Engelbach, R., *The Problem of the Obelisks, From a Study of the Unfinished Obelisk at Aswan*, T. F. Unwin, limited, London (1923), 67.

Chapter 26: Ancient Literary Testimony

1. Pliny, *Natural History*, XXXVI. 8-9.

2. Pliny, *Natural History.* XXXVI, 14.

3. History of Herodotus II, 155.

4. Wilkinson, J.G., *The Manners and Customs of the Ancient Egyptians*, New ed. rev. and corrected by Samuel Birch, London, J. Murray (1879). 307.

5. Wilkinson, J.G., *The Manners and Customs of the Ancient Egyptians*, New ed. rev. and corrected by Samuel Birch, London, J. Murray (1879), 307.

6. Wehausen, J.V., "The Colossi of Memnon and Egyptian Barges," *International Journal of Nautical Archaeology and Underwater Exploration* (1988), v. 17, no. 4., Table 1, p. 297.

7. Clarke, S., Engelbach, R., *Ancient Egyptian Masonry: The Building Craft*, London, Oxford University Press, Milford (1930), 38–40.

8. Wehausen, J.V., "The Colossi of Memnon and Egyptian Barges," *International Journal of Nautical Archaeology and Underwater Exploration* (1988), v. 17, no. 4., Table 1, p. 297.

9. Abdel–Satar, A.M. and Elewa, A.A. "Water quality and environmental assessments of the River Nile at Rosetta Branch." Proceeding of the 2nd International Conference and Exhibition for Life and Environment, April 3–5, 2001, Alexandria, Egypt, 136–164.

10. Pliny, *Natural History*, XXXVI. 8–9.

11. Private correspondence with George Gardiner, September 2002.

12. Thomas Witlam Atkinson, *Travels in the regions of the upper and lower Amoor, and the Russian acquisitions on the confines of India and China*, London, Hurst and Blackett (1860), 117.

13. Arnold, D., *Building in Egypt: pharaonic stone masonry*, New York, N.Y., Oxford University Press (1991), 65–66.

14. *The New Jerusalem Bible*, Doubleday & Company, Inc. Garden City, New York, (1985), 106. The Mosaic Law appears also in Deuteronomy 27:5. "And there you shall build an altar to the Lord your God, an altar of stones; you shall lift up no iron tool." Refer to ibid., 255. The passage reads, "You must build the altar of Yahweh your God of rough stones, and on this altar you will present burnt offerings to Yahweh you God, and immolate communion sacrifices and eat them there, rejoicing in the presence of Yahweh your God. On these stones you must write all the words of this Law; cut them carefully." Note that the ancient word is here translated as "rough stones." Something is lost in the translation. Joshua built an altar of unhewn stones on Mount Ebal (Josh 8:31, p. 294). There, following the instructions of Moses, he "coated stones with lime" and inscribed words of the Law (Deut. 27:1–8, p. 255; Josh. 8:32, p. 294). What has been preserved in present translations is that the sacred altar stones were unhewn and that lime was involved. In the Septuagint, the word is "bomos," meaning a high, raised rectangular altar. A large horned altar used for animal sacrifice, stood in the court of Solomon's Temple. Refer to Kings I 1:50, Kings I 2:28–34. Similar altars have been found and some have been reconstructed. They are made of regular blocks, not rough field stones. A small limestone altar, with stylized horns at the corners and a rectangular base, is thought to have been built by King Solomon. It was excavated from a level of Megiddo dating from the 10th century B.C. It is thought to have been used for offerings of incense, wine, and grain mixed with oil, rather than for animal sacrifice. In the Israelite town of Beer–Sheva, stones of a large altar were found built into the walls of later structures. Many of the stones were identified, allowing the altar to be partially reconstructed. It, too, is made of regular stones that fit together, not "rough stones." Within the Jerusalem Temple was the court of Israel and of the priests, in which stood a 15-foot-high altar of unhewn stones. The altar, built according to Mosaic Law (Ex. 20:25) was 48 feet square at the bottom and 36 feet at the top. Also refer to Isaiah 19:19 for a reference to an altar of the Lord in the midst of Egypt.

15. Herodotus, *The History of Herodotus*, II, 125. Herodotus also uses the word *krossai*, which literally means "altar steps"; refer to W.W. How and J. Wells, *A Commentary on Herodotus* (1989), 472 pp. So, some translators render steps and stairs, but this sacred connotation is not generally stressed.

16. Josephus, *Antiquities of the Jews*, Book 8, William Whiston's translation reads "Now the whole structure of the temple was made with great skill of polished stones, and those laid together so very harmoniously and smoothly, that there appeared to the spectators no sign of any hammer or other instrument of architecture; but as if, without any use of them, the entire materials had naturally united themselves together, that the agreement of one part with another seemed rather to have been natural, than to have arisen from the force of tools upon them." In other words, these were not unhewn or rough field stones. They were building units made without the use of tools. It is logical to suggest the use of agglomerated stone, which was once a sacred technology used in accordance with Mosaic Law.

17. *The New Jerusalem Bible*, Doubleday & Company, Inc. Garden City, New York, (1985), 439. The translation from this source reads, "The building of the Temple was done with quarry-dressed stone; no sound of hammer or pick or any iron tool was to be heard in the Temple while it was being built." Something is lost in the modern translations, given that it defies Mosaic Law (Ex.20: 25), which specifies that no tools shall be lifted upon the sacred altar stones (*bomos, Septuagint*) This compares to the pyramid stones or *bomidas* (see Herodotus).

18. Borekes (Hebrew), emerald (Catholic), carbuncle (King James); Nofek (Hebrew), carbuncle (Catholic), ruby (Josephus); emerald (King James); ihalom (Hebrew), diamond (King James); jasper (Josephus); leshem (Hebrew), agate (Catholic), lingure (Josephus), opal (Protestant); schebo

(Hebrew), hyacinth (Catholic), amethyst (Josephus), agate (Protestant and King James); ahlama (Hebrew), amethyst (Catholic), agate (Josephus), tarchisch (Hebrew), chrysolite (Catholic), beryl (King James), shoham (Hebrew), cornaline (Catholic), onyx (Josephus).

19. Manetho was a 3rd century B.C. Egyptian Ptolemaic priest and historian. His Greek *Aegyptiaca of Manetho* was a history of Egypt, of which only fragments survive. His *Aegyptiaca of Manetho* organized Egypt's pharaohs into thirty dynasties that roughly corresponded to families. Refer to Waddell, W.G., *Manetho, With an English Translation*, Loeb Classical Library, London and New York (1997 edition), 40–41. For the discussion of *xestos (xeston) lithon* by Davidovits J., and Joseph Davidovits, F., refer to the 2001 version of *The Pyramids: An Enigma Solved*, available in e–format from the Geopolymer Institute Web site.

20. Davidovits, J., Morris, M., *The Pyramids: An Enigma Solved*, Hippocrene, N.Y. (1988), 129–130.

21. For Leviticus 2:13, refer to *The New Jerusalem Bible*, Doubleday & Company, Inc. Garden City, New York (1985), 135.

22. For Proverbs 25:20, refer to *The New Jerusalem Bible*, Doubleday & Company, Inc. Garden City, New York (1985), 1001.

23. Diodorus, *Library of History*, Book I, 63 (Oldfather translation).

24. Contendings of Horus and Seth (translated by Edward F. Wente), in *The Literature of Ancient Egypt*, ed. William Kelly Simpson, Yale University Press, New Haven (1972), 108–26. Gardiner, A.H., "*The Contendings of Horus and Seth*," The Chester Beatty Papyri, Oxford (1931). "Contendings of Horus and Seth," James, T.G.H., *Myths and Legends of Ancient Egypt* (1971). "The Contendings of Horus and Seth" as found in the Ramesside Papyrus, Chester Beatty I.

25. Davidovits, J., "Pyramid Man–Made Stone, Myths of Facts, III. The Famine Stele Provides the Hieroglyphic Names of Chemicals and Minerals Involved in the Construction," presented at the 5th International Congress of Egyptology, Cairo, 1988, published in the *Abstracts*, pp. 57–58. For ancient Egyptian minerals, refer to Harris, J.R., *Lexicographical Studies in Ancient Egyptian Minerals*, Akademie–Verlag, Berlin (1961), 262 pp.

26. For Herodotus' report, refer to Herodotus, *The history of Herodotus*, L. MacVeagh, The Dial press, New York, Longmans, Green & company, Toronto (1928), 124-126. We know that the Egyptians were using sulfur in their products resulting from mineral processing, at least in later times. Refer to Pliny, *Natural History*, Book 31, 8, Loeb Classical Library, translation by W.H.S. Jones, p. 447, which reads, "The soda–beds of Egypt used to be confined to the regions around Naucratis and Memphis, the beds around Memphis being inferior. For the soda becomes stonelike in heaps there, and many of the soda piles there are for the same reason quite rocky. From these they make vessels, and frequently by baking melted soda with sulfur."

27. For the Renaissance drawing of Imhotep as The Alchemist, refer to Wildung, D., *Egyptian Saints: Deification in Pharaonic Egypt*, New York University Press, New York (1977), 77.

28. For Ibn Umayl's report concerning Imhotep's temple in Abusir, refer to Wildung, D., *Egyptian Saints: Deification in Pharaonic Egypt*, New York University Press, New York (1977), 78.

29. Great alchemical works were ascribed to Pharaoh Khufu. Khufu's name is also rendered as Cheops, Keops, Suphis, Sophe, Chemmis, etc. Rosalie and Anthony E. David, *A Biographical Dictionary of Ancient Egypt*, Seaby, London (1992) state on page 32 (entry under "Cheops") that "In contrast with his reputation as a tyrant, Cheops was also accredited with great sacred wisdom and knowledge and was stated to be the author of a hermetic book. In fact, few verifiable details have survived…" Georges Posener, *A Dictionary of Egyptian Civilization*, Tudor, N.Y. (1959) p. 41 (entry under "Cheops or Suphis," article by Jean Yoyotte): "He himself boasted of knowing the 'number of caverns in the temple of Thoth,' the god of Wisdom, and the Hellenistic alchemists attributed to 'Suphis the Egyptian' the editorship of a hermetic book." The section concerning the caverns in the temple of Thoth may derive from the narrative in the Westcar Papyrus (ms. 3033 in the Egyptian Museum of Berlin), which contains a text reprinted as "King Cheops and the Magicians." Refer to Simpson, W.K., (ed.), *The Literature of Ancient Egypt*, Yale U Press, New Haven (1972), 22. The text is typical of ancient Egyptian wonder tales, which may

contain some hidden meaning recognizable to an ancient priestly adept. Also refer to the article on alchemy in the *Oxford Classical Dictionary*, p. 53, "Zosimus of Panopolis (mod. Ahmim), in Upper Egypt, fl. ca. A.D. 300, the author of a large work called *Imouth* (Imhotep) in 28 books, each designated by a letter of the alphabet. The Corpora preserve some fairly lengthy sections (the so-called 'authentic memoirs') reorganized on a didactic principle by a Byzantine compiler. The titles of some sections are known: the Book of Sophe' (Pharaoh Cheops)...." Jean Doresse, *Secret Books of the Egyptian Gnostics*, Viking Press, N.Y. (1960), p. 106 reads "In the world to which these writings transport us there were two impressive Wisdoms which claimed to eclipse all the others; one had to endeavour systematically to connect, with one or the other of these, any myth whatever upon which one wanted to confer prestige. Thus, we find an alchemical manuscript entitled A GENUINE DISCOURSE BY SOPHE [Cheops] THE EGYPTIAN, AND BY THE GOD OF THE HEBREWS, THE LORD OF THE LORD OF POWERS SABAOTH, 'for there are two sciences and two wisdoms: that of the Egyptians and that of the Hebrews.'" Refer to the footnote for this quotation referring to page 187 of Reitzenstein, Richard (1861–1931). *Studien zum antiken synkretismus aus Iran und Griechenland*, Leipzig, B. G. Teubner (1926).

30. For Diodorus' record of Khufu's name as Chemmis, refer to Diodorus, *Library of History*, Book I, Ch. 63, lines 6–7.

31. For an illustration of Khufu's name, refer to Davidovits, J., Morris, M., *The Pyramids: An Enigma Solved*, Hippocrene, N.Y. (1988), 115.

32. Wildung, D., *Egyptian Saints: Deification in Pharaonic Egypt,* New York University Press, New York (1977), 76, Fig. 77. For more on the Step Pyramid attributed to Imhotep, refer to Drioton, E., and Lauer, J.P., *Sakkarah, The Monuments of Zoser*, Cairo (1939); Firth, C.M., Quibell, J.E., and Lauer, J.P., *The Step Pyramid,* Volumes 1 and 2.], Cairo (1935–6). For more on Imhotep, refer to Hurry, J.B., *Imnotep, the Vizier and Physician of King Zoser, and Afterwards the Egyptian God of Medicine*, Oxford University Press, H. Milford, London (1926). Cormack, M., *Imhotep, Builder in Stone*, F. Watts, New York (1965), 112 pp.

33. The ancient Egyptian *Books of Thoth*, containing cosmogonic and alchemical writings, were translated (and partially corrupted) into the *Corpus Hermeticum (Hermetica)*. By definition, *Hermeticum* is directly associated with alchemy. Refer to *A New Dictionary of the Italian and English Languages; Based Upon that of Baretti*: comp. John Davenport & Guglielmo Comelati, London, Whittaker (1854), authors Baretti, Giuseppe Marco Antonio, 1719–1789, *Fetonte sulle rive del Po. Componimento drammatico per le nozze delle A.A.R.R. di Vittorio Amedeo duca di Savoja, e di Maria Antonia Ferdinanda infanta di Spagna, da cantarsi nel palazzo di Sua Eccellenza Fra'D. Emanuello De Sada e Antillon*, Torino, Pietro Giuseppe Zappata, e figlio, 1750), under the entry Ermetico [E: Ermétic–o] "pl. ci, che, hermetic, hermetical, belonging to alchemy; adv." Diodorus explained Isis and Osiris in terms of alchemical principles of water and fire. Refer to Diodorus, *Library of History*, Book I, 10.11. Empedocles, who postulated that the universe is made up of the alchemical elements of earth, fire, wind, and water, had access to earlier writings from Egypt. For example, the biographers of Homer, Thales of Milet, Pythagoras, and also Plato all claimed that these sages had visited Egypt. It was claimed that Plato went to Egypt to learn geometry and theology. Refer to Diodorus Siculus, *Library of History*, I, 69 (for Homer); Diogenes Laerce, *Thales*, 43 and 24, Porphyrius, *Life of Pythagoras*, 7; Olympiodorus, *Life of Plato* and Strabo's description of Egypt, XVII, I, 29, for Plato's visit to Heliopolis and how he spent thirteen years with the priests. Also refer to Plato, *Hippias Major, Hippias Minor, Ion, Menexenus, Cleitophon, Timaeus, Critias, Minos, Epinomis*: div1 Tim., section 56b [Timaeus], which reads, "Thus, in accordance with the right account and the probable, that solid which has taken the form of a pyramid shall be the element and seed of fire; the second in order of generation we shall affirm to be air, and the third water." When Auguste Mariette discovered the Serapeum, in the environs of Memphis, he found arranged in a "hemicycle" (semicircle) statues of Protagorus, Plato, and Homer, suggesting that the Serapeum Library was a place of higher learning that inspired Greek thinkers. Also see Wildung, D., *Egyptian Saints: Deification in Pharaonic Egypt*, New York University Press, New York (1977), 77–78.

4. For the worship of Imhotep in Greek times, refer to Wildung, D., *Egyptian Saints: Deification in Pharaonic Egypt*, New York University Press, New York (1977), 47–55.

5. For Imhotep at the head of the Memphite pantheon, refer to Wildung, D., *Egyptian Saints: Deification in Pharaonic Egypt*, New York University Press, New York (1977), 43.

6. Wildung, D., *Egyptian Saints: Deification in Pharaonic Egypt*, New York University Press, New York (1977), 31–32.

7. Egyptologists acknowledge the sudden rise in culture. Refer to Arnold, D., *Building in Egypt: pharaonic stone masonry*, New York, N.Y., Oxford University Press (1991), 66. On ibid., p. 3, Arnold wrote, "In the Third Dynasty (ca. 2700 B.C.), true stone architecture appeared cometlike with the mortuary complex of king Djoser at Saqqara. The existence of other primitive forerunners of this type is possible, but they remain beyond our grasp....Just a few generations after King Djoser, in the reigns of Snofru, Cheops, and Chephren, pyramids and pyramid temples of gigantic dimensions were erected with blocks weighing up to 200 tons. We know the reason neither for the sudden rise of stone architecture nor for its immediate development into superhuman dimensions."

8. During her mention of the museum item she witnessed and the observation of Egyptologists of her time, Blavatsky mentioned Carpenter's assertion. She was referring to Professor W.B. Carpenter, President of the British Association. See Blavatsky, H.P., *Isis Unveiled: A Master Key to the Mysteries of Ancient and Modern Science and Theology*, Theosophical University Press, Vol. I, 519. She gives no other references and does not provide the museum piece number.

9. Campbell, D.H., Folk, R.L., "The Great Pyramid Debate: The Ancient Egyptian Pyramids – Concrete or Rock? The cons of the cast–in–place theory," *Concrete International: Design and Construction*, American Concrete Institute, Detroit, Michigan (August 1991), Vol. 13, No. 8, 28–39. Morris, M., "The Great Pyramid Debate: The Cast–in–Place Theory of Pyramid Construction, the pros of geopolymeric construction" (August 1991), *Concrete International: Design and Construction*, American Concrete Institute, Detroit, Michigan, Vol. 13, no. 29, pp. 33–44; Folk, R.L., Campbell, D.H., "Are the Pyramids of Egypt built of poured concrete blocks?," *Journal of Geological Education*, The National Association of Geology Teachers, Madison, WI (1992), Vol. 40, No. 1, 25–34; Morris, M., "Geopolymeric Pyramids: A Rebuttal to R.L. Folk and D.H. Campbell," *Journal of Geological Education*, The National Association of Geology Teachers, Madison, WI, Vol. 40, No. 1 (January 1992), 35–46. Schoch, R.M., "Comment on the Folk and Campbell Article," *Journal of Geological Education*, Vol. 40, No. 1, 34; Folk, R.L., Letters (to the Editor), *Journal of Geological Education*, Vol. 40, No. 4 (September 1992), 344. Morris, M., Letters: Morris Responds to Folk and Campbell, *Journal of Geological Education*, The National Association of Geology Teachers, Madison, WI, Vol. 40, No. 4 (September 1992), 344–346. Harrell, J.A., Penrod, B.E., "The great Pyramid Debate – Evidence From the Lauer Sample," *Journal of Geological Education*, The National Association of Geology Teachers, Madison, WI, Vol. 41, No. 4 (September 1993), 358–363; "Morris, M., "How Not to Analyze a Pyramid Stone – The Invalid Conclusions of James A. Harrell and Bret E. Penrod," *Journal of Geological Education*, The National Association of Geology Teachers, Madison, WI, Vol. 41, No. 4, September 1993, 364–369; McKinney, R.G., "Comments on the Work of Harrell and Penrod," *Journal of Geological Education*, The National Association of Geology Teachers, Madison, WI, Vol. 41, No. 4, September 1993, 369; Harrell, J.A., Letters (to the Editor): "Harrell's Response to Morris' Article," *Journal of Geological Education*, The National Association of Geology Teachers, Madison, WI, Vol. 42, No. 2 (March 1994), 195–198; Morris, M., "Response (to Harrell in letters to the Editor)," *Journal of Geological Education*, The National Association of Geology Teachers, Madison, WI, Vol. 42, No. 2 (March 1994), 198–203; Ingram, K., Daugherty K., Marshall, J., "The Pyramids – Cement or Stone?" *Journal of Archaeological Science* (December, London 20 (1993), 681–687; Davidovits J., Zeller, E.J., and Morris, M., "Re–Assessing Ingram's Data" (submitted to the *Journal of Archaeological Science* in 1993, but unpublished, see Appendix 2 of this book).

40. Newberry, P.E., *The Life of Rekhmara*, Constable, London (1900), Fig. 1 shows brickmaking. For block cutting, see Plate XX. Mud bricks were made with Nile silt and straw formed in wooden molds and left to bake in the Sun. A cartouche or other inscription was stamped onto the brick before it got too hard. The ancient Egyptian word for brick was "debet," which came into modern English through Spanish as "adobe," meaning Sun–dried brick. Some mud bricks are extremely durable, like those bearing the cartouche of Ramses II incorporated into the Ramesseum. Ramses II reused many bricks bearing the names of his predecessors. Joseph Davidovits suspects that many bricks survived the centuries because natron, lime, and possibly kaolin clay were used. Sand will adhere and protect blocks made in this way.

41. Pliny, *Natural History*, Book 31, Vol. 8, Loeb Classical Library translation by W.H.S. Jones, p. 447, line 111. In Latin, "Nitrariae Aegpri circa Naucratim et Memphim tanturn solebant esse circa Memphim deteriores. Nam et lapidescit ibi in acervis: multique sunt cumuli ca de causa saxei. Faciunt ex his vasa..."

42. Pliny, *Natural History*, Book 37, "Date of the introduction of the murrhine vases and what they commemorated: VII. With this same victory came the introduction to Rome of the murrhine vases. Pompey was the first to dedicate murrhine cups and bowls to Jupiter in the Capitol. These vessels soon passed into daily use, and they were in demand for display and tableware. Lavish expenditure on these items increased daily: An ex–consul drank from a murrhine vessel for which he paid 70 talents although it held just three pints. He was so taken with the vessel that he gnawed its edges. The damage actually caused its value to increase, and today no murrhine vessel has a higher price upon it. The same man squandered vast sums to acquire other articles of this substance, which can be determined by their number, so high that when Nero robbed them from his children for display they filled the private theater in his gardens beyond the Tiber, a theater large enough to satisfy even Nero's urge to sing before a full house as he rehearsed for his appearance at Pompey's theater. It was at this event that I counted the pieces of a single broken vessel included in the exhibition. It was decided that the pieces, like the remains of Alexander the Great, should be preserved in an urn for display, presumably as a token of the sorrows and misfortune of the age. Before dying, the consul Titus Petronius, in order to spite Nero, had a mur-rhine bowl, valued at 30 talents, broken in order to deprive the Emperor's dining table of it. But Nero, as befitted an emperor, surpassed everyone else by paying 100 talents for a single vessel. It is a memorable fact that an emperor, head of the fatherland, should drink at such a high price."

43. Pliny, *Natural History*, Book 37.8.

44. Pliny, *Natural History*, Book 37.8 reads, "The murrhine vases come to us from the East. They are found there in various little–known places, especially in the kingdom of Parthia. The fin-est come from Carmania. They are said to be made of a liquid to which heat gives consistence when covered with earth. Their dimensions never exceed those of a small display stand. Rarely their thickness is no more than that of a drinking vessel such as mentioned. They are not very brilliant. They glisten rather than shine. What makes them fetch a high price is the varieties of shades, the veins, as they revolve, vary repeatedly from pink to white, or a combination of the two, the pink becoming fiery or the milk–white becoming red as the new shade merges through the vein. Some connoisseurs especially admire the edges of a piece, where the colors are reflected as in a rainbow. Others favor thick veins. Any transparency or fading is a flaw. Also there are the grains and the blisters which, like warts on human bodies, start just beneath the surface. The stone is also appreciated for its odor." The French academy study is quoted from a translation by Joseph Davidovits. Refer to Davidovits, J., Morris, M., *The Pyramids: An Enigma Solved*, Hippocrene, N.Y. (1988), 166–171. "The matter of the murrhine vases was discussed for a long time. According to Scaliger, Mariette, Lagrange, et al., it was porcelain that, in Roman times, was only made at the extremities of the known world (China, Japan, and Formosa), and which transported at great cost overland through the hands of twenty different people, must indeed have fetched an enormous price. But porcelain is artificial, and the variety of colors, the play of light on the murrhine surface, the stripes, and the wavy stains of which Pliny speaks, are no traits of porcelain. Moreover ...*humorem sub terra calore densari*...a liquid to which heat give

consistency when covered with earth, i.e., hardens when it is heated in clay, can hardly mean a manmade process analogous to that which transforms kaolin into porcelain. But from his description, the only natural substance with all the features described by Pliny is fluorite." Despite Pliny's description of a material that could only be fabricated, the French academy judged that the vases were natural fluorite. Their comments continue: "To identify fluorite in the midst of so many heterogeneous substances would have been difficult; to extract it, i.e., to isolate it and purify it, impossible. It was thus necessary to find native pieces of heterogeneous material with as little filler as possible. This was rare. Rarer still were pink crystallized samples, for pink is last in the order of abundance: greenish gray, white, yellow, violet, blue, honey yellow, and pink. It should be remembered that, even today, fine specimens of fluorite are used to make beautiful vases. Recently, fluorite was used to give a matte finish to porcelain statues which had become vitrified during firing." The French Academy members were here referring to fluorite use in producing hydrofluoric acid, of importance to ceramic production. When fluorite is dissolved in sulfuric acid, hydrofluoric acid is produced (hydrofluoric acid is useful for etching glass). Members of the French Academy interpreted Pliny's statement as follows: "...for which he paid 70 talents: Such incredible sums (70 talents) are almost beyond belief. Seventy talents equals almost 35,000 sovereigns in our money; and we shall be referring to a sum more than four times as great as this a little later—and all this for a vessel meant for the least auspicious applications. Any transparency or fading are flaws: Semi–transparency: this is confirmed below. The stone is also appreciated for its odor: This is one of the reasons to believe that the murrhine was artificial. Made of a liquid to which heat gives consistence: It is difficult to understand that heat can cause solidification. Normal experience is that when a solid is heated, it melts. Thus, we must consider the possible meanings of the expression, viz.: (1) evaporation followed by condensation, binding together of a magma, and still more likely, crystallization, (2) kinds of stalactites or stalagmites (remembering that there does exist a compact variety composed of small lumps bound together)."

45. Middleton, A. P., Bradley, S. M., "Provenancing of Egyptian Limestone Sculpture" *Journal of Archaeological Science*, London, 16 (5) (September 1989), 475–488.

46. A number of finds are listed in Cremo, M.A., Thompson, R.L., *Forbidden Archeology: The Hidden History of the Human Race*, Govardhan Hill Publishing, Alachua, FL (1995 edition) [344 pages]. Refer to a rebuttal to Cremo by Brass, M., *Antiquity of Man*, PublishAmerica, Baltimore (2002), 220 pp.

47. Clement of Alexandria, *Exhortation to the Heathen*, Ch. 4. (translation by Alexander Roberts and James Donaldson; American Reprint of the Edinburgh Edition, revised and chronologically arranged, with brief prefaces and occasional notes by A. Cleveland Coxe, D.D. T&T Clark, Edinburgh Wm. B. Eerdmans publishing company, Grand Rapids, Michigan).

48. U. Wilcken presented sound argumentation showing that the derivation from the word Sinope (the location of the origin of the famous statue of Serapis) was a misunderstanding based on a term "Sinopites Zeus" applied to Serapis in view of his Memphite origin at "Sinopion," which is explained by Eustathius as a mountain or hill in the Memphite necropolis (*Commentarium in Dionyssii Periegeism*, 255). Refer to Wilcken, U., *Urkunden der Ptolemaerzeit*, Vol. I: Papyri Aus Unteragyptien (1922–27). Wilcken's argument is strengthened by the mention of Sesostris in the account by Clement. Some Egyptologists think Sesostris represents Ramses II, because Herodotus mentioned enormous colossi erected in Memphis (in the village now known as Mit Rahina) by a king known as Sesostris. Herodotus likely saw the gigantic statues of Ramses II. Refer to Herodotus, *Histories*, 2.102–109; Also see Gomaa, F., *Chaemwese Sohn Ramses'II und Hoherpriester von Memphis* (1973), 35; Petrie, W.M.F., *Memphis I*, London Office of School of Archaeology University College (1909), 2.

49. For example, the *Theban Recension of the Book of the Dead*, Chapter clvi, refers to a carnelian amulet intended to allow a person passed over to the netherworld to safely go about that realm. The passage reads, "Let the blood of Isis, and the magical powers (or spirits) of Isis, and the words of power of Isis, be mighty to protect and keep safely this great god [the deceased were

accorded a degree of divinity], and to guard him from him that would do unto him anything which he abominateth."

50. The gold was also observed by geologist Dr. Edward J. Zeller, Head of the Radiation Physics Laboratory of the University of Kansas. Refer to Morris, M., "Geopolymeric Pyramids: A Rebuttal to R.L. Folk and D.H. Campbell," *Journal of Geological Education*, Vol. 40, No. 1 (January 1992), 37, and by investigators in the two European laboratories that analyzed the Lauer sample for Joseph Davidovits. For their results, refer to Davidovits, J., "X–Rays Analysis and X–Rays Diffraction of casing stones from the pyramids of Egypt, and the limestone of the associated quarries," published in David, R.A. (ed.), *Science in Egyptology*, Manchester University Press, Manchester, U.K. (1986), 511–20. The gold was also observed by Dr. Mike Silsbee, at the Materials Science Laboratory of Pennsylvania State University (unpublished). James Harrell tried to argue that the gold was fool's gold, but he was observing the wrong portion of the sample. The gold other researchers observed was embedded in the surface of the rock itself. Harrell destroyed most of the sample during his unauthorized destructive testing, and so it is not surprising that he could not find gold.

Chapter 27: Analysis of Specimens

1. Munier, P., *Technologie des Faience Technologie des faïences*, Préf. de M. P. de Groote, Gauthier–Villars, Paris (1957), 132. Similarly, Rustum Roy, Head of the Penn State Materials Science Department, classified geopolymer technically as very siliceous glass.

2. Nicholson, P.T., *Egyptian Faience and Glass*, Princes Risborough, Shire Publications, Buckinghamshire, U.K. (1993). For Joseph Davidovits' published studies, refer to Davidovits, J., "Détermination de la Provenance des céramiques, par analyse des géopolymères contenus dans les pâtes céramiques cuites à basse température," 20th Archaeometry Symposium, Paris (1980), pub. *Revue d'Archéométrie*, 3 (1981), 53–56; Boutterin, C., Davidovits, J., "Low Temperature Geopolymeric Setting of Ceramics: fabrication of black–surfaced ceramics," Proc. 22nd Symposium on Archaeometry (1982), A. Aspinal and S.E. Warren eds., University of Bradford, U.K., 213–217; Davidovits, J., and James, C., "Low Temperature Geopolymeric Setting of Ceramics (L.T.G.S.) (IV), Dolomite Presence is Proof of L.T.G.S. in Cyprus Amphorae" (1984) Symposium on Archaeometry, Smithsonian Institution, Washington, D.C., *Abstracts*, 24–25.

3. Henri Le Chatelier's work appeared in Munier, P., *Technologie des Faience Technologie des faïences*, Préf. de M. P. de Groote, Gauthier–Villars, Paris (1957), 132–133.

4. For information on molds, refer to Lucas, A., *Ancient Egyptian Materials and Industries*, 4th Edition, Mineola, N.Y., Dover Publications (1962), 77, 158–160, 177–8.

5. Several reports are not published in journals, but can be found at the Mansoor web site: www.amarna.com. Some of the published papers concerning the Mansoor Collection include, Stross, F.H., "Authentication of Antique Stone Objects by Physical and Chemical Methods," *Analytical Chemistry*, Vol. 32, n 3 (1960), 17; Hochfield, S., "The Mansoor Collection: An Insoluble Controversy?" *ARTnews*, Summer (1975), 50–57; Iskandar, Z., Mustafa, Z., "Examination of Sculpture Pieces of El–Armana Type," *Report*, November 28, 1950; Protsch, R, "Expertise of the Mansoor Collection," January 12, 1976; Blanc, P., "Report Mansoor Amarna Collection," May 31, 1986.

6. Mansoor internal report by Hay, R.L., "Report On Two Sculptures From El–Amarna," February 10, 1975. For the other internal reports quoted, visit www.amarna.com.

7. El–Khouli, A., *Egyptian Stone Vessels: Predynastic Period to Dynasty III* typology and analysis, von Zabern, Mainz/Rhein (1978), in Vol. II titled *Manufacture of Stone Vessels – Ancient and Modern*, 796.

8. Wilkinson, J.G., *The Manners and Customs of the Ancient Egyptians, New Edition*, rev. and corrected by Samuel Birch, J. Murray, London [1879], 147–148.

9. For the quote from Caley and other information on the Stockholm Papyrus, refer to Caley, E.R., "The Stockholm Papyrus," *Journal of Chemical Education*, IV, No. 8 (August 1927), 878–1002.

10. Davidovits, J., Courtois, L., "Differential Thermal Analysis (D.T.A.) Detection of Intra–Ceramic Geopolymeric Setting in Archaeological Ceramics and Mortars," 21st Symposium on Archaeometry, Brookhaven N.Y. (1981), *Abstracts*, p. 22.

11. The founding father of zeolite chemistry Richard Maling (1910–1996) published 36 papers, which characterize zeolite microporous frameworks as adsorbents and catalysts. The first paper was "Sorption of Polar and non–Polar Gases by Zeolites," published in *The Proceedings of the Royal Society* in 1938. Barrer demonstrated how zeolites can be synthesized, modified by ion–exchange, and can be converted into extremely strong solid acid catalysts.

12. Hyerdahl, T., *Paa jakt efter Paradiset,* Oslo (1938); Hyerdahl, T., *The Kon–Tiki Expedition,* Oslo (1948); Hyerdahl, T., *American Indians in the Pacific, The Theory Behind the Kon–Tiki Expedition,* Stockholm, London, Chicago (1952); Hyerdahl, T., *Archeological Evidence of PreSpanish Visits to the Galpagos Islands* (With A. Skjoldsvold). Memoir of the Soc. for American Archeology, N. 12. Salt Lake City (1956); Hyerdahl, T., *AKU–AKU. The Secret of Easter Island,* Oslo (1957); Hyerdahl, T., "Reports of the Norwegian Archaeological Expedition to Easter Island and the East Pacific" (With coeditor: E.N. Ferdon, Jr.). Vol. I: *Archeology of Easter Island,* Vol. II: Miscellaneous Papers, Monograph of American School of Research, the Museum of New Mexico and the Kon-Tiki Museum. Santa Fe, London, Chicago, Oslo (1961); Hyerdahl, T., *Vanished Civilizations (coauthor chapter: Navel of the World),* Thames Hudson, London (1963); Hyerdahl, T., *Sea Routes to Polynesia.* London, Chicago (1967), (various translations from the original: *Indianer und Alt-Asiaten im Pazifik,* Vienna 1965); Hyerdahl, T., *The Ra Expeditions,* Oslo (1967); Hyerdahl, T., *Quest for America* (coauthor, chapters: *Isolationist and Diffusionist and The Bearded Gods Speak*), Pall Mall Press Lts., London (1971).

13. Pliny, *Natural History,* Book 31, Ch. 37, titled To Remedy Unfit Water.

14. For the Cosmic Mountain theme, also refer to Widengren, G., *The King and the Tree of Life in Ancient Near Eastern Religion: King and Savior IV,* Lundequistska bokhandeln, Uppsala (1951). 79 pp.; Wheeler, N.F., "Pyramids and their Purpose," *Antiquity,* IX (1935), 172–85. The widespread Cosmic Mountain concept was still being observed thousands of years after the Great Pyramid was built. For example, the Roman Emperor Augustus Caesar's mausoleum in Rome (built between 28 and 23 B.C.) took the form of a large concrete drum surmounted by a mound. It was reminiscent of earthen tumuli of Etruscan times. In about 15 B.C., Caius Cestius (a contemporary of Augustus Caesar) chose a pyramid–shaped tomb for his burial.

15. Fisher, L. E., *Pyramid of the Sun, Pyramid of the Moon,* Macmillan, New York (1988), 32 pp.

16. Lyle, E. (ed.), *Sacred Architecture in the Traditions of India, China, Judaism, and Islam,* Edinburgh University Press, Edinburgh (1992), 220 p; Scully, V. J., *The Earth, the Temple, and the Gods; Greek Sacred Architecture,* Yale University Press, New Haven (1962). 257 pp.

17. Davidovits, J., "X–Rays Analysis and X–Rays Diffraction of casing stones from the pyramids of Egypt, and the limestone of the associated quarries," published in David, R.A. (ed.), *Science in Egyptology,* Manchester University Press, Manchester, U.K. (1986), 511-520. Also refer to the chemical analyses of stone from the pyramid of Teti (ca. 2323-2991 B.C.), provided by Egyptologist J.P. Lauer, in Davidovits, J., *The Book of Stone: Alchemy and Pyramids,* Geopolymer Institute, St. Quentin, France (1983), 246-7, 249.

18. Yoshimira, S., *Studies in Egyptian Culture, no. 6, non-destructive pyramid investigation (1) by Electromagnetic Wave Method,* Waseda University Press, Tokyo (2 volumes), 73-74.

19. R.L. Folk claimed that the coating is limestone, whereas J.A. Harrell argued that it is plaster (I do not take his analysis seriously because he said to me by phone, "today the coating, tomorrow the body of the sample." This suggests an agenda). Refer to Morris, M., Letters: "Morris Responds to Folk and Campbell," *Journal of Geological Education,* The National Association of Geology Teachers, Madison, WI, Vol. 40, No. 4 (September 1992), 344. For Harrell's opinion, refer to Harrell, J.A., and Penrod, B.E., "The Great Pyramid Debate - Evidence from the Lauer Sample," *Journal of Geological Education,* The National Association of Geology Teachers, Madison, WI, Vol. 41 (September 1993), 362; Morris, M., "How Not to Analyze a Pyramid Stone - The Invalid Conclusions of James A. Harrell and Bret E. Penrod," *Journal of Geological Education,* The

National Association of Geology Teachers, Madison, WI, Vol. 41, No. 4 (September 1993), 364-369; McKinney, R.G., "Comments on the Work of Harrell and Penrod," *Journal of Geological Education*, The National Association of Geology Teachers, Madison, WI, Vol. 41, No. 4, (September 1993), 369.

Chapter 28: Supporting Data and Opinions

1. For Zeller's statement, refer to Morris, M., "Geopolymeric Pyramids: A Rebuttal to R.L. Folk and D.H. Campbell," *Journal of Geological Education*, The National Association of Geology Teachers, Madison, WI, Vol. 40, No. 1 (January 1992), 37.

2. For Klemm's study, refer to Klemm, R., and Klemm, D., *Die Stein der pharaonen: Munchen*, Staatliche Sammlung Agyptischer Kunst Munchen (1981), 12-21.

3. Dolphin, L.T., Barakat, N., and others, "Electromagnetic Sounder Experiments at the Pyramids of Giza," Stanford Research International (SRI), Menlo Park, California (1975). 125 pp. Also refer to Alvarez, L. W., et al., "Search for Hidden Chambers in the Pyramids," *Science*, Vol. 167 (6 February 1970), 832-839.

4. Dolphin, L.T., Barakat, N., and others, "Electromagnetic Sounder Experiments at the Pyramids of Giza," Stanford Research International (SRI), Menlo Park, California (1975), 125 pp. Also refer to Alvarez L. W., et al., "Search for Hidden Chambers in the Pyramids," *Science*, Vol. 167 (6 February 1970), 832-839.

5. http://www.noaa.gov/.

6. Zeller's statement of August 23, 1995, is otherwise unpublished in print. It was provided to me for publication in this book.

7. Harrell, J.A., Penrod, B.E., "The great Pyramid Debate - Evidence From the Lauer Sample," *Journal of Geological Education*, The National Association of Geology Teachers, Madison, WI, Vol. 41, No. 4, September 1993, Table 1. We did not compare the salt content with regard to Giza limestone. For a study of salt at Giza, refer to Chikaosa, T., Kiyoshi, K., Onuma, E., Kunio, M. "The Salinization and Slaking of Egyptian Mokattam Limestone," *Journal of the Society of Materials Science*, Japan, Vol. 44, No. 502 (July 1995), 862–868.

8. Robert G. McKinney has a long career with major international oil companies and a major international mining company, in most phases of their operations, but with particular emphasis on organization and management related to exploration and production of natural resources, and in finance and business development. He has 13 years experience in the development and deployment of electronic equipment used to detect leaks from underground storage tanks and the delineation and remediation of released hydrocarbons. He is a Licensed Geologist in the State of North Carolina, License No. 1317. He specializes in hard rock and in limestone. For McKinney's statement, refer to McKinney, R.G., "Comments on the Work of Harrell and Penrod," *Journal of Geological Education*, The National Association of Geology Teachers, Madison, WI, Vol. 41 (1993), 369; Morris, M., "Morris Responds to Folk and Campbell," *Journal of Geological Education*, The National Association of Geology Teachers, Madison, WI, Vol. 40, No. 4 (September 1992), 346; Morris, M., "Geopolymeric Pyramids: A Rebuttal to R.L. Folk and D.H. Campbell," *Journal of Geological Education*, The National Association of Geology Teachers, Madison, WI, Vol. 40, No. 1 (January 1992), 36.

9. For more on the reddish–brown paint, refer to Davidovits, J., Morris, M., *The Pyramids: An Enigma Solved*, Hippocrene, N.Y. (1988), 91–92, 94.

10. Arnold, D., *Building in Egypt: pharaonic stone masonry*, Oxford University Press, New York, N.Y., (1991), 45.

11. McKinney's statement is otherwise unpublished. It was provided as a contribution to this book.

Endnotes 369

Chapter 29: Return to the Pyramid Mystique

. Diodorus Siculus, *Library of History*, Book I, Ch. 63, lines 6–7. (trans. by C. H. Oldfather), the Loeb Classical Library edition, William Heinemann Ltd., London, and G.P. Putnam's Sons, New York (1933), Vol. I, 217.

2. For Gaston Maspero (1846–1916) searching for the cup of King Solomon, refer to Hassan, S., *The Sphinx: Its History in Light of Recent Excavations*, Government Press, Cairo (1949), 22. Solomon's cup–bearers are mentioned in 1 Kings 10:5; 2 Chr. 9:4. The oracular properties of Solomon's cup are traditional, similar to those that circulated about Joseph's cup. A Jewish extrabiblical tradition tells of how Moses caused Joseph's coffin to rise from the waters by throwing in pieces of Joseph's cup while repeating a request for the coffin to emerge, refer to Ginzberg, L., *The Legends of the Jews*, Publication Society of America, Philadelphia (1946), Vol. II, 181–182.

. Ginzberg, L., *The Legends of the Jews*, Publication Society of America, Philadelphia (1968 reprint), Vol. VI, 51, n. 266. Flavius Josephus, *Antiquity of the Jews*, Loeb edition, Vol. 4, 252 (the Josephus reference is II.203). Josephus speaks of Egyptian relations with the Israelites immediately prior Moses' birth, "Thus they ordered them to divide the river into numerous canals, to build ramparts for the cities and dikes to hold the waters of the river and to prevent them from forming marshes when they overflowed its banks; and with the rearing of pyramid after pyramid they exhausted our race, which was thus apprenticed to all manner of crafts and became inured to toil."

. *Who's Who in the Old Testament* places Abraham c. 18–16 centuries B.C. Refer to Comay, J., *Who's Who in the Old Testament, together with the Apocrypha* (Advisory editors for this volume: Michael Graetz and Leonard Cowie), Holt, Rinehart and Winston, N.Y. (1971), 28.

. Kitchen, K.A., *Pharaoh Triumphant: the life and times of Ramesses II, King of Egypt* (edition: 3rd corr. Impression), Warminster, Wiltshire, England, Aris & Phillips, Mississauga, Ont., Canada: Benben (1985, c. 1982), 107.

. Ramses II's East Delta city discovered at Qantir is considered by many scholars to be Pi–Ramesses, in which ruins were found, as well as an ostracon mentioning "Per–Ramesses–Mere–Amun" ("The House of Ramses, Beloved of Amun"), Refer to Uphill, E.P., "Pithom and Raamses: Their Location and Significance," *Journal of Near Eastern Studies,* Vol. 27 (1968), 291 ff; 28 (1969), 15 ff. Some scholars, however, asserted that Pi–Ramesses was a different major city of Ramses II, 15 miles south of Qantir, namely Tanis (modern San el–Hagar), which had been the Hyksos stronghold, refer to Gardiner, A.H., "Tanis and Pi–Ra'Messe: A Retraction," *Journal of Egyptian Archaeology* 19, (1933), 122 ff; Weill, R., "The Problem of the Site of Avaris," *Journal of Egyptian Archaeology*, 21 (1935), 17.

. Ramses II campaigned against the Hittites. The exact borders agreed upon in his Hittite–Egyptian alliance are not clear, but inland areas of the Trans–Jordan were under the control of either the Egyptians or the Hittites. Many people were displaced from their land and crowded into the Egyptian Delta cities to escape the Hittites.

. It was Egyptian policy to allow foreigners refuge in times of need. Many people from Palestine were crowding into northern Egyptian cities to escape the Hittites.

. Herodotus, *The History of Herodotus*, New York, L. MacVeagh, Longmans, Green & company, The Dial press, Toronto (1928), 124–126.

10. Hancock, G., *The Sign and the Seal: A Quest for the Lost Ark of the Covenant,* Simon & Schuster, Inc., N.Y. (1993), 312–355, 510.

11. Davidson, D., *The Great Pyramid, Its Divine Message*, London (1925); Davidson, D., *The date of the crucifixion and the era of new birth; the truth of salvation through belief in Our Lord Jesus Christ confirmed by the great pyramid's scientific revelation, comprising a study showing the origins of the economic crisis and giving the dates of the beginning and ending of the crisis, with explanatory diagrams by David Davidson.* Leeds (1933), x, 73 pp.

12. Smith, C.P., *Our Inheritance in the Great Pyramid*, London, Daldy, Isbister (1877), 626 pp. For Rutherford, A., refer to the series of four books titled *Pyramidology*, Harpenden, Institute of

370   The Great Pyramid Secret by Margaret Morris

Pyramidology (1957, 1962, 1966, 1972). Also refer to Behrend, G., *The Romance and Prophecie* *of the Great Pyramid*, Los Angeles, Calif., DeVorss & Co. (1934), 135 pp,

13. Two mosaics depict the pyramids as Joseph's granaries. They appear in Demus, O., *The Mosaic* *of San Marco in Venice*, University of Chicago Press, Chicago (1984), 4 vols. 1116 pp.

14. Gregory of Tours (540–594) indicated that pyramids were Joseph's granaries. Refer to *Histori* *Francorum*, I. 10. The legend was known to Julius Honorius more than a century earlier.

15. The Palace of Eternity, built at Abydos by the 2nd Dynasty King Khasekhemwy, is made of larg mud brick walls. Until recent times, this site, too, was held in local tradition to be Joseph's silos For various sites associated with Joseph, refer to Jeffreys, D.G., *The Survey of Memphis*, Part with a preface by H.S. Smith, Egypt Exploration Society, London (1985), 44, 52, 55, 56, 61.

16. Ginzberg, A., *The Legends of the Jews*, Vol. II, the Jewish Publication Society of America Philadelphia (1920, 1948), 77–79.

17. Modern grain silos are equipped with heat sensors that detect hot spots and heat given off b insects. Constant humidity and temperature control are maintained by electrical devices to dis courage mold. Eventually, grain loses moisture and becomes infested, so that it is used as anima feed. With these methods, the storage time is about four years (preservatives further increas shelf life). In contrast, agronomists were surprised to learn that ancient containment system successfully stored grain. Archaeologists discovered ancient food storage in Spain, Hungary France, England, Ukrania, Turkestan, India, Africa, and Central and North America.

18. Toth, M., *Pyramid Power: the Secret Energy of the Ancients Revealed*, 1st Quality Paperback Destiny Books Rochester, Vt., (1985), 205 p; Flanagan, P., *Pyramid Power: the Millenniun Science*, Anchorage, Alaska, Earthpulse (1997, 1973), 173 pp. (originally published by Pyrami Publishers, Glendale, California [1973]).

19. Emery, W.B., *Archaic Egypt: Culture and Civilizations in Egypt Five Thousand Years Ago*, 198 rev.), 243.

20. Timaeus and Critias are the only existing ancient records referring to Atlantis. The story o Atlantis appears in Plato's dialogue called the *Timæus*, in the introductory part before Timæus segment about the origins of the universe. Plato's dialogue called the *Critias* is a continuation o the *Timæus*.

21. Lehner, M., *The Egyptian Heritage: Based on the Edgar Cayce Readings*, Virginia Beach, Va. A.R.E. Press (1974), 136 pp.

22. For the quote, refer to Lehner, M., *The Egyptian Heritage: Based on the Edgar Cayce Readings* Virginia Beach, Va. A.R.E. Press (1974), 132. Cayce's idea of the hall of records under th Sphinx could have been elaborated from long–standing tradition about the Sphinx. Fakhry, A. *The Pyramids*, University of Chicago Press, Chicago and London (1969 ed.), page 163 wrote "From early times, even as far back as the Ptolemaic period, tradition held that a sacred chambe or tomb existed under the Sphinx, and that a subterranean passage might even connect the statu with the Second Pyramid."

23. A fundraising brochure titled *Discovering the People of the Pyramids*, Sponsored by: Th Foundation of the Archaeological Record, Inc., page 10, accomplishment C reads: "Participatior in a Nova/WGBH television documentary film with experimental pyramid building. As part of th Nova/WGBH documentary about pyramid building (aired in October 1992), Lehner moderatec and participated in the design of an experimental approach to the topic. With the participatior of GPMP Team architectural consultant, Nicholas Fairplay, various tools and techniques of th ancient Egyptians – pulling blocks on sleds, levering stones up the steps of a pyramid, use o copper tools, etc. – were replicated and tried in building a small version of the pyramid." Othe accomplishments of the Foundation for the Archaeological Record listed are the Giza Mappin Project (page 8), archaeological excavations between 1988–1991 (page 8), radiocarbon datin the pyramids (page 19).

24. For the quote, refer to Lehner, M., *The Egyptian Heritage: Based on the Edgar Cayce Readings* A.R.E. Press, Virginia Beach, Va. (1974), v.

25. Lehner, M., *The Egyptian Heritage: Based on the Edgar Cayce Readings*, A.R.E. Press, Virginia Beach, Va. (1974), 11, 20, 22.

26. Lehner, M., *The Egyptian Heritage: Based on the Edgar Cayce Readings*, A.R.E. Press, Virginia Beach, Va. (1974), 5, 9.

27. Lehner, M., *The Egyptian Heritage: Based on the Edgar Cayce Readings*, A.R.E. Press, Virginia Beach, Va. (1974), v. The book also claims that the Egyptian Book of the Dead was conceived over ten million years ago. Ibid., 20.

28. Hancock, G., Bauval, R., *The Message of the Sphinx: a Quest for the Hidden Legacy of Mankind*, Crown Publishing, Inc., New York (c.1996), 370 pp. Compare their assertions to a study by University of Cambridge Egyptologist Kate Spence titled "Ancient Egyptian Chronology and the Astronomical Orientation of Pyramids," *Nature*, 408 (2000), 20, 324. Spence's study concludes that the Great Pyramid was built during the 4th Dynasty. Spence theorizes that the construction of the Great Pyramid of Giza dates to about 4,478 years ago (or within five years of 2478 B.C.), i.e., within Egypt's 4th Dynasty. The date is reasonably close to the range of dates estimated by Egyptology. Spence arrived at her date by analyzing the relative position of the Earth and two stars, the star named Mizar, in the handle of the Big Dipper, and Kochab, in the bowl of the Little Dipper. Because the Earth wobbles on its axis, over the centuries these two stars gave different indications for north. So, Spence calculated when the two stars would have been in the northern alignment. According to Spence, during the construction of the Great Pyramid, both of these stars orbited nightly around a point over the North Pole. Thus, when one star was seen directly over the other, the priest–astronomers could find north by using a simple plumb line. Spence theorizes that her calculation produces the approximate construction date for the Great Pyramid, which Egyptologists believe was built during the 24–year reign of Pharaoh Khufu.

29. Bauval, R., *The Orion Mystery, Unlocking the Secrets of the Pyramids*, Crown Trade Paperbacks, New York (1995 1994), 325 pp.

30. Hancock, G., Bauval, R., *The Message of the Sphinx: a Quest for the Hidden Legacy of Mankind*, Crown Publishing, Inc., New York (c. 1996), 247–267.

31. For the idea developed by Badawi and Trimble, refer to Virginia Trimble, "Astronomical Investigation concerning the so–called Air Shafts of Cheops' Pyramid," *Mitteilungen der deutschen Akademie*, Berlin, Vol. 10 (1964), 183–187. Edwards, I.E.S., *The pyramids of Egypt*, Rev. and updated, repr. with minor revisions Harmondsworth, Middlesex, England, New York, N.Y., Penguin Books (1988), 279. Badawi, A., "The Stellar Destiny of Pharaoh and the So–called Air–shafts of Cheops' Pyramid," in *Mitteilungen der deutschen Akademie*, Berlin, Band X, Heft 2/3 1964), 189–206.

32. For the positioning toward the Orion belt and Alpha Draconis, refer to Edwards, I.E.S., *The pyramids of Egypt*, Rev. and updated, repr. with minor revisions Harmondsworth, Middlesex, England, New York, N.Y., Penguin Books (1988), 279.

33. Edwards, I.E.S., The pyramids of Egypt, Rev. and updated, repr. with minor revisions Harmondsworth, Middlesex, England; New York, N.Y., Penguin Books (1988), 279. Also refer to Faulkner, R.O., "The King and the Star–Religion in the Pyramid Texts," *Journal of Near Eastern Studies* (1966), 153–161.

34. For instance, in the *Pyramid Texts*, Spell 821 addressed the pharaoh as follows, "Thou wilt regularly ascend with Orion from the eastern region of the sky, thou wilt regularly descend with Orion into the western region of the sky." Spell 882 identifies the pharaoh with Sirius, "O king, thou art this great star, the companion of Orion, who traverses the sky with Orion." Refer to Mercer, S.A.B., *The Pyramid Texts in Translation and Commentary*, Longmans, Green New York (1952) [4 volumes]. Faulkner, R.O., "The King and the Star–Religion in the Pyramid Tests," *Journal of Near Eastern Studies*, XXV (1966), 153–161.

35. Bauval, R., *The Orion Mystery: Unlocking the Secrets of the Pyramids*, Crown Trade, New York (1995), 325 pp.

36. E.C. Krupp is an astronomer and Director of Griffith Observatory in Los Angeles. He is the author and editor of several books on ancient, prehistoric, and traditional astronomy, including *In Search of Ancient Astronomies* (Doubleday & Co. Inc., 1978), *Archaeoastronomy and the*

Roots of Science (AAAS/Westview Press, 1984), and *Echoes of the Ancient Skies* (Harper & Row, 1983). *Beyond the Blue Horizon* (HarperCollins, 1991) is a worldwide comparative study of celestial mythology. He also writes astronomy books for children illustrated by his wife, Robin Rector Krupp, including *The Comet and You, The Big Dipper and You, and The Moon and You. The Rainbow and You*, published in 2000. He is a contributing editor *for Sky & Telescope* and writes a monthly column that emphasizes the cultural component of astronomy for this nationally distributed magazine. In 1989, he received a national prize from the Astronomical Society of the Pacific: Klumpke–Roberts Award for outstanding contributions to public understanding and appreciation of astronomy. In 1996 he received the G. Bruce Blair Medal for substantive contributions to amateur and public astronomy from the Western Amateur Astronomers. He has visited nearly 1,600 ancient and prehistoric sites throughout the world, and his book, *Skywatchers, Shamans, & Kings: Astronomy and the Archaeology of Power*, published by John Wiley & Sons. Inc. (1997). He has published very brief criticisms of the *Orion Mystery* in *Skywatchers, Shamans, & Kings* and in *Sky & Telescope*. Lehner also remarked about Bauval's theory, refer to Lehner, M., *The Complete Pyramids: Solving the Ancient Mysteries*, Thames and Hudson (1997), 107. "A theory of Robert Bauval suggests that the Giza diagonal is inspired by the stars in the belt of the constellation Orion, which the Egyptians saw as a symbol of Osiris. But when the map of Orion is positioned over that of Giza and nearby pyramids, it is clear that there are stars in Orion for which there are no matching pyramids, and pyramids for which there are no stars in Orion, or any other constellation."

37. West, J.A., *Serpent in the Sky: the High Wisdom of Ancient Egypt*, Quest Books, Wheaton, Ill (1992), 266 pp. Also refer to the film titled *Mystery of the Sphinx*, Livonia, MI, Magical Eye/North Tower Films [producer]; The Sphinx Project [distributor] (1993), Audiovisual: 1 videocassette (95 min., VHS, sound, color). An expanded version of the program was originally broadcast on the NBC Television Network. "Based on original research by John Anthony West" (videocassette label). Executive producer: Boris Said, producer: Robert Watts, directors: Bill Cotes, Charlton Heston.

38. Schoch, R.M., "Redating the Great Sphinx of Giza," *KMT, A Modern Journal of Ancient Egypt* (Summer 1992), Vol. 3, No. 2, 56–58. Schoch, R. M., and West, J.A., "Redating the Great Sphinx of Giza, Egypt," *Geological Society of America abstracts with programs* (1991), v. 23, no. 5, p. A253. Schoch, R. M., "How old is the Sphinx?" *Abstracts for the 1992 Annual Meeting of the American Association for the Advancement of Science*, Chicago (1992), p. 202. Schoch, R.M., "Redating the Great Sphinx of Giza," *KMT, A Modern Journal of Ancient Egypt*, v. 3, no. 2 (Summer 1992), pp. 52–59, 66–70; Coxill, D., "The Riddle of the Sphinx," *Inscription: Journal of Ancient Egypt*, Papyrus Publishing, Stafford, England, Issue 2 (Spring 1998), 13–19; Schoch, R.M., Dobecki, T.L., "Seismic Investigations in the Vicinity of the Great Sphinx of Giza, Egypt," *Geoarchaeology*, v. 7, no. 6 (1992), 527–544. With regard to the issue of a cavity under the Sphinx, Yoshimura et al. used ground penetrating radar and microgravity techniques. They first utilized a frequency of 150MHz for a ground penetrating radar experiment and identified two possible cavities in front of the Sphinx. But in their second attempt, using the same techniques with a reduced frequency of 80MHz, they found no significant anomalies. They determined that they would not be able to confirm the existence of a cavity without boring into the ground. Refer to Yoshimura, S., Nakagaua, T., Tonuchi, S., Seki, K., *Non-destructive Pyramid Investigation (1)*, Studies in Egyptian Culture No. 6, Waseda University Press, Tokyo (1987); and Yoshimura, S., Nakagaua, T., Tonuchi, S., *Non-destructive Pyramid Investigation (2)*, Studies in Egyptian Culture No. 8, Waseda University Press, Tokyo (1988).

39. Schwaller de Lubicz (1891-1962), who inspired West, was not the first to notice severe erosion on the Sphinx. One of the founders of Egyptology, Auguste Mariette (1821-1881), studied erosion on the Sphinx that is generally considered to be water damage. Mariette recognized that the 1st Dynasty Pharaoh Menes (c. 2770 B.C.), Egypt's first king, reclaimed land for the construction of Egypt's original capital of Memphis. To do this, Menes had a dike built to divert the Nile's course. Mariette believed that the dike could still be seen near Kafr el–Aiyat. Geological evidence

supports this contention. The Nile's course originally ran closer to the edge of the Libyan Desert. With the founding of Memphis, the main channel next to and extending its artesian network under the Giza Plateau dried up. The operation diverted the river eastwards to run its present course. Mariette suggested that the rock formation from which the Sphinx was formed could have, before the 1st Dynasty, protruded into the waters of the Nile's main channel. For many years, Egyptologists assumed that high Nile run-off caused the water damage on the Sphinx. For more on observations at Giza, refer to Reisner, G.A., *A History of the Giza Necropolis*, Vol. 1, Harvard University Press, Cambridge (1942), 580 pp. Smith, W.S., "Inscriptional Evidence for the History of the Fourth Dynasty," *Journal of Near Eastern Studies*, XI (1952), 113–28.

40. Rains, highly damaging to the Cairo area, are recorded in the annals of modern weather reporting. Former director of the Geological Survey of Egypt W.F. Hume described the violent rains in his *Geology of Egypt* (1925). Hume describes "sheet floods" in Cairo and its suburbs, "It must not be forgotten that the rains in the desert produce what MacGee has termed sheet floods; the vast amount of water falling cannot be dealt with in many cases by the channels already existing, and as a result it makes new passages for itself along lines of least resistance. The deep grooves are cut through the more friable strata, and serious damage may result when the storm takes place in an inhabited area. The district of Zeitun and Helmiya, north of Cairo, was suddenly flooded in 1913, the railway being destroyed in many places, and shallow 'ravines' excavated in the soft deposits bordering the cultivation. On January 17, 1919, much of the suburb of Manshiyet el Sadr was destroyed by a flood due to heavy rainfall in the hills to the east of Cairo. The disaster arose from the concentration of the rain waters which fell on a surface of not less than 162–5 kilometres....The total fall was reckoned by the late M. Fourtan at about 7,000,000 cubic metres. Cairo itself received some 1,500,000 cubic metres of this amount. In order that serious results may happen from this rainfall, it is necessary that the downfall should be very heavy during a short interval. In the present case, the whole 43 millimetres fell between 11 a.m. and 3 p.m. Much of the rain falling on a sun–dried surface does not sink in, but at once forms torrents. As the air is saturated with humidity, evaporation plays no important role." Hume, W.F., *Geology of Egypt*, Cairo, Pub. Ministry of Finance, Egypt, Survey of Egypt Government Press (1925 1937), p. 221–288. Hume reported other instances of severe flooding in and around Cairo. One cloudburst occurred on January 14, 1891, after which boats navigated the streets of Cairo. Another downpour took place on December 7, 1891. On April 14, 1895, a little more than 22.8 million gallons of water fell from the sky. After a flood on November 14, 1895, a local paper reported, "The rain fell with extraordinary violence on the Mokattam." The current's force razed some 50 houses to the ground. Another newspaper reported that during this flood Cairo formed lakes. The day after the storm, the center of the city resembled an enormous lake dotted with islands. Another cloudburst, on February 25, 1900, produced water 16 to 20 inches high in some of Cairo's streets. On April 24, 1908, a torrent destroyed 75 houses. The violent rain completely razed the village of Arab el Mohammadi, and this happened three times in this area. There has been a general trend of desiccation in the Cairo region since remotely ancient times. But Hume reminds us that, "This narrative of events will recall many a similar occurrence to those long resident in Egypt, but cause surprise to those who regard this country as one of perpetual sunshine." Southern Egypt, too, which has a dryer climate than the Giza area, has been bombarded with rare heavy downpours that have damaged tombs. Chapter 175 of the *Theban Recension of the Egyptian Book of the Dead* indicates that the concept of severe flooding was known in ancient Egypt. The chapter relates that the god Thoth, in his role as the universal demiurge, resolves to send a raging flood to cleanse the Earth of the sinful. Refer to *The Chapters of Coming Forth by Day or, The Theban Recension of the Book of the Dead: the Egyptian Hieroglyphic*. New York, AMS Press (1976 1910), Ch. 175. For thousands of years, people built houses of mud brick, a highly perishable material. Because these houses have vanished, we do not know how common waterspouts may have been in northern Egypt. Petrie observed a stone waterspout leading from the roof of a 5th Dynasty tomb at Giza. See Petrie, W.M.F., Sir, *Pyramids and Temple of Gizeh*, Field, London, Histories and Mysteries of Man, Ltd., London (1883 reprint 1990).

41. Emery, K.O., "Weathering of the Great Pyramid," *Journal of Sedimentary Petrology*, 30 (1) (1960), p. 140–143. An excerpt from the abstract reads: "Since the facing was removed 1,000 years ago, products of weathering have formed talus slopes overflowing the blocks and banking against the base of the pyramid. An estimate of the rate of talus formation indicates that the pyramid annually loses only 0.01 percent of its total volume and could remain standing for 100,000 years."

42. Gauri, K.L., "Geological Study of the Sphinx," *Newsletter American Research Center in Egypt*, No 127 (1984), 24–43. A combination of weathering factors may partially explain the erosion on the body of the Sphinx during historical times. One mode of weathering is exfoliation. K. Lal Gauri explains that dew dissolves salts within the stone and on its surface. This salt solution seeps into pores in the rock by capillary action. As this salt solution evaporates during the day, salt crystals form. They cause a minute amount of pressure that weaken the rock by expanding existing fissures. The process causes the Sphinx to flake off. Robert Schoch agrees that this is one of the weathering factors involved in the erosion of the Sphinx. But Schoch points out that there is more intense erosion, weathering and degradation at the western end of the Sphinx's enclosure that cannot be accounted for by this process alone.

43. Aigner, T., "Facies and Origin of Nummulitic Buildups: An Example from the Giza Pyramids Plateau (Middle Eocene, Egypt)," *Neues Jahrbuch für Geologie und Paläontologie, Abhandlung*, V. 166 (1983), 347–368.

44. Davidovits, J., Morris, M., *The Pyramids: An Enigma Solved*, Hippocrene, N.Y. (1988), 106.

45. For Giza's cults dedicated to guarding and maintaining the sepulchres of dead pharaohs, refer to Zivie, C., "Giza au deuxième millénaire," *Bibliothèque d'étude, Fouilles de l'Institut francais, d'Archaeologie oriental*, Cairo (1976), 185 ff; for Teti's cult, refer to Yoyotte, J., "A Propos De La Parente Feminine Du Roi Teti (VI Dynastie)," *Bulletin de l'institut d'archeologie orientale*, 57 (1958), 96, n. 4; for Sahure, refer to Martin, G.T., *The tomb of Hetepka and Other Reliefs and Inscriptions from the Sacred Animal Necropolis, North Saqqâra, 1964–1973* (with chapters by Alan B. Lloyd and J.J. Wilkes, and a contribution by R.V. Nicholls), Egypt Exploration Society, London (1979), pl. 55. Fakhry, A., *The Pyramids*, University of Chicago Press, Chicago and London (1969 ed.), 18–19. Fakhry cites Junker, H., Giza, VI (*Gîza. Bericht über die von der Akademie der Wissenschaften in Wien auf gemeinsame Kosten mit Dr. Wilhelm Pelizaeus unternommenen Grabungen auf dem Friedhof des Alten Reiches bei den Pyramiden von Gîza*, Wien, Leipzig Hölder–Pichler–Tempsky A.G., (1929–1955)), 6–25 for a study of priests and officials of the pyramid cult.

46. Kha–em–waset cleared the Sphinx and set up a stele in front of that of Thuthmosis IV. Refer to Hassan, S., *The Sphinx: Its History in Light of Recent Excavations*, Government Press, Cairo (1949), 8, 11. Hassan's book, which describes several seasons of excavation, provides some idea of the tremendous amount of work that must have been involved in Kha–em–waset's project.

47. Private discussion with Folk.

48. With regard to the ancient Egyptian concept of portrait statuary, refer to Scharff, A., "On the Statuary of the Old Kingdom," *Journal of Egyptian Archaeology*, Vol. XXVI, 41–50. In the 1930s Scharff studied the issue of portrait statuary and wrote, "…we can say with certainty that the ancient Egyptians had no idea of what we call a real portrait of a person." Unfortunately, surviving statues from the reign of Khafra are few in number, ibid., 46; therefore, there are not many examples for a comparison study.

49. Lehner, M., *The Complete Pyramids: Solving the Ancient Mysteries*, Thames and Hudson, New York (1997), 38.

50. For instance, by the New Kingdom, temple columns had evolved to a variety of stylized hybrids, lacking in the naturalistic forms and devoid of the original paradisal theme. Kha–em–waset's use of the papyriform columns harks back to the mythological primordial swamp by depicting plant clusters exhibiting bud–and umbel–shaped capitals of composite plants that are bound by annual rings imitating vegetal forms. Kha–em–waset copied these vegetal columnar styles from the much earlier architecture, like those adorning Zoser's pyramid complex. These forms recapitulate the symbolic ambience of the "First Time" (Primeval Time) emergence of life from

the primal swamp, i.e., creation mythology. One of Kha–em–waset's columns was found in his brother Merneptah's temple built a little later at Memphis, refer to Petrie, W.M.F., et al., *Memphis*, Vol. I, School of Archaeology in Egypt, London (1909), 10.

51. For the erosion on limestone blocks in Khafra's Valley Temple, refer to Schoch, R.M., "Redating the Great Sphinx of Giza," *KMT, A Modern Journal of Ancient Egypt* (Summer 1992), Vol. 3, No. 2, 55–58. Lehner mentions the restorations of Ramses II's reign, Lehner, M., *The Complete Pyramids: Solving the Ancient Mysteries*, Thames and Hudson, New York (1997), 38, which reads: "In fact, there is evidence that they [Kha–em–waset et al. of Ramses II's administration] removed the fine limestone, alabaster and granite of Khafre's pyramid temples at the same time that they restored the Sphinx in the form of the god Horemakhet. Perhaps they had to remove a certain amount of old material to restore the temples."

52. Dolphin, L.T., Barakat, N., and others, "Electromagnetic Sounder Experiments at the Pyramids of Giza," Stanford Research International (SRI), 1975, Menlo Park, California, 125 pp. Also refer to Alvarez, L. W., et al., "Search for Hidden Chambers in the Pyramids," *Science*, Vol. 167, (6 February 1970), 832–839.

53. Allen, R.H., *Star Names: Their Lore and Meaning*, Dover edition, General Publishing Company, Ltd., Toronto, Ontario, Canada (1963), 123.

54. For the Cosmic Mountain theme, also refer to Widengren, G., *The King and the Tree of Life in Ancient Near Eastern Religion: King and Savior IV*, Lundequistska bokhandeln, Uppsala (1951), 79 pp.

55. Arnold summarizes the Cosmic Mountain concept, "They not only turned their conception of kingship into stone, but also animated these stone replicas by rituals and magic spells written on the walls. They also linked the buildings to phenomena such as the rise of the original hill from the primeval waters and the daily rise of the sun. Only a proper conjuration in stone seems to have been a guarantee for the functioning of the Egyptian universe." Arnold, D., *Building in Egypt: pharaonic stone masonry*, Oxford University Press, New York, N.Y., (1991), 4. For the obelisk (which has a pyramidal top) as a Sun symbol, refer to Breasted, J.H., *Development of Religion and Thought in Ancient Egypt*, lectures delivered on the Morse Foundation at Union Theological Seminary, C. Scribner's Sons, New York (1912), 11, 15, 71.

56. Nibley, H.W., "Looking Back," *The Temple in Antiquity: Ancient Records and Modern Perspectives*, edited with an introductory essay by Truman G. Madsen, Provo, Utah, Religious Studies Center, Brigham Young University, Salt Lake City, Utah, Produced and distributed by Bookcraft (1984), 49, 26. Lundquist, J.M., "The Common Temple Ideology of the Ancient Near East," *The Temple in Antiquity: Ancient Records and Modern Perspectives*, edited with an introductory essay by Truman G. Madsen, Provo, Utah, Religious Studies Center, Brigham Young University, Salt Lake City, Utah, Produced and distributed by Bookcraft (1984), 69.

57. Nafilyan, G., *Angkor Vat, description graphique du temple (Avec la collaboration de Alex Turletti, Mey Than, Dy Proeung, Vong Von), Ècole française d'Extrême–Orient*, A. Maisonneuve Paris (1969), 32 pp, Series: Publications de l'Ecole française. Dumont, R., *Angkor Vat par la règle et le compas: analyse du plan de ce temple par les moyens de la g ̂om ̂trie l mentaire*, P ̂ninsule, Metz (1996), 89 pp.

58. For more on cosmology and sacred architecture, refer to Lyle, E. (ed.), *Sacred Architecture in the Traditions of India, China, Judaism, and Islam*, Edinburgh University Press, Edinburgh (1992), 220 pp.; Snodgrass, A., *Architecture, Time and Eternity: Studies in the Stellar and Temporal Symbolism of Traditional Buildings*, Aditya Prakashan, New Delhi (1990) (2 volumes), 622 pp.; Spence, K., "Ancient Egyptian Chronology and the Astronomical Orientation of Pyramids," *Nature*, 408 (2000), 20, 324.

59. Lyle, E. (ed.), *Sacred Architecture in the Traditions of India, China, Judaism, and Islam*, Edinburgh University Press, Edinburgh (1992), 220 p; Scully, V. J., *The Earth, the Temple, and the Gods; Greek Sacred Architecture*, Yale University Press, New Haven (1962), 257 p.

50. Herodotus, *The History of Herodotus*, II, 124.

376 The Great Pyramid Secret by Margaret Morris

61. Nibley, H.W., Nibley, H.W., "Looking Back," *The Temple in Antiquity: Ancient Records and Modern Perspectives*, edited with an introductory essay by Truman G. Madsen, Provo, Utah, Religious Studies Center, Brigham Young University, Salt Lake City, Utah, Produced and distributed by Bookcraft (1984), 19-37; Nibley, H.W., "What is a Temple?," in *Mormonism and Early Christianity*, edited by T.M. Compton and S.D. Ricks. *The Collected Works of Hugh Nibley, 4* Salt Lake City, Utah, Deseret Book (1987), 355-390; Lundquist, J.M., "The Common Temple Ideology of the Ancient Near East," *The Temple in Antiquity: Ancient Records and Modern Perspectives*, edited with an introductory essay by Truman G. Madsen, Provo, Utah, Religious Studies Center, Monograph Series 9, Brigham Young University Press, Salt Lake City, Utah (1984), 53-76.

Chapter 30: Geopolymers: Past, Present, and Future

1. Lime (CaO) can be made by burning dolomite, limestone or magnesite. They each yield different limes that produce cement of different qualities. Some plant materials are also useful for making lime. The ashes of some wood and certain other plants have a high amount of lime, between 50 and 70 percent by weight of the ashes.

2. The use of lime to plaster floors and walls in Jericho was discovered during the Garstang excavations of the early 1930's. The floors proved to be quite durable and have survived. For a description of the floors and their construction, refer to Garstang, J., and Garstang, J.B.E., *The Story of Jericho*, New Edition (Revised 1948), Marshall, Morgan and Scott, Ltd., London and Edinburgh, 58–59, 67–68. *The Oxford Companion to Archaeology*, Brian M. Fagan, Editor in Chief, Oxford University Press, Oxford, New York (1996), p. 364 (under "Jericho," by Ian Kuijt), indicates that in the period between 9300–8000 B.C., villagers in Jericho "lived in rectangular thirteen–by–twenty–six–foot (4 by 8 m) houses with painted red and white lime plaster floors."

3. For the Neolithic basalt vases, refer to Lucas, A., "Egyptian Prehistoric Stone Vessels," *Journal of Egyptian Archaeology*, XVI (1930), 210, n.9. Some of the rock types are known to be unusual. El–Khouli, A., *Egyptian Stone Vessels: Predynastic Period to Dynasty III typology and analysis*, von Zabern, Mainz/Rhein (1978). In Vol. II titled *Manufacture of Stone Vessels – Ancient and Modern*, 796.

4. For the diorite palette, refer to Lucas, A., "Egyptian Prehistoric Stone Vessels," *Journal of Egyptian Archaeology*, XVI (1930), 210 (note No. 9).

5. For the imitation basalt, refer to Stone, E.C., Lindsley, D.H., Pigott, V., Harbottle, G., Ford, M.T. "From Shifting Silt to Solid Stone: The Manufacture of Synthetic Basalt in Ancient Mesopotamia," *Science*, Vol. 280, No. 5372. (June 1998), pp. 2091–93. For basalt in Egyptian monuments, refer to Hoffmeier, J.K., "The Use of Basalt in Floors of Old Kingdom Pyramid Temples," *Journal of the American Research Center In Egypt*, XXX (1993), 117–123. Note that very tiny beads were also found in the ruins of Mesopotamia. Compare Lucas' remarks, "In the Cairo Museum there are a number of very tiny beads of Middle Kingdom date made respectively of carnelian, lapis lazuli, and turquoise which vary in diameter from about 0.58 to 0.64 millimeter (approximately 0.028 to 0.031 inch). In what manner these beads were bored is not known. Tiny beads of much the same size have been found in India and Mesopotamia," refer to Lucas, A., *Ancient Egyptian Materials and Industries*, Dover Publications, Mineola, N.Y (1999 1962), 44.

6. Davidovits, F., "Les mortiers de pouzzolanes artificielles chez Vitruve, évolution historique et archirtecturale, DEA thesis by Frédéric Davidovits, Université de Nanterre – Paris X (1993). Davidovits, F., "A la recherche du Carbunculus," *Revue Voces*, Vol. 5, (1994), 33–46. Marcus Vitruvius Pollio, *The Ten Books on Architecture*, (ed. Morris Hicky Morgan): Book 5, Chapter 11, Section 4: The Palaestra. Not all Roman cement is geopolymeric. *Opus signinum*, the most high–quality cement, was needed for complex designs that required rapid setting. The Coliseum and Pantheon were made with *opus signinum*. *Opus signinum* is waterproof and was used for structures in which preventing leakage was important. At Leptiminus, for instance, *opus signi*

num is found mainly in aqueduct channels, garum tanks, and a variety of structures at the public baths.

7. For the deteriorated modern structures, refer to Davidovits, J., "Ancient and Modern Concretes: What is the Real Difference?" *Concrete International: Design and Construction*, American Concrete Institute, Detroit, Michigan, Vol. 9, No. 12 (Dec. 1987) 23–28.

8. Pozzuoli was named after the powdered volcanic rock from near Mt. Vesuvius called pozzolan. Pozzolan is a finely divided siliceous, or siliceous and aluminous, material that chemically reacts with slaked lime at ambient temperature to make good–quality hydraulic cement.

9. In 1978, archaeologists discovered concrete blocks near the breakwater offshore at Caesarea, built for Augustus Caesar by Herod the Great. Hydraulic concrete, which hardens underwater, had been employed to build the harbor at Caesarea, and the breakwaters extended into the sea. The discoveries at Caesarea showed the use of hydraulic concrete on a massive scale.

10. Davidovits, J., "Ancient and Modern Concretes: What is the Real Difference?" *Concrete International: Design and Construction*, American Concrete Institute, Detroit, Michigan, Vol. 9, Nr 12 (Dec. 1987) 23–28.

11. GÉOPOLYMÈRE '99, International Conference. Friday, July 2, 1999, Session F: Application to Archaeology, *Archaeological Analogues and long–term stability of geopolymeric materials* (Results from the European research project GEOCISTEM), Joseph Davidovits, Geopolymer Institute, France and Frédéric Davidovits, Université de Caen, France. Published in the Proceedings, available online at the Geopolymer Institute web site.

12. Frederic Davidovits, "A la Recherche du Carbunculus," *Voces*, Vol. 5 (1994), 35–46. Also refer to in Frederic Davidovits' thesis titled *Les Mortiers de Pouzzolanes Artificles chez Vitruve*, D.E.A. Thesis, Univ. of Paris X - Nanterre (1993).

13. Today's portland cement is a proportioned chemical combination of calcium, silicon, iron and aluminum. About 85% of its mass is lime and silica. These pulverized materials are burned into clinker (stony matter fused together or slag), in a rotating, cylindrical kiln. A small amount of gypsum is added and the clinker is ground into finished cement.

14. In 1972, Joseph Davidovits received his first patent for the polycondensation of kaolinite with NaOH, titled *Sintered composite panels*. Refer to Davidovits, J., Coordination et Developpement de l'Innovation S. A., Patent ZA7308383 - 740808.

15. Davidovits, J., "Ancient and Modern Concretes: What is the Real Difference?" *Concrete International: Design and Construction*, American Concrete Institute, Detroit, Michigan, Vol. 9, Nr 12 (Dec. 1987) 23–28.

16. For efforts to rescue the Sphinx, refer to International Symposium on the Great Sphinx 1st: 1992, Cairo, Book of proceedings: The First International Symposium on the Great Sphinx, Cairo, Ministry of Culture, Egyptian Antiquities Organization (1992), 390 pp.; International Symposium on the Great Sphinx 1st (1992), Cairo, The First International Symposium on the Great Sphinx: towards global treatment of the Sphinx: prospectus, programme, and abstracts held Cairo, 29 February–3 March 1992. Ministry of Culture, Egyptian Antiquities Organization (1992), 51 pp.

17. For a study of the salt deterioration, refer to Chikaosa, T., Kiyoshi, K., Onuma, E., Kunio, M., "The Salinization and Slaking of Egyptian Mokattam Limestone," *Journal of the Society of Materials Science*, Japan, v 44 n 502 (July 1995), 862–868. The Abstract reads as follows, "The Great Sphinx–Giza, Egypt was carved out of Middle Eocene limestone formations. The upper part of the statue,...including the neck and the head, consists of soft and marly formations (named Maadi Formation). They are highly porous and cavernous showing the evidence of having been greatly affected by water erosion. At present, the Great Sphinx as one of the most important World Heritages is being seriously subjected to aggressive deterioration of limestone members. Since it was not possible to employ any specimen sampled from the immediate site of the Sphinx, it was tried to investigate the process of deterioration of marly limestone in terms of Mokkatam Limestone (called Pyramid Stone) which is considered to be a little older than Maadi Formation. In the present study the process of recrystallization of salt substance on limestone surface and

378   The Great Pyramid Secret by Margaret Morris

the transportation of salt and water through micropores were observed for the period of three months. The electron microscopic scanning was used to illustrate the pore size, pore distribution and recrystallization of salt. The same test as described in this paper is recommended to be applied to the Maadi Formation for the feasibility study on the preservation of the Great Sphinx." In ancient times, Egypt did not suffer from salination because the Nile floods leached salts from the soil and added layers of fresh silt. The construction of the Aswan High Dam in the 1960s halted that process. So, now salt levels build up, and salt works its way into the soft sandstone Theban monuments. The salt constantly dissolves and recrystallizes within the rock pores, and the continued stress degrades the monuments.

18. Davidovits, J., "Ancient and Modern Concretes: What is the Real Difference?" *Concrete International: Design and Construction*, American Concrete Institute, Detroit, Michigan, Vol. 9, Nr 12 (Dec. 1987), 23–28.

19. Modern geopolymers are routinely tested for freeze-thaw cycles in modern testing. To determine the general properties of geopolymers, the U.S. Army Corps of Engineers conducted tests in the mid 1980s. Refer to Malone, P.G., Randal, C.A., Kirkpatrick, T., "Potential for Use of Alkali-Activated Silicoaluminate Binders in Military Applications" *Miscellaneous Paper No. GL85–15*, U.S. Army Engineer Waterways Experiment Station, Vicksburg (Nov. 1985).

20. The mortar formula was published in Davidovits, J., Morris, M., *The Pyramids: An Enigma Solved*, Hippocrene, N.Y. (1988), 107–108.

21. For Arnold's remarks, refer to Arnold, D., *Building in Egypt: pharaonic stone masonry*, New York, N.Y., Oxford University Press (1991), 291.

22. The mortar formula was published in Davidovits, J., Morris, M., *The Pyramids: An Enigma Solved*, Hippocrene, N.Y. (1988), 107–108. Klemm, D., Klemm, R., "Mortar Evolution in the Old Kingdom of Egypt," *Archaeometry '90*, Birkhäuser Verlag, Basel, Switzerland (1990), 445–454. In this report, Klemm opposed the geopolymer theory based on his study of lime. According to Joseph Davidovits, Klemm's objection is invalid because the amount of lime in pyramid blocks is much lower than Klemm could detect. According to Joseph Davidovits, although the mortar Klemm studied contained about 30–40 percent by weight of recarbonated lime, the blocks would at most contain only 3–4 percent. This smaller amount would not be easy to detect by the method Klemm developed. Egyptologists were initially reluctant to accept Klemm's findings of lime in ancient Egyptian mortar. His discovery went against the consensus of Egyptology at that time. The supposed absence of lime in Egyptian mortar and the supposed absence of the knowledge of working with lime was a major reason Egyptologists rejected the geopolymer theory when it was introduced much earlier than Klemm's study. Now that Klemm has shown lime in early Egyptian mortar, Egyptologists have not updated their opinion on the geopolymer theory. Klemm also chemically analyzed samples of pyramid stones, and he objected to the geopolymer theory based on his analyses. But Klemm carried out only bulk chemical analyses, methodology insufficient for detecting geopolymerization.

23. Lucas, A., *Ancient Egyptian Materials and Industries*, Mineola, N.Y., Dover Publications (1999 1962), 469.

24. Romer, J., *Damage in the Royal Tombs in the Valley of the Kings*. With Rutherford and Chekene, Privately published, San Francisco (1977); Romer, J., "Physical Deterioration of the Royal Tombs in the Valley of the Kings: A Progress Report on the 1977–1978 Season of the Brooklyn Museum Theban Expedition." The Brooklyn Museum, Brooklyn (1978).

25. The King's Chamber of the Great Pyramid must always be kept very secure so that it never caves in on tourists. Earthquakes have taken their toll. Petrie was very concerned, "...extremely severe in wrenching, as all the deep beams of granite over the King's chamber in the Great Pyramid are snapped through at the south end, or else dragged out in the upper chambers. The whole roof hangs now by merely catching contact..."; refer to Petrie, W.M.F., *Egyptian Architecture*, London (1938), 67. For the rate at which the Great Pyramid decays from weathering, refer to Emery, K.O., "Weathering of the Great Pyramid," *Journal of Sedimentary Petrology, Society of Economic Paleontologists and Mineralogists*, Tulsa, OK (1960), Vol. 30, No. 1, 140–143.

26. Campbell, D.H., and Folk, R.L., "The Ancient Pyramids – Concrete or Rock?," *Concrete International: Design and Construction*, American Concrete Institute, Detroit, Michigan, Vol. 13, No. 8 (1991), 38.

27. Modern geopolymers endure intense acid leaching tests. Leachate tests were conducted according to Regulation 309, Ontario Ministry of the Environment. Refer to Davidovits, J., Comrie, D., Paterson, J., and Ritcey D., "Geopolymer Concrete for Environmental Protection," *Concrete International: Design and Construction*, American Concrete Institute, Detroit, Michigan (July 1990), Vol. 12, No. 7. Modern geopolymers are routinely tested for freeze–thaw cycles.]]]For general properties of geopolymers, see the U.S. Army Corps of Engineers study by Malone, P.G., Randal, C.A., Kirkpatrick, T., "Potential for Use of Alkali–Activated Silico–Aluminate Binders in Military Applications," The tests were made on geopolymer mixed with portland cement, i.e., Pyrament, manufactured by Lone Star Industries, Inc. (the combination allows portland to withstand freeze thaw cycles). *Miscellaneous Paper No. GL85–15*, U.S. Army Engineer Waterways Experiment Station, Vicksburg (November, 1985).

28. Davidovits J., "Geopolymers: Inorganic Polymeric New Materials," *Journal of Thermal Analysis*, Vol. 37, (1991), 1633–1756; Davidovits, J., Davidovics, M., Orlinski, J., "Geopolymer inorganic resins. Their uses in the composite industry," *Composites*, Paris (ISSN 0754–0876VOL), 31, (1991), 76–89.

29. Refer to Lyon, R., "Fire Response of Geopolymer Structural Composites," *Report DOT/FAA/AR-TN95/22*, Federal Aviation Administration (January 1996); Foden, A., Balaguru, P.N., Lyon, R., Davidovits, J., "High Temperature Inorganic Resin For Use in Fiber Reinforced Composites," ICCI'96, Fiber Composites in Infrastructure, Tucson (1996) USA, 166–177; Lyon, R., Sorathia U., Balaguru, P.N., Foden, A, Davidovics, M., Davidovits, J., "Fire Response of Geopolymer Structural Composites," ICCI'96, Fiber Composites in infrastructure, Tucson (1996) USA, 972–981; Lyon, R, Balaguru, P.N., Foden, A., Sorathia, U., Davidovics, M., Davidovits, J., "Fire–resistant Aluminosilicate Composites," *Fire and Materials*, Vol. 21 (1997), 67–73.

30. Davidovits, J., "Global warming impact on the cement and aggregates industries," *World Resource Review*, Vol. 6, No 2 (1994), 263–278; Davidovits, J., "CO2–Greenhouse Warming: what future for Portland Cement?," Emerging Technologies on Cement and Concrete in the Global Environment, Symposium (1993–03–10), Chicago, IL, Skokie, IL: PCA, USA (1993), 21 pp., SYM.147; Davidovits, J., "Geopolymer Cements to minimize Carbon–dioxide greenhouse–warming," *Ceramic Transactions*, Vol. 37 (1993), 165-182; M. Moukwa et al (eds.). *Cement–Based Materials: Present, Future, and Environmental Aspects*, American Ceramic Society (1993), 165–182.

31. For the Wismut program, refer to Hermann, E., Kunze, C., Gatzweiler, R., Kiessig, G. Davidovits, J., "Solidification of various radioactive residues by Geopolymere with special emphasis on long–term stability," in Géopolymère '99, Proceedings of the Second International Conference on Geopolymers (1999), 211–228. For general information on the potential of geopolymerization for nuclear waste remediation, refer to Davidovits, J., "Recent Progresses in Concretes for Nuclear Waste and Uranium Waste Containment," *Concrete International: Design and Construction*, Vol. 16, N°12, (1994), 53–58. A product called 'geopolymer' is being used at Chernobyl. It is not geopolymer chemistry as discovered or developed by Joseph Davidovits. Instead, the company who makes it decided to name it 'geopolymer.' The engineering properties of geopolymers at the time of this writing are as follows: Specific heat: 900 J/KgK°; Thermal conductivity: 0,7 W/mK°; Coefficient of Thermal Expansion: 7 10–6/°C; Flexural Strength: 35–50 Mpa; Flexural Modulus: 15 Gpa; Compressive Strength: 115–130 Mpa; Shrinkage: 0,1 per cent at 500C. For developments, see Davidovits' web site. Also refer to Davidovits, J., "New Confinement Concepts based on geopolymeric materials, Geology and Confinement of Toxic Wastes," Arnould, M., and Barres, M., Eds., International Symposia; Balkema, A.A., Rotterdam, P., 499–504 (1993). For the Battelle Institute testing, refer to Rolf–Erhard Schmitt and Volker Friehmelt, Battelle Institut, Germany. Ceramic Transactions, Vol. 36, "Microwaves: Theory and Application in Materials Processing II" (1993), 61–72, Presented at the International Symposium on Microwave Processing, the

95th Annual Meeting of the American Ceramic Society, held in Cincinnati, April 19–22, 1993. Also see A. D. Chervonnyi and N. A. Chervonnaya, "Geopolymeric Agent for Immobilization of Radioactive Ashes after Biomass Burning" *Radiochemistry,* Volume 45, Number 2, March (2003), 182-188. The abstract reads, "Solidification of low-level radioactive wastes obtained after biomass burning was studied. Two solidification modes using Portland cement and geopolymeric binder were tested experimentally. The strength at various hardening times, compacting efficiency, and leaching rate of the resulting monolithic concretes were analyzed. The compacting efficiency in concretes prepared by two different modes is similar. At the same time, geopolymeric binder is solidified in significantly shorter period and its compression strength is several times higher, but its main advantage is chemical immobilization of strontium cations. The leaching rate under the static conditions after 28-day hardening is nearly 10- 6 g cm- 2 day- 1. Thus, substitution of geopolymerization of the clay component (in general case, aluminosilicate material) for common solidification of low-level wastes using Portland cement is economically promising due to significant energy and resource saving. The geosynthesis can be easily realized as an environmentally safe process, yielding no liquid waste and involving no high-temperature stages with radioactive materials."

32. Diamond Microcircuitry was invented by physicist Dr. Gisela A. Dreschhoff and geophysicist Dr. Edward J. Zeller. Diamond microcircuitry is a method for making electrical components within single crystal diamond film. The electricity-conducting channels (separated by electrically insulating diamond) can be made into any desired three-dimensional configuration, including whole circuit boards (including small ones that can be connected together). While pure diamond is not a good conductor of electricity, this creation of electrically conductive graphite zones within diamond offers excellent conductivity in combination with the advantages of diamond's superior properties. The graphite is embedded below the unaffected diamond surface, i.e., by using a proton beam to etch patterns within diamond film. Diamond microcircuitry is an excellent conductor of heat. It is fireproof, strong, impact-resistant, light-weight, and durable. Such a device, having its electrically conductive components embedded within the protective diamond layers, allow it to withstand ionizing radiation far better than today's electronic components. Diamond drill bits have long been in use, and only recently have been improved by embedding the diamonds (industrial diamonds) into a particularly hard matrix, such as titanium. For more on diamond microcircuitry, see: margaremorrisbooks.com/diamond_microcircuitry.html

Appendix 1: Tier Heights of the Great Pyramid

1. Goyon, G., "Les Rangs d'assises de la Grande Pyramide," *Bulletin de l'Institut Francais d'Archeologie Orientale*, Cairo, 1978, Vol. 78, No. 2, 405-413.

Appendix 2: The Great Pyramid Debates

1. The quote by John Locke is from his *An Essay Concerning Human Understanding*, dated 1690.

2. Campbell, D.H., Folk, R.L., "The Great Pyramid Debate: The Ancient Egyptian Pyramids – Concrete or Rock? The cons of the cast–in–place theory," *Concrete International: Design and Construction,* American Concrete Institute, Detroit, Michigan (August 1991), Vol. 13, No. 8, 28–39. Morris, M., "The Great Pyramid Debate: The Cast–in–Place Theory of Pyramid Construction, the pros of geopolymeric construction" *Concrete International: Design and Construction,* American Concrete Institute, Detroit, Michigan, Vol. 13, no. 29 (August 1991), 33–44; Folk, R.L., Campbell, D.H., "Are the Pyramids of Egypt built of poured concrete blocks?," *Journal of Geological Education*, The National Association of Geology Teachers, Madison, WI (1992), Vol. 40, No. 1, 25–34; Morris, M., "Geopolymeric Pyramids: A Rebuttal to R.L. Folk and D.H. Campbell," *Journal of Geological Education*, The National Association of Geology Teachers, Madison, WI, Vol. 40, No. 1 (January 1992), 35–46. Schoch, R.M., "Comment on the Folk and Campbell Article," *Journal of Geological Education*, Vol. 40, No. 1, 34; Folk, R.L., Letters (to the Editor), *Journal of Geological Education*, Vol. 40, No. 4 (September 1992), 344. Morris,

M., Letters: "Morris Responds to Folk and Campbell," *Journal of Geological Education*, The National Association of Geology Teachers, Madison, WI, Vol. 40, No. 4 (September 1992), 344–346. Harrell, J.A., Penrod, B.E., "The great Pyramid Debate – Evidence From the Lauer Sample," *Journal of Geological Education*, The National Association of Geology Teachers, Madison, WI, Vol. 41, No. 4, September 1993, 358–363; Morris, M., "How Not to Analyze a Pyramid Stone – The Invalid Conclusions of James A. Harrell and Bret E. Penrod," *Journal of Geological Education*, The National Association of Geology Teachers, Madison, WI, Vol. 41, No. 4, September 1993, 364–369; McKinney, R.G., "Comments on the Work of Harrell and Penrod," *Journal of Geological Education*, The National Association of Geology Teachers, Madison, WI, Vol. 41, No. 4, September 1993, 369; Harrell, J.A., Letters (to the Editor): "Harrell's Response to Morris' Article," *Journal of Geological Education*, The National Association of Geology Teachers, Madison, WI, Vol. 42, No. 2 (March 1994), 195–198; Morris, M., "Response (to Harrell in letters to the Editor)," *Journal of Geological Education*, The National Association of Geology Teachers, Madison, WI, Vol. 42, No. 2, March 1994, 198–203; Ingram, K., Daugherty K,, Marshall, J., "The Pyramids – Cement or Stone?" *Journal of Archaeological Science*, London 20 (1993), 681–687. Joseph Davidovits, J., Zeller, E.J., and Morris, M., "Re–Assessing Ingram's Data" (submitted to the *Journal of Archaeological Science* in 1993 and unpublished).

3. Folk, R.L., Campbell, D.H., "Are the Pyramids of Egypt built of poured concrete blocks?," *Journal of Geological Education*, The National Association of Geology Teachers, Madison, WI (January, 1992), Vol. 40, No. 1, 25. Robert L. Folk examined the pyramid blocks and stated that their deep hollows are clam burrows made during the formation of the limestone, a feature that would not be present in concrete. He did not test the depth or shape of any of the hollows. Another geological study concentrated on the hollows in the main blocks, which are commonly held to be the result of differential erosion. J. Walther, in his study of the deep hollows, determined that they form due to sand action. Blowing sand gets into the pores of the rocks, and once inside it twirls around (because of the wind) until holes form. The periodic action causes the hollows to gradually deepen. Refer to Walther, J., *Das Gesetz der Wustenbilung* (1912), pp. 111–121, Figs. 45–56. If the Egyptians used cut stones, it is not logical to think that they would select limestone that is full of holes when there is so much weather-resistant limestone at Giza (the bottom geological layer).

4. Folk, R.L., Campbell, D.H., "Are the Pyramids of Egypt built of poured concrete blocks?" *Journal of Geological Education*, The National Association of Geology Teachers, Madison, WI (1992), Vol. 40, No.1, 29.

5. Morris, M., "Geopolymeric Pyramids: A Rebuttal to R.L. Folk and D.H. Campbell," *Journal of Geological Education*, The National Association of Geology Teachers, Madison, WI, Vol. 40, No. 1 (January 1992), 39.

6. Folk, R.L., Campbell, D.H., "Are the Pyramids of Egypt built of poured concrete blocks?" *Journal of Geological Education*, The National Association of Geology Teachers, Madison, WI (1992), Vol. 40, No.1, 29–30.

7. Folk, R.L., Campbell, D.H., "Are the Pyramids of Egypt built of poured concrete blocks?" *Journal of Geological Education*, The National Association of Geology Teachers, Madison, WI (1992), Vol. 40, No. 1, 29–30. A SEM (scanning electron microscope) and TEM (transmission electron microscope are used to analyze geopolymeric cements.

8. These reactions are of the poly(sialate), poly(sialate–siloxo/ disiloxo) types. Geopolymerization involves a chemical reaction between various aluminosilicate oxides (Al_3+ in IV–V fold co-ordination) with silicates, yielding polymeric Si–O–Al–O sialate bonds like the following: $2(Si_2O_5,Al_2O_2) + K_2(H_3SiO_4)_2 + Ca(H_3SiO_4)_2 \rightarrow (K_2O,CaO)(8SiO_2,2Al_2O_3,nH_2O)$. Davidovits, J., "GEOPOLYMERS: Inorganic Polymeric New Materials," presentation at Real Advances in Materials Symposium, Washington, D.C., Sept. 26, 1994, published in the *Journal of Materials Education*, Vol. 16 (2,3) (1994), 91–138.

9. Folk, R.L., Campbell, D.H., "Are the Pyramids of Egypt built of poured concrete blocks?" *Journal of Geological Education*, The National Association of Geology Teachers, Madison, WI (1992),

Vol. 40, No. 1, 29; Morris, M., "Geopolymeric Pyramids: A Rebuttal to R.L. Folk and D.H Campbell," *Journal of Geological Education*, The National Association of Geology Teachers, Madison, WI, Vol. 40, No. 1 (January 1992), 37–38.

10. Folk, R.L., Campbell, D.H., "Are the Pyramids of Egypt built of poured concrete blocks?" *Journal of Geological Education*, The National Association of Geology Teachers, Madison, WI (1992) Vol. 40, No. 1, 29.

11. Folk, R.L., Campbell, D.H., "Are the Pyramids of Egypt built of poured concrete blocks?" *Journal of Geological Education*, The National Association of Geology Teachers, Madison, WI (1992) Vol. 40, No. 1, 25.

12. Our work plan was important because it required studying the transition between the natural bedrock steps of Khafra's pyramid and the blocks extending from them to form tiers. In other words, Folk and Campbell agreed before our trip to investigate the difference between scrambled shells in the blocks and the natural sedimentation in the adjoining bedrock steps. Our work plan required comparing the enormous blocks on the outer walls of Khafra's Valley Temple with the Giza quarries, too. Our plan also required a systematic comparison of pyramid and temple blocks with the Giza quarries.

13. Morris, M., "Geopolymeric Pyramids: A Rebuttal to R.L. Folk and D.H. Campbell," *Journal of Geological Education*, The National Association of Geology Teachers, Madison, WI, Vol. 40 No. 1 (January 1992), 43.

14. Morris, M., "Geopolymeric Pyramids: A Rebuttal to R.L. Folk and D.H. Campbell," *Journal of Geological Education*, The National Association of Geology Teachers, Madison, WI, Vol. 40 No. 1 (January 1992), 43.

15. Folk, R.L., Campbell, D.H., "Are the Pyramids of Egypt built of poured concrete blocks?" *Journal of Geological Education*, The National Association of Geology Teachers, Madison, WI (1992) Vol. 40, No. 1, 31; Morris, M., "Geopolymeric Pyramids: A Rebuttal to R.L. Folk and D.H Campbell," *Journal of Geological Education*, The National Association of Geology Teachers Madison, WI, Vol. 40, No. 1 (January 1992), 44–45.

16. Aigner, T., "Facies and Origin of Nummulitic Buildups: An Example from the Giza Pyramids Plateau (Middle Eocene, Egypt)," *Neues Jahrbuch für Geologie und Paläontologie, Abhandlung* V. 166 (1983), 347–368.

17. For the study by Joseph Davidovits and Hisham Gaber, refer to Davidovits, J., Morris, M., *The Pyramids: An Enigma Solved*, Hippocrene, NY (1988), 97–112.

18. Jomard, M. (Edme–François), *Description de l'Egypte*, ou, Recueil des observations et des recherches qui ont été faites en Egypte pendant l'expédition de l'armee française, Paris, Pub. Imprimerie Imperiale (1809 1828), 26 v. Their drawing of the jumbled shells is shown in Davidovits, J., Morris, M., *The Pyramids: An Enigma Solved*, Hippocrene, NY (1988), Fig. 14 on page 89.

19. Morris, M., "Geopolymeric Pyramids: A Rebuttal to R.L. Folk and D.H. Campbell," *Journal of Geological Education*, The National Association of Geology Teachers, Madison, WI, Vol. 40 No. 1 (January 1992), 43.

20. Folk, R.L., Campbell, D.H., "Are the Pyramids of Egypt built of poured concrete blocks?" *Journal of Geological Education*, The National Association of Geology Teachers, Madison, WI (1992) Vol. 40, No. 1, 26, 27, 31, 32; Morris, M., "Geopolymeric Pyramids: A Rebuttal to R.L. Folk and D.H. Campbell," *Journal of Geological Education*, The National Association of Geology Teachers, Madison, WI, Vol. 40, No. 1 (January 1992), 44.

21. Morris, M., "Geopolymeric Pyramids: A Rebuttal to R.L. Folk and D.H. Campbell," *Journal of Geological Education*, The National Association of Geology Teachers, Madison, WI, Vol. 40 No. 1 (January 1992), 41.

22. Morris, M., "Geopolymeric Pyramids: A Rebuttal to R.L. Folk and D.H. Campbell," *Journal of Geological Education*, The National Association of Geology Teachers, Madison, WI, Vol. 40 No. 1 (January 1992), 44.

23. Folk, R.L., Campbell, D.H., "Are the Pyramids of Egypt built of poured concrete blocks?" *Journal of Geological Education*, The National Association of Geology Teachers, Madison, WI (1992), Vol. 40, No. 1, 25–34.

24. For the misuse of the unfinished granite casing blocks on Menkaure's pyramid, refer to Folk, R.L., Campbell, D.H., "Are the Pyramids built of poured concrete blocks?" *Journal of Geological Education*, The National Association of Geology Teachers, Madison, WI (1992), Vol. 40, 26. Reisner examined these blocks and found no tool marks on them except for those made by the Arabs in the 12th and 13th centuries, refer to Reisner, G.A., *Mycerinus, The Temples of the Third Pyramid at Giza*, Cambridge, MA (1931), 71. The shapes of the front faces of these blocks show that they are not the product of sanding. The most logical explanation is that they were built up like sculptures with extra stock on their front faces, which for some reason hardened before it could cut away with simple tools. Folk and Campbell reported no veins in these blocks. A scientific study could help settle the issue. For hard stone in general, Folk and Campbell refer to evidence of tool marks to claim that the Egyptians cut stone in the hard state. They write, "Joseph Davidovits and Morris suggest that the Old Kingdom technicians were even able to make imitation granite, porphyry, diorite and so forth, by agglomerating igneous minerals and pouring them into molds. This follows their hypothesis that the early Egyptians did not have the technology to cut hard stones; therefore, they must have agglomerated them like concrete. This is preposterous;..." To support this, Folk and Campbell allude to many Old Kingdom statues, vases, and granite blocks, and their textures, which they observed with a pocket microscope. Folk and Campbell reported that all the examples they saw in Egypt are "normal crystallized igneous rocks, not of a crystal mush bonded by geopolymeric cement. Of course, we have not been able to sample these art objects for thin sectioning." In fact, they would need to use a scanning electron microscope and understand what geopolymers can look like. They continue, "The fact that large granite blocks in Old Kingdom temples contain occasional dikes, veins, and xenoliths did not convince Ms. Morris of their geologic origin." Refer to Folk, R.L., Campbell, D.H., "Are the Pyramids of Egypt built of poured concrete blocks?" *Journal of Geological Education*, The National Association of Geology Teachers, Madison, WI (1992), 32. The comments of Folk and Campbell show their willingness to trample evidence rather than try to understand the geopolymeric paradigm: For them, fabricated granite mixed with a geopolymeric binder should necessarily look like a cemented crystalline mush. So, refer to my chapter concerning "geopolymieric metamorphism." They cite occasional veins, which may represent restoration material or to geopolymeric self healing (similar to self healing in lime plaster). A great many veins will be apparent with natural granite masonry. They report xenoliths (fragment of a rock included in another rock) as evidence against the theory, but xenoliths are to be expected in a synthetic rock made with a liquid. They fail to report that they saw absolutely no veins in the hundreds of blocks inside Khafra's Valley Temple, which would be an extraordinary circumstance for natural granite. The Valley Temple exhibits merged blocks that cannot be the result of cutting natural stone. Folk and Campbell proved that they were unable to distinguish between geopolymerized rock and natural rock.

25. For the restoration operations during Ramses the Great's reign, refer to Kitchen, K.A. *Pharaoh Triumphant: the life and times of Ramesses II, King of Egypt* (edition: 3rd corr. Impression), Warminster, Wiltshire, England: Aris & Phillips; Mississauga, Ont., Canada, Benben, (1985, ca. 1982), 107.

26. For the horizontal crack, refer to Folk, R.L., Campbell, D.H., "Are the Pyramids of Egypt built of poured concrete blocks?" *Journal of Geological Education*, The National Association of Geology Teachers, Madison, WI (1992), Vol. 40, No. 1, 31.

27. Campbell, D.H., Folk, R.L., "The Great Pyramid Debate: The Ancient Egyptian Pyramids – Concrete or Rock? The cons of the cast–in–place theory," *Concrete International: Design and Construction*, American Concrete Institute, Detroit, Michigan (August 1991), Vol. 13, No. 8, 33–34.

28. Given that Joseph Roder (Roder, J., "Zur steinbruchgeschichte des rosengranits von Assuan," *Archalogischer Anzeiger 3*, Jahrbuch des Deutschen Archaeologischen Instituts (1965), 523)

showed that fins and wedges were not used to quarry rock until Ptolemaic times, Egyptologists assume that the blocks were pried out of the bedrock with long levers, as suggested by Reisner *Mycerinos*, 70. The process involves creating separations trenches large enough for a man to stand in and use long levers. This contradicts Campbell's description of a uniform crack running through the blocks, a fine feature that cannot survive the quarrying techniques investigated by Egyptology.

29. Lucas, A., *Ancient Egyptian Materials and Industries*, Mineola, N.Y., Dover Publications (1999, 1962), 469. Also refer to Davidovits, J., "Ancient and Modern Concretes: What is the Real Difference?" *Concrete International: Design and Construction*, American Concrete Institute. Detroit, Michigan, Vol. 9, No. 12 (December 1987) 23–28.

30. Morris, M., "Geopolymeric Pyramids: A Rebuttal to R.L. Folk and D.H. Campbell," *Journal of Geological Education*, The National Association of Geology Teachers, Madison, WI, Vol. 40, No. 1 (January 1992), 38; Folk, R.L., Campbell, D.H., "Are the Pyramids of Egypt built of poured concrete blocks?" *Journal of Geological Education*, The National Association of Geology Teachers, Madison, WI (1992), Vol. 40, No. 1, 30.

31. For Folk requiring a scanning electron microscope, Folk, R.L., Campbell, D.H., "Are the Pyramids of Egypt built of poured concrete blocks?" *Journal of Geological Education*, The National Association of Geology Teachers, Madison, WI (1992), Vol. 40, No. 1, 29.

32. For their shrill remarks, refer to Folk, R.L., Campbell, D.H., "Are the Pyramids of Egypt built of poured concrete blocks?" *Journal of Geological Education*, The National Association of Geology Teachers, Madison, WI (1992), Vol. 40, No. 1, 25.

33. For Folk and Campbell insisting that geopolymers should exhibit at least 25% of cement between the rock particles, Folk, R.L., Campbell, D.H., "Are the Pyramids of Egypt built of poured concrete blocks?" *Journal of Geological Education*, The National Association of Geology Teachers. Madison, WI (1992), Vol. 40, No.1, 29.

34. Folk, R.L., Campbell, D.H., "Are the Pyramids of Egypt built of poured concrete blocks?" *Journal of Geological Education*, The National Association of Geology Teachers, Madison, WI (1992), Vol. 40, No. 1, 29; Morris, M., "Geopolymeric Pyramids: A Rebuttal to R.L. Folk and D.H. Campbell," *Journal of Geological Education*, The National Association of Geology Teachers, Madison, WI, Vol. 40, No. 1 (January 1992), 40; also refer to Klemm, D., and Klemm, R., *Steine und Stein–Burche im Alten Agypten*, Springer–Verlag, Berlin, 1993 (in German), 60–71.

35. Morris, M., "Geopolymeric Pyramids: A Rebuttal to R.L. Folk and D.H. Campbell," *Journal of Geological Education*, The National Association of Geology Teachers, Madison, WI, Vol. 40, No. 1 (January 1992), 43. Also Klemm, D., Klemm, R, "Mortar Evolution in the Old Kingdom of Egypt" (unpublished version presented at the Heidleberg Congress, Heidleberg University. West Germany, and then received by Folk from Klemm in January 1991. Folk sent the paper to me, and I sent it to Edward J. Zeller. The needle–shaped crystals appear in Klemm's Fig. 13 of that paper). Also refer to Klemm, D. D., and R.Klemm, "Mortar evolution in the Old Kingdom of Egypt," *Archaeometry '90*, ed. E.Pernicka and G. A.Wagner. Basel: Birkhäuser Verlag (1991). 445–54.

36. In addition to the published microphotographs in *Concrete International*, a scanning electron microphotograph of the Lauer sample is in the possession of Robert Schoch of Boston University. He had the SEM photograph taken and showed it to participants, including Folk, at a meeting of the American Geological Society. Folk had apparently forgotten that he viewed this microphotograph when he claimed that the Lauer sample is plaster.

37. Morris, M., "Geopolymeric Pyramids: A Rebuttal to R.L. Folk and D.H. Campbell," *Journal of Geological Education*, The National Association of Geology Teachers, Madison, WI, Vol. 40, No. 1 (January 1992), 37. We published the microphotograph with the oval bubbles in Davidovits. J., Morris, M., *The Pyramids: An Enigma Solved*, Hippocrene, NY (1988), 90. For the microphotographs of the Lauer sample at 200 x, refer to Morris, M., "The Great Pyramid Debate: The Cast–in–Place Theory of Pyramid Construction, the pros of geopolymeric construction" *Concrete*

International: Design and Construction, American Concrete Institute, Detroit, Michigan, Vol. 13, no. 29, (August 1991), 41, 43.

38. Folk sent me a photocopy of pages 83–84 from Lepre, J.P., *The Egyptian Pyramids: A Comprehensive Illustrated Reference*, McFarland & Co., Inc., Jefferson, NC and London (1990). Folk wrote on the photocopy he sent to me, "Hah! I think the Lauer mystery is solved. Page 84 shows a drawing of an inset stone in the Grand Gallery with mortar around it. I'll bet this is what Lauer sampled." But the Lauer sample is limestone and it came from the Ascending Passageway. Page 83 describes the mortar, "As to the so–called Flag Stones which comprise inverted L–shapes, they are, in reality, inverted L–shaped cavities filled in with mortar. Yet this is not mortar in the typical sense of the word, but an incredibly solid and durable type which is certainly as strong as the surrounding limestone. It is indeed the very same cement which was used extensively by the original builders throughout the external portions of the monument to obtain a more solidified bond between the huge blocks of coarse, nummulitic limestone." In other words, in his zeal to debunk the geopolymer theory, Folk not only reinvented the place of sampling for the Lauer specimen, but he also reinvented the kind of material it is made out of. Folk and Campbell published their wholly unscientific reinvention of the Lauer sample in Campbell D.H. and Folk R.L., "The Ancient Pyramids – Concrete or Rock?," *Concrete International: Design and Construction*, American Concrete Institute, Detroit, Michigan, Vol. 13, No. 8 (1991), 38. After Campbell submitted his article to Concrete International, he sent a letter to Joseph Davidovits asking him not to allow me to rebut (Campbell's letter proposed that my rebuttal would only further embarrass geopolymeric research). Campbell's effort, if successful, would have allowed their shameful misinformation to stand on record in *Concrete International* without correction.

39. For the microphotographs, Morris, M., "Geopolymeric Pyramids: A Rebuttal to R.L. Folk and D.H. Campbell," *Journal of Geological Education*, The National Association of Geology Teachers, Madison, WI, Vol. 40, No. 1 (January 1992), 37. The microphotographs of the Lauer sample are published in Morris, M., "The Great Pyramid Debate: The Cast–in–Place Theory of Pyramid Construction, the pros of geopolymeric construction" *Concrete International: Design and Construction*, American Concrete Institute, Detroit, Michigan, Vol. 13, No. 29 (August 1991), 41, 43.

40. Folk commented that the microphotographs look like ordinary limestone in private communication with me.

41. Folk taught sedimentary geology at the University of Texas from 1953–1988. Folk developed widely used classification systems for limestones and sandstones, and published papers that help to establish the groundwork for studying those rocks.

42. Folk, R.L., Letters (to the Editor), *Journal of Geological Education*, Vol. 40, No. 4 (September 1992), 344.

43. McKinney countered Folk's arguments in my part of this debate, refer to Morris, M., "Letters: Morris Responds to Folk and Campbell," *Journal of Geological Education*, The National Association of Geology Teachers, Madison, WI, Vol. 40, No. 4 (September 1992), 346.

44. For the quote by Folk, refer to Morris, M., "Letters: Morris Responds to Folk and Campbell," *Journal of Geological Education*, The National Association of Geology Teachers, Madison, WI, Vol. 40, No. 4 (September 1992), 344.

45. For the slide showing the cuts on the unfinished granite sarcophagus of Prince Dedef Hot, refer to Campbell D.H., Folk R.L., "The Ancient Pyramids – Concrete or Rock, The cons of the cast–in–place theory," *Concrete International: Design and Construction*, American Concrete Institute, Detroit, Michigan, Vol. 13, No. 8 (1991), 34 and Fig. 8 on page 33.

46. Harrell, J.A., and Penrod, B.E., "The Great Pyramid Debate –Evidence from the Lauer Sample," *Journal of Geological Education*, The National Association of Geology Teachers, Madison, WI, Vol. 41 (September 1993), 358–363.

47. Harrell, J.A., "An inventory of ancient Egyptian quarries," *Newsletter of the American Research Center in Egypt*, No. 146 (1989) 1–7; Harrell, J.A., "Misuse of the term 'alabaster' in Egyptology," *Göttinger Miszellen, Beiträge zur Ägyptologischen Diskussion*, No. 119 (1990), 37–42; Harrell,

J.A., "Ancient Egyptian limestone quarries – a petrological survey." *Archaeometry*, Vol. 34, No. 2 (1992), 195–212. See more at his web site.

48. Davidovits, J., "X–Rays Analysis and X–Rays Diffraction of casing stones from the pyramids of Egypt, and the limestone of the associated quarries," published in David, R.A. (ed.), *Science in Egyptology*, Manchester University Press, Manchester (1986), 511–520.

49. For Harrell's chemical analysis, refer to Harrell, J.A., and Penrod, B.E., "The Great Pyramid Debate – Evidence from the Lauer Sample," *Journal of Geological Education*, The National Association of Geology Teachers, Madison, WI, Vol. 41, No. 4 (September 1993), 360–361.

50. Tite's chemical analysis is not published to my knowledge. It is rebutted in Davidovits, J., "X–Rays Analysis and X–Rays Diffraction of casing stones from the pyramids of Egypt, and the limestone of the associated quarries," published in David, R.A. (ed.), *Science in Egyptology*, Manchester University Press, Manchester (1986), 511–520.

51. Refer to Tite's chemical analysis in Davidovits, J., "X–Rays Analysis and X–Rays Diffraction of casing stones from the pyramids of Egypt, and the limestone of the associated quarries," published in David, R.A. (ed.), *Science in Egyptology*, Manchester University Press, Manchester, (1986), 511–520.

52. For the chemical analysis, refer to Davidovits, J., "X–Rays Analysis and X–Rays Diffraction of casing stones from the pyramids of Egypt, and the limestone of the associated quarries," published in David, R.A. (ed.), *Science in Egyptology*, Manchester University Press, Manchester (1986), 511–520.

53. For Harrell's testing for chemically bound water, refer to Harrell, J.A., Penrod, B.E., "The Great Pyramid Debate – Evidence from the Lauer Sample," *Journal of Geological Education*, The National Association of Geology Teachers, Madison, WI, Vol. 41, No. 4 (September 1993), 358–363.

54. For Harrell's unprofessional libelous remarks, refer to Harrell, J.A., "Letters (to the Editor): Harrell's Response to Morris' Article," *Journal of Geological Education*, The National Association of Geology Teachers, Madison, WI, Vol. 42, No. 2 (March 1994), 198.

55. For Harrell's abuse of the Lauer sample, refer to Morris, M., "Response (to Harrell in letters to the Editor)," *Journal of Geological Education*, The National Association of Geology Teachers, Madison, WI, Vol. 42, No. 2 (March 1994), 202.

56. Dolphin, L.T., Barakat, N., and others, "Electromagnetic Sounder Experiments at the Pyramids of Giza," *Stanford Research International* (SRI), 1975, Menlo Park, California, 125 pp. Also refer to Alvarez, L.W., et al., "Search for Hidden Chambers in the Pyramids," *Science*, Vol. 167 (6 February 1970), 832–839.

57. Dolphin, L.T., Barakat, N., and others, "Electromagnetic Sounder Experiments at the Pyramids of Giza," *Stanford Research International* (SRI), 1975, Menlo Park, California, 125 pp. Also refer to Alvarez, L.W., et al., "Search for Hidden Chambers in the Pyramids," *Science*, Vol. 167 (6 February 1970), 832–839.

58. http://www.noaa.gov/

59. Dr. Edward Zeller's comments were provided for publication in this book.

60. To support this statement, Harrell cites the following sources: Hume, W.F., *The Building Stones of Cairo Neighbourhood and Upper Egypt*, Egyptian Geological Survey, Cairo (1910), 92 pp.; Kabesh, M.L.A., Hamada, M.M., *Limestones of the Cairo Neighborhood*, Egyptian Geological Survey, Cairo (1956), 24 pp; el–Hinnawi, E.E., Loukina, S.M., "Petrography and Chemistry of Some Egyptian Carbonate Rocks," *Neues Jahrbuch für Geologie und Palaontologie*, Abhandlungen, Vol. 138 (1971), 284–312. Klemm, R., Klemm, D., *Die Steine der Pharaonen*, Munich Staatliche Sammulung Agyptischer Kunst (1981), 48 pp.; Botros, G. (ed.), *Limestone and Dolomite in Egypt – A Commodity Package*, Geological Survey of Egypt, Cairo (1986), 76 pp.

61. Dolphin, L.T., Barakat, N., et al., "Electromagnetic Sounder Experiments at the Pyramids of Giza," *Stanford Research International* (SRI), 1975, Menlo Park, California, 125 pp. Also refer to Alvarez. L.W., et al., "Search for Hidden Chambers in the Pyramids," *Science*, Vol. 167 (6 February 1970), 832–839.

2. El–Baz, F., "Finding a Pharaoh's Funeral Bark," *National Geographic*, Vol. 173, No. 14, April 1988.

3. Yoshimura, S., et al., *Studies in Egyptian Culture, no. 6: Non–Destructive Pyramid Investigation (1) By Electromagnetic Wave Method*, Tokyo, Factor Corp. (1987) (2 volumes).

4. See a listing in Lakshmanan, J., Montlucon, J., "Microgravity Probes the Great Pyramid," *Geophysics: The Leading Edge of Exploration*, Tulsa, Soc. of Exploration Geophysicists (January 1987), 20–17.

5. Breck, D.W., *Structure of Zeolites by Infra–Red Spectroscopy, Zeolite Molecular Sieves*, John Wiley & Sons, New York (1974), 415–425.

6. Yoshimura, S., et al. *Studies in Egyptian Culture, no. 6: Non–Destructive Pyramid Investigation (1) By Electromagnetic Wave Method*, Tokyo, Factor Corp. (1987) (2 volumes).

7. Dolphin, L.T., Barakat, N., et al., "Electromagnetic Sounder Experiments at the Pyramids of Giza," *Stanford Research International* (SRI), 1975, Menlo Park, California, 125 pp. Also refer to Alvarez, L.W., et al., "Search for Hidden Chambers in the Pyramids," *Science*, Vol. 167 (6 February 1970), 832–839.

8. Davidovits, J., "X–Rays Analysis and X–Rays Diffraction of casing stones from the pyramids of Egypt, and the limestone of the associated quarries," published in David, R.A. (ed.), *Science in Egyptology*, Manchester University Press, Manchester (1986), 511–520.

9. Mark Lehner questioned Joseph Davidovits about the mortar between pyramid core blocks in the original 1992 Nova *This Old Pyramid* film, which aired repeatedly over PBS stations.

70. Lucas, A., *Ancient Egyptian Materials and Industries*, Mineola, N.Y., Dover Publications (1999 1962), 75.

71. For the 200–ton temple blocks at Giza, refer to Reisner, G.A., *Mycerinus, The Temples of the Third Pyramid at Giza*, Cambridge, MA (1931), 70.

72. For Lehner asserting that he can match places in Giza quarries where blocks were removed to build Khafra's Valley Temple, refer to Lehner, M., *The Complete Pyramids: Solving the Ancient Mysteries*, New York, Thames and Hudson (1997), 206–7.

73. Arnold, D., *Building in Egypt: pharaonic stone masonry*, New York, N.Y., Oxford University Press (1991), 33.

74. For the photograph of the ditch behind the Sphinx, refer to Lehner, M., *The Complete Pyramids: Solving the Ancient Mysteries*, New York, Thames and Hudson (1997), 207.

75. Morris, M., "Geopolymeric Pyramids: A Rebuttal to R.L. Folk and D.H. Campbell," *Journal of Geological Education*, The National Association of Geology Teachers, Madison, WI, Vol. 40, No. 1 (January 1992), 43.

76. Another series of geological debates between myself and geologist Colin Reader is posted on the web: http://www.margaretmorrisbooks.com/eye/maes/concrete_pyramids2.html

Appendix 3: Comments by Gelogist James Shelton

1. Private correspondence dated December 7, 1999.

Index

Moon Base and Beyond
by Margaret Morris

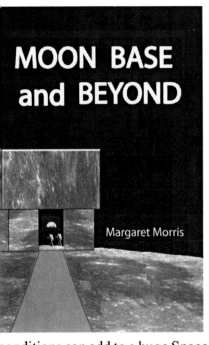

MOON BASE and BEYOND

Margaret Morris

Explore a system for building a highly-economical, highly-functional, massive, virtually permanent Moon Base. The technology for accomplishing this is called the GEO-DMF System.

Experts advocate that mining rare and precious metals from our solar system would be so lucrative as to solve all economic problems on Earth many times over. Studies predict that a robust Space Economy could grow global economies enough to support a quadrillion people under very ideal conditions.

Manufacturing in lunar microgravity conditions can add to a huge Space Economy that can enrich the Earth. Many products cannot be manufactured without prolonged microgravity conditions, such as exists on the Moon. The GEO-DMF System can help enable these important endeavors.

Owing to major obstacles, experts assume that building a Moon Base will only be practical many years in the future. Some consider the retirement of the Space Shuttle in 2011 as the end of the human spaceflight era for the foreseeable future. *Moon Base and Beyond* presents a new technological approach to the hurdles of building a Lunar Base—and, therefore, a new way forward:

Based on existing technology, explained in *Moon Base and Beyond*, a Moon Base can be established years in advance of present expectations. The usual barriers to erecting massive, sturdy architecture and space super-computing capabilities and functionality do not apply.

Humankind is poised to embrace an incredible new era as a spacefaring civilization. The achievement belongs to us all and comes with a special duty to ensure that prosperity and justice uplifts everyone and solves environmental problems—and does not just further enrich the ultra rich.

LaVergne, TN USA
19 January 2010
170524LV00004B/45/P